Latin American Democratic Transformations: Institutions, Actors, and Processes

Edited
by

William C. Smith

WILEY-BLACKWELL

Blackwell Publishing was acquired by John Wiley & Sons in February 2007. Blackwell's publishing program has been merged with Wiley's global Scientific, Technical, and Medical business to form Wiley-Blackwell.

Registered Office
John Wiley & Sons Ltd, The Atrium, Southern Gate, Chichester, West Sussex, PO19 8SQ, United Kingdom

Editorial Offices
350 Main Street, Malden, MA 02148-5020, USA
9600 Garsington Road, Oxford, OX4 2DQ, UK
The Atrium, Southern Gate, Chichester, West Sussex, PO19 8SQ, UK

For details of our global editorial offices, for customer services, and for information about how to apply for permission to reuse the copyright material in this book please see our website at www.wiley.com/wiley-blackwell.

The right of William C. Smith to be identified as the author of the editorial material in this work has been asserted in accordance with the Copyright, Designs and Patents Act 1988.

Library of Congress Cataloging-in-Publication Data

Latin American democratic transformations : institutions, actors, and processes / edited by William C. Smith.
   3 v. cm.
   ISBN 978-1-4051-9758-8
   1. Democratization–Latin America. 2. Democracy–Latin America. 3. Latin America–Politics and government–1980– I. Smith, William C., 1946–
   JL966.L356 2009
   320.98–dc22
                              2009022485

A catalogue record for this book is available from the British Library.

Set in 10 on 12 pt A Garamond Light by SNP Best-set Typesetter Ltd., Hong Kong

01—2009

For María de Lourdes and Gabriela Lucía.

LATIN AMERICAN DEMOCRATIC TRANSFORMATIONS: INSTITUTIONS, ACTORS, AND PROCESSES

Edited
by

William C. Smith
University of Miami

About the Editor and Contributors

Editor

William C. Smith is Professor of International Studies at the University of Miami. His current research focuses on transnational social movements and contentious politics in Latin America, with particular emphasis on Argentina and Brazil. He is the author of *Authoritarianism and the Crisis of the Argentine Political Economy* (1991) and the editor and contributor to numerous edited volumes, including *Latin American Political Economy in the Age of Neoliberal Reform* (1994); *Democracy, Markets and Structural Reform in Latin America* (1994); *Security, Democracy, and Development in U.S.–Latin American Relations* (1994); *Latin America in the World-Economy* (1996); and *Politics, Social Change, and Economic Restructuring in Latin America* (1997). His articles have appeared in the *Latin American Research Review, Political Power and Social Theory, América Latina Hoy, Desarrollo Económico, Dados, Studies in Comparative International Development*, and other journals. Smith is the editor of *Latin American Politics and Society*.

Contributors

Ariel C. Armony is an associate professor of government and co-director of the Goldfarb Center for Public Affairs and Civic Engagement at Colby College. His research interests are comparative democratization, authoritarianism, and Latin American politics. His latest book is *The Dubious Link: Civic Engagement and Democratization* (2004). He is currently at work on a book-length manuscript, *Daring More Democracy: Citizenship, Identity, and Difference in Latin America*.

Víctor Armony is an associate professor in the Department of Sociology at the University of Québec at Montreal. He is a past president of the Canadian Association of French-Language Sociologists and Anthropologists and the current editor of the *Canadian Journal of Latin American and Caribbean Studies*. Author of *L'Énigme argentine* (2004), he is currently conducting a study on citizenship and subjectivity in Latin America with a grant from the Social Sciences and Humanities Research Council of Canada.

Michelle D. Bonner is an assistant professor in the Department of Political Science at the University of Victoria, Canada, where she is a member of the Latin American Research Group. Her research specializes in Argentine politics, social movements, human rights, gender and politics, and state–society relations. She is the author of *Sustaining Human Rights: Women and Argentine Human Rights Organizations* (2007). Bonner is a member of the board of the Canadian Association of Latin American and Caribbean Studies.

Maxwell Cameron is Professor of Political Science at the University of British Columbia and in 2005 he held the Canadian Bicentennial Visiting Professorship at Yale University. His research interests focus on issues in comparative democratization and international political economy. Among his books are *Democracy and Authoritarianism in Peru* (1994); *The Peruvian Labyrinth* (1997); *To Walk Without Fear: The Global Movement to Ban Landmines* (1998); and *The Making of NAFTA: How the Deal Was Done* (2000). He is currently completing a manuscript on democracy without checks and balances in Latin America.

John M. Carey is the John Wentworth Professor in the Social Sciences in the Department of Government at Dartmouth College. His interests are comparative politics, constitutional design, elections, and Latin American politics. His publications include *Presidents and Assemblies: Constitutional Design and Electoral Dynamics* (1992); *Term Limits and Legislative Representation* (1996); *Executive Decree Authority* (1998); *Term Limits in the State Legislatures* (2000); and *Legislative Voting and Accountability* (2008).

Kent Eaton is an associate professor in the Department of National Security Affairs at the Naval Postgraduate School. He is the author of *Politics Beyond the Capital* (2004) and *Politicians and Economic Reform in New Democracies* (2002). His articles have appeared in many journals, including *Comparative Politics, Comparative Political Studies*, and the *Latin American Research Review*. His current research focuses on political obstacles to police reform, decentralization in postwar settings, and conflict between subnational regions in Latin America.

Jodi S. Finkel is an associate professor in the Department of Political Science at Loyola Marymount University. Currently, she is investigating the Ombudsman's Office (human rights office) in Mexico and Peru. Her previous research focused on judicial reform in Latin America, with articles on Argentina and Mexico published journals such as the *Latin American Research Review* and the *Journal of Latin American Studies*. She is the author of *Judicial Reform as Political Insurance: Argentina, Peru, and Mexico in the 1990s* (2008). Finkel is also a founder of MUJER (a literacy program for sex workers in Guatemala) and a founding board member of HOY (a volunteer organization in Mexico).

Joe Foweraker is Director of SIAS, Professor of Latin American Politics, and a Professorial Fellow of St. Antony's College, Oxford University. His research interests include grassroots politics, democratic citizenship, and the comparative performance of democratic governments. His publications include *Theorizing Social Movements* (1995); *Citizenship Rights and Social Movements* (2000); *Encyclopedia of Democratic Thought* (2001, as editor); *The Struggle for Land: a Political Economy of the Pioneer Frontier in Brazil* (2002); *Making Democracy in Spain: Grass-roots Struggle in the South* (2003); *Popular Mobilization in Mexico: The Teachers' Movement 1977–87* (2002); and *Governing Latin America* (2003).

Roman Krznaric did his doctoral studies at Essex University. His numerous publications on Guatemala include *What the Rich Don't Tell the Poor: Conversations in Guatemala* (2006) and articles in the *Bulletin of Latin American Research* and the *Journal of Refugee Studies*. He also is the author of *The Oxford Muse: Guide to an Unknown University* (2006). His articles on liberal democratic performance have appeared in *Democratization, Latin American Politics and Society*, and *Political Studies*. Krznaric has served as the Project Director at The Oxford Muse, the foundation established by the avant-garde thinker Theodore Zeldin, and a consultant to Oxfam and the United Nations on education and human development.

Steven Levitsky is Associate Professor of Government and Social Studies at Harvard University. His areas of research include political parties and party change, informal institutions and organizations, and political regimes and regime change in Latin America, with a particular focus on Argentina and Peru. He is author of *Transforming Labor-Based Parties in Latin America: Argentine Peronism in Comparative Perspective* (2003) and *Informal Institutions and Democracy: Lessons from Latin America* (2006), as well as numerous articles in leading journals, including *Journal of Democracy, Comparative Politics, Latin American Politics and Society, East European Politics and Societies,* and the *Annual Review of Political Science.*

Raúl L. Madrid is an associate professor of government at the University of Texas at Austin. He is the author of *Retiring the State: The Politics of Pension Privatization in Latin America and Beyond* (2003). His articles on economic and social reform and on indigenous political behavior in Latin America have been published by *Electoral Studies, Journal of Latin American Studies,* and *Latin American Research Review.* He is currently working on a book on the voting patterns of the indigenous population in Latin America, and he has published recent articles on this topic in *Comparative Politics, Latin American Politics and Society,* and *Electoral Studies.*

Anthony W. Pereira is Professor and Chair of the Department of Political Science at Tulane University. Before coming to Tulane, he held positions at Harvard, the New School University, Tufts University, and the University of East Anglia (U.K.). His research interests include the issues of economic development, state institutions, democracy and human rights, particularly in Brazil and the southern cone of Latin America. Among his publications are *The End of the Peasantry: The Rural Labor Movement in Northeast Brazil, 1961–1988* (1997), *Irregular Armed Forces and Their Role in Politics and State Formation* (2003), and *Political (In)justice: Authoritarianism and the Rule of Law in Brazil, Chile and Argentina* (2005).

Paul W. Posner is an assistant professor in the Department of Government and International Relations at Clark University. His current research focuses on democratization and political participation in Latin America. He is also interested in the impact of economic globalization and related state reforms on social organization and collective action in both developing and developed countries. His work has appeared in the *Journal of Inter-American Studies and World Affairs, Latin American Politics and Society,* and *Democratization.* He is the author of *State, Market, and Democracy in Chile: The Constraint of Popular Participation* (2008).

Kenneth M. Roberts is Professor of Government at Cornell University. His research interests focus on comparative and Latin America politics, with an emphasis on the political economy of development, party systems, and political representation. His research on Latin American populism, electoral volatility, party system change, and the social bases of political representation has been published in a number of scholarly journals, including *American Political Science Review, World Politics, Comparative Political Studies, Comparative Politics, Studies in Comparative International Development, Politics and Society,* and *Latin American Politics and Society.* He is the author of *Deepening Democracy? The Modern Left and Social Movements in Chile and Peru* (1998) and a forthcoming book entitled *Changing Course: Parties, Populism, and Political Representation in Latin America's Neoliberal Era.*

David Samuels is Benjamin E. Lippincott Associate Professor in the Department of Political Science at the University of Minnesota. His research focuses on Brazilian politics, political parties, federalism, the separation of powers, and the relationship between institutional context and the nature of political representation and accountability. He is the author of *Ambition, Federalism, and Legislative Politics in Brazil* (2003), *Decentralization and Democracy in Latin America* (2004), and *Presidents, Prime Ministers, and Parties: How the Separation of Powers Affects Party* (forthcoming). His articles have appeared in *American Political Science Review, Comparative Political Studies, Comparative Politics, The Journal of Politics, The British Journal of Political Science, The Journal of Democracy, Latin American Politics and Society*, and *Legislative Studies Quarterly*.

Peter H. Smith is Distinguished Professor of Political Science and Simón Bolívar Professor of Latin American Studies at the University of California, San Diego. His main research interests are in long-term patterns of political change. Among his many books are *Politics and Beef in Argentina: Patterns of Conflict and Change* (1969), *Argentina and the Failure of Democracy: Conflict among Political Elites, 1904–1955* (1974), *Labyrinths of Power: Political Recruitment in Twentieth-Century Mexico* (1979), *Modern Latin America* (5th edition 2005), and *Democracy in Latin America* (2005) and *Talons of the Eagle* (3rd edition 2008). Smith is a former president of the Latin American Studies Association.

Fredrik Uggla is a researcher in the Department of Government at Uppsala University. His early work focused on the comparative study of the politics of Chile and Uruguay during and after the transition to democracy. He has subsequently done research on legal reform, democratic development, and political protest in Latin America and Western Europe. His scholarly articles have appeared in *Journal of Latin American Studies, Mobilization, World Development, Latin American Politics and Society, Comparative Politics, World Development*, and *Comparative Political Studies*.

Donna Lee Van Cott was an associate professor in the Department of Political Science at the University of Connecticut. She died recently at the height of her scholarly productivity. Her research interests included the politics of Bolivia and other Andean countries, indigenous peoples' movements, ethnic conflict, constitutional reform, and political parties. Van Cott was author of *From Movements to Parties in Latin America: The Evolution of Ethnic Politics* (2005), *The Friendly Liquidation of the Past: The Politics of Diversity in Latin America* (2000), and *Radical Democracy in the Andes* (2008). Her articles appeared in scholarly journals such as *Comparative Political Studies, Studies in Comparative International Development, The Journal of Democracy, Latin American Politics and Society*, and *Latin American Research Review*. She was the founding chair of the section on Ethnicity, Race, and Indigenous Peoples of the Latin American Studies Association.

Brian Wampler is associate professor of political science at Boise State University. His research interests focus in the comparative study of Brazilian participatory institutions. He is the author of *Participatory Budgeting in Brazil: Contestation, Cooperation, and Accountability* (2007), and his articles have been published in numerous scholarly journals, including *Comparative Politics, Studies in Comparative International Development, Journal of Development Studies, Latin American Research Review, Latin American Politics and Society*, and *Journal of Latin American Urban Studies*.

Kurt Weyland is Lozano Long Professor of Government at the University of Texas, Austin. His research interests focus on democratization, market reform, social policy and policy diffusion, and populism in Latin America. He is the author of *Democracy without Equity: Failures of Reform in Brazil* (1996), *The Politics of Market Reform in Fragile Democracies: Argentina, Brazil, Peru, and Venezuela* (2002), and *Bounded Rationality and Policy Diffusion: Social Sector Reform in Latin America* (2007). His numerous articles have appeared in the *Latin American Research Review, Studies in Comparative International Development, Latin American Politics and Society, World Politics, Comparative Politics, Comparative Political Studies, International Studies Quarterly, The Journal of Democracy, Foreign Affairs,* and *Political Research Quarterly.*

León Zamosc is Associate Professor of Sociology at the University of California, San Diego. His research interests include Latin American societies, political economy, development, social movements, ethnicity, and rural sociology. He is the author of *The Agrarian Question and the Peasant Movement in Colombia: Struggles of the National Peasant Association, 1967–1981* (1986), *The Struggle for Indigenous Rights in Latin America* (2004); and *Civil Society and Democracy in Latin America* (2006). Zamosc is the founding editor of the journal *Latin American and Caribbean Ethnic Studies.*

Melissa R. Ziegler is a Ph.D. candidate in the Department of Political Science at the University of California, San Diego. Her dissertation examines relative effectiveness of provincial governments in Argentina. Her scholarly articles have appeared in the *Taiwan Journal of Democracy* and *Latin American Politics and Society.*

Preface and Acknowledgements

Latin American Democratic Transformations is the first volume in a series making available some of the articles originally featured in *Latin American Politics and Society* (LAPS), a peer-reviewed journal published under the auspices of the Center for Latin American Studies at the University of Miami. The idea for this project originated during a pleasant lunch with Augusto Varas in Miami accompanied by bottle of Argentine Malbec. At the time with the Ford Foundation in Santiago, Chile, Varas praised the transformation of LAPS (previously published as the *Journal of Interamerican Studies and World Affairs*) into one of the leading venues for research on contemporary Latin America by political scientists, sociologists, historians, and scholars from allied disciplines.

Varas suggested publishing a series of volumes on major themes such as democracy, political economy of market reforms, social movements and contentious politics, as well as volumes on countries, including Argentina, Brazil, Chile, and Mexico, regularly analyzed in contributions to our journal. I am grateful to Augusto Varas for the inspiration and to the Ford Foundation for its support in launching this project.

I originally recruited colleague and friend Felipe Agüero as my co-editor of the planned series. Unfortunately for me and for LAPS, the opportunity to return to his native Chile for a position at the Ford Foundation enticed Felipe away from the University of Miami. I thank him for his counsel in the early stages of this volume's preparation. I would also like to express my appreciation to Ana Morgenstern, my graduate research assistant, for her invaluable help in preparing the manuscripts, to Laura Gómez-Mera, my Miami colleague, for her encouragement, and to Eleanor T. Lahn, the journal's managing editor, for her tireless work in preparing the original articles published in LAPS. My gratitude goes to the colleagues whose work is collected in this volume who collaborated enthusiastically in revising and updating their chapters. I also thank the anonymous peer reviewers for their selfless service on behalf of our journal. Finally, I want to mention Michael Streeter and Teresa Huang, at Wiley-Blackwell in Boston, for their constant support for LAPS and for the publication of this volume.

William C. Smith
Editor, *Latin American Politics and Society*
Department of International Studies
Center for Latin American Studies
University of Miami

Chapter 1

Institutions, Actors, and Processes in the Transformation of Latin American Democracy

William C. Smith

Major transformations in recent decades have had far-reaching consequences for Latin American politics and the region's struggle for democracy. The most significant of these transformations have been the tectonic shifts wrought by the traumatic changes in development paradigm associated with the rise of neoliberalism in the 1980s, and the equally dramatic changes in the region's international relations following the end of the Cold War. These transformations formed the backdrop to the ascent, and perhaps equally rapid eclipse, of unchallenged U.S. power, signified by the events of September 11, 2001, and their complex aftermath and culminating in the global financial and economic crisis initiated in 2008.

In the wake of these changes, the old antinomies of (capitalist) reform versus (socialist) revolution have been all but extinguished. Contemporary "security threats" have nothing to do with old-fashioned ideological conflicts couched in the discourse of superpower rivalries. Instead, the new democracies confront *sui generis* challenges to state power and governance stemming from the accelerating globalization of production, trade, and labor flows; the volatility of international financial markets; the scourges of drug trafficking and transnational criminal organizations; and unchecked environmental degradation, to mention a few of the more salient aspects of the contemporary context of politics in the region.

In this new context, the military dictatorships and authoritarian regimes that proliferated in the 1960s and 1970s have given way to unstable civilian rule. The "lost decade" of the 1980s was characterized by the debt crisis, economic stagnation, hyperinflation, deepening poverty, and inequality, during what many analysts perceived as a neoliberal critical juncture (for my views on this period, see Acuña and W. Smith 1994; W. Smith and Korzeniewicz 1997; and Korzeniewicz and W. Smith 2000). In the 1990s, democratic politics became more firmly entrenched, and the market-oriented reforms associated with the Washington Consensus restored macroeconomic stability in most countries, albeit without guaranteeing sustained economic growth or much progress in ameliorating deeply rooted patterns of social exclusion.

By the beginning of the twenty-first century, a significant "left turn" was under way, with center-left politicians and parties of a social democratic orientation in countries like Brazil, Chile, Uruguay, and more problematically, Argentina, striving to strengthen democratic institutions, respect for human rights, the rule of law, and accountability to citizens. Elsewhere in the region, most notably in Venezuela but also in Ecuador and Bolivia and, with different nuances, in Peru, the collapse of traditional party systems opened the way for "outsider" politicians committed to ambitious reform projects. These new-style populist projects claimed to represent ideological and policy alternatives to neoliberalism and "formal" democracy. Predictably, however, these projects frequently exacerbated the normal (and desirable) uncertainties of electoral politics by challenging the logic of liberal democratic and representation of conflicting interests via political parties.

Beyond the heterogeneity of their ideological differences, specific institutional features, and leadership styles, none of the problematic "really existing democracies" have escaped vexing problems, old and new, about how much they respect the varieties of democratic institutional design, the protection of human rights, the imperative of strengthening the rule of law, and the necessity of promoting citizenship and combating poverty, egregious inequality, and widespread social exclusion. More democratic and competitive politics means that, although still plagued by endemic inequalities and deeply entrenched authoritarian values and practices, dynamic civil societies, characterized by a plethora of new organizations and social movements, are emerging in most Latin American countries. Contemporary democracies must contend not only with the pathologies of inherited systems of class stratification but also with the consequences of new cleavages, the result of perplexing struggles over the place and limits of differences defined along racial, ethnic, gender, and sexual dimensions, together with conflicts stemming from multiculturalism and the problematic coexistence of plurinational identities.

These multifaceted transformations have opened a *nueva época* for the Americas. They also have initiated a rethinking of social science paradigms and an impressive outpouring of theoretically sophisticated and empirically rich studies of Latin American politics, political sociology, and political economy. As a journal and as part of a broader intellectual community, *Latin American Politics and Society* has sought to constitute itself as a forum for leading political scientists, sociologists, and colleagues from other disciplines to share their research on a broad range of themes and issues, including the various dimensions of democratic politics. To showcase and further contribute to this burgeoning literature, *Latin American Democratic Transformations: Institutions, Actors, and Processes* brings together recent analyses by scholars who share the common objective of exploring the diverse and contradictory ways Latin America is confronting democratic challenges, both across and within countries. Selected from among the most-read articles originally published in *Latin American Politics and Society*, these studies have all been revised in light of the latest theoretical debates and significant events in the region and the specific countries. In doing so, the participants in this volume wish not only to address their fellow Latin America specialists but also to contribute to ongoing theoretical debates in the social sciences.

This volume is organized in four sections, beginning with an overview of recent debates on liberal and illiberal democracy and the complex and contradictory connections between democratic politics and neoliberal, market-oriented reforms. The chapters in the second section examine a wide array of institutional features, from electoral reform and constitutional change to subnational politics, participatory institutions, and the opportunities for ethnic representation. The picture presented emphasizes problems and opportunities, roadblocks to institutionalizing a more inclusive, expansive, and more competitive way of practicing politics.

The volume's third section focuses on issues related to mass politics, with chapters on party system fragmentation and indigenous mobilization, human rights organizations and the state, party identification and partisanship, agrarian reform and the persistence of oligarchic control in the countryside, and popular participation in local government. The fourth and final section, on unstructured political mobilization, probes new dilemmas stemming from citizen protests in the context of legitimation deficits and institutional fragility, the crumbling of party systems, and the erosion of institutionalized options for political participation and representation. The tentative lesson may be that in lieu of a more permanent reorganization of linkages between the state and the citizenry, for the foreseeable future, democratic institutions and practices will survive but are likely to remain subject to constant flux without necessarily leading to consolidated, high-quality equilibrium combining growth, equity, and democratic deepening.

DEMOCRACY AND NEOLIBERALISM

In chapter 2, Peter H. Smith and Melissa R. Ziegler interrogate the burgeoning literature in comparative politics, focusing on the conceptualization of democracy and democratization, as well as empirical issues concerning the kind of democracies that have emerged during the "Third Wave." They argue that in Latin America, transitions from authoritarian rule toward more competitive politics have most often led not to the emergence and consolidation of liberal democracy but rather to illiberal democracy, which combines free and fair elections with systematic constraints on citizens' rights (see P. Smith 2005). Although illiberal democracies may have become the norm, this regime type may not be a stable suboptimal equilibrium. Indeed, employing rigorous statistical techniques, Smith and Ziegler find that hyperinflation and presidential elections have had a significant impact on the movement toward deepening democracy. Hyperinflation, interpreted as a short-term economic shock, generates widespread mass discontent. In the postauthoritarian context of a broadening of the franchise and relatively unrestricted opportunities to vote, citizens are free to elect reformist opposition candidates who, once in office, tend to dismantle controls on civil liberties. This scenario substantially increases the likelihood of transition from illiberal to liberal democracy.

Kurt Weyland, in chapter 3, elucidates the complexities and controversies regarding the compatibility and tensions between democratic politics and market-oriented neoliberal restructuring in Latin America. Building on his previous work (1996a, 1996b, 2002), Weyland challenges many commonplace assumptions, and argues that neoliberalism has strengthened the sustainability of democracy in Latin America while simultaneously limiting the quality of democratic governance. (For his analysis of Brazil, see Weyland 2005.) His analysis here demonstrates that the domestic and international repercussions of far-reaching market reform have contributed to the survival of competitive civilian rule. By opening up the region to the world economy, neoliberalism has exposed Latin American societies more fully to the international pressures for preserving democracy that intensified with the end of the Cold War.

Concomitantly, the move to market economics has weakened leftist parties, labor unions, and other proponents of more radical projects of socioeconomic reform while reassuring dominant classes, the military, and traditional political elites, thereby giving them less incentive to undermine democracy. But tighter external economic constraints limit the latitude of democratically elected officials and their policy teams. Restrictions on the effective range of democratic choice, together with the weakening of parties, subaltern class organization, and civic associations, have depressed political participation and eroded government accountability. Weyland concludes that in light of the available evidence, neoliberalism has been a decidedly mixed blessing for Latin American democracies.

Probing further into this mixed record, in chapter 4, Joe Foweraker and Roman Krznaric employ an original database of quantitative indicators (see Foweraker and Krznaric 2000, 2001, 2003) to flesh out and operationalize a conceptual model of the core elements of liberal democratic government, with which to explore the uneven performance of the new democracies (see also Foweraker et al. 2003). They argue that democratic performance is uneven in two main ways. First, in markedly disjunctive fashion, the institutional attributes of democratic government advance while individual and minority rights languish. Second, particular institutional attributes coexist uncomfortably, as do particular rights. Complementing their large-N statistical analysis, a comparison of Brazil, Colombia, and Guatemala traces the specific contextual conditions that shape the political contours of contemporary democracies in the region. The evidence leads to the conclusion that uneven democratic performance, particularly the imperfect reach of the rule of law, is mainly explained by the persistence of oligarchic power in combination with a largely unaccountable military. Converging with analyses of Weyland and Smith and Ziegler, however, Foweraker and Krznaric find that uneven performance, and the imperfect rule of law in particular, does not necessarily prevent democratic survival.

THE INSTITUTIONS OF COMPETITIVE POLITICS

A close examination of the role of institutions and accountability is crucial to understanding the dynamics of liberal and illiberal democracies. One prominent aspect of current debates on the quality of democratic rule is the problematic accountability of hyperpresidentialist executives, tenuously held in check by the "delegative" legitimacy derived from their electoral mandate. In chapter 5, the key issue of presidential reelection is taken up by John M. Carey, a leading scholar of presidential and legislative politics (Shugart and Carey 1992; Carey 1998, 2008). In the mid-1990s, the debate over presidential reelection reappeared with the approval of constitutional changes permitting an immediate second term for Carlos Menem in Argentina, Fernando Henrique Cardoso in Brazil, and Alberto Fujimori in Peru. The polemic over *continuismo* still roils politics in the region, particularly in the unstable Andean region, where Hugo Chávez, Rafael Correa, and Evo Morales, in Venezuela, Ecuador, and Bolivia, respectively, are embroiled in ongoing conflicts over the constitutional rules of the game. Arguments in favor of these constitutional changes contend that the possibility of immediate reelection increases politicians' responsiveness to citizen demands and allows voters the freedom to retain popular incumbents. The case against reelection highlights the risk of abuse of power by incumbents who seek to prolong their tenure. Carey's chapter illustrates the parallels between these arguments and those made historically regarding the issue. Carey suggests that the means by which provisions to allow reelection are adopted can provide valuable signals of their political and institutional consequences.

Experiments in institutional design dealing with political and administrative decentralization have elicited considerable attention in recent years. In chapter 6, Kent Eaton challenges the common view that authoritarianism has been an unambiguously centralizing experience. Building on his previous research on subnational institutions and economic reform (1998, 2004), he investigates the subnational reforms that military regimes actually introduced in Latin America and argues that the decision by military authorities to dismiss democratically elected mayors and governors opened a critical juncture with strong elements of path dependence, which has continued to shape the subsequent development of subnational institutions under democracy. His analysis reveals that once they centralized political authority, the generals were in a position to enact changes that expanded the institutional, administrative, and governing capacity of subnational governments.

Eaton thus shows how cross-national variations gave rise to quite distinct subnational institutional configurations. In each country, these decentralizing reforms profoundly shaped the democracies that reemerged in the 1980s and 1990s. Eaton further argues that, perhaps paradoxically, policy reforms under authoritarian rule sometimes contributed to greater subnational autonomy than in the neoliberal period. In Brazil, for example, the post-1964 military regime maintained electoral politics at the subnational level, which, in the long run, further empowered local actors relative to central authorities. This chapter thus is crucial to understanding rising tensions between national governments and subnational actors who had been empowered by decentralizing reforms before the recent wave of democratization.

The capacity of competitive political institutions to "democratize democracy" by expanding citizenship and incorporating previously excluded sectors of society raises obvious questions about the role of political parties. In chapter 7, Donna Lee Van Cott extends her pioneering research (2005) to ask why and how indigenous social movements formed electorally viable political parties in Latin America in the 1990s. She demonstrates that these new parties represented a new phenomenon in Latin America, where ethnic parties had previously been both rare and unpopular among voters. Using a structured-focused comparison, Van Cott examines institutional reforms in six South American countries—Argentina, Bolivia, Colombia, Ecuador, Peru, and Venezuela—to see if the emergence and success of these parties is related to changes in electoral systems, political party registration requirements, or the administrative structure of the state. She concludes that institutional changes are likely to be necessary but not sufficient conditions for the emergence and electoral viability of ethnic parties, especially in the volatile Andean region (see also Van Cott 2008).

Turning from parties and the electoral arena, Brian Wampler, in chapter 8, focuses on the role of participatory institutions at the local level in Brazil. The construction of new political institutions provided Brazilians with unprecedented access to policymaking and decisionmaking venues, thereby potentially breaking from that country's perverse tradition of *política fisiológica,* characterized by patrimonialism, clientelism, and oligarchic domination. In recent years, politicians and activists have undertaken reform efforts to promote institutional arrangements partly designed to expand accountability. But while the expansion of participatory decisionmaking venues may grant citizens greater authority, these institutions may simultaneously undermine municipal councils' ability to curb the prerogatives of mayors.

Wampler addresses these complex relationships through an analysis of the politics of participatory budgeting in São Paulo, Recife, and Porto Alegre. This comparison allows him to probe the differing capacities of mayors to implement their policy preferences. Wampler finds that the effectiveness of participatory budgeting is crucially shaped by the institutional arrangements in which it is embedded, as well as by the local demands articulated in the public sphere. Participatory budgeting, Wampler finds (see also Wampler 2007), can therefore best be seen as a complement to rather than as a substitute for the construction of broader participatory institutions and new, innovative practices by both parties and civil society actors.

Frequent rewriting of constitutions is a time-honored tradition in many Latin American countries. Relatively few scholars, however, have analyzed constitution-making in the context of the recent transitions from authoritarian rule. In chapter 9, Fredrik Uggla examines Chile's 1980 Constitution, which embodied the political aspirations of the military regime led by General Augusto Pinochet to refashion permanently that nation's politics and fundamental institutions. Uggla demonstrates that before democratization, the Pinochet dictatorship carried out a process of constitutional reform that did away with some of the charter's most blatantly authoritarian provisions while creating and preserving a legacy of authoritarian enclaves and institutional constraints that would haunt a future democratic Chile. His account of that process juxtaposes two theoretical perspectives: one that sees the results as determined primarily by the power relationship of the participants, and one that stresses contextual factors, such as institutional traditions. Uggla's important contribution is to argue that while the Chilean case largely affirms the importance of the existing constitution for the outcome, the final institutional configuration depended nonetheless on the participants' assessment of the relations of power, and therefore might have been open to arrangements closer to the preferences of those parties and interests that would make up the Concertación coalition, which has dominated electoral politics in the postauthoritarian period.

The courts and the judicial system are understudied institutional components of the new models of democratic governance emerging in Latin America. Jodi S. Finkel, in chapter 10, focuses on judicial autonomy as a critical but often overlooked arena of transition politics in Mexico. After seven decades of subordination to the ruling Institutional Revolutionary Party (PRI), the judicial branch saw reforms, introduced by President Ernesto Zedillo (1994–2000), that expanded its independence and judicial review powers. The deliberate creation of a judiciary capable of checking the power of the president and the heretofore dominant PRI seems to contradict elementary political logic. As Finkel shows, however, by the 1990s, PRI politicians had begun to lose control over political outcomes at state and local levels, and therefore were unsure if they would continue to dominate the national government in the future. President Zedillo and his team perceived that a more autonomous judiciary might function as a political "insurance policy" to protect the ruling party from its rivals. Consequently, they opted to empower the Mexican Supreme Court as a hedge against the loss of office. Finkel's chapter demonstrates that in Mexico, the likelihood of the reforms' producing an empowered judiciary increases as the ruling party's probability of reelection declines. Extending Finkel's thesis to other countries in the region (see Finkel 2008 for analyses of Argentina, Peru, and Mexico), it might be argued that autonomy-enhancing judicial reforms also will be a function of the expectations of incumbent elites regarding the probability of retaining office in future electoral contests.

ACTORS AND MASS POLITICS

The construction of democratic institutions simultaneously constrains and empowers political actors to pursue their interests and advance their goals. In contemporary Latin America, one of the key challenges to democratic institutions is to incorporate and extend citizenship to previously excluded subaltern populations. In chapter 11, Raúl L. Madrid turns from his previous focus on pension reform (2003) to offer a new perspective on democracy and the indigenous political parties that have emerged in the last several decades. Unlike many analysts who view this development with trepidation, Madrid persuasively argues that the indigenous parties in Latin America are unlikely to exacerbate ethnic conflict or to create the kinds of problems that have been sometimes associated with ethnic parties in other regions. To the contrary, Madrid contends that the emergence of major indigenous parties in Latin America may actually contribute to the consolidation and deepening of democracy. His analysis suggests that these parties improve the representativeness of the party system in the countries where they arise. He also cites evidence that these parties should increase political participation while concomitantly reducing party system fragmentation and electoral volatility in indigenous areas. Madrid concludes that indigenous parties may even increase the acceptance of democracy and reduce political violence in countries with large indigenous populations (see also Madrid 2005).

Political rights are not just codified in constitutions and laws; they are also defined in the process of political struggle. In chapter 12, Michelle D. Bonner advances the study of contentious politics and human rights. She argues that defining the rights that must be protected in a democracy is a fundamental dimension of democratization. Examining the case of Argentina, Bonner's research finds that the definition of these rights resulted partly from important debates between human rights organizations and the state. In Argentina, these human rights organizations initially framed their demands for state guarantees protecting human rights in terms of the need to protect women and the family (see Bonner 2007). Yet the success of human rights organizations in using international courts as arbiters, Bonner contends, may subsequently lessen their need to present their demands in this family framework, thus opening the way for a broader and more expansive notion of rights.

Scholars have long taken for granted that mass partisanship in most Latin American countries is comparatively weak. In a major contribution to the sparse literature on this topic, in chapter 13 David Samuels builds on his extensive research on Brazil (2001, 2004, 2006) to argue that the aggregate level of party identification in that country actually falls only slightly below the world average, and exceeds levels of identification prevalent in many newer democracies. Yet a simple reading of this finding is misleading, Samuels argues, because the distribution of partisanship is skewed toward only one party, the Workers' Party (PT), led by Luiz Inácio Lula da Silva. Samuels demonstrates that this trend results from a combination of party organization and recruitment efforts and individual motivation to acquire knowledge and become involved in politicized social networks (see also Samuels and Hellwig 2007).

Partisanship for parties other than the PT, however, derives substantially from personalistic attachments to party leaders. As the PT reckons with the aftermath of the 2005 corruption scandals, and as President Lula concludes two terms in office with the 2010 presidential succession uncertain, Samuels's findings have significant implications for current debates about parties and electoral politics in Brazil and other countries confronting the challenges of globalization (see also Samuels and Hellwig 2007).

Brazil also illuminates the importance of rural actors in shaping state policies related to the pursuit of social justice under conditions of democratic governance. Anthony W. Pereira's research, reported in chapter 14, extends his previous contributions to the study of the peasantry and the rule of law (1997, 2005). He finds that the governments of Fernando Henrique Cardoso (1995–2002) and Lula (2003–10) redistributed a surprising amount of land to Brazil's landless. Assessing that reform, Pereira argues that an adequate appreciation of land redistribution must transcend the debate about the number of beneficiaries and place the reform in the larger context of state policies toward land and agriculture. He questions to what extent such policies under Cardoso and Lula have actually contributed to effective dismantling of past state practices in the countryside. Although both the Cardoso and Lula administrations enacted some significant democratizing changes, Pereira's analysis finds that they both failed to take full advantage of opportunities to benefit the rural poor. Pereira concludes that despite advances in land titling, agricultural credit, taxation, and land expropriations, the Cardoso and Lula governments essentially maintained the agricultural model of oligarchic exclusion of recent decades. In view of the recent commodity export booms in much of the region, the implications of Pereira's analysis raise troubling prospects for efforts to achieve greater equity in the countryside.

In chapter 15, León Zamosc, a leading scholar on the peasantry and indigenous movements in the Andes (Zamosc 1986; Postrero and Zamosc 2004), returns to the question of indigenous politics raised by Van Cott and Madrid. In contrast to Madrid's more optimistic assessment for Latin America in general, however, he offers a somewhat different interpretation of the implications of the Ecuadorian Indian movement for democracy. His research finds that during the 1990s, various movements successfully

fostered indigenous and popular participation in the public sphere, exercised significant influence over government policies, and became an important contender in power
struggles. But in the institutional domain, the participatory breakthrough had mixed
effects. While the movement fulfilled functions of interest representation and control of
state power, its involvement in coup attempts demonstrated that its political socialization had not nurtured a strong commitment to democracy. Civil society actors, including
indigenous movements, do not necessarily have either fixed identities or stable pro- or
antidemocratic orientations. Consequently, their participation may or may not contribute
to democracy. Zamosc's important conclusion (see also Feinberg et al. 2006) is that the
study of indigenous politics and, more generally, the democratic spinoffs of civil activism require a context-specific approach that considers the particularistic orientations of
civil associations, the definition of means and ends, the institutional responses evoked
by movement initiatives, and the unintended consequences of movement actions.

Paul W. Posner, in chapter 16, critically examines the case of popular participation in Chile. His concern is how structural reforms, institutional arrangements, and the
dominant mode of political party-base linkage may militate against effective participation
in local democracy. Posner argues that structural reforms in Chile limited the resources
available to local leaders while constraining their policymaking prerogatives. Similarly,
he finds that prevailing institutional arrangements limit both the accountability of local
public officials to their constituents and the opportunities for citizens to contribute to
decisionmaking. Posner contends that the parties of the center-left Concertación actually
reinforced this vicious cycle by pursuing a mode of linkage with civil society designed
to promote their electoral success, with only minimal organization and participation by
their grassroots constituents. He finds that such conditions reinforce the desire of elites
of the Concertación parties and the Right to depoliticize civil society in order to preserve
macroeconomic and political stability. He concludes that these conditions question the
efficacy of popular participation and the strength of local democracy in Chile. (For further
analysis of Chile, see Posner 2008.)

UNSTRUCTURED POLITICAL MOBILIZATION

Processes of relatively spontaneous, unstructured political mobilization can potentially
contribute to the erosion or even the collapse of fragile institutions, particularly political
parties, with unpredictable consequences for democratic politics. In this context, politics
is constituted as particularly fluid, and rapid fluctuations in the public sphere are highly
likely. Ariel C. and Víctor Armony depict this transformational potential in chapter 17.
They contend that most accounts of the social and political turmoil that shook Argentina
in 2001–02 focus on the harmful impact of the financial environment, imprudent policymaking, and institutional weaknesses, with scant attention to the cultural frames and
cognitive patterns that inform and animate the complex articulations between civil society
and political society (see also A. Armony 2004 and V. Armony 2004). To fully grasp the
significance of the Argentine crisis, they argue, demands careful tracing of the linkages
between collective behavior and ingrained conceptions of national identity. Based on a
discourse analysis of Internet forums and presidential speeches, the Armomys' innovative
interpretation finds that national myths and definitional questions of national purpose
are key factors in shaping how citizens behave in junctures of deep and pervasive social
upheaval and political and economic crisis (see Armony 2008 for a comparative analysis).

Fujimori's Peru and the prospects of democracy without political parties are the subjects of chapter 18, by Steven Levitsky and Maxwell A. Cameron. Based on their previous

work on Argentina (Levitsky 2003; Levitsky and Murillo 2005) and Peru (Cameron 1994, 1997), their analysis departs from the recognition that political parties are critical to the stability and quality of governance in Latin American democracies. This was demonstrated in Peru, where an atomized, candidate-centered party system emerged following Alberto Fujimori's 1992 presidential *autogolpe*, or self-coup. Levitsky and Cameron show how the decomposition of the party system fatally weakened the democratic opposition against the advance of an increasingly aggressive authoritarian regime. Since that regime collapsed in 2000, prospects for party rebuilding have been mixed. Structural changes, such as the growth of the informal sector and the spread of mass media technologies, have provided scant incentive or capacity for weakened politicians to invest in the construction of effective parties, leaving many spheres of political life in Peru (and elsewhere; see Levitsky and Helmke 2007) largely to regulation by informal institutions.

Levitsky and Cameron conclude that although these transformations were not the only cause of party system collapse, they continued to play an important role during the governments of Alejandro Toledo and Alan García, thereby inhibiting the reconstruction of a meaningful system of political representation and electoral competition.

The volume concludes with chapter 19, on party system collapse and populist resurgence in Venezuela, by Kenneth M. Roberts. Congruent with his work on parties and social movements in the era of neoliberalism (1998, 2002a, b, 2006), this chapter reminds us that, given its strong, institutionalized two-party system, Venezuela once was seen as one of the least likely countries in Latin America to experience a party system breakdown. Probing beyond the formal institutional arrangements of the post-1958 democratic political system, however, Roberts contends that the traditional party system was founded on a mixture of corporatist and clienteles linkages that rested on the distribution of petroleum rents. This system proved unexpectedly vulnerable to the secular decline of the oil economy and the consequences of several aborted attempts at market liberalization. Successive administrations led by the two dominant parties, Acción Democrática and COPEI, failed to reverse the economic slide, with devastating consequences for the party system as a whole. When its social moorings crumbled as the 1990s advanced, the party system collapsed, and the populist movement of Hugo Chávez emerged to fill the political void. Roberts's chapter persuasively demonstrates (see Robert's forthcoming for comparative analysis) how this populist resurgence both capitalized on and accelerated the institutional decomposition of the old order, thereby ushering in the transformations associated with Chávez's controversial project for "twenty-first-century socialism."

AN INVITATION

From a variety of theoretical perspectives, ranging from institutional analysis to survey research and discourse analysis, the participants in this volume have in common the hope that their contributions will inform debates on Latin American politics and the region's democratic present and future. In this regard, these chapters seek to elucidate some of the complexities of contemporary democratic politics in the region. Moving beyond the earlier discussions of transition and consolidation, with their primary focus on institutional questions, the social sciences are now exploring new themes, requiring a reassessment of theories, concepts, and methods. The challenges are many, from persistent patterns of social and economic exclusion to new forms of social stratification, ethnic and gender hierarchies, and flawed institutional arrangements. Yet the region still offers reasons for cautious optimism. Social movements and collective actors striving to expand the logic of citizenship beyond the confines of the electoral arena continue to demand farther-reaching social and economic reforms. With the impetus from the intrinsic logic of electoral competition, moreover, there is hope that the fluid context of institutional change may progressively compel recalcitrant elites and ossified parties and state bureaucracies to become more accountable, thereby improving the quality of democracy and democratic governance. Hopefully the perspectives in this volume will inform future research on Latin America's democratic future.

REFERENCES

Acuña, Carlos, and William C. Smith. 1994. The Political Economy of Structural Adjustment: The Logic of Support and Opposition to Neoliberal Reform. In *Latin American Political Economy in the Age of Neoliberal Reform: Theoretical and Comparative Perspectives,* ed. William C. Smith, Carlos H. Acuña, and Eduardo A. Gamarra. New Brunswick/Coral Gables: Transaction/ North-South Center. 17–66.

Armony, Ariel. 2004. *The Dubious Link: Civic Engagement and Democratization.* Stanford: Stanford University Press.

———. 2008. Disharmony and Civil Society: A View from Latin America. In *Governance for Harmony in Asia and Beyond,* ed., Julia Tao. New York: Routledge.

Armony, Víctor. 2004. *L'énigme argentine - Images d'une société en crise.* Montréal: Athéna.

Bonner, Michelle. 2007. *Sustaining Human Rights: Women and Argentine Human Rights Organizations.* University Park: Penn State University Press.

Cameron, Maxwell. 1994. *Democracy and Authoritarianism in Peru: Political Coalitions and Social Change.* New York: Palgrave Macmillan.

Cameron, Maxwell, and Philip Mauceri, eds. 1997. *The Peruvian Labyrinth: Polity, Society, Economy.* University Park: Penn State University Press.

Carey, John M. 1998. *Term Limits and Legislative Representation.* New York: Cambridge University Press.

———. 2008. *Legislative Voting and Accountability.* New York: Cambridge University Press.

Eaton, Kent. 1998. *Politicians and Economic Reform in New Democracies: Argentina and the Philippines in the 1990s.* University Park: Penn State University Press.

———. 2004. *Politics Beyond the Capital: The Design of Subnational Institutions in Latin America.* Stanford: Stanford University Press.

Feinberg, Richard, Carlos H. Waisman, and León Zamosc. 2006. *Civil Society and Democracy in Latin America.* New York: Palgrave Macmillan.

Finkel, Jodi. 2008. *Judicial Reform as Political Insurance: Argentina, Peru, and Mexico in the 1990s.* Notre Dame: Notre Dame University Press.

Foweraker, Joe, and Roman Krznaric. 2000. Measuring Liberal Democratic Performance: An Empirical and Conceptual Critique. *Political Studies* 48: 759–787.

———. 2001. How to Construct a Database of Liberal Democratic Performance. *Democratization* 8, 3 (Autumn): 1–25.

———. 2003. Differentiating the Democratic Performance of the West. *European Journal of Political Research* 42: 3.

Foweraker, Joe, Todd Landman, and Neil Harvey. 2003. *Governing Latin America.* London: Polity Press.

Levitsky, Steven. 2003. *Transforming Labor-Based Parties in Latin America: Argentine Peronism in Comparative Perspective.* New York: Cambridge University Press.

Levitsky, Steven, and M. Victoria Murillo, eds. 2005. *Argentine Democracy: The Politics of Institutional Weakness.* University Park: Penn State University Press.

Levitsky, Steven, and Gretchen Helmke, eds. 2007. *Informal Institutions and Democracy: Lessons from Latin America.* Baltimore: Johns Hopkins University Press.

Korzeniewicz, Roberto Patricio, and William C. Smith. 2000. Poverty, Inequality, and Growth in Latin America: Searching for the High Road to Globalization. *Latin American Research Review* 35, 3 (October): 7–54.

Madrid, Raúl L. 2003. *Retiring the State: The Politics of Pension Privatization in Latin America and Beyond.* Stanford: Stanford University Press.

———. 2005. Ethnic Cleavages and Electoral Volatility in Latin America. *Comparative Politics* 38, 1 (October): 1–20.

Pereira, Anthony W. 1997. *End of the Peasantry: The Rural Labor Movement in Northeast Brazil.* Pittsburgh: University of Pittsburgh Press.

———. 2005. *Political (In)justice: Authoritarianism and the Rule of Law in Brazil, Chile, and Argentina.* Pittsburgh: University of Pittsburgh Press.

Posner, Paul. 2008. *State, Market, and Democracy in Chile: The Constraint of Popular Participation.* New York: Palgrave Macmillan.

Postero, Nancy Grey, and León Zamosc. 2004. *The Struggle for Indigenous Rights in Latin America.* Sussex: Sussex Academic Press.

Roberts, Kenneth M. 1998. *Deepening Democracy? The Modern Left and Social Movements in Chile and Peru.* Stanford: Stanford University Press.

———. 2002a. Social Inequalities Without Class Cleavages: Party Systems and Labor Movements in Latin America's Neoliberal Era. *Studies in Comparative International Development* 36, 4 (Winter): 3–33.

———. 2002b. Party-Society Linkages and the Transformation of Political Representation in Latin America. *Canadian Journal of Latin American and Caribbean Studies* 27, 53: 9–34.

———. 2006. Populist Mobilization, Socio-Political Conflict, and Grass-Roots Organization in Latin America. *Comparative Politics* 38, 2 (January): 127–48.

———. Forthcoming. *Changing Course: Parties, Populism, and Political Representation in Latin America's Neoliberal Era.* Cambridge: Cambridge University Press.

Samuels, David. 2001. Money, Elections, and Democracy in Brazil. *Latin American Politics and Society* 43, 2 (Summer): 27–48.

———. 2004. From Socialism to Social Democracy? The Evolution of the Workers' Party in Brazil. *Comparative Political Studies* 37, 9 (November): 999–1024.

———. 2006. *Ambition, Federalism, and Legislative Politics in Brazil.* Cambridge: Cambridge University Press.

Samuels, David, and Timothy Hellwig. 2007. Electoral Accountability and the Variety of Democratic Regimes. *British Journal of Political Science* 37: 1–26.

Samuels, David, and Matthew Shugart. Forthcoming. *Presidents, Prime Ministers and Parties: How the Separation of Powers Affects Party Organization and Behavior Around the World.* Cambridge: Cambridge University Press.

Shugart, Matthew Soberg, and John M. Carey. 1992. *Presidents and Assemblies: Constitutional Design and Electoral Dynamics.* New York: Cambridge University Press.

Smith, Peter H. 2005. *Democracy in Latin America: Political Change in Comparative Perspective.* Oxford: Oxford University Press.

Smith, William C., and Roberto Patricio Korzeniewicz. 1997. Latin America and the Second Great Transformations. In *Politics, Social Changes, and Economic Restructuring in Latin America,* ed. William C. Smith and Roberto Patricio Korzeniewicz. Boulder: Lynne Rienner. 1–20.

Van Cott, Donna Lee. 2005. *From Movements to Parties in Latin America: The Evolution of Ethnic Politics.* New York: Cambridge University Press.

———. 2008. *Radical Democracy in the Andes.* New York: Cambridge University Press.

Wampler, Brian. 2007. *Participatory Budgeting in Brazil: Contestation, Cooperation, and Accountability.* University Park: Penn State University Press.

Weyland, Kurt. 1996a. *Democracy without Equity: Failures of Reform in Brazil.* Pittsburgh: Pittsburgh University Press.

———. 1996b. Neo-Populism and Neo-Liberalism in Latin America: Unexpected Affinities. *Studies in Comparative International Development* 32, 3 (Fall): 3–31.

———. 2002. *The Politics of Market Reform in Fragile Democracies: Argentina, Brazil, Peru, and Venezuela.* Princeton: Princeton University Press.

———. 2005. The Growing Sustainability of Brazil's Low-Quality Democracy. In *The Third Wave of Democratization in Latin America,* ed. Frances Hagopian and Scott Mainwaring. New York: Cambridge University Press. 90–130.

Zamosc, León. 1986. *The Agrarian Question and the Peasant Movement in Colombia: Struggles of the National Peasant Association, 1967–1981.* New York: Cambridge University Press.

Chapter 2

Liberal and Illiberal Democracy in Latin America

Peter H. Smith
Melissa R. Ziegler

Latin America has embarked on an era of democracy—democracy with adjectives (Collier and Levitsky 1997). While national elections have become competitive, democratic polities throughout the region are frequently described as incomplete, partial, hollow, or shallow (depending on the choice of metaphor). Decisionmaking authority appears to be overconcentrated, hyperpresidentialist, or delegative; popular representation suffers from fragmented political parties and "inchoate" party systems; legal orders and judicial institutions tend to be subservient, biased, or incompetent; policy responses to key issues of the day—poverty, inequality, criminality—seem utterly inadequate (O'Donnell 1994; Mainwaring and Scully 1995; Lustig 1995; Diamond 1999). Throughout this cacophony of qualifiers, there exists a common concern: assessing the quality of democratic life (O'Donnell et al. 2004; Diamond and Molino 2005). All of which tempts one to ask: What kind of democracy has been taking shape in contemporary Latin America?

This issue is here addressed by focusing on the distinction between "liberal" and "illiberal" democracy. As described by Fareed Zakaria, "liberal" democracy requires not only free and fair elections but also constitutional protection of citizens' rights; "illiberal" democracy occurs when free and fair elections combine with systematic denial of constitutional rights. Scanning the world in the late 1990s, Zakaria discovered a pervasive phenomenon:

> Democratically elected regimes, often ones that have been reelected or reaffirmed through referenda, are routinely ignoring constitutional limits on their power and depriving their citizens of basic rights and freedoms. From Peru to the Palestinian Authority, from Sierra Leone to Slovakia, we see the rise of a disturbing phenomenon in international life—illiberal democracy (Zakaria 1997; see also Schedler 2002, 2006).

What has been the situation in contemporary Latin America? This article approaches that question in several ways. It begins with an explication and application of the concepts of liberal and illiberal democracy. Focusing on the period from 1978 to 2004, elsewhere defined as the third and final "cycle" of democratization in twentieth-century Latin America (Smith 2004, 2005; Hagopian and Mainwaring 2005), this study proceeds to measure the incidence and evolution of liberal and illiberal democracy (and nondemocracy). It identifies and traces transitional routes between different kinds of political regime; in particular, it explores the possibility that illiberal democracy might provide a recurrent pathway to liberal democracy. Finally, to assess the logic and circumstances of regime transition, the study examines structural correlates of movements toward political democracy. Are there observable relationships between changes of regime and economic, social, and political variables?[1]

This approach has limitations. One of the principal deficits in contemporary Latin American democracy concerns the rule of law. As described below, the treatment of citizen rights here deals with this question, but only indirectly, as one of several components in a broad operational definition. We recognize that state capacity, governance, and the legal order represent key issues for the assessment of democratic quality. The dissection of liberal versus illiberal democracy can make an important contribution to this enterprise, but it cannot resolve all meaningful questions.

SETTING UP THE PROBLEM: VARIATIONS OF DEMOCRACY

The inquiry begins by exploring the empirical relationship between electoral processes and citizen rights. What will here be called "electoral democracy" refers to the existence of free and fair elections—no more and no less. Most adult citizens must have the right to vote, and there must be genuine competition among rival candidates for national office. In contrast, the notion of "citizen rights" entails a panoply of basic liberties—the freedom to form and join organizations, freedom of expression, access to alternative sources of information (through freedom of the press), and so on. Such protections not only enable groups and individuals to present their views and ideas, they also provide the basis for true competition among power contenders. According to conventional usage, elections constitute a procedural component of democracy; rights make up a substantive component.

The analysis embraces 19 countries of Latin America—all those countries conventionally thought to belong to the region, with the conspicuous exception of Cuba.[2] For each year from 1978 through 2004, electoral systems have been classified according to a threefold scheme. Elections that were free and fair, with open competition for support among the voting-age population, qualify as "democratic." Elections that were free but not fair—when only one candidate had a realistic prospect of winning, when any major candidate or party was effectively prevented from winning, or when elected leaders were obliged to share effective power with or cede it to nonelected groups—are considered to be "semidemocratic." Elections that were nonexistent, openly fraudulent, conducted by authoritarian regimes, or held under military occupation by a foreign power were viewed as "nondemocratic."

To operationalize the concept of citizen rights, multiple sources have been consulted: annual assessments of "civil liberties" by Freedom House, the recently developed Cingranelli-Richards (CIRI) database on human rights, and documentary narratives. This process created an ordered-nominal variable with three values: extensive, limited, and minimal. Extensive citizen rights correspond to "liberal" democracies or semidemocracies; partial but systematic limitations on rights characterize "illiberal" polities; and minimal rights reflect hard-line levels of repression. (See appendix 1 for a detailed explanation of the methodological apparatus.)

The research utilized annual results for each of the 19 countries for every year from 1978 through 2004. To obtain a composite picture of elections and citizen rights,

Table 1. Democracy, Elections, and Citizen Rights: A Typology

Citizen Rights	Character of Elections		
	Free and Fair	Free not Fair	None
Expansive	Liberal Democracy	Liberal/Permissive Semidemocracy	(Null)
Limited	Illiberal Democracy	Illiberal/Restrictive Semidemocracy	Moderate *Dictablanda*
Minimal	(Null)	Repressive Semidemocracy	Hard-Line *Dictadura*

Table 2. Profile of Political Regimes in Latin America, 1978–2004

	Character of Elections		
Civil Liberties	Free and Fair	Free not Fair	None
Expansive	108	6	0
Limited	194	69	41
Minimal	0	25	70
Total	302	100	111

as shown in table 1, the two variables were cross-tabulated. Instead of concocting cumulative scores, that is, the study explored the relationship between these separate dimensions. On theoretical and empirical grounds, two of the nine cells constituted null categories—repressive democracy and liberal dictatorship. This procedure yielded a sevenfold typology.

For the most part, liberal democracies meet the widely accepted criteria for full-fledged democracy (Dahl 1971, 1–3); a case in point would be Chile under the Concert-ación. Regimes that combine free and fair elections with partial but systematic restrictions on citizen rights constitute "illiberal" democracies: Bolivia since the early 1980s and Argentina under Carlos Menem offer illustrative examples. As a matter of definition, regimes without elections—or without meaningful elections—are authoritarian. Hard-line autocracies or *dictaduras* (such as Chile under Augusto Pinochet or Guatemala under Efrain Rios Montt) impose relentless repression on citizen rights; traditional dictatorships, sometimes known as *dictablandas*, often allow the partial enjoyment of civil rights, but only within prescribed limits (as in Brazil during the early 1980s). Autocracies do not promote extensive civil liberties; if they did, they would not be truly autocratic.

Partly because of their interim status, electoral semidemocracies could tolerate varying degrees of civil liberties; some were liberal and some were repressive, but they were most frequently "illiberal." As demonstrated elsewhere (Smith 2005), semidemocracies were often short-lived; under the facade of rigged elections, they furnished convenient exits for authoritarian rulers.

To demonstrate the practical implications of the typology, table 2 presents a cross-tabulation of all country-years from 1978 through 2004. The display reveals an empirical profile of political practice during the "third wave" of political change in Latin America. Democracy (of one sort or another) appeared about 60 percent of the time, semidemocracy 19 percent of the time, and nondemocracy 21 percent of the time. (Appendix 2 contains a country-by-country listing of regimes.) The most striking result is that illiberal democracy, combining free and fair elections with restrictions on citizen rights, was the most common of all types, appearing almost 40 percent of the time. Illiberal democracy proved to be the modal regime.

Moves, Paths, and Transitions

Movement across these categories provides the foundation for the statistical analysis. The typology offers a suggestive opportunity to interpret regime change as a form of political hopscotch, as countries migrate from cell to cell. Mexico, for instance, went from being a soft-line authoritarian regime (under the PRI) to an illiberal semidemocracy (under Carlos Salinas and Ernesto Zedillo) to an illiberal democracy (2000–2001) to a liberal democracy (2002–2004). Chile and Argentina both moved quickly from hard-line dicta-torships through brief illiberal interludes to liberal democracies; Brazil, meanwhile, went from moderate military rule through semidemocracy to illiberal democracy. In contrast, Venezuela and Colombia have moved in the opposite direction, from liberal to illiberal democracy (Colombia) or to illiberal semi-democracy (Venezuela). Utilized this way, the typology allows us to trace political pathways over time.

In many instances, movement across these categories is much more modest in scale than the grand "transitions" described in the prevalent literature, which tends to focus on far-reaching changes from authoritarian to democratic outcomes. Some of the cells in this typology, especially those under electoral semidemocracy, actually depict "moments," "situations," or "arrangements" rather than established "regimes." Under authoritarian rule, back-and-forth changes from "hard-line" to "moderate" usually reflect oscillations, fluc-tuations, or tactical decisions rather than systemic transformations. Indeed, many move-ments between cells can be better understood as shifts, steps, switches, modifications, or changes, rather than full-blown transitions. At the same time, this classification opens up the step-by-step process of democratic transition, allowing the detection and analysis of its component parts. Democracy, as we will see, has often come on the installment plan.

LIBERAL AND ILLIBERAL DEMOCRACY: RHYTHMS, INCIDENCE, AND CHANGE

Competitive elections have clearly become the instrument of choice for allocating politi-cal power in Latin America. Figure 1 demonstrates the steady rise of electoral democracy from 1972 through 2004. In the mid-1970s, an era of stark military repression, only three countries could boast sustained records of free and fair elections: Colombia, Costa Rica, and Venezuela. What became a persistent cycle of democratization first took root in the

Figure 1. The Rise of Electoral Democracy in Latin America, 1972–2004

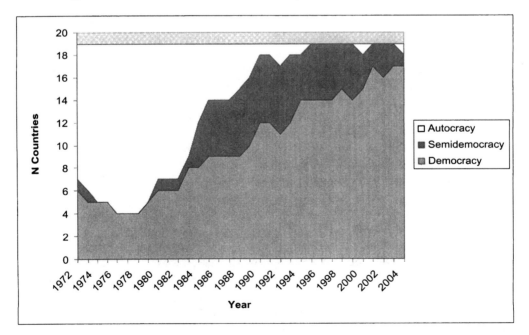

Andes, in Ecuador and Peru, bringing the number of electoral democracies by 1980 up to a total of 6. The ensuing decade witnessed the restoration of democracy throughout much of South America, with the addition by 1985 of Argentina and Uruguay and by 1990 of Brazil and Chile. The 1990s then heralded the installation of essentially new democracies in Mexico, Central America, and the Caribbean. By 2004, 17 out of 19 countries were holding free and fair elections, the sole exceptions being Haiti and Venezuela.

Outright autocracy had all but vanished from the region by 2004. So had semidemocracy, which had served as a "halfway house" between autocracy and democracy from the mid-1980s through the late 1990s and thereby aided the overall process of transition. As electoral democracy continued its spread, however, semidemocracy faded from the picture.

What of the quality of these democracies? Regarding this question, figure 2 displays the year-by-year incidence of liberal and illiberal democracy from 1978 through 2004. Notably conspicuous is the expansion of illiberal democracy. In 1980 there were 3 liberal democracies and 3 illiberal democracies; by 1990 there were 4 liberal democracies and 9 illiberal democracies; during the late 1990s there were as many as 12 illiberal democracies; by the year 2000, there were 6 liberal democracies and 9 illiberal democracies.

Illiberal democracy thus became the most common, pervasive, and visible form of political organization in contemporary Latin America. As noted above, it accounted for 40 percent of all country-years from 1978 through 2004. By the year 2004, more than 310 million people (nearly 60 percent of the regional total) in ten countries were living under illiberal democracy. About 177 million people (in seven countries) were enjoying the fruits of liberal democracy. And 20 million people in two countries (Haiti and Cuba) were enduring nondemocracy. No matter what the criterion—number of countries, millions of people, or accumulated country-years—illiberal democracy emerged as the dominant type of political regime throughout the region.

Figure 2. Liberal and Illiberal Democracy in Latin America, 1978–2004

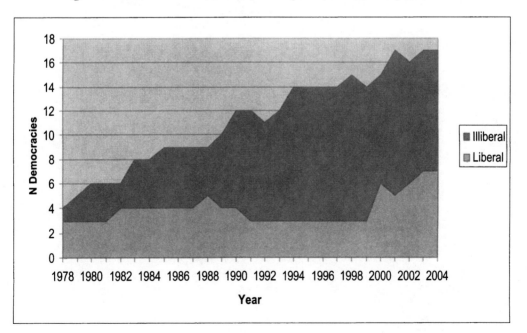

Yet there were subtle signs, starting about the year 2000, that liberal democracy was making incremental gains. Might this become a major trend? How, and under what conditions?

TRANSITIONS: TYPES, RATES, AND DIRECTIONS

Do patterns of political transition reveal identifiable routes from one kind of regime to another? Were there observable pathways toward liberal democracy?

Table 3 presents information on 54 regime changes between 1978 and 2004. It breaks down the data by "origin" and "endpoint," showing the raw number of switches from each kind of regime to all the others. (For the sake of parsimony, the table has combined all versions of semi-democracy into one grouping and has merged hard-line and moderate versions of authoritarianism into a single category of "nondemocracy.") Of 20 departures from nondemocratic rule, for example, 12 moved toward semidemocracy, 6 toward illiberal democracy, and 2 toward liberal democracy.

The array reveals some fascinating tendencies. One is that, as already suggested, illiberal democracy provided the most common form of exit for both nondemocracies and semidemocracies. Only in rare instances did the autocrats cede power directly to full-fledged democracies.[3] Understandably, they preferred to leave power under the protective umbrella of semidemocracy or illiberal democracy.

As a category, illiberal democracy shows considerable staying power. It constitutes the most frequent destination, accounting for no fewer than 22 out of the 54 endpoints.

Table 3. Regime Transitions: Origins and Endpoints, 1978–2004

	To	
From	Regime	N
Nondemocracy	Nondemocracy	—
	Semidemocracy	12
	Illiberal Democracy	6
	Liberal Democracy	2
	Subtotal	20
Semidemocracy	Nondemocracy	4
	Semidemocracy	—
	Illiberal Democracy	9
	Liberal Democracy	1
	Subtotal	14
Illiberal Democracy	Nondemocracy	2
	Semidemocracy	3
	Illiberal Democracy	—
	Liberal Democracy	8
	Subtotal	13
Liberal Democracy	Nondemocracy	0
	Semidemocracy	0
	Illiberal Democracy	7
	Liberal Democracy	—
	Subtotal	7
	Total	54

Among the 15 illiberal democracies in place at any time during the 1990s, moreover, 8 were still going strong by 2004, and 2 others would return to the fold after detours elsewhere.[4] (Cases in point were Ecuador and Peru, the countries that initiated this whole cycle in the first place!) Illiberal democracy was not merely a stopping point for transitions toward fuller democracy; it was a distinct subtype of political regime.

At the same time, illiberal democracy would provide an identifiable gateway to liberal democracy: out of 13 exits, 8 moved in the direction of liberal democracy. (On the other 5 occasions, illiberal rule slipped back to nondemocracy or semidemocracy.) To put it another way, of 11 transitions leading to liberal democracy, 8 came through illiberal democracy, only 2 emerged from nondemocracy, and just 1 from semi-democracy. To this degree, illiberal democracy provided a common precondition—neither necessary nor sufficient, but nonetheless recurrent—for the achievement of liberal democracy.

This relationship functioned in reverse, as well. Liberal democracy reverted to illiberal democracy on eight occasions, but it never—not once—gave way to nondemocracy or semidemocracy. One implication is obvious: the most secure context for the survival of liberal democracy is liberal democracy itself. Another implication concerns plausible courses of action: democratic leaders could curb citizen rights with relative impunity, but they could not so easily renege on the basic promise of free and fair elections.

Through basic arithmetic, table 3 conveys additional messages. One is that regime changes are rare events. Among the 513 country-years in the analysis, regime alterations (of any kind) occurred just over 10 percent of the time. Transitions are less frequent than we sometimes think; and democratic transitions, as a subtype, have been especially uncommon. Changes in democratic directions took place in less than 8 percent of all country-years, while shifts toward liberal democracy occurred only 2.5 percent of the time. Regime transitions ended up in liberal democracy in only 11 out of 47 transitions from other starting points (that is, 24 percent of the time), while illiberal democracy was the outcome of 54 percent of potential transitions. In this sense, liberal democracy has been a *rara avis*; it did not mark the end of most regime changes. Still a further implication is that full democracy often results from an incremental process, rather than appearing all at once; democratization arrived one step at a time.

The data reveal yet another point: teleological conceptions of "democratic transitions" run a substantial risk of empirical error. According to table 3, 70 percent of all regime changes moved in a democratic direction while no less than 30 percent moved in an undemocratic or authoritarian direction. There was substantial and repeated backsliding. With regard to Latin America, at least, there is absolutely no reason to assume either that all transitions end up in democracy, or even that all transitions move toward democracy. The time has come to dispense with the "transition paradigm" (Carothers 2002). It does not fit the facts.

CORRELATES OF CHANGE: SEARCHING FOR DETERMINANTS

Under what conditions do regimes move toward full democracy? This question is explored through a statistical analysis of political transitions. The analysis thus raises a crucial issue of special importance for Latin America: what are the structural conditions that facilitate transitions from illiberal to liberal democracy?

Organizing the Analysis

To operationalize these concerns, two dichotomous dependent variables were constructed. The first, Alldem, is coded 1 for all transitions in the direction of liberal democracy, including movements from non-democracy or semidemocracy toward electoral democracy (illiberal or liberal) and from illiberal democracy to liberal democracy; it is otherwise coded as zero. This variable is designed to capture overall dynamics of democratic transition and expansion. Its correlates should reflect conditions encouraging Latin American countries to expand the scope of democratic governance over the past quarter century.

The second variable, Illibtolib, focuses exclusively on transitions from illiberal to liberal democracy. It is designed to illuminate conditions that lead illiberal democracies in Latin America to broaden the civil liberties of citizens. Taken together, these two variables make it possible to compare transitions toward fuller democracy from any starting point with the more restricted cases of illiberal to liberal democracy.[5]

The independent variables include those economic and political factors most commonly associated with the likelihood of regime transition. To explore potential effects of socioeconomic development, the study examined the effects of current GDP, of percentage of the workforce in agriculture, and of school enrollment rates. The inquiry also constructed dummy variables for subregion–Central America versus South America–considering that U.S. pressure and civil war during the 1980s may have exerted exceptional pressures on political arrangements throughout the beleaguered isthmus. Their conceptual appeal notwithstanding, none of these variables revealed significant relationships with regime change in the battery of tests.[6]

After considerable experimentation, parsimonious models were developed, with a carefully selected subset of economic and political factors. To begin, it was assumed that all regimes benefit from economic stability and prosperity. A primary function of the state in modern times is to cushion citizens from global economic fluctuations through prudent fiscal policies; when regimes are unable to control inflation or encourage economic growth, we would expect a weakened mandate to govern. Accordingly, the analysis examined changes in Gross Domestic Product (GDP Growth), GDP per capita (GDP/capita), and inflation (Inflation, using the lagged inflation deflator) to see if these economic indicators helped predict regime transition.

Further explored was the impact of social upheaval—measured as the number of general strikes (Strikes), riots (Riots), and antigovernment demonstrations (Demonstrations). On the one hand, such developments could reflect (or intensify) demands for full democracy and lead to elections or liberalization. On the other hand, they might pose grievous threats to the socioeconomic order and encourage rulers to clamp down on citizen rights; or, alternatively, they might provoke nondemocratic actors to seize the reins of government. Either way, strikes and demonstrations seem likely to foster instability and change.

In the political realm, it is commonly argued that the likelihood of democratic transition depends on the existence, nature, and extent of prior democratic experience. The underlying hypothesis suggests that earlier experience with democracy reduces uncertainty about the new regime, thus assuaging anxiety among weary and wary elites. The research explored this idea with a variable measuring the simple number of previous experiences with democracy (Previous). Similarly, it tested whether democracies are more or less likely to undergo transition the longer they stay in power, using the duration of electoral democracy (DemDuration) as an empirical measure.

The study also examined whether electoral cycles, specifically presidential elections (Election), make changes in expansion of citizen rights more likely. In all but the most repressive regimes, presidential elections can provide focal points for political change. In particular, opposition candidates who campaign for less corruption and greater citizen participation have strong incentives to fulfill such promises. (Appendix 3 presents operational definitions for all our independent variables.)

As table 3 shows, regime change was a rare occurrence. Because the dependent variables are dichotomous, furthermore, logit estimates offer the appropriate techniques. Given the relative scarcity of transition years, however, logit standard errors for these dependent variables would be skewed. To correct for this bias, the correlates were analyzed with Rare Events Logit, hereafter referred to as ReLogit (Tomz et al. 1999; King and Zeng 2001). ReLogit's corrections are most important when sample size is around or under 500 and observation of event (coded 1) occurs no more than 5 percent of the time, both of which apply to this analysis.

Modeling Regime Change

The basic results appear in table 4. Here let us focus on the direction of associations (positive or negative) and on their statistical significance, measured through standard errors and p values. (The magnitude of ReLogit coefficients has no meaningful interpretation.) "First difference" results also are presented to show how movement in one variable changes the likelihood of transitions.

Cursory examination reveals that the independent variables have limited explanatory power. Neither model generates overwhelmingly accurate predictions of regime transition.[7] This is not entirely surprising; transitions often occur unexpectedly, or fail to happen when we might think they should. Nonetheless, the analysis found some significant values in the models, and the signs of the coefficients were mostly consistent with expectations.

The Alldem model shows that inflation, prior duration of democracy, and presidential election years are significant predictors of movements toward democracy. Illiberal to liberal transitions are clearly related to inflation and, to a lesser extent, to presidential election years (with a positive but not quite significant coefficient).

Table 4. Correlates of Democratization: ReLogit Results

	Dependent Variables	
Independent Variables	Transitions Toward Liberal Democracy (Alldem)	Illiberal to Liberal Transitions (Illibtolib)
Socioeconomic Variables		
GDP Growth	.0238 (.0342)	.0100 (.0499)
GDP/capita	.0001 (.0001)	.0002 (.0002)
Inflation	.0002 (.0001)[c]	.0016 (.0004)[a]
Strikes	−.0726 (.2705)	.2326 (.4097)
Demonstrations	−.0121 (.0951)	.0216 (.1359)
Riots	.0033 (.2420)	.1486 (.4642)
Political Variables		
Previous	.1856 (.1729)	−.0240 (.2869)
DemDuration	−.0799 (.0366)[b]	−.0065 (.0214)
Election	1.5392 (.4875)[a]	1.1841 (.7417)
N	513	513

[a]Significant at .01 level.
[b]Significant at .05 level.
[c]Significant at .10 level.
Standard errors in parentheses.

Table 5. Key Predictors of Transitions: First Difference Results

Independent Variables (Starting value, First difference value)	Transitions Toward Fuller Democracy (Alldem)	Illiberal to Liberal Transitions (Illibtolib)
Inflation (Median value = 16, Argentina in 1984 = 382)	.03 (0% to .07%)[a,c]	1% (.02% to 3%)[b]
DemDuration (Median value = 19, Costa Rica = 52)	−1% (−3% to −.1%)[b]	−.2% (−1% to 3%)[c]
Election (No presidential Election = 0, Presidential election = 1)	15% (2% to 27%)[b]	3% (.01% to 13%)[c]

[a]Significant at .05 level.
[b]Significant at .01 level.
[c]Confidence intervals estimated at .10 level.

To gauge the relative strength of associations, table 5 displays first-difference analysis for those socioeconomic and political variables found to have statistically significant relationships with Alldem and Illibtolib. As presented here, values in the table identify, for a given change in an independent variable, how much more or less likely is a transition, all else held constant at the median level. Economic indicators, except for inflation, performed poorly in the models. The social upheaval indicators were not significant in the models, but their contrasting relationships to the dependent variables merit close examination. We return to this later.

The common-sense expectation is that the ability of any type of regime to promote the economic well-being of its citizens should be linked to its staying power. This relationship has generally been shown to be true, although the current wave of democratization may differ from earlier transitional periods (Remmer 1990; Gasiorowski 1995; Smith 2005). A related analysis has shown that the relationship between GDP growth and transitions away from democracy is negative at a statistically significant level: the greater the increase in GDP, the lower the incidence of democratic collapse (Smith and Ziegler 2006). And as shown in table 4, economic growth is positively associated with transitions toward fuller democracy (Alldem) and with the expansion of civil liberties in democracy (Illibtolib), although these relationships are not statistically significant. Similarly, levels of development, proxied by GDP per capita, bear no observable relationship with either transition variable. Democracies do not live or die by bread alone.

Like low levels of economic growth, high levels of inflation would be expected to have destabilizing effects (Gasiorowski 1995; Kaufman 1979; Epstein 1984). Hyperinflation is the quintessential short-term economic shock. It is devastating to citizens who see the value of their earnings plummet and face the future with tremendous uncertainty. It exacerbates poverty and inequality. It evaporates savings, discourages investment, and promotes extensive capital flight. It is especially tough on the working poor and salaried sectors of the middle class, who, understandably, begin to question the ability of incumbent regimes to manage the economy and protect them from sudden fluctuations.

Inflation is a scourge on all leaders: it undermines whatever regime happens to be in power at the time. Outraged citizens are likely to press their economic demands by engaging in public demonstrations, throwing their support to opposition parties, or clamoring for firm and effective leadership. Leaders might respond in various ways. In nondemocratic or semidemocratic settings, they might attempt to quell unrest by modestly expanding outlets for the expression of discontent and grievances; alternatively, they might resort to repression, raising the cost of dissent for the sake of regime continuance. Under illiberal democracy, they might have to confront the unsettling but unavoidable prospect of free and fair elections. Wherever support for regimes is contingent on the provision of economic stability, high inflation would be more likely to spur transition.

The relationship between inflation and transition, weak but significant in the Alldem model, takes explicit form in the Illibtolib analysis: the greater the level of inflation, the greater the likelihood of expansion in citizen rights. Yet the link between inflationary spirals and transitions from illiberal to liberal democracy is deceptively modest at moderate levels of inflation. A change from the median inflation rate to a high value increases the likelihood of illiberal to liberal transition by merely 1 percent. Hyperinflation tells another story. At the highest values of the inflation deflator variable, the statistical likelihood of transition ranges from 10 percent to 82 percent! Although this result is based on a small number of observations, it has compelling interpretive significance.[8]

Three social upheaval variables were tested: general strikes, antigovernment demonstrations, and riots. As stated earlier, the association of these variables to democratic transitions could theoretically go in either direction. Governments could expand civil liberties to appease the discontented, or they could restrict citizen freedom and halt the democratic process to promote domestic stability. The opposite effect of the general strikes and antigovernment demonstrations variables commands attention. It is possible that nondemocratic rulers see general strikes and antigovernment demonstrations as threats to public safety and respond by repressing civil liberties. These social upheaval independent variables thus showed a negative, although insignificant, relationship to Alldem in the model. In democratic settings, by contrast, general strikes and antigovernment demonstrations (especially orderly ones) seemed to give democratically elected leaders of illiberal democracies the impression that repression would be ineffective or counterproductive. Antigovernment demonstrations and general strikes are positively related to transitions from illiberal to liberal democracy (IllibtoLib). The most destabilizing social protest of all, riots, are positively associated with both dependent variables. These results suggest caution in the use of aggregated "social disturbance" variables for the analysis of political transformation.

As shown in table 5, the duration variable DemDuration shows a significant and negative coefficient in the Alldem model. (This argument might at first seem circular, but not in light of the number and frequency of the transitions observed.) A change in the survival of electoral democracy variable (DemDuration) from the median value of 19 years to Costa Rica's 2004 value of 52 years would decrease the likelihood of a transition toward fuller democracy by 1 percent. Such a finding provides modest evidence for the notion of regime "consolidation"; the longer regimes last, whether democratic or authoritarian, the less susceptible they are to transition. Previous studies have found no observable relationship between length of democracy and likelihood of transition (Przeworski et al. 1996). Although the results here are hardly conclusive, they suggest that regime inertia or "momentum" might make alteration less likely. On the other hand, the findings produced no supporting evidence for the proposition that prior experience with democracy (Previous) increases the likelihood of greater democracy.

The results for the presidential election variable are robust for transitions to fuller democracy. Its relationship to Alldem is positive and statistically significant at the .01 level. As argued here, presidential campaigns can lead to subsequent improvements in degrees of democratic practice. Conspicuous cases of crucial elections coincided with the collapse of authoritarian regimes in Ecuador in 1979, Uruguay in 1985, and Chile in 1989. Other key elections occurred in Argentina in 1989 and 2003, Brazil in 1989, Guatemala in 1995, Honduras in 1981, Mexico in 2000, and Nicaragua in 1990.[9]

The strength of the relationships between the presidential election year and the transition variables emerges with sharp clarity. States are 15 percent more likely to experience a transition in a democratic direction (not necessarily ending in liberal democracy but going up the scale) in a presidential election year than in a year off the election cycle, all else equal. This is the strongest result in the Alldem model. This relationship is positive (and virtually significant) for Illibtolib transitions as well, with a predicted 3 percent improvement in chances for a shift to liberal democracy.

This study has argued that high degrees of inflation encourage transitions from illiberal to liberal democracy. We can surmise that high levels of inflation place stress on illiberal democracies, often provoking such orderly forms of protest as general strikes, and that the response to these popular demands frequently consists of a relaxation of state-imposed controls, which, by definition, leads to an expansion of citizen rights.

That expansion, in turn, might help explain the coincidence between electoral cycles and changes from illiberal to liberal democracy. Most of these transitions took place around the time of national elections: Argentina in 1983–84 and 2000, Ecuador in 1988, the Dominican Republic in 1982 and 2000, Chile in 1989–90, and Panama in 1999–2000.[10] In addition, it took Vicente Fox just over one year to bring Mexico into the fold of liberal democracy. A conspicuous feature of these elections is that they resulted in victory for the political opposition: one thinks not only of Alfonsín, Aylwin, and Fox, but also of Fernando de la Rúa, Rodrigo Borja, Leonel Fernández Reyna, even Mireya Moscoso. Running on platforms against incumbent (illiberal) regimes, antiestablishment candidates were obliged to fulfill campaign promises for greater freedom of speech, press, political affiliation—and for the impartial rule of law. Moreover, this kind of policy reform incurs only modest short-term costs: it is much easier to lift controls on dissent than to impose them. (In the longer term, public debates and transparent disclosure might make it more difficult for the incumbent president or party to win re-election, but that is a separate matter.) One thing seems surprisingly clear: elections and leadership can bring about substantial changes in the political lives of the citizens. To put it in a nutshell, free and fair elections are the Achilles' heel of illiberal democracies.

CONCLUSIONS

During the course of the "third wave," political change in Latin America bore a distinctive signature: it was an era of illiberal democracy. Almost everywhere, the combination of free and fair elections with partial but systematic repression of citizen rights became a dominant and defining trend. According to a broad variety of measures—number of countries, shares of population, percentages of total country-years—illiberal democracy has reigned supreme. To be sure, liberal democracy has made incremental gains in recent years, but there is no self-evident reason to believe that it will displace illiberal democracy in the foreseeable future.

Changes of regime are moments of maximum uncertainty. The data in this study show that teleological presumptions about the "democratic" direction of political change are wholly unwarranted. Since the late 1970s, most regime changes have led to something other than liberal democracy. The most common destination has been illiberal democracy. While illiberal democracy has helped to forge a path toward liberal democracy, a good deal of backsliding has occurred as well. Even after long periods in power, as revealed by the quantitative data, liberal democracy has often succumbed to illiberal democracy.

What brings about liberal democracy? This analysis reveals that correlates between transitions to liberal democracy and a host of independent variables—ranging from changes in GDP to antigovernment demonstrations—do not meet basic levels of statistical significance. These nonresults are very meaningful, however, in that they allow us to rule out—and discard—a large array of plausible hypotheses. This work has cleared away the underbrush.

The most prominent structural determinant of transition from illiberal to liberal democracy has proven to be high levels of inflation. It is the interpretation of this study that under illiberal democracy, citizens are willing to accept constraints on dissent in exchange for the promise of economic security. By their nature, inflationary spirals rupture this quasi-authoritarian bargain. Protest mounts and pressure increases.

Social disturbance lurks in the minds of all leaders. Politicians of any kind would prefer to avoid antigovernment demonstrations and economic strikes; they are high-profile demonstrations of regime failures, and they can have notable economic consequences. This analysis demonstrates that such social behavior can have meaningful political effects. Under authoritarian rule, democratization of any kind is less likely when general strikes and antigovernment demonstrations occur. Once free elections are in place, however, expansion of citizen rights is more likely when citizens express these political and economic demands. The detection of these differential effects of popular mobilization in this study makes a significant contribution to scholarly work on democratic transitions.

In illiberal democracies, citizens can vote for leaders and parties of the opposition. Once in power, newly elected leaders can repeal constraints on civil liberties. This combination of grassroots activism with electoral opportunity and elite leadership paves the way toward liberal democracy. In this scenario, the achievement of full-fledged democracy depends on three factors: the strength of civil society, the availability of channels for expression, and the responsiveness of leadership, especially presidential leadership.

Such developments lay bare the internal contradictions of illiberal regimes: the inherent tension between freedom of elections and restrictions on expression. This paradox defines the core of contemporary politics in Latin America. As so often occurs, such logical inconsistency does not necessarily require effective resolution. It formed a keystone for the process of democratic change, and it might well endure into the future.

APPENDIX 1: CLASSIFICATION AND MEASUREMENT

The purpose of this essay is to apply Fareed Zakaria's notion of "illiberal democracy" to political realities in contemporary Latin America and to see what we can learn from this exercise. In pursuit of this goal, the study offers ways to improve on Zakaria's own methods of empirical measurement.[11] It seeks to "unpack" the concept of democracy and explore the interplay of key component parts. To borrow a phrase from Adam Przeworski et al., the association between these facets of democracy "is best left open for investigation, rather than resolved by definition" (2000, 33–34). For this reason, composite scales of degrees of democracy, such as POLITY IV, were of no use for this enterprise.

Electoral Democracy

This analysis begins with a rigorously minimalist definition of electoral democracy. It regards elections as "democratic" if they were free and fair: if adult suffrage was more or less universal, if all serious candidates could run, if any candidate could win, if votes were counted accurately, if victory went to the contender with the highest number of votes (according to transparent decision rules), and if the winner acquired effective authority as a result.

Every year from 1978 through 2004 for 19 countries of Latin America was coded according to those criteria. The categorization is based on qualitative judgments deriving from firsthand observation, secondary sources, news reports, and in-depth consultations with professional colleagues. Also scrutinized were quantitative data on voter eligibility, voter turnout, and victory margins.

Numerous instances were encountered of formal elections (often considered "democratic") that met some but not all of the criteria. These were classified as "semidemocratic." Such cases occurred when

- Only one candidate had a reasonable prospect of winning—as in Mexico (1988–99), Peru (1993–2000), and Venezuela (1999–2004).
- Constraints were placed on candidacies—as in Brazil (1985–89) and Argentina (2002).
- The armed forces held true power—as in El Salvador (1984–93), Guatemala (1986–95), and Honduras (1981–96).
- A foreign presence exerted undue influence—as in Panama (1990–93).

These subcategories are analytically distinct from one another. In principle, they might deserve separate coding; in practice, they tend to overlap. Yet they were relatively infrequent, so all such occurrences were grouped under a single semidemocratic rubric.

The initiation of "democratic" or "semidemocratic" periods was coded according to year of first national election. Nondemocracy was a residual category, except for years of military coups, which are positively coded as nondemocratic. Years of military occupation by a foreign power (e.g., Haiti 2004) were also coded as nondemocratic.

Citizen Rights

The second task was to obtain a suitable indicator for citizen rights. After many trials and much error, a composite variable was constructed. The first step was to consult annual ratings from Freedom House (FH) on "civil liberties," which focus on the presence of "freedoms to develop views, institutions, and personal autonomy apart from the state." The FH checklist includes such items as

- Freedom of expression and belief, including freedom of the press.
- Rights of assembly, association, and organization.
- An impartial rule of law and the protection of human rights.
- Personal autonomy and economic rights, including choice of residence and occupation.

This inventory spans an extremely broad range, including some phenomena (such as criminal warfare or economic bondage) that do not necessarily reflect the designs, intentions, or capacities of state authorities.

Through assessment by experts, countries received scores ranging from 1 (most extensive) to 7 (virtually nonexistent). FH scores thus represent real-time judgments by well-informed and fair-minded observers. Zakaria himself relied on FH measures in his original article.

As scholars have observed, Freedom House indicators for "civil liberties" tend to be highly correlated with separate FH measures for "political rights." Within our set of Latin American country-years, for example, the Pearson's r coefficient for the seven-point scales comes out to +.821. It comes as no surprise to learn that the relationship is positive.

Indeed, this feature works to our advantage, because the notion of "illiberal democracy" concerns constraints not only on civil liberties but also on "political rights"—free participation in the political process, unfettered expression of political opinions, the right to join political organizations, and so on.[12]

Given the breadth of the FH definition, the ratings were collapsed into three categories:

- Scores of 1 or 2 indicate "extensive" civil liberties corresponding to liberal polities.
- Scores of 3 and 4 reflect "moderate" civil liberties characteristic of illiberal systems.
- Scores of 5 to 7 reveal "minimal" or nonexistent liberties under repressive regimes.[13]

Contrary to conventional wisdom, a deliberate decision was made to move from a higher to lower level of measurement. This was done for technical and conceptual reasons. From the beginning, the notion of citizen rights was construed as a three-point ordered nominal variable.

The second step was to check the validity of the FH-based variable against the recently developed Cingranelli-Richards (CIRI) database on human rights, which encompasses polities around the world from 1980 to the present. This exercise focused on two composite measures: the CIRI "physical integrity" index (0 through 8, from worst to best), based on quantitative measures of political imprisonment, torture, disappearance, and extrajudicial killing; and an "empowerment rights" index (0 through 10, worst to best), based on quantitative measures of freedom of movement and speech, workers' rights, political participation, and freedom of religion (Cingranelli and Richards 1999). The concern here was straightforward: how does the Freedom House civil liberties measure compare with the CIRI indicators?

They turn out to be closely related. The correlation between the seven-point Freedom House civil liberties scale and the eight-point CIRI physical integrity scale comes out to +.554 (with one scale inverted); the correlation with empowerment rights is +.588. It is interesting that both of these correlations are higher than the association between the two CIRI measures, which comes out, for this study's cases, to +.343. The FH civil liberties variable occupies a middle ground between the two CIRI scales and thus constitutes a valid foundation for an omnibus indicator of what this study refers to as citizen rights.

As a further test, the CIRI data were collapsed into a three-point scale and the results cross-tabulated with the three-point FH indicator. Tables 6 and 7 display the outcomes.

The correspondence is very close. The gamma coefficients for the two tables are nearly identical: +.689 for physical integrity, +.685 for personal empowerment. Equally important, very few observations (4 for physical integrity, 7 for personal empowerment) are in contrasting cells (extensive–low, minimal–high). These discrepancies were explored with care and, for selected country-years; appropriate adjustments were made in scores for citizen rights.[14]

Table 6. FH Civil Liberties and CIRI Physical Integrity Index (N = 456)

Freedom House Score	CIRI Score		
	Low (0–2)	Medium (3–5)	High (6–8)
Minimal (5–7)	33	38	2
Moderate (3–4)	77	145	54
Extensive (1–2)	2	38	67

Table 7. FH Civil Liberties and CIRI Empowerment Rights Index (N = 455)

Freedom House Score	CIRI Score		
	Low (0–3)	Medium (4–7)	High (8–10)
Minimal (5–7)	13	52	7
Moderate (3–4)	5	79	194
Extensive (1–2)	0	13	92

As a third and final step, the notion of citizen rights was bolstered with qualitative evidence from two key sources: the Committee to Protect Journalists' annual *Attacks on the Press* and the U.S. State Department's *County Reports on Human Rights Practices*. It should also be noted that the annual FH reports contain summary descriptions of the events and developments that could precipitate a move from one category of civil liberties to another: release of political prisoners, lifting of press censorship laws, legalization of labor unions, prosecution of corrupt judges, allowance for manifestations, and so on. This documentary evidence proved to be essential both for confirming the face validity of the citizen rights scale and for providing an empirical window into the practical meaning of illiberal democracy (Smith 2005, chap. 10).

With such reassurances, the analysis proceeded. One unavoidable inconvenience was that coding procedures are not neatly synchronized: assessments of electoral democracy are based on qualitative observation of periodic events occurring in short periods of time, whereas evaluations of civil liberties are based on annual reviews of cumulative processes stretching over entire years. Changes in electoral scores are clearly traceable to specific occurrences (i.e., elections); in contrast, changes in civil liberties scores might be due to gradual alterations in objective conditions (e.g., tolerance of political opposition). This disjuncture can produce apparent "hiccups" and inconsistencies in coding. They are infrequent, however, and they do not distort the overall results.

APPENDIX 2: POLITICAL REGIME BY COUNTRY, 1978–2004

Argentina
1978–1980 Hard-line nondemocracy
1981–1982 Moderate nondemocracy
1983 Illiberal democracy
1984–1989 Liberal democracy
1990–2000 Illiberal democracy
2000 Liberal democracy
2001 Illiberal democracy
2002 Illiberal semidemocracy
2003–2004 Liberal democracy

Bolivia
1978–1979 Moderate nondemocracy
1980 Hard-line nondemocracy
1981–1982 Moderate nondemocracy
1983–2004 Illiberal democracy

Brazil
1978–1984 Moderate nondemocracy
1985–1987 Liberal semidemocracy
1988 Illiberal semidemocracy
1989 Liberal semidemocracy
1990–2004 Illiberal democracy

Chile
1978–1987 Hard-line nondemocracy
1988 Moderate nondemocracy
1989 Illiberal democracy
1990–2004 Liberal democracy

Colombia
1978–2004 Illiberal democracy

Costa Rica
1978–2004 Liberal democracy

Dominican Republic
1978 Liberal democracy
1979–1980 Illiberal democracy
1981–1983 Liberal democracy
1984–1999 Illiberal democracy
2000–2004 Liberal democracy

Ecuador
1978 Moderate nondemocracy
1979–1984 Liberal democracy
1985–1987 Illiberal democracy
1988–1990 Liberal democracy
1991–1995 Illiberal democracy
1996–1999 Illiberal semidemocracy
2000 Moderate nondemocracy
2001–2004 Illiberal democracy

El Salvador
1978 Hard-line nondemocracy
1979 Moderate nondemocracy
1980 Illiberal semidemocracy
1981–1983 Hard-line nondemocracy
1984 Repressive semidemocracy
1985–1993 Illiberal semidemocracy
1994–2004 Illiberal democracy

Guatemala
1978 Moderate nondemocracy
1979–1984 Hard-line nondemocracy
1985 Moderate nondemocracy
1986–1990 Illiberal semidemocracy
1991–1995 Repressive semidemocracy
1996–2004 Illiberal democracy

Haiti
1978–1985 Hard-line nondemocracy
1986 Moderate nondemocracy
1987–1989 Hard-line nondemocracy
1990 Illiberal democracy
1991–1994 Hard-line nondemocracy
1995–2003 Repressive semidemocracy
2004 Hard-line nondemocracy

Honduras
1978–1980 Moderate nondemocracy
1981–1996 Illiberal semidemocracy
1997–2004 Illiberal democracy

Mexico
1978–1987 Moderate nondemocracy
1988–1999 Illiberal semidemocracy
2000–2001 Illiberal democracy
2002–2004 Liberal democracy

Nicaragua
1978–1983 Hard-line nondemocracy
1984–1987 Repressive semidemocracy
1988 Illiberal semidemocracy
1989 Repressive semidemocracy
1990–2004 Illiberal democracy

Panama
1978–1979 Hard-line nondemocracy
1980–1983 Moderate nondemocracy
1984–1985 Illiberal semidemocracy
1986 Moderate nondemocracy
1987–1989 Hard-line nondemocracy
1990–1991 Liberal semidemocracy
1992–1993 Illiberal semidemocracy
1994–1999 Illiberal democracy
2000–2004 Liberal democracy

Paraguay
1978–1988 Hard-line nondemocracy
1989 Moderate nondemocracy
1990–1992 Illiberal semidemocracy
1993–2004 Illiberal democracy

Peru
1978–1979 Moderate nondemocracy
1980–1991 Illiberal democracy
1992 Hard-line nondemocracy
1993 Repressive semidemocracy
1994–2000 Illiberal semidemocracy
2001–2004 Illiberal democracy

Uruguay
1978–1980 Hard-line nondemocracy
1981–1984 Moderate nondemocracy
1985–2004 Liberal democracy

Venezuela
1978–1988 Liberal democracy
1989–1998 Illiberal democracy
1999 Illiberal semidemocracy
2000–2001 Repressive semidemocracy
2002–2004 Illiberal semidemocracy

APPENDIX 3: VARIABLES, DATA, AND SOURCES

	Coding	Source
Dependent Variables		
Transitions toward Liberal democracy (Alldem)	0 = No transition in that year 1 = Any transition in the direction of liberal democracy in that year (e.g. a transition from semidemocracy to illiberal democracy is coded 1)	Smith and Ziegler 2006
Transitions from Illiberal to liberal Democracy (Illibtolib)	0 = No transition from illiberal to liberal democracy 1 = Transition from illiberal to liberal democracy	Smith and Ziegler 2006
Independent Variables: Political		
Previous experience with democracy (Previous)	Number of Democratic Experiences (e.g., 0 = Never Democratic; 4 = 4 transitions to electoral democracy)	Smith 2005, appendix 1
Duration of Regime (RegimeLength)	Regime duration in years, coded each year	Smith and Ziegler 2006
Duration of democracy (DemDuration)	Democratic duration in years, coded each year (e.g., Costa Rica = 1 in 1953. 21 in 1973)	Smith and Ziegler 2006; Smith 2005
GDP Per Capita (GDPPerCap)	GDP / Population	World Bank 2004
Presidential election year (Election)	0 = No presidential election in that year; 1 = Presidential election year. Where alldem or illibtolib transition preceded the election, cases excluded	Smith and Ziegler 2006; Smith 2005
Prior experience with democracy (Prior)	0 = No prior experience with democracy 1 = Any prior experience with democracy	Smith and Ziegler 2006; Smith 2005
Subregion	0 = South America 1 = Central America and Caribbean	World Bank 2004
Independent Variables: Socioeconomic		
Antigovernment demonstrations (Demonstrations)	Number of antigovernment demonstrations	Banks 2006
Riots (Riots)	Number of riots	Banks 2006
General strikes (Strikes)	Number of general strikes	Banks 2006
GDP growth (GDP Growth)	Annual 1%	World Bank 2004
Lagged inflation Deflator (Inflation)	Annual 1%, 1 year lag	World Bank 2004
Current GDP (GDP)	GDP in current U.S. dollars	World Bank 2004

	Coding	Source
Agriculture, value added (Agriculture)	% of GDP	World Bank 2004
Secondary school enrollment (Enrollment)	Enrollment as % of age group	World Bank 2004

NOTES

1 In method and approach, this study bears a distinct resemblance to the path-breaking 2005 essay by Scott Mainwaring and Aníbal Pérez-Liñan. The principal difference is that Mainwaring and Pérez-Liñan seek to explain the origins and timing of the post-1978 cycle of democratization, whereas the attempt here is to understand political alterations within the cycle itself. The classification of political regimes here is therefore more refined than theirs. And while they conclude that changes in the international political environment were essential to the upsurge of democracy in Latin America, that factor was more or less constant during the entire period of the present study.

2 Cuba is excluded because it did not hold competitive elections for national executive office during this period (Smith 2005, 24).

3 Argentina and Chile present ambiguous instances, since key transitional years—1983 and 1990, respectively—are classified as "illiberal democracies" as a result of coding conventions. Reconsideration of these moments as direct transitions from autocracy to liberal democracy would not seriously affect the overall result.

4 Not counting Mexico, which became an electoral (illiberal) democracy in the year 2000.

5 An earlier version of this article also tested all transitions of any type, transitions away from democracy, transitions to liberal democracy from any starting point, transitions to illiberal democracy from any starting point, and transitions from liberal to illiberal democracy (Smith and Ziegler 2006).

6 Other variables not included because of missing observations: unemployment rate, public sector wages, and percent of government expenditure on the military.

7 The ReLogit program does not provide a "goodness-of-fit" test akin to an R2 in OLS. It is possible to calculate "pseudo R2" values, as in logit, but it is not recommended (private communication with Gary King). The closest way to judge goodness of fit in ReLogit is to test its predictive value from the number of correctly predicted transitions.

8 The upper value used in the first difference analysis, 382, is the inflation deflator value for Argentina in 1984. This is high, but does not approach the highest values in the sample, 12,339 (Bolivia 1985) and 13,611 (Nicaragua 1988). The first difference values are larger even for middle-range higher values, such as Argentina in 1989 (inflation deflator value of 3,057), but the prediction range is quite large in these extreme values.

9 In some cases, the transition occurred in the year following the presidential election. A lagged version of the presidential election variable yields statistically significant relationships with both Alldem and Illibtolib, thus emphasizing the importance of this electoral phenomenon. Yet it has the disadvantage of reducing the significance of the inflation variable, which is essential for this study's overall interpretation.

10 Argentina and Chile were special cases, because their times of "illiberal democracy" in 1983 and 1989 were one-year periods of political transition rather than established illiberal regimes (see note 3 above).

11 Zakaria considers all countries with combined Freedom House scores between 5 and 10 to be "democratizing," and regards those instances where "political rights" scores are better than "civil liberties" scores as "illiberal democracies." This means that a country with a 4 on political rights and a 5 on civil liberties would qualify as an illiberal democracy. In contrast, this study insists

that countries must hold genuinely free and fair elections in order to be any kind of democracy, liberal or illiberal.

12 The FH political rights measure itself was not used, however, because it embraces the electoral process, which was scored according to this study's own scale.

13 In effect, these are equal-size intervals, because FH scores of 7 appeared in only three instances among the 513 country-years (in Haiti under Cedras)

14 These discrepancies tend to result from sharp variation between the two CIRI measures. In table 6, for example, Paraguay 1988 received a positive score on physical integrity—given the relative infrequency of torture and disappearances, hence the inconsistency with Freedom House— along with a low rating on empowerment. In table 7, Peru 1991 scored well on the empowerment index but very poorly on physical integrity, given the violent, state-led campaign against Sendero Luminoso. In our judgment, such outliers offer additional evidence that a composite measure based on FH scores for civil liberties provides an appropriate measure of citizen rights.

REFERENCES

Banks, Arthur. 2006. Cross-National Time-Series Data Archive. Databanks International. <www.databanks.sitehosting.net/Default.htm>.

Carothers, Thomas. 2002. The End of the Transition Paradigm. *Journal of Democracy* 13, 1: 5–21.

Cingranelli, David L., and David L. Richards. 1999. Measuring the Level, Pattern, and Sequence of Government Respect for Human Rights. *International Studies Quarterly* 43, 2: 407–18.

Collier, David, and Stephen Levitsky. 1997. Democracy with Adjectives: Conceptual Innovation in Comparative Research. *World Politics* 49, 3: 430–51.

Committee to Protect Journalists. Various years. Attacks on the Press: A Worldwide Survey by the Committee to Protect Journalists. New York: Committee to Protect Journalists.

Dahl, Robert A. 1971. *Polyarchy: Participation and Opposition.* New Haven: Yale University Press.

Diamond, Larry. 1999. *Developing Democracy: Toward Consolidation.* Baltimore: Johns Hopkins University Press.

Diamond, Larry, and Leonardo Molino, eds. 2005. *Assessing the Quality of Democracy.* Baltimore: Johns Hopkins University Press.

Epstein, Edward. 1984. Legitimacy, Institutionalization, and Opposition in Exclusionary Bureaucratic Authoritarian Regimes. *Comparative Politics* 17: 37–54.

Gasiorowski, Mark J. 1995. Economic Crisis and Political Regime Change: An Event History Analysis. *American Political Science Review* 89, 4: 882–97.

Hagopian, Frances, and Scott Mainwaring, eds. 2005. *The Third Wave of Democratization in Latin America: Advances and Setbacks.* Cambridge: Cambridge University Press.

Kaufman, Robert. 1979. Industrial Change and Authoritarian Rule in Latin America: A Concrete Review of the Bureaucratic-Authoritarian Model. In *The New Authoritarianism in Latin America*, ed. David Collier. Princeton: Princeton University Press. 165–253.

King, Gary, and Langche Zeng. 2001. Logistic Regression in Rare Events Data. *Political Analysis* 9, 2: 137–63.

Lustig, Nora, ed. 1995. *Coping with Austerity: Poverty and Inequality in Latin America.* Washington, DC: Brookings Institution Press.

Mainwaring, Scott, and Aníbal Pérez-Liñan. 2005. Latin American Democratization Since 1978: Democratic Transitions, Breakdowns, and Erosions. In Francis Hagopian and Scott Mainwaring, eds. *The Third Wave of Democratization in Latin America: Advances and Setbacks.* Cambridge: Cambridge University Press. 14–59.

Mainwaring, Scott, and Timothy R. Scully, eds. 1995. *Building Democratic Institutions: Party Systems in Latin America.* Stanford: Stanford University Press.

O'Donnell, Guillermo. 1994. Delegative Democracy. *Journal of Democracy* 5, 1 (January): 55–69.

O'Donnell, Guillermo, Jorge Vargas Cullell, and Osvaldo M. Iazzatta, eds. 2004. *The Quality of Democracy: Theory and Applications.* Notre Dame: University of Notre Dame Press.

Przeworski, Adam. 2000. *Democracy and Development: Political Institutions and Well-Being in the World, 1950-1990.* Cambridge: Cambridge University Press.

Przeworski, Adam, Michael Alvarez, Jose Antonio Cheibub, and Fernando Limongi. 1996. What Makes Democracies Endure? *Journal of Democracy* 7, 1: 39–55.

Remmer, Karen. 1990. Debt or Democracy? The Political Impact of the Debt Crisis in Latin America. In Debt *and Transfiguration? Prospects for Latin America's Economic Revival*, ed. David Felix. Armonk, NY: M. E. Sharpe. 63–78.

Schedler, Andreas. 2002. Elections Without Democracy: The Menu of Manipulation. *Journal of Democracy* 13, 1: 36–50.

Schedler, Andreas, ed. 2006. *Electoral Authoritarianism: The Dynamics of Unfree Competition.* Boulder: Lynne Rienner.

Smith, Peter H. 2004. Los ciclos de democracia electoral en América Latina, 1900–2000. *Política y Gobierno* 11, 2: 189–228.

———. 2005. *Democracy in Latin America: Political Change in Comparative Perspective.* New York: Oxford University Press.

Smith, Peter H., and Melissa Ziegler. 2006. Illiberal and Liberal Democracy in Latin America. Paper presented at the 26th International Congress of the Latin American Studies Association, March 15–18, San Juan, Puerto Rico.

Tomz, Michael, Gary King, and Langche Zeng. 1999. *ReLogit: Rare Events Logistic Regression.* Stata Version 1.1: 10/29/99.

U.S. State Department. Various years. Country Reports on Human Rights Practices. Washington, DC: U.S. Government Printing Office.

World Bank. 2004. World Development Indicators Database 2004. Washington, DC: World Bank. <http://devdata.worldbank.org/dataonline/>

Zakaria, Fareed. 1997. The Rise of Illiberal Democracy. *Foreign Affairs* 76, 6 (November–December): 22–43.

Chapter 3

Neoliberalism and Democracy in Latin America: A Mixed Record

Kurt Weyland

How compatible are neoliberalism and democracy in Latin America? How do eco-nomic adjustment and market reform affect political liberty and competitive civil-ian rule? This question is highly relevant for the future of the region. The experience of First World countries might suggest that democracy and the market system tend to go together; after all, no democracy has existed in nations that did not have the basic contours of capitalism; namely, a large extent of private ownership and competition as the main mechanism of economic coordination (Lindblom 1977, 161–69). Latin America's experience, however, used to differ from this happy convergence. Given the severe social inequality plaguing the region, political liberalism historically tended to trigger calls for social redistribution and state interventionism; that is, for significant deviations from economic liberalism. The free-market system, by contrast, used to be an elitist project that was often associated with support for or acquiescence to authoritarian political rule. During long stretches of Latin American history, therefore, a clear tension existed between political democracy and economic liberalism (Sheahan 1987, Chapter 12; Gibson 1992, 168–71). Furthermore, even if the free-market system—that is, the end product of neoliberal reform—is compatible with democracy, the process of neoliberal reform might not be; after all, it involves the forceful dismantling of the established develop-ment model, and may therefore require a significant concentration of political power. Indeed, Latin America specialists used to have strong concerns that neoliberalism would destroy democracy. These fears reflected the experience of the 1980s, when many new democratic regimes in the region postponed economic stabilization and structural adjust-ment. Governments in fragile, unconsolidated democracies feared that neoliberal reforms, which impose high short-term costs on important, powerful sectors and large segments of the population, would trigger social turmoil and political conflict and thus endanger the survival of democracy.

By contrast, radical market reforms were pushed through in Chile, but by dictator Augusto Pinochet with the force of arms. The received wisdom therefore used to claim that democracy and neoliberalism were incompatible. Democracies would avoid painful structural adjustment; and where external pressures—especially from the International Monetary Fund and the World Bank—forced them to enact neoliberalism, they could do so only by resorting to repression, thus turning into authoritarian regimes (Foxley 1983, 16, 102; Pion-Berlin 1983; Sheahan 1987, 319–23; see also the discussion in Armijo et al. 1994).

Surprisingly, however, a large number of Latin American democracies did enact drastic, painful market reforms from the late 1980s on. To end hyperinflation and sta-bilize the economy, they imposed harsh budget austerity, dismissed many government employees, privatized public enterprises, opened their economies to foreign trade, and removed myriad regulations and controls. These draconian measures created tremen-dous short-term costs for influential, well-organized sectors of business and labor (see

Haggard and Kaufman 1995, parts 2–3; Murillo 2001; Stokes 2001a; Teichman 2001; Corrales 2002; Weyland 2002).

How did these profound reforms, which revamped the development model of many countries, affect democracy? Did they really threaten the survival of competitive civilian rule? Did they undermine the quality of democracy, as governments used autocratic means to impose draconian changes, restrict popular participation, and thus limit opposition and protest against these controversial measures? In sum, how compatible have democracy and neoliberalism been in contemporary Latin America?

The available evidence suggests that the record has been mixed, but overall more favorable than many observers feared. Neoliberalism clearly has not destroyed competitive civilian rule in the region; it has actually helped to secure the survival of democracy, as defined in minimal procedural terms. Drastic market reform, however, seems, on balance, to have limited and weakened the quality of democracy in Latin America.

This essay develops these arguments in turn, stressing that the same external and internal repercussions of drastic market reform have contributed to these divergent outcomes. Thus, it seeks to put together different pieces of the puzzle by stressing the double-sided nature of neoliberalism's impact on democracy in Latin America.[1] After discussing these two sides in depth, it concludes by explaining the paradoxical connection of these discrepant developments. Specifically, the populist political strategy often used to advance neoliberalism under democracy helped to avoid the dreaded destruction of competitive civilian rule, but simultaneously diminished the quality of democracy.

Two initial caveats are in order. First, in arguing that neoliberalism has bolstered the survival of democracy in Latin America but helped to limit its quality, this essay by no means claims, of course, that drastic market reform has been the only cause of these outcomes; it has probably not even been the single most important factor. But the essay will try to show that radical market reform seems to have made a significant contribution to the strengthening of democratic stability and the weakening of democratic quality.

Second, this essay intends to stimulate debate and research, not to "settle" any of the topics under discussion. The claims it advances are meant as conjectures that deserve and require more systematic investigation. Also, the essay deliberately paints with a broad brush, trying to stress some underlying commonalities behind the great variety of country experiences. Obviously, analyses of specific issues in certain nations arrive at more nuanced and precise findings. But occasionally, it may be useful to step back from such detailed studies and consider the big picture, which may help elucidate the significance and meaning of the results unearthed by more circumscribed analyses.

WHY NEOLIBERALISM HAS NOT DESTROYED DEMOCRACY

Contrary to the received wisdom, neoliberalism did not destroy democracy in Latin America; the available evidence suggests that it actually helped to guarantee the maintenance of democracy. Why did competitive civilian rule in most cases survive the enactment of drastic, costly, and risky market reforms? Perhaps the most crucial reason for democracy's surprising resilience was that most Latin American countries enacted neoliberalism only when they faced dramatic crises, and the population was therefore prepared to swallow the bitter pill of tough stabilization. In particular, structural adjustment often was a last-ditch response to hyperinflation—that is, to price rises above 50 percent per month.

The tremendous costs of exploding inflation commonly induce large segments of the population to support tough, risky stabilization plans that hold the uncertain prospect of overcoming the crisis. When facing the danger of a catastrophe, many people are willing to shoulder considerable short-term losses in the hope of receiving payoffs from restored stability and renewed growth in the medium and long run. Thus, in crisis situations, people do not dig in their heels and strenuously defend their immediate material well-being; instead, they are willing to make sacrifices and trust their leaders' plans for straightening out the economy. They are willing to accept substantial risks by supporting adjustment plans that promise to turn the country around, but that—for economic and, especially, political reasons—have uncertain prospects of success. Thus, people's economic calculations are much more complicated and sophisticated—and more susceptible to persuasion and leadership—than the literature used to assume (see Stokes 2001b; Graham and Pettinato 2002; Weyland 2002). As a result, governments that combated profound crises often managed to muster sufficient political backing to enact bold, painful market reforms under democracy (Armijo and Faucher 2002).

Democracy therefore survived neoliberalism in many Latin American countries, such as Argentina, Brazil, and Bolivia, that had unstable civilian regimes when they initiated market reform. Even in Peru, where President Alberto Fujimori governed in an autocratic fashion, these deviations from democratic norms and principles were not directly caused by or "required for" the enactment of neoliberalism (McClintock 1994). Instead, the longstanding postponement of determined adjustment, combined with large-scale guerrilla insurgencies and terrorism, had discredited the country's "political class," and Fujimori took advantage of this opportunity to concentrate power and disrespect liberal–democratic safeguards. Thus, market reform as such did not destroy democracy in Latin America.

HOW NEOLIBERALISM HAS STRENGTHENED THE EXTERNAL PROTECTION OF DEMOCRACY

Rather than undermining democracy, neoliberalism actually seems to have strengthened its survival in a couple of important ways. First, market reform has enhanced the international protection for democracy in Latin America. Second, the internal socioeconomic transformations resulting from profound market reform have helped to forestall domestic challenges to democratic stability.

Structural adjustment and its corollary, the deeper integration of Latin American countries into the global economy, have made the region more susceptible to international pressures for maintaining democracy. Since the end of the Cold War, the United States, other First World countries, and international organizations have put much more emphasis on preserving pluralistic, civilian rule in the region (Mainwaring and Pérez-Liñán 2005, 40–43; see in general Levitsky and Way 2005; Pevehouse 2002). As the concern over communism faded away, the promotion of democracy, which often took a back seat during the preceding decades, became a first-order priority from the early 1990s on. The disappearance of threats to its strategic interests has made U.S. support for democracy in Latin America much more unconditional. As a result, when the danger of a military coup or some other interruption of democracy threatens, the U.S. government most often has sought to prevent it.[2] And when democracy actually is interrupted or overthrown, the U.S. government has typically threatened or enacted sanctions.

Neoliberalism has increased the exposure of Latin American countries to these forms of international pressure. By lowering barriers to trade, Latin American countries have become more involved in the world economy. By opening up to foreign investors, they have become much more dependent on international capital markets. By submitting, however grudgingly, to greater supervision from the IMF and other international financial institutions, they have seen their autonomy in economic policymaking shrink. Because the U.S. government has considerable direct and indirect influence over these international economic flows, it now has greater leverage for protecting democracy in the region.

Thus, when President Fujimori closed the Peruvian congress with his *autogolpe* of April 5, 1992, the U.S. government protested and intervened. This pressure, which was exerted unilaterally and through the Organization of American States, quickly made clear to Peru's autocratic leader, who had recently initiated neoliberal reform, that he was facing a stark trade-off. If he wanted to reschedule the country's external debt and reestablish good relations with the IMF—relations that his predecessor, Alan García, had destroyed—he needed to accommodate the U.S. demand for restoring minimal, procedural democracy. If he sought to attract foreign capital and thus reignite growth in his crisis-plagued nation, he needed to be in good standing with the advanced industrialized countries, especially the United States. Therefore, Fujimori reluctantly and grudgingly backed away from his effort to install an openly authoritarian regime and started a process of redemocratization (Boloña 1996; De Soto 1996). Thus, by increasing the economic costs of a move to open dictatorship, neoliberalism helped to restore the basic outlines of democracy in Peru.

To what extent neoliberalism and its result, the greater integration of Latin American economies into the world market, have facilitated the external protection of democracy is evident in the case of Guatemala. In 1977, President Jimmy Carter told Guatemala's military dictators that he would cut off aid unless they began to respect human rights. Because the country was not highly involved in foreign trade at the time, the military government canceled collaboration with the United States and continued to commit egregious atrocities (Martin and Sikkink 1993, 331–38). In the 1980s and early 1990s, however, Guatemala opened its economy to foreign trade and capital and significantly increased its exports of agricultural products to the United States.[3] When President Jorge Serrano in 1993 followed Fujimori's example and tried to assume dictatorial powers, the Clinton administration threatened to impose sanctions, and domestic business leaders worried about the resulting disturbance of trade flows. These threats and concerns contributed to the failure of Serrano's self-coup and the restoration of democracy.

Indeed, societal opposition to the *autogolpe*, which had a significant impact on the outcome of the crisis, was "led by major business elites" (Torres-Rivas 1996, 58). By contrast, "Guatemalan business organizations were uniformly conservative and supportive of the repressive policies of the government during the 1970s" (Martin and Sikkink 1993, 346). The comparison of these two episodes from Guatemala suggests with particular clarity that market reform has strengthened the hand of external powers that seek to protect democracy in Latin America and has helped to transform the stance of the societal groups that are most directly affected by these external pressures.

This external support for democracy emerges not only from First World countries but also from other Latin American nations.[4] It is being institutionalized, moreover, through the inclusion of democracy clauses in trade agreements, which have flourished as a result of neoliberal reform. For instance, the South American Common Market (MERCOSUR), which received its most important impulse from the decisions of Argentine President Carlos Menem (1989–99) and his Brazilian counterpart, Fernando Collor de Mello (1990–92), to enact market–oriented reform and therefore to reduce trade barriers (Cason 2000, 208–10), has provisions that make membership conditional on the preservation of competitive civilian rule. Accordingly, when Paraguay faced serious challenges to democracy in the mid- to late 1990s, its neighbors encouraged that nation to maintain its established regime, and these pressures contributed to the survival of competitive civilian rule (Valenzuela 1997, 50–54; Mainwaring and Pérez-Liñán 2005, 42–43). While the inclusion of Hugo Chávez's semi-democratic Venezuela may weaken MERCOSUR's commitment to upholding liberal democracy, other mechanisms of international economic integration, such as the Central American Free Trade Agreement (CAFTA–DR), have as one of their purposes the preservation of civilian competitive rule.

Neoliberalism and the resulting move to international economic integration furthered not only the maintenance but also the promotion of democracy during the 1990s, as the Mexican case suggests. The decision to open Mexico's economy and seek a close association with the United States constrained the margin of maneuver of Mexico's authoritarian regime, making electoral fraud and political repression much more costly and therefore less likely. For instance, when the established regime faced a rebellion in Chiapas in early 1994, it first responded with traditional means (as applied against a similar rebellion in Guerrero in the early 1970s); namely, brute military force. But the international outcry provoked by the resulting human rights violations quickly made the government change course and pursue negotiations with the insurgents, because a "dirty war" could have jeopardized its close relations with its partners in the North American Free Trade Agreement. Similarly, directly after NAFTA took effect, the Mexican government, for the first time, invited international observers to certify the honesty of its elections. Thus, neoliberal reform and its direct effect, economic integration with the United States, helped to advance democratization in Mexico (Levy and Bruhn 2006, 194–201; Pastor 2001, 278; Remmer 2003, 33).

In sum, neoliberalism and the resulting advance in economic globalization have increased the exposure of Latin American countries to the international pressures for the promotion and preservation of democracy that have become much more intense with the end of the Cold War. While this change in geostrategic context clearly was the major reason for the increased sustainability of democracy in the region, market reform and its product, Latin America's greater openness to the world economy, have contributed to this outcome. As Domínguez notes, "Involvement in international markets, especially if guaranteed by free–trade agreements, increases the leverage that external actors can apply in defense of constitutional government" (1998, 72; similar Remmer 2003, 33, 52).

HOW NEOLIBERALISM HAS WEAKENED INTERNAL THREATS TO DEMOCRACY

In addition to enhancing the effects of external support for democracy, neoliberalism has also stabilized competitive civilian rule by weakening internal challenges to its survival. To explain this argument, it is important to explore how threats to democracy often emerged in Latin America before the wave of neoliberalism, especially in the 1960s and 1970s.

On several occasions, the region's large-scale poverty and tremendous inequalities of income and wealth triggered calls for redistribution and other deep-reaching social reforms. These problems also allowed for the rise of radical populists, who used fiery rhetoric to win backing from masses of discontented citizens, left-wing parties, and trade unions and thereby to advance their political ambitions. The variegated demands and proposals for profound socioeconomic and political change led to mobilization and countermobilization; as a result, polarization intensified. All this conflict and turmoil further diminished the capacity of governments to solve problems and maintain economic and political stability. The growing disorder, in turn, frightened established political and economic elites, leading them to ask the military to intervene. In many cases, important groups inside the armed forces felt that social polarization and political conflict threatened the military's own institutional interests. Therefore, they eventually used force to restore order, thereby interrupting or abolishing democracy.[5]

Across most of Latin America, wherever neoliberalism has firmly taken hold, it has largely blocked this dynamic by sealing the political defeat of radical populists and socialists and by hindering the emergence of mass movements that socioeconomic and political elites perceive as serious threats. What the enactment of market reform means, essentially—above and beyond all its specific reforms—is that capitalism and the market economy are here to stay. Communism, socialism, and radical populism are dead or greatly weakened wherever the new development model is in place.[6] International economic integration has made challenges to the established economic and social order much less feasible. Even advancing such demands now has a prohibitive cost by scaring away domestic and foreign investors, who have more "exit" options as a result of market reform, especially the easing or elimination of capital controls.

Neoliberalism has also changed the balance of power between domestic socioeconomic and political forces. Leading business sectors have gained greater clout; they now have better access to international capital markets; they have stronger links to transnational corporations; they have bought up many public enterprises, often at rock-bottom prices; and therefore they own a greater share of the economy. At the same time, thoroughgoing market reform has weakened the sociopolitical forces that used to support radicalism. As a result of trade liberalization, labor market deregulation, privatization, and the shrinking of the public administration, unions have lost members in most countries, are often internally divided, and have generally reduced their militancy. Because of the fall of communism and the worldwide victory of capitalism, most of Latin America's socialist and Marxist parties are on the defensive. A number of them have given up socialist programs and radical–populist rhetoric, and many have accepted the basic outlines of the market model. Therefore, the recent capture of the presidency by leftist parties in a number of Latin American countries, such as Brazil, Chile, and Uruguay, has rarely threatened the basic interests of economic and political elites. In fact, several political leaders of the neoliberal era have used populist political tactics not to attack neoliberalism but to promote, enact, and preserve it (Roberts 1995; Weyland 1996).

Latin America's economic, social, and political elites are therefore much more secure nowadays than they were during the decades preceding the recent neoliberal wave. While this shift in the domestic balance of power precludes any bold equity-enhancing reforms designed to combat Latin America's pronounced social inequality, it favors the preservation of political democracy. Economic and political elites no longer feel the need to knock at the barracks door. Because the risk of mass mobilization, polarization, and turmoil is relatively low, moreover, the military itself is disinclined to roll out the tanks and impose order. Thus, by putting economic and political elites at greater ease, neoliberalism has substantially lowered internal challenges to democracy in Latin America (for Brazil, see Weyland 2005, 115–19; for Chile, Kurtz 2004b).[7]

The exceptional experience of Venezuela under the regime of Hugo Chávez corroborates this rule. Throughout the 1990s, Venezuela instituted the neoliberal program only partially and in a confusing stop-and-go pattern, giving the country a relatively low score on the "general reform index" (Morley et al. 1999, 29; see also Weyland 2002, chaps. 5, 6, 8). The economy therefore never attained stability and remained highly dependent on volatile oil revenues. Popular discontent with the failure of the established political class to stop Venezuela's continuing economic and political deterioration allowed radical outsider Chávez to win the presidency in a landslide.[8]

The belligerent rhetoric of this radical populist leader scared domestic and foreign investors, the church, sectors of the military, and even most trade unions (Ellner and Hellinger 2003). In a pattern resembling the experience of many Latin American countries from the 1940s to the 1970s, these sectors coalesced to oppose the president with all means, culminating in an abortive military coup in April 2002. Thus, precisely where market reform has not firmly taken hold, the old sequence of radical populism, stubborn elite-led opposition, and threats to the survival of democracy still gets under way. In most other Latin American countries, however, thoroughgoing market reform has prevented such dangerous polarization from emerging. Thus, the Venezuelan contrast provides interesting corroboration for the argument.

In sum, neoliberalism seems to have boosted the sustainability of democracy in Latin America, both by exposing the region more to external pressures for maintaining competitive civilian rule and by forestalling internal challenges to its survival.

HOW NEOLIBERALISM HAS TIGHTENED EXTERNAL CONTRAINSTS ON DEMOCRATIC QUALITY

There is, however, another, darker side to the relationship of neoliberalism and democracy in Latin America. At the same time that drastic market reform has furthered the survival of democracy in the region, it seems to have helped erode and limit the quality of democracy.[9] The quality of democracy can be assessed in terms of citizen participation; the accessibility, accountability, and responsiveness of government; and political competitiveness (see Schmitter 1983, 888–90).

Ironically, this negative impact is, in many ways, the corollary of the positive repercussions that this essay has stressed so far. First, the external constraints intensified by market reform seem to have limited the exercise of popular sovereignty, one of the basic principles of democracy. Elected governments do not have a great deal of latitude in their economic and social policymaking. Therefore, citizens' choices are effectively restricted and cannot "make much difference" without violating clear demands of economic and political prudence that reflect powerful external constraints. The resulting frustration seems to have contributed to the decline in electoral participation and the growing dissatisfaction with governmental performance in the region.

Second, as neoliberalism has further tilted the internal balance of forces by strengthening elite sectors, it seems to have weakened important organizations of civil and political society, including political parties. Intermediary organizations, which are crucial for stimulating meaningful popular participation and for holding governments accountable, have grown feebler in most countries of the region and have atrophied or collapsed in some nations. As a result, problems such as the betrayal of campaign promises, demagoguery, and corruption seem to have grown in contemporary Latin America.

Latin American democracies face increased external constraints in the neoliberal era. By opening up their economies, these nations have become more exposed to the vicissitudes of international financial markets. They need to attract and retain capital that could, in principle, leave the country easily and quickly. Investors can use these enhanced "exit" options to gain bargaining leverage. In order to win major productive investments, countries—or states and provinces inside countries—often engage in competitive bidding. They promise free infrastructure, tax breaks, and a number of other benefits. These subsidies for investors limit the resources available for other programs, such as social improvements. One of the central tasks of democracy is decision-making over the budget, but a good part of Latin American budgets is "occupied" by investors. This limits the influence that democratic choice can exert on the country's priorities.

More important, openness to the world economy constrains the options that Latin American democracies can pursue with the resources they retain (see Remmer 2003, 35–38, 51; and in general, Strange 1996, chaps. 4–5). For instance, the renationalization or tight regulation of recently privatized firms would scare away domestic and foreign investors and therefore is not feasible. Substantial tax increases designed to finance additional social spending might trigger capital flight. Therefore, such changes are difficult to enact, and even dangerous to consider. Only under exceptional circumstances, such as the current boom on international markets for raw materials, can Latin American countries have greater latitude. For instance, Chile and Peru have recently imposed higher royalty payments on foreign mining companies without suffering negative consequences. Under more normal conditions, however, external constraints are fairly tight. For instance, investors responded with great nervousness—even panic—to the rise of socialist Luiz Inácio Lula da Silva in vote intentions during the 2002 presidential election campaign in Brazil (Martínez and Santiso 2003). The threat of capital flight practically forced this candidate to offer strong reassurances during the campaign (Faust 2002, 6), appoint a rather orthodox economic team on taking office, and pursue a moderate economic policy course throughout his government (Hunter and Power 2005: 130–32). Ecuador's president, Lucio Gutiérrez, who emerged as a left-wing populist resembling Venezuela's Chávez in the 2002 elections, acted in a similarly accommodating fashion and submitted to IMF recommendations, although this compliance with external pressures triggered increasing popular unrest, which contributed to his downfall in 2005.

Thus, the external pressures intensified by market reform seem to have effectively limited the policymaking latitude of democratic governments. As a result, only 10.5 percent—2 out of 19—of the governments elected during the 1990s that Stokes (2001a, 14–15) analyzes pursued a "security-oriented" (that is, non-neoliberal) approach, whereas 32 percent of the governments elected during the 1980s did so. A full 89.5 percent of governments during the 1990s enacted market-oriented ("efficiency-oriented") policies, compared to 68 percent during the 1980s, which suggests the diminishing latitude for economic policy choice in the neoliberal era. For instance, Chile's Concertación, which had criticized the neoliberal policies imposed by the Pinochet dictatorship during the 1980s, pursued a notably cautious economic policy course after assuming government power in 1990. While the new administrations did enact significant economic and social improvements, they did not go nearly as far as expected, so as not to antagonize the domestic and external supporters of the country's new market system (Arriagada and Graham 1994, 243, 265–66, 272–73, 282). Other opposition leaders who came to power after a neoliberal administration, such as Alejandro Toledo in Peru (2001–2006) and Fernando de la Rúa in Argentina (1999–2001), proceeded with similar caution (Barr 2003, 1163–65; Pousadela 2003, 136–53; Epstein 2006, 101).

Along with its political leaders, the general population is aware of the limitations facing contemporary governments. For instance, when asked "who has most power," 50 percent of respondents in the region-wide Latinobarómetro poll named "large enterprises," which nowadays tend to have strong transnational links; this score ranked right behind "the government" (56 percent) (Latinobarómetro 2000, 7). Thus, Latin Americans see big business—the sector most responsive to international economic pressures and constraints—as almost equal in power to the democratically elected government.

These effective limitations on governments' range of policy options emerge from forces that lack democratic representativeness. To put it in stark terms, Latin American governments have two distinct constituencies: the domestic citizenry, voters, and interest groups on the one hand; and foreign and domestic investors with strong transnational links on the other (see, in general, Lindblom 1977, chaps. 13–16).[10] According to most democratic theories, the first constituency should be decisive; but in reality, the second constituency has considerable influence as well.

In a number of situations, moreover, these two constituencies pull in different directions. When governmental decisions diverge from "the will of the people," the quality of democracy is limited. Certainly these regimes are full democracies, as the "popular sovereign," of course, retains the right to disregard the direct and indirect pressures of investors.[11] But such imprudence would carry considerable costs in the neoliberal era of increasing global market integration. The citizenry can, in principle, exert its full range of democratic rights and, for instance, vote for whatever candidate it pleases, but concentrated control over economic resources often leads to a clear self-restriction. Thus, as a result of pronounced socioeconomic inequality and of exit options amplified by market reform, "all full citizens" do *not* "have unimpaired opportunities . . . to have their preferences weighed *equally* in the conduct of the government," as Robert Dahl stipulates in his famous explication of the ideal type of democracy (1971, 2; emphasis added).

Increased constraint on the range of viable political options seems to diminish public trust in and accountability of democratically elected governments and politicians. For instance, candidates must appeal to their first constituency, the people, to win office. They therefore make promises designed to increase their vote share; for example, by pledging to introduce new social benefits. But after the victorious candidates take office—and before the next election approaches—the citizenry becomes politically less important and the investment community more important. As a result, the new government officials often do not pursue with much zeal the promises they made during the campaign.[12] In the extreme, they execute a drastic policy switch—an experience that has not been uncommon in contemporary Latin America, especially during the initiation of neoliberal reform (see especially Stokes 2001a).

Limited government responsiveness seems to breed diminishing political participation. If governments dispose of only a narrow range of options, if citizens' choices therefore cannot have that much effect, why should the people bother to vote or participate in politics in other ways? Citizens feel betrayed, voters turn more cynical, and the "political class" falls into even deeper disrepute (see, e.g., Epstein 2006, 101). Politics itself becomes devalued; and politics is, of course, the lifeblood of democracy. Democracy therefore risks becoming more anemic and less vibrant.

No wonder electoral abstention has increased in many Latin American countries while satisfaction with democracy and trust in democratic institutions has diminished. For instance, Ryan (2001, 15–20) shows that electoral participation has declined over the last three decades (see also Payne et al. 2002, 55–60) and that this decline has been associated with the depth of the neoliberal reforms enacted in different countries. Surveys conducted by Duch (2002, 10–22) demonstrate that perceptions of economic problems, which respondents disproportionately attribute to external pressures and constraints, diminish trust in politicians, democratic institutions, and the competitive civilian regime as such. Similarly, the massive Latinobarómetro surveys suggest that "poor economic performance in the region as a whole," which results partly from the external constraints and vulnerabilities exacerbated by neoliberal reform, "has significantly impacted the legitimacy of democracy," which experienced "a striking drop" at the beginning of the new millennium (Lagos 2003, 150; see also *Economist* 2001; Latinobarómetro 2002). Indeed, the congress—the main deliberative body in a democracy—was "the democratic institution that . . . lost most popular trust" from 1996 to 2001 (Latinobarómetro 2001, 5).

In sum, neoliberalism seems to have limited the quality of democracy in Latin America by tightening external constraints and thus diminishing the range of feasible political options and restricting effective political competitiveness. While the region has long been subject to external economic pressures and structural limitations emerging from "global capitalism," as the old dependency school (over-)emphasized, market reforms have further intensified these pressures and limitations. As a result, the space for democratic citizenship and meaningful participation appears to have narrowed.

HOW NEOLIBERALISM HAS WEAKENED THE ORGANIZATIONAL INFRASTRUCTURE OF DEMOCRACY

The internal effects of neoliberalism also seem to have limited the quality of democracy in Latin America. As mentioned above, drastic adjustment and thorough market reform have further tilted the balance of power in society and politics. Specifically, they have helped to weaken many of the established intermediary organizations that, in principle, could give democracy a firm and vibrant infrastructure. The organizational landscape in Latin America has become more fragmented and atomized; although it is certainly not the only cause, neoliberalism has contributed significantly to this outcome (see especially Hagopian 1998; Oxhorn 1998). While market reform has also had some positive effects by helping to undermine undemocratic parties and associations and by triggering the emergence of new organizations, such as consumer movements (Rhodes 2006), on balance it has done more harm than good, at least for the time being.

Trade unions nowadays tend to be more divided, to have fewer effective members, and to command lower political influence than they did before the wave of market reform. This decline in union strength has resulted partly from trade liberalization, the deregulation of the labor market, the dismissal of government employees, and the privatization of public enterprises. These reforms have often increased unemployment and underemployment in the short-run and have reduced the legal protection for workers in the long-run. At the same time, financial liberalization has fortified employers' bargaining position by enhancing their exit options. As a result, unions face greater difficulty in organizing and have less clout (Murillo 2003, 104–8; Roberts 2002, 21–23).

Similarly, social movements, which were quite vibrant in the 1980s and which used to advance broader political demands, have often had to concentrate primarily on immediate survival issues. Nowadays, they tend to have less voice on political questions that go beyond their basic needs (Roxborough 1997, 60–62; Portes and Hoffman 2003, 76–77).[13] Indeed, the social costs of neoliberalism have induced many movements to accept the handouts that market reformers provided to bolster their popular support. Where these social emergency programs were heavily politicized and used systematically for patronage purposes, as in Mexico under Carlos Salinas de Gortari (1988–94) and in Peru under Fujimori (1990–2000), they served to co-opt or divide social movements, thereby weakening their capacity for autonomous demand making, especially on general political issues (see Haber 1994 on Mexico; Tanaka 1998b on Peru).

Political parties, for their part, have grown weaker in many countries, and their reputation in the eyes of the citizenry has dropped further. While certainly not solely responsible for this decline, market reform has contributed to it in several ways. As a result of state shrinking and other austerity measures, party organizations, which often used to be sustained through patronage and clientelism, now have fewer resources to distribute and therefore greater difficulty maintaining their membership base. The external constraints intensified by neoliberalism make it more difficult for parties that win government office to fulfill their electoral promises and deliver on popular expectations for social improvements. Furthermore, conflicts over painful neoliberal reforms have led to tensions and divisions inside parties and thus have exacerbated the fragmentation of party systems. In some countries, such as Peru and Venezuela, they have even contributed to party system collapse, and Argentina avoided this fate only narrowly in the period 2001–2003 (Levitsky 2005: 83–86; Epstein and Pion-Berlin 2006).

Of course, not all of these tendencies toward involution have resulted from neoliberalism alone. Party decline, for instance, began before the recent wave of market reforms. In a number of countries, parties lost popular support during the 1980s, when they proved unable to fulfill the high—and frequently excessive—hopes engendered during the transition to democracy. Many Latin Americans had unrealistic expectations about the improvements that the restoration of democracy would bring. When these hopes were frustrated, parties were assigned the blame. Furthermore, the very economic crises that neoliberalism was meant to combat contributed greatly to the enfeeblement of Latin America's civil societies, especially devastating trade unions and social movements, but also parties. Indeed, it is often difficult to ascertain how much the debt crisis and hyperinflation (the "disease") or structural adjustment and market reform (the "medicine") are to blame.[14] It seems undeniable, however, that the substantial transitional costs of neoliberalism and the tighter external constraints that it imposed contributed significantly to the discrediting of parties and especially the weakening of trade unions and social movements (see recently Kurtz 2004a; Roberts 2002).

It is also important to remember that the intermediary organizations that existed before the neoliberal wave were not always very democratic; in reality, internal democracy was often conspicuous by its absence. Personalistic leaders or small elite groups used to control many parties and interest groups. Unions, professional associations, and business organizations often had captive audiences through obligatory membership, which made it difficult for the rank and file to hold their leaders accountable. Parties and other organizations, moreover, frequently used patronage and clientelism to get backing. By obtaining support through the distribution of particularistic benefits, leaders gained a fairly free hand to pursue their own goals, with minimal real input from their "bases." Thus, in the decades before the recent advance of market reform, Latin America's civil societies certainly were not perfectly democratic; they were not even consistently civil.

It would have been better for the quality of democracy, however, if these intermediary organizations had been reformed rather than weakened and divided.[15] At present, civil society and the party system are too weak in several countries—most glaringly, Peru in the late 1990s—to provide a counterweight to the government. Governments therefore have excessive latitude to deviate from their campaign promises, to give in to the real demands or anticipated pressures of investors, to use their offices for private benefit (for instance, through egregious corruption), and to disregard the demands, needs, and interests of citizens. In several instances, government leaders have used their ample margin of maneuver to govern the country as they see fit, rather than being responsive and accountable to the citizenry (see the seminal analyses in O'Donnell 1994, 1998).

NEOPOPULISM, NEOLIBERALISM AND THE QUALITY OF DEMOCRACY

That personalistic, populist leadership, which claims an electoral mandate from "the people" but determines the content of this mandate at will, went hand in hand with neoliberal reform in a number of Latin American countries. The most outstanding cases of such neoliberal neopopulism were Menem in Argentina (1989–99), Fujimori in Peru (1990–2000), Collor de Mello in Brazil (1990–92), Abdalá Bucaram in Ecuador (1996–97), and currently Alvaro Uribe in Colombia (2002–present). All these presidents who adapted populism to the neoliberal age (Roberts 1995; Weyland 1996) stressed their personalistic, charismatic leadership and based their governments to a considerable extent on unorganized and therefore fickle mass support. Their connection to "the people" had the character of plebiscitarian acclamation rather than liberal representation.

As a result, these neopopulist leaders used their popular mandate to run roughshod over institutional checks and balances. They sought and often managed to strengthen the powers of the presidency and to weaken the congress and the courts (Palermo and Novaro 1996, 256–66; Cotler and Grompone 2000, 22–35; Kingstone 1999, 159–69). They imposed their will through decrees and the threat of plebiscites (Carey and Shugart 1998). Several of them tried to intimidate or control the media. All of these strong-arm tactics diminished the quality of democracy.

Neoliberal reform provided these neopopulist presidents with useful instruments for enhancing their autonomy and power, thereby boosting their leadership. Trade liberalization, privatization, and labor market deregulation weakened trade unions, which used to restrict presidential latitude with their demands and pressures. Trade liberalization also put some powerful business sectors on the defensive, while the sale of public enterprises allowed presidents to buy support from select groups of big business through favorable privatization deals (see, for example, Corrales 1998). The dismissal of public employees enabled neopopulist leaders to eliminate their predecessors' appointees, who might use their bureaucratic power to block presidential initiatives.

In all these ways, neopopulist leaders used neoliberalism for their own political purposes (see Weyland 1996; Roberts 1995). Where structural adjustment eventually restored economic stability and reignited growth, and where neopopulist leaders therefore attained lasting political success, as in Argentina and Peru, neoliberalism indeed strengthened the political predominance of neopopulist leaders (Weyland 2002, chaps. 6–7). This reinforcement of neopopulism constitutes another way market reform has reduced the quality of democracy in Latin America.

THE INVERSE RELATIONSHIP BETWEEN DEMOCRATIC STABILITY AND DEMOCRATIC QUALITY

With the preceding argument, the discussion comes full circle. It is important to recognize a paradox: while neopopulist leadership has diminished the quality of democracy in Latin America, it actually seems to have helped ensure democracy's survival. Remember that many observers during the mid- to late 1980s believed that only a dictator like Chile's Pinochet could enact neoliberal reform.

One significant reason why this prediction proved wrong and why democracies managed to survive the imposition of neoliberal reform was the emergence of neopopulist leaders who realized that they could use neoliberalism to advance their own political goals. This convergence of neopopulism and neoliberalism arose from the deep crises that afflicted many Latin American countries in the late 1980s. Hyperinflation and other dramatic problems made many citizens willing to support painful stabilization and market reform. Neopopulist leaders therefore won political backing by enacting the adjustment plans their predecessors had postponed for fear of provoking unrest. Neopopulists' courage in combating the crisis head-on gave them popular support and proved their charisma, while market reforms ultimately enhanced their power. Thus, the surprising compatibility—even affinity—of neoliberalism and neopopulism is one of the important reasons for the survival of democracy despite neoliberalism. Viewed from this perspective, the reduction in democratic quality produced by neopopulism may have been the price for guaranteeing the survival of democracy during the enactment of neoliberalism.[16]

The positive and negative sides of the mixed record that this essay has discussed are intrinsically linked. While neoliberalism has intensified the external restrictions on democratic choice and governmental decisionmaking and has thereby diminished the quality of democracy, those very restrictions also expose Latin American countries to diplomatic pressures to maintain democracy. Such constraints limit the effective exercise of popular sovereignty and thereby discourage political participation, but they also preclude highly pernicious options, especially the overthrow of democracy by the military or its abrogation by the people themselves, who may elect and support autocratic populists like Fujimori.

In a similarly paradoxical twist, the further weakening and fragmentation of popular sector organizations, which detracts from the quality of democracy, bolsters the survival of democracy by putting socioeconomic and political elites at ease, which prevents them from resorting to extra constitutional means to protect their core interests. Popular sector weakness limits democratic representation and governmental accountability, but by foreclosing the danger of radicalism, it forestalls an elite backlash against competitive civilian rule. Altogether, both the external and internal effects of neoliberalism diminish the range of political choice, but precisely in this way, they contribute to the persistence of democracy itself.

The available evidence suggests that neoliberalism has affected Latin American democracy in opposite, even contradictory ways. By exposing the region's countries to greater external pressures and by changing the internal balance of forces so as to preclude threats to domestic elites, market reform has bolstered the survival of democracy. Yet in exactly the same ways, namely by imposing stronger external constraints and by changing the internal balance of forces through a weakening of domestic intermediary organizations, market reform has abridged the quality of democracy. As is so often the case, politics poses real dilemmas and painful trade-offs.

NOTES

I would like to thank Jonathan Hartlyn, Wendy Hunter, Raúl Madrid, Christopher Sabatini, Joseph Tulchin, Arturo Valenzuela, Eliza Willis, three anonymous reviewers, and Bill Smith, the editor of the present volume, for many valuable comments.

1 This argument about the double-sided impact of neoliberalism on Latin American democracy does not necessarily claim that the two sides are of equal strength and significance. Actually, the strength of these two effects would be methodologically very difficult to compare, given their qualitative difference and, therefore, the absence of a common underlying metric.

2 The equivocal U.S. response to the temporary ouster of Venezuela's Hugo Chavez in April 2002 constitutes a partial exception. After this populist president was reinstalled and Washington's stance drew strong criticism from Latin American governments, the Bush administration stressed very clearly that it would not support any further military adventures, despite the continuing political crisis in Venezuela.

3 On the significant extent of trade and financial liberalization in Guatemala, see the measurements in Morley et al. 1999, 30–32.

4 For analyses of the strengths and limitations of this international democracy-promotion regime, see Cooper and Legler 2001 and Levitt 2006.

5 While many military coups emerged in this way, not all did; the 1968 coup in Peru, undertaken by nationalist, left-leaning officers who wanted to bring reform to their country, constitutes an exception.

6 Venezuela's radical populist Hugo Chávez emerged precisely in a country that has enacted comparatively little neoliberal reform.

7 For a general argument along similar lines that emphasizes the importance of increasing capital mobility, see Boix 2003.

8 Similarly, the mass mobilization that led to the January 2000 coup in Ecuador occurred in a country that had not pushed the neoliberal agenda very consistently or very far (Pion-Berlin 2001, 8–10; Lucero 2001, 59–68).

9 Although this essay focuses on the repercussions of neoliberalism, other aspects of globalization, such as the increasing traffic in drugs and small arms, have certainly contributed to the problems plaguing Latin American democracies, such as a rising crime wave (Tulchin and Frühling 2003) and the virtual implosion of state authority in large swaths of Colombia and in Rio de Janeiro's urban slums. Globalization is, however, a multifaceted process, which has also had important positive effects on Latin American democracies; for instance, through transnational activism, which has supported civil society groups in many countries of the region (see, for example, Keck and Sikkink 1998). These complex and complicated issues, which are tremendously important for the quality of Latin American democracies, are far larger than the limited scope of this essay.

10 Lindblom depicts the "privileged position of business," which market reforms have strengthened in contemporary Latin America, as not very democratic.

11 Thus, Latin American democracies in the neoliberal age should not be classified as "diminished subtypes" of democracy. This essay does not mean to contribute to the conceptual problems that Armony and Schamis (2005) correctly criticize.

12 For instance, one important reason for the drastic popularity decline of Peru's president Alejandro Toledo has been the difficulty of fulfilling his campaign promises while maintaining investor confidence (Barr 2003, 1163–65). Disillusionment with the new president's performance, in turn, seems to have exacerbated citizens' distrust of politicians in general.

13 Brazil's Movement of Landless Rural Workers (MST) constitutes a partial exception to this general tendency. Still, the MST's tremendous expansion during the 1990s was triggered not by neoliberalism and its effects, such as exacerbating employment problems in the countryside, but by the reformist background and officially social-democratic orientation of President Fernando Henrique Cardoso (1995–2002), which restricted government repression and rewarded the MST's mobilization efforts, as Ondetti's thorough study (2002) clearly shows.

14 While it would be difficult to disentangle the causal impact of these different factors, careful analysis of the timing of party system decline could provide important clues. For instance, Tanaka (1998a) argues that the collapse of Peru's party system was not predetermined by the economic and political crisis of the 1980s but was contingent on President Fujimori's antiparty maneuvers, which accompanied the president's enactment of neoliberalism.

15 This argument applies at least in the short and medium run. In the long run, the weakening of the existing, not-so-democratic intermediary organizations could create a clean slate for the formation of new, more democratic parties and interest groups. But several factors—erratic economic growth, fluid, rapidly shifting socioeconomic alignments, and the tremendous political importance of the mass media—make such a rebuilding of strong parties and associations unlikely.

16 The fact that in recent years some plebiscitarian leaders, especially Hugo Chávez in Venezuela and Evo Morales in Bolivia, have risen to government power by attacking neoliberalism and have significantly diverged from market-oriented principles while in office may foreshadow greater challenges and risks for prudent economic policies as well as for liberal democracy in the region. At present, for instance, Bolivia seems to be headed toward a dangerous polarization and confrontation over the future course of the country (*La Razón* 2006).

REFERENCES

Armijo, Leslie Elliot, and Philippe Faucher. 2002. 'We Have a Consensus': Explaining Political Support for Market Reforms in Latin America. *Latin American Politics and Society* 44, 2 (Summer): 1–40.

Armijo, Leslie Elliot, Thomas Biersteker, and Abraham Lowenthal. 1994. The Problems of Simultaneous Transitions. *Journal of Democracy* 5, 4 (October): 161–75.

Armony, Ariel, and Hector Schamis. 2005. Babel in Democratization Studies. *Journal of Democracy* 16, 4 (October): 113–28.

Arriagada, Genaro, and Carol Graham. 1994. Chile: Sustaining Adjustment During Democratic Transition. In *Voting for Reform: Democracy, Political Liberalization, and Economic Adjustment*, ed. Stephan Haggard and Steven Webb. Oxford: Oxford University Press. 242–89.

Barr, Robert. 2003. The Persistence of Neopopulism in Peru? From Fujimori to Toledo. *Third World Quarterly* 24, 6 (December): 1161–78.

Boix, Carles. 2003. *Democracy and Redistribution*. Cambridge: Cambridge University Press.

Boloña, Carlos. 1996. Former Minister of Economy and Finance (1991–92), Peru. Author interview. Lima, August 14.

Carey, John, and Matthew Shugart, eds. 1998. *Executive Decree Authority*. Cambridge: Cambridge University Press.

Cason, Jeffrey. 2000. Democracy Looks South: Mercosul and the Politics of Brazilian Trade Strategy." In *Democratic Brazil: Actors, Institutions, and Processes*, ed. Peter Kingstone and Timothy Power. Pittsburgh: University of Pittsburgh Press. 204–16.

Cooper, Andrew, and Thomas Legler. 2001. The OAS Democratic Solidarity Paradigm: Questions of Collective and National Leadership. *Latin American Politics and Society* 43, 1 (Spring): 103–26.

Corrales, Javier. 1998. Coalitions and Corporate Choices in Argentina, 1976–1994. *Studies in Comparative International Development* 32, 4 (Winter): 24–51.

———. 2002. *Presidents Without Parties, The Politics of Economic Reform in Argentina and Venezuela in the 1990s*. University Park: Pennsylvania State University Press.

Cotler, Julio, and Romeo Grompone. 2000. *El fujimorismo: ascenso y caída de un régimen autoritario*. Lima: Institute de Estudios Peruanos.

Dahl, Robert A. 1971. *Polyarchy: Participation and Opposition*. New Haven: Yale University Press.

De Soto, Hernando. 1996. Former Special Adviser to President Alberto Fujimori, Peru. Author interview. Lima, August 20.

Domínguez, Jorge. 1998. Free Politics and Free Markets in Latin America. *Journal of Democracy* 9, 4 (December): 70–84.

Duch, Raymond. 2002. State of the Latin American Political Economy. Paper presented at the conference "The Political Consequences of Economic Turmoil in Latin America," Americas Project, Baker Institute, Rice University, October 29–30.

Economist. 2001. An Alarm Call for Latin America's Democrats. <www.economist.com/display/Story.cfm?storyJd=709760>. July 26.

Ellner, Steve, and Daniel Hellinger, eds. 2003. *Venezuelan Politics in the Chávez Era: Class, Polarization, and Conflict*. Boulder: Lynne Rienner.

Epstein, Edward. 2006. The Piquetero Movement in Greater Buenos Aires. In *Broken Promises? The Argentine Crisis and Argentine Democracy*, ed. Edward Epstein and David Pion-Berlin. Lanham, MD: Lexington Books. 95–115.

Epstein, Edward, and David Pion-Berlin. 2006. The Crisis of 2001 and Argentine Democracy. In *Broken Promises? The Argentine Crisis and Argentine Democracy*, ed. Edward Epstein and David Pion-Berlin. Lanham, MD: Lexington Books. 3–26.

Faust, Jörg. 2002. Brasilien: Nach den Wahlen ist vor den Wahlen? *SWP–Aktuell* 50 (November): 1–8.

Foxley, Alejandro. 1983. *Latin American Experiments in Neoconservative Economics*. Berkeley and Los Angeles: University of California Press.

Gibson, Edward. 1992. Conservative Parties and Democratic Politics: Argentina in Comparative Perspective. Ph.D. diss., Columbia University.

Graham, Carol, and Stefano Pettinato. 2002. *Happiness and Hardship: Opportunity and Insecurity in New Market Economies*. Washington, DC: Brookings Institution Press.

Haber, Paul. 1994. The Art and Implications of Political Restructuring in Mexico: The Case of Urban Popular Movements. In *The Politics of Economic Restructuring: State–Society Relations and Regime Change in Mexico*, ed. Maria Lorena Cook, Kevin Middlebrook, and Juan Molinar Horcasitas. San Diego: Center for U.S.–Mexican Studies, University of California. 277–303.

Haggard, Stephan, and Robert Kaufman. 1995. *The Political Economy of Democratic Transitions.* Princeton: Princeton University Press.

Hagopian, Frances. 1998. Democracy and Political Representation in Latin America in the 1990s. In *Fault Lines of Democracy in Post-Transition Latin America,* ed. Felipe Aguero and Jeffrey Stark. Coral Gables: North–South Center Press. 85–120.

Hunter, Wendy, and Timothy Power. 2005. Lula's Brazil at Midterm. *Journal of Democracy* 16, 3 (July): 127–39.

Keck, Margaret E., and Kathryn Sikkink. 1998. *Activists Beyond Borders: Advocacy Networks in International Politics.* Ithaca: Cornell University Press.

Kingstone, Peter R. 1999. *Crafting Coalitions for Reform: Business Preferences, Political Institutions, and Neoliberal Reform in Brazil.* University Park: Pennsylvania State University Press.

Kurtz, Marcus. 2004a. The Dilemmas of Democracy in the Open Economy: Lessons from Latin America. *World Politics* 56, 2 (January): 262–302.

———. 2004b. *Free Market Democracy and the Chilean and Mexican Countryside.* Cambridge: Cambridge University Press.

Lagos, Marta. 2003. Public Opinion. In *Constructing Democratic Governance in Latin America,* 2nd ed., ed. Jorge I. Domínguez and Michael Shifter. Baltimore: Johns Hopkins University Press. 137–61.

Latinobarómetro. 2000. Gráficos informe de prensa 2000. Santiago de Chile: Latinobarómetro.

———. 2001. Informe de prensa: encuesta Latinobarómetro 2001. Santiago de Chile: Latinobarómetro.

———. 2002. Informe de prensa: Latinobarómetro 2002. Santiago de Chile: Latinobarómetro.

Levitsky, Steven. 2005. Argentina: Democratic Survival amidst Economic Failure. In *The Third Wave of Democratization in Latin America,* ed. Frances Hagopian and Scott Mainwaring. Cambridge: Cambridge University Press. 63–89.

Levitsky, Steven, and Lucan Way. 2005. International Linkage and Democratization. *Journal of Democracy* 16, 3 (July): 20–34.

Levitt, Barry. 2006. A Desultory Defense of Democracy: OAS Resolution 1080 and the Inter–American Democratic Charter. *Latin American Politics and Society* 48, 3 (Fall): 93–123.

Levy, Daniel, and Kathleen Bruhn. 2006. *Mexico: The Struggle for Democratic Development,* 2nd ed. Berkeley: University of California Press.

Lindblom, Charles. 1977. *Politics and Markets: The World's Political–Economic Systems.* New York: Basic Books.

Lucero, Jose. 2001. Crisis and Contention in Ecuador. *Journal of Democracy* 12, 2 (April): 59–73.

Mainwaring, Scott, and Aníbal Pérez-Liñán. 2005. Latin American Democratization since 1978. In *The Third Wave of Democratization in Latin America,* ed. Frances Hagopian and Scott Mainwaring. Cambridge: Cambridge University Press. 14–59.

Martin, Lisa, and Kathryn Sikkink. 1993. U.S. Policy and Human Rights in Argentina and Guatemala, 1973–1980. In *Double-Edged Diplomacy: International Bargaining and Domestic Politics,* ed. Peter B., Evans, Harold K. Jacobson, and Robert D. Putnam. Berkeley: University of California Press. 330–62.

Martínez, Juan, and Javier Santiso. 2003. Financial Markets and Politics: The Confidence Game in Latin American Emerging Economies. *International Political Science Review* 24, 3 (August): 363–95.

McClintock, Cynthia. 1994. The Breakdown of Constitutional Democracy in Peru. Paper presented at the 18th International Congress of the Latin American Studies Association, Atlanta, March 10–12.

Morley, Samuel, Roberto Machado, and Stefano Pettinato. 1999. *Indexes of Structural Reform in Latin America.* Economic Reform series, no. 12. Santiago de Chile: United Nations Economic Commission for Latin America and the Caribbean.

Murillo, María Victoria. 2001. *Labor Unions, Partisan Coalitions, and Market Reforms in Latin America.* Cambridge: Cambridge University Press.

———. 2003. Latin American Labor. In *Constructing Democratic Governance in Latin America,* 2nd ed., ed. Jorge I. Dominguez and Michael Shifter. Baltimore: Johns Hopkins University Press. 100–17.

O'Donnell, Guillermo. 1994. Delegative Democracy. *Journal of Democracy* 5, 1 (January): 55–69.
——. 1998. Horizontal Accountability in New Democracies. *Journal of Democracy* 9, 3 (July): 112–26.
Ondetti, Gabriel. 2002. Opportunities, Ideas, and Actions: The Brazilian Landless Movement, 1979–2001. Ph.D. diss., University of North Carolina, Chapel Hill.
Oxhorn, Philip. 1998. Is the Century of Corporatism Over? Neoliberalism and the Rise of Neopluralism. In *What Kind of Democracy? What Kind of Market? Latin America in the Age of Neoliberalism*, ed. Oxhorn and Graciela Ducatenzeiler. University Park: Pennsylvania State University Press. 195–217.
Palermo, Vicente, and Marcos Novaro. 1996. *Política y poder en el gobierno de Menem*. Buenos Aires: Grupo Editorial Norma.
Pastor, Robert A. 2001. *Exiting the Whirlpool: U.S. Foreign Policy Toward Latin America and the Caribbean*. 2nd ed., rev. Boulder: Westview Press.
Payne, J. Mark, Daniel Zovato G., Fernando Carillo Flórez, and Andrés Allamand Zavala. 2002. *Democracies in Development: Politics and Reform in Latin America*. Washington, DC: Inter-American Development Bank.
Pevehouse, Jon. 2002. Democracy from the Outside–In? International Organizations and Democratization. *International Organization* 56, 3 (Summer): 515–49.
Pion-Berlin, David. 1983. Political Repression and Economic Doctrines: The Case of Argentina. *Comparative Political Studies* 16 (April): 37–66.
——. 2001. The Armed Forces and Economic Adjustment in Latin America. Unpublished mss. Department of Political Science, University of California, Riverside.
Portes, Alejandro, and Kelly Hoffman. 2003. Latin American Class Structures. *Latin American Research Review* 38, 1: 41–82.
Pousadela, Inés. 2003. La oposición progresista frente al consenso neoliberal. In *De la ilusión reformista al descontento ciudadano. Las elecciones en Argentina, 1999–2001*, ed. Isidoro Cheresky and Jean-Michel Blanquet. Rosario: Homo Sapiens. 117–55.
(La) Razón. 2006. La tension de 2 bloques acerca el enfrentamiento. 22 September <www.la–razon.com/versiones/20060922_005672/nota_249_335627.htm>
Remmer, Karen. 2003. Elections and Economies in Contemporary Latin America. In *Post-Stabilization Politics in Latin America: Competition, Transition, Collapse*, ed. Carol Wise and Riordan Roett. Washington, DC: Brookings Institution Press. 31–55.
Rhodes, Sybil. 2006. *Social Movements and Free-Market Capitalism in Latin America: Telecommunications Privatization and the Rise of Consumer Protest*. Albany: State University of New York Press.
Roberts, Kenneth. 1995. Neoliberalism and the Transformation of Populism: The Case of Peru. *World Politics* 48, 1 (October): 82–116.
——. 2002. Social Inequalities Without Class Cleavages in Latin America's Neoliberal Era. Studies in *Comparative International Development* 36, 4 (Winter): 3–33.
Roxborough, Ian. 1997. Citizenship and Social Movements Under Neoliberalism. In *Politics, Social Change, and Economic Restructuring in Latin America*, ed. William C. Smith and Roberto P. Korzeniewicz. Coral Gables: North–South Center Press. 57–77.
Ryan, Jeffrey. 2001. 'Painful Exit': Electoral Abstention and Neoliberal Reform in Latin America. Paper presented at the 22nd International Congress of the Latin American Studies Association, September 6–8.
Schmitter, Philippe. 1983. Democratic Theory and Neocorporatist Practice. *Social Research* 50, 4 (Winter): 885–928.
Sheahan, John. 1987. *Patterns of Development in Latin America: Poverty, Repression, and Economic Strategy*. Princeton: Princeton University Press.
Stokes, Susan. 2001a. *Mandates and Democracy. Neoliberalism by Surprise in Latin America*. Cambridge: Cambridge University Press.
Stokes, Susan, ed. 2001b. *Public Support for Market Reforms in New Democracies*. Cambridge: Cambridge University Press.
Strange, Susan. 1996. *The Retreat of the State: The Diffusion of Power in the World Economy*. Cambridge: Cambridge University Press.

Tanaka, Martin. 1998a. *Los espejismos de la democracia: el colapso del sistema de partidos en el Peru*. Lima: Instituto de Estudios Peruanos.

———. 1998b. From Movimientismo to Media Politics. In *Fujimori's Peru: The Political Economy*, ed. John Crabtree and Jim Thomas. London: Institute of Latin American Studies. University of London. 229–42.

Teichman, Judith. 2001. *The Politics of Freeing Markets in Latin America: Chile, Argentina, and Mexico*. Chapel Hill: University of North Carolina Press.

Torres-Rivas, Edelberto. 1996. Guatemala: Democratic Governability. In *Constructing Democratic Governance: Mexico, Central America, and the Caribbean in the 1990s*, ed. Jorge I. Domínguez and Abraham Lowenthal. Baltimore: Johns Hopkins University Press. 50–63.

Tulchin, Joseph, and Hugo Frühling, eds., with Heather Golding. 2003. *Crime and Violence in Latin America: Citizen Security, Democracy, and the State*. Washington, DC: Woodrow Wilson Center Press.

Valenzuela, Arturo. 1997. Paraguay: The Coup that Didn't Happen. *Journal of Democracy* 8, 1 (January): 43–55.

Weyland, Kurt. 1996. Neo-Populism and Neo-Liberalism in Latin America: Unexpected Affinities. *Studies in Comparative International Development* 32, 3 (Fall): 3–31.

———. 2002. *The Politics of Market Reform in Fragile Democracies: Argentina, Brazil, Peru, and Venezuela*. Princeton: Princeton University Press.

———. 2005. The Growing Sustainability of Brazil's Low-Quality Democracy. In *The Third Wave of Democratization in Latin America*, ed. Frances Hagopian and Scott Mainwaring. Cambridge: Cambridge University Press. 90–120.

Chapter 4

The Uneven Performance of Third Wave Democracies: Electoral Politics and the Imperfect Rule of Law in Latin America

Joe Foweraker
Roman Krznaric

The number of democracies in the world has rapidly increased over the past three decades, but the quality of these democracies is uneven.[1] It is alleged that many of the new democracies are being "hollowed out" (for example, Diamond 1999, 49). The consequence is the spread of electoral democracy, where political parties compete for control of the government through relatively free and fair elections (O'Donnell 1997); but not liberal democracy, with an effective rule of law underpinning individual and minority freedoms and protections (Diamond 1999, chaps. 1, 2). A claim to liberal democracy may serve to legitimate state authority nearly everywhere, but the reality falls far short of the global triumph of liberal democratic government.[2]

This essay sets out to investigate the uneven quality of the new democracies of the third wave; that is, those formed from 1970 through 1998. It demonstrates that the institutional attributes of democratic governance advance while individual and minority rights languish. But this is not the whole story. Distinct institutional attributes may coexist uncomfortably in many emerging democracies, and this is also true of different democratic rights. Thus, this study will show that the vertical accountability implicit in electoral politics does not necessarily entail an equal degree of horizontal accountability (O'Donnell 1997, 1999; Schedler 1999). The latter is often checked by military prerogatives and military influence over civilian government. Equally, the political rights required for electoral politics can promote more intense political contestation, but civil rights may suffer as a result.[3] Yet the continuing fragility of civil rights in general does not prevent the reinforcement of property rights in particular. Indeed, civil and minority rights violations may flow directly from the lack of horizontal accountability and from the violent defense of private property in conditions of poverty and social exclusion.

The inquiry is framed by a conceptual model of liberal democratic performance that serves as the blueprint for a Database of Liberal Democratic Performance. The model specifies the distinct aspects of democratic performance that should be measured, and is therefore a model of how precisely liberal democratic governments are expected to perform. The new democracies of the third wave can then be described by the uneven or incomplete presence of these distinct aspects of democratic performance. One resulting observation is that governments are indeed voted in and voted out through elections that are reasonably free and fair, but that the "institutional environment of elections" (Riker and Weimer 1993, 79, n.2) is far from fully established.[4] The model specifies the ways and degrees in which this environment is lacking.

By differentiating distinct aspects of performance, the model can suggest the dynamic and interactive effects that help shape the political contours of the third wave. But it is not a formal model that requires trade-offs across different measures of performance in logical fashion. On the contrary, the uneven democratic performance of the new democracies whether structured by trade-offs or not, can only be explained by the political context and the political culture. For this reason, the general account of the political contours of the third wave derived from the database is complemented by a particular but still comparative inquiry into the contextual conditions of the wave in Brazil, Colombia, and Guatemala. On the basis of the contextual inquiry, this study will argue that it is in these kinds of conditions (but not uniquely in these conditions) that democratic performance is likely to be uneven, with a tendency for specific aspects of performance to trade off against each other.

INVESTIGATING THE THIRD WAVE

The conceptual model assumes that liberal democratic government is founded on the two key principles of liberty and equality, which must be upheld by the rule of law and the sovereignty of the people. Furthermore, the model specifies that these two principles are achieved in practice through the operation of eight core liberal democratic elements, and that these elements comprise two main axes that combine the individual experience of democracy (rule of law) with the institutional efficacy of democratic government (sovereignty of the people). The first axis contains the legal elements of civil rights, property rights, political rights, and minority rights. These rights and the rule of law are important guarantees of individual freedoms and protections, and thus help to deliver the substance of democracy to the citizenry at large. The second axis contains the institutional elements of accountability, representation, constraint, and participation. These are the elements that protect the rule of law by making government accountable to the people.[5]

The model is designed to reflect the broad consensus that exists on the foundational principles of liberal democracy. The intellectual grounds for the consensus were created by long traditions of both liberal and democratic thought, beginning in seventeenth-century England, and in the encounter and conversation between them. The classic statement of liberal principles is found in Locke's Second Treatise, and his defense of the constitutional protection of individual liberty and equality under the rule of law has remained central to liberal theory ever since (Locke 1924, 180–83).

The first strands of modern democratic thought were skeptical of the ability of the law to protect liberty and equality unless each citizen could "exercise an equal right of participation in the making of the laws" (Skinner 1998, 69–70). By making government accountable to the people, self-rule provides a guarantee that it will uphold the law, thereby supplying the essential democratic link to liberal democracy. Over time, the consensus was extended to include the main institutional and legal means for achieving and defending the principles of liberty and equality, and each of the model's elements can be justified by arguments from mainstream liberal democratic theory (see Foweraker and Krznaric 2000).

The Database of Liberal Democratic Performance collates measures of these 8 elements (see Foweraker and Krznaric 1999) and covers the years 1970 to 1998, inclusive, in order to capture the full shape of the third wave. Its 21 variables were chosen to provide serviceable time-series measures that are sensitive (sufficient variation), diverse (in sources and substance), and scaled in more than one way (ordinal and interval). At the same time, the objective was to use tried and tested measures wherever possible to maximize reliability and economy of effort. All the measures have been employed in mainstream comparative work on democracy and democratic institutions (see appendix).[6]

The Database is global in scope, and its universe comprises 40 country cases. The criteria for their selection can be found in the appendix. The selection was made from democratic governments only, with a minimal and procedural threshold for democracy sufficient to warrant inclusion. Thus, the database includes both "electoral" and "liberal" democracies, in Diamond's language (1997a, 1999), because the difference between the two is a matter of democratic performance, and this is precisely what the database sets out to measure. It is assumed that the better and the more consistently a democratic government performs (across distinct liberal democratic elements), the more liberal it is likely to be.

Within this broad democratic universe, case selection turned mainly, if not exclusively, on questions of data availability and geographical scope and consistency. For example, countries with less than one-and-a-half million inhabitants were excluded, partly on grounds of data scarcity and partly to increase comparability across cases.

Once assembled in this way, the database can be deployed to describe the political contours of the third wave. But it does so differently from the extant studies. Previous measures of democracy, such as those of Polity III or Freedom House, tend to subsume different aspects of performance into a single score, thereby obscuring variations in performance across distinct democratic elements or attributes.[7] This database, in contrast, provides a differentiated picture of the third wave. The picture is drawn from selected variables for the 23 cases of the 40 in the database that are new democracies; that is, that became democratic in or after 1970, with average scores presented from 1970 to 1998 for every year that data are available.[8]

Four variables were selected to capture competitive, electoral politics and political representation (figure 1). All four variables show the same pattern of little change until 1982, with a marked rise from the mid-1980s that accelerates in subsequent years before

Figure 1. Scaled Mean Institutional Scores for 23 New Democracies

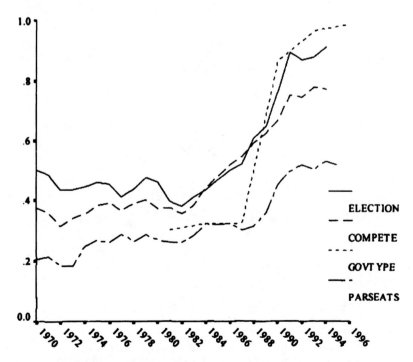

ELECTION: vertical accountability
COMPETE: political rights of competition
GOVTYPE: civilian or military control
PARSEATS: breadth of representation in the political system

flattening again in the 1990s. In effect, they all reproduce the conventional shape of the third wave that is familiar from Freedom House and Polity III, and tell the same story of a third wave that has succeeded in spreading the formal institutions of procedural democracy across the globe.[9]

A different picture emerges, however, for the six variables selected to reflect the practical performance of civil and minority rights over the same years (figure 2). In stark contrast to the rising trajectory of the political–institutional variables, all these variables remain flat throughout the period of the third wave. In other words, despite the rapid dissemination of competitive electoral politics across the new democracies, civil and minority rights are still fragile, suggesting that the citizens of these democracies remain unprotected and vulnerable. The electoral and representative institutions of government are fully present, but individual and minority rights are absent or ineffective.[10]

The story of a differentiated third wave that enshrines Schumpeterian competitive politics at the expense of civil and minority rights can be seen to correspond to main-stream accounts of democratic transition that focus on the "short-term maneuvering" and negotiation of elite actors (Levine 1988, 385). Elite decisionmaking is required to establish the terms of the pacts and settlements that will found the new democratic regime (see, for example, Higley and Gunther 1992; Hagopian 1990). Competitive electoral politics are central to the institutional arrangements that will underpin the pacts and establish the boundary conditions for procedural consensus among the elite actors. Broadly speaking,

Figure 2. Scaled Mean Rights Scores for 23 New Democracies

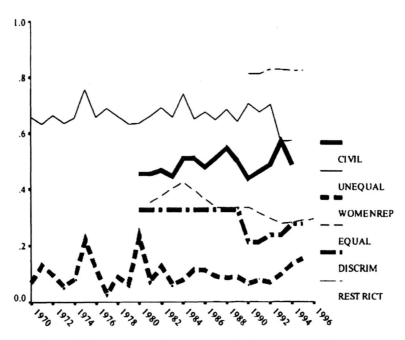

CIVIL: civil rights
UNEQUAL: income inequality as proxy for equality before law
WOMENREP: percentage of women in the lower legislative chamber
EQUAL: women's legal equality of access to social goods
DISCRIM: political discrimination against minorities
RESTRICT: cultural restrictions on minorities

this is the "Lockean" approach to democratic constitutionalism, which, in the contemporary context, is imagined as a process of "institutionalizing uncertainty" (Przeworski 1986, 58–59). Unwittingly, these accounts accurately reflect the political content of third wave democracies that appear to ignore "the citizenry at large" and its "wish to be rid of tangible evils" (Rustow 1970, 354–57). Democracy is a matter of mass as well as elite; but without the real practice of civil liberties and minority rights, the secure substance of democracy cannot be delivered to the individuals who compose the polity. The uneven quality of these new democracies therefore means that democratic constitutionalism often has little to do with the citizens' lived experience.

CONTEXTUALIZING THE MEASURES

The database draws a big picture of a third wave characterized by advancing electoral politics combined with retarded civil and minority rights. But it does not and cannot describe the historical and contextual conditions that—taken together—may begin to explain the big picture. This is one aspect of the classic methodological trade-off between large-N comparative research and a close-focus, hermeneutic style of analysis.

The inquiry therefore now moves to complement the big picture with a small-N comparison that explores particular variables in particular contexts. Its purpose is twofold. First, it seeks to ground the global measures and see whether the big picture conforms to what is happening on the ground. If the measures succeed in characterizing the political content of the third wave, then those characteristics should be evident in the country cases that provide the raw scores. Second, it seeks to reveal some possible reasons for the uneven quality of third wave democracy and to suggest the characteristic ways that distinct aspects of democratic performance may trade off against each other. The small-N comparison cannot demonstrate general relationships, but it may provide the raw material for specific causal inferences.

In this regard, it must be recognized that the general political characteristics of the third wave may have different causes in different contexts. It cannot be argued that the cases selected for the small-N inquiry, namely Brazil, Colombia, and Guatemala, are representative of the global sample in any statistical sense. Nor are they necessarily exemplary of the characteristic conditions of uneven democracy in Latin America overall, or even of the nine Latin American cases in the database. On the contrary, they simply illustrate, in clear and often dramatic fashion, how specific contextual conditions can contribute to creating the general political effects described by the big picture.

These are considerable differences across these three cases. Brazil went through a gradual transition, Guatemala a rapid one in conditions of civil war, while Colombia has employed elite pacts to restore and secure a restricted democracy by ensuring the alternation of the two main parties in government.[11] Yet their comparison does reveal the continuing impact of oligarchic power and military prerogatives on their overall democratic performance.

Electoral Politics versus Civil and Minority Rights

The first step is to ascertain whether these three cases conform to the big picture of institutional advance with retarded rights. The country measures for vertical accountability (figure 3) appear successful in tracking the main institutional changes.[12] Brazil goes through a "stepped" process of liberalization and transition, with a significant political opening in 1974 and legislative and indirect presidential elections in 1985 (Weffort 1989,

Figure 3. Vertical Accountability (ELECTION) in Brazil, Colombia, and Guatemala

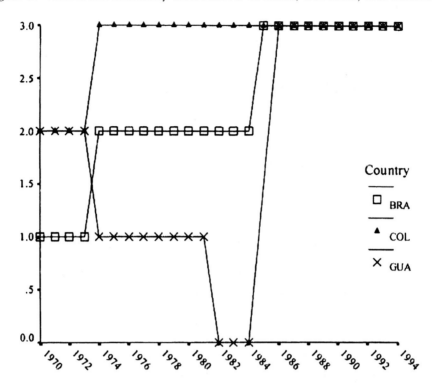

339; Lamounier 1989, 113; Skidmore 1989, 33).[13] The Guatemala measure drops with the fraudulent election of 1974 and hits zero with the military coup of General Ríos Montt in 1982. The rapid rise to a top score (indicating free and fair elections) in 1986 records the election of a civilian president, ending 30 years of more or less continuous military rule. The score nevertheless seems somewhat optimistic.[14]

Colombia has been free of direct military rule since 1958, but competitive party politics was constrained by the National Front coalition that shared all offices between the two major parties, including alternating presidencies (Kline 1996, 182). The measure marks the end of the coalition in 1974 and gives Colombia a top score for a free electoral system since that time (Archer 1995, 165; Deas 1986, 642).[15]

The country measures for civil and minority rights, in contrast, suggest that these are certainly no stronger in Colombia and Guatemala, while they appear to have weakened yet further in Brazil (figures 4 and 5). Brazil's civil rights score for 1994 indicates "high levels of political murder and disappearance," while its minority rights score comes to reflect "social ostracism." Brazil saw persistent abuse of civil rights by both civil and military police throughout the 1980s and into the 1990s, including torture, death squads, and the murder of street children. The failures of the judicial system leave many perpetrators unpunished. Indigenous minorities have suffered years of abuse, while black Brazilians experience consistent discrimination by the police, the judicial system, and the labor market (Mitchell and Wood 1997, 14; Reichmann 1995, 36; Amnesty International 1980–92; Pedone 1996, 86).[16]

Civil rights abuses continued unchecked in Guatemala despite the democratic transition. Groups targeted for torture and "disappearance" included journalists, trade unionists,

Figure 4. Civil Rights (CIVIL) in Brazil, Colombia, and Guatemala

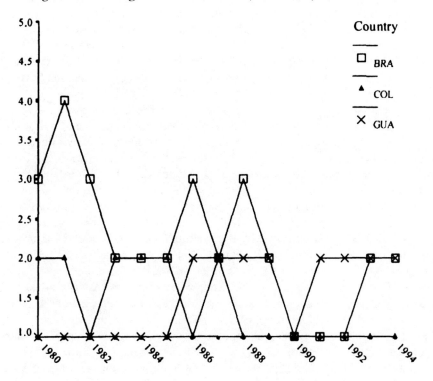

Figure 5. Minority Rights (DISCRIM) in Brazil, Colombia, and Guatemala

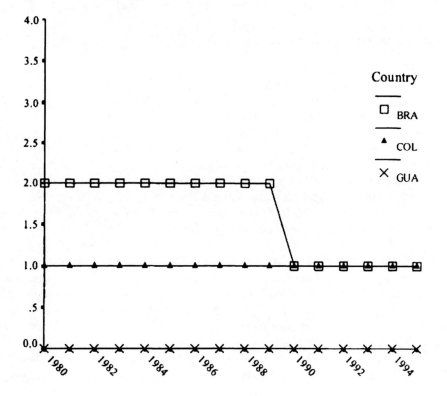

lawyers, judges, students, academics, lay workers, priests, party activists, and human rights campaigners. Until the mid-1990s, many leftist candidates could not run for office without fearing for their lives. The judicial system, moreover, systematically failed to bring the guilty to justice (Krznaric 1997, 64–65; Amnesty International 1980–1998; La Rue 1995, 76). Indigenous peoples have been forcibly recruited into self-defense patrols while their own organizations have been repressed; displaced populations have suffered some of the worst military violence (Krznaric 1997, 64–65).[17]

In Colombia, the military's counterinsurgency campaigns in response to guerrilla groups such as the Revolutionary Armed Forces of Colombia (FARC) and the proliferation of paramilitary organizations have led to similar abuses. Elections have been especially violent and marked by hundreds of assassinations of left-wing activists and candidates. Disappearances and death squads are a commonplace of political life. The government has ruled under an almost continuous state of siege since 1949, restraining civil authority and expanding the legal range of military control. Since 1991, public order courts have damaged due process and reinforced military impunity. Colombia's small indigenous minorities are treated as "subversive" by the security forces and routinely murdered over land disputes (Amnesty International 1980, 1982, 1991, 69; Molano 1992, 216; Chernick 1998, 29; Lee 1995, 29).[18]

This brief contextual account of the three cases confirms that the advances made in political rights and parliamentary representation have not been matched by improvements in the record of civil and minority rights. There are strong indications, furthermore, especially in Colombia and Guatemala, that a more open or intense process of political competition (and the extension of political rights) may lead to infringements of civil and minority rights. The oligarchy has little compunction about resorting to violence if it perceives its vital interests to be threatened. It must be conceded, however, that the state does not always perpetrate the abuses and may not necessarily be able to prevent them. In short, there are problems of government here as well as of democracy.

Vertical versus Horizontal Accountability

The degree of vertical accountability achieved through the electoral process may not be matched by a similar degree of horizontal accountability within the newly minted civilian and democratic government. Military accountability, in particular, is especially difficult in Latin America, where democratic constitutions are all imbued with special military prerogatives that reflect its "constitutional and supraconstitutional mission as guardian of national security and sovereignty" (Loveman 1998, 123). The military has recurrently invoked this mission when destroying democratic government. Despite the spate of democratic transitions of the 1980s, the military still demands "a formal constitutional and statutory role in the new regimes" (Loveman 1998, 121–27). As a virtual fourth branch of government, the military enjoys a wide range of privileges and immunities, including impunity for past and, often, present civil rights abuses (Cruz and Diamint 1998, 17).

Despite the spread of civilian government (GOVTYPE), the rate of military spending (MILITARY) in third wave democracies does not diminish (see figure 6).[19] Although continued high spending may relate to the demands of external defense in particular cases, it is remarkable that spending holds constant across all 23 new democracies in the database. This suggests that the third wave has failed to curtail the autonomy of many military establishments, which continue to extract institutional "rents" as their price for staying out of democratic politics.

The exception to this rule among the country cases is Brazil, where military spending fell steadily throughout the 1980s (see figure 7). This may properly be interpreted

Figure 6. Scaled Mean Horizontal Accountability Scores for 23 New Democracies

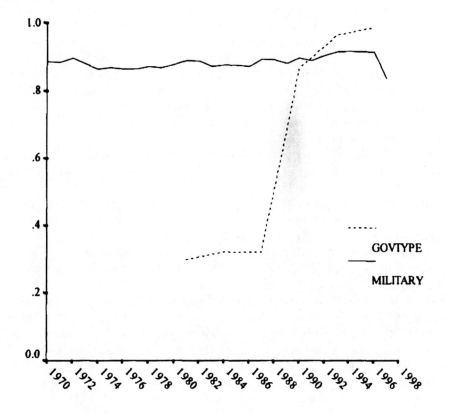

Figure 7. Horizontal Accountability (MILITARY) in Brazil, Colombia, and Guatemala

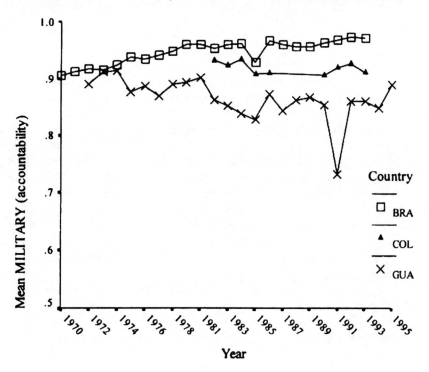

as reflecting a reduction in the military influence on civilian government (Hunter 1995, 425).[20] Still, many military prerogatives continue intact.[21] The military retains autonomy in the management of its own corporate business and continues to act "constitutionally" in the defense of law and order (Acuña and Smulovitz 1996, 26). It is in this role that the military and its police frequently infringe basic civil rights and liberties.

In Guatemala, by contrast, military spending continued to increase throughout the democratic transition of the mid-1980s. War against the guerrillas continued unabated and military control of the countryside was comprehensive as ever (Wilson 1993, 136). At least 50,000 people were resettled in model villages and 725,000 placed in civilian "defense patrols" (Dunkerley 1994, 79).

The new democratic constitution contained 40 clauses of military immunities and prerogatives (Amnesty International 1987; Jonas 19891), including impunity for past rights violations, with the military intelligence apparatus intact and the military role in internal security unmitigated (Zur 1995, 56). There was no democratic scrutiny of either the military's political autonomy or its economic–corporate power, and the military threatened the government at the first sign of civilian interference in its affairs (Trudeau 1993, 131; Sieder and Dunkerley 1994). The almost complete lack of accountability is apparent in the feeble mandate of the Truth Commission which finally began its hearings in 1996, and the persistence of military violations of civil rights.

Military spending in Colombia remains high and constant, reflecting the steady expansion of the military's legal mandate to wage war on the guerrillas (Hartlyn 1989, 317). The military has made full use of its enhanced powers in the "Special Public Order Zones" (such as those created by government emergency decrees in 1997) where some of the most flagrant abuses of civil rights have occurred (Amnesty International 1997, 122). Furthermore, the military's use of paramilitary groups removes any vestige of accountability and reinforces its impunity (Vargas Meza 1998, 25; Chernick 1998, 29; Pearce 1990, 214).[22] Thus, the problem of horizontal accountability is quite as serious in Colombia as it is in war torn Guatemala and certainly more acute than in Brazil. In all three cases, the problem explains much of the failure to establish secure civil rights under the rule of law.

Property Rights versus Civil and Minority Rights

All liberal democratic constitutionalism encompasses specific individual rights that provide a bulwark against unbridled majority control and thereby act to protect democracy (Sunstein 1993, 342). Liberal theory sees this as a virtue of all private rights, both civil and economic. But property rights are considered to be distinct from civil rights in general, since they directly constrain government power (Nedelsky 1993, 242) and underpin the protection of civil rights by diffusing political power (Dahl 1989, 252). Property rights are also understood to contribute to system stability by limiting the policy dimensions that are subject to democratic choice and by preventing recurrent struggles over the distribution of wealth in particular (Riker and Weimer 1993, 80). Yet despite their virtuous contribution to constraint and stability, property rights are still seen as ambivalent and potentially antidemocratic. For, in contrast to the inclusive quality of most civil rights, property rights have come to be "exclusive" (Macpherson 1978, 199), and sometimes violently so.

The graphic description of the third wave democracies drawn from the database shows that the rise of electoral politics and vertical accountability is closely tracked by the measure of protection of property rights (see figure 8), while civil and minority rights remain unprotected. This synchronicity is strengthened in some degree by the "dual transition" in Central and Eastern Europe to democratic systems and market-

Figure 8. Scaled Mean Vertical Accountability and Property Rights for
23 New Democracies

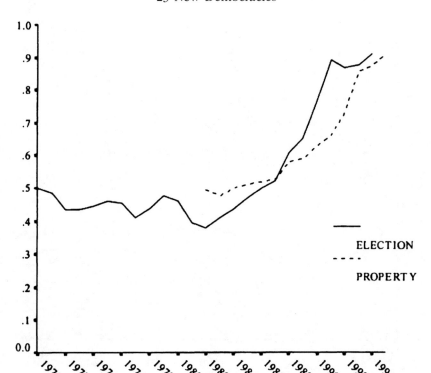

based economies (5 out of 23 cases in the database). But in the elite-centered view of
democratic transition, the pacts and settlements that underpin the process are designed
first and foremost to protect elite interests and thus bind elite actors to the democratic
outcome (Karl and Schmitter 1991, 281). Property rights therefore have an "overriding
importance" in all new democracies (Schmitter 1995, 23), while the extension of political rights that accompanies the transition may encourage challenges to those rights. It
is often the violent vindication or defense of property rights that links the increases in
political rights to the infringements of civil rights. In the three Latin American cases, the
property rights that are most keenly contested are those of landed property.[23]

The country case variables all suggest that property rights became better protected
in the late 1980s and 1990s (see figure 9). In Brazil the landowning oligarchy mobilized
sufficient support within the National Constituent Assembly (1987–88) to resist calls for an
agrarian reform during the process of democratic transition (Payne 2000; Hagopian 1996,
251). The Rural Democratic Union in particular fought hard to protect landed property
from the threat of "reformist" governments in the 1980s (Payne 2000), and the titling of
Indian lands in the 1990s favored the private landowners (Schwartzman et al. 1996, 37).
By 1995 there was little or no perceived risk of land expropriation in Brazil. Legal and
constitutional protections have consistently been backed by force, and landowners have
enjoyed the support of civil and military police in suppressing the claims of peasants
and indigenous minorities (Amnesty International 1980–92; Payne 2000). Land disputes
have led to widespread killing in the countryside; most of the victims have been leaders
of rural trade unions and peasant movements (especially the Landless Movement) and

Figure 9. Property Rights (PROPERTY) in Brazil, Colombia, and Guatemala

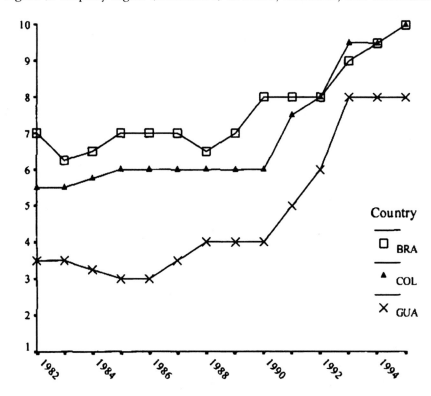

priests, lawyers, and environmentalists working with them. Indeed, the democratic transition has hardly mitigated the violent defense of landed property that was commonplace
under the military governments (Foweraker 1981), and may even have exacerbated it.

In Guatemala, too, the rural oligarchy's traditional political dominance has continued
through the period of democratic transition. But here, the popular organizations pressing
for agrarian reform were explicitly linked to guerrilla activity, and treated accordingly.
Peasant and indigenous groups were routinely evicted from the land by private or state
security forces (Schirmer 1997), including both the police and specialized "rapid reaction" units (Amnesty International, 1997, 25), frequently using illegal and violent means.
The judicial system tended to favor the landowners in land disputes and to ignore the
landless (Bastos and Camus 1995, 117–18; Gidley 1996, 34; Amnesty International 1997,
25–26). When the issue of land reform was eventually debated as part of the peace
process, landowning interests successfully lobbied for a pattern of modernization based
on respect for private property (Krznaric 1999, 12–13).

The defense of landed property by the traditional oligarchy in Colombia (Pearce
1990, xii; Kline 1996, 177) has been bolstered by the creation of a "narco-oligarchy"
that has used the profits from the illicit drug trade to amass some eight million acres of
land since the 1970s. Old and new oligarchies alike employ private armies to repel land
claims by both guerrilla and peasant groups, often with extreme violence (Vargas Meza
1998, 23; Restrepo 1992, 289). The attacks on indigenous groups during land disputes
have often led to tortures and assassinations (Pearce 1990, 134).

Colombia is distinctive in further securing the regime of private property in land
by pursuing successful peace accords with a number of guerrilla organizations, such as

M–19. But the overall pattern of protecting property rights through violent violation of civil rights is very similar to that of Brazil and Guatemala. The three cases differ only in degree, and in every case the lack of accountability of military and police and the fierce defense of property rights lead inexorably to the assaults on civil and minority rights.[24]

EXPLAINING UNEVEN PERFORMANCE

The small-N comparison of the three Latin American cases confirms the big picture of the uneven performance of third wave democracies drawn from the database. In particular, it shows how political party competition through electoral politics can take hold even while civil arid minority rights remain fragile and uncertain. It also suggests specific causes that may produce this particular pattern of uneven performance; namely, the unchanging nature of oligarchic power and the constitutional and political prerogatives that render the military largely unaccountable. It shows how the oligarchy and military often work hand in hand, with military police and paramilitary organizations acting to protect oligarchic power, especially in the form of private property in land.[25] Thus, the evidence of the small-N inquiry points plausibly to the conclusion that it is the combination of oligarchic power and military prerogatives that explains the patchy and imperfect rule of law and the failure to achieve a stable rights regime.

This conclusion must remain speculative on at least two counts. First, although the case materials reveal different ways that the oligarchy and military undermine the rule of law, they still fall short of specifying the key causal mechanisms that produce this effect. Second, it is impossible to "test" this conclusion using statistical methods of any kind because there are no comparative measures of oligarchic power, and hence no easy way of operationalizing the causal mechanisms at work, whatever they are. It is possible, however, to offer a brief theoretical statement of these causal mechanisms—a statement that is consistent with both previous field research and the mainstream literature but that must remain subject to further testing through the inductive method.

The main theoretical claim can be briefly stated. Oligarchic power produces an imperfect rule of law through the structural support it provides to clientelist politics. The pervasive presence of clientelism, in turn, has two major political effects. First, it underpins what Weber terms a patrimonial pattern of politics, which shows no clear and enduring distinction between the private and public spheres (Weber 1968, 1028) and therefore no cultural defense of a *res publica* that requires the rule of law. Second, clientelism assumes and promotes a particularistic style of politics that produces and reproduces power through particular relationships of favor and loyalty that are inimical to the general claims of individual rights. The tension between the particularism of clientelism and the universalism of an effective regime of individual rights has been explored elsewhere (Foweraker 1993, chap. 10, 1995, chap. 5; Foweraker and Landman 1997, chap. 2). These studies support the assertion that particularistic politics impair the rule of law in many third wave democracies and that this "particularism vigorously inhabits most formal political institutions" (O'Donnell 1997, 49).

Thus, in Brazil, regional oligarchies have retained their traditional powers through deeply embedded systems of patronage, while clientelist political machines in national government, especially the national congress, have operated to protect military autonomy and landed property (Hagopian 1996, 222, 247, 249; De Souza Martins 1996, 196, 204, 209; Mainwaring 1995, 387–90; Weffort 1989, 340). In Guatemala, party politics is patronage politics, where the traditional oligarchic families have continued to exert a powerful influence over the elected executive (Rosada Granados 1992, 103; Casaus Arzu

1992, 106; Dosal 1995, 188). In Colombia, national politics is divided among oligarchic domains that encompass local and regional politics and severely constrain the reach of political parties and political representation (Abel and Palacios 1991, 674–76; Archer 1995, 190–91; Melo 1998, 66; Restrepo 1992, 282; Hartlyn 1988, 172–76; Pecaut 1992, 220; Leal Buitrago 1990, 35; Kline 1996, 173; García Márquez 1997).

The theoretical assertion is that it is conditions like these that subvert the rule of law and prevent judicial reform; that typically promote trade-offs between political rights and civil rights, property rights and minority rights, and vertical and horizontal accountability; and that therefore go a long way to explain the differentiated contours of the third wave, at least in these particular cases.

Oligarchic power is not abstract or invisible; it operates through the interrelationships among powerful political families. In Brazil, the principal families of the political elite of Minas Gerais remain especially strong, and have successfully colonized political parties and maintained control of local politics, in addition to preventing agrarian reform (Hagopian 1996, 222, 247, 249). Moreover, "no group or political party is today in a position to govern Brazil except by means of alliances with those traditional groups, and therefore, without large concessions to the needs of political clientelism" (De Souza Martins 1996, 196). In Guatemala, the networks of the Castillo, Novella, Gutiérrez, and Herrera families enjoy government protection and incentives to their areas of economic interest—brewing, cement, chicken, and sugar, respectively. Family members and high-level employees frequently occupy government jobs, including ministerial posts (Casaus Arzu 1992, 106). In Colombia, apart from the new "narco-oligarchy," traditional families dominate politics and the press, "the sons of ex-presidents [appear] as candidates for the presidency or other political posts in disproportionate numbers, [arid so do] the sons of senators and regional leaders" (Melo 1998, 66).

The Rule of Law and the Survival of Third Wave Democracies

This inquiry into the political context of the third wave is very far from complete. It takes a selection of measures from the database in order to examine just three relationships in three country cases. This summary inquiry, furthermore, may recognize, but cannot explore in detail, the impact of contextual differences on the uneven quality of democracy: regional political traditions and the strength of federalism in Brazil, the militarization of the countryside and genocide in Guatemala, the drug trade and the state's renunciation of its monopoly on violence in Colombia. Yet this study does reveal striking similarities across the cases. Electoral politics appear to persist in the absence of civil and minority rights. The armed forces and the police remain largely unaccountable to elected civilian government. The landed oligarchy frequently resorts to violence to protect its private property. Consequently, oligarchic actors are free to pursue political power through competitive party politics; but the poor, the powerless, and the minorities remain unprotected and subject to abuse.

What is at issue here is the rule of law. In some degree, this rule is imperfect because of the incomplete or contradictory nature of the law itself. The special immunities and protections of the military or police clearly contribute to damaging the integrity of civil and minority rights. (The residual problem here is the often long-term suspension of constitutional guarantees in specious conditions of domestic strife or national emergency.)

The main problem, however, is simply that the law is bypassed or subverted, and this is a problem of accountability. In principle, democratic government is designed to safeguard the rule of law by making government accountable to the people. But in conditions of continuing oligarchic power and clientelistic control, the principles and practice of accountability are fractured or enfeebled. The result is freely elected governments that "either do not respect or do not maintain the state based on the rule of law" (Merkel 1999, 10; compare Zakaria 1997). The governments enjoy the democratic legitimacy of popular election, but the people are not sufficiently sovereign to defend the rule of law and prevent the violation of their liberties and protections.

The mainstream accounts of these new democracies argue, however, that they will never be "consolidated"—will not survive—without an effective "rule of law to ensure legal guarantees for citizens' freedoms and independent associational life" (Linz and Stepan 1996, 7). It is the rule of law that underpins consolidated democracy by its specific effects on political attitudes and political behavior.[26] Without the rule of law, democracy will have no routine and ingrained expectations that make it the "only game in town" (Linz and Stepan 1996, 15–16).[27] It will not, therefore, achieve the "widespread legitimation" (Diamond 1997b, xix) so essential to consolidation.[28] Thus, consensus and active consent will enable new democracies to endure. But these conditions will only obtain if the new democratic governments are capable of defending the integrity of the rule of law.

Still, the historical reality of the third wave and the increasing longevity of many third wave democracies cast doubt on these assumptions. The evidence suggests, on the contrary, that third wave democracies can and do survive without a fully effective rule of law. The law has a formal presence but is not fully established, because it has to contend continually with the informal rules that coalesce in clientelism (O'Donnell 1997, 47). The result is an imperfect rule of law that is repeatedly subverted by the informal rules that favor the oligarchy and discriminate systematically against the powerless. What survives is a form of democracy that is only partially constrained by Rechtstaat (Linz 1964; for more detail, see Foweraker 2001).

The salient exception to this institutionalized informality (partial or complete, depending on the country in question) is the electoral arena, which remains protected or "ring-fenced" (O'Donnell 1997, 49). This relative immunity may be achieved through the measure of accountability implicit in political party competition. It may also be buttressed by international monitoring and stimulated by the requirements of international legitimacy and finance. After all, membership in the democratic club brings privileges and serves to assuage sanctions, and governments can claim membership only so long as elections proceed regularly and unhindered.

The database provides graphic evidence of the imperfect rule of law in third wave democracies and of the enduring division between ring-fenced electoral politics and the fragility of civil and minority rights and liberties. It may be conjectured that the uneven quality of these new democracies is simply a consequence of being new, and that, given time, they will come to fit the more even profile of the old democracies. The evidence is not yet in, however. Whether the electoral principle alone is sufficient to promote a fully effective rule of law over the longer term is an open question, one that will no doubt receive different answers in different political contexts and at different historical moments.

APPENDIX: VARIABLES AND CASES

The Database of Liberal Democratic Performance was designed to capture the third wave, and therefore covers the years 1970 to 1998, inclusive. It comprises 21 variables and 40 cases. Because scores do not exist for each variable for each year, the database contains just 8,958 observations out of a potential total of 24,360.

Variables

Variables were chosen according to their geographic and temporal range, their affinity with the values to be measured, and their empirical quality. The database was designed for both balance and texture, with an even distribution of measures to values, a mixture of ordinal and interval level indicators, and a variety of scale ranges. The following list classifies the variables according to the distinct aspects of democratic performance and references their sources.

Accountability

> ELECTION executive recruitment competition, Polity III (Jaggers and Gurr 1995)
> GOVTYPE civilian versus military government, Binghamton (Cingranelli and Richards 1999)
> MILITARY military spending as percentage of total central government spending (IMF 1997)

Representation

> DISPORP electoral disproportionality, Gallagher's least-squares (Lijphart 1994; Zelaznik 1999)
> PARSEATS size of legislature/number of seats held by largest party (Banks 1997)

Constraint

> EXECONST executive constraints, Polity III (Jaggers and Gurr 1995)
> LOCALTAX local and state government tax revenue as percent of central tax revenue (IMF 1997)

Participation

> LEGIVOTE legislative votes as percent of voting-age population (International IDEA 1997)
> PRESVOTE presidential vote as percent of voting-age population (International IDEA 1997)

Political Rights

> COMPETE competitiveness of participation, Polity Ill (Jaggers and Gurr 1995)
> UNION trade union rights, Binghamton (Cingranelli and Richards 1999)
> CENSOR government media censorship, Binghamton (Cingranelli and Richards 1999)

Civil Rights

> CIVIL Amnesty International human rights reports (Poe and Tate 1994; Poe et al. 1999)
> UNEQUAL income inequality, Gini coefficient (Deininger and Squire 1996)
> PRISON prisoners per 100,000 population (Walmsley 1996; SPACE/Council of Europe)

Property Rights

>   ECONFREE Index of Economic Freedom, Heritage Foundation (Johnson et al. 1998)
>   PROPERTY risk of expropriation, Political Risk Services (Knack and Keefer 1995)

Minority Rights

>   WOMENREP percent of women in lower house of legislature (Inter-Parliamentary Union 1995)
>   EQUAL women's equal rights, Binghamton (Cingranelli and Richards 1999)
>   DISCRIM political discrimination, Minorities at Risk (Haxton and Gurr 1997)
>   RESTRICT cultural restrictions, Minorities at Risk (Haxton and Gurr 1997)

All 21 variables have been used in some form in published work (although this study has often varied their geographical scope and temporal range). ELECTION, EXECONST, and COMPETE are taken directly from the Polity III dataset created and analyzed by Jaggers and Gurr (1995). GOVTYPE, UNION, CENSOR, and EQUAL are all found in the Binghamton Human Rights dataset applied by Cingranelli and Richards (1998). DISCRIM and RESTRICT come from the Minorities at Risk dataset and appear in a number of studies by Haxton and Gurr (1997). The CIVIL variable is an updated version of the one used by Poe and Tate (1994).

Table 1. Democracies Compared

Old Democracies (17)	
USA, Canada, Japan	Highly developed capitalist states
Costa Rica, Venezuela, Colombia	Latin America's three "old" institutional democracies
Denmark, Netherlands, Switzerland	"Consensual" democracies[a]
UK, France, Italy	Nonconsensual democracies[a]
Australia, New Zealand, India, Sri Lanka	Shared British colonial heritage: in Asia/Oceania
Israel	Only Middle Eastern old democracy
New Democracies (23)	
Chile, Argentina, Brazil	Southern Cone dictatorships
El Salvador, Nicaragua, Guatemala	Central American cases with civil wars
Poland, Hungary	Economically advanced Central European, non-Ottoman
Bulgaria, Romania, Albania	Economically less advanced Central European, Ottoman heritage
Spain, Portugal, Greece	Southern European dictatorships
South Korea, Philippines, Taiwan	East, Southeast Asian
Pakistan, Bangladesh, Turkey	Islamic influence
South Africa, Malawi, Ghana	African states with British colonial experience

[a]As classified by Lijphart (1984, 219).

The variables DISPROP, LOCALTAX, LEGIVOTE, PRESVOTE, UNEQUAL, PRISON, and WOMENREP all derive from Lijphart's work (1994, 1999); he uses them to create proxy measures of representation, constraint, participation, civil rights, and minority rights. In some cases, these variables were extended by calculating new scores (for example, DISPROP) or importing new information (for example, PRISON). Hunter (1995) provides the inspiration for the MILITARY variable. Vanhanen's (1997) Index of Democratization uses an indicator very similar to PARSEATS. The Heritage Foundation's ECONFREE is analyzed in Johnson et al. (1998), while Knack and Keefer (1995) use PROPERTY for their study of property rights.

Cases

Cases were selected on both methodological and practical grounds. The initial population was the 118 countries described as either "liberal" or "electoral" democracies by Diamond (1997a) and as reaching a minimum threshold of procedural democracy by Freedom House standards. Countries with fewer than 1.5 million inhabitants were eliminated (leaving 82 cases), as were countries formed or reformed as nation–states since 1970, including both Germany and the Czech Republic (leaving 67 cases). Countries were also eliminated if they did not appear in either the Minorities at Risk database (Haxton and Gurr 1997), the Binghamton Human Rights database, or the Political Risk Services database on property rights (Knack and Keefer 1995). This left 56 cases, of which 17 were "established" democracies.

Additional countries were eliminated in order to balance the number of "established" and "new" democracies and to achieve an appropriate geographic spread. This left 40 countries, distributed into selected clusters on historical, geographical, economic, or institutional grounds. Clusters such as the three former Central American dictatorships (Guatemala, El Salvador, and Nicaragua) were included, whereas cases like Papua New Guinea or Mali were excluded.

NOTES

We wish to acknowledge the support of the Economic and Social Research Council of the United Kingdom for our research project, "Comparative Democratic Performance: Institutional Efficacy and Individual Rights."

1 Twenty-five years ago there were some 35 democracies in the world, most of them wealthy and industrialized nations in the West. Today this number has grown to about 120. Huntington argues that at least 30 countries turned democratic between 1974 and 1990 (1993, 3), while Diamond takes Freedom House data to show that the number of democracies increased from 39 in 1974 to 118 in 1996 (Diamond 1997a, 22). Consequently, democratic governments now outnumber all others. Jaggers and Gurr (1995) claim that the proportion of democracies rose from 27 percent in 1975 to 50 percent in 1994.

2 The "remarkable consensus concerning the legitimacy of liberal democracy" served as the premise of Fukuyama's thesis on "the end of history" (1992, xi). Doubts about the quality of the new democracies imply that the new democratic constitutions may enshrine democratic principles that fail to operate in practice, and that the populations of new democratic states do not therefore enjoy liberal democratic freedoms. But it is also the case that some of the most populous states are not democracies (China, Indonesia).

3 In other words, as political rights advance, civil rights decline and deteriorate. This was as true of Europe after World War I as it is of many countries of the third wave. Civil rights are often violated by traditional oligarchies in their fight to maintain property and privileges.

4 The degree to which a political system is democratic depends on the practical effectiveness and political relevance of voting in terms of participation (the promotion of popular choice), liberty (the freedom to pursue one's goals), and equality (the facilitation of self-respect and self-realization)" (Riker and Weimer 1993, 79, n. 2).

5 Any model will necessarily reduce the political complexity of the real world, and it is recognized that none of the distinct elements of this model constitutes a pristine category. For example, the model distinguishes between political and civil rights, in keeping both with mainstream democratic theory and with most extant measures of democratic performance. Yet the distinction may easily be overdrawn, insofar as free and fair elections clearly require effective civil liberties. For the practical purposes of comparative analysis, however, it is still possible to separate the basic rights and procedures of electoral politics (regular elections, universal suffrage, the right to form political parties, and so on) from civil rights violations, even though the latter will often impair both the "freedom" and "fairness" of elections. The blurred boundary between civil and political rights is recurrently evident in the small-N comparison presented here, but the distinction continues to create considerable analytical leverage.

6 A full account of the construction of the database and the decisions governing the rejection and selection of variables, in particular, can be found in Foweraker and Krznaric (2001). Overall, we sought to diversify data sources as much as possible and to review measures from the cognate disciplines of international relations, economics, and even criminology, as well as political science; to strike a balance between ordinal and interval-level measures, varying scale ranges to increase overall sensitivity; to leave all the measures unweighted, since weightings are so difficult to justify; to avoid measures derived from either events data, owing to inconsistencies of reporting and recording, or survey data, owing to the intractable problems of applying them comparatively; and to include at least two and no more than four measures for each of the eight liberal democratic values—to increase confidence in the validity of the measures.

7 The Polity III Democracy Scale (Jaggers and Gurr 1995) and the Freedom House Index of Political Freedom (Freedom House 1997) are the standard aggregate indices of democracy that both place country cases on a single, ordinal scale. In principle, the Polity III scale encompasses electoral and representative institutions, while the Freedom House Index reflects both institutions and political rights, such as freedom of opposition and association.

8 All variables have been scaled from 0 to 1 for ease of presentation, despite the distortions that different scale ranges may introduce.

9 The annual average scores from Polity III (1970–94) and Freedom House (1972–98) were plotted for the 40 cases in this database, with both variables scaled from zero to one. They show a third wave that builds slowly in the 1970s, gains momentum in the 1980s, and accelerates rapidly in the late 1980s and early 1990s. This is the "global trend in the direction of democratization" (Jaggers and Gurr 1995, 477) that reaches a "high-water mark" in the early 1990s (Diamond 1997a, 23). But although the number of "electoral democracies" rapidly increased in this way, the number of "liberal democracies" (with higher scores from Freedom House) expanded more slowly (Diamond 1997a, 25).

10 In the 17 old democracies of the database, both the institutional variables and the rights variables remain flat and constant over time. Since these are all liberal democracies where individual and minority rights are mainly protected under the rule of law, this picture of "no change" (not shown here) conforms to our expectations.

11 By a minimal and strictly procedural definition, Colombia is an old democracy. But its electoral politics became fully competitive again only in 1974—at the beginning of the third wave—and this makes it appropriate for the small-N inquiry.

12 Raw scores rather than scales will be used for all individual country measures.

13 The measure does not reflect the turning point of 1982, when the opposition gained a majority in the lower chamber and the government permitted direct election of state governors.

14 The return to civilian rule was tightly controlled by the armed forces, which have continued to dominate Guatemalan political life and subvert the electoral process (Jonas 1991, 157). But the electoral system has survived a number of difficult challenges since 1986 (coup attempts in 1988 and 1989 and a "self-coup" by the president in 1993), and an end was negotiated to the

civil war (Jonas 1991, 167). So there is some good reason for the measure to remain constant during this time.

15 Even after 1974, however, all cabinet ministers, governors, mayors, and other administrative positions not part of the civil service were still divided equally between the main parties. It was not until 1986 that the system changed to something resembling government and opposition (Kline 1996, 182–83).

16 Improvements include the prohibition of torture in the 1988 Constitution, some prosecutions for rights abuse in 1992, and government endorsement of international agreements to protect rights (Amnesty International 1989, 1993). But these are changes more in principle than in practice.

17 The measure does not reflect some improvements. Human rights procurators have played an important role in the fight against impunity. The demobilization of military commissioners in 1995 reduced military control of justice in the countryside. The presence of the UN Mission to Guatemala (MINUGUA), as part of the peace process, has been a deterrent to human rights abuses (Krznaric 1999, 10).

18 By the mid-1990s, public order court cases accounted for half of Colombia's prison inmates, 90 percent of whom were still awaiting trial (Weiner 1996, 35).

19 This variable has been inverted for the purposes of presentation; for example, if military spending is 8 percent of total central government expenditure, the inverted score is 0.92. Less military spending represents higher democratic performance.

20 Hunter shows a decline in spending similar to our database, but her absolute levels of military spending are higher because she excludes the government's internal debt in her calculations of government expenditure (Hunter 1995, 437, n. 46).

21 When civilian replaced military government in 1985, the armed forces retained six cabinet posts and a majority on the National Security Council (CSN) and National Information Service (SNI) (Hagopian 1996, 226; Acuña and Smulovitz 1996, 24–25), but lost some ground in the 1990 restructuring of these two bodies.

22 A measure of accountability may possibly be restored through a negotiated peace process with guerrilla groups. Success has been patchy. One of the principal groups, M–19, was brought into electoral politics, and other accords have been signed on a piecemeal basis. But the issues of military reform, judicial reform, and rights guarantees have not been addressed (Leal Buitrago 1990, 41; Hartlyn 1988, 224–28; McDonald 1997, 11).

23 In this regard, the small-N comparison tends to confirm Barrington Moore's general thesis that the presence of a strong rural oligarchy impedes the emergence of "the Western version of democracy" (1966, 418).

24 It may be objected that property owners are quite "within their rights" to defend their property and do not infringe civil or minority rights in the process. But property rights, especially landed property rights, are legally moot and highly contested throughout much of Latin America, and their defense by the oligarchy is often nothing more or less than a raw assertion of oligarchic power. For a full account of the legal complexities of land titling and tenure in Brazil see Foweraker 1981, chaps. 4, 5.

25 Military prerogatives are clearly important in these cases, but may not be so everywhere. In the new democracies of Eastern Europe, the consolidated privileges of the nomenclatura may have the same salient role. In the same way, property rights are likely to have a different impact on democratic performance in these two contexts (Borneman 1997, 24).

26 It emerges from Linz and Stepan's argument that the rule of law is central to the other four "arenas" of consolidated democracy. On the one hand, "the necessary degree of autonomy and independence of civil and political society must be embedded in and supported by the rule of law." On the other, the rule of law is integral to a "useable state bureaucracy" and a regulated "economic society" (Linz and Stepan 1996, 10–11).

27 This sense of consensus about the rules of the game is clearly linked to Przeworski's notion of "institutionalizing uncertainty" (Przeworski 1986, 58) because the political actors must be convinced of the institutional guarantees that minimize the threat to their longer-term interests. But the notion refers most directly to the reiterative game of electoral democracy, in which today's losers must be able to think of themselves as tomorrow's winners.

28 It is not always clear, however, "who must accept formal democratic rules, and how deep must this acceptance run" (O'Donnell 1997, 48) and, in particular, whether it is just the oligarchy or the mass of the population that must support democracy. Although most survey data seek out the general attitudes of the population, the Latin American historical record demonstrates that "democracies are overthrown by elite conspiracies, not popular revolt," with loss of popular support neither "a necessary nor sufficient condition for democratic breakdown" (Remmer 1995, 113).

REFERENCES

Abel, Christopher, and Marco Palacios. 1991. Colombia Since 1958. In *The Cambridge History of Latin America, Volume 3, Latin America Since 1930: Spanish South America*, ed. Leslie Bethell. Cambridge: Cambridge University Press. 629–86.

Acuña, Carlos H., and Catalina Smulovitz. 1996. Adjusting the Armed Forces to Democracy: Successes, Failures, and Ambiguities in the Southern Cone. In *Constructing Democracy: Human Rights, Citizenship, and Society in Latin America*, ed. Elizabeth Jelin and Eric Hershberg. Boulder: Westview Press. 13–38.

Amnesty International. 1986–97. Annual Report. London: Amnesty International.

Archer, David. 1995. Party Strength and Weakness in Colombia's Besieged Democracy. In *Building Democratic Institutions: Party Systems in Latin America*, ed. Scott Mainwaring and Timothy R. Scully. Stanford: Stanford University Press. 164–99.

Banks, Arthur S. 1997. Cross-Polity Time-Series Data. Binghamton: State University of New York.

Bastos, Santiago, and Manuela Camus. 1995. *Abriendo caminos: las organizaciones mayas desde el novel hasta el Acuerdo de Derechos Indígenas*. Guatemala City: FLACSO.

Borneman, John. 1997. *Settling Accounts: Violence, Justice, and Accountability in Postsocialist Europe*. Princeton: Princeton University Press.

Casaus Arzu, Marta. 1992. *Guatemala: linaje y racismo*. Guatemala City: FLACSO.

Chernick, Marc W. 1998. The Paramilitarization of the War in Colombia. *NACLA Report on the Americas* 31, 5 (March–April): 28–33.

Cingranelli, David L., and David L. Richards. 1998. Human Rights Dataset. Binghamton: State University of New York.

———. 1999. Measuring the Level, Pattern, and Sequence of Government Respect for Physical Integrity Rights. *International Studies Quarterly* 43, 2: 407–17.

Cruz, Consuelo, and Rut Diamint. 1998. The New Military Autonomy in Latin America. *Journal of Democracy* 9, 4 (October): 115–27.

Dahl, Robert. 1989. *Democracy and Its Critics*. New Haven: Yale University Press.

Deas, Malcolm. 1986. The Troubled Course of Colombian Peacemaking. *Third World Quarterly* 8, 2: 639–57.

Deininger, Klaus, and Lyn Squire. 1996. A New Data Set for Measuring Income Inequality. *World Bank Economic Review* 10, 3: 565–91.

De Souza Martins, Jose. 1996. Clientelism and Corruption in Contemporary Brazil. In *Political Corruption in Europe and Latin America*, ed. Walter Little and Eduardo Posada–Carbo. London: Institute of Latin American Studies, University of London. 195–218.

Diamond, Larry. 1997a. The End of the Third Wave and the Global Future of Democracy. Reihe PolitikwiBenschaft/Political Science Series No. 45. Vienna: Institute for Advanced Studies. July.

———. 1997b. Introduction: In Search of Consolidation. In *Consolidating the Third Wave Democracies: Themes and Perspectives*, ed. Larry Diamond, Marc F. Plattner, Yun–han Chu, and Hung–mao Tien. Baltimore: Johns Hopkins University Press. xv–xlix.

———. 1999. *Developing Democracy: Toward Consolidation*. Baltimore: Johns Hopkins University Press.

Dosal, Paul. 1995. *Power in Transition: The Rise of Guatemala's Industrial Oligarchy, 1987–1994*. Westport: Praeger.

Dunkerley, James. 1994. *The Pacification of Central America*. London: Verso.

Foweraker, Joe. 1981. *The Struggle for Land: A Political Economy of the Pioneer Frontier in Brazil from 1930 to the Present Day*. Cambridge: Cambridge University Press.

———. 1993. *Popular Mobilization in Mexico: The Teachers' Movement, 1977–87*. Cambridge: Cambridge University Press.

———. 1995. *Theorizing Social Movements*. London: Pluto Press.

———. 2001. Transformation, Transition, Consolidation: Democratisation in Latin America. In *The Blackwell Companion to Political Sociology*, ed. Kate Nash and Alan Scott. Oxford: Blackwell. 355–65.

Foweraker, Joe, and Roman Krznaric. 1999. Database of Liberal Democratic Performance. Computer file and codebook. Study Number 4046. National Data Archive, University of Essex. <www.data–archive.ac.uk>

———. 2000. Measuring Liberal Democratic Performance: An Empirical and Conceptual Critique. *Political Studies* 48, 4: 759–87.

———. 2001. How to Construct a Database of Liberal Democratic Performance. *Democratization* 8, 3: 1–25.

Foweraker, Joe, and Todd Landman. 1997. *Citizenship Rights and Social Movements: A Comparative and Statistical Analysis*. New York: Oxford University Press.

Freedom House. 1997. *Comparative Survey of Freedom*. New York: Freedom House.

Fukuyama, Francis. 1992. *The End of History and the Last Man*. London: Penguin.

García Márquez, Gabriel. 1997. *News of a Kidnapping*. London: Jonathan Cape.

Gidley, Ruth. 1996. The Politics of Land in Guatemala, 1985–1995. Master's thesis. Institute of Latin American Studies, University of London.

Hagopian, Frances. 1990. Democracy by Undemocratic Means? Elites, Political Pacts, and Regime Transition in Brazil. *Comparative Political Studies* 23, 2: 147–70.

———. 1996. Traditional Politics and Regime Change in Brazil. Cambridge: Cambridge University Press.

Hartlyn, Jonathan. 1988. *The Politics of Coalition Rule in Colombia*. Cambridge: Cambridge University Press.

———. 1989. Colombia: The Politics of Violence and Accommodation. In *Democracy in Developing Countries*, ed. Larry Diamond, Juan J. Linz, and Seymour Martin Lipset. Boulder/London: Lynne Rienner/Adamantine Press. 291–334.

Haxton, Michael, Ted Robert Gurr, et al. 1997. Minorities at Risk. Dataset. College Park: University of Maryland.

Higley, John, and Richard Gunther, eds. 1992. *Elites and Democratic Consolidation in Latin America and Southern Europe*. Cambridge: Cambridge University Press.

Hunter, Wendy. 1995. Politicians Against Soldiers: Contesting the Military in Postauthoritarian Brazil. *Comparative Politics* 27, 4 (July): 425–43.

Huntington, Samuel P. 1993. Democracy's Third Wave. In *The Global Resurgence of Democracy*, ed. Larry Diamond and Marc F. Plattner. Baltimore: Johns Hopkins University Press. 3–25.

International IDEA. 1997. Voter Turnout from 1945 to 1997. A Global Report. Stockholm: International Institute for Democracy and Electoral Assistance.

International Monetary Fund (IMP). 1997 and various years. *Government Finance Statistics Yearbook*. Washington, DC: IMF.

Inter-Parliamentary Union. 1995. Women in Parliaments, 1945–1995 A World Statistical Survey. Geneva: Inter-Parliamentary Union.

Jaggers, Keith, and Ted Robert Gurr. 1995. Tracking Democracy's Third Wave with the Polity III Data. *Journal of Peace Research* 32, 4: 469–82.

Johnson, Bryan, Kim R. Holmes, and Melanie Kirkpatrick. 1998. Index of Economic Freedom 1998. Washington, DC/New York: Heritage Foundation/Wall Street Journal.

Jonas, Susanne. 1989. Elections and Transitions: The Guatemalan and Nicaraguan Cases. In *Elections and Democracy in Central America*, ed. John A. Booth and Mitchell A. Seligson. Chapel Hill: University of North Carolina Press. 126–57.

———. 1991. *The Battle for Guatemala: Rebels, Death Squads, and U.S. Power*. Boulder: Westview Press.

Karl, Terry Lynn, and Phillipe C. Schmitter. 1991. Modes of Transition in Latin America and Eastern Europe. *International Social Science Journal* 28: 269–84.

Kline, Harvey F. 1996. Colombia: The Attempt to Replace Violence with Democracy. In *Latin American Politics and Development*, ed. Howard Wiarda and Kline. Boulder: Westview Press. 173–99.

Knack, Stephen, and Phillip Keefer. 1995. Institutions and Economic Performance: Cross-Country Tests Using Alternative Institutional Measures. *Economics and Politics* 7, 3 (November): 207–27.

Krznaric, Roman. 1997. Guatemalan Returnees and the Dilemma of Political Mobilization. Journal of Refugee Studies 10, 1: 61–78.

———. 1999. Civil and Uncivil Actors in the Guatemalan Peace Process. *Bulletin of Latin American Research* 18, 1:1–16.

Lamounier, Bolivar. 1989. Brazil: Inequality Against Democracy. In *Democracy in Developing Countries*, ed. Larry Diamond, Juan J. Linz, and Seymour Martin Lipset. Boulder/London: Lynne Rienner/Adamantine Press. 111–57.

La Rue, Frank. 1995. The Right to Truth in Central America. In Sieder, Rachel, ed. 1995. *Impunity in Latin America*. London: Institute of Latin American Studies, University of London. 73–81.

Leal Buitrago, Francisco. 1990. Estructura y coyuntura de la crisis política. In *Al filo del caos: crisis política en la Colombia de los años 80*, ed. Leal Buitrago and León Zamosc. Santafé de Bogotá: Instituto de Estudios Políticos y Relaciones Internacionales/Tercer Mundo. 27–56.

Lee, Susan. 1995. Colombia: A Case Study in Impunity. In In Sieder, Rachel, ed. 1995. *Impunity in Latin America*. London: Institute of Latin American Studies, University of London. 25–31.

Levine, Daniel. 1988. Paradigm Lost: Dependency to Democracy. *World Politics* 40, 3: 377–94.

Lijphart, Mend. 1984. *Democracies: Patterns of Majoritarian and Consensus Government in Twenty-one Countries*. New Haven: Yale University Press.

———. 1994. *Electoral Systems and Party Systems: A Study of 27 Democracies, 1945–1990*. New York: Oxford University Press.

———. 1999. *Patterns of Democracy: Government Forms and Performance in Thirty-Six Countries*. New Haven: Yale University Press.

Linz, Juan J. 1964. An Authoritarian Regime: Spain. In *Cleavages, Ideologies, and Party Systems*, ed. Erik Allardt and Yjro Littunen. New York: Academic Bookstore.

Linz, Juan J., and Alfred Stepan. 1996. *Problems of Democratic Transition and Consolidation: Southern Europe, South America, and Post-Communist Europe*. Baltimore: Johns Hopkins University Press.

Locke, John. 1924. *Of Civil Government: Two Treatises*. n.d. With an introduction by William S. Carpenter. Everyman Library no. 751. London: J. M. Dent.

Loveman, Brian. 1998. When You Wish Upon the Stars: Why the Generals (and Admirals) Say Yes to Latin American "Transitions" to Civilian Government. In *The Origins of Liberty: Political and Economic Liberalization in the Modern World*, ed. Paul W. Drake and Matthew D. McCubbins. Princeton: Princeton University Press.

Macpherson, C. B. 1978. Liberal-Democracy and Property. In *Property: Mainstream and Critical Positions*, ed. C. B. Macpherson. Oxford: Basil Blackwell.

Mainwaring, Scott. 1995. Brazil: Weak Parties, Feckless Democracy. In *Building Democratic Institutions: Party Systems in Latin America*, ed. Scott Mainwaring and Timothy R. Scully. Stanford: Stanford University Press, 354–98.

McDonald, Geraldine. 1997. Peacebuilding from Below: Alternative Perspectives on Colombia's Peace Process. London: Catholic Institute for International Relations.

Melo, Jorge Orlando. 1998. The Drugs Trade, Politics, and the Economy: The Colombian Experience. In *Latin America and the Multinational Drugs Trade*, ed. Elizabeth Joyce and Carlos Malamud. London: Institute of Latin American Studies, University of London. 63–96.

Merkel, Wolfgang. 1999. Defective Democracies. Working Paper 1999/132. Madrid: Centro de Estudios Avanzandos en Ciencias Sociales, Instituto Juan March de Estudios e Investigaciones. March.

Mitchell, Michael J., and Charles H. Wood. 1997. Ironies of Citizenship: Skin Color, Police Brutality, and the Challenge of Democracy in Brazil. Unpublished mss.

Molano, Alfredo. 1992. Violence and Land Colonization. In Bergquist, Charles, Ricardo Penaranda, and Gonzalo Sanchez, eds. 1992. *Violence in Colombia: The Contemporary Crisis in Historical Perspective.* Wilmington: Scholarly Resources. 195–216.

Moore, Barrington, Jr. 1966. *The Social Origins of Dictatorship and Democracy.* Harmondsworth: Penguin.

Nedelsky, Jennifer. 1993. American Constitutionalism and the Paradox of Private Property. In *Constitutionalism and Democracy,* ed. Jon Elster and Rune Slagstad. Cambridge: Cambridge University Press.

O'Donnell, Guillermo. 1997. Illusions About Consolidation. In *Consolidating the Third Wave Democracies Themes and Perspectives,* ed. Larry Diamond, Marc F. Plattner, Yun-han Chu, and Hung–mao Tien. Baltimore: Johns Hopkins University Press. 40–57.

———. 1999. Horizontal Accountability in New Democracies. In *The Self-Restraining State: Power and Accountability in New Democracies,* ed. Andreas Schedler, Larry Diamond, and Marc F. Plattner. Boulder: Lynne Rienner. 29–51.

Payne, Leigh. 2000. *Uncivil Movements: The Armed Right-Wing and Democracy in Latin America.* Baltimore: Johns Hopkins University Press.

Pearce, Jenny. 1990. *Colombia: Inside the Labyrinth.* London: Latin American Bureau.

Pecaut, Daniel. 1992. Guerrillas and Violence. In Bergquist, Charles, Ricardo Penaranda, and Gonzalo Sanchez, eds. 1992. *Violence in Colombia: The Contemporary Crisis in Historical Perspective.* Wilmington: Scholarly Resources. 217–39.

Pedone, Luiz. 1996. Worsening of Poverty, Human Rights, and Public Policies: Crucial Questions in the Consolidation of Brazilian Democracy. In *Problems of Democracy in Latin America,* ed. Roberto Espindola. Stockholm: Institute of Latin American Studies, University of Stockholm.

Poe, Steven, and C. Neal Tate. 1994. Repression of Human Rights to Personal Integrity in the 1980s: A Global Analysis. *American Political Science Review* 88, 4 (December): 853–72.

Poe, Steven, C. Neal Tate, and Linda Camp Keith. 1999. Repression of Human Rights to Personal Integrity Revisited: A Global Cross-National Study Covering the Years 1976–1993. *International Studies Quarterly* 43: 291–313.

Przeworski, Adam. 1986. Some Problems in the Study of Transition to Democracy. In *Transitions From Authoritarian Rule: Comparative Perspectives,* ed. Guillermo O'Donnell, Phillipe C. Schmitter, and Laurence Whitehead. Baltimore: Johns Hopkins University Press. 47–63.

Reichmann, Rebecca. 1995. Brazil's Denial of Race. *NACLA Report on the Americas* 28, 6 (May–June): 35–42.

Remmer, Karen L. 1995. New Theoretical Perspectives on Democratization. Review article. *Comparative Politics* 28, 1 (October): 103–22.

Restrepo, Luis Alberto. 1992. The Crisis of the Current Political Regime and Its Possible Outcomes. In Bergquist, Charles, Ricardo Penaranda, and Gonzalo Sanchez, eds. 1992. *Violence in Colombia: The Contemporary Crisis in Historical Perspective.* Wilmington: Scholarly Resources. 273–92.

Riker, William H., and David L. Weimer. 1993. The Economic and Political Liberalization of Socialism: The Fundamental Problem of Property Rights. *Social Philosophy and Policy* 10, 2: 79–102.

Rosada Granados, Hector. 1992. Parties, Transitions, and the Political System in Guatemala. In *Political Parties and Democracy in Central America,* ed. Louis W. Goodman, William M. LeoGrande, and Johanna Mendelson Forman. Boulder: Westview Press.

Rustow, Dankwart A. 1970. Transitions to Democracy: Toward a Dynamic Model. *Comparative Politics* 2, 3 (April): 337–64.

Schedler, Andreas. 1999. Conceptualizing Accountability. In *The Self-Restraining State: Power and Accountability in New Democracies,* ed. Schedler, Larry Diamond, and Marc F. Plattner. Boulder: Lynne Rienner. 13–28.

Schirmer, Jennifer. 1997. Prospects for Compliance: The Guatemalan Military and the Peace Accords. Paper presented at the conference "Guatemala After the Peace Accords," Institute of Latin American Studies, University of London, November 6–7.

Schmitter, Philippe C. 1995. Transitology: The Science or the Art of Democratization? In *The Consolidation of Democracy in Latin America,* ed. Joseph S. Tulchin with Bernice Romero. Boulder: Lynne Rienner. 11–41.

Schwartzman, Stephen, Ana Valeria Araujo, and Paulo Pankararu, 1996. The Legal Battle over Indigenous Land Rights. *NACLA Report on the Americas* 29, 5 (March–April): 36–42.

Sieder, Rachel, ed. 1995. *Impunity in Latin America*. London: Institute of Latin American Studies, University of London.

Sieder, Rachel, and James Dunkerley. 1994. The Military in Central America: The Challenge of Transition. Institute of Latin American Studies Occasional Papers no. 5. London: Institute of Latin American Studies, University of London.

Skidmore, Thomas. 1989. Brazil's Slow Road to Democratization. In *Democratizing Brazil: Problems of Transition and Consolidation*, ed. Alfred Stepan. New York: Oxford University Press. 5–42.

Skinner, Quentin. 1998. *Liberty Before Liberalism*. Cambridge: Cambridge University Press.

SPACE/Council of Europe. Various years. Council of Europe Annual Penal Statistics. Strasbourg: SPACE/Council of Europe.

Sunstein, Cass R. 1993. Constitutional Democracies: An Epilogue. In *Constitutionalism and Democracy*, ed. Jon Elster and Rune Slagstad. Cambridge: Cambridge University Press. 327–53.

Trudeau, Robert. 1993. *Guatemala: The Popular Struggle for Democracy*. Boulder: Lynne Rienner.

Vanhanen, Tatu. 1997. *Prospects for Democracy: A Study of 172 Countries*. New York: Routledge.

Vargas Meza, Ricardo. 1998. The FARC, the War, and the Crisis of the State. *NACLA Report on the Americas* 31, 5 (March–April): 22–27.

Walmsley, Roy. 1996. *Prison Systems in Central and Eastern Europe*. Helsinki: Heuni, European Institute for Crime Prevention and Control.

Weber, Max. 1968. *Economy and Society: An Outline of Interpretive Sociology*, eds. Guenther Roth and Claus Wittich. New York: Bedminster Press.

Weffort, Francisco. 1989. Why Democracy? In *Democratizing Brazil: Problems of Transition and Consolidation*, ed. Alfred Stepan. New York: Oxford University Press. 327–50.

Weiner, Robert. 1996. Colombia's Faceless Courts. *NACLA Report on the Americas* 30, 2 (September–October): 31–36.

Wilson, Richard. 1993. Continued Counterinsurgency: Civilian Rule in Guatemala. In *Low Intensity Democracy: Political Power in the New World Order*, ed. Barry Gills, Joel Rocamora, and Richard Wilson. London: Pluto Press.

Zakaria, Fareed. 1997. The Rise of Illiberal Democracy. *Foreign Affairs* (November–December): 22–43.

Zelaznik, Javier. 1999. Electoral Disproportionality Dataset. Wivenhoe Park: University of Essex, Department of Government.

Zur, Judith. 1995. The Psychological Effects of Impunity: The Language of Denial. In Sieder, Rachel, ed. 1995. *Impunity in Latin America*. London: Institute of Latin American Studies, University of London. 57–72.

Chapter 5

The Reelection Debate in Latin America

John M. Carey

At the close of a century in which it was largely prohibited throughout the region, presidential reelection returned to center stage in Latin America. Beginning in 1993, President Alberto Fujimori of Peru pushed through a constitutional reform to allow for his consecutive reelection. Carlos Menem followed suit in Argentina the next year, and both were reelected in 1995. Then President Fernando Henrique Cardoso of Brazil engineered a reform that allowed him to run, successfully, for reelection in 1998. In 1999, newly elected Venezuelan president Hugo Chávez convoked a constituent assembly that declared itself sovereign, displaced the sitting congress, and drafted a new charter of government that extended the presidential term from five to six years and allowed for consecutive reelection. President Chávez stood for reelection the next year and renewed his mandate. Also in 2000, Fujimori, the modern pioneer of presidential reelection, stood for a third consecutive term and won a disputed contest, only to be subsequently unseated by a corruption scandal sufficiently fantastic as to defy brief description.

The question of reelection also played a small but significant part in Argentina in December 2001. The Argentine Congress appointed San Luis Province governor Adolfo Rodríguez Saá as temporary replacement for President Fernando de la Rúa, who was resigning, on the understanding that interim elections for a successor would be held in a few months. Rodríguez, however, immediately alienated supporters and skeptics alike by announcing his intention to stand as a candidate in the planned presidential elections. Having selected him on the understanding that he would not use the office as a platform from which to launch a presidential candidacy, Peronist copartisans abandoned Rodríguez, who resigned a week later.

In the aftermath of the Fujimori debacle, Peruvians re-reformed their constitution to prohibit once again consecutive reelection of the president. When, in 2003, Argentine voters failed to rally to a Menem comeback candidacy, one might have concluded that the high tide of reelection had ebbed. But then, in 2005, Colombian President Alvaro Uribe negotiated a reelection amendment, then won a second term in a landslide in May 2006. Hugo Chávez, moreover, won reelection for a second time in December 2006.

Is presidential reelection a problem? Reelection has been at the center of regime crises in Peru and Venezuela, but has (so far, at least) been well received in Brazil and Colombia, and barring a dramatic fall from grace, Argentines may welcome the opportunity to reelect another widely popular president, Néstor Kirchner, in 2007. This essay reviews the historical context in which restrictions on presidential reelection were first widely adopted, along with the recent wave of changes in these rules, and concludes by evaluating the arguments both for and against reelection.

THE HISTORICAL ROOTS OF "NO REELECTION"

Concerns about presidential perpetuation in office are as old as presidentialism itself; they followed naturally from the preoccupation among the founders of America's many republics with maintaining political stability in the absence of monarchy.

In Philadelphia in 1787, delegates to the U.S. constitutional convention considered limiting presidents to a single six- or seven-year term (Madison 1787 [1966], 322–29, 356–61). The idea attracted substantial support but criticism as well, most thoroughly articulated by Alexander Hamilton in Federalist 72 with a series of arguments still echoing through present-day debates over presidential term limits. Hamilton elaborates the rationale behind the combination of a four-year presidential term and reelegibility for election.

> The first is necessary to give the officer himself the inclination and the resolution to act his part well, and to the community time and leisure to observe the tendency of his measures, and thence to form an experimental estimate of their merits. The last is necessary to enable the people, when they see reason to approve of his conduct, to continue him in the station in order to prolong the utility of his talents and virtues (Hamilton 1789 [1961], 436).

Hamilton argued, in addition, against enshrining in the Constitution a prohibition on returning successful and popular presidents to office, on the grounds both that this would impinge on voters' freedom and that it would prevent stability in the executive branch. Given Hamilton's initial support for a monarchy—the most stable executive imaginable, in his mind—his appeals to democratic principles with regard to presidential selection may have been somewhat disingenuous. They did, at any rate, carry the day.

Although the Constitution provided for a renewable presidency, however, those distrustful of executive authority continued to advocate an informal norm that no president should serve more than two terms, citing as precedent George Washington's refusal to stand for reelection in 1796. No incumbent challenged this informal rule until Franklin Delano Roosevelt ran for, and won, a third term in 1940, and then a fourth in 1944, in the midst of World War II. The U.S. Constitution was subsequently amended in 1951 to prohibit any subsequent president serving more than two terms. The main rationale was to prevent the personalization of the executive branch through its prolonged occupation by any individual.

The idea of ¡No reeleccionismo! was emblazoned on Latin America's political consciousness most famously as the rallying cry of Francisco Madero's campaign in 1910 to unseat Porfirio Díaz after 34 years in which Díaz dominated the Mexican executive. Controversy over presidential continuismo and over constitutional restrictions on reelection, however, has historical roots that go far deeper. Díaz's own campaign slogan as he challenged Benito Juárez in 1871 was "Effective suffrage and no reelection." Further back still, at the birth of the Latin American republics, there were advocates both of limiting presidential terms and of extending them. Simón Bolívar enthusiastically endorsed both positions at different times. Delivering a constitutional plan to the Venezuelan Congress in 1819, he wrote,

> Nothing is more perilous than to permit one citizen to retain power for an extended period. The people become accustomed to obeying him, and he forms the habit of commanding them; herein lays the origins of usurpation and tyranny. . . . Our citizens must with good reason learn to fear lest the magistrate who has governed them long will govern them forever (Quoted in Bierck 1951, 175).

Seven years later, however, in delivering a constitutional plan to the Congress of the Republic of Bolivia, his position had changed completely.

> The President of the Republic, in our Constitution, becomes the sun which, fixed in its orbit, imparts life to the universe. This supreme authority must be perpetual, for in non-hierarchical systems, more than in others, a fixed point is needed about which

leaders and citizens, men and affairs can revolve. . . . For Bolivia, this point is the
lifetime presidency [presidencia vitalicia] (Quoted in Bierck 1951, 598).

The change in Bolívar's position with respect to presidential perpetuation was part of a
broader change in his theory of constitutional design. Whereas initially, for Venezuela,
he advocated a concentration of power in the executive and short terms, his *presidencia
vitalicia* for Bolivia was endowed with limited constitutional authority. As Bolívar put it,
"his hands have been tied so that he can do no harm," on the premise that constitutional
limitations on presidential power could guarantee stability while preventing tyranny
(Bierck 1951, 599).

In practice, Latin American prohibitions on presidential reelection appear to have
been motivated both by theory and by experiences of individual politicians who endeav-
ored to entrench themselves in power.[1] All countries adopted prohibitions on immediate
reelection during the nineteenth century, in most cases early in their national histories.
Summoning the recent memories of Juan Manuel de Rosas's rule in Argentina during
the 1830s and 1840s, Juan Bautista Alberdi successfully endorsed a ban on consecutive
reelection in the 1853 charter as follows:

> To allow reelection is to extend to twelve years the presidential term. The president
> always has the means to secure his own reelection, and only rarely would refrain
> from doing so. Any reelection sows controversy, because it will be fought based upon
> actions taken in the first period in preparation for the effort (1915, 276).

Peruvian constitutions prohibited reelection after independence in 1822, with the
brief exception of an 1826 charter, which established a presidencia vitalicia for Bolívar
himself but which lasted only 54 days. The Colombian Constitution of 1821 allowed one
consecutive reelection, but was replaced nine years later with a charter that prohibited
consecutive reelection, as did all Colombian charters until Uribe's 2005 amendment.
With the exception of the period 1869–78, all Ecuadorean constitutions have banned
consecutive reelection.

Chilean presidents were allowed one consecutive reelection until 1871, but not
since. Costa Rica's early constitutions allowed two consecutive terms. In 1857, however,
President Juan Rafael Mora attempted to change the rule to allow for a third period, and
was ousted as a result. Both subsequent constitutions, 1869 and 1871, included prohibitions on consecutive reelection. Cleto González Víquez, who served two nonconsecutive
terms as president himself, described a fundamental distrust of continuismo among Costa
Ricans by the late nineteenth century (González Víquez 1958).

The first republican constitution of Brazil, promulgated in 1891, replaced the emperor
with a president as head of state and banned consecutive reelection. In his account of
the constituent assembly, Rui Barbosa, the constitution's principal intellectual author,
reflected on the examples of two contemporary republics, France and the United States—
neither of which imposed formal restrictions at the time—and the relevance of their
precedent for Brazil. Anticipating arguments by Juan Linz 60 years later in his rationale
for deviating from the French example, Barbosa reasoned that parliamentarism would
ensure the selection of executives only from among those with long and honorable
political careers—a model not relevant to Brazil's presidential system. With respect to
the United States, Barbosa (1933, 161–65) cited the unwritten norm limiting presidential
tenure, which he ascribed to George Washington and believed was inviolable. On these
grounds, then, Brazil's no reelection rule was regarded as consistent with the theory that
presidential power must be checked.

CONTINUISMO AND REACTION IN THE TWENTIETH CENTURY

Although constitutional restrictions on reelection were common, so also were efforts to avoid or overturn them. Juan Rafael Iglesias managed to suspend the Costa Rican restrictions and win a second term in 1897. In the twentieth century, a number of South American presidents who rose to power on combinations of popular and military support disdained constitutional obstacles to their continued rule.

Augusto Leguía forced through amendments to the Peruvian Constitution that allowed his reelection to second and then third consecutive terms in the 1920s. Getúlio Vargas pursued a similar strategy in establishing his Estado Novo in Brazil in the 1930s. In Bolivia, Víctor Paz Estenssoro attempted to prolong his 1960–64 presidency, securing a constitutional amendment to allow consecutive reelection from a congress dominated by his Movimiento Nacional Revolucionario (MNR), then winning the 1964 election. Splits in the MNR, however—most notably opposition to Paz Estenssoro among organized labor—forced the president to rely increasingly on the military to support his administration. Within a few months of his reelection, the generals dispensed with the civilian executive altogether, removing Paz Estenssoro in a coup.

Restrictions on reelection were also abolished during the first presidency of Juan Domingo Perón in Argentina. As late as 1948, Perón himself argued against presidential reelection as follows:

> Although it may well be that everything depends on men, history shows us that they are not always evenhanded or honorable in judging their own merits and taking into consideration the common good, subordinating this to personal or factional interests. To my mind, reelection would be an enormous danger to the political future of the republic and a threat to public service (Congreso de Argentina 1948, 17).

By the next year, however, the president had evidently changed his mind; and he convened a constituent assembly that established reelection without restrictions. His party's Consejo Superior appealed to the democratic principle of maximizing voter choice, arguing, "the prohibition on reelection presents an offense to the Argentine citizen. . . . It is as equally undemocratic to require a voter to vote for an unwanted choice as to prevent a vote for the desired option" (Serrafero 1997, 123). Peronist leaders in the assembly invoked Argentina's particular historical circumstances, which, they argued, required Perón to continue in office.

> If the fortune of this Argentine enterprise depends on the constitutional possibility that General Perón is reelected president of the republic by the free vote of its citizens, then we should remove the constitutional impediment that is consistent with neither political wisdom nor the historical circumstance in which the country finds itself (Sampay 1949, 289).

In all the cases reviewed here, disillusionment with the performance of these presidencies and the upheaval with which they ended fueled a reaction against continuismo and the reestablishment of constitutional prohibitions on reelection. Meanwhile, the success of the PRI regime and the Constitution of 1917 in bringing stability to Mexican politics while tempering personalism served as an endorsement for strong prohibitions on presidential reelection.

Constitutional restrictions, then, were common throughout Latin America from early on, although they were enforced with varying degrees of success. By the middle of the twentieth century, however, the principle of restricting reelection had gained widespread currency and—during periods of civilian rule, at least—had become the norm in most of Latin America.

OPENING PANDORA'S BOX?

As the twentieth century yielded to the twenty-first, the tide appeared to be turning once more in favor of incumbent presidents. Longstanding prohibitions on immediate reelection were overturned in Peru (1993), Argentina (1994), Brazil (1996), Venezuela (1999), and Colombia (2005). Both the reforms and their chief proponents enjoyed substantial popular support, at least initially. In all five cases, the presidents who secured the reforms were subsequently reelected by large margins.

Before rushing to conclude that we are witnessing a definitive historical trend, however, we should look at the broader perspective. Restrictions on reelection were relaxed in five of Latin America's largest countries. It must be noted, however, that the restriction was subsequently reinstated in Peru, and that during the same period, the Dominican Republic, Nicaragua, and Paraguay placed various sorts of restrictions on reelection where none had previously existed. In Panama, moreover, voters rejected then-president Ernesto Pérez Balladares's 1998 referendum to amend the constitution and allow consecutive reelection by a margin of almost 2 to 1.

Other countries made smaller adjustments to the restrictions associated with presidential terms, with no clear pattern visible. Colombia in 1991 disallowed reelection after an intervening term out of office, which had previously been permitted. Panama in 1994 increased the required "sitting out" period from one to two terms. Ecuador in 1998 allowed reelection after one intervening term, which it previously had not permitted.

In Costa Rica, nonconsecutive reelection was prohibited by constitutional amendment in the 1970s, after the third presidency of José Figueres Ferrer. In 2000, former president Oscar Arias proposed removing the lifetime prohibition and allowing nonconsecutive reelection once again. Opinion polls showed broad popular support for the idea, but critics labeled it as self-serving, given the source. Arias, in turn, complained that prominent politicians had originally approached him with the idea and encouraged him privately, then betrayed him once he went public, torpedoing the prospects for the reform.

As this brief review of recent reforms suggests, there has been an overall movement toward allowing reelection, but it is far from uniform. Table 1 shows its current status. The details of provisions regulating presidential reelection, moreover, such as whether

Table 1. Rules on Presidential Reelection, as of 2006

No Reelection	After One Interim Term	After Two Interim Terms	Two Consecutive Terms, Then No Reelection	Two Consecutive Terms, Then One Interim Term
Costa Rica	Bolivia	Panama	Brazil	Argentina
Guatemala	Chile		Colombia	
Honduras	Dominican Republic		Venezuela	
Mexico	Ecuador			
Paraguay	El Salvador			
	Nicaragua			
	Peru			
	Uruguay			

restrictions are permanent or interim, are potentially important, and warrant serious consideration.

THE PROMISE OF REELECTION: DEMOCRACY AND LEADERSHIP

What does immediate reelection mean for presidencies in Latin America? In the most straightforward sense, eliminating restrictions allows voters an increased measure of discretion to retain a popular incumbent in office. This is an argument that reelection enhances choice, and therefore the quality of democracy. In his influential work on presidentialism, Juan Linz (1994) suggests that one of the system's central flaws is that the no reelection rule prevents the retention of a competent and popular chief executive, should a country be fortunate enough to have found one. The point would appear to be ratified by the resounding reelection victories won by presidents Carlos Menem in Argentina in 1995 and Fernando Henrique Cardoso in Brazil in 1998. Even their critics, moreover, must acknowledge the extent of Fujimori's support in Peru in 1995 and Chávez's in Venezuela in 2000.

An even more powerful argument in favor of reelection is that it should improve democratic responsiveness and accountability by aligning the incentives of incumbent presidents more closely with those of voters. To realize this happy outcome, voters must reward politicians who promise and deliver popular policies, such that presidents who aspire to reelection will be more attentive to citizens' preferences than those who are constitutional lame ducks. Although these premises are regarded as practically axiomatic by many political scientists (particularly North Americans), however, the real situation invites skepticism. Research by Susan Stokes (2001) presents the puzzle that Latin American presidents who flagrantly violated their own campaign promises have subsequently been rewarded at the polls—either personally, if reelection is allowed, or through their parties—provided that their policy switches yielded strong macroeconomic performance.

Another argument occasionally offered in favor of reelection is that lame duck status weakens presidents as leaders of their parties. The logic here is that legislators and other politicians will be less inclined to support an executive whose time remaining in office is limited. Thus, allowing reelection may enhance presidential ability to construct and sustain legislative coalitions and to bargain effectively with politicians at other levels of government. It is worth keeping in mind, however, that presidential strength is a double-edged sword, and executive dominance can undermine the broader goal of enhancing democracy within parties. For example, in the months preceding the 2000 Venezuelan elections, the prospect that Chávez could hold the presidency for 12 more years bolstered his personal influence in the Movimiento Quinta República (MVR), encouraging lower-level politicians to defer to his edicts. When Chávez announced preferences for candidates to lower offices that contradicted nomination decisions the MVR's executive committee had already made, the committee scrambled to amend its list and ratify the presidential choices (*El Universal* 2000). In Costa Rica, by contrast, where presidential reelection is proscribed completely, incumbent presidents exercise far more limited control over the fates of lower-level politicians, contributing to parties' greater independence from presidential control (Carey 1996).

In short, there are a number of strong arguments for allowing presidential reelection, but the relative lack of experience with reelection in democratic regimes in Latin America makes it difficult to evaluate the validity of those arguments against hard evidence. The relationships among citizen preferences, presidential performance, electoral responses, and party politics in Latin America are complex, and we are only just beginning to understand them.

THE RISK: MORE *CONTINUISMO*

The argument against presidential reelection that continues to hold the most currency is simply that presidents will abuse the powers of the executive branch to ensure their own perpetuation in office. Each of the countries that banned presidential reelection during the 1990s endured extreme cases of such continuismo earlier in its recent history—under Alfredo Stroessner in Paraguay, various Somozas in Nicaragua, and Joaquin Balaguer in the Dominican Republic. Before the abrupt collapse of Fujimori's presidency, Peru appeared to be moving along this path, and the extraordinary circumstances surrounding the president's removal in November 2000 should not obscure the danger of continuismo that the case represented. It is worthwhile, therefore, to review in somewhat greater detail the issues surrounding Fujimori's attempt to hold on to his office.

Fujimori's very candidacy in 2000 violated the limit of two consecutive terms embodied in the constitution he introduced in 1993. He justified his third candidacy by declaring that his first term as president (1990–95) did not count, because it began under the previous constitution (which allowed no consecutive reelection at all!). When a plurality of Peru's Constitutional Tribunal objected to Fujimori's creative interpretation of his own charter, the president's compliant congressional majority fired the offending judges.[2]

During the 2000 campaign, Fujimori's supporters systematically intimidated opposition candidates and disrupted their campaign rallies; his administration used state resources to pressure the Peruvian media to slant their campaign coverage; and the vote count harbored irregularities—particularly in the first round. Had it not been for the extraordinary leak of videotapes that exposed his administration's attempts to change the outcome of the congressional election retroactively by purchasing a compliant majority, Fujimori might well have retained control of the executive for another five years.[3]

Peru's 2000 election must serve as a warning that presidential continuismo by means of intimidation and fraud has not been relegated decisively to the past. Yet continuismo is far from inevitable. The case of Argentina's Carlos Menem suggests that the same political bargains by which presidents pursue their ambitions can strengthen the checks and balances that limit presidential abuse of power.

In his initial term, 1989–95, Menem successfully stacked the Argentine Supreme Court with compliant justices, who subsequently ratified a number of constitutionally dubious expansions of presidential power. To secure legislative support for constitutional reform allowing reelection, however, Menem acquiesced to opposition demands to restore the court to its original size, removing many of his cronies and thus restoring balance. One result was that Menem's attempt to interpret the "two consecutive term" clause favorably, as Fujimori had, faced multiple institutional obstacles. Many politicians in Menem's own Peronist Party (Partido Justicialista) preferred the president's rival, Eduardo Duhalde, as their candidate.

Emboldened by the political opposition to the president's overtures, the Supreme Court in March 1999 ruled unanimously against appeals that would have allowed a third consecutive Menem candidacy. The court's action, which was supported by a congressional majority consisting of pro-Duhalde Peronists and all other parties, thus deterred Menem from openly pursuing the Peronist nomination. In short, the bargain Menem struck in 1994 secured his first reelection, but the longer-term effect was to restore the potential for judicial independence from the executive, balancing power more evenly among the executive, the legislature, and the courts than it had been earlier in the decade (Jones 1997).

A final observation regarding institutional design has to do not with consecutive reelection but with the rules governing eligibility for non-consecutive reelection and the potential problem associated with "punctuated" eligibility. In most cases in which reelection is limited, former presidents must sit out one term before they are eligible to run again. This opens up the possibility that an incumbent president prohibited from immediate reelection may be privately inclined to undermine his own party's immediate electoral success. If another politician from the incumbent's own party wins control of the executive—with all the policymaking and patronage powers that entails—then the outgoing president will almost certainly be eclipsed as the party's leading figure. If the incumbent's party loses the next election, however, the outgoing president may retain prominence as leader of the opposition, along with an aura as the champion capable of winning a national election.

Punctuated eligibility therefore presents potential problems in political parties. One is the garden-variety tension between former presidents angling to return to office and the current administration. In Venezuela, for example, where the 1961–99 Constitution allowed reelection after two interim terms, President Jaime Luscinchi's term was marked by a struggle between his supporters and former president Carlos Andrés Pérez over control of the Acción Democrática organization and the party's next presidential nomination (Coppedge 1994, 102–3). More interesting, from the perspective of constitutional design, is the possibility of moral hazard between parties and incumbent presidents under punctuated eligibility, whereby the incumbent's incentives with respect to his own party's electoral success may be compromised by ambitions to regain the presidency in the future. It was widely believed, for example, that Menem failed to support his party's nominee, Duhalde, in 1999 partly because Menem aspired to regain control of the Peronist Party and recapture the presidency in 2003.

The problem is particularly acute in the Peruvian and Argentine formats because an outgoing incumbent whose party retains the presidency will confront a copartisan who is eligible for reelection, too, at the end of the required sitting-out period. The perverse incentives within parties generated by punctuated eligibility suggest that if presidents are to be barred from reelection at all, whether after multiple terms or only one, they should be barred permanently.

REELECTION TO OTHER OFFICES

The matter of punctuated eligibility highlights the tension between reelection of current and former presidents and the progressive ambitions of other politicians. This, in turn, suggests the importance of considering the presidency in the context of reelection more generally. Do prohibitions on reelection to other offices mirror those on the presidency? Are restrictions for other offices based on the same rationale? The answer to the first question is, for governors, generally yes; for others, no. The empirical asymmetry implies, moreover, that the matter of reelection for chief executives is distinct, theoretically and politically, from other elected positions.

When the positions are popularly elected, restrictions on subnational governors are common. In Mexico, state governors are constitutionally limited to a single six-year term, just as the president is (Article 116). Venezuelan state governors are limited to two consecutive terms, as is the president, although gubernatorial terms are only four years long, whereas the presidency is six (Article 160). In Colombia, departmental governors serve three-year terms and cannot be reelected (Gómez Albarello 2001). In Brazil, state governors were, like the president, ineligible for reelection, until the 1997 constitutional reform allowed one consecutive reelection for each office (Article 82). In Argentina, the federal constitution does not stipulate rules; and heterogeneity prevails across provincial charters, with many, but not all, allowing consecutive reelection (Eaton 2001).

Prohibitions on legislative reelection are much rarer; three Latin American countries currently impose constitutional limitations. Venezuela's 1999 Constitution (Article 192) allows two, or possibly three, consecutive terms.[4] Mexico and Costa Rica prohibit all consecutive reelection for legislators—a provision slightly less restrictive than their permanent bans on presidential reelection. In both countries, however, there is discussion of relaxing or abolishing restrictions on legislative reelection, with the goal of enhancing members' expertise and strengthening Congress as a policymaking institution in regard to the executive.

Apart from these cases, legislators are eligible for unlimited reelection. Constitutional restrictions on municipal executives are rarer still. Mexico (Article 115) prohibits immediate reelection; Venezuela (Article 174) limits mayors to two consecutive terms. Prohibitions are absent in other cases.

Whereas presidents in every country face at least some restriction on reelection, restrictions on other major elected offices are more varied. Restrictions on governors— where they are elected—are common; on legislators and mayors, they are rare. Why do we observe this particular brand of asymmetry, but not the reverse (for example, cases in which legislative reelection is restricted but presidential is not)? The issue is not explicitly discussed in any constitutional debates of which I am aware, but there are at least two plausible explanations, one based on principle, the other on the alignment of politicians' ambitions.

First, to the extent that prohibitions are necessary to guard against manipulation of the electoral processes, this principle is more compelling the greater the capacity of the office to act unilaterally and, perhaps, secretly to usurp power and perpetuate tenure in office by illicit means. Alternatively, even if chief executives could be expected not to tamper with the electoral process, politicians farther down the political ladder have every reason to support constitutionally mandated turnover at the top, which ensures that the most sought-after offices will periodically be available. It would be difficult to secure acquiescence among those who draft constitutions to an arrangement that allows unrestricted presidential reelection while it compels turnover for lower posts.

REALIZING THE BOLIVARIAN IDEAL?

Clearly, the general contours of the debate over presidential reelection have remained remarkably stable over time. Arguments in favor emphasize a number of points. One is that the prospect of reelection and, conversely, the threat of its denial, induces politicians to be responsive to the demands of citizens. Another is that in principle, restrictions on reelection are restrictions on voter choice, and in that sense are antidemocratic. A third is that reelection lengthens the president's time horizon, as well as those of the other political actors with whom the president interacts, thus mitigating the problem of ineffectual, lame duck executives.

The most compelling counterargument continues to be, as it has been since the founding of the American republics, that allowing reelection invites the abuse of executive power and, ultimately, tyranny. Bolívar's argument, that long terms are unproblematic as long as the office is weak, appears to assume away the central problem—that presidents may seek to expand and manipulate executive power in the pursuit of the presidencia vitalicia. Bolívar's basic insight suggests, nevertheless, that reforms to allow presidential reelection may be distinguished according to how they are engineered.

For example, when reforms are brought about by negotiations between the president and political opponents, these deals tend to involve concessions that limit presidential power, mitigating the danger that presidential perpetuation will transform itself into presidential tyranny. This is a variant of the Bolivarian ideal, and among the recent cases of presidential reelection, it is best approximated in Argentina, Brazil, and Colombia. To secure reforms that allowed for reelection, Menem, Cardoso, and Uribe all had to make concessions to their opponents, the effects of which ultimately limited the power of their office. In these cases, the threat of continuismo through the subversion of democracy appears to have been allayed, and the potential advantages of presidential reelection may have been realized.

When reforms to allow reelection are brought about by plebiscite, in contrast, concessions to other political actors tend to be absent, and subsequent constraints on presidential authority are weaker as a result. This is the antithesis of the Bolivarian ideal, in that even the Liberator acknowledged the danger of tyranny inherent in prolonged rule by a powerful chief executive. Brazil's experience under the first Vargas regime, Argentina's under Perón, and Peru's under Fujimori all conform to this model, and Chávez's Venezuela appears to be headed squarely along this path.

NOTES

Some of the ideas developed in this chapter were first developed for a project of the Inter-American Dialogue and in Carey (2003) *Constructing Democratic Governance*, Thanks to the following for sharing their historical expertise on presidential reelection in specific countries: on Brazil, Octavio Amorim Neto; on Costa Rica, Kevin Casas; on Peru, Gregory Schmidt; and also Brian Crisp, Juan Gabriel Gómez Albarello, Kent Eaton, Jorge I. Domínguez, Mark Jones, and Kathleen O'Neill.

1 Much of the specific information about constitutional prohibitions on reelection in the following section is drawn from Nohlen 1993 and Serrafero 1997.

2 Fujimori's majority in Congress had ratified language specifically approving two consecutive presidential terms under the current constitution. The Constitutional Tribunal voted 3–0 (but with the remaining four members abstaining) that the law was inapplicable to Fujimori. The abstentions rendered the decision dubious. The doubts themselves were rendered moot, however, by Congress's ensuing impeachment of the antireelection judges. I thank one of the anonymous reviewers for *LAPS* for clarifying the specific sequence of events here and the legal and constitutional issues at play.

3 It is not surprising that in the wake of Fujimori's fall, the issue of presidential reelection has been opened to debate once again in Peru. A reform to prohibit immediate reelection was considered in Congress in 2001, but as of January 2002 it had yet to be ratified as a constitutional amendment. See Congreso del Perú 2001.

4 Article 192 states that deputies "may be reelected for two periods, maximum." This could be read to mean that two periods are the maximum period of service allowed. The language, however, leaves open the possibility of reelection to two subsequent periods after a deputy's first period.

REFERENCES

Alberdi, Juan Bautista. 1915. *Bases y puntos de partida para la organización política de la República Argentina*. Buenos Aires: La Cultura Argentina.

Barbosa, Rui. 1933. *Comentários à constituição federal brasileira*, vol. 3. São Paulo: Livraria Acadêmica.

Bierck, Harold A., Jr., ed. 1951. *Selected Writings of Bolívar.* New York: Colonial Press.

Carey, John M. 1996. *Term Limits and Legislative Representation.* New York: Cambridge University Press.

Carey, John M. 2003. Presidentialism and Representative Institutions in Latin America at the Turn of the Century. In *Constructing Democratic Governance: Latin America,* ed. Jorge I. Domínguez and Michael Shifter. Baltimore: The Johns Hopkins University Press. 11–42.

Congreso de Argentina. 1948. Diarios de sesiones de la Cámara de Diputados de la Nación. Buenos Aires.

Congreso del Perú. 2001. Diario de los debates, June 14, session no. 27, Comisión Permanente <www.congreso.gob.pe/index.asp>.

Coppedge, Michael. 1994. *Strong Parties and Lame Ducks: Presidential Partyarchy and Factionalism in Venezuela.* Stanford: Stanford University Press.

Eaton, Kent. 2001. Personal communication. January 14.

Gómez Albarello, Juan Gabriel. 2001. Personal communication. January 14.

González Viquez, Cleto. 1958. *Personal del poder ejecutivo de Costa Rica,* 1821–1936 Updated by Ricardo Fernández Peralta [1974?]. San José.

Hamilton, Alexander. 1789 [1961]. *The Federalist Papers.* New York: Signet.

Jones, Mark P. 1997. Evaluating Argentina's Presidential Democracy. In *Presidentialism and Democracy in Latin America,* ed. Scott Mainwaring and Matthew Soberg Shugart. New York: Cambridge University Press. 259–99.

Linz, Juan J. 1994. Presidentialism or Parliamentarism: Does It Make a Difference? In *The Failure of Presidential Democracy: The Case of Latin America,* vol. 2, ed. Juan J. Linz and Arturo Valenzuela. Baltimore: Johns Hopkins University Press. 3–87.

Madison, James. 1787 [1966]. *Notes of Debates in the Federal Convention of 1787, Reported by James Madison.* Columbus: Ohio University Press.

Nohlen, Dieter, ed. 1993. *Enciclopedia electoral latinoamericana y del Caribe.* San José, Costa Rica: CAPEL.

Sampay, Arturo. 1949. *Convención nacional constituyente.* Buenos Aires: Congreso de la Natión.

Serrafero, Mario D. 1997. *Reelección y sucesión presidencial: poder y continuidad. Argentina, América Latina, y EE. UU* Buenos Aires: Belgrano.

Stokes, Susan C. 2001. *Mandates and Democracy: Neoliberalism by Surprise in Latin America.* New York: Cambridge University Press.

El Universal (Caracas). 2000. March 6: 1–10.

Chapter 6

Decentralization's Nondemocratic Roots: Authoritarianism and Subnational Reform in Latin America

Kent Eaton

One of the common definitional stances adopted in the now sizable literature on decentralization is to distinguish between its two main forms: deconcentration and devolution. Deconcentration refers to changes that empower the subnational offices of national government ministries, dispersing central agents throughout the country and endowing them with greater resources and responsibilities (Rondinelli 1989; Parker 1995). Devolution, in contrast, refers to the transfer of resources and responsibilities to subnational authorities who are "largely or wholly independent of higher levels of government" (Manor 1999). Scholars generally agree that for devolution to occur, subnational elections are a necessary but not sufficient condition (Heller 2001; Hutchcroft 2001; Manor 1999).

As this simple distinction suggests, the politics surrounding these two forms of decentralization are likely to be quite distinct. For example, whereas deconcentration often appeals to central state actors seeking to penetrate interior regions more completely (Migdal 1988), devolution poses a more direct challenge to these actors because it empowers subnational officials they do not control.

By examining important cases that do not readily fit into either category, this chapter problematizes the distinction between deconcentration and devolution. It does not question the importance of subnational elections as signal events that alter the calculations of would-be decentralizers at the center. In Latin America and other regions, the spread of subnational elections in the last two decades has set in motion deep changes in the political careers that politicians pursue, the lobbying strategies that interest groups adopt, and the demands that are now emerging from subnational governments. Indeed, in many countries, using electoral mechanisms rather than appointment procedures to constitute subnational governments is one of the most significant features that distinguishes democracy's third wave from earlier waves (Eaton 2004).

Placing too much emphasis on elections, however, overlooks reforms that expand the institutional capacity of subnational officials who are not elected but who still cannot be described accurately as agents of central government bureaucracies. Salient examples of such reforms include changes that give unelected subnational governments greater statutory control over the provision of education and health care, additional taxing authority, and the right to operate their own banks and state-owned enterprises. The conceptual distinction between deconcentration and devolution cannot account for these changes because they transcend the mere empowerment of central bureaucrats located below the national level (deconcentration), but do not meet the higher standard set by separate elections for subnational officials (devolution). This study explores this middle ground by investigating the subnational reforms that authoritarian governments introduced in Latin America in the third quarter of the twentieth century. In the cases examined here, military-led governments at the center canceled subnational elections and then proceeded to modify subnational governments in ways that went far beyond bureaucratic deconcentration. Herein lies the core puzzle: Why did authoritarian regimes regarded as highly centralist expand the governing capacity of subnational governments?

The decision by military authorities to terminate prior experiences with direct subnational elections opened up a critical juncture for the subsequent development of subnational governments. In earlier democratic periods, the separate election of subnational officials often encouraged those who controlled the national government to guard governing capacity jealously and to resist expanding subnational authority. When, in contrast, military authorities dismissed elected officials at the subnational level and gave these jobs to appointees who enjoyed their confidence, they could contemplate deep changes in the capacity of subnational governments. Once they had asserted political control over mayors and governors, military authorities could and did use subnational governments in the service of the far-reaching economic and political goals that motivated the coups of the 1960s and 1970s. Because the military authorities chose to strengthen the capacities of unelected subnational governments rather than rely exclusively on the efforts of central government bureaucrats placed in subnational jurisdictions, neither devolution nor deconcentration successfully captures the logic of these military-led reforms.

The military regime's decision to do other than deconcentrate power within the central bureaucracy is not merely of academic interest. When democracy was restored at the subnational level in the end phase of authoritarian rule, newly elected officials were returned to gubernatorial and mayoral offices whose capacity had been considerably expanded. The simple return to subnational elections immediately brought new political significance to the changes that had been introduced in the period of military rule. From the standpoint of incoming, democratically elected national politicians, the reversal of bureaucratic deconcentration would have been much easier to effect than the recentralization of governing authority from separately elected subnational governments. In this sense, the form taken by the generals' subnational engineering helps explain why intergovernmental conflict—that is, conflict between separately constituted levels of government—has become so pronounced in the postauthoritarian period.

To explore the logic of subnational reforms by military authorities, the research here focuses on the three countries in Latin America that have received the most scholarly attention from students of military government: Argentina, Brazil, and Chile. For Argentina, the focus is on two distinct periods of military rule: the so-called *Revolución Argentina* between 1966 and 1973 and the subsequent *Proceso de Reorganización Nacional* between 1976 and 1983. The relevant period in Brazil is the lengthy experience with military rule that began with the coup of 1964 and terminated more than two decades later in the indirect presidential election of 1985. In Chile, the military government was led by Augusto Pinochet, who took power in the wake of the 1973 coup and left the presidency in 1990.

These four regimes shared many traits. Together they represent the closest real-world approximations of bureaucratic authoritarianism (BA) as an ideal type (O'Donnell 1973; Collier 1979). At the same time, scholars have also noted that the BA label masks a significant degree of cross-national variation in the actual economic and political reforms pursued by authoritarian rulers in these three countries (Hagopian 1993; Hirschman 1979; Schamis 1991). The discussion of subnational reforms that follows takes its cues from both strands in the literature on BA regimes. At one level, what is striking are the commonalities that led each of these regimes—despite their strongly centralizing profiles—to expand subnational roles. The purpose of these regimes was not simply to clean house and hold a new round of democratic elections. Instead, military leaders in each case engaged subnational governments in the pursuit of ambitious attempts to transform their country's society, polity, and economy. Considering the relevant counterfactual here, major changes in subnational government would have failed to interest military authorities with shorter time horizons, as in the more traditional military interventions that took place so frequently in Latin America earlier in the twentieth century.

At another level, while longer time horizons and transformative ambitions explain these regimes' common interest in subnational governments, the content of their subnational reforms varied considerably. This cross-national variation can be explained by emphasizing differences in the economic policy orientation of the generals in each country. Specifically, differences in national economic development strategies translated into distinct changes in the mix of rights and responsibilities that the generals decided to assign to subnational actors, again with important implications for postauthoritarian politics. Whether the regime attempted to promote economic development through statist or neoliberal programs directly shaped the quality of the subnational reforms it proposed and implemented. The contrast is clearest in the Brazilian and Chilean cases. While the statist approach of the Brazilian generals accelerated the expansion of subnational authority over public sector banks, industries, and universities, the neoliberal approach in Chile resulted largely in the offloading of what were previously central government responsibilities in the absence of accompanying resources. Simply put, statism generated greater increases in autonomy for subnational governments than did neoliberalism.

The two Argentine regimes suggest that, in addition to the content of economic policy goals, the relative consistency with which generals pursued these goals is equally critical in understanding whether military rule actually put subnational governments on a new footing. Governed at different moments by the statist logic of the *Revolución Argentina* and the neoliberal logic of the *Proceso*, authoritarian governments in Argentina did propose ambitious subnational reforms but lacked the coherence necessary to turn those proposals into reality.

By emphasizing the content and consistency of the generals' economic policy goals in all four regimes, this study adopts a plainly top-down approach. Different goals at the top explain much of the variation in subnational reforms, but a more complete explanation would certainly require greater attention to the various strategies of subnational officials, who defined their own goals within the distinct development frameworks that were imposed from above.

To set up the argument about how and why military-era subnational reforms differed, this chapter proceeds by investigating what these four military regimes had in common; namely, political centralization. It then analyzes the differential impact of distinct development strategies on the changes that military governments decided to introduce in the four cases. These reforms had particular consequences for politics in the postauthoritarian period. The analysis concludes with comments on the relationship between regime type and subnational reform.

THE LOGIC OF POLITICAL CENTRALIZATION IN FOUR MILITARY REGIMES

For the military governments with transformative projects that came to power in Argentina, Brazil, and Chile, it was not enough simply to close the national legislature or dismiss politicians from national offices. Unlike most other Latin American countries where subnational officials had been appointed by national politicians in earlier democratic periods, military leaders in these three countries confronted long histories of subnational elections. Independent political space at the subnational level posed obvious problems for the new de facto authorities at the center, who responded in short order by removing, and in some cases repressing, subnational politicians.

Respect for independent subnational politics might not have been problematic for the type of short-lived military government that took power simply to dismiss "objectionable" national politicians, but military leaders with more foundational goals viewed unfettered subnational democracy as incompatible with the pursuit of these goals. Because subnational elections were canceled, none of the subnational changes that followed can accurately be considered "devolution." Yet the story does not end here. The decision to centralize political authority operated as the necessary condition for a myriad of decisions in the subsequent period that increased the governing roles of local and intermediate governments, in effect making such increases politically palatable.

Beyond the similarly ambitious goals that brought each of these regimes to power, a distinct political logic guided subnational interventions in each case. For example, while all the regimes included in this study disrupted democratic procedures at the subnational level, the reasons for and extent of the disruption differed considerably. In Chile, the chief targets of military repression were the directly elected municipal councils, which, before 1973, were charged with electing the country's mayors. In contrast to subnational jurisdictions in Argentina and Brazil, the municipalities in Chile did not wield much governing authority before the coup.[1]

As a result, worries that the municipalities might use their authority over resources in ways that would challenge the military were not the dominant concern facing the new de facto authorities. Instead, the need to terminate the municipal democratic process reflected the municipalities' status as important sites of political contestation (Valenzuela 1977). Intervening in municipal government was thus an important component of the regime's broader attempt to rid Chile of the cancer of party politics. Municipal officeholders had few responsibilities and fewer independent revenues, but municipal elections themselves were an important element in what the military viewed as a failed democracy. The important victory of Salvador Allende's Popular Unity government in the municipal elections of 1971 (Dornbusch and Edwards 1990) provided further partisan motivation for the extreme political centralization experienced in Chile.

In contrast to Chile, political repression at the subnational level in both Argentine regimes focused on the provincial rather than the municipal level. As in Chile, however, the political logic of subnational interventions in Argentina also reflected a clear anti-party agenda—specifically the anti-Peronism of military reformers. After the military regime barred the Peronists from participating in the presidential elections that it held three years after the 1955 overthrow of Juan Perón, the Peronist Party's electoral successes in the provinces proved to be critical evidence of Perón's continuing support in the 1960s. For example, Peronist victories in the provincial elections in 1962 encouraged the military to depose President Arturo Frondizi; and four years later, a similar victory in the important province of Mendoza inspired the June 1966 coup (McGuire 1997, 89, 146).

For the authoritarian government of Juan Carlos Onganía, which took power that month, maintaining democracy in the provinces would have been fundamentally at odds with the *Revolución Argentina* through which he sought to steer the country toward a non-Peronist future. The more brutal and radical authoritarian coalition that took power a decade later had even greater cause to abolish provincial elections. In the brief democratic interregnum between the military's departure in 1973 and its return in 1976, the Peronists swept gubernatorial elections throughout Argentina. After the March 1976 coup, the military moved aggressively to repress the governors, then divided up responsibility for the provinces between officers of the army, navy, and air force (Gibson 1997, 79).

If hostility to subnationally successful political parties led to the sharp centralization of political authority in Argentina and Chile, Brazil represents a different dynamic. Political parties were much less established in Brazil before the 1964 coup (Mainwaring 1999; Schwartzman 1982), and attempts to root them out were consequently much less central to the authoritarian project than in the other countries. In contrast to the immediate halting of subnational democracy in Argentina and Chile, at first the Brazilian generals went ahead with direct gubernatorial elections scheduled for 1965. Later, however, they shifted to indirect elections, due to the concern that direct elections would not install politicians who supported a substantial period of military rule (Abrúcio and Samuels 2000). Some leading governors had supported the coup in 1964 not because they wanted extended military rule, but because they hoped to compete in new presidential elections expected to be held in the wake of João Goulart's overthrow (Camargo 1993).

Direct gubernatorial elections would have given these governors a major foothold with which to oppose the military's continued stay in power, in contrast to the indirect electoral procedures that the generals were better able to manipulate. Indirect elections certainly gave traditional elites in the states greater room to demand advantageous treatment from the center than their counterparts enjoyed in Argentina and Chile (Hagopian 1996). Considering the military authorities' ability to manipulate indirect elections, however, the termination of direct elections is appropriately understood as a centralizing rupture—one that was simply not as extreme as that effected by the Argentine and Chilean militaries (Kugelmas 2001).[2] Ultimately, because it requires politically independent subnational governments, devolution is not an accurate label for the subnational reforms that Brazil's generals would subsequently introduce.

STATISM AND NEOLIBERALISM AT THE SUBNATIONAL LEVEL

If the canceling of elections (Argentina and Chile) or altering of electoral procedures (Brazil) lessened the threat posed by independent subnational governments, the scale of the socioeconomic transformations sought by military leaders provided them with the incentive to enlist these governments as allies and partners. All four regimes searched for successful economic development strategies in response to broadly similar economic crises, and in all four cases this search convinced the generals of the need to do more than redistribute authority within the bureaucracy of the central government (that is, bureaucratic deconcentration). To understand how the character of subnational government changed over the course of authoritarian rule, the generals' economic policy orientation is the single most important factor to consider.

While the Brazilian regime and the first Argentine regime (1966–73) sought to facilitate industrial deepening through the maintenance or expansion of state-led industrialization (Stepan 1973; Smith 1989), the Chilean regime and the second Argentine regime (1976–83) embraced neoliberal policies in the attempt to move away from statist models (Foxley 1983; Lewis 1990; Schamis 1991).[3] That national strategies differed along a core neoliberal-statist dimension is well accepted in the literature on Latin American political economy. Less understood is the differential impact these national strategies had on subnational governments and on the nature of the intergovernmental conflicts that raged subsequent to redemocratization.

The case studies that follow address a broad set of functional changes that the generals designed and introduced. These changes altered both the roles assigned to subnational governments and the resources they could use in performing those roles. With respect to the assignment of new roles, the literature has tended to emphasize changes in the division of expenditure responsibilities, including the transfer of education, health care, and other services to subnational governments (Manor 1999; Rondinelli 1989). But the narrow focus on expenditure responsibilities is problematic because subnational roles also expand when, as in the Brazilian case, governments below the national level are allowed to create their own state-owned enterprises and to adopt their own industrial policies (Montero 2002).

With respect to changes in the resources at the disposal of subnational governments, this study focuses on fiscal as opposed to administrative resources.[4] Fiscal resources include the tax revenues that subnational officials are empowered to raise in their own districts and through their own effort, along with the tax revenues they receive from the national government in the form of unconditional transfers, matching grants, and earmarked funds. Also in this category are nontax revenues that subnational officials can borrow from a variety of sources, including foreign and national governments, private holders of debt at home and abroad, and state-owned banks under the control of subnational governments themselves.

Table 1 documents the major changes that affected subnational governments during each of the four military governments.[5] The four military governments did not introduce changes in all of the functional categories described above, which renders a systematic comparison across these cases somewhat difficult. For example, revenue-sharing arrangements were reformed by military authorities in Argentina and Brazil but not in Chile; and education and health care responsibilities were explicitly transferred downward in Chile and in the second Argentine regime but not in Brazil. Nevertheless, table 1 summarizes the changes examined in greater detail in the country-specific analyses that follow.

Table 1. Changes in Subnational Government During Military Rule

Military Regimes	Changes in the Distribution of Fiscal Authority	Changes in the Distribution of Policy Responsibilities
Argentina 1966–1973	• Decrees in 1967 and 1968 cut revenue transfers to provinces and Buenos Aires • 1973 law increases transfers by giving provinces and federal government equal shares of revenue	
Argentina 1976–1983	• Decrees in 1976 cut provincial transfers in half to finance social security reform • Buenos Aires removed from revenue-sharing system	• 1979, 1982, and 1983 laws enhance provincial authority over regional industrial policies • 1981 decree transfers primary education and some health care to provinces
Brazil 1964–1985	• 1967 centralization of tax bases reduces subnational fiscal autonomy • Increases in revenue transfers to states and municipalities after the electoral defeat of the ARENA party in 1974	• Creation of more than 200 parastatals controlled by state and municipal governments • Expansion of banks and universities run by state governments
Chile 1973–1990		• 1974 creation of regional governments; regional authorities given input in expenditure decisions • 1981 decree transfers responsibility for schools and hospitals to municipalities

State-led Development in Brazil

In the study of Brazilian federalism during military rule, scholars have focused on two distinct periods: the sharp centralization of taxing authority in 1967, and the steady decentralization of tax revenues after the 1974 electoral defeat of the pro-military party (Abrúcio and Samuels 2000; Rezende 1996; Selcher 1989). These important tax and revenue changes symbolize the distinct dynamics at play in the first and second decades of military rule. Beyond tax policy, however, once the generals eliminated direct gubernatorial elections, their commitment to statism as an economic ideology led them to introduce a series of changes that were, in some senses, deeper and more structural.

For example, military authorities chose to expand state universities, state-owned enterprises (*estatais estaduais*), and state-owned banks, all at Brazil's intermediate level of government (Britto 1995; Prado 1996; Tendler 1968). As Montero (2002) demonstrates, the military in Brazil presided over the expansion of industrial policymaking by subnational authorities. Some states (for example, Minas Gerais) responded by delegating authority to technocrats in developmental agencies, producing increased levels of public investment; while in others (such as Rio de Janeiro), populism undermined the effective use of industrial policymaking authority.

For the purpose of categorizing these changes relative to the concepts of deconcentration and devolution, it is important to note that what the generals in Brazil did not do was assign exclusive authority over industrial policy to the deconcentrated agents of the central government. Instead, they shared this authority with subnational governments. The shift from direct to indirect electoral procedures reduced the potential threat posed by this phenomenon of "subnational statism," facilitating its expansion considerably beyond what had been contemplated in the earlier democratic period by the government of President Juscelino Kubitschek (1956–60).

While the growth of the parastatal sector under the Brazilian generals has been subject to extensive study, most scholars of this period have focused exclusively on those new state-owned enterprises that were controlled by the federal government (Abranches 1980; Evans 1979; Werneck 1987). Yet in the first years of the military government, 175 state-owned enterprises (SOEs) were created in the states, in contrast to only 39 at the federal level. Between 1970 and 1976, the numbers were more equal, with the establishment of 70 federally controlled SOEs and 60 SOEs at the state level (Rezende 1980, 47). The available data clearly demonstrate nevertheless that the aggressive pursuit of statism reached far below the national level. Fifteen years into the military period, according to data presented in table 2, the share of state-owned enterprises controlled by subnational spheres of government—both state and municipal—far exceeded those controlled by the federal government. Of the 654 SOEs in place in 1979, 456 were owned by subnational governments.

Beyond the growth in the number of subnationally owned enterprises in the 1960s and 1970s, it is also evident that Brazilian states and municipalities derived valuable revenues from these enterprises over the course of military rule. According to several scholars, revenues from the parastatal sector served as partial compensation to the states for the centralizing changes in taxing authority that the generals had instituted in 1967 (Lopreato 1997, 95; Prado 1996, 34). It also bears noting that subnational statism was particularly significant in the area of banking and insurance, and that subsequent to redemocratization; this expansion would trigger attempts by later generations of federal politicians to assert control over state finances through the privatization of state-owned banks.

Table 2. Distribution of State Enterprises by Sector and Sphere of Government, 1979

Sectors	Federal Government	State Government	Municipal Government	Total
Agriculture and Mining	20	11	1	32
Manufacturing	56	33	3	92
Services	122	312	96	530
Utilities	41	51	11	103
Transport, storage, commerce	40	29	8	77
Planning, research, development	7	70	57	134
Technical/administrative services	19	64	16	99
Construction, engineering	8	9	4	21
Banks, insurance	7	89	—	96
Total	198	356	100	654

Source: Trebat 1983, 38.

Table 2 shows that the phenomenon of subnational statism was a cross-sectoral one, but the weight of state-controlled SOEs relative to federally controlled SOEs varied across sectors. Although it federalized decisionmaking authority in all sectors by the late 1960s, the military government allowed a much greater degree of participation by the states in some sectors (for example, transportation and electricity) than in others (oil and telecommunications). The impact of statism on subnational governments was particularly striking in the strategic electricity sector (Tendler 1968). According to Villela (1984, 41), whereas only 7 percent of Brazil's electricity was generated by parastatals that were owned by the states in 1962, that percentage steadily increased to nearly 50 percent under military rule.[6] Considering the numerous decisions that a government is called on to make when it runs its own enterprises, banks, and universities, it is possible to conclude that statism produced much greater autonomy for subnational authorities than the more liberal approaches adopted elsewhere.

Liberal Development Strategies in Chile

The dominance of neoliberalism as the Chilean regime's guiding ideology generated a set of changes that were much less advantageous for subnational governments than those in Brazil. These changes have received far less attention from scholars relative to other reforms, like privatization and financial liberalization, but the changes that Pinochet referred to as "decentralization" were an important part of the new regime's neoliberal program. Having suppressed local democracy, Pinochet was able to reconfigure subnational governments profoundly in the attempt to institutionalize this radically new policy orientation.

The key change at the municipal level occurred in the early 1980s and involved shifting responsibility for education and health care to the municipalities, but without giving these governments additional control over revenue. As table 3 shows, by the end of the dictatorship, municipal spending as a percentage of total spending had experienced a significant increase without a concomitant change in the share of revenues collected by municipalities (Marcel 1994). Endowing municipalities with important responsibilities marks a major departure, given the insignificance of this level of government in the decades before the coup. Pinochet also created an entirely new tier of 13 regional governments between the municipalities and the national government, and instructed his

Table 3. Indicators of Fiscal Decentralization in Chile, 1970 and 1992

	1970	1992
National government spending as a percentage of total spending	95.3	87.3
Municipal government spending as a percentage of total spending	4.7	12.7
National revenue as a percentage of total revenue	97.5	97.2
Municipal revenue as a percentage of total revenue	2.5	2.8

Source: Yáñez and Letelier 1995, 187.

national ministries to channel their spending through these new regional governments (Gleisner 1988; Zavala 2001).

These regional and municipal reforms clearly bear the imprint of the military's drive to reverse decades of statism in Chile. The creation of the regions and the transfer of important expenditure items to the municipalities were two different ways of achieving the same result: a central state that would be less relevant in the national political economy. Reducing the importance of the central state was important to the military as a means of limiting the damage to its interests that could be done by the victory of left-wing parties in future national elections. In this respect, military engineering at the subnational level proved to be quite advantageous to the Chilean right. Having lost every presidential election since the transition in 1989, the subnational offices reconfigured by Pinochet served as important political bases for the parties of the right in the postauthoritarian period. Considering the particular strength of national unions in the education and health sectors and their hostility to the authoritarian project, moreover, Pinochet's special interest in transferring responsibility for schools and hospitals to the municipalities was no accident. What is clear is that the desire to transform Chile's political economy in a profound way encouraged Pinochet to look beyond bureaucratic deconcentration. Because it could have been more easily undone by his democratic successors, bureaucratic deconcentration represented a less attractive option for Pinochet than these more fundamental changes in the roles assigned to subnational governments.

Besides redistributing functions away from Santiago and toward regional and municipal governments, the Pinochet regime also used subnational reforms in the attempt to reduce the overall size of Chile's consolidated public sector (Boisier 1994). By forcing new expenditure responsibilities onto municipal governments while failing to give them either additional tax bases or sufficient revenue transfers from the center, the Pinochet government set the stage for a sharp decline in the quality of governmental services in education and health care. The goal, according to some critics of the authoritarian-era reforms, was to encourage Chileans "voluntarily" to shift out of the public sector and into the private market for these services (Caro 2001).

Yet if municipal decentralization appealed to neoliberals in the military government as a form of privatization through the back door, in the end, education and health care were starved of public resources but never completely privatized. Because full-scale privatization never happened, municipal governments emerged from the authoritarian period overburdened and impoverished, but much more important than they had been in the period before authoritarian rule, thanks to their new statutory responsibility for some of the most critical services government can provide.

The contrast with Brazil is instructive. Whereas many states in Brazil emerged from the military period stronger than ever and with enhanced access to revenue from subnational parastatals, Chilean municipalities emerged with new responsibilities but subject to tight fiscal control from Santiago. According to the analysis here, then, statism and neoliberalism produced sharply divergent outcomes in these two cases: subnational actors in Brazil received revenues in excess of their obligations, while in Chile new responsibilities for local officials far exceeded their revenue authority. Thus the capacity of Chilean municipalities certainly increased under military rule because they were called on to deliver services that were much more important than anything they had done in the past. Relative to Brazil, however, the scope for autonomy in decision making was much more limited because of the continued and extreme financial centralization associated with the overarching pursuit of neoliberalism.

Economic Policy Incoherence in Argentina

The pursuit of distinct economic development strategies in Brazil and Chile generated very different proposals for subnational reform, but in each country the design and implementation of these different proposals was reasonably coherent. The same cannot be said of either of the two Argentine military governments considered here. Debates over the appropriate economic policy course certainly took place in the Brazilian and Chilean militaries, but studies of both the *Revolución Argentina and Proceso* regimes demonstrate the failure of the Argentine military to coalesce in a consistent fashion behind any one approach (Peralta Ramos 1990; Smith 1989).

Incoherence and volatility were problems not just in the national debate between economic nationalists and economic liberals; the provinces also functioned as tools in the fierce and ultimately unresolved conflicts over economic policy that took place within the Argentine military. The subnational reforms proposed in Argentina's authoritarian interludes were just as significant as those proposed in the other two cases, but most of them were either reversed or undermined by rival factions in the military before the generals withdrew from power.[7] Thus, unlike its counterparts in the other countries, the military failed to take advantage of the closing of the national legislature—historically a key arena for provinces to defend their prerogatives relative to the national government—to introduce consistent provincial reforms.

The extreme policy swings that characterized Argentina's revenue sharing system between 1966 and 1973 illustrate the inconsistency of the regime's attitudes toward provincial governments and the development role they could be expected to play. As shown in table 4, this period witnessed harsh cuts in fiscal transfers to the provinces, only to be followed by the most generous increases in revenue sharing in Argentine history. While the attempt to deepen industrialization was central to President *Onganía's* developmental plans, his economy minister, Adalberto Krieger Vasena, introduced nevertheless a very liberal program, sponsored by the International Monetary Fund, to control the federal budget deficit. This program involved sharp reductions in automatic provincial revenue transfers in March 1967 and further cuts for the city of Buenos Aires the following year.

Table 4. Contradictory Changes in Revenue Sharing During the 1966–1973 Regime

1967	1968	1973
Increase in federal share of revenues from 54% to 59%, decrease in subnational shares of revenues from 46% to 41%	Further 22% decrease in revenue shares for the federal capital city of Buenos Aires	Decrease in federal share of revenues from 59% to 48.5%, increase in subnational share of revenues to 48.5%

Source: Nuñez Miñana and Porto 1982.

Considering their huge dependence on transfers from the center, cuts in revenue sharing had powerfully centralizing outcomes, and put provinces on the defensive relative to the federal government. In 1973, however, the military reversed course and decreed a new revenue-sharing law that was highly advantageous to the provinces (Luna 1975; Saiegh and Tommasi 1998). The law's most important effect was that it incorporated the provinces' historical demand for a share in tax revenues that would be equal to the federal government, a demand they had failed to secure under previous democratic governments. According to the new law decreed by the military in 1973, any new taxes created by the federal government would necessarily form part of the revenue pool subject to provincial transfers, and provinces would be free to devote these transfers to the expenditure items they chose (that is, transfers were not earmarked). In other words, the *Revolución Argentina* began by reducing the revenue autonomy of the provinces relative to the earlier democratic period, but ended by increasing it beyond anything that earlier democratic governments had been willing to grant.

An examination of military rule during the subsequent *Proceso* regime reveals the play of these same contradictory impulses. The neoliberal impulse that dominated in the years following the 1976 coup led to cuts in provincial revenue transfers that mirrored the changes in 1967 and 1968 and that undid the 1973 revenue-sharing legislation that had been advantageous for the provinces. The Videla government used these provincial revenue cuts to finance an expensive reform of the social security system, through which the government sought to excuse employers from contributing to their employees' retirement funds (Núñez Miñana and Porto 1982). As in Chile, neoliberalism and the attempt to marginalize powerful national labor unions led the Argentine military government in the early 1980s to transfer expenditure responsibilities for primary education and health care to the provinces. Also as in Chile, these new responsibilities did not come with any extra revenue (FIEL 1993). All these changes reflect the neoliberal approach to subnational reform that Carlos Menem would pick up on in the 1990s.

Even as the provinces bore the brunt of attempts by the *Proceso* generals to liberalize Argentina's economy, however, they also benefited from a series of highly illiberal changes in tax policy that significantly expanded provincial autonomy. In 1979, 1982, and 1983, the federal government delegated to interior provinces the right to grant federal tax breaks, a policy departure that clashed fundamentally with the austerity measures the generals were then enacting (Azpiazu and Basualdo 1990; Eaton 2001). According to the data presented in table 5, the provinces moved aggressively to take advantage of this new authority over federal taxes, resulting in heavy losses to the federal treasury for years to come (Macón 1985, 161). So long as national authorities exercised political control over the governors, as was the case under the *Proceso*, provincial governments could be seen as mere extensions of the national government. For this reason, delegating authority over federal tax policy to the provinces did not threaten the interests of the generals who controlled the federal government. After provincial and national elections were reintroduced in 1983, however, this military-era reform would produce a significant

Table 5. Fiscal Cost of Provincial Tax Breaks Granted by the Military Government in Argentina (in millions of US dollars)

	1990	1991	1992	1993	1994	1995
Fiscal cost	2,661	2,888	3,085	3,521	3,232	3,256

Source: World Bank 1993, 59.

loss of control for the national government. Thus, as under the earlier military period, the provinces under the *Proceso* experienced a bewildering mix of changes that reduced provincial autonomy in some dimensions but enhanced it substantially in others.

In Argentina, the generals proposed reforms that moved subnational governments simultaneously in statist and neoliberal directions. The conflicting reforms, however, did not merely cancel each other out. Although internally contradictory, these reforms are as important for understanding intergovernmental struggles in postauthoritarian Argentina as are the more coherent subnational changes introduced in Brazil and Chile.

THE IMPACT OF MILITARY-LED REFORMS ON CONTEMPORARY DEMOCRACIES

In all four cases, despite important cross-national differences, changes in the roles ascribed to subnational governments were made politically possible by the prior cancellation of direct subnational elections. Once direct subnational elections were reinstituted as part of the return to democracy, particular institutions, actors, and interests reproduced the military reforms over time. In each of the three countries, military-era subnational engineering—whether this engineering was internally consistent or not—had implications for politics once the military withdrew from power. Following their victories in the "founding" subnational elections of Brazil (1982), Argentina (1983), and Chile (1992), mayors and governors used the newly regained independence of these offices to defend those military-era changes that had expanded the importance of subnational governments.[8] This opportunity to defend acquired capacities would not have been open to subnational actors if the military had chosen simply to deconcentrate power within the central government bureaucracy.

As Hagopian has argued, when Latin America redemocratized in the 1980s, its new democracies did not merely pick up where preceding democracies had left off (Hagopian 1993). One of the most important illustrations of this point from the four cases is that the simple reintroduction of subnational elections in the course of the national transition immediately infused new political meaning into the functional changes that the military governments had introduced at the subnational level.

The timing of the reintroduction of subnational elections (that is, when these elections took place within the timetable of the broader democratic transition) did differ significantly across the three countries. In Brazil, subnational elections preceded the direct election of the president by seven years; in Argentina, provincial and national elections were held in the same year (1983); and in Chile, subnational elections were held three years after national elections. But in each case, when direct subnational elections were once again held, their reintroduction altered overnight the significance of the manipulation of the system by the preceding military government. So long as the generals appointed subnational officials (Argentina and Chile) or controlled their indirect election (Brazil), the central government retained ultimate authority over how subnational officials used the additional powers that the military had decided to transfer. The return to separate electoral procedures to constitute national and subnational authorities directly increased the potential for conflict between these authorities over such disparate issues as provincial banks, municipal schools, and state universities. Statism and neoliberalism created distinct legacies for subnational governments once the military returned to the barracks in the 1980s and 1990s.

That military-era subnational reforms shaped postauthoritarian politics is well established in the Brazilian case. According to Abrúcio and Samuels (2000), subsequent to their defeat in the 1974 elections, the generals used their discretionary control over revenue transfers to subnational governments as a resource that enabled them to delay and control the terms of the democratic transition. Playing to the governors in the area of revenue sharing exacted a heavy and well-documented toll on the federal government (Samuels 2003; Seabra 1997; Shah 1991). The successful demands of state-based politicians for increases in revenue transfers, which were accompanied by no equally explicit redistribution of expenditure responsibilities, proved disastrous for rational public budgeting in the late 1980s and clearly fueled the hyperinflationary episodes of the early 1990s (Lopreato 1997; Rezende 1996).

Beyond the story of revenue transfers, however, Brazil's generals put subnational governments on a new footing in another sense. Precisely because the generals had presided over a sharp increase in the number and size of banks and enterprises owned by state governments, the position of subnational actors in Brazil's new democracy was much more advantageous than in other countries. Because of the generals' statism, governors in the post-1982 period wielded a greater set of policy tools than had their pre-1964 predecessors, particularly in the larger Brazilian states (Dias 2002; Kugelmas 2002). In states like Minas Gerais, democratically elected governors now presided over state-level developmental agencies that had been created or strengthened during military rule (Montero 2002, 69–71). Changes introduced under the military period, however, did more than expand the governors' own policy relevance. In the fiscal struggles that have taken place in the contemporary democratic period between the federal and state governments, subnational statism created "facts on the ground" in the form of thousands of state government employees who resisted privatization and adjustment in the 1990s.

The legacy of subnational statism therefore deserves to be included to the already sizable list of obstacles, including fragmented parties, federalism, and weak party discipline, that have complicated the pursuit of fiscal balance and economic stability in Brazil (Mainwaring 1997; Sallum 1996). Simply put, conflict between the states and the federal government over the prerogatives of each has been critically important in recent years; and it was the military government that set the parameters of this conflict by expanding the administrative and institutional capacity of subnational governments.

If the task facing governors in Brazil was to defend an advantageous position inherited from the military period, subnational actors in Chile did not want simply to continue down the path set by the previous authoritarian government. Reversing those military-era changes that they found problematic, however, has been an uphill struggle, and the military period has indeed cast a long shadow on subnational politics in post-authoritarian Chile. The challenges facing municipal and regional officials alike are a direct result of the neoliberal logic that pervaded Pinochet's subnational reforms and of the paramount concern with fiscal stability that is still one of the chief legacies of his rule.

At the municipal level, mayors have attempted (with little success) to secure levels of revenue authority commensurate with the additional responsibilities they took on under the dictatorship. But the national government continues to control the calculation of property values, the chief determinant of the property tax revenues that are the most important municipal tax base (Abalos 1994; Yáñez and Letelier 1995). Since Pinochet's departure from the executive branch, national politicians have kept mayors on a tight fiscal leash, continuing to exert much heavier control over municipal finances than is now common in most countries of the region. If anything, democratization has given the politicians who control the national government additional reason to prefer this imbalance between municipal expenditure responsibilities and revenue authority. In the years since 1990, as in the democratic period before 1973, revenue-starved municipalities have been the necessary condition that enables national legislators to claim credit for brokering additional revenue transfers from Santiago (Valenzuela 1977).

Authoritarian engineering at the regional level has also had a significant impact on Chile's new democracy. Given the six failed attempts to create regional governments before the coup in 1973 (Valenzuela 1999), each of which failed as a result of opposition from the national congress, it is unlikely that Chile would have regional governments today if it had not experienced the breakdown of democracy. Imposed by Pinochet, regional governments since 1990 have become quite institutionalized, largely because of the creation of a new set of socioeconomic and political actors identified with regional interests (Tobar 2001). While regional governments are there to stay, their revenue authority is even more anemic than that of the municipalities. This, too, is a direct reflection of the neoliberal concern with fiscal restraint that guided subnational reforms in Chile. Unlike most intermediate-level governments in Latin America, the regions in Chile have no statutory authority to raise any revenues on their own, nor do they receive any form of automatic revenue sharing from the national government. The continued revenue dependence of subnational governments in Chile stands in contrast with other unitary countries in Latin America such as Colombia and Bolivia, which introduced automatic transfer systems in the 1980s and 1990s for departmental (Colombia) and municipal (Bolivia) governments. In Chile, national politicians decide every year, in the course of annual budget negotiations, how much money to send to the regions. During the presidency of Eduardo Frei (1994–2000), the regions' share of public investment increased from 21 percent in 1994 to 43 percent by 2000; but virtually all of these investment funds are closely earmarked, controlled, and monitored by the national government (SUBDERE 2001).

While the generals in Brazil and Chile forged distinctive and consistent subnational changes that were reproduced subsequent to redemocratization, the impact of military-era reforms on Argentina's democracy is more ambiguous. The contradictory changes that were implemented—slashing revenue transfers from the federal government and then enabling provinces to grant federal tax exemptions—generated their own institutional legacy. In the post-1983 period, governors sought to advance and build on those military-era changes that had expanded provincial authority, while presidents drew on military-era reforms that sought to shift the intergovernmental balance of power in the opposite direction.

Argentina's most recent experience with democracy thereby reproduced the same inability to find stable institutional equilibria that had characterized military rule. Consider, for example, the repeated waves of decentralization and recentralization that have affected revenue sharing in the two decades since the transition. In 1987, governors secured a major increase in provincial revenue transfers in order to finance the unfunded transfer of responsibility for primary schools and health care that took place under the *Proceso*. Several years later, President Menem championed the need for the type of revenue cuts associated with military-era economy ministers Krieger Vasena and José Martínez de Hoz, slashing provincial revenue shares even as he successfully shifted responsibility for an additional set of expenditures onto the provinces. Later in the decade, this reversal was itself reversed in the form of successful attempts by governors to secure increased revenue transfers, even as total tax revenues were collapsing in the late 1990s. To the extent that provincial fiscal institutions in the 1980s and 1990s have experienced the same volatility and incoherence that characterized both the 1966–73 and 1976–83 periods of military rule, the generals' failure to fashion coherent subnational changes has indeed been reproduced in Argentina.

CONCLUSIONS

In the last quarter of the twentieth century, most countries in Latin America both democratized and decentralized. In some cases, the very transition to democracy incorporated decentralizing changes, often as a result of prodemocracy advocates who inserted decentralization into the agreements that governed the transition because they understood it to be an inherently democratizing reform. In other countries, transitions from authoritarian rule included no explicit decentralizing measures, but democratization nevertheless set in motion changes that increased the stature of subnational governments. The timing of decentralization, either in the course of the democratic transition or in its aftermath, suggests that democratization has played an important causal role in the shift toward more decentralized patterns of governance (Diamond 2000; Eaton 2004; Montero and Samuels 2003). The complicated and important connections between democratization and decentralization certainly deserve much attention from Latin Americanists and comparativists more generally.

At the same time, while many episodes of decentralization can doubtless be traced to democratization, fuller explanations of the decentralizing changes under way in developing countries must look to the predemocratic period. In many countries, the nondemocratic regimes that governed before the contemporary wave of democracy introduced significant and often surprising changes that had the effect of strengthening subnational governments. In no case do these earlier changes count as "devolution," since de facto authorities at the center controlled subnational officials for most of their rule (Manor 1999). These changes, however, cannot be dismissed as mere window dressing by authoritarian leaders. The uneven but undeniable expansion of subnational capacity on the military's watch—including subnational statism in Brazil, provincial control over federal tax breaks in Argentina, and the devolution of schools and hospitals in Chile—suggests that democracy is not a necessary condition for reforms that increase the governing relevance of subnational governments. Though these reforms fall well short of "devolution," their adoption does challenge the view of authoritarianism as an exclusively centralizing experience. It was, ironically, an act of political centralization in the form of disruptions in subnational democracy that subsequently enabled military authorities in each of the four cases to increase the stature of subnational governments.

The military-era reforms examined here also show that "deconcentration" as a concept fails to exhaust the variety of subnational changes that authoritarian actors can introduce. If military governments had opted mostly for deconcentration in their attempts to promote economic development, postauthoritarian politics would have looked quite different. In each case, military authorities decided not simply to redistribute power downward within the bureaucracy but to endorse structural changes in subnational governments themselves. While national politicians could opt to "reconcentrate" power within the bureaucracy via unilateral executive action, the structural changes introduced by the military were harder to undo. In effect, these changes shaped the contours of conflict between national and subnational governments in the years following the restoration of democracy.

In Chile, for example, municipalities emerged as important centers of political gravity after the withdrawal of Pinochet not simply because elections were reintroduced in 1992, but because mayors were now being elected to offices with real governing capacity. In Brazil, military rulers expanded the set of policy tools at the disposal of state-level governments, and this expansion subsequently made it more difficult for democratically elected federal authorities to rein in the states. Some of these attempts to rein in the states succeeded and some did not, but all of them occupied a salient position in the national policy agenda and consumed significant amounts of political capital. In Argentina, thanks to the failure of democratically elected politicians in the last 20 years to negotiate a comprehensive new system of revenue transfers, revenue sharing still bears the imprint of unilateral changes introduced by the generals in the 1960s and 1970s. The generals' introduction of a highly redistributive system of revenue sharing in 1973 has proven to be a particularly important innovation, one that fiscal reform advocates have been singularly unable to touch. According to the research presented here, it would be quite difficult to understand these contemporary phenomena without reference to the different development strategies that military governments articulated after the last round of democratic collapse.

NOTES

1 Important taxing powers were devolved in the wake of the 1891 civil war, but these powers were mostly recentralized in the 1925 Constitution.

2 Like that in Chile but unlike that in Argentina, the municipal level in Brazil also experienced important changes during the military period, with the generals holding elections in many municipalities and (later) expanding municipal revenue sharing. For reasons of space, this study focuses on state-level dynamics.

3 It is important to note that both Argentine regimes comprised at least three distinct subperiods, each of which partly reversed the objectives of the earlier ones. This makes it difficult to ascribe a single economic development strategy to either of these two regimes. The research for this study therefore focused on the initial, distinguishing phases of each: the Onganía presidency (1966–70) and the Videla presidency (1976–81).

4 Examples of potentially important changes in administrative resources include transferring to subnational officials authority over personnel decisions (such as hiring and firing workers) and requiring bureaucrats in subnational jurisdictions to report to subnational policymakers rather than to superiors in the national-level bureaucracy. Here, the focus is on changes in fiscal rather than administrative resources because the former experienced far greater change under military rule.

5 Table 1 lists changes that both increased and decreased subnational autonomy. Given the centralizing reputations of the governments in question, the former set of changes are more surprising; indeed, they prompted this attempt to understand why and how subnational governments acquired additional relevance despite the centralizing logic of military rule. It would be misleading, however, to overlook the more expected set of changes that limited subnational autonomy.

6 Three state-level SOEs were particularly significant in the electricity sector: Companhia Paranaense de Energia Elétrica, Centrais Elétricas de Minas Gérais, and Companhia Energética de São Paulo.

7 The same conflict and lack of cohesion that undermined the generals' economic development goals in Argentina was also reflected in the regimes' political objectives. In the *Revolución Argentina*, liberal factions vetoed Onganía's corporatist proposals, according to which "provincial governors and local notables would erect new political structures to link the state and society by means of so-called 'intermediate groups'" (Smith 1989, 63). Under the *Proceso*, conflict developed between softliners willing to engage in conversations with conservative provincial politicians and hardliners uninterested in dialogue with any elements of political society (Gibson 1997, 81, 82).

8 This analysis focuses only on the second of the two Argentine regimes. The democracy that was initiated in Argentina in 1983 has lasted much longer than the ill-fated democracy born in 1973, making it easier to assess the impact of military reforms in the post-1983 period. Though the 1973 fiscal decentralization law did strengthen the position of governors between 1973 and 1976, that development pales in comparison to the much more serious problems of political polarization and social unrest that led to the breakdown of democracy in 1976.

REFERENCES

Abalos, José Antonio. 1994. La descentralización en Chile: antecedentes históricos y reformas actuales. *Serie Azul* 4, 1–36. Santiago: Instituto de Estudios Urbanos, Pontificia Universidad Católica de Chile.

Abranches, Sérgio Henrique, ed. 1980. *A empresa pública no Brasil: uma abordagem multidisci-plinar.* Brasilia: Instituto de Planejamento Econômico e Social.

Abrúcio, Fernando, and David Samuels. 2000. The New Politics of the Governors: Subnational Politics and the Brazilian Transition to Democracy. *Publius: The Journal of Federalism* 30, 1: 1–28.

Azpiazu, Daniel, and Eduardo M. Basualdo. 1990. *Cara y contracara de los grupos económicos: estado y promoción industrial en la Argentina.* Buenos Aires: Cántaro Editores.

Boisier, Sergio. 1994. Perspectivas político-administrativas en Chile. In *Regionalización, descentral-ización y desarrollo regional.* Valparaíso: Centro de Estudios y Asistencia Legislativa. 15–38.

Britto Alvares Affonso, Rui de. 1995. A federação no Brasil: impasses e perspectivas. In *A fed-eração en perspectiva,* ed. de Britto Alvares Affonso and Pedro Luiz Barros Silva. São Paulo: FUNDAP. 57–75.

Camargo, Aspasia. 1993. La federación sometida: nacionalismo desarrollista e inestabilidad democrática. In *Federalismos latinoamericanos:México/Brasil/Argentina,* ed. Marcello Carma-gnani. Mexico City: Fondo de Cultura Económica. 300–62.

Caro, Jorge. 2001. Chief, Division of Regionalization Policy, Subsecretariat for Regional Develop-ment, Chile. Author interview. Santiago, August 24.

Collier, David, ed. 1979. *The New Authoritarianism in Latin America.* Princeton: Princeton University Press.

Diamond, Larry. 2000. *Developing Democracy: Toward Consolidation.* Baltimore: Johns Hopkins University Press.

Dias, Luciano. 2002. Researcher, Fundação Getulio Vargas. Author interview. Rio de Janeiro, January 25.

Dornbusch, Rudiger, and Sebastian Edwards. 1990. Macroeconomic Populism. *Journal of Develop-ment Economics* 32: 247–77.

Eaton, Kent. 2001. The Logic of Congressional Delegation: Argentine Economic Reform. *Latin American Research Review* 36, 2: 97–117.

——. 2004. *Politics Beyond the Capital: The Design of Subnational Institutions in South America.* Stanford: Stanford University Press.

Evans, Peter. 1979. *Dependent Development: The Alliance of Multinational, State, and Local Capital in Brazil.* Princeton: Princeton University Press.

Foxley, Alejandro. 1983. *Latin American Experiments in Neoconservative Economics.* Berkeley: University of California Press.

Fundación de Investigaciones Económicas Latinoamericanas (FIEL). 1993. *Hacia una nueva orga-nización del federalismo fiscal en la Argentina.* Buenos Aires: Ediciones Latinomericanas.

Gibson, Edward. 1996. *Class and Conservative Parties: Argentina in Comparative Perspective.* Baltimore: Johns Hopkins University Press.

Gleisner, Hagen. 1988. *Centralismo en Latinoamérica y descentralización en Chile.* Concepcion: G.A.T.

Hagopian, Frances. 1993. After Regime Change: Authoritarian Legacies, Political Representation, and the Democratic Future of South America. *World Politics* 45, 3: 464–500.

——. 1996. *Traditional Politics and Regime Change in Brazil.* Cambridge: Cambridge University Press.

Heller, Patrick. 2001. Moving the State: The Politics of Democratic Decentralization in Kerala, South Africa, and Porto Alegre. *Politics and Society* 29, 1: 131–63.

Hirschman, Albert. 1979. The Turn to Authoritarianism in Latin America and the Search for Its Economic Determinants. In Collier 1979. 61–98.

Hutchcroft, Paul. 2001. Centralization and Decentralization in Administration and Politics: Assessing Territorial Dimensions of Authority and Power. *Governance* 14, 1: 23–53.

Kugelmas, Eduardo. 2001. A evolução recente do regime federativo no Brasil. In *Federalismo na Alemanha e no Brasil*, ed. Wilhelm Hofmeister and José Mário Brasiliense Carneiro. São Paulo: Konrad Adenauer Stiftung. 29–49.

———. 2002. Professor, Universidade de São Paulo. Author interview. São Paulo, January 31.

Lewis, Paul. 1990. *The Crisis of Argentine Capitalism*. Chapel Hill: University of North Carolina Press.

Lopreato, Francisco Luiz. 1997. Um novo caminho do federalismo no Brasil? *Economia e Sociedade* (Universidade de Campinas) 9: 95–114.

Luna, Félix. 1975. *Argentina: De Perón a Lanusse, 1943–1973*. Buenos Aires: Biblioteca Universal Planeta.

Macón, Jorge. 1985. *Finanzas públicas argentinas*. Buenos Aires: Ediciones Macchi.

Mainwaring, Scott. 1997. Multipartism, Robust Federalism, and Presidentialism in Brazil. In *Presidentialism and Democracy in Latin America*, ed. Mainwaring and Matthew Shugart. New York: Cambridge University Press. 55–109.

———. 1999. *Rethinking Party Systems in the Third Wave of Democratization: The Case of Brazil*. Stanford: Stanford University Press.

Manor, James. 1999. *The Political Economy of Democratic Decentralization*. Washington, DC: World Bank.

Marcel, Mario. 1994. Decentralization and Development: The Chilean Experience. In *En Route to Modern Growth: Essays in Honor of Carlos Díaz-Alejandro*, ed. Gustav Ranis. Washington, DC: Johns Hopkins University Press. 79–121.

McGuire, James. 1997. *Peronism Without Perón: Unions, Parties, and Democracy in Argentina*. Stanford: Stanford University Press.

Migdal, Joel. 1988. *Strong Societies and Weak States: State-Society Relations and State Capabilities in the Third World*. Princeton: Princeton University Press.

Montero, Alfred P. 2002. *Shifting States in Global Markets: Subnational Industrial Policy in Contemporary Brazil and Spain*. University Park: Penn State University Press.

Montero, Alfred P., and David Samuels, eds. 2003. *Decentralization and Democracy in Latin America*. Notre Dame: University of Notre Dame Press.

Núñez Miñana, Horacio, and Alberto Porto. 1982. Coparticipación federal de impuestos: distribución primaria. *Jornadas de Finanzas Públicas* 15: 1–73.

O'Donnell, Guillermo. 1973. *Modernization and Bureaucratic Authoritarianism*. Berkeley: Institute of International Studies.

Parker, Andrew. 1995. Decentralization: The Way Forward for Rural Development? World Bank Policy Research Paper no. 1475. Washington, DC: World Bank.

Peralta-Ramos, Mónica. 1990. *The Political Economy of Argentina*. Boulder: Westview Press.

Prado, Sergio. 1996. Aspectos federativos do investimento estatal. In *Empresas estatais e federação*, ed. Rui de Britto Alvares Affonso and Pedro Luiz Barros Silva. São Paulo: Fundação do Desenvolvimento Administrativo. 11–71.

Rezende, Fernando. 1980. A empresa pública e a intervenção do estado na economia. In Abranches 1980. 31–85.

———. 1996. Federalismo fiscal en Brasil. In *Hacia un nuevo federalismo?* ed. Alicia Hernández Chávez. Mexico City: Fondo de Cultura Económica. 45–73.

Rondinelli, Dennis. 1989. Decentralizing Public Services in Developing Countries: Issues and Opportunities. *Journal of Social, Political and Economic Studies* 14, 1: 77–97.

Saiegh, Sebastian, and Mariano Tommasi. 1998. *Argentina's Federal Fiscal Institutions*. Buenos Aires: Centro de Estudios para el Desarrollo Institucional.

Sallum, Brasilio. 1996. *Labirintos: dos generais à Nova República*. São Paulo: Editora Hucitec.

Samuels, David. 2003. *Ambition, Federalism, and Legislative Politics in Brazil*. New York: Cambridge University Press.

Schamis, Hector. 1991. Reconceptualizing Latin American Authoritarianism in the 1970s: From Bureaucratic-Authoritarianism to Neoconservatism. *Comparative Politics* 23, 2: 201–20.

Schwartzman, Simón. 1982. *Bases do autoritarismo brasileiro*. 2nd ed. Rio de Janeiro: Editora Campus.

Seabra Fagundes, Miguel. 1997. Aspectos da trajetória histórica do regime federativo no Brasil. In *Reforma constitucional*, ed. Mario Brockmann Machado. Rio de Janeiro: Rui Barbosa. 105–35.

Selcher, Wayne. 1989. A New Start Toward a More Decentralized Federalism in Brazil? *Publius: The Journal of Federalism* 19: 167–83.

Shah, Anwar. 1991. The New Fiscal Federalism in Brazil. World Bank Discussion Papers 124. Washington, DC: World Bank.

Smith, William C. 1989. *Authoritarianism and the Crisis of the Argentine Political Economy*. Stanford: Stanford University Press.

Stepan, Alfred. 1973. *Authoritarian Brazil: Origins, Policies, and Future*. New Haven: Yale University Press.

Subsecretaría de Desarrollo Regional y Administrativo (SUBDERE). 2001. *El Chile descentralizado que queremos: un proyecto de todos*. Santiago: SUBDERE.

Tendler, Judith. 1968. *Electric Power in Brazil: Entrepreneurship in the Public Sector*. Cambridge: Harvard University Press.

Tobar, Manuel. 2001. President, National Association of Regional Councilors, Chile. Author interview. Valparaíso, August 20.

Trebat, Thomas. 1983. *Brazil's State-Owned Enterprises: A Case Study of the State as Entrepreneur*. Cambridge: Cambridge University Press.

Valenzuela, Arturo. 1977. *Political Brokers in Chile: Local Government in a Centralized Polity*. Durham: Duke University Press.

Valenzuela, Esteban. 1999. *Alegato histórico regionalista*. Santiago: Ediciones Sur.

Villela, Aníbal. 1984. *Empresas do governo como instrumento de política econômica*. Rio de Janeiro: Instituto de Planejamento Econômico e Social.

Werneck, Rogério. 1987. *Empresas estatais e política macroeconômica*. Rio de Janeiro: Editora Campus.

World Bank. 1993. *Argentina: From Insolvency to Growth*. Washington, DC: World Bank.

Yáñez, José, and Leonardo Letelier. 1995. Chile. In *Fiscal Decentralization in Latin America*, ed. Ricardo López Murphy. Washington, DC: Inter-American Development Bank. 137–88.

Zavala, Jaime. 2001. Director of Municipal Administration, Subsecretariat for Regional Development (1984–90), Chile. Author interview. Las Condes, August 22.

Chapter 7

Institutional Change and Ethnic Parties in South America

Donna Lee Van Cott

The literature on political parties recognizes ethnic cleavages as among the cleavages most likely to generate political parties and to organize political competition in multiethnic societies. The more socially and culturally diverse the society, the larger the number of parties necessary to fill these representational needs (Harmel and Robertson 1985, 503). Yet until the 1990s, political parties organized around ethnicity were rare in Latin America, despite the region's ethnic and racial diversity. Of the few that had been formed, none enjoyed enduring electoral success or had much impact on the political party system or the representation of their constituency in formal politics (Stavenhagen 1992, 434). Given the persistence of strong indigenous identities after the extension of full suffrage in multiethnic Latin American societies, and the existence of indigenous social organizational structures at community, regional, and even national levels in most of them, the absence of ethnic parties in most of the region was curious.

The sudden emergence in the 1990s of indigenous peoples-based political parties in some Latin American countries is equally curious. The author became aware of this phenomenon while conducting research on constitutional reform and indigenous rights in Bolivia, Colombia, Ecuador, and Venezuela during the last decade. In all four countries, indigenous peoples' social movement organizations formed political parties following the codification of special indigenous constitutional rights or changes in electoral laws that lowered barriers to party system entry (see table 1).

This study seeks to analyze why indigenous peoples formed political parties in the 1990s and why some of those parties have been electorally viable. These are distinct research questions, because we cannot assume that the conditions necessary for party formation and electoral viability are the same (Harmel and Robertson 1985, 502). Parties with poor prospects for electoral success may form in order to gain attention for a political issue or to provide a platform for a particular personality (Harmel and Robertson 1985, 507). Nevertheless, there is some relationship between formation and viability, inasmuch as the decision to expend the resources necessary to form a party will incorporate a calculation as to the likely electoral result. The broader theoretical questions the research illuminates are: Under what conditions do ethnic parties form, endure, and succeed? And under what conditions will a new cleavage emerge in a party system?

Ethnic party is defined here as an organization authorized to compete in local or national elections; the majority of its leadership and membership identify themselves as belonging to a nondominant ethnic group, and its electoral platform includes demands and programs of an ethnic or cultural nature. While using the broader term *ethnic party* to relate the research to the literature on ethnic parties, this study focuses on parties based on an ethnic identity as "indigenous," as that term is understood in the Americas.

This study does not claim that the political behavior of indigenous peoples differs in any way from that of other nondominant ethnic groups. The definition here includes entities that call themselves "political movements" in order to distance themselves rhetorically from the negative connotations associated with political parties in their societies,

Table 1. Electorally Viable Ethnic Parties

Country/Percent Indigenous[a]	Year Formed
Argentina 1.1%	None
Bolivia 50.51%	Movimiento Revolucionario Tupaj Katari de Liberación (MRKTL), 1985
	Asamblea de la Soberanía del Pueblo (ASP) 1995, uses valid registration of Izquierda Unida because of difficulty with registration.
	Instrumento Político de la Soberanía de los Pueblos (IPSP), 1999, splinter of ASP, uses the valid registration of the Movimiento al Socialismo.
Colombia 2.7%	Organización Nacional Indígena de Colombia (ONIC), the largest national indigenous social movement organization, founded in 1982. Competed in 1990 National Constituent Assembly elections and 1991 national elections. Retired from electoral politics in 1993.
	Autoridades Indígenas de Colombia (AICO), created as a social movement organization in 1977 under different name. First competed in 1990 National Constituent Assembly elections.
	Alianza Social Indígena (ASI), created by Consejo Regional Indígena del Cauca in 1991.
	Movimiento Indígena Colombiano (MIC), 1993. Formed to secure reelection for ONIC's 1991–1994 indigenous senator after ONIC retired from electoral competition.
Ecuador 24.85%	Movimiento de Unidad Plurinacional Pachakutik (MUPP), created by Confederación de Nacionalidades del Ecuador in 1995.
Peru 38.39%	None
Venezuela 1.48%	Pueblo Unido de Multiétnico de Amazonas (PUAMA), created by Organización Regional de Pueblos Indígenas de Amazonas in 1997.

[a]All figures except those of Colombia are from Deruyttere (1997, 1). These figures may be considered low/conservative estimates. Colombian figure is from 1993 Census.

but which otherwise meet the definition. It also includes parties that incorporate nonindigenous candidates and form electoral alliances with nonindigenous social movements, provided that ethnic rights and recognition remain a central part of the party's platform and Indians constitute at least half the party's leadership. The definition excludes from this category parties formed as dependent clients of nonindigenous parties.

Party formation is defined as the legal registration of a political party or movement and its participation in two consecutive elections. The requirement of two consecutive elections connotes the intention to form an enduring political organization, as opposed to a temporary electoral alliance. *Electoral viability* is defined as the demonstrated ability of a political party to win a seat in two consecutive elections at any level of government (municipal, regional, national). In addition, an electorally viable party must win a sufficient number of votes to maintain its registration.

Little comparative research has been done on the new ethnic parties in Latin America, despite the current intense interest among political scientists in the poor representativity of Latin American parties and the weak institutionalization of the region's party systems (for example, Cantón 1995; Coppedge 1998; Dominguez 1995; Mainwaring 1999, Mainwaring and Scully 1995; Roberts and Wibbels 1999). A few monographic studies of individual parties or countries have been published. Ecuador, having the indigenous party with the most stunning electoral success, has received the most attention from political scientists (Andolina 1999; Beck and Mijeski 2001; Collins 2001; Selverston-Scher 2001).

Work on Colombia has been undertaken mainly by anthropologists rather than political scientists. Bolivian anthropologists have published descriptive, interpretive research on the new Indianist parties and new alliances between indigenous candidates and nonindigenous parties (Albó 1994; Ticona et al. 1995; Ministerio de Desarrollo Humano 1997). Two new political science dissertations compare indigenous political activity in Bolivia and Ecuador; these studies focus attention on the new political parties as part of a broader interest in representation and social movement issues (Andolina 1999; Lucero 2002). A third recent political science dissertation links clientelism with the emergence of new indigenous movement-related parties in Bolivia and Ecuador (Collins 2006). A comparative study of the impact of ethnic cleavages on party systems in Latin America— as part of a larger effort to understand how societal cleavages determine party system evolution—is long overdue (Coppedge 1997).

This article is an initial attempt to organize empirical data and to investigate this phenomenon. Following an explanation of the research design, case selection, and preliminary hypotheses, it presents findings regarding the impact of institutional change on the emergence and electoral viability of ethnic parties. Then, brief case studies of Bolivia and Colombia illustrate the impact of institutional change.

RESEARCH DESIGN

The research design is a "structured focused comparison" of six cases (King et al. 1994, 107) designed to avoid both the Scylla of large-N macro political party research—which is devoid of complex, contextual nuances unique to individual political systems—and the Charybdis of single-case studies, which explicate the uniqueness of one case but fail to test theoretical propositions generalizable to more cases. Here, a carefully selected, manageable set of cases includes various outcomes on the dependent variable while controlling for variation in the proportional size of the indigenous population. The cases are six political systems, each of which constitutes a unique political environment where ethnic parties may or may not form and, if they form, may or may not prove electorally viable. Thus, each case produces a single dependent variable that can have one of three values: no ethnic party formed, ethnic party formed but not electorally viable, or ethnic party formed and electorally viable.[1]

The cases under study needed to be limited because a full understanding of the emergence of indigenous parties requires intensive fieldwork. Although it would have been relatively easy to compile information on institutional change for all 13 Latin American countries with indigenous populations larger than 1 percent, it would have been necessary to conduct field research in most of them to ascertain the value of the dependent variable. This is because some important ethnic parties are active only at the regional or local level and would not show up in the secondary literature on each country or in the various regional databases that have been compiled of election results for national elections. Without some fieldwork, moreover, it would be difficult to distinguish indigenous social movement-based parties from those created by and dependent on nonindigenous, clientelist parties, or parties whose platforms use indigenous-sounding names to appeal to indigenous voters but contain no ethnic content. Thus a representative sample was chosen.

The selection process began by choosing all the cases where new electorally viable ethnic parties were known to have been formed: Bolivia, Colombia, Ecuador, and Venezuela. It then eliminated countries where indigenous populations numbered less than 1 percent of the total population (Brazil and Uruguay) and which had less than ten years of democratic rule (Paraguay), to allow for analysis of party system and electoral law changes over time. In addition to the four cases selected, this left Argentina, Chile, and Peru. The absence of electorally viable ethnic parties was expected in all three of these cases; Peru was selected to include a case with a proportionally significant indigenous population but no electorally viable ethnic party.

This left two cases with small indigenous populations where the dependent variables could be negative. Argentina was chosen over Chile for several reasons. Argentina has a federal system, which allows the researcher to observe the operation of decentralizing measures in promoting the emergence of new parties. The nation achieved a comprehensive constitutional reform in 1994 that included reforms affecting indigenous peoples. Provincial parties also exist; and these, we can suspect, are potentially an important vehicle for geographically concentrated indigenous peoples. Chile, in contrast, has a shorter period of democratic rule since 1980 and a rigid constitutional structure imposed by the outgoing Pinochet regime, which limits the extent to which we would be able to observe the effects of institutional change on party formation. This later proved to be the right decision, because a Mapuche Indian multiparty coalition was contesting national elections at least as early as 1993 (FBIS-LAT 1993).

These six cases provide a diverse sample of South American countries where indigenous peoples are politically organized, significant institutional reform has occurred in the last decade, and multiple elections have been held. Three countries in the sample have federal or quasi-federal systems (Argentina, Colombia, Venezuela); all three unitary systems in the sample (Bolivia, Ecuador, Peru) undertook decentralizing or centralizing reforms in the 1990s that enable us to observe the impact of changes in state structure on the dependent variables. The sample also includes a wide variety of party systems: two cases in which traditional party systems collapsed in the 1990s (Peru, Venezuela), two noted for their extreme fragmentation since the transition to democracy (Bolivia, Ecuador), and two with two-party-dominant systems (Argentina, Colombia). Finally, the sample includes cases with variation on the dependent variable. In Bolivia, Colombia, Ecuador, and Venezuela, ethnic parties proved electorally viable; in Argentina and Peru, regional indigenous parties, or factions within parties, recently formed but have yet to achieve electoral viability. It should be noted that the author was not aware that any indigenous parties had formed in Argentina and Peru until after selecting these countries for the study and beginning to gather information on the two cases.

The cases in the sample can be divided into two subsets according to indigenous population size, the better to hold constant this potentially important variable (see table 1). This will facilitate observation of how the proportional size of the indigenous population might affect the design of electoral systems, requirements for party registration, the capacity of indigenous populations to mobilize, the propensity of non-Indians to vote for indigenous parties, and the likelihood that non-indigenous political elites would enact reforms giving electoral advantages to indigenous populations. Argentina, Colombia, and Venezuela have minuscule indigenous populations. All cases in this subset also are federal or quasi-federal and traditionally have had two-party-dominant party systems. That two of the cases score positively on the dependent variables and one case scores negatively enables us to examine more closely the impact of electoral and party registration rules. Similarly, the remaining three cases constitute a subset of significantly sized indigenous populations in unitary political systems with fragmented, volatile political party systems in which the dependent variables are positive in two cases and negative in the third.

The time period under study is 1980 to 2002. These 22 years encompass multiple national and subnational elections in all six cases. Colombia and Venezuela held competitive elections throughout this period; Argentina and Bolivia resumed elections in 1983 and 1980–82, respectively; Ecuador and Peru resumed elections in 1979 and 1980, respectively. The resumption of elections is a particularly important starting point for Ecuador and Peru because it coincided with the elimination of literacy requirements that had disenfranchised the majority of indigenous voters.

HYPOTHESES

There are two ways of looking at the formation of ethnic parties in the 1990s. Either we assume, as the literature does, that political parties will automatically form around ethnic cleavages (Harmel and Robertson 1985, 503; Horowitz 1985, 293–94); or we assume that ethnic parties form when political actors make strategic decisions to form them. A model can be derived from each assumption.

If we assume that ethnic parties form automatically, then in the absence of ethnic parties we should look for formal or informal barriers that might have impeded the formation of political parties by indigenous peoples. Accordingly we can look for the removal (or not) of those barriers in the individual cases, followed by the formation of electorally viable ethnic parties. Two types of barriers are likely independent variables: institutional change; that is, changes in constitutional provisions, laws, and rules that structure the political system, particularly the electoral system; and party system change that significantly lowers barriers to new entrants.

In the alternative, we could assume that ethnic parties are not the natural, automatic result of the existence of ethnic cleavages in a society. In the absence of institutional barriers to party formation or a "frozen" party system (Lipset and Rokkan 1967, 50; Mair 1997, 13–14), we cannot assume that ethnic parties automatically will form. Party formation may require political actors to make a conscious, strategic decision, which may occur only under particular conditions. Electoral rules and party system change may be intervening variables or even necessary conditions for party formation and viability; but they may not be sufficient to explain our dependent variables.

Under this assumption, we could use the social movement literature to examine changes in the political environment or within social movements themselves that might cause them to decide to form political parties and might make them more likely to achieve electoral viability. Social movement analysis is crucial for a full understanding of ethnic party formation because that step always was preceded by an unprecedented level of political organization and mobilization by indigenous peoples' social movements. The most successful parties were social movement organizations that participated in elections, or parties that maintained strong ties to their "parent" social movement organization.

The expectation here is that all four independent variables—institutional change, political party system change, changes in the political opportunity structure external to social movements, and factors internal to social movements themselves—are important in explaining the emergence and electoral viability of ethnic parties. The hypotheses tested here relate to the first variable, institutional change, based on a review of the comparative electoral institutions literature and research in the six cases under study.

Hypothesized Impact of Institutional Change

Historical institutional approaches demonstrate how "the stability of certain types of institutions effectively constrains the range of outcomes on the dependent variable" (Lieberman 2001, 1015). Electoral institutions create an underlying structure that "both supports and constrains the evolution of party systems" and that partly explains the variation among party systems in different countries. As Coppedge argues, this structure "will never completely explain outcomes . . . , but it is an indispensable part of the picture" (Coppedge 1997, 184).

The literature on electoral systems and political parties suggests that several types of rule changes should lower the barriers to the formation of new parties, "challenger" parties, or ethnic minority parties. Such changes should therefore encourage ethnic parties. The discussion that follows will specify when the changes considered are particularly relevant for ethnic parties. At this point in the development of the theory, it is not known to what extent it will be generalizable to new nonethnic parties or other types of cleavages.

Proportional representation. Electoral systems based upon proportional representation (PR) are more likely than other forms to encourage the formation and ensure the success of new parties. The introduction of PR removes barriers to party system entry by creating a more proportional vote-to-seat calculation and by giving voters more choices (Sartori 1986, 58). Single-member-district systems, in contrast, tend to produce a two-party system and make it difficult for new parties to form (Lijphart 1986b, 113; Riker 1986). Proportionality is particularly important for minorities "who tend to be severely underrepresented or excluded by non-PR systems" (Lijphart 1986b, 113; see also Mozaffar 1997, 149). PR is also more likely to encourage the institutionalization of antiestablishment political parties, which most of the new ethnic parties are, because PR presents lower barriers to small parties' gaining seats (Schedler 1996, 305). Pressure to switch to PR tends to follow the emergence of new issue dimensions or party fragmentation (Taagepera and Shugart 1989, 150).

Lower threshold of representation. Three types of electoral rules combine to present a "threshold of representation:" the seat allocation formula, the threshold for apportionment of seats, and district magnitude.[2] Seat allocation formulas that award seats to parties winning small proportions of the vote should be correlated with the formation and electoral viability of new parties. Formulas favoring larger parties should inhibit new party formation and electoral viability.

According to Lijphart, the consensus in the literature is that the d'Hondt formula tends to favor larger parties and to be relatively less proportional than the other electoral formulas used under PR. D'Hondt is a "highest averages formula" that "awards seats sequentially to parties having the highest average numbers of votes per seat until all seats are allocated. Each time a party receives seats its average goes down" (Birnir 2000, 15). The Largest Remainders formula tends to treat larger and smaller parties equally and thus provides a more proportional result. Sainte-Lague, while using a highest averages formula, tends to produce a result that is closer to Largest Remainders in terms of proportionality (Lijphart 1986a, 173–75).

Thresholds refer to minimum vote requirements for the allocation of seats and are usually based on nationwide vote shares (Taagepera and Shugart 1989, 133). If we assume that new parties will have relatively fewer votes, lower thresholds will enable them to gain access to political power and the resources appertaining thereto, which can be used to enhance the new party's share in the next election.

In a study of 62 elections between 1914 and 1995 in Argentina, Bolivia, Colombia, Peru, and Venezuela, Coppedge found that neither the seat-to-vote electoral formula, vote threshold to win a seat, signatures required to register a party, nor percentage of the vote required to maintain party registration had any independent impact on the effective number of parties for seats, when controlling for effective number of parties for votes (Coppedge 1997). Coppedge did find that district magnitude (DM) was "the only electoral institution that has a distinguishable, separate impact on [party system] fragmentation" (Coppedge 1997).

District magnitude has both mechanical and psychological effects. The mechanical effect is that the larger the magnitude of the district, the more proportional will be the translation of votes into seats. Larger DMs help challenger parties because they do not have to win a plurality to gain seats, even in plurality districts, provided that there is more than one seat (Taagepera and Shugart 1989, 115). Psychologically, small DMs discourage voters from "wasting" their votes on smaller parties that are unlikely to win seats (Taagepera and Shugart 1989, 119). The extent to which smaller parties are helped by a given seat allocation formula depends on DM and the size of divisors and remainders used in the allocation formula (Taagepera and Shugart 1989, 29–35).

The impact of DM depends on whether the system is PR or plurality. Under PR, the larger the DM, the closer to proportionality the allocation of votes will be, and thus the more favorable the system is to new party formation and electoral viability. Under plurality, increasing DM decreases proportionality (Taagepera and Shugart 1989, 19, 112; Sartori 1986, 53). DM is decisive because it "has a stronger impact on proportionality than almost any other factor" (Taagepera and Shugart 1989, 112).

Coppedge (1997) found that a significant change in DM is required to increase the effective number of parties for seats by just one party. According to his statistical regression, average DM would have to increase by 58.8 seats to have this effect, an increase that was present in only 3 of the 62 observations in his study. On the basis of this finding, Coppedge concluded that changes in DM significant enough to affect the number of parties in the system are rare. Coppedge's data, however, included only chamber of deputies and constituent assembly elections, and his study period ended in 1995. His data therefore do not include at least four additional cases of significant changes in DM that occurred after 1995 or in senate elections.[3]

Constituent assembly elections are particularly important in observing the link between institutional and party system changes. Constituent assemblies are typically elected from single national districts with more than 70 members; smaller parties, and even civil society organizations in some cases, can thereby secure representation in them. The reciprocal effect, of course, is lower-than-usual representation for the system's most dominant parties. Five of our six cases experienced constituent assemblies between 1980 and 2002 (a sixth was underway in Bolivia in late 2006). In five cases (Bolivia's underway Assembly, Colombia, Ecuador, Peru, and Venezuela), for different reasons, the representation of the major parties was unusually reduced, allowing potential party system entrants and challengers the opportunity to change electoral laws that had favored the major parties and to open the system to new parties.

For all these reasons, DM is recognized in the parties literature as "the critical institutional variable influencing the formation and maintenance of parties" (Ordeshook and Shvetsova 1994, 105). Its impact may be particularly important to ethnic parties. On the basis of data from stable Western industrialized democracies, Ordeshook and Shvetsova concluded, "if the effective number of ethnic groups is large, political systems become especially sensitive to district magnitude" (1994, 122). The difficulty of observing DM's impact at the aggregate level is that DM varies, sometimes significantly, within countries and can have different effects in different districts throughout the country. DM often reflects the density of the population in a district rather than a conscious effort to affect party formation (Taagepera and Shugart 1989, 125).

Variations in DM interact with variations in the geographic dispersion and concentration of ethnic minorities. Where minorities are proportionally small and highly dispersed, they are more likely to win seats in districts with a high number of seats. Where minorities are concentrated geographically, they are more likely to win seats in districts that correspond to the boundaries of their settlement patterns, where they may be a numerical majority. Variations in DM and in the geographic concentration of ethnic minorities may generate distinct likelihoods of formation and electoral viability in the same country. For example, in Venezuela, with its federal system, where Indians constitute less than 2 percent of the population, in 2000 the indigenous party PUAMA (in coalition with other parties) won the governorship of Amazonas state, which is 43 percent indigenous. PUAMA's base in Amazonas is so strong that it also won a seat in the National Assembly elections in 2000, outside the reserved indigenous district. It is less likely, however, that indigenous parties will succeed in statewide elections in other Venezuelan states where the indigenous population is minuscule.

Indigenous peoples, like most ethnic minorities, typically are not evenly distributed in a population. Instead, they tend to be concentrated geographically, because sufficient numbers must exist in one place to constitute a self-reproducing cultural community and because minorities, surrounded by people different from themselves and sometimes victims of discrimination or worse, prefer to settle in areas where their numbers are greatest and bonds of solidarity can protect them. Indigenous peoples, like many ethnic minorities, feel a particular attachment to specific locales and prefer to settle there to protect or advance longstanding territorial claims. States may also create laws and norms that require or encourage indigenous peoples to live in certain places and not others; for example, Colombia's 1991 Constitution exempts Indians from military service provided that they live in constitutionally recognized *resguardos* or *reservas*.

Ballot access. Given the meager financial resources of indigenous populations in Latin America, political party laws that place a high financial or logistical burden on registration of new parties inhibit the formation of indigenous parties. Conversely, low registration requirements and the absence of penalties for poor electoral performance should help new parties.

Decentralization. Federal or highly decentralized political systems that allow for regional and local elections may be more likely to generate ethnic parties, to the extent that ethnic minorities are geographically concentrated, particularly where districts are designed to create ethnic majorities. Harmel and Robertson found that regional parties are more likely to develop in decentralized federal systems (1985, 507; see also Hauss and Rayside 1978). We may assume that new parties will be more successful in countries that are decentralized rather than centralized because new parties have the opportunity to develop at geographical levels where the cost of party formation is lower—that is, lower transportation and advertising costs, a smaller campaign organization, fewer signatures on the candidate's petition to appear on the ballot. As Dalton et al. observe, "[a] political movement first may win subnational elections where its strength is concentrated, and these bases can provide the infrastructure for further political action" (1984, 467).

Ethnic groups are particularly disposed to benefit from local and regional elections because they are usually concentrated geographically. They may comprise a majority in local and regional districts in a country where their overall numbers are relatively minuscule. Once parties become established at the local or regional level, they may be able to project themselves onto the national level. If local and regional elections are held separately from national ones, moreover, the gap may reduce the electoral advantages of larger parties and thereby help challengers.

Reserved seats or ethnic electoral rolls. Lijphart argues that the creation of electoral districts along ethnic rather than geographic lines is the simplest way to guarantee ethnic representation. This usually involves creating ethnic voting rolls, which exist in Cyprus, New Zealand, and Zimbabwe (Lijphart 1986b, 116). The review of the parties literature enables us to form six hypotheses. The formation and electoral viability of ethnic parties will follow any of the following events:

1. A shift to proportional representation
2. A shift to a more proportional electoral formula
3. A reduction in requirements for ballot access
4. Increased district magnitude under proportional representation
5. Administrative and political decentralization
6. The allocation of reserved seats for indigenous representatives

Findings with Respect to Institutional Change

The research results for each of the various factors were as follows.

Proportional representation. We cannot test the impact of a shift to PR because all six cases began with PR systems. Bolivia and Venezuela shifted, in 1994 and 1993, respectively, to a mixed, German-style system in which half the lower chamber of a bicameral legislature is elected by single-member district (SMD). The 1998 Ecuadorian Constitution shifted from PR to a multiseat, candidate-based majoritarian system in which only 20 of 121 seats are elected on national party lists. The 1999 Venezuelan Constitution shifted to a unicameral legislature that retained the mixed system used for the lower chamber.

Threshold of representation. D'Hondt is the most common seat allocation formula in Latin America and has been used throughout the period under study in Argentina and Peru for the lower chamber. Venezuela used d'Hondt until 1993, when half the lower house was elected by SMD, while the remaining half is still elected by d'Hondt. Venezuela during the period under study also allocated compensatory seats to under-represented parties winning at least one quota (Jones 1997, 14). Colombia has used the Largest Remainders—Hare system since 1974 (on electoral formulas in Latin America, see Jones 1995, 1997).[4]

Ecuador has used Largest Remainders—Hare since 1978, with the exception of districts that have two deputies, where d'Hondt is used (Jones 1997, 15). The 1998 Constitution adopted an open-list panachage system, in which voters have as many votes as there are seats in their district, enabling them to vote for multiple parties. The shift from closed to open lists was chosen by voters in a 1998 referendum on a variety of political reform issues. For the 1997 constituent assembly elections, voters could vote for any candidate on the ballot, at anyplace on a list, and had as many votes as there were seats in that voter's district. This enabled voters to divide votes among parties (Birnir 2000, 12). This change may help indigenous parties win votes from strategic voters who might otherwise not choose to "waste" a single congressional vote. According to Lijphart, it is logical to expect that when voters have more than one choice they are more likely to vote their sincere preferences, which tends to encourage multipartism (Lijphart 1986b, 120). In only one case (Bolivia) did a shift occur to a formula more favorable to small parties, and this shift was reversed in the next election cycle.

With respect to seat thresholds, in no case were they lowered. Argentina since 1983 has required a threshold of 3 percent of the registered voters in a district to receive seats. In Bolivia, a one-quota threshold was in place between 1989 and 1993, the 1996 electoral law makes no mention of this quota. In Ecuador until 1987, the threshold for parties to receive seats in the legislature was one-half a quota. In 1987 this was raised to 0.6 unless no party receives more than a half-quota (Jones 1995, 15).

District magnitude. In two cases, DM under PR increased significantly when a chamber of the legislature shifted from multiple districts to a single national district: Colombia's national constituent assembly in 1990 and senate in 1991, and Peru's legislature in 1993. Peru shifted back to multiple districts in 2001 (Birnir 2001). In Colombia, as DM for the senate increased, the lower chamber was reduced from 199 to 161 seats, causing average DM to decrease from 8 to 5. The negative impact on small parties was offset by a law establishing up to 5 additional seats for ethnic and political minorities and Colombians living abroad (Dugas 2001, 16). A 1993 law (Law 70) used this provision to create two seats for Afro-Colombians; the law was overturned in 1996 for technical reasons (Van Cott 2000b, 96–98).

As expected, all these shifts were followed by a higher effective number of parties in the legislature. District magnitude increased in Ecuador as well. The size of the unicameral legislature increased from 82 to 121 seats following the 1998 constitutional reform. Of those 121, 20 are elected in a single national district and the remainder uninominally from provincial districts. The number of seats in both the national district and the provincial districts increased from 12 to 20 and from 70 to 101, respectively (Birnir 2000, 12). In Bolivia and Venezuela, DM decreased with the shift to a mixed system in 1997 and 1993, respectively; now half the lower house is elected in single-member districts. In Venezuela, average DM decreased from 8 to 6 with the move from the Chamber of Deputies to a national assembly in 2000. As Molina observes, this, together with other institutional changes, resulted in a less proportional vote-to-seat ratio that helped the larger parties and reduced the effective number of parties in the legislature (V. Molina 2002).

An increase in DM was followed by the formation and electoral success of ethnic parties only in Colombia. There, Indians have twice won a senate seat (in addition to their two reserved seats) since the shift to a single, hundred-member district. They also won two seats in the single-district constituent assembly elections of 1990, their first electoral outing. In Ecuador, the already-formed MUPP achieved the same number of seats after the change as before, which translated to a smaller proportion of seats because of the increased size of the legislature. Thus, an increase in DM alone cannot explain either dependent variable.

Ballot access. Barriers to party registration historically have been highest in the three Andean countries with the greatest party system fragmentation (Bolivia, Ecuador, and Peru). Those barriers have been employed to limit the number of personalist and populist electoral vehicles. During the period under study, registration barriers were maintained in Bolivia (where, since 1979, parties must win 3 percent of the vote to maintain registration and avoid paying fines). However, before the December 2004 local elections, constitutional changes allowed "citizens groupings" and "indigenous peoples" to register for elections according to less-stringent criteria. This led many indigenous communities and regional organizations to compete independently from the new indigenous parties in the 2004 municipal and 2005 national elections. This change mainly drew voters away from the weaker, faltering indigenous party, the Movimiento Indígena Pachakutik, while the surging MAS expanded its vote share and seized national power. Registration barriers were increased in Peru in 1995 (when signature requirements for registering national parties were raised from one hundred thousand to four hundred thousand) and decreased in Ecuador in 1995 (by allowing social organizations and independents to participate in elections). The author's interview subjects, along with experts on the Ecuadorian indigenous movement-based MUPP, believe the 1995 change was crucial to the decision to form an electoral vehicle that year (Andolina 1999, Collins 2001; Lluco 1999).

In Colombia and Venezuela, ballot access was improved: Colombia's 1991 Constitution allows social movements to contest elections without formal registration as a party, while Venezuela's 1999 Constitution allows Indians to run in local elections without forming a party. No change was made in ballot access in Argentina.

Decentralization. In Bolivia, Colombia, and Venezuela, decentralization increased significantly in the 1990s. Direct municipal and regional elections were instituted in Colombia (in 1988 and 1991, respectively), Bolivia (municipal 1995), and Venezuela (municipal 1989). Whereas Bolivian Indians formed a party to compete in the first-ever municipal elections in 1995, Indians in Colombia and Venezuela formed parties after the codification of constitutional rights, in 1991 and 1999, respectively, and after they had achieved surprising success in National Constituent Assembly elections. Indigenous parties were particularly successful in departments or states where they constituted a significant minority or a majority, even in countries where they were a minuscule minority nationwide. The PUAMA victory in Amazonas noted above is an example.

In Argentina, decentralization was slightly increased in an already-federal system. In Ecuador, decentralization had occurred in 1980, and the status quo was maintained. In Peru, recentralization occurred following a brief experiment with regional government (1989–93).

As the data in the appendix illustrate, indigenous parties that established a foothold in local elections in Bolivia, Colombia, and Ecuador expanded their electoral participation with some success to higher levels of government in subsequent elections. Thus, as one reviewer of this article pointed out, decentralization need not increase to encourage the formation of ethnic parties. Its mere existence tends to help new parties with geographically concentrated potential supporters. Decentralization may operate in conjunction with other variables, such as the reservation of special seats for Indians (Colombia, Venezuela) or the availability of resources for new parties (Colombia).

Special ethnic districts or reserved seats. Special districts for indigenous candidates were created in Colombia and Venezuela. In Colombia, Indians are guaranteed two seats in the senate. In Venezuela, Indians compete for three seats in the national unicameral legislature and for seats in municipal and state assemblies where indigenous populations are concentrated. Although the districts significantly increased the electoral viability of indigenous candidates and thus the incentive to form indigenous parties, it should be emphasized that in both cases the special districts were achieved after indigenous social movements had already demonstrated their ability to elect candidates against enormous odds in competition with nonindigenous candidates in National Constituent Assembly elections. Indians won two seats in the Colombian assembly and two in Venezuela (in addition to three seats allocated by President Hugo Chávez).

Once achieved, the special districts not only guaranteed a legal minimum of representation but provided resources to expand representation above this minimum level.

Indigenous parties in Colombia have used the resources allocated to their indigenous senators to build parties at other nonreserved levels of government. They also have benefited from the national media platform provided to national senators. For example, the notoriety gained by former indigenous senator Floro Tunubalá enabled him to capture the governorship of Cauca in 2000. In both Colombia and Venezuela, immediately following the allocation of reserved seats, indigenous parties successfully contested elections for nonreserved seats in order to maximize representation.

It should be noted that in both Colombia and Venezuela, too, constitutional reforms allowed indigenous organizations to contest reserved seats and any local office without forming a political party, eliminating the party registration barrier. Indigenous organizations may also contest elections in Ecuador since the 1995 electoral reform, which allows any social movement or independent candidate to contest elections. This provision was upheld in the 1998 constitutional reform. As of early 2002, the Bolivian congress was considering a proposal, generated by a national dialogue held the previous year, to allow candidates unaffiliated with registered political parties (*agrupaciones de ciudadanos*) to contest municipal elections as well as uninominal seats in the lower chamber of congress (see Bolivian Congress 2001).[5]

In sum, it was impossible to test hypotheses 1 and 2 (shift to PR and more proportional electoral formula) for lack of observations on these independent variables. There is some evidence to support hypothesis 3, considering that in the only country where ballot access requirements were lowered, an ethnic party formed. The results for hypothesis 4, regarding increased district magnitude, are mixed: the Colombian case supports, while the Ecuadorian and Peruvian cases disconfirm it. Similarly, the results for hypothesis 5 were mixed: Bolivia, Colombia, and Venezuela support the hypothesis; in Ecuador there was no change on this independent variable; and in Peru, the hypothesis was disconfirmed. Hypothesis 6, regarding reserved seats, was supported by the evidence, because in both cases ethnic parties formed and became electorally viable.

The information compiled on institutional changes is presented in table 2. A timeline matching institutional changes favorable to ethnic party formation and electoral viability is found in table 3. As this information illustrates, the number of favorable institutional changes made in Bolivia, Colombia, Ecuador, and Venezuela ranges from 2 to 5, while only one change favorable to new parties occurred in Argentina and Peru. This suggests that the combined effect of multiple types of institutional change may be more important than the presence of any particular type of change. The electoral results achieved by the ethnic parties are also found in the appendix.

CASE STUDIES

Bolivia and Colombia are useful examples to illustrate the effects of changes in electoral rules on the formation and success of indigenous political parties. They show these effects in countries with both significantly large and minuscule indigenous populations. (For details on the much-studied Ecuadorian case, see Andolina 1999; Beck and Mijeski 2001; Collins 2001; Selverston-Scher 2001; Van Cott 2005. On Venezuela, see Van Cott 2005.)

Bolivia

Bolivia has the largest indigenous population among the countries in the sample, with 37 distinct ethnic groups, including a 30,000-member Afro-Bolivian group the government treats as "indigenous." It is the only country in the sample where indigenous identity-based political parties formed before the 1990s. Indian-led parties began to form during the transition to democracy (1978–82) as a result of two factors. One was the deteriorating relations between the peasant population and the Movimiento Nacional Revolucionario (MNR), which had represented this population since the 1952 revolution. The other was the rise of ethnic consciousness and educational attainment among Indians, particularly among urban Aymara. Three such parties contested the 1978 presidential elections.

Although most indigenous parties formed between 1978 and 1985 invoked the Katarista name and shared a critique of the Bolivian state as colonial, exclusionary, and discriminatory, they represented two distinct ideological camps: Indianismo and Katarismo.[6] Indianismo emphasizes the ethnic basis of the subordination of the indigenous population; it is overtly anti-Western and anti-white. Its most famous proponent was Fausto Reynaga, who tried to form an indigenous political party, the Partido Indio de Bolivia, in the late 1960s. Indianismo had its greatest electoral success with the Movimiento Indio Tupak Katari (MITKA), which elected two militants to Congress in 1980 (Bonfil Batalla 1981, 214; Apaza 2001; Cárdenas 2001; Mamani 2001; R. Molina 1997; Ticona 2001).

Kataristas espouse an ideology that blends class consciousness with ethnic revindications and calls for the reconstruction of the Bolivian state along ethnic criteria. The state it envisions tolerates ethnic diversity and incorporates both indigenous and Western cultures and forms of government. Kataristas have sought alliances with nonindigenous social movements and leftist and populist political parties. Their less ethnicist, more liberal-democratic and classist orientation has gained them many nonindigenous adherents, and thereby greater access to political and financial resources than the Indianistas (Mamani 2001).

The Katarista tendency became dominant in the mid-1980s and throughout the administration of Gonzalo Sánchez de Lozada (1993–97). Its most successful party was the Movimiento Revolucionario Tupaj Katari de Liberación (MRTKL), which first competed in 1985, winning two deputies' seats in the national legislature (Patzi Paco 1999, 40). One of these seats was held between 1985 and 1989 by Victor Hugo Cárdenas, who brought the MRTKL into an electoral alliance with the MNR in 1993. After helping the MNR win the presidency with a significant plurality of the vote, the MRTKL "cogoverned" between 1993 and 1997.

Critics say that Cárdenas himself restricted the MRTKL's opportunity to consolidate itself as a political party by marginalizing its militants from the government—for example, by appointing nonindigenous, non-MRTKL advisers to important government positions; by excluding MRTKL congressional representatives from policy meetings; and by prohibiting the party from competing in the 1997 elections, when state campaign funds were available based on the party's strong showing in 1993, because Cárdenas himself was barred from seeking the presidency (Van Cott 2000b, 292, n12; interviews, Cárdenas 2001).[7]

In the summer of 2001, Cárdenas sought alliances to enable the MRTKL to compete in the 2002 national elections; but in the end, he did not register for those elections. To participate, he would have had to pay fines imposed on the party for its poor showing in the 1999 municipal elections, when it gained two municipal council seats in the department of Oruro (Cárdenas 2001; Ticona 2001).[8] Thus, the substantial symbolic and legislative achievements of the Sánchez de Lozada administration notwithstanding, MRTKL leader Victor Hugo Cárdenas failed to institutionalize his political party, to make Katarismo a viable electoral alternative, or to maintain its independence from nonindigenous parties, such as the MNR.

Table 2. Selected Electoral Laws and Institutional Reforms Compared

	Argentina	Bolivia	Colombia	Ecuador	Peru	Venezuela
Representation Threshold						
Seat allocation threshold raised?	No	No	No	No	No	No
More favorable seat allocation formula adopted?	No	No	No	No	No	No
District magnitude increased under PR?	No	No	Yes, senate	Yes, 1998	Yes,1993	No
Legislature	Bicameral	Bicameral	Bicameral	Unicameral	Shift to unicameral	Shift to unicameral
Change in ballot access?	No	No	Yes	Yes	No	Yes
Decentralization	Yes, marginal increase	Yes, municipal since 1995	Yes, municipal since 1988, departmental since 1991	No	No	Yes, municipal and state since 1989
Creation of special ethnic districts or seats?	No	No	Yes	No	No	Yes

Table 3. Favorable Institutional Change and Formation of Viable Ethnic Parties

	1980	1985	1990	1995	2000
Argentina					
Ethnic parties formed					
Institutional Change					
Small increase in decentralization				1994	
Bolivia					
Ethnic parties formed					
Institutional Change		MRKTL ('85)		ASP('95) IPSP('99)	
Shift to Sainte-Lague				1993–1996	
Municipal decentralization				1995	
Shift to ½ Senate elected in single-member districts				1997	
Colombia					
Ethnic parties formed			ONIC, AICO ('90) ASI('91), MIC('93)		
Institutional Change		1988			
Municipal decentralization			1991		
Increase in DM			1991		
Departmental decentralization			1991		
Reserved seats			1991		
Improved ballot access					

Indianista and Katarista parties splintered along personalistic lines during the 1980s, and their candidates have been unable to compete with the patronage powers of their populist rivals (Van Cott 2005; on the Katarista parties see Rolón Anaya 1999, 681–90; Tapia 1995; and Patzi Paco 1999, 40–41). The parties had difficulty expanding their narrow geographic base; their lack of financial resources was exacerbated by the fines imposed by the National Electoral Court. Failure to pay the fines, for example, resulted in the MITKA's disqualification during the 1985 elections-a fate now threatening the MRTKL (Tapia 1995, 375–443). Another challenge has been the larger parties' attempts to coopt individual indigenous leaders and to create electoral vehicles with Katarista names in order to confuse indigenous voters and disperse the indigenous majority's votes (Cárdenas 2001; Ticona 2001).[9]

The next attempt to form ethnic parties occurred in the mid-1990s. In March 1995, mostly Quechua-speaking coca growers, who by then had control of the national peasant Confederación Syndical Unica de Trabajadores Campesinos de Bolivia (CSUTCB), launched their own political party to participate in the first-ever direct municipal elections, which were held that December. The Asamblea de la Soberanía de los Pueblos (ASP) was formed at a meeting that brought together CSUTCB leaders with roots in Marxist parties and the lowland organization Confederación Indígena del Oriente Boliviana (CIDOB) (Buitrago 1997; Patzi Paco 1999, 116–19). The idea of forming an electoral vehicle had been discussed at many previous CSUTCB conferences. It became a viable option, pushed mainly by the coca growers, after the creation of elected municipal offices throughout the country, providing support for those who argued that the campesino movement could transform the Bolivian state by occupying established spaces of power (Patzi Paco 1999, 118). In addition, the collapse of the Indianista and Katarista parties opened the field for a new contender to represent the indigenous majority.

ASP president Alejo Véliz denies that the 1994–95 constitutional reforms had any influence on the decision to form a party. This decision was, Véliz insists, the next logical step in the maturation of the peasant movement. By 1994 the coca growers' movement had achieved a certain level of political consensus and mobilization. Movement leaders decided that the purely syndical form of struggle would not be sufficient to achieve their demands, and that for the "final conquest" it would be necessary to gain access to democratic political space (Véliz 2001). In contrast, ASP national deputy Roman Loaza, elected in 1997, gives the municipal decentralization credit for the ability of the national campesino union to form its first successful political party ever (Loaza 1997).

Whatever may have been the motivation to create the ASP, it is clear that the 1994 municipal decentralization—in a country where, previously, most of the rural areas had no formal local government, elected or appointed—made electoral activity more viable while providing a platform from which to pursue national representation in 1997. After 1997, the electoral eclipse of the traditional parties allied with the rural poor (the MNR and the leftist Movimiento Bolivia Libre, MBL, did poorly in the 1997 national elections) also helped to clear the field for the ASP. In its first outing—listed on the ballot under the name of the nearly defunct Izquierda Unida because of technical problems with its own registration—the ASP swept municipal elections in the coca-growing Chapare district and won 10 mayors' offices, 49 municipal council seats, and 6 department-level *consejeros* in Cochabamba, as well as 5 council seats in other highland departments (Patzi Paco 1999, 119; Van Cott 2000b, 189).

The 1994 constitutional reform also created uninominal single-member-district seats in one-half of the 130-member lower chamber of congress (there also are 27 senators). In 1997 the ASP won 4 of the new uninominal congressional seats, representing its base in the Chapare. The coca growers' leader, Evo Morales, won a larger percentage of the vote in his district than any other candidate in the country.[10]

In 1997–98 a deep, personal rift emerged in the national peasant movement between the two most important leaders of the ASP, national deputy Evo Morales, who is Aymara, and party president Alejo Véliz, who is Quechua. This led to the division of the ASP, with Morales starting his own party, the Instrumento Político para la Soberanía de los Pueblos (IPSP), while Véliz remained president of a rump ASP. The two parties competed separately in the 1999 municipal elections. The ASP won 28 municipal councilors and 5 mayoralties in 1999, all in Cochabamba. The IPSP, using the registration of the moribund Movimiento al Socialismo, won 79 municipal council seats in 7 of Bolivia's 9 departments, a total of 3.27 percent of the vote nationwide. The largest number of seats was won in La Paz (18) and Cochabamba (40), where, in 5 municipalities, IPSP won a majority of seats on the council (see Corte Nacional Electoral).

Even given the promising results for indigenous parties in the 1990s, the results achieved in 2002's national election are truly astounding, with revolutionary implications for Bolivia's party system. The IPSP, now using only the name Movimiento al Socialismo (MAS) and led by presidential candidate Evo Morales, came in second in the unified presidential—congressional elections with 20.94 percent of the vote, less than two percentage points behind the leader. This garnered MAS 8 seats in the senate and 27 deputies in the lower chamber. MAS finished first in the highland departments of La Paz, Oruro, and Potosí and its base in Cochabamba. It also picked up support throughout the country, including 9.6 percent of the vote in Santa Cruz, where lowland indigenous leader Jose Bailaba earned the MAS a seat in the lower house. The much-weakened ASP did not run, but its leader, Alejo Véliz, won a seat on the list of the populist Cochabamba-based party Nueva Fuerza Republicana, and immediately pledged his support to the MAS coalition. The MAS finished first in the 2004 municipal elections, with 18.48 percent of the vote, and in 2005, as the Bolivian party system collapsed, Morales won the presidency with 53.74 percent of the vote—the most convincing presidential victory since the transition from military rule. The party won a majority of seats—54 percent—in the July 2006 National Constituent Assembly elections—far ahead of its closest competitor, which won 24 percent (www.cne.org.bo).

The party of Aymara leader Felipe Quispe, Movimiento Indígena Pachakutik, a bitter rival of Morales and Véliz, formed in 2000, won 6.09 percent of the vote in the 2002 national contest, netting 6 seats in the chamber of deputies. Compared to a previous high of 3.7 percent of the vote, indigenous parties had garnered 27.03 of the vote (*La Razón* 2002; *Los Tiempos* 2002). Quispe's movement lost steam after 2002. It failed to meet requirements to maintain registration in 2004, when it won only .66 percent of votes, and in 2005 elected only one legislative representative, with 2.16 percent of the vote. It did not compete in 2006.

The experience of these parties demonstrates some significant effects of changes in electoral rules and institutional design on the propensity of indigenous populations to form political parties and to achieve electoral success. Electoral and political party rules intended to reduce party system fragmentation have presented obstacles to party registration. Since its return to democracy in 1982, Bolivia has had one of the most fragmented party systems in the region, with five parties typically sharing 90 percent of the vote (Mainwaring and Scully 1995). Seat allocation formulas that favor larger parties have prevailed: d'Hondt until 1986, when a double quotient of participation and allocation was implemented that further restricted congressional representation of small parties. This had the intended affect of reducing the representation of smaller parties for the 1989 elections.

Before the 1993 elections, the Sainte-Lague formula was established, which resulted, as expected, in increased representation of small parties. The system shifted back to d'Hondt in 1996, when a 3 percent threshold was established for representation in the PR half of the chamber of deputies. Party registration requirements also have been used to restrict party fragmentation. Various laws have instituted a de facto 3 percent threshold to maintain party registration since 1979, when an electoral law was enacted that required parties not receiving 50,000 votes to share the costs of printing ballots (Birnir 2000, 21).

The 1994 constitutional reform changed the system from closed-list, single-national-district PR (which had prevailed during democratic periods since 1956, the first elections following the extension of suffrage to the illiterate) to a German-style mixed PR-SMD formula for the chamber of deputies.[11] Intended to respond to voters' desires for more accountability from politicians, the reform may have the predicted effect of reducing the number of viable parties. Nevertheless, the SMD formula may give an advantage to smaller, regionally based parties like the ASP, which would be less competitive against the centrally organized national parties in nationwide PR contests (ASP's national share of the vote in 1997 was less than 4 percent).

Counteracting the tendency of the electoral and party laws to discourage the formation of new parties, the 1994 Law of Popular Participation encouraged more indigenous leaders to run for political office. The law resulted in the country's first nationwide municipal elections in 1995, and enabled the newly formed ASP to achieve electoral success in its sociogeographic base. Elsewhere, rather than undertake the financial burden and risk of forming new political parties, local indigenous organizations formed pragmatic electoral alliances with major national parties, most of which lacked local organizations in much of the territory.[12] These conjunctural alliances resulted in the election of 464 indigenous or campesino municipal councilors (out of a national total of 1,624, or 28.6 percent); approximately half of the indigenous-campesino councilors had close ties to indigenous social movement organizations. In 73 of 311 municipalities, indigenous or campesino council members constituted a majority (Van Cott 2000b, 188).

Alliances between indigenous organizations and large parties were necessary until 2005 because only formally registered political parties could compete in elections. The constitutional change that enabled civil society organizations and indigenous peoples to launch candidates for local offices without joining political parties attracted new competitors. In 2004 newly registered indigenous peoples elected 105 indigenous municipal councilors in 60 municipalities.

A continuing hurdle for all parties seeking to represent Indians is the continued low level of voter registration among the indigenous majority, despite intensified efforts during the Sánchez de Lozada administration to provide the necessary identity cards to Indians. CIDOB estimated in 1996 that cards had yet to be distributed in approximately half of the communities (Patzi Paco 1999, 124). Registration has since improved but remains a problem in rural areas particularly among women.

Colombia

Compared to Bolivia, Colombia represents the opposite end of the demographic spectrum, with an indigenous population of 2.7 percent, according to a 1993 census conducted with the cooperation of the indigenous movement (see Padilla 1996, 93). The 81 distinct indigenous groups, speaking 64 languages, are widely dispersed throughout the country, particularly in the southwestern departments of Cauca and Tolima and in lowland border areas. Indians are a numerical majority in the three sparsely populated Amazonian departments of Guainia, Vaupes, and Vichada (Van Cott 2000b, 44–45).

Colombia has one of the most stable and most exclusionary two-party systems in the region, a situation that has tended to impede the emergence of new parties. In 1991, a new constitution was written, partly to weaken the stranglehold of the traditional Liberal and Conservative parties on access to political representation. Several electoral law reforms were made to encourage the creation of new parties (see Dugas 2001; García Sánchez 2001). Although the results of these reforms were not as strong as expected, indigenous peoples have dramatically increased their representation at all levels of government through the creation of their own political parties. Their achievements in constitutional reform and their electoral success in the early 1990s served as a model for indigenous movements elsewhere.

Colombia's indigenous social movement emerged from the peasant land movement of the 1960s and 1970s in the department of Cauca. The Consejo Regional Indígena del Cauca (CRIC), formed in 1971, created the Organización Nacional Indígena de Colombia (ONIC) in 1982. ONIC today represents approximately 90 percent of the country's organized indigenous population (Laurent 1997, 67). A rival, more traditional movement, also based in Cauca, now called the Autoridades Indígenas de Colombia (AICO; formerly Southwest Indigenous Authorities, AISO), formed in 1977. AICO's geographical extension is more limited, with activities concentrated in Cauca, Nariño, and the Sierra Nevada de Santa Marta (Laurent 1997, 67). In 1990, ONIC and AISO ran candidates in the National Constituent Assembly elections. Their expectations were low, given the minuscule size of the indigenous population, its low level of voter registration, and the virtual lack of financial resources. Everyone was surprised—including the indigenous movement—when the movements won two seats. The single-district PR rules for those elections were intended to give representation to dispersed minorities (Van Cott 2000b, chap. 2).

The two indigenous delegates, in an alliance with a surging new leftist party representing the demobilized M-19 guerrillas, Alianza Democrática M-19 (ADM-19), successfully lobbied for the constitutional recognition of a wide spectrum of indigenous rights, including the creation of two seats reserved for Indians in the Colombian senate.[13] As prescribed in the 1991 Constitution, the senate is elected in a single list. The 1991 Constitution also provides state financing and free media time for political parties and movements with political representation. After 1991, Indians took advantage of the new laws allowing social movements to contest elections and launched indigenous candidacies.

Both AICO and ONIC ran candidates in the 1991 congressional elections; each won one of the two designated senate seats. ONIC retired from elections in 1993 in order to heal the internal conflicts that electoral competition had caused and to focus on its social role. In 1994 AICO again won a senate seat in the reserved district and elected one departmental deputy and 6 municipal councilors in Cauca. In 1997 it won 5 mayoralties, and in 1998 it won 1 of the 2 indigenous senatorial seats. Gradually expanding beyond its base in the Guambiano ethnic group and the southwestern departments of Cauca and Nariño, in 2000 AICO won 4 mayors' offices, distributed among the departments of Antioquia, Cauca, and Nariño; 74 municipal councilors in 11 departments (Caldas, Cauca, Córdoba, Huila, Nariño, Sucre, Guajira, Guainia, Meta, Putumayo, Vichada); and 3 deputies in departmental assemblies (Antioquía, Cauca, Vichada). In 2002, for the fourth consecutive time, AICO claimed 1 of the 2 reserved indigenous seats, and also picked up 1 seat in the Chamber of Deputies reserved for Indians, Afro-Colombians, and Colombians living abroad (*El Tiempo* 2002).

ONIC's 1991–94 senate representative, Gabriel Mujuy Jacanamejoy, founded a new party in 1994 to secure his reelection after ONIC retired from electoral activity. The

Movimiento Indígena Colombiano (MIC) attempted to build alliances with nonindigenous campesinos and poor urban workers, but its strength comes mainly from Indians in the western lowland departments. The MIC reelected Mujuy in 1994 and secured 4 departmental deputies and 23 municipal council seats, mainly in the lowland departments with proportionally large indigenous populations. In 1997 MIC won one mayorship (Van Cott 2000b, 286, n. 7). In 1998 the MIC failed to recapture a seat in the indigenous senatorial district; no results for this party could be found after that loss, which cost the party crucial funding and its legal registration.

Another indigenous party proved more successful than AICO, ONIC, or MIC. In 1991 the CRIC, today one of the country's strongest and most institutionalized department-level indigenous organizations, formed a political party named the Alianza Social Indígena (ASI) in alliance with local nonindigenous popular organizations. In contrast to the other three indigenous parties, ASI sought alliances with nonindigenous popular sectors, emphasizing class solidarity as well as ethnic bonds (Laurent 1997, 68). In 1991, ASI launched a candidate for senator in the regular national district (not the special two-seat district created by the 1991 constitution). ASI won this "third," unreserved indigenous senate seat in 1991, 1998, and 2002. In 1992 ASI contested local and departmental elections in Cauca and some additional departments. In 1994 the party elected 8 mayors, 84 municipal councilors, and 2 departmental deputies each in Cauca and Vichada, and 1 departmental deputy in Antioquia (Laurent 1997, 74). In coalition with another party, it elected Afro-Colombian leader Zulia Mena to the lower chamber of congress in a reserved Afro-Colombian district. It should be noted that not all ASI candidates were indigenous. Nevertheless, ASI's results for 1994 brought the total for indigenous parties to 8 mayors, 170 municipal councilors, and 11 departmental deputies (Laurent 1997, 76).

In 1997 ASI won the first governorship for an indigenous party (Guainía) and finished second in gubernatorial contests in Cauca and Vaupés. That year an ASI assembly deputy in the department of Antioquia, Eulalia Yagary, earned reelection with more votes than any other candidate and twice as many as her closest competitor (Van Cott 2000b, 227). ASI also won 6 mayoral posts in 1997. In 1998, former CRIC president Jesús Piñacué, representing the ASI in alliance with a progressive opposition coalition, finished 15th in a field of more than three hundred national senatorial candidates. Piñacué had been vice presidential candidate for the leftist Alianza Democrática M-19 in 1994 (see Laurent 1997, 71–73 for a discussion of the controversy this alliance with the ADM-19 engendered within the ASI). In addition, ASI won a senate seat in the indigenous district and two national deputy seats in two majority-indigenous departments (the sparsely populated Amazonian departments of Guainía and Vaupés).

In 2000 ASI joined with AICO to elect the first indigenous governor of Cauca, Floro Tunubalá, who had been elected to one of the indigenous reserved senate seats in 1991. That year ASI won 11 mayorships in 4 departments (Cauca, Cundinamarca, Chocó, Risaralda); 146 municipal councilors in 20 departments (Antioquía, Caldas, Cauca, Córdoba, Cundinamarca, Chocó, Huila, Nariño, Risaralda, Norte de Santander, Santander, Sucre, Tolima, Valle de Cauca, La Guajira, Guainía, Amazonas, Putumayo, Vaupés, Vichada); and 8 departmental deputies in 5 departments (Antioquía, Cauca, Guainía, Vaupés, Vichada). In 2002, Senator Piñacué won reelection in the nonindigenous district, this time finishing 12th among the hundreds of candidates in contention. Senator Rojas Birry, who had won election in the indigenous district in 1998 as an ASI candidate, broke with ASI before the elections; he was reelected to his seat representing the Valle-based regional party Movimiento Huella Ciudadana (*El Tiempo* 2002).

In a study of the success of nontraditional parties following the 1991 constitutional reform, García Sánchez found that only 5 of 48 such parties had gained power in more than 2 percent of the country's 1,100 municipalities between 1988 and 2000. ASI was among this elite group, winning in 2.6 percent of the country's municipalities. AICO was among the 12 that had won more than 1 percent. ASI and AICO were among only 8 parties that had been reelected (García Sánchez 2001, 7). ASI is among the most endur- ing nontraditional parties: of the five parties that won in more than 2 percent of the country's municipalities, only ASI and the Movimiento Cívico Independiente (MCI) were formed before 1997. Only ASI and MCI, moreover, have a regional and national political presence (García Sánchez 2001, 13).

In Colombia, thus, we can see that a number of institutional changes enabled ethnic parties to form, maintain their registration, and achieve electoral viability. The first change was the creation of a single district for the National Constituent Assembly elections (1990) and the National Senate (since 1991). This change was made to better represent dispersed minorities of all kinds; it facilitated indigenous representation in both bodies at least proportional to that representation in the population. While DM declined in the lower chamber to an average of five seats, indigenous parties still have a fair chance of winning seats in a two-party dominant system.

The second change, setting aside two seats in the national senate, provided financial and media resources to indigenous political parties and enabled them to motivate and mobilize their constituents. The indigenous senators became national figures—one was subsequently elected governor of the Department of Cauca.

Third, a number of changes were made to help new parties. The 1991 Constitution and implementing legislation provided financial support and free access to state-run media to legally recognized political parties and movements. Even though most of the funds go to the larger parties on the basis of seats won, modest financial subsidies to parties with representation in Congress and departmental assemblies have enabled new indigenous parties to construct party organizations. Although the number of signatures required for party registration was raised from 10,000 to 50,000 signatures or votes in the previous election, this is still a low barrier for registration and unregistered parties may run for local office (Dugas 2001, 16). The state now supplies official ballots, removing the logistical and financial challenge for political parties of having to print and distribute their own ballots.

A fourth change was that the constitution finally eliminated the requirement, in effect since the 1957 National Front pact, that an "adequate and equitable" proportion of administrative posts be given to the second-largest party, a mandate that "had limited the political participation of third parties in Colombia by perpetually reinforcing the two- party system" (Dugas 2001, 16).

Fifth, municipal decentralization, with direct election of mayors, was instituted in 1988, followed by election of departmental governors and assemblies, pursuant to the 1991 Constitution. Decentralization has enabled indigenous movements to become strong challengers in municipal and departmental races where indigenous peoples are concen- trated and well organized. The timing of the decentralization, which coincided with the creation of special reserved seats for Indians and party subventions, enabled indigenous parties to contest these newly created political spaces. Thus, although a few indigenous candidates ran in the 1988 municipal elections, they ran as independents or as members of nonindigenous political parties (Laurent 1997, 63). Only after 1991 did they run with indigenous parties.

The impact of these institutional changes was distorted by a sharp increase in political violence, in particular, assassinations and threats against local elected officials (García Sánchez 2001, 2). Guerrillas now are present in more than 60 percent of Colom- bian municipalities (Hartlyn and Dugas 1999, 286), while the number of paramilitaries increased by 960 percent between 1992 and 2000 (García Sánchez 2001, 2). Indians have been among the hardest hit by the violence. Guerrillas and paramilitaries are present in the majority of the municipalities governed by ASI and AICO; at least two ASI mayors were assassinated (García Sánchez 2001, 14). Nevertheless, parties and movements not associated with the Liberal or Conservative parties have increased their share of mayors every year since 1994. The best showing for "third forces" was 29.69 percent of mayors in 1992. This dropped to 9 percent in 1994, but increased to 13.8 percent and 19.8 percent in 1997 and 2000. Approximately half (549 of 1,100) of Colombian municipalities have been governed by a "third force" party (García Sánchez 2001, 4).

CONCLUSIONS

This study has examined the operation of a number of institutional changes the comparative parties literature associates with the formation and electoral viability of new parties representing underrepresented groups, particularly ethnic minorities. Given the multiplicity and diversity of such laws across the case sample, it is difficult to discern a systematic causal effect of any one particular law or regulation. The full impact of these changes may not yet be visible, moreover, considering that most of them are quite recent and it should take several electoral cycles for actors to adapt. Nevertheless, three tendencies may be identified.

Regulations intended to reduce the number of parties—particularly thresholds and fines with respect to party registration—have the intended affect of making it difficult for indigenous peoples to form and sustain political parties. It is no accident that such thresholds are highest in the three countries with significant indigenous populations. As I have argued elsewhere, highly fragmented, personalistic, weakly institutionalized party systems are likely to emerge in Latin American countries with deep ethnic cleavages (Van Cott 2000a). Thresholds are likely to be instituted in such polities in order to reduce fragmentation and to exclude indigenous political movements.

Decentralized political systems provide an opportunity for ethnic parties to form and to be electorally viable. They present the opportunity of local or regional electoral campaigns, which are relatively cheaper, while bringing the contest to geographical districts where indigenous populations may constitute a majority. New parties that manage to build a local base can expand to gain regional and national power-provided that electoral laws allow them to gain office based on geographically concentrated support.

Finally, reserving elected offices for indigenous candidates is enormously effective in stimulating political mobilization among indigenous populations. Not surprisingly, reserved seats are found only in the systems with the smallest proportional indigenous populations, where they pose less of a threat to established parties. Once established, however, indigenous movements have made impressive electoral gains outside the set-aside seats. It must be emphasized that special indigenous districts have been instituted where well-organized indigenous movements have successfully mobilized for them. In both Colombia and Venezuela, minuscule indigenous populations produced social movement organizations that won seats in constituent assemblies over better-financed and more experienced traditional parties. Those effective social movement organizations—and the constituencies they mobilized during the constitutional reforms—may be the main reason for the electoral success that follows the creation of indigenous political parties.

These findings lead to the conclusion that institutional change is likely to be a necessary but not sufficient condition for the emergence and electoral viability of ethnic parties. Future research will investigate what other variables might interact with institutional change to produce this outcome.

The formation and electoral success of ethnic parties constitutes an improvement in the level of representation of Indians and their interests within the formal political system. It remains to be seen whether their representatives will more effectively address their concerns than the populist and clientelist parties that continue to compete for their votes. The preponderant view in the political parties literature is that ethnic parties tend to exacerbate ethnic conflict "by bolstering the influence of ethnically chauvinist elements within each group" while making it more difficult to convert narrow group claims into the public interest (Horowitz 1985, 291).

It is equally possible that the parties may constitute a democratizing trend. As Roberts (2001) argues, Latin American parties are becoming less linked to social structures and more devoted to enabling a small elite caste to access state power. The emergence of parties with clear, coherent programmatic agendas, parties that are deeply rooted in a vibrant, dense network of social organizations, may signify that the trend toward self-serving electoralism may be reversible. A review of municipal institutional innovations that indigenous parties in Bolivia and Ecuador have instituted in the past 10 years presents some positive, albeit modest, results (Van Cott 2006).

APPENDIX: INDIGENOUS POLITICAL PARTIES AND THEIR ELECTORAL ACHIEVEMENTS

Argentina

Successful indigenous parties: None. Indigenous *sublemas* or *agrupaciones* within the Partido Justicialista.
1996 An Ona indigenous leader became the first Indian to serve in the Argentine congress after the first-listed candidate resigned.

Bolivia

Movimiento Indio Tupak Katari (MITKA), 1980.
1980 Elected two deputies to lower chamber of national congress.
Movimiento Revolucionario Tupaj Katari de Liberación (MRTKL), 1985.
1985 Elected two deputies to lower chamber of congress.
1993 Leader Victor Hugo Cárdenas elected vice president on MNR-MRTKL ticket.
1995 Municipal elections won 33 municipal councilors.
1999 Municipal elections won 2 municipal council seats in Oruro.
Asamblea de la Soberanía del Pueblo (ASP), 1995.
1995 Municipal elections won 10 mayoralties, 49 municipal council seats, and 11 department-level consejeros.
1997 National elections won 4 uninominal seats in the 130-seat lower chamber of congress, 17.5 percent of proportional vote in its base in the department of Cochabamba, 3.7 percent nationwide.
1998 Party split.
1999 Municipal elections: rump ASP won 28 council seats and 5 mayoralties all in Cochabamba, total 1.12 percent of seats nationwide. (The National Electoral Council lists 22 seats won by ASP, which borrowed the registration of the Partido Comunista Boliviana [PCB] for these elections.)
Instrumento Político por la Soberanía de los Pueblos (IPSP), 1999. Uses valid registration of the Movimiento Al Socialismo.

1999 IPSP (MAS-U) won 79 municipal council seats in 7 departments, total 3.27 percent of the vote nationwide.

2002 MAS won 20.94 percent of the vote in national elections, coming in second, less than 2 percentage points behind the leader, and winning 8 senators and 27 deputies in the lower chamber.

2004 MAS won 18.48 percent Council seats in municipal elections.

2005 MAS won 53.74 percent of the vote in national elections, 84 seats in Congress.

2006 MAS won 54 percent of seats in the Constituent Assembly elections.

Movimiento Indígena Pachakutik (MIP).

2002 In its first election, won 6.09 of the vote, netting 6 deputies in the lower chamber.

2004 won. 66 percent of the vote in municipal council elections.

2005 attracted 2.16 percent of the vote in national elections, electing one deputy.

Colombia

Organización Nacional Indígena de Colombia (ONIC), 1990.

1990 Elected 1 ANC representative.

1991 Elected 1 national senator, both of these in reserved indigenous district.

1993 Retired from electoral politics.

Autoridades Indígenas de Colombia (AICO), 1990.

Created as social movement organization in 1977 under different name.

First competed in 1990 ANC elections.

1990 Elected 1 ANC representative.

1991, 1994, 1998, 2002 Elected 1 national senator in the reserved indigenous district.

1994 Elected 1 departmental deputy and 6 municipal councilors in Cauca.

1997 Won 5 mayoralties.

2000 Won four mayoralties in 3 departments, 74 municipal councilors in 11 departments, and 3 departmental deputies in 3 departments. (Colombia has 27 departments.)

2002 Won one seat in Chamber of Deputies.

Alianza Social Indígena (ASI), 1991.

1991, 1998, 2002 Elected 1 senator in open competition with nonindigenous candidates and parties.

1998 Won an additional reserved indigenous seat.

1994 Elected 8 mayors, 84 municipal councilors, 2 departmental deputies in the Department of Cauca, its base; 1 departmental deputy in Antioquia (other non-Cauca results not known).

1994 In coalition with another party, elected Afro-Colombian leader Zulia Mena to lower chamber in the reserved black district.

1997 Repeated election of a senator in the nonindigenous district in national elections, also winning 2 national deputy seats and 6 mayors.

1997 Won its first governorship, finishing second in two other departments.

2000 Joined with AICO to elect first Indian governor of Cauca; won 11 mayoralties in 4 departments, 146 municipal councilors in 20 departments, and 8 departmental deputies in 5 departments.

Movimiento Indígena Colombiano (MIC), 1993.

1993 Formed to secure reelection for ONIC's 1991–94 indigenous senator after ONIC retired from electoral competition.

1994 He won reelection; MIC also won 4 departmental deputies and 23 municipal council seats.

1997 Won 1 mayoralty.

1998 Lost its indigenous senate seat.

2000 Ran no candidates.

Ecuador

Movimiento de Unidad Plurinacional Pachakutik (MUPP), 1995.

1996 Won 8 seats in 82-seat national congress, becoming fourth-largest bloc; won 68 seats in local elections, 7 of every 10 races entered.

1997 Won 7 of 70 ANC seats.

1998 Won 8 seats in 121-seat national congress; 27 mayors.

2000 Won 5 of 22 prefectures, 25 of 215 mayoralties, 60 percent of seats on parish advisory councils.

2002 In alliance with Patriotic Society, won presidency in second round with 54.79 percent of the vote; elected 14 of 100 deputies.

2004 Elected 20 of 219 mayors, 3 of 22 prefects.

Peru

Movimiento Indígena de la Amazonia Peruana (MIAP), 1999. A party formed in 1999. by the Asociación Interétnica de Desarrollo de la Selva Peruana (AIDESEP), which formed in 1980 as a social movement organization.

2000 Won 12 mayoralties (Source: AIDESEP 2000).

Venezuela

Pueblo Unido Multiétnico de Amazonas (PUAMA), 1997.

A regional party in Amazonas State, which is 43 percent indigenous.

1998 Unable to compete in elections because of obstruction by state electoral officials.

1999 Elected 1 of Amazonas's ANC representatives to the National Constituent Assembly. In coalition with leftist Patria Para Todos, became the third force in Amazonas (Perez 1999, 9).

2000 Following the 1999 constitutional reform, PUAMA indigenous leader Liborio Guarulla won the Amazonas state governorship (in coalition with the PPT).

2000 Won 1 deputy in Amazonas state legislative assembly; 1 seat in National Assembly, outside the reserved 3-seat indigenous senate district. Won 10 municipal council seats in 4 of the state's 7 municipalities. (Each council has an average 4 to 5 seats, half elected by list, half nominally. PUAMA won 3 seats by list, 7 nominally.)

Consejo Nacional Indio de Venezuela (CONIVE), 1989.

The 1999 Constitution allows social movement organizations such as CONIVE to contest reserved indigenous seats.

1999 Won all 3 reserved indigenous seats in the National Constituent Assembly.

2000 Won all 3 reserved seats in the National Assembly. Competitors were mainly indigenous vehicles established by nonindigenous political parties. The CONIVE list was closely associated with the Chavez coalition. CONIVE member Noeli Pocaterra is second vice president of the National Assembly.

NOTES

The author wishes to thank Johanna Kristin Birnir, Andrew Grain, Dieter Meinen, and José E. Molina V. for their generous help with acquiring data and materials necessary for this project; and Raul Barrios, Brian Crisp, Kevin Healy, and Mark P. Jones for comments on a previous draft. Research in Bolivia and Colombia in 1997 was funded by a Fulbright dissertation scholarship; in Ecuador in 1999 and Venezuela in 2000 by a University of Tennessee Professional Development Award; in Bolivia in 2001 by a University of Tennessee Cordell Hull Fund award.

1 The exception to this rule is significant variation within a political system. For example, if district magnitude (the number of seats available in an electoral district) or the geographic concentration of indigenous populations varies significantly in a particular country, ethnic parties may form or be electorally viable in one district but not another.

2 I thank Mark P. Jones for his suggestion to combine these elements.

3 These cases were the shift to a single-member district for the Colombian Senate, which took effect in 1991 following the 1991 constitutional reform; the 1997 Ecuadorian Constituent Assembly elections and the subsequent expansion of its unicameral legislature from 82 to 121 seats; and Peru's shift to multiple-member districts in 2001.

4 The Hare quota is the total number of valid votes cast divided by the total number of seats in the district (Lijphart 1986a, 172).

5 Citizens' groups would have to collect signatures of 0.5 percent of citizens inscribed on the electoral roll in the relevant district.

6 The parties take their name from the eighteenth-century Indian rebel leader Tupaj Katari.

7 In Bolivia, Article 252 of Law 1779 (March 1997) provides for public financing of electoral campaigns. Fifty percent of the total budget appropriated is distributed 60 days before the election "in a form proportional to the number of votes each party, front, or alliance had obtained in the latest general or municipal elections, provided that they obtained the minimum 3 percent of the total valid votes at the national level and gained at least one seat in the Chamber of Deputies in the general elections. The other 50 percent will be distributed in the same manner, based on results in the corresponding general or municipal election, an amount to be disbursed in the same period of 60 days from the date of the election." (Translation by the author.)

8 As a result of his collaboration with the neoliberal traditional parties, Cárdenas gained stature among nonindigenous Bolivians and in the international community, but he and his MRTKL lost legitimacy with the campesino movement (Patzi Paco 1999, 41–42, 115–16). The national peasant organization CSUTCB officially declared Cárdenas "an enemy and a traitor" at its 6th Congress in 1994 (Patzi Paco 1999, 116).

9 The MNR did this in 1978–79; the ADN (Acción Democrática Nacional) did it in 1993 by creating the Movimiento Katarista Nacional, led by Fernando Untoja (the current name is Movimiento Katarista Democrática).

10 Morales was expelled from Congress in mid-January 2002 after charges that he was the "intellectual author" responsible for the murder of two Bolivian security officials during clashes with his coca growers' movement in Cochabamba. *La Prensa* 2002; Healy 2002.

11 Half of the 130 deputies are elected in uninominal districts, the other half on departmental party lists—headed by presidential, vice presidential, and senatorial candidates—with seats allocated proportionally by each party's share of the vote. Currently, the country's 9 departments are its electoral districts for the purpose of allocation of legislative seats. Each department has 3 senators and 5 deputies in the chamber, plus an additional deputy for each 50,000 inhabitants. The first-voted party in each department wins 2 senate seats, the second-voted wins 1.

12 For example, for the 1997 presidential and legislative elections, the lowland indigenous confederation CIDOB formed an electoral alliance with the MBL. CIDOB president Marcial Fabricano ran for vice president on the MBL ticket. The pairing garnered less than 4 percent of the vote and failed to win a single national deputy. The much-weaker-than-expected results led to severe fragmentation of the lowland indigenous movement (Van Cott 2000b, 216).

13 A third indigenous delegate was appointed, without voting rights, as a representative of the armed indigenous movement Quintin Lame.

REFERENCES

Albó, Xavier. 1994. And from Kataristas to MNRistas? The Surprising and Bold Alliance Between Aymaras and Neoliberals in Bolivia. In *Indigenous Peoples and Democracy in Latin America*, ed. Donna Lee Van Cott. New York: St. Martin's Press. 55–82.

Andolina, Robert. 1999. Colonial Legacies and Plurinational Imaginaries: Indigenous Movement Politics in Ecuador and Bolivia. Ph.D. diss., University of Minnesota.

Apaza, Jaime. 2001. Consejo Nacional de Ayllus y Markas de Qullasullo. Author interview. La Paz, July 17.

Asociación Interétnica de Desarrollo de la Selva Peruana (AIDESEP). 2000. Primer Boletín de la Asociación Interétnica de Desarrollo de la Selva Peruana. August.

Beck, Scott H., and Kenneth J. Mijeski. 2001. Barricades and Ballots: Ecuador's Indians and the Pachakutik Political Movement. *Ecuadorian Studies* 1 (September): 1–23.

Birnir, Jóhanna Kristín. 2000. The Effect of Institutional Exclusion on Stabilization of Party Systems in Bolivia, Ecuador, and Peru. Paper presented at the 22d International Congress of the Latin American Studies Association. Miami, March 16–18.

———. 2001. Personal communication, August 7.

Bolivia. Congress. 2001. Anteproyecto de ley de necesidad de reforma constitucional, Article 224. April.

Bolivia. Corte Nacional Electoral, n.d. Website. <www.cne.org.bo>.

Bonfil Batalla, Guillermo, comp. 1981. *Utopía y revolución. El pensamiento político de los indios en América Latina.* Mexico: Editorial Nuevo Imagen.

Buitrago, Jaime E. 1997. Alejo Véliz cree en Cristo y en Túpac Katari. *Presencia* (La Paz). May 4: 4–5.

Canton, Santiago. 1995. *Partidos políticos en las Américas: desafíos y estrategias.* Washington: National Democratic Institute.

Cárdenas, Víctor Hugo. 2001. Former vice president of Bolivia. Author interview. La Paz, July 14.

Collins, Jennifer N. 2001. Opening Up Electoral Politics: Political Crisis and the Rise of Pachakutik. Paper prepared for presentation at the 23d Congress of the Latin American Studies Association, Washington, DC, September 6–8.

———. 2006. Democratizing Formal Politics: Indigenous and Social Movement Political Parties in Ecuador and Bolivia, 1978–2000. Ph.D. dissertation, University of California, San Diego.

Coppedge, Michael. 1997. District magnitude, economic performance, and party-system fragmentation in five Latin American countries. *Comparative Political Studies* 30, 2 (April): 156–85.

———. 1998. The Evolution of Latin American Party Systems. In *Politics, Society and Democracy: Latin America*, ed. Scott Mainwaring and Arturo Valenzuela. Boulder: Westview Press. 171–206.

Dalton, Russel J., Scott C. Flanagan, and Paul Allen Beck. 1984. Political Forces and Partisan Change. In *Electoral Change in Advanced Industrial Democracies: Realignment or Dealigment?* ed., Dalton, Flanagan, and Beck. Princeton: Princeton University Press. 451–76.

Deruyttere, Anne. 1997. Indigenous Peoples and Sustainable Development: The Role of the Inter-American Development Bank. Forum of the Americas, April 8. Washington: Inter-American Development Bank.

Domínguez, Jorge I. 1995. Los desafíos de los partidos políticos en América Latina y el Caribe. Paper prepared for the conference on political parties in Latin America and the Caribbean under the auspices of PNUD y la Fundación F. Ebert, Cartagena, Colombia. July.

Dugas, John C. 2001. Sisyphus in the Andes? The Pursuit of Political Party Reform in Colombia. Paper prepared for delivery at the 23d Congress of the Latin American Studies Association, Washington, DC, September 6–8.

Foreign Broadcast Information Service-Latin America (FBIS-LAT). 1993. 93–081 (April 20): 31.

García Sánchez, Miguel. 2001. La democracia colombiana: entre las reformas institucionales y la guerra. Una aproximación al desempeño de las terceras fuerzas en las alcaldías municipales, 1988–2000. Paper prepared for presentation at the 23d Congress of the Latin American Studies Association, Washington, DC, September 6–8.

Grofman, Bernard, and Arend Lijphart, eds. 1986. *Electoral laws and Their Political Consequences.* New York: Agathon Press.

Harmel, Robert, and John D. Robertson. 1985. Formation and Success of New Parties: A Cross-National Analysis. *International Political Science Review* 6, 4 (October): 501–23.

Hartlyn, Jonathan, and John Dugas. 1999. Colombia: The Politics of Violence and Democratic Transformation. In *La democracia en América Latina. Actualidad y perspectivas*, ed. Pablo González Casanova and Marcos Roitman Rosenmann. Mexico City: La Jornada. 249–307.

Hauss, C., and D. Rayside. 1978. The Development of New Parties in Western Democracies Since 1945. In *Political Parties: Development and Decay*, ed. L. Maisel and J. Cooper. Beverly Hills: Sage. 31–57.

Healy, Kevin. 2002. Personal communication. February 16.

Horowitz, Donald L. 1985. *Ethnic Groups in Conflict*. Berkeley: University of California Press.

Jones, Mark P. 1995. A Guide to the Electoral Systems of the Americas. *Electoral Studies* 14, 1: 5–21.

———. 1997. A Guide to the Electoral Systems of the Americas: An Update. *Electoral Studies* 16, 1: 13–15.

King, Gary, Robert O. Keohane, and Sidney Verba. 1994. *Designing Social Inquiry: Scientific Inference in Qualitative Research*. Princeton: Princeton University Press.

Laurent, Virginie. 1997. Población indígena y participación política en Colombia. *Análisis Político* 31 (May–August): 63–81.

Lieberman, Evan S. 2001. Causal Inference in Historical Institutional Analysis. *Comparative Political Studies* 34, 9 (November): 1011–35.

Lijphart, Arend. 1986a. Degrees of Proportionality of Proportional Representation Formulas. In Grofman and Lijphart 1986. 170–79.

———. 1986b. Proportionality by Non-PR Methods: Ethnic Representation in Belgium, Cyprus, Lebanon, New Zealand, West Germany, and Zimbabwe. In Grofman and Lijphart 1986. 113–23.

Lipset, Seymour Martin, and Stein Rokkan. 1967. *Party Systems and Voter Alignments: Cross-National Perspectives*. New York: The Free Press.

Lluco, Miguel. 1999. Leader, Movimiento Unido Pluricultural Pachakutik. Author interview. Quito, August 2.

Loaza, Román. ASP national deputy. Author interview. La Paz, 1997.

Lucero, José Antonio. 2002. Arts of Unification: Political Representation and Indigenous Movements in Bolivia and Ecuador. Ph.D. diss., Princeton University.

Mainwaring, Scott. 1999. *Rethinking Party Systems in the Third Wave of Democratization: The Case of Brazil*. Stanford: Stanford University Press.

Mainwaring, Scott, and Timothy Scully, eds. 1995. *Building Democratic Institutions: Party Systems in Latin America*. Stanford: Stanford University Press.

Mair, Peter. 1997. *Party System Change: Approaches and Interpretations*. Oxford: Clarendon Press.

Mamani, Carlos. 2001. Member, Taller de Historia Oral Andina. Author interview. La Paz, July 16.

Mayorga, René Antonio. 2001. Director, Centro Boliviano de Estudios Multidisciplinarios. Author interview. La Paz, July 18.

Ministerio de Desarrollo Humano, Secretaria Nacional de Participación Popular. 1997. Indígenas en el poder local. La Paz.

Molina R., Ramiro. 1997. Anthropologist. Author interview. La Paz, April 28.

Molina V., José E. 2002. The Presidential and Parliamentary Elections of the Bolivarian Revolution in Venezuela: Change and Continuity (1998–2000). *Bulletin of Latin American Research* 21, 2 (April 2002): 219–47.

Mozaffar, Shaheen. 1997. Electoral Systems and Their Political Effects in Africa: A Preliminary Analysis. *Representation* 34, 3–4: 148–56.

Ordeshook, Peter C., and Olga V. Shvetsova. 1994. Ethnic Heterogeneity, District Magnitude, and the Number of Parties. *American Journal of Political Science* 38, 1 (February): 100–123.

Padilla, Guillermo. 1996. La ley y los pueblos indígenas en Colombia. *Journal of Latin American Anthropology* 1, 2 (Spring): 78–97.

Patzi Paco, Felix. 1999. *Insurgencia y sumisión. Movimientos indigenocampesinos (1983–1998)*. La Paz: Muela del Diablo.

Pérez, Benjamín. 1999. Participación en el Movimiento Político Indígena Pueblo Unido Multiétnico de Amazonas (PUAMA). *La Iglesia en Amazonas* 85 (September): 8–9.

La Prensa (La Paz). 2002. February 8. Via Internet.

La Razón (La Paz). 2002. July 9. <www.la-razon.com>.

Riker, William H. 1986. *The Art of Political Manipulation.* New Haven, CT: Yale University Press.

Roberts, Kenneth M. 2001. Political Cleavages, Party-Society Linkages, and the Transformation of Political Representation in Latin America. Paper prepared for delivery at the 23d Congress of the Latin American Studies Association. Washington, DC, September 6–8.

Roberts, Kenneth M., and Erik Wibbels. 1999. Party Systems and Electoral Volatility in Latin America: A Test of Economic, Institutional, and Structural Explanations. *American Political Science Review* 93, 3 (September): 575–90.

Rolon Anaya, Mario. 1999. *Política y partidos en Bolivia.* 3d edition. La Paz: Librería Editorial Juventud.

Sartori, Giovanni. 1986. The Influence of Electoral Systems: Faulty Laws or Faulty Method? In Grofman and Lijphart 1986. 43–68.

Schedler, Andreas. 1996. *Antipolitical-establishment Parties.* Party Politics 2, 3: 291–312.

Selverston-Scher, Melina. 2001. *Ethnopolitics in Ecuador: Indigenous Rights and the Strengthening of Democracy.* Coral Gables: North-South Center Press.

Stavenhagen, Rodolfo. 1992. Challenging the Nation-State in Latin America. *Journal of International Affairs* 34, 2 (Winter): 421–40.

Taagepera, Rein, and Matthew Soberg Shugart. 1989. *Seats and Votes: The Effects and Determinants of Electoral Systems.* New Haven: Yale University Press.

Tapia, Luciano. 1995. *Ukhamawa Jakawisaxa (Así es nuestra vida). Autobiografía de un aymara.* La Paz: Hisbol.

Ticona, Esteban. 2001. Professor, Universidad de la Cordillera. Author interview. La Paz, July 18.

El Tiempo (Bogotá). 2002. March 11. <www.eltiempo.com>.

Los Tiempos (Cochabamba). July 9. <www.lostiempos.com>.

Van Cott, Donna Lee. 2000a. Party System Development and Indigenous Populations in Latin America: The Bolivian Case. *Party Politics* 6, 2 (April): 155–74.

———. 2000b. *The Friendly Liquidation of the Past: The Politics of Diversity in Latin America.* Pittsburgh: University of Pittsburgh Press.

———. 2005. *From Movements to Parties in Latin America: The Evolution of Ethnic Politics.* New York: Cambridge University Press.

———. 2006. "Radical Democracy in the Andes: Indigenous Parties and the Quality of Democracy in Latin America." Notre Dame: Helen Kellogg Institute for International Studies. Working Paper.

Véliz, Alejo. 2001. Member, Asamblea de la Soberanía del Pueblo. Author interview. La Paz, July 17.

Chapter 8

Expanding Accountability Through Participatory Institutions: Mayors, Citizens, and Budgeting in Three Brazilian Municipalities

Brian Wampler

Citizens and civil society organizations (CSOs) play a more prominent role in Latin America's new democratic regimes than under previous democratic experiences. Efforts to promote transparency, accountability, and participation have led citizens, community organizations, social movements, and nongovernmental organizations to demand a more expansive role in decisionmaking venues. Brazil, Latin America's most populous and most decentralized democracy, has witnessed the proliferation of participatory institutions at the municipal level, granting citizens access to decisionmaking venues as well as the right to engage in oversight activities. Participatory institutions, such as participatory budgeting (PB), represent an effort to devolve and broaden decisionmaking venues with the potential to place a check on the prerogatives of mayors.

The functioning of and outcomes from participatory institutions appear to be intimately related to the breadth and intensity of support extended by mayoral administrations. Mayors must be willing to delegate authority to citizens. Likewise, citizens and CSOs interested in the expansion of participatory institutions must work closely with mayoral administrations to ensure that the rules are followed and public policy projects are implemented. The delegation of authority to citizens has the potential to expand accountability at the local level as citizens contribute to policymaking decisions and work on third-party oversight committees. Yet there is also the risk that the insertion of CSOs into participatory policymaking venues based on their close political connections to elected mayors may subvert the development of "checks and balances." This article analyzes the opportunities created by participatory institutions to expand accountability and the concurrent intertwining sets of interests among the relevant actors that may actually limit that expansion.

In Brazil, participatory institutions have been implemented at the behest of political strategies promoted by "participatory" or leftist sectors of Brazil's political and civil societies. These institutions are designed to overcome numerous social and political problems, such as low levels of accountability, inefficiencies in social service provisions, and corruption, all of which hamper efforts to improve the quality of democratic governance. Brazilian democracy is plagued by a "private" state, where most mayors continue to treat their municipal administrations as personal fiefdoms (García Canclini 1995; Leal 1997; Diniz 1982). In many municipalities, the policymaking process is undertaken far from the prying eyes of politicians and civil society organizations. Participatory institutions, their advocates often argue, will make a dent in Brazil's social and political inequalities by allowing citizens to deliberate in public, negotiate over the distribution of public resources, and hold government officials accountable (Wampler and Avritzer 2004).

This article considers Brazil's best-known participatory experience, participatory budgeting (PB, orçamento participativo), in the municipalities of São Paulo, Recife, and Porto Alegre. This innovative institutional format incorporates citizens and municipal administrative officials into a policymaking process in which citizens directly negotiate over the distribution of public resources. In the most successful cases, PB has had the power to transform basic state—society relations, redistribute resources to underserviced neighborhoods, and create transparency in the budgetary process (Baiocchi 2001; Abers 1998, 2001; Marquetti 2003; Fung and Wright 2001; Fedozzi 1998). In less successful cases, PB creates opportunities for activists to raise awareness of public policies, which is still a desirable outcome but has a much more limited impact on policymaking (Nylen 2002; Wampler 1999).

To address the interplay of institutions and interests, this article addresses the following questions: Why would a mayor delegate authority to decisionmaking bodies dominated by citizens? And, once a mayor initiates a participatory decisionmaking process, what influences the mayor's capacity to implement particular policy preferences? The first question taps into the mayor's willingness and preference to redesign policymaking processes. The second question situates mayors in the municipality's broader political environment to demonstrate how Brazilian mayors face a series of constraints that limit their ability to implement their desired policies.

This study emphasizes the role of mayors because the office of mayor holds most legal, budgetary, and administrative authority at Brazil's municipal level. While authority has devolved from the federal government to state and local institutions, no corresponding deconcentration of authority at the municipal level has occurred (Rodríguez 1997). At Brazil's municipal level, legislatures act as a negative check or veto on the mayor, doing little to contribute to policymaking, because of the concentration of authority in the mayor's office (Wampler 2000). Municipalities nevertheless increased their importance in Brazil's federal structure with the 1988 Constitution and now account for 16 to 20 percent of all government spending (Couto and Abrúcio 1995; Montero 2000).

Most research on Brazil's participatory institutions has utilized a single-case study methodology, which limits the generalizability of the theoretical insights that can be gleaned from the cases (Abers 2001; Fedozzi 1998; Baiocchi 2001). The bulk of studies have focused on citizen participation or on the organizing efforts of municipal administrations (Nylen 2002; Abers 1998). Thus, we know a great deal about who, how, and why people participate, but much less about how that participation affects outcomes. Comparative studies have appeared in more limited numbers, but these often have been based on the most successful cases, Porto Alegre and Belo Horizonte (Jacobi and Teixeira 1996a; Avritzer 2002b). The three cases analyzed here produced markedly different policy outcomes, specifically regarding how PB affected the extension of accountability.

The concept of accountability has been employed by political scientists to account for variations in the quality of Latin America's new democratic regimes. Theorizing about diverse arenas, such as institutional authority, citizen participation, and political contestation, is a central concern as political scientists seek to move beyond the "consolidation" debates to assess the processes that generate political renewal. This article draws on the three variants of the "accountability" debates: societal, vertical, and horizontal.

THREE TYPES OF ACCOUNTABILITY

Does the expansion of decisionmaking venues limit mayoral authority? Does it undermine the responsibilities and duties of legislative bodies? Is accountability enhanced if citizens must still depend on mayoral administrations? The focus of the accountability debates has been on how one agent (the voters, the courts) can control another agent (elected officials, the executive branch). One weakness of such a focus is that the conceptual variants—horizontal, vertical, and societal—tend to run on parallel tracks, unable to show how citizens, CSOs, politicians, and institutions may place interlocking checks on the ambitions of other actors.

Participatory institutions, by contrast, tap into all three dimensions of the debates. Participatory institutions have the potential to act as a check on the prerogatives and actions of mayoral administrations (horizontal), to allow citizens to vote for representatives and specific policies (vertical), and to rely on the mobilization of citizens into political process as a means to legitimate the new policymaking process (societal).

Vertical accountability, generally framed as the control of public officials by citizens primarily via elections, has received significant attention as scholars have analyzed how citizens can use elections to exercise control over public officials (Przeworski et al. 1999). Horizontal accountability, the distribution of authority among different departments or branches of government, has also received attention as scholars have sought to evaluate the consequences of institutional arrangements that were designed to strengthen democratic practices and rights (O'Donnell 1998). Societal accountability, the pressures placed on state agencies by CSOs to encourage elected officials and bureaucrats to abide by the rule of law, has emerged as a counterbalance to the other two approaches; it can directly link ongoing political activity in civil society to formal political institutions (Smulovitz and Peruzzotti 2000).

Przeworski, Stokes, and Manin's book *Democracy, Accountability, and Representation* (1999) set the tone for the debate on vertical accountability. It engages a classic theme of democratic politics: how can citizens control their governments? Working in the rational choice tradition and employing a principal—agent model to explain outcomes, Przeworski et al. analyze how elections influence the choices of public officials in new democracies, concentrating on the inability of the electoral process to produce binding decisions or guarantee that public officials will remain virtuous. Unfortunately, Przeworski et al. reduce the range of political roles that citizens can play to one: the voter. "Governments make thousands of decisions that affect individual welfare; citizens have only one instrument to control these decisions: the vote" (Przeworski et al. 1999, 50).

Although most citizens may not be actively engaged or interested in policymaking processes, that assertion is greatly overstated. It ignores the vast range of political strategies and actions that activists use to influence public officials and policy outcomes. Citizens now have access to a range of legal and political resources to pressure public officials, including lawsuits, public demonstrations, public hearings, and participatory institutions. Democratic regimes allow citizens to seek redress in a number of decision-making venues, including executive, legislative, and judicial branches. In Brazil, groups demanding political reform have utilized municipal and state levels of government to challenge traditional mechanisms of control, which suggests that electoral analysis (especially of national elections) is not a sufficient indicator for how CSOs affect policymaking (Dagnino 1994; Jacobi 2000; Hochstetler 2000).

Przeworski et al.'s approach assumes the absence of political and social organizing. Elections are only one avenue for citizens to encourage increased accountability and improvements in public policies. The citizen as activist, the citizen as community organizer, and the active citizen does not appear in their analysis. This analytical focus ignores the role that CSOs play in democratic politics.

Smulovitz and Peruzzotti (2000) recognize the drawbacks of relying on elections to show how citizens might influence elected officials. They introduce the concept of societal accountability to complement vertical accountability, and they demonstrate how CSOs can act as watchdogs by monitoring the actions of elected officials and bureaucrats.

> Societal accountability is a nonelectoral, yet vertical mechanism of control that rests
> on the actions of a multiple array of citizens' associations and movements and on the
> media, actions that aim at exposing governmental wrongdoing, bringing new issues
> onto the public agenda, or activating the operation of horizontal agencies (Smulovitz
> and Peruzzotti 2000, 150).

This concept moves beyond a narrow conceptualization of citizen participation to show how some citizens and CSOs are engaged in continual efforts to influence the actions and behaviors of state actors.

Smulovitz and Peruzzotti demonstrate how CSOs have taken advantage of the partial extension of civil and political liberties to develop new strategies to pressure elected officials. Yet their approach is also limited, because it depends on CSOs' putting sufficient pressure on elected officials rather than showing how new actors can contribute to policy outcomes. CSOs are transformed into interest groups rather than active agents that participate in policymaking venues where binding decisions are made. Their empirical examples show how CSOs do not have the authority or ability to make binding decisions, but merely to influence powerholders. The case study for this article, PB, by contrast, offers the opportunity to overcome this theoretical impasse by demonstrating the effects of delegating authority to citizens. Citizens are neither limited to roles as "voters" or "watchdogs" but become real, meaningful players in the policymaking process.

O'Donnell's work on horizontal accountability opened up this line of analysis as it focused on another classic dilemma of politics: how can state agencies act as effective checks on the actions and ambitions of other state agencies? Horizontal accountability "depends on the existence of state agencies that are legally empowered—and factually willing and able—to take actions ranging from routine oversight to criminal sanctions or impeachment in relation to possibly unlawful actions or omissions by other agents or agents of the state" (O'Donnell 1998, 117). State agents must be able to exert effective oversight to ensure that other state agents—elected and appointed officials or bureaucrats—can be held accountable for the violation of rules and laws.

The system of checks and balances requires that third parties be able to make binding decisions, which means that third parties must be able to carry out and enforce these decisions. "Effective horizontal accountability is not the product of isolated agencies, but of networks of agencies (up to and including high courts) committed to upholding the rule of law" (O'Donnell 1998, 119). This is an important advance to the work of Przeworski et al. and Smulovitz and Peruzzotti because O'Donnell includes formal, binding decisions, which indicate the distribution of authority as well as the length to which the rule of law has been extended.

While O'Donnell's approach highlights the importance of the judicial branch and the legislature in acting as checks on the potential misuse of authority by executives, this approach, too, is limited because it fails to address how different interests are represented within state agencies. O'Donnell argues that contemporary polyarchies include "various oversight agencies, ombudsmen, accounting offices, *fiscalías*, and the like" (1998, 119), but he does not demonstrate how these institutions incorporate new actors that seek to use their authority to promote alternative institutional formats or alternative policies. These new institutions have the potential to place the political ambitions of different actors into direct competition with one another, thereby promoting interlocking sets of authority. Horizontal accountability, as O'Donnell frames it, does not sufficiently treat how the ambitions of different actors may be pitted against one another to produce different outcomes; institutions seemingly float above political and civil society rather than being occupied by specific actors with particular interests.

The case studies analyzed in this article cut across the three types of accountability. Participatory budgeting, as it has been created in São Paulo, Recife, and Porto Alegre, was initially implemented to allow citizens to deliberate over issues of public policy. The purpose of each program was to incorporate interested citizens and CSOs into decisionmaking bodies (that is, to expand checks and balances) so as to enhance the quality of policy outcomes while limiting corruption. PB can be viewed as offering the opportunity to allow citizens to promote societal and vertical accountability, but it can also be understood as a policymaking institution that competes with other state agencies over the distribution of authority, power, and resources.

As an innovative policymaking institution, PB provides a unique opportunity for interested citizens and activists to select policy outcomes. PB is not a representative case of urban politics in Brazil or in Latin America, but its exceptional nature provides the opportunity to demonstrate how citizens exert influence over elected municipal administrations.

The outcomes of PB in São Paulo, Recife, and Porto Alegre were quite varied, ranging from marginal to highly significant. Elected mayors sought to delegate authority even with few clear short-term political benefits. How to explain the emergence of new preferences held by reformist coalitions and reformist mayors? To find out why mayors would embark on this potentially risky path, we must turn to the historical precedents.

BUILDING BRAZIL'S CIVIL SOCIETY

Civil society activism reemerged in Brazil during the 1970s and 1980s (Avritzer 2002a; Doimo 1995; Alvarez et al. 1998a). Its new expansion led CSOs and activists to develop new political preferences that challenged the political and social exclusion experienced by many Brazilians (Wampler and Avritzer 2004; Doimo 1995). The new political actors utilized innovative strategies as they sought to influence government officials during Brazil's transition to democratic rule. The "explosion" of demands based on rights since then has transformed the institutional format of municipal and state institutions, and also the means by which citizens have sought to negotiate their demands with public officials (Baierle 1998; Avritzer 2002a; Dagnino 1998). The expansion of the number of actors and the type of CSOs during the late 1970s and throughout the 1980s helped to create new strategies for engaging politics (Wampler and Avritzer 2004).

The expansion of civil society had an important direct effect on political society. Civil society leaders reached out to and worked with politicians to help elect candidates and to influence public policy. Conversely, public officials sought CSO support to mobilize potential voters.[1] The willingness of elected mayors to support and implement participatory institutions is intimately linked to mayors' political connections to the new CSOs. These observations—mayors respond to constituents and potential voters, and interest groups seek to influence policy outcomes—add little to ongoing political science debates, but they provide a necessary corrective to earlier analyses of PB that emphasize the primacy of social movements in creating participatory institutions or the benevolent policies enacted by the Workers' Party (PT) to induce citizens to participate.

During the 1990s, CSO activists became directly engaged in election campaigning, monitoring public officials, and creating new public politics. CSOs proposed new institutional formats and types of policies to help them overcome the legacies of political, social, and economic exclusion faced by vast numbers of Brazil's population (Wampler and Avritzer 2004). Activists paid more attention to how government officials designed and implemented public policies. That led to demands by CSOs for direct involvement in policymaking venues. Proposing alternative policies often requires that citizens build close ties to politicians, often especially with state and local legislators, so that their proposed policies can be introduced into policy debates. Proposing new institutional types suggests that movement activists are attempting to situate themselves and their issues in a broader political and social context. Neighborhood leaders and reformist politicians created political alliances based on the idea that citizens should be directly incorporated into the policymaking process.

The growth of civil society led to the emergence of activists who functioned as political operatives for reformist politicians and as participants in new policymaking venues. The initial expansion of civil society helped to form new types of leaders and eased the way for new political coalitions to be built. Although the high-water mark of citizen mobilization was achieved in the 1984 *diretas já* (direct elections now) movement, which centered on the demand for direct elections for Brazil's presidency, and the 1992 movement to impeach President Fernando Collor de Mello, CSOs continued to organize throughout the 1990s, albeit in new ways. During the late 1980s and throughout the 1990s, many CSO leaders worked for and on behalf of leftist party candidates, especially from the Workers' Party and the Brazilian Socialist Party (PSB).

The institutionalization and the routinization of elections also suggest that politicians will seek out community leaders who can deliver new constituencies or maintain old ones. The leaders of CSOs now occupy dual roles. First they are catalysts for groups in civil society who work to educate and inform their citizens, as well as strategists using classic mass mobilization tactics, such as public demonstrations, to pressure public officials (that is, seeing societal accountability). Their second role is often as political operatives of a single party or politician, engaged in constituency service, fundraising, and campaigning.

Civil society activists no longer occupy a niche as political outsiders, but often act as intermediaries between political and civil societies. They now mediate between local neighborhood organizations and reformist politicians, between individual citizens and new policymaking venues. How community leaders exercise this role is particularly important to the creation of vibrant participatory venues. In the three cases analyzed in the following section, activists were able to align themselves to mayoral candidates before the candidates' first election, thereby giving the activists the leverage to demand that participatory institutions be established.

PARTICIPATORY BUDGETING IN THREE CITIES

To learn about PB, mayors, and municipal councils, this study conducted 30 months of research between 1995 and 2001 in the three subject cities. Budgets, election results, legislative proposals, and the internal memoranda of parties and social movements all were analyzed, and nearly two hundred interviews were conducted with municipal council members, appointed officials, bureaucrats, and civil society activists. Many hours of ethnographic observation were conducted in PB meetings and municipal council offices.

PB has received considerable attention from academics, policymakers and citizen-activists, both within and beyond Brazil. Initiated in Porto Alegre during the late 1980s, PB has now been implemented in more than one hundred municipalities (Teixeira 2003). While the range of outcomes has been correspondingly wide, most studies focus on the most successful cases, Porto Alegre and Belo Horizonte (Santos 1998; Avritzer 2002b; Baiocchi 2001).

PB depends on the mutual participation of civil society and state officials in the selection and implementation of policies and public works (Fedozzi 1998; Abers 2001).

Civil society is represented by a myriad of private persons, social movement activists, and community leaders. The state is represented by the municipal administration, the mayor's office in particular. PB is designed to bridge the gap between the municipal administration and the nascent civil society that has been developing in Brazil since the late 1970s.

Implementing PB is a potential risk for mayors if the program does not provide positive results, as interpreted by the administration's political allies, interested CSOs, and voters (most of whom are nonparticipants). PB has the potential to redistribute authority and resources, which places institutional reformers on a collision course with entrenched interests. Understanding the political interests of different groups is vital to explaining the risk involved when delegating authority is used as a political strategy.

Certain CSOs have an incentive to participate in PB and promote it as a vital new policymaking institution if the specific organization is likely to benefit from the particular set of rules that govern PB. If a specific organization favors public decisionmaking processes, which require extensive deliberation and negotiation as well as the mobilization of an organization's followers at several key moments throughout the year, then it is likely that an organization will support PB. PB rewards "participatory" CSOs that develop a specific set of political skills: public deliberation and negotiation, mobilization, and the capacity to analyze government data. CSOs that rely on more traditional forms of organizing, such as clientelism and patronage, will not seek to take advantage of this new form of policymaking because their political resources do not easily mesh with this new system. "Traditional" CSOs, which rely on private exchanges and networks, will not actively support the implementation of PB, and they are not likely to participate in high numbers.

Likewise, some, but not all, elected officials also have specific incentives for supporting this new type of policymaking. First, elected officials who rely on participatory CSOs to help campaign, mobilize voters, and provide their educational material are more likely to support the implementation of a participatory process. Second, elected officials who seek to change how political resources are distributed are more likely to support the implementation of this new policymaking institution. The potential for the transparent implementation of public resources will undermine the private exchanges between elected officials, bureaucrats, and leaders of "traditional" CSOs, thereby enhancing the ability of political reformers to limit the influence of their political opponents.

Third, reformist politicians may seek to use PB as a means to create new bases of political support. The risk, of course, is that the new participatory institutions will produce weak results, or that the mayoral administration will not be able to generate sufficient participation to create a dynamic process. Initiating a new participatory experience is a time-consuming process that does not necessarily offer short-term policy or electoral benefits. Administrations must be willing to commit time, energy, and resources to reforming the policymaking process. Citizens and political opponents can potentially use the new participatory institutions to promote policies, strategies, and outcomes that are not beneficial to the mayor's interests.

Budgetary processes are excellent proxies with which to understand efforts to limit and disperse authority because the process depends on the distribution of basic technical and financial information, debate, and negotiation among interested parties, and the eventual implementation of public works. Budgetmaking and service provision processes incorporate bureaucrats, appointed and elected public officials, and interested citizens. Because budgets and resource allocation are often the center of political disputes, a focus on new budgetary processes should illuminate the extent to which political strategies and relationships have been modified.

Initiating Participatory Budgeting: Mayoral Elections

Porto Alegre, Recife, and São Paulo in the 1980s elected mayors with deep roots in the participatory sectors of civil society. This helps to explain why participatory decisionmaking bodies were initiated. Elected mayors sought to transform governing and policymaking processes not merely to promote their own political careers but to reward their supporters and reach out to potential supporters.

In Porto Alegre, Olivio Dutra was elected in 1988 with support from the Workers' Party, trade unions, social movements, and community associations. Dutra had matured as a political leader in social movements and labor unions where the ideas and values of direct citizen and worker participation in government were emphasized. Dutra's victory was a surprise come-from-behind win, abetted by being part of a first-past-the-post election. In the 1988 elections, the candidate with the highest number of votes won; there was no runoff between the two highest vote getters. Dutra was elected mayor with just over 3.3 percent of the vote.

In São Paulo the same year, Luiza Erundina was elected mayor with support from the Workers' Party, social movements, trade unions, and middle-class progressives. Trained as a social worker, Erundina first emerged as a political leader in São Paulo's East Side (Zona Leste) housing movement. She was an early crossover between civil and political societies as she was elected to São Paulo's municipal council in 1982 and the state legislature in 1985 before becoming mayor in 1988. Like Dutra, she, too, won with only one-third of the total valid votes.

Recife elected Jarbas Vasconcelos mayor in 1985 and again in 1992. Vasconcelos was affiliated with the Catholic church's efforts to organize groups around land-use issues. Throughout this period, he was a member of the centrist, catchall PMDB (Party of the Brazilian Democratic Movement), although he was briefly associated with the leftist PSB in 1985.

The three mayors followed similar political trajectories. Each had strong ties to social movements, progressive sectors of the Catholic church, and labor unions. All three had been vocal and public opponents of the military dictatorship, and all had advocated the return to democratic rule. In each municipality, therefore, the mayor's willingness to initiate innovations was high. Dutra, in Porto Alegre, was affiliated with an umbrella organization of community associations (UAMPA), which laid out the first ideas for participatory budgeting in 1986 (Avritzer 2002b). Vasconcelos, in Recife, had ties to the liberation theology-inspired Commission for Justice and Peace, which advocated citizens' direct participation in issues pertaining to land use. While this organization did not develop specific political strategies focused on budgets, it did insist on direct citizen participation. In São Paulo, Erundina was involved in housing and healthcare movements that sought to establish citizen councils (*conselhos*), through which activists could present their demands in public venues (Jacobi 1989; Erundina 1990). Erundina's election was ideal for advocates of participatory programs because the conventional wisdom suggested that a mayor with deep roots in the new civil society could greatly increase citizens' decisionmaking authority.

Table 1 situates the individual mayors in their broader political and institutional context. While authority is concentrated in the mayor's office, the table highlights the different pressures the mayors must contend with to implement their preferred policy outcomes. The third row indicates that the intensity of the mayor's willingness to implement new policymaking venues was roughly similar in the three municipalities. The fourth row suggests that the mayor's governing coalition affects the degree to which decisionmaking authority can be delegated to citizens. The fifth row suggests that mayors must craft a

Table 1. Political Climate for Participatory Budgeting

	São Paulo	Recife	Porto Alegre
Year PB initiated	1990	1995	1989
Mayor Political Party	Luiza Erudina, PT	Jarbas Vasconcelos, PMDB	Olivio Dutra, PT
Participatory civil society associations' importance to the mayor's base of support	High	Moderate to High	High
Governing coalition support for delegation of decisionmaking authority	Moderate	Low	High
Support for mayor in municipal council	Low	Moderate	Moderate

stable voting majority in the municipal council to establish sufficient political capital to implement a radical overhaul of decisionmaking processes.

All three mayors were reformers with strong political links to organized sectors of the emergent civil society. This is a finding that is assumed but not explicitly accounted for in many accounts of PB; mayors have specific ties to CSOs that are likely to benefit from the creation of participatory, deliberate policymaking bodies. To determine and measure each mayor's particular allegiance to participatory CSOs, each mayor's personal political trajectory, their official statements regarding how they would govern, internal documents of CSOs, and multiple interviews were analyzed. Variation between the three mayors can be accounted for by analyzing each mayor's personal and political connections to the new CSOs.

In Recife, Mayor Vasconcelos was the least supportive of delegating decisionmaking authority; he preferred that the participatory institution receive and channel citizens' demands rather than being a deliberative body. In Porto Alegre and São Paulo, Mayors Dutra and Erundina supported the delegation of authority to citizens in these new decision making venues. Each mayor's intense involvement in the municipality's civil society suggests that this was a necessary condition for the implementation of a new institutional format. The table's fourth and fifth rows, however, indicate that factors beyond the direct and immediate control of the mayor affect the ability to implement a new (and potentially radical) PB program. This suggests that mayors operate in a constrained environment, unable simply to govern as they might want. Political risk therefore can be assessed by analyzing how different factions might use competing institutional authority to check the power of other branches.

Table 1 shows that the mayor's governing coalition (that is, municipal council members, appointed officials, and interest groups) affected the extent to which decisionmaking authority was delegated to citizens. The intensity was measured from low to high. Low indicated that the mayor's governing coalition would not support the delegation of authority; high would indicate that the mayor had a green light to innovate. To measure this factor, this study analyzed the percentage of seats that the mayor's party held in the municipal council, the percentage of seats held by potential allies, and the political trajectories of the key municipal and party officials.

In Recife, the governing coalition relied heavily on the centrist PMDB and, later, the conservative PFL (Party of the Liberal Front). Reformist wings in the PMDB supported innovation through the delegation of authority, but traditional political sectors viewed this as a threat to their resources. Mayor Vasconcelos and his closest allies promoted

PB, but other groups in his coalition did not support expanding citizens' access to decisionmaking venues. In São Paulo, the support for participatory institution was strong in the governing party (the PT) but ultimately was hampered by disagreements over how to delegate authority. These disagreements led a significant potential base of support to remain neutral to the idea of PB. In Porto Alegre, the governing coalition threw its weight and support behind PB as party and state officials worked to promote PB as a vibrant institutional venue.

Table 1 indicates that the mayor must craft a stable voting majority in the municipal council to establish sufficient political capital to implement a radical overhaul of how decisions are made. PB, as a new policymaking institution, would flounder without direct involvement by the mayor's office. While mayors do hold the most authority, they must negotiate with the legislative branch to govern. Thus, the capacity to build a new decisionmaking body depends on circumstances that extend far beyond the confines of the participatory institution. In order to measure this, the study analyzed the percentage of seats the mayor's party held in the municipal council, the percentage of seats held by potential allies, the percentage of the vote received by the mayor's party in the mayoral election, and a series of legislative debates and votes.

In São Paulo, Erundina faced a hostile municipal council that nearly impeached and removed her from office. She had difficulty getting her legislative proposals passed because of her party's minority position and its inability to negotiate with potential supporters (Couto 1995). In Porto Alegre, Dutra was also in a minority position, but managed to craft a stable voting coalition by working with political rivals (namely the leftist-populist PDT). The municipal council was neither a thorn in his side nor a strong asset; instead, it was neutralized as a political actor. Vasconcelos's party in Recife nearly had an outright voting majority. Vasconcelos was able to add the support of rival parties (namely the rightist PFL). The support for the mayor was strong, although Vasconcelos had to pay attention to the interests of elected officials who did not share his emphasis on participatory decisionmaking. Recife aptly demonstrates the differences between rows 4 and 5 of table 1: Mayor Vasconcelos's support in the municipal council was partly contingent on his being unable to delegate real decisionmaking authority.

Table 1 highlights the embedded character of Brazilian mayors. Individual mayors rely on the support of their political supporters and parties to build a coherent administrative strategy, which, in turn, allows them to build support in the municipal council while simultaneously delegating authority. When the mayor's broader coalition did not support delegation (Recife) or squabbled over the type of delegation (São Paulo), the mayor's efforts to promote PB were thwarted. When, on the other hand, the mayor enjoyed unified support (Porto Alegre), it increased the likelihood that PB would be implemented. Thus PB as a participatory institution has a potential impact on the ambitions and interests of mayors, municipal council members, and citizens. PB has the potential to alter the distribution of authority among these three institutions, which will affect how accountability can be extended.

OUTCOMES: THE RIGHT TO DECIDE, PUBLIC DEBATES, AND LEGAL IMPLEMENTATION

To establish an empirical litmus test for accountability, this study analyzed three factors: the right to make decisions based on access to transparent information (vertical), public debate and mobilization (societal), and legal implementation (horizontal). The right to make decisions creates a link between the participants and the government, which is a necessary first step; it establishes citizens' ability to contribute directly to the governing process. Participants in the policymaking process may make decisions on specific policy issues, generalized policy trends (for example, basic infrastructure over health care), or representatives in the process. The ability to debate in public and to mobilize citizens to participate in debates and decisionmaking processes are features of societal accountability. Citizens have the opportunity to influence their fellow citizens and government officials by using the public venues to press their claims.

The implementation of projects, as selected by citizens, touches on two aspects of horizontal accountability. If decisions made by PB delegates are included in a municipality's budget, are the projects being implemented? If so, then horizontal accountability will be extended, because municipal administrations are implementing projects selected in one institution (PB), ratified by a second (municipal council), and implemented by a third (municipal administration). In addition, most PB programs have oversight committees, so that projects cannot be considered completed (and, by extension, final payment to contractors cannot be made) until committees approve them. If municipal administrations follow the rules that govern the oversight committees, then it will be possible to confirm that horizontal accountability is being extended.

Porto Alegre

Porto Alegre's PB was initiated in 1989 and is often considered the most successful case in Brazil to date. The municipal administration, as a result of its close ties to activists in civil society, has actively promoted governing practices that encourage the delegation of authority. After nearly 15 years of PB, the municipal administration continues to promote the values embedded in PB and, equally important, follows the rules established by PB. Responsibility for the selection and implementation of public works is shared by the municipal administration and the citizens; citizens have a larger role in the selection of projects, while the administration plays a much larger role in the implementation of the projects.

When PB was initiated in Porto Alegre, the municipal government enjoyed a favorable political context that allowed it to experiment with a new institutional format. The government relied on "participatory" CSOs, which demanded an active role in policymaking. The Workers' Party (PT) led the electoral coalition, and most of its members supported direct citizen involvement in decisionmaking venues (Fedozzi 1998). The PT was able to cobble together support in the municipal council, based on the support of an opposition party (the Democratic Labor Party, PDT). The governing coalition led by the PT controlled 10 of the 33 seats. Centrist parties with similar ideologies, most important the PDT, controlled 12 additional seats, while the political and ideological opposition controlled 10 seats. The PT government could negotiate with the centrist parties to secure a relatively positive atmosphere in which to initiate reform efforts. For example, during Mayor Dutra's administration (1989–92), the PT passed a series of progressive taxation laws, which demonstrates the broad support the administration could achieve. This indicates that the PT found highly favorable conditions to initiate and implement a participatory venue.

How has Porto Alegre's PB affected the extension of accountability? First, citizens have the right to make decisions about general policy trends and specific public works. Citizens have access to vital technical and financial information that helps them during decisionmaking processes. Information about public policies and budgeting is available to citizens in a coherent and easily understood form. Through the auspices of PB, the government holds meetings to provide basic information on issues such as tax revenues, budget allocation, and debt servicing. For example, each specific project selected by the PB participants receives a tracking number that enables municipal bureaucrats to inform any interested party about the project's current status. This transparency serves as the basis for informed deliberation and dialogue. After PB participants select projects, the implementation process is more administrative than political.

Second, the municipal administration honors decisions made by the PB participants by implementing the public works they select in a timely and transparent manner. Implementation is at the discretion of the mayor, because line items in the budget do not necessarily have to be implemented. In Porto Alegre, decisions made through PB have become binding decisions, as the municipal administrations have implemented projects selected by PB participants.[2] By honoring the decisions made in PB, the government signals to the population that important public policy decisions are now made in this institutional sphere. This shifts decisionmaking processes away from the private spheres of the government and into the PB meetings (Genro 1995).

The municipal administration has taken a third step that has increased horizontal accountability and public trust by submitting its own policy initiatives for approval by PB participants. Without formal approval in the citizens' forum, the government's specific public works initiatives could not be included in the municipal budget and therefore could not be implemented. This step represents a fundamental change in Brazilian policymaking, because Porto Alegre's government must publicly defend its specific projects and submit these projects to a project-specific vote.

Porto Alegre's PB has made extensive efforts to create a new public arena for deliberation and negotiation (Avritzer 2002a). Citizens are mobilized for a series of local, regional, thematic, and municipal meetings that enable them to interact with each other as well as with public officials. This allows interested and engaged citizens to maintain pressure on the mayoral administration. It also allows mayoral administrations that support PB participants' demands to argue for the "inversion of priorities" based on the participation of increasing numbers of citizens.

Porto Alegre's municipal budget is much closer to a real budget than the "black box" (*caixa preta*) that budgets tend to be at other levels of government. An accurate budget makes it easier for citizens to understand the budget process and to work to include their own items. Under these conditions, items included in the budget enjoy a much higher likelihood of being implemented than under the more familiar "black box" method. This also gives all factions the opportunity to know what the government is actually doing.

In many ways, Porto Alegre provides the most paradoxical results among the three cases studied. It has simultaneously strengthened and weakened efforts to expand accountability. Citizens have been directly incorporated into decisionmaking bodies that exercise authority, transparency has been increased, participation has steadily increased, and the implementation of public works follows legal means. This has been accomplished under the auspices of a unified government led by the PT that increased the authority of the mayor's office while simultaneously marginalizing the municipal council.

Porto Alegre's PB took the municipal council out of the decisionmaking process by having citizens make all budgetary decisions that fall within the purview of "discretionary spending." This undermined horizontal accountability, because one branch of government (the municipal council) received a smaller, weaker role in the budgetary process. PB still has not been legally constituted, which means that it is technically and legally part of the municipal administration (mayor's office). While successive Workers' Party mayors in Porto Alegre have gone to considerable lengths to ensure that citizens in public venues make most budgetary decisions, final legal authority still rests with the mayor's office. If

PB is considered from the vantage point of horizontal accountability, it is apparent that the mayor's office remains firmly in control of the policymaking process. The municipal administration provides information, allocates the political and bureaucratic staff to conduct meetings, and implements projects. PB is a success in Porto Alegre because it has the firm support of the municipal administration.

If we analyze PB from the vantage point of vertical accountability, we must note that the PB contributes to limits on mayoral authority because citizens are making real, important decisions. PB, however, is intimately associated with the PT's success in winning four successive mayoral elections. Citizens may have greater authority via PB, but the party that implemented it has managed to benefit handsomely from this new institutional type.

From the standpoint of societal accountability, it is clear that through PB, citizens can engage in meaningful deliberation and negotiation. This allows citizens to pressure their government to implement changes in public policies. The groups most likely to benefit from PB are those skilled in mobilization and deliberation, which tend to be supporters of the PT. Again, societal pressures may help to strengthen the mayoral administration by creating short-term benefits for the PT and the party's supporters. There is no evidence, however, that PB creates a permanent set of checks and balances that can be utilized by citizens or opposition parties.

It is not clear whether citizens can legally force the mayor's hand to provide information or implement projects. This means that PB participants must depend partly on the good will and benevolence of the municipal government, which indicates that PB has only partly promoted restrictions on mayoral authority in Porto Alegre. PB in Porto Alegre is noteworthy for how it has modified and expanded decisionmaking processes, but the outcomes continue to be limited because the PB's positive results depend on intense support from the municipal government. It is hoped that citizen involvement may decrease the power of the mayor's office over the long term, but for the present the mayor's office remains the most important political actor in Porto Alegre.

Recife

The capacity to place real limits on mayoral authority or to create public and citizen-controlled decisionmaking venues through PB has been much weaker in Recife than in Porto Alegre. Yet societal accountability may be somewhat stronger, because Recife's PB was, during the mid- to late 1990s, an institutional venue occupied by groups that opposed successive mayors' inattention to the program. The conditions under which PB was initiated in Recife were much less favorable than in Porto Alegre. The popular mayor, Jarbas Vasconcelos, had a long history of working directly with community organizations, but the relationship with activists was rather personalistic. Vasconcelos channeled the demands for public works through his administrative structure, but he was less interested in delegating decisionmaking authority to citizens (Soler 1991; Soares 1998).

Vasconcelos was a member of the PMDB, a catchall centrist political party whose elected representatives in Recife were suspicious of PB. City council members and state deputies feared that this new institutional sphere would decrease their influence over the distribution of scarce resources, and therefore sought to undermine Recife's PB at every turn (Wampler 2000). Theirs was a legitimate concern for municipal council members, because PB has the potential to transfer decisionmaking authority to citizens and to limit council members' ability to influence policy outcomes.

In Recife, the PMDB municipal council members did not support the delegation of authority to citizens and sought to be personally involved in the distribution of public works projects. Few members of Recife's PMDB had strong commitments to participatory CSOs, and therefore wanted to maintain control of resources as part of the exchange between the mayoral and legislative branches.

At the time that PB was initiated, Mayor Vasconcelos enjoyed a broad base of support in the municipal council. While his coalition held just 16 of 41 seats, 18 centrists were willing to work with the mayor. Only 7 municipal council members could plausibly be identified as opposition. This support gave Vasconcelos sufficient flexibility to experiment with a new institutional type. Municipal council members affiliated with centrist and center-right parties in Recife had few connections to the participatory civil society, which gave prevalence to longstanding political preferences based on clientelistic exchanges, as opposed to support for the delegation of authority. How did this affect the outcome?

First, the municipal administration only partially ceded decisionmaking powers. Thus, citizens lacked the right to make policy decisions, and vertical accountability was not extended through PB. Participants had the right to decide only a small fraction of the projects to be implemented by the municipal administration (10 percent of all discretionary funding, as opposed to 100 percent in Porto Alegre). Two administrations, led by Vasconcelos (1992–96) and Roberto Magalhaes (1997–2000), did not dedicate their full attention or resources to PB. Vasconcelos's links to the groups that most strongly advocated PB weakened over time, while Magalhães's ties to these groups were based on his political alliance with Vasconcelos. Over time, the two administrations began to use the PB structure for other purposes, such as the distribution of money during Carnival, in a manner more reminiscent of clientelism than of an innovative policymaking institution. Decisionmaking authority was not delegated to citizens, and mayoral authority was not checked.

Second, the administrations of Vasconcelos and Magalhaes did not guarantee that the projects selected by PB participants would be prioritized for implementation. The municipality's internal administrative structure was not substantially modified to ensure that the decisions made in PB would be implemented. The binding decisions that have begun to emerge in Porto Alegre were absent in Recife.

Third, PB had a slightly positive effect in that it helped to foster increased transparency in Recife's municipal administration. Administrations had to provide information to citizens and bureaucrats in order to set up and manage the program. Information about public policies and budgeting was not readily available to PB participants, however; nor were the programs promoted in such a way as to involve the general public. The budget remained a black box; no one was really sure what projects went in or what would come out. The information provided to citizens, moreover, contained multiple inaccuracies, making it virtually impossible for PB participants to make informed decisions related to how the municipal budget and policymaking processes actually worked.

Yet there is one important caveat to this case: negotiations over the distribution of resources, as well as the oversight meetings, which analyzed the administration's performance, were held in public. This gave PB participants the opportunity to work directly with government officials. Denunciations of the administration's actions (or inactions) allowed activists to hold administration officials accountable in a public format. Recife had few other venues that allowed a public discussion of the administration's policy outputs. Confrontations and arguments between participants and the government officials in public meetings were a vital part of the learning process that leads to the increasing openness and transparency of the state. These meetings forced the mayor or his representatives to explain their policies, while also permitting traditionally excluded citizens to enter into discussions and debates that had long been held in the private realms of the state.

This development suggests that societal accountability is being extended in Recife. It also suggests that Recife's PB is a "demand-receiving" institution that depends on societal pressure, rather than an institutional venue in which binding decisions are made. This "success" reflects one of the basic conceptual problems of societal accountability: the concept itself rests on the pressure that can be applied to government officials by civil society actors, while the civil society actors themselves have no authority to make decisions.

The structure of Recife's PB, which coincided with many of the leaders' political beliefs and ideologies, offered opportunities to CSOs to demand rights that could not be guaranteed by other institutional means. Yet participants were caught between demanding that the government fulfill its commitments and asking for compliance; between the demands of rights-bearing citizens and goods-receiving clients (Sales 1994). While these are not ideal conditions in which to develop a new decisionmaking venue, PB did provide an institutional format for citizens to join a public debate.

Recife's PB placed few limits on the mayor's authority and failed to develop into a real decisionmaking venue. Yet PB was an official part of the government's agenda, which gave activists opportunities to raise contentious issues in official, municipally sponsored public meetings. This provided an opportunity to hold administrative officials publicly accountable for their failures. Innovative policymaking institutions are valuable to the process of building the foundations for accountability, as in the case of Porto Alegre; but the short-term impact may be weak if government officials do not support incorporating traditionally excluded actors into the policymaking process.

São Paulo

Limiting mayoral authority and creating new decisionmaking venues were weakly established through PB in São Paulo during Luiza Erundina's administration (1989–92). Erundina, a member of the PT, was closely aligned to São Paulo's participatory civil society, especially the social movements that had grown rapidly during the 1970s and 1980s. Erundina sought to initiate reform, but her government proved incapable of implementing a vibrant participatory policymaking venue. This suggests that the mere existence of the PT in power is not a sufficient condition to guarantee the success of the program.

Within the PT-led governing coalition, Erundina faced a difficult political struggle over the type of participatory institution that would be created. Discussion centered on "deliberative" versus "consulting" bodies, as well as territory-based versus sectoral bodies (Couto 1995). The intense divisions in the governing coalition made it difficult for Erundina to dedicate her administration's full attention to PB. The demand for PB came from the social movement sector of the PT, but was not necessarily shared by other factions in the party. As Erundina was forced to concentrate on a more limited range of reforms than the PT had originally proposed, she chose to forgo the delegation of authority to citizen bodies (Singer 1996).

Erundina also faced a hostile municipal council that was unwilling to rubber-stamp her proposals. Erundina was forced to dedicate considerable time and energy to building the necessary majority in the council to pass the budget and other legislation. During the 1988–92 legislative period, the PT's governing coalition held 20 of 55 seats in the municipal council. They needed the support of 8 centrist legislators, many of whom were unwilling to negotiate or support the PT's policy initiatives. Ten of the 16 centrists were from the PMDB and would become members of the conservative governing coalition for the 1992–96 period. The political capital Erundina expended to build a stable voting majority undermined her ability to delegate decisionmaking authority, as she was forced to support the political projects of potential supporters in the municipal council. This support, both administrative and resource-oriented, meant that fewer resources were available for PB.

Another important factor is that many of the opposition council members did not support the delegation of authority to citizen decisionmaking bodies. The creation of a parallel decisionmaking process, if successful, could emasculate the authority of the municipal council. Many council members relied on clientelistic exchanges to deliver goods and resources to their constituents, acting as intermediaries between the municipal administration and community organizations. As one council member stated,

> You need to have clientelism, radio, and TV because the vote is not an informed vote. Right? . . . I am currently a municipal council member, do I want to continue? If I want to continue, and if I follow the rules of the game, then it is likely that I will not have success, that I will not be reelected (Author interview, São Paulo, February 18, 1997).

Municipal council members not affiliated with the "participatory" civil society eschewed calls for transparency, openness, deliberation, and public negotiation because it was not to their advantage. The internal strife in the PT-led governing coalition, as well as the hostile opposition, made conditions for launching a PB program very unfavorable. How did this affect PB's outcomes?

Citizens were given the opportunity to present their demands in PB, but few institutional mechanisms guaranteed negotiation and deliberation over the selection of public works. While PB has the potential to expand the number of decisionmaking venues, the administration's difficulties in implementing selected public works curtailed any positive impact.

PB in São Paulo did not produce a transparent municipal administration, given that it yielded few concrete results. PB increased direct public contact between citizens and the municipal government, but meetings were sparsely attended (Jacobi and Teixeira 1996b). While PB did increase the amount of information available to interested citizens, most participants sympathized with the municipal government. This did little to provide a check on the policy prerogatives of the municipal administration.

PB as an institution and as a means of limiting mayoral authority was therefore unsuccessful in the municipality of São Paulo. The government that implemented PB had deep roots in civil society; CSOs and citizen activists demanded that government officials delegate decisionmaking authority; but the government could not do so because pressure from the municipal council proved to be far greater than pressure from CSOs.

São Paulo's PB experience suffered from the administration's lack of support, suggesting that heightened civil society mobilization is not sufficient to extend accountability. CSOs proved too weak as partners for an embattled administration. Sao Paulo's PB therefore had weak impact on the extension of vertical or societal accountability. Yet municipal council members, in the context of a divided government, acted as a check on the prerogatives of the municipal administration. While the reasons many municipal council members rejected the delegation of authority to citizens may have been politically undesirable (for example, the wish to maintain existing clientelistic networks), it is rather ironic that the municipal council might actually have helped to extend horizontal accountability by not allowing a mayor to do as she pleased. PB did not have a direct effect on the extension of horizontal accountability, but the mayor's inability to promote this new institutional venue suggests that at least one branch of government may be able to check another branch. This is quite different from Porto Alegre, where the Workers'

Party-led governing coalition was rarely checked by the municipal council; or Recife, where mayors sought to appease demands from municipal council members and PB participants through the distribution of targeted resources.

CONCLUSIONS

Political innovations in Brazilian municipalities demonstrate how CSOs, political activists, and reformist politicians have, at times, forged political coalitions to place limits on mayoral authority. By imposing such limitations, CSOs and their political allies have attempted to extend accountability. At Brazil's municipal level, this process has been based on the delegation of authority to participatory, citizen-dominated decisionmaking bodies. Participatory institutions increase citizens' access to government and encourage public debate, both of which intensify pressure on municipal administrations to implement policy projects selected by citizens.

The line of analysis pursued in this article has two broader implications for the study of democratic politics in Brazil and Latin America. First, the vitality of participatory institutions that delegate authority to citizens builds on the intense support of mayoral administrations. If mayors and their political allies have significant ties to participatory CSOs, then it is far more likely that mayors will seek to promote the delegation of authority. In Recife, São Paulo, and Porto Alegre, mayors had deep connections to the new civil society, which helps to explain why they all were willing to experiment with the delegation of authority. The form of delegation differed in each municipality, largely based on the degree to which the mayor sought to include citizens in the decisionmaking process.

Mayors with strong connections to participatory CSOs are also more likely to hold political preferences that may be transformed into policies that support extending accountability. Using public decisionmaking venues, reorienting public spending, and allowing citizens to make binding decisions may contribute to that extension. Yet the intense involvement of municipal administrations in support of these institutions may have the paradoxical result of undermining accountability, because support for an institution such as participatory budgeting has come at the expense of the municipal council's participation. Participatory budgeting has allowed citizens to wield great authority partly because the institution partly replaces the municipal council's role in policymaking.

A second lesson from these case studies is that mayors cannot govern without the support of their main constituencies, whether these are in the same party or part of the broader governing coalition. This conclusion runs counter to much of the conventional wisdom in Brazil, where governors and mayors are often analyzed as being able to govern with few constraints. A key factor that helps to explain the mayor's capacity to delegate authority is the willingness of the municipal council members to support that action. If municipal council members are unwilling to support participatory institutions, it becomes extremely difficult for the mayor to dedicate the necessary resources to doing so. This was clearly the case in Recife and São Paulo. Participatory budgeting was weakly implemented in both municipalities. On the other hand, if the municipal council members are willing to support participatory institutions, then it increases the likelihood that the mayor will be able to implement preferred institutional reforms. This was the case in Porto Alegre. Mobilizing citizen support, therefore, is insufficient for mayors to successfully implement participatory programs. Mayors must, in the best-case scenario, hope for a majority of council members who are willing to support the delegation of authority. If mayors do not have broad support in the council, they must devise other payoffs to induce recalcitrant council members to support innovative policymaking institutions.

Participatory budgeting helped partly to extend accountability in Porto Alegre and Recife; São Paulo's PB had a negligible impact on this outcome. The paradoxical results from Porto Alegre, which indicated that vertical and societal accountability was being extended through the new institutional type while horizontal accountability was being weakened, suggest that PB may only partially contribute to the redistribution of authority at Brazil's subnational levels of government. PB is by no means a magic bullet to extend accountability and deepen democratic practices. While PB does offer new opportunities for participation and decisionmaking, it continues to bear the risk that authority will be concentrated in the mayor's office, which has the potential to undercut efforts to establish a system of checks and balances at Brazil's local level of government.

NOTES

The author would like to thank the Social Science Research Council, the Ford Foundation, and the David Boren NSEP Program for their generous support of predissertation and dissertation research over a five-year period in Brazil. The author also thanks Lawrence S. Graham, Henry Dietz, Sonia E. Alvarez, Raúl Madrid, Todd Lochner, Ross Burkhart, and four anonymous reviewers for their timely and insightful suggestions. Any remaining errors, of course, are the author's responsibility.

1 Although voting is mandatory in Brazil, political parties and politicians spend considerable resources on election day to remind their supporters to vote, as well as to "win over" voters with weak or no preferences.

2 It is difficult to define "binding" decisions narrowly in the case of Brazilian budgets. Because approved budget lines do not necessarily have to be spent, it is left to the executive's discretion to allocate resources (beyond personnel and debt payments) where appropriate. For PB in Porto Alegre, however, all the PB decisions are entered into the budget. Evidence demonstrates that the executive spent all available discretionary funds on the projects selected by the participants.

REFERENCES

Abers, Rebecca. 1998. From Clientelism to Cooperation: Local Government, Participatory Policy, and Civic Organizing in Porto Alegre, Brazil. *Politics and Society* 26 (October): 511–37.
———. 2001. *Inventing Local Democracy. Grassroots Politics in Brazil*, Boulder: Westview Press.
Alvarez, Sonia E., Evelina Dagnino, and Arturo Escobar. 1998a. Introduction: The Cultural and the Political in Latin American Social Movements. In Alvarez et al. 1998b. 1–29.
Alvarez, Sonia E., Evelina Dagnino, and Arturo Escobar, eds. 1998b. *Cultures of Politics/Politics of Cultures: Re-visioning Latin American Social Movements*. Boulder: Westview Press.
Avritzer, Leonardo. 2002a. *Democracy and the Public Space in Latin America*. Princeton: Princeton University Press.
———. 2002b. O orçamento participativo: as experiências de Porto Alegre e Belo Horizonte. In *Sociedade civil e espaça público*, ed., Evelina Dagnino. São Paulo: Cortez. 17–46.
Baierle, Sergio Gregorio. 1998. The Explosion of Experience: The Emergence of a New Ethical-Political Principle in Popular Movements in Porto Alegre, Brazil. In Alvarez et al. 1998b. 118–38.
Baiocchi, Gianpaolo. 2001. Participation, Activism, and Politics: The Porto Alegre Experiment and Deliberative Democratic Theory. *Politics and Society* 29 (January): 43–72.
Couto, Claudio Gonçalves. 1995. *O desafio de ser governo: o PT na prefeitura de São Paulo (1988–1992)*. Rio de Janeiro: Paz e Terra.
Couto, Claudio Gonçalves, and Fernando Luiz Abrúcio. 1995. Governando a cidade? A força e a fraqueza da câmara municipal. *São Paulo em Perspectiva* 9, 2: 57–65.
Dagnino, Evelina. 1994. *Os anos 90: política e sociedade no Brasil*. São Paulo: Brasilense.
———. 1998. Culture, Citizenship, and Democracy: Changing Discourse and Practices of the Latin American Left. In Alvarez et al. 1998b. 33–63.

Diniz, Eli. 1982. *Voto e máquina política: patronagem e clientelismo no Rio de Janeiro.* Rio de Janeiro: Paz e Terra.

Doimo, Ana Maria. 1995. A vez e a voz do popular: movimentos sociais e participação pós-70. Rio de Janeiro: ANPOCS.

Erundina, Luiza. 1990. Sem medo de ser governo. *Teoria e Debate* 11, 3: 13–15.

Fedozzi, Luciano. 1998. *Orçamento participativo: reflexões sobre a experiência de Porto Alegre.* Porto Alegre: Tomo Editorial.

Fung, Archon, and Erik Olin Wright. 2001. Deepening Democracy: Innovations in Empowered Participatory Governance. *Politics and Society* 29 (January): 5–41.

García Canclini, Néstor. 1995. *Hybrid Cultures: Strategies for Entering and Leaving Modernity.* Minneapolis: University of Minnesota Press.

Genro, Tarso. 1995. Reforma do estado e democratização do poder local. In *Poder local, participação popular, construção da cidadania,* ed. René Villas-Boas and Vera Telles. São Paulo: Fórum Nacional de Participação Popular nas Administrações Municipais. 19–27.

Hochstetler, Kathryn. 2000. Democratizing Pressures from Below? Social Movements in the New Brazilian Democracy. In *Democratic Brazil: Actors, Institutions, and Processes,* ed. Peter R. Kingstone and Timothy J. Power. Pittsburgh: University of Pittsburgh Press: 167–82.

Jacobi, Pedro. 1989. *Movimentos sociais e políticas públicas: demandas par saneamento básico e saúde.* São Paulo, 1974–84. São Paulo: Cortez.

———. 2000. *Políticas sociais e ampliação da cidadania.* São Paulo: Fundação Getúlio Vargas.

Jacobi, Pedro, and Marco Antonio Carvalho Teixeira. 1996a. Orçamento participativo: co-responsabilidade na gestão das cidades. *São Paulo em Perspectiva* 10, 3: 119–28.

———. 1996b. Orçamento participativo: o caso de São Paulo (1989–1992), a luz das experiências de Porto Alegre e Belo Horizonte. Mimeograph. São Paulo: Centro de Estudos de Cultura Contemporânea.

Leal, Victor Nunes. 1997. *Coronelismo, enxada e voto: o município e o regime representativo no Brasil.* 3rd edition. São Paulo: Nova Fronteira.

Marquetti, Ademir. 2003. Democracia, equidade e eficiência, o caso do orçamento participativo em Porto Alegre. In *A inovação democrática no Brasil: o Orçamento participativo,* ed. Leonardo Avritzer and Zander Navarro. São Paulo: Cortez. 129–56.

Montero, Alfred P. 2000. Devolving Democracy? Political Decentralization and the New Brazilian Federalism. In *Democratic Brazil: Actors, Institutions, and Processes,* ed. Peter R. Kingstone and Timothy J. Power. Pittsburgh: University of Pittsburgh Press. 58–76.

Nylen, William R. 2002. Testing the Empowerment Thesis: The Participatory Budget in Belo Horizonte and Betim, Brazil. *Comparative Politics* 34 (January): 127–45.

O'Donnell, Guillermo. 1998. Horizontal Accountability in New Democracies. *Journal of Democracy* 9, 3: 112–26.

Przeworski, Adam, Susan C. Stokes, and Bernard Manin. 1999. *Democracy, Accountability, and Representation.* New York: Cambridge University Press.

Rodríguez, Victoria E. 1997. *Decentralization in Mexico: from Reforma Municipal to Solidaridad to Nuevo Federalismo.* Boulder: Westview Press.

Sales, Teresa. 1994. Raízes da desigualdade social na cultura política brasileira. *Revista Brasileira de Ciências Sociais* 25, 9: 26–37.

Santos, Boaventura de Sousa. 1998. Participatory Budgeting in Porto Alegre: Toward a Redistributive Democracy. *Politics and Society* 26, 4: 461–510.

Singer, Paul. 1996. *Um governo de esquerda para todos: Luiza Erundina na prefeitura de São Paulo (1989–1992).* São Paulo: Editora Brasiliense.

Smulovitz, Catalina, and Enrique Peruzzotti. 2000. Societal Accountability in Latin America. *Journal of Democracy* 11, 4: 147–58.

Soares, José Arlindo. 1998. *Os desafios de gestão municipal democrática: Recife.* Recife: Centro Josué de Castro.

Soler, Salvador. 1991. O PREZEIS: um processo de participação popular na formação da cidade. Master's thesis. Universidade Federal de Pernambuco.

Teixeira, Ana Claudia. 2003. Experiências de orçamento participativo no Brasil, 1997–2000. In *A inovação democrática no Brasil: o orçamento participativo,* ed. Leonardo Avritzer and Zander Navarro. São Paulo: Cortez. 189–216.

Wampler, Brian. 1999. Orçamento participativo: os paradoxos da participação e governo no Recife. *Cadernos de Estudos Sociais* 15, 2: 343–73.

———. 2000. Private Executives, Legislative Brokers, and Participatory Publics: Building Local Democracy in Brazil. Ph.D. diss. University of Texas.

Wampler, Brian, and Leonardo Avritzer. 2004. Participatory Publics: Civil Society and New Institutions in Democratic Brazil. *Comparative Politics* 36(3): 291–312.

Chapter 9

"For a Few Senators More"?
Negotiating Constitutional Changes
During Chile's Transition to Democracy

Fredrik Uggla

Of all the events that constituted the Chilean transition to democracy, few were as decisive for the character of the ensuing democratic regime as the negotiation of constitutional reforms in 1989. These reforms were important for two reasons. They did away with the most authoritarian elements of the constitution that the military regime had promulgated in 1980; and the negotiation process was the first instance of agreement between the opposition coalition Concertación de los Partidos por la Democracia (CPD) and the rightist supporters of the regime, Renovación Nacional (RN). In this sense, the negotiations preceded the politics of agreement that would come to characterize Chilean democracy in the 1990s.

While these were positive effects for the consolidation of the postauthoritarian system, other consequences of these negotiations were more problematic. This is because this process and the referendum that it led to also entailed the CPD's endorsement of a reformed version of Pinochet's 1980 Constitution, along with its remaining authoritarian elements. (In the words of one critical observer, the reform "whitewashed" the regime's constitution. Moulian 1997, 355). In perhaps no other recently democratized country has a set of institutions inherited from the previous regime come to impose such constraints on democratic politics as in Chile (Linz and Stepan 1996). The strong contingent of nonelected "designated" senators that have hampered representation in the upper chamber has probably been the most notable feature, but it is not the only one. Very strong presidential power (Siavelis 1997), autonomy from civilian control enjoyed by the military, and an electoral system that systematically favors runners-up (which, in most cases, has meant the political right), among other features, were also part of the institutional heritage of the Pinochet regime.

Thus, if the first effect of these negotiations was to consolidate the transition, their second effect puts in doubt whether this transition actually led to full democracy or not (Whitehead 2002). It has been noted that "the peculiarity of the Chilean redemocratization has been the consolidation of a mix of democratic institutions and authoritarian institutions, a product of the 54 reforms to the 1980 Constitution that were put to a plebiscite in 1989" (Riquelme 1999, 276).

In spite of its prominence, there have been few attempts to study the negotiation process that led to the maintenance of the 1980 Constitution, albeit in a reformed version.[1] Therefore it would seem worthwhile to ask the question, how did the CPD (which had, a few years earlier, called for the derogation of what it saw as an illegitimate creature of the dictatorship) end up endorsing a constitution that would severely constrain its opportunities in the regained democracy?

Another question also must be added: why does an outgoing authoritarian regime, still intact and with a constitution made to its measure, subject that charter to a process of negotiations and alterations? The Chilean transition to democracy was not brought about by any collapse or uprising. On the contrary, it followed the regime's timetable as set down in the constitution itself. What did the regime hope to gain by altering that institutional framework?

Although the question of the regime's motives is purely empirical, the issue of the CPD's calculations lends itself to a theoretical discussion with implications for political science and, in particular, for theories of democratic transitions. More concretely, this article juxtaposes two theoretical perspectives on what factors condition the outcomes of transitional negotiations. One view, akin to game-theoretical approaches, presents such processes as open-ended processes in which the relative distribution of power among the participants determines the outcome. Another theoretical perspective, closer to a "path-dependent" view of political development, critiques such a view as being too voluntaristic and disregarding contextual factors. In other words, the crucial difference between the two perspectives lies in the importance they attribute to formative moments, such as a transition to democracy, and in the relative autonomy they confer on the actors involved.

Given the actual outcome of the 1989 negotiations, it might be tempting to view the CPD as entirely constrained in its scope of action, which would support the latter perspective. But on the basis of the evidence to follow, it is possible to advance a picture with more nuances. On the one hand, it is obvious that the institutions set down by the Pinochet regime in the 1980 Constitution provided a general framework for the 1989 negotiations that the participants found it impossible to escape, a point that clearly indicates the weight of institutional factors. On the other hand, the following account indicates that the CPD did, until the end, debate the possibility of not agreeing to the regime's reform proposals, and that its final embrace owed much to the hope of enacting rapid future reforms in the constitution.

DEMOCRATIZATION AND CONSTITUTION MAKING

Constitutional negotiations and reforms often play a major role in democratic transitions. Andrea Bonime-Blanc, in her study of the Spanish transition, notes,

> . . . constitution making is at once the most varied and the most concentrated form of political activity during the transition. In it, political maneuvering, bargaining and negotiating take place and the political positions, agreements, and disagreements between groups and leaders come to the fore. How the constitution drafters handle these issues may tell us crucial things about the transition and the regime it leads up to. (Bonime-Blanc 1987, 13).

Theoretically, the institutional agreements and foundational pacts that make up such processes are often indicated as a way out of the central dilemma of a transition, which is how to get to democracy without stirring violent opposition to the process. The framework developed by scholars such as Guillermo O'Donnell and Philippe Schmitter (1986) and by Adam Przeworski (1988) centers on how these events are shaped by the interaction of four groups. On the regime side are hardliners and softliners; that is, those who advocate the necessity of negotiating with the democratic opposition and those who refuse such compromise. This division parallels a similar split on the side of the democratic opposition, between moderates (who could accept making a deal with representatives of the regime) and radicals (who press for all-out change without compromises). In cases of negotiated transitions, democratization follows from a compromise struck between softliners and moderates, leaving the maximalists on each side behind. Hence the importance of constitutional negotiations; it is then that the democratic opposition can choose to give guarantees to the old rulers sufficient to ensure that the softliners' strategy can prevail in the regime (Przeworski 1988, 1992). The establishment of democracy thus hinges on the willingness of the democratic opposition to provide assurances to the regime's supporters.

This perspective, however, has not eluded criticism. Scholars working from a more structural perspective have denounced it as being too voluntaristic and disregarding the conditions in which such a negotiation takes place. Against the rational, calculating players freely interacting in "games of transition" (Przeworski 1992; see also Whitehead 2002), the opposing perspective contrasts the socioeconomic conditions and institutional legacies that, according to this view, shape the institutional outcome of the democratization process. As one of its exponents notes,

> Even in the midst of the tremendous uncertainty provoked by a regime transition, where constraints appear to be most relaxed and where a wide range of outcomes appear to be possible, the decisions made by various actors respond to and are conditioned by the types of socioeconomic structures and political institutions already present (Karl 1991, 170).

In other words, the transition is not the kind of open-ended formative moment depicted by the first theory, but instead is contingent on more fundamental and unalterable factors. This second view narrows the range of choices available to participants in the negotiating and constitution-making processes during a transition, and thus portrays these actors as relatively constrained in their preferences and calculations (see, for example, Haggard and Kaufman 1995, 5).

Of course, from the standpoint of the individual participant, all social interactions include constraints and limitations; processes of negotiation especially so. Authors such as Przeworski do not deny this. Where the two perspectives differ, however, is in the nature of the constraints. In Przeworski's view, the outcome of the process depends on "whether the relation of forces is known" and "whether this relation is uneven or balanced" (1991, 81). In other words, the final result can be deduced from the distribution of power between the actors involved. But against this view, critics such as Karl posit the importance of factors beyond the participants that preclude or favor certain outcomes. If the first view comes closer to game-theoretical perspectives, this second view can be said to be closer to a "path-dependent" approach.

The two perspectives also differ in the relative weights they assign to the transition as a potentially formative moment of political importance. Whereas the former perspective tends to see the transitional negotiations as fundamental for the character of the ensuing regime, exponents of the latter perspective usually view the transition as an event that, however important, cannot actually change much in the resultant regime, because existing institutions impose severe limitations on the opportunities for actors in the transition. (As Paul A. Davies has noted, path dependency basically amounts to the simple idea that "one damn thing follows another" once an institution has been set up. 1985, 332.) Typically, underlying explanatory factors or the general mode of transition itself are portrayed as more important in determining the character of the following regime than choices made during transitional negotiations (see, for example, Rueschemeyer et al. 1992; Karl 1991).

Obviously, the Chilean case gives particular reason for doubt regarding the possibilities open during a transition. More than any other democracy, Chile would remain characterized by the institutions inherited from the previous regime, and it is tempting to see in this evidence of the constrained nature of the Chilean transition (compare

Linz and Stepan 1996).[2] That the CPD, even though it had just beaten the regime at the polls, acquiesced to giving the regime formidable guarantees would seem to indicate the importance of factors beyond the relative power of the two opposing factions. One hypothesis might be that the institutional setup established by the 1980 Constitution itself could have imposed constraints on the negotiations.

If this were so, it would reveal the limits of a view that portrays the actors as relatively unfettered in their institutional choices and the transition as a crucial moment of choice. If, on the other hand, the CPD's acquiescence was simply the result of an assessment of the distribution of power between the opposition and the regime, then the calculations that underlay such a choice would have to be specified in order to explain why the coalition agreed to such a thwarted outcome of the transition.

HISTORICAL CONTEXT: 1986–1988

The Chilean transition to democracy proceeded through two phases. A first period comprised the great mobilizations between 1983 and 1986. Indeed, that process looked quite like the textbook example of a transition to democracy (see O'Donnell and Schmitter 1986). The incipient liberalization of the regime in the early 1980s opened a political space that opposition groups (unions, organizations of *pobladores*, and so on) could use to mobilize against the regime. As mobilizations escalated with the monthly protest days, the first accords were reached between the democratic parties, which allowed them to present a united front in calling for democratization. Thus, in 1983, Socialists and Christian Democrats, united in the Alianza Democrática, called for the end of dictatorship and a constituent assembly; and two years later, Cardinal Juan Francisco Fresno brought together the two sectors with some elements of the right in the Acuerdo Nacional (Otano 1995). This is the stage at which the theoretical model would lead one to expect that the regime would crumble under the pressure of internal conflicts between hardliners and softliners, with the latter striking an eventual compromise with the democratic opposition to proceed to democratization.

This did not happen in Chile. Instead, the regime (in which power was so centralized in General Pinochet as to make any divisions between hard- and softliners relatively insignificant for the outcome) responded with increased repression of the popular mobilizations and paid scant attention to the opposition parties' clamor. By 1986, the opposition appeared defeated.

One potential opening for the democrats, however, was included in the constitution that the regime had enacted in 1980: a provision stating that a plebiscite should be held in 1988 on the continuation of Pinochet's rule. Since the mid-1980s, voices such as Patricio Aylwin's had been arguing that the opposition should try to make use of this provision to defeat the regime at the polls, if not in the streets (Otano 1995; Cumplido 1989). Yet this "juridico-political solution" was not without problems. The Constitution of 1980 embodied the military regime. It was stuffed with authoritarian elements, such as a powerful national security council dominated by the military commanders; a number of senators designated by that council and by other nonelected organs; and a strong constitutional court named by the outgoing regime. Playing by these rules could be seen as an endorsement of them, if not of the regime that had created it to serve as its legacy.

As it became increasingly clear that the regime would not be defeated in the streets, however, Aylwin's view won the argument, and in 1988 the opposition defeated the regime in the referendum. The road to democracy lay open, but among the primary obstacles on the way was the constitution itself.

THE REGIME'S CONSTITUTION

The constitution that the military enacted in 1980 contained the provisions that would establish military rule until at least 1990, along with rules designed to ensure that any future democracy would not escape a narrow set of limits and constraints. Pinochet therefore instructed the framers of the constitution that "its conception of the State and of the exercise of sovereignty should protect the Nation from another Marxist–Leninist infiltration of the governing apparatus and the social fabric, and also suppress the dema-gogic vices which have become prevalent in the last decades."

These demands were met in the constitution. For instance, the role of the president of the republic was substantially strengthened with relation to the legislature. The president would have the ability to dissolve the lower chamber and to exercise important preroga-tives in the areas of economic and social policy. The upper chamber of the legislature would be composed partly (9 out of 35) of senators named by institutions, such as the armed forces and the Supreme Court. The constitutional court would have the ability to censure motions by legislators and thus force them out of office; it would also be able to outlaw organizations, parties, or even persons on the basis that they had "tended" toward totalitarian doctrines or merely "threatened the family."

The most formidable power, however, was given to the military. The constitution made it impossible to dismiss the commanders of the armed forces during their tenure of office. With the creation of a national security council (made up of representatives from the four branches of the armed forces, together with the president and two other civilians), the abstract idea of the military as guardians of national security attained a highly tangible form. This was spelled out in Article 96(b), which stated that the council would have the right "To express to any authority established by the constitution, its opinion regarding any fact, action, or matter which in its judgment gravely threatens the foundations of institutionality or which might affect national security." This was indeed a card that the military could play at any time in the future, if it believed that its interests were threatened.

Thus the 1980 Constitution served two purposes for the military regime. Its enactment (and the timetable for a return to democracy that it laid out) was the cornerstone of a general strategy to construct a basis of legitimacy for the regime (Huneeus 2000). The constitution could therefore be said to manifest the regime's view of itself as a legitimate government governing according to a rule of law (see Barros 2002). The constitution also contained the legacy the regime wished to bestow on the future democracy. In that respect it was characterized by the wish of "binding the future out of fear of the past" (Barros 2002, 226), because it was designed to ensure that the precoup experience could not be repeated. In the words of one of the regime's staunchest supporters, the constitution was "the primary juridical, political, and institutional product of the Pinochet regime" (Fernández 1997, 300).

FEARS AND STRATEGIES

On the verge of transition, the democratic opposition had to consider what to do about the constitution. Basically, two alternatives were present: to wait until after assuming power to reform the constitution (and then possibly write a completely new one) or to try to amend the constitution, even if only partially, before taking office (Zaldívar 1995; Viera-Gallo 1989). The second option was strengthened in that a constitutional reform was technically easier to effect before democracy returned, as the so-called "transitional articles" stipulated an easier procedure for amendment than the one that would apply after March 11, 1990 (Verdugo 1990).

The CPD expressed few reservations regarding its preferences in this regard. The coalition, even before the plebiscite, had proclaimed its willingness to ensure that "this transition should mean to agree with the armed forces [on] the terms of change that will lead to the full exercise of popular sovereignty without producing a vacuum either institutional or legal" (CPD 1988, 47). On the other hand, the CPD's proposal for constitutional amendment included far-reaching reforms, including the elimination of Article 8 (which outlawed Marxist thoughts and practices), the abolishment of the designated senators, the establishment of civilian control over the military, easier terms for amending the constitution, and stronger protection of human rights.

Soon after the 1988 referendum, leadership of the Ministry of the Interior passed to Carlos Cáceres, who, although he did not initially believe in constitutional reform, soon came to see it as a means to an end (Cáceres 1994).[3] His primary ends were to ensure that the transition was orderly and to avoid forcing the regime out of power ahead of the timetable. He also wanted to make certain that the constitution would not become an issue in the upcoming elections (Cáceres 1994). The idea of constitutional reforms was not totally embraced within the regime, however; among its opponents was the minister of justice, Hugo Rosende. As for Pinochet himself, the general appeared to vacillate throughout the transition process. Immediately after the 1988 plebiscite he had stated that the constitution could be "perfected" (Andrade 1991, 2). At the same time, he is said to have told Cáceres, as he held two fingers of his hand close together, "Minister, concerning all this with constitutional reforms, you have this much of a space" (Cáceres 1994).

To understand why the regime would even begin to consider amendments to its constitution, the question of the future of the charter has to be taken into account. Above all, the regime wanted to rule out the possibility of the constitution being dismantled in the future, and a referendum on a limited set of reforms backed by a broad consensus might actually preclude that possibility (Godoy 1994). This idea might explain the regime's constant refusal to consider reforms unless full consensuses were achieved. Therefore, while discussing matters of relatively minor importance, the regime was set on preserving some key institutions, such as the political role conceded to the military, military autonomy, and the designated senators.

There was also an important lapse in the original constitution. The requirements of substantial quorums and the condition that reforms had to be approved by two subsequent congresses made many of its chapters virtually unchangeable. But the 14th chapter, which established the process of amendment, could itself be amended with a simple legislative majority of 60 percent and presidential approval. This meant that the incoming civilian administration could choose to reform this chapter first and then move on to make whatever other changes it liked (Cavallo 1992). Obviously, this could constitute a way to unravel the entire constitution. The regime saw this as a dangerous mistake that had to be corrected (Cáceres 1994; Allamand 1999a, 180).[4]

Of course, the constitutionalists in the opposition had noticed this loophole too, and debated whether it presented a real opportunity to make future changes, and to avoid negotiations with the regime at this point. This strategy also carried its risks, however, as the military might then reply by convoking the National Security Council. This, in turn, would bring about a crisis and perhaps even a military intervention (Viera-Gallo 1989). "We had to choose between running the risk of planting the reforms with a low quorum and having a military intervention, [thereby] having a problem of instability at the very beginning of the government, or bringing the [negotiated] reforms to the maximum" (Cumplido 1994).

ALTERNATIVE PROPOSALS: OCTOBER–DECEMBER 1988

Immediately after the plebiscite, CPD launched a reform proposal that explicitly aimed at "fully restoring popular sovereignty" (Andrade 1991, 260). The most urgent reforms proposed dealt with the process for constitutional amendment and the composition of Congress. In addition, the coalition proposed to repeal Article 8, place the armed forces under presidential control, and add three civilian members to the national security council while diminishing its authority. No mention was made of diminishing presidential power, nor was the constitutional court discussed. In any case, such limitations mattered little to the regime, which saw in this proposal little less than an unacceptable full-scale dismantling of the constitution (Cáceres 1994).

At the beginning of December, the CPD suddenly received support from the RN for the idea of reforming the constitution when this party presented its own proposal. The RN's version, although it recognized the legitimacy of the constitution and even went so far as to describe it as "fundamentally democratic," replicated the CPD's demands with proposals that included modifying Article 8, establishing a proportional system of representation, abolishing the designated senators, adding two civilian members to the national security council, and facilitating the process of amendment (*El Mercurio* 1988).[5] In addition, and in contrast to the opposition coalition, the RN proposed to diminish the powers of the constitutional court and the president.

Apparently, the RN (which had supported Pinochet in the plebiscite and would, in principle, continue to do so in the future) had become convinced that the opposition would prevail, and had therefore begun to discuss possible reforms even before the October plebiscite (Amunátegui 1994). Furthermore, an RN source claims that the regime had been unaware of these initiatives, which would have spelled treason in its eyes (Amunátegui 1994).[6] If so, the regime's fears were heightened just before Christmas 1988, when the CPD and RN met to appoint a joint technical committee to study further reforms. According to Cáceres himself, the regime now began to fear that it would be left out of the process altogether (Cáceres 1994).

A SUMMER OF NEGOTIATIONS: DECEMBER 1988–APRIL 1989

The technical committee consisted of politicians and constitutionalists from both sides along with three independent members, in all a dozen persons. In spite of the stakes in play, it appears that work in the group went surprisingly smoothly. There were differences, however, most notably regarding Article 8, the election system, the future composition of the congress (that is, the future of the designated senators), and according to some members, the future political role of the military (Viera-Gallo 1994; Cea 1994; Cumplido 1994; Godoy 1994). In relation to the last point, one of the independent members would later recall, "In some way [the RN representatives] reflected the idea that, given the historical situation of the country, some kind of political intervention of the armed forces was inevitable and that it was necessary to preserve this within the institutional system. But this was never very explicit" (Godoy 1994).

In spite of such opinions, the CPD appears to have viewed the RN as a trustworthy partner in this enterprise (Correa 1994; Cumplido 1994). In this regard, it is possible that the previous experience of the Acuerdo Nacional probably weighed in as well, as parts of the RN (most notably the sectors around the party's second-in-command, Andrés Allamand) had been party to that agreement, which had included a far-reaching proposal for constitutional reform (Allamand 1999a). Still, it bears noting that the RN's stance on constitutional matters was never very clear, because the party was riddled with internal divisions over these questions. For now, though, the reformers held the upper hand. But even they shared with the more reluctant sectors and with the regime itself one motive for participating in these negotiations: to reform the constitution in order to preserve it and to make sure that the issue of constitutional reform would come off the political agenda (Amunátegui 1994; Allamand 1999a).

Even so, discussions in the committee proceeded rapidly and in an atmosphere relatively propitious for agreement. In this regard, it is important to note that the CPD's delegates seem to have acted with great caution; they viewed a reversion of the reform process as a real possibility. As one of the CPD members later remarked, if the reforms had been blocked, "anything could have happened" (Viera-Gallo 1994). Actually, as one of the independent members later noted, the CPD could possibly have gained more in the negotiations but "they would not, under any circumstance, risk the transition. In the end, the negotiations were ruled by fear" (Barros 1994).

Meanwhile, the regime had begun to harbor fears of its own. It clearly wanted to have a say in the process, and on March 11, 1989, Pinochet once again stated that the constitution could be "perfected" (the regime's pet phrase); he mentioned the possibility of softening Article 8, abolishing the president's right to dissolve the lower chamber, diminishing the powers of the executive during states of exception, and adding a civilian member to the National Security Council (*El Mercurio* 1989a). But, the general added, consensus on these issues would be a condition for reforms.

On April 5, though, the CPD and RN again appeared to bypass the regime when the technical committee presented its proposal for constitutional reform. Among the most important reforms were proposals to give international treaties ratified by Chile precedence over national law, to add two civilian members to the National Security Council and to turn it into a advisory body to the president, to shorten the terms of office of the military commanders to three years, to soften Article 8 so that only antidemocratic parties were proscribed, to abolish the right of the constitutional court to force members of congress out of office, to lower the quorums required for constitutional reform, and to establish a system of proportional representation for the entire congress (thereby abolishing the designated senators).[7]

The CPD had previously approved the entire package. The RN was more hesitant, but the party's political commission finally approved it two weeks later, albeit with some minor alterations (such as keeping ex-presidents as senators and keeping the electoral system outside the constitution). Thus, the proposal represented a broad political consensus on the issue of constitutional reform and a strong position from which to negotiate with the regime. Furthermore, RN's leader, Sergio Onofre Jarpa, remarked in an interview just before the proposal was presented, "Let it be clear: we will always support, now and in the future congress, the same ideas and the same constitutional proposals no matter who the president is" (Jarpa 1989). Thus it seemed that even if reform would not be accomplished at this time, the proposals would eventually be approved in the future democracy. And this was exactly the regime's foremost worry: reforms it could not control.

The proposal, moreover, included a number of propositions that were by themselves unacceptable to the regime, primarily those regarding the designated senators, the electoral system, and the National Security Council (Pérez de Arce 1994). Still, Cáceres held more meetings with Aylwin and Jarpa and was said to be working on a counterproposal from the regime. In late April he was reported to have discussed his proposals with Pinochet, and it seemed as if the general would accept limited reforms (*¿Qué Pasa?* 1989a).

END OF THE ROAD? APRIL–MAY 1989

So far the process had gone rather smoothly, and a final agreement must have appeared within reach. But in the last few days of April, everything seemed to be reversed when Pinochet suddenly told Cáceres that there would be no modifications to the constitution because he considered them "not appropriate" (Cáceres 1994; Cavallo 1992). Committed to the process of reform, the interior minister resigned the next day, followed by a large portion of the cabinet (Cáceres 1994; ¿Qué Pasa? 1989a). For the moderate sectors in the regime this must have appeared catastrophic; by the following day they had apparently managed to swing Pinochet's opinion, and Cáceres was back in office. The day after that he presented the regime's constitutional proposal.

Presented as "the conservation of a democracy whose institutions are not left to the grace of occasional majorities," the proposal included the repeal of Article 8, lowering the quorums for constitutional reforms (but keeping the need for them to be approved by two subsequent congresses), adding one civilian member to the National Security Council while slightly diminishing its authority, and diminishing the power of the president and the constitutional court in relation to the congress (El Mercurio 1989b). On the other hand, the proposal also increased the constitution's rigidity by raising the quorum for amending Chapter 14, thereby closing the 60 percent loophole.

The answer from the CPD came quickly. Apparently, the coalition had viewed Cáceres's fall from power with alarm, fearing that the whole process of transition might be at considerable risk if no reform was achieved (Correa 1994). Still, the CPD would not acquiesce to what it saw as an insufficient reform. On May 1, Ricardo Lagos, leader of the Partido por la Democracia (PPD), urged voters to reject these reforms in a future plebiscite (El Mercurio 1989c). At a meeting with the entire coalition, Francisco Cumplido from the Christian Democrats outlined the foremost objections to the proposal. Among these were that the electoral system would not be changed, that the designated senators would be kept, that the National Security Council would still be composed of civilians and military in equal portions, and that the constitutional amendment process would signify that "a strong consensual majority, such as the one that the agreement between RN and the CPD politically signifies, would be inhibited from making definite reforms . . . before 1995" (Hoy 1989).

Therefore the coalition declared on May 2 that it could not give its consent to the proposal, which was still unsatisfactory and even represented a retreat because it would make future reforms more difficult. Apparently, the CPD was confident that the RN's cautious opposition to the regime's proposal provided extra backing, and this made the CPD believe that it could get more out of the negotiations (Correa 1994). Two days later, however, such hopes received a severe blow, when Cáceres officially declared that because no consensus could be reached on the question, "no reform will be promoted" (El Mercurio 1989d).

The end of the reform process put the entire transition at risk because it threatened to bring about a much more confrontational political climate. Apparently both sides were surprised by the outcome. Cáceres never thought the opposition would flatly turn down his proposal, and the CPD did not think the regime would actually close the door on reform altogether (Cáceres 1994; Cumplido 1994).

As the regime seemed unwilling to continue the negotiations, the CPD tried to devise an alternative strategy based on the realization that any reforms would have to wait until the return of democracy (Cumplido 1994). According to one source, representatives from the coalition met with the two RN leaders, Allamand and Jarpa, and agreed to go ahead with the reforms anyway (Correa 1994). An RN source claims, however, that this promise to go ahead with reforms in the future was primarily designed to get the regime to return to the negotiating table, a view that is actually supported by the first source (Amunátegui 1994).) But for the reasons already discussed, the idea of postponing the reforms was not much favored in either camp.

"FOR A FEW SENATORS MORE": MAY 1989

With the process stalled, it was the RN that made the first move to get it started again. About a week after the interruption, the party presented a new proposal regarding the designated senators and the process of amendment. A couple of days later, the technical committee was once more called together to prepare a report on the regime's proposal. In its judgment, the committee accepted most of the regime's proposals but insisted on a few, such as the authority of the national security council, the process of amendment, guarantees for political pluralism, and a stronger position for international treaties (Andrade 1991, 298ff). No mention was made of the designated senators, however.

The negotiations were now drawing to a close. On May 16, Aylwin met with Cáceres, and the latter proposed to increase the number of elected senators, smooth the political proscription clauses, and make constitutional reform in some areas easier (Andrade 1991, 156f; *Analisis* 1989a; *¿Qué Pasa?* 1989b).[8] But the minister also seems to have demanded that all designated senators be kept and that the quorums for amendment be increased for certain areas (what one journalist called "the pillars of authoritarianism"— the armed forces, the National Security Council, and the constitutional court), where any constitutional reform would be postponed until three years into the democratic period. Furthermore, the regime flatly refused to back down from its demand that the law regulating promotions and retirements in the armed forces be elevated to the rank of organic constitutional law, ensuring the military a great deal of autonomy from civilian influence in the future. Apparently, this was among the most important points in the final negotiations (Correa 1994).

This proposal was fiercely debated among the opposition coalition and, according to one version, future president Lagos argued that accepting it would make the CPD appear to have sold out "for a few senators more" (*¿Qué Pasa?* 1989b; Cumplido 1994). He was not alone, though, as several opposition politicians harbored misgivings about the possible freezing of certain areas, the provisions regarding the National Security Council, and the retention of the designated senators (*¿Qué Pasa?* 1989b; Andrade 1991, 160). Most of the CPD politicians, however, had already come to accept the idea of making a negotiated (and therefore gradual) reform, and the discussion now centered on technicalities (Cumplido 1994).[9] According to press reports, the RN, meanwhile, tried to persuade the coalition to accept, arguing that the more complicated themes could wait until further reforms could be enacted after the return of democracy (*Análisis* 1989a).

The endgame was played out in at least three different forums: within the CPD; in a new joint technical committee formed by the CPD, the RN, and the government; and among Jarpa, Aylwin, and Cáceres. Regarding the themes for discussion, it appears that what now occurred was basically logrolling between the parties. The regime agreed to diminish the authority of the National Security Council in return for giving it equal civilian and military representation, and the CPD agreed to retain the designated senators in return for an increase in the number of elected ones. In addition, the opposition accepted the organic constitutional law of the armed forces (assuring them of their future autonomy), while the regime accepted giving international treaties precedence over national law.

The final negotiations took place within the CPD. Some factions wanted to try to get more out of the negotiations or, according to one source, still considered the idea of using the low quorum for amending Chapter 14 in order to force through future reforms (Cumplido 1994). Aylwin tried to convince those groups that the final point had been reached, that the regime would not concede anything more, and that further delays could put the whole process at risk (*Análisis* 1989b). The Christian Democrats and the Radicals had already opted to accept the bid and, after heavy internal debate, Aylwin could, on May 31, finally tell Cáceres that the CPD gave the green light to the reform proposal (Andrade 1991, 1640). That same night, Pinochet appeared on television to present the agreement in a speech packed with references to God, the fatherland, national security, and whatever he himself thought convenient (*El Mercurio* 1989e).

Eventually, 54 reforms were subjected to a referendum in late July. In addition to those proposed in late April, the concerted agreement included retention of the nine designated senators but with an increase in the number of elected ones (from 26 to 38), Guarantees for political pluralism were introduced. The process of constitutional amendment was simplified to require qualified majorities of 60 percent for all matters except for certain chapters (most prominently the ones regulating the constitutional court, the armed forces, the national security council, and the amendment process in Chapter 14), for which a two-thirds majority would be necessary. The laws regulating the armed forces were elevated to the rank of "organic constitutional law." Article 8 was fully eliminated (although new provisions were added elsewhere against antidemocratic forces), and Article 5 was rewritten to give stronger guarantees to human rights and international treaties. Authority of the National Security Council was restricted in line with CPD proposals.

In its public statements before the eventual plebiscite, the CPD stressed that these changes were far from enough but that the coalition embraced them nevertheless as an important step forward (*El Mercurio* 1989f; Andrade 1991, 167ff). Indeed, with the exception of the Communists, who argued that the constitution "is and will continue to be illegitimate" (quoted in Andrade 1991, 182), some minor parties, and odd characters on the right, all portions of the political spectrum embraced the reforms, and in the end these were approved by 86 percent of the voters.[10]

GAINS AND LOSSES

The Chilean case appears to correspond rather well to the general concepts employed by theories about constitution making as a crucial part of a process of democratization. An institutional agreement was found that provided the regime with a number of political guarantees, and it was the result of agreement between the moderates or softliners on each side. Conversely, maximalists (the Communists and the "bunker sector" in the regime) on both sides lost out in the process.

The agreement gave all parties involved something of what they wanted. The CPD managed to do away with some of the most blatantly authoritarian provisions of the constitution. The coalition would go on to govern Chile in a way that would probably have been impossible if the CPD had tried to force through a major constitutional reform after the transition. The RN, for its part, showed that it was an actor to reckon with; it would participate in more negotiations and deals with the CPD after the transition to democracy. It clearly played a key role in the negotiations: on the one hand, it acted together with the opposition to put the regime under pressure; on the other hand, it defended parts of the constitution and acted as a moderating element in the process of reform.

But the regime also managed to extract favors from the agreement. Not only did it maintain some of its pet provisions, it also definitively closed the loophole in Chapter 14. Moreover, it made sure that the 1980 Constitution—albeit reformed—was still in force. It may be tempting to regard the last point as little more than a formality, but that would overlook Pinochet's constant demand that the constitution as such had to stay in place and that any reform would primarily serve to ensure that the constitution would continue in force. As one source from within the regime remarked, the reforms ensured that "the specter of large-scale modifications [being introduced] after the military government had left power had gone away" (Ballerino 1994). Even if the constitution was amended in the process, the reforms also served to ensure the regime's primary objective; namely, that this constitutional legacy would remain (compare Angell 2002). As Cáceres stated in reference to the overwhelming approval in the plebiscite, this meant "the consolidation of the Fundamental Charter from 1980" (quoted in Andrade 1991, 192).[11]

THE PROBLEM WITH GUARANTEES

Actually, Cáceres's remark would prove more farsighted than most people would have believed at that time. The first signs of this appeared soon after the CPD had given its consent to the reforms, as it became clear that RN would not make good on the agreements to promote further amendments (Cumplido 2002; Correa 1994). One of the CPD's chief politicians would later recall that as the coalition met with RN to discuss how to go about making the remaining reforms, the RN strongman, Jarpa, refused to attend; "then we realized that Jarpa had made agreements with the military not to go beyond [the 54 amendments]" (Correa 1994).[12] The same source also stresses that if Jarpa had not done so, the regime would not have lent its agreement to the reforms, either.

Thus, the further reforms the CPD had constantly stressed as a reason for accepting those 54 amendments failed to materialize for the next 15 years. In 1992, the government did introduce two packages of additional constitutional reforms in Congress, but apparently did so primarily to make the opposition pay the political price of resisting them (Cumplido 2002). Thus, among other themes, these reforms included agreements from 1989, such as eliminating the designated senators, adding the president of the lower chamber to the National Security Council, and establishing a proportional election system (Boeninger 1997; for the actual text of the proposals see Aylwin 1992a, b).

But the RN refused to lend its agreement to any of these reforms and declared that it now considered them "inconvenient, unnecessary, and inopportune" (Galilea 1992). Regarding the agreements of 1989, the RN deputies mostly evaded references to these in the debate in favor of more technical criticism of the proposals. Without support from the center-right, neither these proposals nor the ones that followed would succeed. A dozen years after Pinochet left the presidential palace, the first minister of justice of the regained democracy would still complain, "if one believes that the transition ends with an entirely democratic constitution, we are still in transition. . . . There is yet no full democracy. What we have now is the least bad [alternative]" (Cumplido 2002).[13] Not until an agreement between government and opposition was struck in late 2004 would the last of these constitutional curbs on Chilean democracy be dissolved.

DID THE CPD HAVE A CHOICE?

Because the 1980 Constitution continued to cast its shadow over politics in Chile, the constitutional negotiations of 1989 might be dismissed as relatively insignificant talks with no real power to change the conditions that ultimately shaped the transition. This would, in turn, be consistent with the criticism that has been levied against the whole theory of pactmaking and its importance during transitions: that it is too voluntaristic and dismissive of the crucial underlying factors that shape the outcome of a transition (see, for example, Haggard and Kaufman 1995).

Indeed, the account presented here seems to vindicate such a critique in that it shows how one institutional factor in particular, the very constitution itself, was a crucial element in the negotiations. In contrast to the situation during most transitions, the regime's constitution was not simply a dead letter.[14] Instead, the foregoing account has shown how both government and opposition at this time were playing strictly by the rules laid down in the constitution, and how the constitution formed the basis for all discussions. Although this arrangement primarily favored the regime—whose creation it was—certain elements also benefited the CPD, primarily the low quorum required to reform the process of amendment, which the regime was very anxious to augment.

Theoretically, this point confirms the observation that contextual factors shape outcomes even during the fluid political situation of a transition. In particular, it shows how a previously created institution serves as a master frame that later participants find impossible to escape from. Indeed, not even the regime thought it possible simply to decree an increase in the quorum for reforming Chapter 14. Reform, whether it came from the regime or the opposition, would have to be done by the book, and the relevant text in this regard was the constitution itself.

On the other hand, this was far from the only determinant in the process. The relationship among the participants was crucial in shaping the outcome within the general limits set by the constitution. In particular, it is clear that all sides feared each other's power. The regime was alarmed about the possibility that a future democratic government would unravel the entire constitution, and the opposition feared a possible reversal of the entire democratization process. In these circumstances, an agreement on limited reforms to the constitution seemed better for both sides.

Such reasoning lends itself better to Przeworski's game-theoretical model. Furthermore, a closer consideration of the CPD's motives for striking an agreement clearly indicates that the coalition, in spite of the limitations imposed by the regime's power and its constitution, did consider alternatives to the final compromise. After all, it refused to lend its support to the regime's first reform proposal, and up to the end, the members of the coalition discussed the possibility of forcing through an overall constitutional revision after transition as an alternative to limited negotiated reforms. Moreover, proposals and institutional alternatives were fiercely and freely debated within the coalition. Granted that the coalition believed that it actually had an alternative, however, the question is, what calculations did the CPD make to choose an outcome in which such formidable guarantees were offered to the regime?

It is evident that the opposition coalition would not under any circumstances put the transition at risk, and it is fully possible that a number of CPD politicians understood that lasting guarantees would be the price for an orderly return to democracy. In that sense, it is clear that the opposition's political calculations were strongly influenced by the fear of a reversal in the transition.

Still, this was not presented as the main rationale for the reforms at the time. In its statements before the plebiscite, the CPD repeatedly stressed that this vote was only a first step toward further reforms (*El Mercurio* 1989e, f). In a telling remark that would later seem highly ironic, one leading CPD official stated, "We gave the green light to the agreement because it is a step toward being able to amend the constitution with two-thirds next year and not waiting ten years, as was initially stated" (Correa 1989). Furthermore, one of the primary reasons the CPD turned down the regime's first bid for reform was exactly that it would make the constitution much too rigid (Andrade 1991, 124). Making it possible to reform the constitution without having to wait for a second congress to sit was one of the CPD's foremost objectives all along (Cumplido 1994; *La Epoca* 1989). Thus it appears that the acceptance of these guarantees was conditioned on a calculation that they would not last for as long as they did.

To make further reforms to the Chilean constitution, however, the CPD would have needed either to gain a large majority in the upcoming elections or to rely on the votes of the future RN legislators. The question is therefore whether the opposition coalition believed that it had assurances that any of these conditions would be fulfilled, and it appears that this was the case. As one of the protagonists in this process would later complain,

> Look, we thought two things. First, that we would do better in the election, that we would get a sufficiently large majority to do the reforms practically by ourselves, wouldn't we? And that did not happen. And, second, there was a tradition among the Chilean political parties of fulfilling political agreements. . . . We thought about those two aspects and in both we were wrong. There is no doubt about it. We were wrong (Cumplido 2002).

Expressed differently, the CPD believed that the relation of power would change in the proximate future. The coalition expected either to do well in the upcoming elections or to count on the support of the RN.[15] In both cases it would come to possess a parliamentary majority sufficient to realize the constitutional reform that the regime denied it at this point. Such considerations were clearly influenced more by assessments of the political power of the participants than by the weight of any structural or institutional factor.

Hence, even if the account above shows the importance of a factor such as the constitution itself, it also demonstrates that there was nothing inevitable about the outcome of the process. At the time, moreover, the CPD did not appear resigned to maintaining the authoritarian elements of the constitution for very long. One could even speculate that if the opposition politicians in the CPD had not trusted their own electoral attractiveness and the RN as much as they did, they might have refused to accept the final reforms as well, and then Chile would have had a very different transition.[16]

CONCLUSIONS

Since democracy returned to Chile in 1990, scholarly views on the Chilean transition have undergone a notable shift (Joignant and Menéndez-Carrión 1999). In the mid-1990s, Chile was commonly seen as a country that had produced a model transition and had managed to return to a high degree of political normalcy. Since then, the description has become considerably bleaker. Various authors have come to point out both the shortcomings of the Chilean transition and the restricted character of politics that followed it. Although it is beyond the scope of this article to enter that debate, the issue has at least distinguished with more clarity how one of the core elements of Chilean democracy came about.

This chapter has indicated the importance of one particular institutional factor—the Constitution of 1980—to the outcome. The constitutional negotiations of 1989 did not take place in a vacuum but were influenced by the existing institutions provided in the regime's constitution. At the same time, developments and choices within that institutional framework were the result of an interaction in which the relative political power of each side mattered greatly. A proper understanding of the transitional process therefore has to include both sets of factors.

In the end, the question arises as to what possibilities the democratic opposition actually had to alter the constitutional framework imposed by the regime. The account shows that such opportunities were indeed slim. Nevertheless, the CPD's acceptance of the reformed constitution was not a foregone conclusion. The coalition appeared quite ready to consider other alternatives, and in the end its acquiescence to the final agreement appears to have been influenced by its hope that further reforms were imminent once democracy returned.

Thus, in spite of the importance of an institutional factor such as the 1980 Constitution for the outcome of the transitional negotiations (and its continued importance under democracy), this account should perhaps not lead to a overdeterministic view in which the transitional negotiations become a relatively unimportant station along the road from dictatorship to democracy. Instead, the description presented here indicates how choices and calculations made during such an event, temporary and provisional as they may have seemed at the time, may leave a lasting mark on the resultant democracy.

NOTES

Material for this chapter was gathered as the author benefited from a Minor Field Study grant from the Swedish International Development Cooperation Agency. The paper was written during a postdoctoral scholarship from the Swedish Foundation for International Cooperation in Research and Higher Education (STINT). The author would like to express his gratitude to Tomás Moulian, Alejandro San Francisco, Felipe Agüero, and three anonymous reviewers for their suggestions and remarks on this piece. Of course, faults and shortcomings are entirely his own responsibility.

1 The best study regarding this process is by Carlos Andrade (1991), who was a member of the CPD's team of negotiators. This study, however, is solely descriptive, and does not attempt to explain the different positions of the involved parties or why the agreement was reached. The same can be said of another valuable study that treats these reforms, that of Francisco Geisse and José Antonio Ramírez Arrayes (1989). The work of Ascanio Cavallo (1992) also gives an extremely interesting and insightful journalistic account of the process and the context in which it took place. In English, one article has been published (Ensalaco 1994), but it is largely limited to a presentation of the changes made and how they relate to the concept of democracy in general. Robert Barros (2002) does not particularly focus on these negotiations in his exhaustive and valuable recent study of the role of the 1980 Constitution during the dictatorship. He does, however, discuss this theme on pages 308–10. With relation to all these works—all of which have been indispensable for this work—the aim is not to contradict them, but rather to attempt to treat the theme from a slightly different perspective, one that may add to our understanding of the process.

2 The contrast with cases such as South Africa and Poland is stark. In those countries, formidable guarantees were also conferred to the regimes, but only temporarily. In South Africa, the "sunset clauses" and constitutional guarantees would last only until 1999 at the latest, and in Poland the favored status of the Communists would end four years after the transition, when completely free elections would be held (Ebrahim 1998; Garton Ash 1990).

3 One should note that ten years earlier, during the elaboration of the constitution, Caceres, then a member of the consultative Consejo de Estado, had supported a minority position of a rather authoritarian inspiration, basically denying popular suffrage and sovereignty as principles of value (Huneeus 2000). According to both Cáceres himself and a close collaborator, however, he had changed position since then (Pérez de Arce 1994).

4 Andrés Allamand was RN general secretary at this time and would go on to become president of the party after the transition. In his autobiography he stresses the importance for these negotiations of this "incredible error" in the original constitution (Allamand 1999a).

5 Contrary to common belief, the electoral system has never formed part of the 1980 Constitution but is regulated in a special law. The RN's proposal (along with the later suggestions in this regard) was based on the premise that it should be included, which ultimately did not happen.

The 1925 Constitution, which was in force until the 1973 military coup, included a provision in its Article 25 stating that the electoral system should result in an "effective proportionality" (Constitutión político, de la República de Chile [1966]).

6 The same point is supported by Cáceres (1994), although he claims that he may have met RN leader Allamand or Jarpa to discuss the theme in general terms after assuming his post. In his autobiography, Allamand (1999a, 174) claims to have presented this proposal to Caceres before it became public exactly in order not to be seen as going behind the regime's back.

7 This last point constituted the only visible discord on the committee, as the RN wanted to include ex-presidents as members of the senate.

8 Cáceres himself would later mention the first two of these points, together with the status of international treaties, as especially important themes in these discussions (1994).

9 At the same time, the CPD was trying to bring in the Communist Party as an observer at the talks, an offer that was turned down. As it seemed, the primary reason for the CPD's eagerness in this regard was to avoid future criticism of having sold out to the regime and to defuse the possibility of the Communists' winning over broader parts of the left with their approach of no surrender (APSI 1989; Correa 1994; Inzunza 1994).

10 According to anecdotal evidence, Pinochet himself was not very content with the reforms. At a reception held for the regime's team of negotiators immediately after he had signed the final draft of reforms, the dictator entered and, pointing at them, yelled, "You are the ones responsible for all this!" (Pérez de Arce 1994). For a more eloquent criticism of the reforms from within the regime, see Fernández 1997.

11 One could, of course, question whether this actually matters. Was the 1980 Constitution principally important as a symbol or for the concrete guarantees it would impose on Chilean democracy (the secure tenure of the commanders of the armed forces, the designated senators, and so forth)? The correct answer is probably both, but the tacit endorsement of the constitution also made substantial reforms harder to achieve. Indeed, as one former politician from the RN remarked, as the problem of legitimacy was solved and all democratic forces agreed to and voted in favor of the reforms, the Chilean political process has [since then] developed under the umbrella of an institutional framework that, although it is highly controversial in some aspects, everybody recognizes and respects (Allamand 1999b). From then on, the CPD did indeed embrace the reformed constitution, and this general endorsement of the charter and its peculiarities has possibility contributed to the difficulties in forcing through further reforms.

12 There is some confusion as to when such a meeting would have occurred. According to Correa (1994), it apparently took place shortly after the plebiscite. Much later, however, Cumplido (2002) would tell how he and Edgardo Boeninger (Ministro Secretario General de la Presidencia at the time) were sent to discuss the theme with RN after Aylwin's government had already assumed power. Of course, this may refer to two separate meetings. In his autobiography, Andrés Allamand (1999a, 185ff) supports Correa's description when he recounts how, instead of signing a formal agreement regarding future reforms, representatives from RN and the CPD were supposed to celebrate their accord with a private dinner on June 7, 1989, at which Jarpa ominously failed to turn up.

13 Furthermore, the 1980 Constitution's very persistence still in force has made it harder to exorcise other ghosts from that time, most notably the human rights violations.

14 The same point has actually been made for the Chilean dictatorship in general. See Barros 2002.

15 In relation to the plebiscite, one leading RN politician had actually stated that although no formal pact existed on further reforms, the parts of the RN-CPD compromise that had not been included at this stage could well be implemented in the future (declarations by Carlos Reymond, quoted in Andrade 1991, 192). Similarly, in his autobiography, Allamand (1999a, 186) is very clear that he personally made promises to the CPD that the RN would proceed with reforms after the transition.

16 In discussing this possibility, one should keep in mind that the CPD did not consist solely of consensus seekers such as Patricio Aylwin but also of more radical sectors, and that the latter were by no means unimportant at that time.

REFERENCES

Allamand, Andrés. 1999a. *La travesía del desierto*. Santiago: Aguilar.

——. 1999b. Las paradojas de un legado. In *El modela Chileno: democracia y desarrollo en los noventa*, eds. Paul Drake and Ivan Jaksic. Santiago: LOM Ediciones. 169–90.

Amunátegui, Miguel Luis. 1994. Former Member (RN), intraparty joint technical committee to discuss constitutional reforms. Author interview. Santiago, January 20.

Análisis (Santiago). 1989a. No. 281, May 29.

——. 1989b. No. 282, June 5.

Andrade, Carlos. 1991. *Reforma de la constitutión política de la República de Chile de 1980*. Santiago: Editorial Jurídica de Chile.

Angell, Alan. 2002. The Pinochet Factor in Chilean Politics. Bicentenario: *Revista de Historia de Chile y América* 1: 53–73.

APSI (Santiago). 1989. No. 307, June 5–11.

Aylwin, Patricio. 1992a. Mensaje de S.E. el Presidente de la República: proyecto de reforma constitucional en material electoral. Cámara de Diputados, legislatura 324a ordinaria, sesión 6:a, June 9.

——. 1992b. Mensaje de S.E. el Presidente de la República que modifica diversas disposiciones de la constitución política. Cámara de Diputados, legislatura 324a ordinaria), sesión 2:a, June 2.

Ballerino, Jorge. 1994. Former Secretary of the Government. Author interview. Santiago, April 8.

Barros, Enrique. 1994. Former Member (independent) of the technical committee. Author interview. Santiago, January 21.

Barros, Robert J. 2002. *Constitutionalism and Dictatorship: Pinochet, the Junta, and the 1980 Constitution*. Cambridge: Cambridge University Press.

Boeninger, Edgardo. 1997. *Democracia en Chile: lecciones para la gobernabilidad*. Santiago: Andrés Bello.

Bonime-Blanc, Andrea. 1987. *Spain's Transition to Democracy: The Politics of Constitution-making*. Boulder: Westview Press.

Cáceres, Carlos. 1994. Former Minister of the Interior. Author interview. Santiago, April 13.

Cavallo, Ascanio. 1992. *Los hombres de la transición*. Santiago: Andrés Bello.

Cea, José Luis. 1994. Former Member (independent) of the technical committee. Author interview. Santiago, January 12.

Concertación de los Partidos por la Democracia (CPD). 1988. Compromiso con la futura democracia. *Política y Espíritu* (Santiago), September: 43–47.

Constitución política de la República de Chile. 1925 [1966]. Santiago: Editorial Jurídica de Chile.

Correa, Enrique. 1994. Former Executive Secretary, CPD. Author interview. Santiago, March 31.

Correa, Germán. 1989. Declarations. *APSI* no. 307 (June 5–11).

Cumplido, Francisco. 1989. Presentation. In Geisse and Ramírez Arrayes 1989. Santiago: ChileAmerica/CESOC. 9–10.

——. 1994. Former Member (CPD) of the technical committee; Minister of Justice. Author interview. Santiago, April 14.

——. 2002. Author interview. Santiago, March 19.

Davies, Paul A. 1985. Clio and the Economics of QWERTY. *American Economic Review* 75: 332–37.

Ebrahim, Hassen. 1998. *The Soul of a Nation: Constitution-making in South Africa*. Cape Town: Oxford University Press.

Ensalaco, Mark. 1994. In with the New, Out with the Old? The Democratising Impact of Constitutional Reform in Chile. *Journal of Latin American Studies* 26, 2 (May): 409–29.

La Epoca (Santiago). 1989. June 2.

Fernández, Sergio. 1997. *Mi lucha por la democracia*. Santiago: Los Andes.

Galilea, Pablo. 1992. Declaraciones. Cámara de Diputados, legislatura 325a extrordinaria, session 7:a, October 20: 484.

Garton Ash, Timothy. 1990. *Folket, del ar vi* [We, the people]. Stockholm: Bonnier. Translation of *We the People: The Revolution of '89 Witnessed in Warsaw, Budapest, Berlin and Prague*. Cambridge: Granta.

Geisse, Francisco, and José Antonio Ramírez Arrayes. 1989. *La reforma constitutional.* Santiago: ChileAmerica/CESOC.

Godoy, Oscar. 1994. Former Member (independent) of the technical committee. Author interview. Santiago, January 18.

Haggard, Stephan, and Robert R. Kaufman. 1995. *The Political Economy of Democratic Transitions.* Princeton: Princeton University Press.

Hoy (Santiago). 1989. No. 616, May 8–14.

Huneeus, Carlos. 2000. *El régimen de Pinochet.* Santiago: Sudamericana.

Inzunza, Jorge. 1994. Member, Political Committee, Chilean Communist Party. Author interview. Santiago, April 8.

Jarpa, Sergio Onofre. 1989. Interview. *APSI* No. 298, April 3–9.

Joignant, Alfredo, and Amparo Menéndez-Carrión. 1999. De la "democracia de los acuerdos" a los dilemas de la polis: ¿transición incompleta o ciudadanía pendiente? In *La caja de Pandora: el retorno de la transición chilena,* ed. Menéndez-Carrión and Joignant. Santiago: Planeta. 13–48.

Karl, Terri Lynn. 1991. Dilemmas of Democratization in Latin America. In *Comparative Political Dynamics: Global Research Perspectives,* ed. Dankwart A. Rustow and Kenneth Paul Erickson. New York: Harper Collins. 163–91.

Linz, Juan J., and Alfred Stepan. 1996. *Problems of Democratic Transition and Consolidation: Southern Europe, South America, and Post-Communist Europe.* Baltimore: Johns Hopkins University Press.

El Mercurio [Santiago]. 1988. December 2.

———. 1989a. March 12.

———. 1989b. April 29.

———. 1989c. May 2.

———. 1989d. May 4.

———. 1989e. June 1.

———. 1989f. June 2.

Moulian, Tomás. 1997. *Chile actual: anatomía de un mito.* Santiago: LOM.

O'Donnell, Guillermo, and Philippe C. Schmitter. 1986. *Transitions from Authoritarian Rule: Tentative Conclusions About Uncertain Democracies.* Baltimore: Johns Hopkins University Press.

Otano, Rafael. 1995. *Crónica de la transición.* Santiago: Planeta.

Pérez de Arce, Hermógenes. 1994. Former Member, Advisory Committee to the Secretary of the Interior. Author interview. Santiago, March 17.

Przeworski, Adam. 1988. Democracy as a Contingent Outcome of Conflicts. In *Constitutionalism and Democracy,* ed. Jon Elster and Rune Slagstad. Cambridge: Cambridge University Press. 59–80.

———. 1991. *Democracy and the Market.* Cambridge: Cambridge University Press.

———. 1992. The Games of Transition. In *Issues in Democratic Consolidation: The New South American Democracies in Comparative Perspective,* ed. Scott Mainwaring, Guillermo O'Donnell, and J. Samuel Valenzuela. Notre Dame: University of Notre Dame Press. 105–52.

¿Qué Pasa? (Santiago). 1989a. No. 943, May 4.

———. 1989b. No. 948, June 8.

Riquelme Segovia, Alfredo. 1999. ¿Quiénes y por qué "no están ni ahí"? Marginación y/o automarginación en la democracia transicional. Chile. 1988–1997. In *El modela Chileno: democracia y desarrollo en los noventa,* ed. Paul Drake and Iván Jaksic. Santiago: LOM Ediciones. 261–79.

Rueschemeyer, Dietrich, Evelyne Huber Stephens, and John D. Stephens. 1992. *Capitalist Development and Democracy.* Cambridge: Polity Press.

Siavelis, Peter M. 1997. Executive-Legislative Relations in Post-Pinochet Chile: A Preliminary Assessment. In *Presidentialism and Democracy in Latin America,* ed. Scott Mainwaring and Matthew Soberg Shugart. Cambridge: Cambridge University Press. 321–62.

Verdugo, Mario. 1990. Modificaciones al procedimiento de reforma constitucional. *Cuadernos de Análisis Jurídico* (January): 77–81.

Viera-Gallo, José Antonio. 1989. El acuerdo constitucional. In Geisse and Ramírez Arrayes 1989. 15–19.

———. 1994. Former Member (CPD) of the technical committee. Author interview. Santiago, January 17.

Whitehead, Laurence. 2002. *Democratization: Theory and Experience*. Oxford: Oxford University Press.

Zaldívar, Andrés. 1995. *La transición inconclusa*. Santiago: Los Andes.

Chapter 10

Judicial Reform as Insurance Policy: Mexico in the 1990s

Jodi S. Finkel

Immediately on taking office in December 1994, President Ernesto Zedillo delivered to the Mexican Congress a comprehensive judicial reform package, including dramatic institutional changes that would affect the independence and authority of the judicial branch. The Supreme Court was granted the power of judicial review (the right to declare unconstitutional laws null and void) in specifically defined circumstances and was also empowered to settle political controversies between and among the branches of government at federal, state, and local levels. As a result of the reforms, the Mexican judiciary, subordinate to the Mexican president and his Institutional Revolutionary Party (PRI) since the 1930s, apparently was now being positioned as an independent and effective counterweight capable of checking the power of the ruling party. Indeed, in 1998, four years after the reforms took effect, Mexico's restructured Supreme Court ruled against the PRI on a key political issue, clearly demonstrating that the reforms had fundamentally altered the traditional balance of power between Mexico's executive and judicial branches. During the administration of Vicente Fox, the Court proved both willing and able to rule against the Mexican president.

The question that arises from these developments is why would the Mexican president seek to create a Supreme Court capable of declaring the laws enacted under his administration unconstitutional? Furthermore, why would the president seek to create a court capable of resolving disputes over the rightful boundaries of political power between government offices held by opposition parties and those held by the ruling party?

This study argues that while Mexico's 1994 judicial reform appears puzzling on the surface, it makes sense when understood as a political "insurance policy" designed to protect a weakening ruling party operating in an increasingly insecure political arena. When political players are uncertain about the future division of power, even if they currently hold the reins of power, they may seek to increase the availability of institutional checks on political authority as a hedge against their possible loss of political dominance. Judicial reform thereby becomes a trade-off in which ruling parties are willing to accept short-term costs in exchange for long-term security.

In Mexico more specifically, increases in judicial power presented a potential short-term cost to the PRI, as the more autonomous and newly empowered court could decide cases against the interests of the ruling party during the period of the Zedillo administration. Yet the court's new powers of judicial review could also serve to protect the ruling party against the threats posed by the increasing power of its political rivals, and thereby provide protection for a ruling party that found itself unable to control political outcomes as it had in the past.

The changes in Mexico's judiciary should be understood in the context of the nature of judicial power, the differences between Mexico's common law and civil law tradition, and contemporaneous judicial reforms in Latin America. Mexico's comprehensive 1994 judicial reform package gave the judiciary's new "rules of the game," and subsequent

Supreme Court rulings demonstrated the empowerment of the judicial branch. The Mexican experience, moreover, has implications for institutional reforms in other transitioning democracies. Mexico's judicial reform may owe a greater debt to the political calculations of politicians seeking to maximize their own interests than to an altruistic homage to democratic principles; but apparently its long-term consequences may be an autonomous judiciary both willing and able to serve as a true check on Mexico's separation of powers.

JUDICIAL POWER AND THE CIVIL LAW TRADITION

Judicial power is defined in this study by four interrelated concepts: impartiality, insularity, institutionalization, and jurisdiction.[1] The first two are concerned with independence (the quality of being unbiased and free from external manipulation), the latter two with authority (rightful exercise of power with claim to be obeyed). Impartiality refers to the making of judicial decisions according to the relevant laws and facts. It is the extent to which judges decide cases based on expressed rules rather than preferences of interested parties. Insularity is the degree to which judges are protected from political retribution, and is the lynchpin that enables judges to decide cases in an impartial manner. The formal arrangements that operationalize insularity include tenure (security in office), appointment procedures (career advancement), and salary (financial compensation, which may not be diminished while in office).

Besides independence, judicial power also encompasses institutionalization and jurisdiction, the concepts required for judicial authority. Institutionalization refers to "the relationship of the courts to other parts of the political system and society" (Larkins 1996, 10) and relates to the legitimacy and stability of the judicial branch. An institutionalized judiciary is seen as the legitimate determiner of legal values. Judicial rulings are accepted and complied with by the affected parties and by those who hold power in the larger political structure.

Jurisdiction is the range of subject matter on which the courts may rule. It is a necessary component of judicial independence because it is the factor that gives independence its value. For example, if the court could make impartial decisions yet by law was permitted to make decisions on only a narrow set of issues, then the concept of independence would be meaningless in practice. The jurisdiction of an independent court envelops political, social, and economic questions. Judicial power therefore refers to insulated and impartial judges who make decisions on a wide range of issues based on expressed laws that are obeyed by political and societal interests.

Civil versus Common Law: The Role of the Judiciary

While the judiciary is the cornerstone of any legal system, it plays distinct roles in different legal traditions. In civil law traditions, such as those found in Western Europe and Latin America, the understanding is that the judiciary is to be independent—but to lack the power to declare laws unconstitutional. (See Merryman 1985 for an overview of civil law systems.) Civil law systems, whose roots developed in eighteenth-century post-revolutionary France, when society was wary of the power of judges, have sought to limit that power. In civil law systems, sovereignty, or the power of lawmaking, is delegated by the people to the legislature, and therefore only the legislature may make laws. In such a system, the judge's role is limited to the application (extended over time to the interpretation) of law. Judges may neither make law (through precedent) nor unmake it (by declaring a law null and void). A judge's decision affects only the individuals involved and does not apply to the rest of the population. Thus, while a judge may declare a law unconstitutional in a particular case, the law itself is not invalidated, and it remains in effect.

In contrast to the civil law tradition, judges in common law systems have the power of *stare decicis* ("the power and obligation of courts to base decisions un prior decisions"), as well as the power of judicial review (the authority to declare a law or government act null and void should that law or act be found unconstitutional). Under common law, judges' decisions are said to have "general effects," meaning that a court's ruling applies to all citizens and political entities in the country. The extended effect of judicial decisions under common law allows for the total invalidation of the law; the law may no longer be applied and is therefore null and void.

While traditionally civil law rejected both *stare decisis* and judicial review, modern civil legal systems have increasingly accepted these two common law principles. While precedent may not be obligatory for civil law judges, "the practice is for judges to be influenced by prior decisions" (Merryman 1985, 47). Also, "the trend toward judicial review of the constitutionality of legislation in the civil law world has been strong, particularly in this [twentieth] century" (Merryman 1985, 139). In continental Europe, such review has often been instituted with the establishment of special constitutional tribunals that are separate from the ordinary judiciary and are exclusively empowered to determine the constitutionality of legislation. The creation of constitutional tribunals in the developing world has lagged behind Europe, but the trend of increasing the judiciary's role as a source of constitutional control in non-European civil law countries is growing.

Judicial Reform in Latin America

Judicial reform became a buzzword in Latin America during the final decade of the twentieth century, and many nascent democracies in the region engaged in dramatic constitutional reforms with the stated intent of increasing judicial power. In general, the reform packages centered on changes affecting the supreme court (and constitutional tribunals where they existed) and changes affecting judicial administration (often via the creation of specialized national judicial councils).[2] Since the 1990s, scholarly writings on the judiciary in Latin America have blossomed. Much of this literature has focused on the importance of establishing a strong judiciary as part of the process of democratization (Stotzky 1993; Schedler et al. 1999). Additional scholarly work has examined the international promotion of other aspects of judicial reform, such as access to justice and judicial efficiency in Latin America (USAID 2002; Domingo and Sieder 2001).

There are now also a number of academic studies describing a particular country's judiciary (Peru: Hammergren 1998; El Salvador: Popkin 2000; Chile: Hilbrink 2003). Research analyzing the political role of Argentine courts has been especially abundant (Helmke 2002; Iaryczower, Spiller, and Tomassi 2002, Bill-Chávez 2004; and Finkel 2004). Mexico, too, has also been the focus of much new judicial research. Domingo examines the role of the Supreme Court in Mexico's political development (2000) and argues that the 1994 reform significantly altered the incentive system faced by Supreme Court justices. Finkel examines all Mexican Supreme Court decisions addressing the constitutionality of electoral rules—rules that are inherently contentious because they determine the chances for obtaining power—during Zedillo's sexenio and demonstrates a fundamental change in the balance of power between Mexico's executive and judicial branches (2003). Staton (2006), analyzing the Mexican Supreme Court, argues that supreme courts selectively issue press releases to publicize specific decisions as a strategy to bolster judiciary authority.

Thus, the field of judicial reforms in Latin America is enjoying much new attention. Yet, current scholarship still remains limited in its ability to explain why some judicial reforms are successfully implemented and others are not. This examination of the Mexican case seeks to shed light on the conditions under which reform succeeds.

THE 1994 MEXICAN JUDICIAL REFORM BILL

Although the last two decades of the twentieth century marked a period of democratic transition in Mexico, culminating in the election of the opposition candidate Vicente Fox in the 2000 presidential election, Mexico at the time of the 1994 judicial reform was perhaps best described as a "semiauthoritarian democracy."[3] The Mexican Constitution of 1917, from which the past and current federal government derives its authority, formally establishes a democratic government based on a tripartite separation of powers. Historically, however, the president was the key political actor, and the judiciary was the weakest branch. President Zedillo's 1995 State of the Union Address, in which he declared, "I reiterate that the times of political naming of the Court and presidential influence over the Supreme Court have ended," is a clear and revealing assessment of the traditional relationship between the executive and judiciary in Mexico (Zedillo 1995).[4]

The 1994 reforms altered the composition of the Supreme Court and included dramatic constitutional and statutory changes that redefined the independence of the judicial branch and the powers and limitations of the Supreme Court. President Zedillo stated, "while changes are not wrought overnight . . . [t]he Constitutional Reform promulgated last December creates the basis for an independent Federal Judiciary, an impartial power, of transparent operations, growing professionalism, and better capacity to fulfill its responsibilities" (Zedillo 1995). Were these latest changes truly substantive? Or did they prove to be purely cosmetic, as some critics have claimed?

Institutional Changes

The 1994 judicial reform bill replaced the entire membership of the Supreme Court and restructured the federal judiciary, creating the Federal Judicial Council (CFJ) to oversee judicial administration and to foster the independence of judges. The reforms also sought to develop a new political understanding of the Supreme Court, codified in the explicit definition of its new powers as a "constitutional court."

The reform reduced the Supreme Court from 26 to 11 justices, thereby returning it to the number originally established by the 1917 Constitution. Before the 1994 reform bill, the president nominated one candidate to fill a vacant seat on the court, and Senate confirmation of the nominee required the approval of a simple majority of senators. Now the Senate selects one candidate from a list of three names sent by the president, and the confirmation of this nominee requires the approval of two-thirds of the Senate. The prerequisites for nominating justices are now more rigorous, and nominees must possess more extensive professional experience. Prospective justices must also face Senate interviews before confirmation and cannot have held a major political post in the year preceding their nomination. Justices' life tenure was replaced by 15-year, staggered terms.

Judicial administration had previously been the Supreme Court's responsibility, but the 1994 reform created the CFJ. The first judicial council was established in France in

1946, and the concept spread throughout Europe in the second half of the twentieth century. The membership and functions of these councils vary across countries. Council composition may include judicial representatives, members of the three branches of government, or some mixture of these, along with lawyers and academics. A council's range of responsibilities may include the naming of judges (all lower-level judges in general and supreme court justices less frequently); the establishment of a judicial career path; the territorial division of the country into judgeships, along with their number and specializations; discipline, suspension, and firing of judges; preparation of the judiciary's budget; the establishment of internal regulations, such as working conditions and business hours; the collection of data to monitor and evaluate the quality of judicial services; and the publication of judicial decisions. Judicial councils were established throughout Latin America in the 1990s.[5] While Latin America's judicial councils vary in their functions, in general they are charged with the selection of lower-level judges, the establishment of judicial career paths, and the preparation of the judicial budget.

Mexico's CFJ is a seven-member body composed of the country's chief justice, one judge, two district magistrates, two members chosen by the Senate, and one member appointed by the president. They serve four year, nonrenewable terms. The CFJ is vested with key responsibilities over judicial careers, including the appointment, promotion, and discipline of all judges below the supreme court level. The CFJ's powers also include the establishment of territorial divisions and the number of circuits; as a result, the CFJ determines the total number of judges. Furthermore, the council is charged with the professionalization of the national judiciary and the establishment of prerequisites for judicial careers (university curriculum and standards for advancement based on experience and merit evaluations). Responsibility for preparing the judicial branch's budget was also transferred from the Supreme Court to the council.[6] The CFJ submits its budget to the president, who then refers it to Congress as part of the national budget proposal. While the Supreme Court does retain some administrative functions, the CFJ is now the main body charged with judicial administration, and the court is primarily responsible for issuing rulings to resolve disputes and to determine the constitutionality of laws.[7]

The most significant changes brought about by Mexico's 1994 judicial reform bill involve the political understanding surrounding the Supreme Court's role as a check on the separation of powers. This change is embodied in the court's right to resolve "constitutional controversies" and to determine the "unconstitutionality of laws."[8] Supreme Court decisions in these two areas have the potential to have "general effects"; in other words, they may declare government acts (in the first instance) or laws (in the second) as null and void. Before the reform, the Mexican legal system considered only cases of *amparo*, or protection of individual guarantees. Under *amparo*, a court's ruling has effect only for the individual bringing the case, not for the entire population. According to Chief Justice Juventino Castro y Castro, "There is no such thing as *amparo* against unconstitutional laws; there is only *amparo* against the application of such laws to a specific case which has been raised by an individual who has been diligent enough to request it from the Federal Judiciary" (quoted in Estrada Samano 1995, 44). Thus, by establishing the general effects of Supreme Court decisions in cases involving "constitutional controversies" or "unconstitutionality of laws," Mexico's 1994 judicial reform granted the Supreme Court the right to act as a constitutional court capable of controlling the constitutionality of government actions and laws.

"Constitutional controversies" refers to the Supreme Court's right to resolve conflicts between public entities in which one entity alleges the other's infringement on a mutual jurisdiction. These conflicts include disputes between the president and Congress, between the federal government and states or cities, between two states, between political organs within states, and between states and cities. Any of these entities may petition the court to hear its case. Although the Supreme Court did previously enjoy the ability to decide such controversies, its decisions did not have any affect beyond the immediate parties involved. Now, the Supreme Court may void an act or law if it is found to violate the jurisdiction of another official public entity.

The explicit inclusion of cities on the list of entities with legal standing to request review is another innovation. In the past, the status of cities under this clause was ambiguous, and varied depending on the prevailing political winds. With formal inclusion in the constitutional controversies clause, cities now possess a clearly defined right to seek legal recourse against presumed unconstitutional acts contrary to their interests.

The 1994 reform also granted the Mexican Supreme Court a second, entirely new function as a constitutional court via the "unconstitutionality of laws" clause. Mexico's Supreme Court may now invalidate laws passed by Congress, state legislatures, and Mexico City's legislative assembly. Before the reform, the court could grant an individual protection if it found a law to be unconstitutional; but now laws found to be unconstitutional under this clause can be declared null and void. The court may examine the constitutional validity of a law if one-third of the members of the legislature that passed the law petition the court to do so. In addition to legislative petitions, under the unconstitutional laws clause, the Senate may request the court to review the constitutionality of treaties, and the attorney general may request Supreme Court examination of any law passed by national, state, or local legislatures.[9]

Both the constitutional controversies and the unconstitutionality of laws clauses enable the Supreme Court to limit governmental authority and define political boundaries, thereby increasing the importance of the judiciary as a mechanism for constitutional control. However, the court's new power to check unconstitutional government action is severely limited in several ways. First, the agreement of a supermajority of justices (8 out of 11, or 72 percent) is required to invalidate an unconstitutional act or law under either of the two constitutional control clauses.[10] With respect to constitutional controversies, furthermore, the court's ruling will have general effects only when a higher body challenges a lower-level one; for example, when a federal body challenges a state or municipal one. Should a lower body challenge a higher body and win with the approval of at least 8 justices, the court ruling will apply only to the lower body involved in that particular case, as was the norm before the reforms. Likewise, the supermajority stipulation applies to unconstitutional laws; the Supreme Court can declare a law null and void only when 8 out of 11 justices agree on the unconstitutionality of the law in question. Thus, even if a majority of justices (6 or 7) on the court were to declare a law in violation of an individual's constitutional rights, the law would continue in effect.

The 1994 reform placed two additional restrictions on the court's power to invalidate laws via the unconstitutional laws clause. First, members of any legislature who desire to question the constitutionality of a law passed by their assembly have only 30 days from the publication of the law to file a petition with the court. Second, the court is explicitly prohibited from using the unconstitutionality of laws clause to determine the constitutionality of laws with respect to "electoral matters." The 1994 judicial reform specifically states that the court cannot decide whether electoral laws are constitutional. The opposition therefore would be unable to challenge electoral rules constructed to provide advantages to the PRI. (For example, such rules allocated 74 percent of the seats in the Senate to the PRI even though it had received only 48 percent of the vote.)[11] Mexico's 1996 electoral reform, passed two years after Mexico's judicial reform was promulgated, partly removed this limitation by allowing for electoral cases to be taken under the unconstitutional laws clause.[12]

Analysis

What have been the effects of this reform package on the Mexican judiciary? This question can be answered by examining changes to the judiciary's neutrality (impartiality and insulation) and authority (institutionalization and jurisdiction).

On the whole, the reforms improve the neutrality of the judicial branch. They promote the development of judicial impartiality; and in particular, the new appointment procedures decrease the opportunities for partisan selection of justices and judges. At the Supreme Court level, the requirement of a two-thirds majority rather than a simple majority for Senate confirmation of nominees makes it difficult for any one party single-handedly to choose its own candidate, and they promote the selection of nonpartisan justices.

The weakened insulation of Supreme Court justices, however, is cause for concern. The decrease in the security of office for Supreme Court justices from life tenure to 15-year terms undermines a key safeguard of justices' impartiality. While life tenure was the norm in the Mexican judicial system before the reform, it had little value, because justices saw the court as a stepping-stone to a better political post, not an end in itself. Thus the structure of the incentive system discouraged impartial rulings, as judges were rewarded with better job placement in exchange for decisions amenable to the ruling party. Before the 1994 reform, justices remained on the court about 10 years on average; only 20 percent of justices served for longer periods. Justices chosen from outside the judicial branch were particularly likely to abandon the court for more attractive political positions (Cossío 1998a). The new 15-year limit institutionalizes this problem because younger justices will be compelled to retire from the court at an age when they may still be in the job market and seeking career advancement.

On the other hand, two nonstructural variables have significant implications for the independence of the Supreme Court in Mexico and must be addressed in any analysis of Mexico's high court. The first is the country's changing domestic political environment. The demise of one party politics alters the incentive structure for Supreme Court justices (Domingo 2000). A justice can no longer be certain that a future president, at a time when the justice might seek another political office, will belong to a particular party. Similarly, rulings that appear partial to a particular party and that do not appear to represent an impartial decision based on the law and the facts could eventually cost a Supreme Court justice political standing. Because of this contingency, the best course of action for a justice may no longer be to issue legal rulings in the hope of currying favor with the government.

The second important nonstructural change is the selection of justices who are dedicated to a career in the judiciary. The naming of justices who view a seat on the Supreme Court as the pinnacle of their career rather than as a strategic move toward a coveted political office provides justices with an incentive to foster the prestige of the Mexican Supreme Court.

With respect to lower-level federal judges, the creation of the CFJ furthers both impartiality and insulation. Before the reform, the selection and career advancement of lower-level judges was in the hands of the Supreme Court. Particularly since 1980, when the federal judiciary began to expand and the number of judicial appointments per year increased dramatically, the selection of judges was marred by corruption and the importance of personal ties.[13] As a result of the reform, a nonpartisan council determines the selection and promotion of judges. The council's mixed membership, a majority of which is chosen from the judicial branch, makes it difficult for any external influence to manipulate the council's decisions for political gain.[14]

The CFJ's use of established merit evaluations to determine career advancement means that a judge's prospects will depend on a demonstrated competency and the use of sound legal reasoning to decide cases, rather than on connections or political ties. The CFJ's responsibility for the discipline and life tenure ratification of lower-level judges also provides for improved judicial insulation, thereby allowing judges to decide cases contrary to the wishes of those with political power or social influence without fear of retribution. As before, constitutional provisions continue to prohibit decreasing judicial salaries while a judge holds office. (It must be noted, however, that the power to raise salaries may still be used to wield influence over judges, particularly in an inflationary economy in which raises do not keep up with inflation.)

Besides neutrality, an evaluation of judicial reform must also analyze changes to judicial authority. How do the changes of 1994 affect the legitimacy of the judiciary and its position in regard to the other branches of government? While respect for the judicial branch will not take hold overnight, the reform package does include changes necessary to induce it to develop. The increasing regard for professionalization and greater experience require- ments for advancement should lead to a more qualified cadre of judges. As for Supreme Court justices, more demanding credentials required of nominees and public scrutiny of their qualifications during Senate hearings will favor candidates with greater expertise.

The creation of a special council to oversee the judiciary's administrative functions is also a positive step in the development of judicial autonomy. The CFJ has the poten- tial to promote greater efficiency within the judiciary and frees the Supreme Court to concentrate its resources solely on the resolution of constitutional issues and socially important legal concerns. The establishment of a judicial career path and specialized curriculum under the CFJ should result in better-trained judges who provide consistent and higher-quality decisions. At the same time, one important weakness with respect to the CFJ concerns its control over the budget. The CFJ prepares the budget and thereby oversees the setting of priorities and allocation of resources within the judicial branch; but Congress is not bound to appropriate the amount of funding the CFJ requests. A better method to guarantee judicial funding would be to specify its amount more explicitly, such as a fixed percentage of gross domestic product.

Jurisdictional changes may perhaps be the most significant feature of the reform. The Mexican Supreme Court's explicit empowerment to act as a constitutional court is a fundamental change in Mexico's separation of powers. Via the constitutional controversies and unconstitutional laws clauses, the Supreme Court has the potential to define political boundaries and declare unconstitutional laws null and void. Nevertheless, the requirement of a supermajority to achieve a ruling with general effects means that the court's ability to overturn government acts and laws is still discouraged rather than encouraged. Yet this constraint does not preclude such an outcome. On the other hand, if an act or law continues to have legal authority even though seven Supreme Court justices find that it vio- lates constitutional principles, this outcome may undermine respect for judicial authority.

The 30-day limit for members of the legislature to petition the Supreme Court to examine the constitutionality of a law is a very short time, both to prepare a legal chal- lenge and simply to discover the law's effects. This time constraint makes it impossible to challenge laws that result in unfair consequences over time. More important, this time limit effectively favors the PRI, because all laws passed during the period of PRI dominance before the 1994 judicial reform were excluded from challenges of unconsti- tutionality because they were, by definition, outside the 30-day time period.[15]

The Supreme Court's power also depends on its willingness to rule on issues it may have avoided addressing in the past. In this regard, the reformed court has greatly expanded the range of its jurisdictional powers. The court has been ruling on a wide range of issues that are hotly contested and highly controversial—issues that previously would have been decided behind closed doors by the ruling party elite. The justices have ruled on political matters, including boundaries between the president and Congress and the president and the Mexico City mayor. The court has also ruled on electoral laws, the naming of state electoral tribunals, and illicit campaign financing. Indeed, some of the Supreme Court justices who took office after the 1994 reforms publicly questioned the limitations on their right to rule on electoral issues—even before the 1996 electoral reform allowed them to do so.[16] The high court has also ruled on a broad array of economic and social issues, including allowing the capitalization of interest on bank debt; the unconstitutionality of the luxury tax; the right of entrepreneurs to refuse membership in government-sponsored chambers of commerce; the federal government's right to audit the national university; the fining of the state-owned oil company, PEMEX, for a spill on the Gulf coast; the denial of extradition to the United States of alleged criminals who could face the death penalty (capital punishment is illegal in Mexico); the right of living individuals to sell their organs for transplants; the decriminalization of abortion in cases of rape or severe fetal deformity, and whether former PRI leaders could be tried for human rights abuses committed during Mexico's "Dirty War"of the 1960s and 1970s.

On balance, the new institutional rules laid the groundwork for the development of an independent judiciary with the potential to play an active role in Mexico's separation of powers. A look at the specifics of some of the post-1994 decisions provides concrete evidence that Mexico's new Supreme Court is both willing and able to rule against the ruling party and the president on extremely salient political issues.

Postreform Court Rulings Opposing the PRI and the President

The first exercise of the court's new judicial review powers against the PRI occurred in 1998, only four years after Mexico's judicial reform, when the Supreme Court declared unconstitutional an electoral law intended to maintain PRI dominance in the state of Quintana Roo.[17]

PRI legislators, realizing that they would lose control over the Quintana Roo state legislature in the next election, enacted a new state electoral law, known as the governability clause that would have awarded a majority of legislative seats to the plurality vote winner. Because the PRI expected to garner the largest share of the vote but still under 40 percent, the clause would have guaranteed the PRI's continued unilateral control over the Quintana Roo legislature even though the party polled less than a majority of the vote. In response to the passage of the governability clause, legislators from the opposition Party of the Democratic Revolution (PRD) filed an unconstitutional laws petition with the Supreme Court in August 1998 to challenge the legality of the state's new electoral code. In a unanimous ruling, all 11 justices declared the clause to be unconstitutional. As a result, the law was struck from the state's electoral code, and the PRI's monopoly over political power in Quintana Roo was broken.[18]

Not only has the court been willing to challenge the PRI at the state level, but the justices have also used their newly acquired judicial review powers to rule against the political elite at the federal level, including the previously sacrosanct presidency. The first challenge to be filed against a Mexican president under the judiciary's new constitutional control powers was brought by the federal congress against Zedillo under constitutional controversies in 1999. At that time, members of Congress from the National Action Party (PAN) and the PRD were attempting to conduct an investigation of alleged illicit bank financing of PRI candidates during the 1994 election, including the funding of Zedillo's presidential campaign. They were stymied by a recalcitrant executive branch.[19] PAN and PRD legislators petitioned the court to determine whether the president was obligated to deliver the requested secret banking data to Congress. On August 25, 2000, in another unanimous decision, the justices ordered Zedillo to remand the relevant documents to Congress within 30 days. Zedillo, now at the end of his sexenio, complied with the ruling; the secretary of the treasury and the head of the National Banking Commission delivered the requested files on time. In this case it may be argued that a lame duck president was too weak to ward off judicial encroachment. But the Supreme Court has been just as able to counter the interests of Vicente Fox, even at the beginning of his presidential term.

The first major judicial challenge faced by Fox began with a dispute between the PAN president and the PRD mayor of Mexico City, Andrés Manuel López Obrador, over the implementation of daylight saving time. Annual presidential decrees had established daylight saving time in Mexico since 1996. The executive branch justified the time change by arguing that the additional hour of daylight saved hundreds of millions of pesos in energy costs and also brought Mexico in line with the United States, the country's most important economic partner. López Obrador, stating that daylight saving disrupted people's biological clocks, announced in March 2001 that Mexico City would not implement the time change and used constitutional controversies to challenge the president's right to do so. In an 8–2 decision (only 10 of the 11 justices voted in this ruling) on April 6, the justices ruled against the mayor, claiming that the setting of time was a federal prerogative. However, the decision left unresolved the question of which federal branch was legally empowered to determine the Mexican timetable. In a second ruling on this issue, on September 4, 2001, the court unanimously decided against the Mexican president, with all 11 justices agreeing that the setting of the clocks was a congressional responsibility. Congress did pass daylight saving legislation the following February, although its version of the law implemented the time change for seven months rather than the six months originally established by presidential decree.

Another Supreme Court ruling worth examining declared unconstitutional a presidential decree allowing for private participation in the provision of electrical energy for public use. President Fox had made reforming Mexico's energy sector a key priority of his administration. His Public Service Electric Energy Law, decreed on May 22, 2001, would have allowed large corporations producing electricity for their own use to sell any surplus they generated to the state for redistribution to the general public. However, Article 28 of the Mexican constitution reserves energy as a state monopoly, with the state solely responsible for the generation, transmission, and distribution of electricity. In addition, energy privatization is strongly opposed by both the PRD and elements of the PRI, and it was congressional members of these two parties who filed a constitutional controversies petition challenging the legality of the decree law. In an 8–3 ruling on April 25, 2002, the Supreme Court held that the presidential decree was unconstitutional, thereby ruling out the possibility that the Federal Electricity Commission could purchase surplus from private providers and dealing a blow to one of the top issues on Fox's agenda.

Furthermore, by the end of Fox's administration, political leaders in Mexico were increasingly calling upon the Mexican Court to decide contentious disputes over political power. For example, in December 2005 President Fox asked the Court to decide whether the executive possessed the right to veto the congressional budget. Although the Mexican constitution explicitly states that the president may veto congressional legislation, it remained unclear as to whether that right extended to the congressional budget as well. In a May 2006 decision, the Court resolved the existing executive—legislative stalemate by ruling that the president did enjoy the right to veto the congressional budget. Additionally, as congress was not in session at that time, the Court ordered congress to convene a special session to discuss the president's budget recommendations.[20] Another example of a Mexican politician asking the Court to resolve a struggle over political power comes from Mexico's southern state of Oaxaca. A June 2006 teachers' strike erupted into months of civil unrest that resulted in the deaths of several protestors and took a heavy toll on the state's tourism-driven economy. On October 30, 2006, the Mexican congress passed resolutions declaring that the Oaxacan governor should resign. In response, the governor of Oaxaca, Ulises Ruiz, announced his intent to challenge the congressional resolutions before the Mexican Supreme Court.

The court's decisions, as well as the broad range of issues on which it has ruled, provide evidence of a fundamentally restructured relationship between Mexico's traditional wielders of political power and its judicial branch. With rulings against the PRI as well as against PRI and PAN presidents, Mexico's postreform Supreme Court has clearly demonstrated both an ability and a willingness to enter the political fray. Yet the paradox of a ruling party willfully engaging in meaningful judicial reform has a rationale: judicial empowerment served the interests of a weakening ruling party in an increasingly insecure political environment.

A THEORETICAL ARGUMENT TO EXPLAIN JUDICIAL REFORM

Institutions provide the "rules of the game"; they define the procedures that govern social, economic, and political behavior. They serve as the mechanisms that constrain the initiation, implementation, and sustainability of policy choices and as the mechanisms that structure political interaction. They thereby establish opportunities for and place constraints on political leaders. Those political actors who have the power to restructure political institutions will seek to do so if such a course of action enables them to replace existing institutions with those that better serve their interests. These ideas underlie the argument to explain judicial reform presented here.

The argument begins by determining the preferences and capabilities of the political actors who oversee judicial changes. With respect to preferences, political parties have interests that are specific to their position in the balance of power. A ruling party, defined here as the party that controls the apparatus of government, will seek to maintain or create institutional structures that minimize or eliminate constraints on its ability to exercise political authority. The opposition, conversely, seeks to check the ruling party's ability to wield political power. The political interests of the ruling and opposition parties depend on the roles they occupy, not ideology or interests.

Capability refers to the relative bargaining power of political parties. It determines whether a ruling party is able to enact changes on its own or must build a coalition to implement reform. In the former scenario, institutional reform will reflect solely the interests of the ruling party; in the latter, the ruling party will have to make compromises in order to garner the support necessary to pass reforms, but will retain the advantage of setting the agenda and defining the set of possible outcomes.

While it is obvious that political actors take actions to increase their current political power, it must be emphasized that they also try to protect their future interests. The inclusion of future interests in a party's cost-benefit calculation may have significant consequences for the outcome of reform, particularly when uncertainty exists about the party's future standing in the domestic political arena. Should the ruling party foresee that it may no longer dominate a political system in which it has previously exercised arbitrary powers, then it is in the ruling party's interest to make sure that those who may come to power in the future are unable to change arbitrarily the rules of the political game in ways detrimental to the former ruling party's political position. In such a scenario, it makes sense for the ruling party to try to establish institutional limits on power, either by directly constraining the use of power or by creating or strengthening political counterweights.

Applying this argument to the specific case of judicial reform, we may assume that a ruling party will generally prefer a judiciary that is less rather than more capable of limiting the government's ability to achieve its interests. This is because a ruling party prefers to wield political power without having to contend with judicial constraints on its actions. Assuming that politicians are self-interested and that they seek to maximize their power, the ruling party would not be expected willfully to initiate reforms to increase the judiciary's potential to limit government authority. On the other hand, the opposition—by definition, those who do not hold power—will want to increase the independence of the judiciary in order to check presidential and legislative power (because they do not control these), as well as to protect the political rights of the opposition (themselves). Ruling parties prefer constraints on judicial independence, while opposition parties prefer to increase judicial neutrality and authority.

The distribution of power not only determines the political players' interests, it also determines the power to achieve those interests. If the ruling party can single-handedly implement reforms and is considering only the current time period, reforms will not include increases in the judiciary's ability to limit government actions. If a coalition is required to pass judicial reform, then the game becomes how to provide the opposition with incentives so as to obtain the number of votes necessary to approve the reform. Thus, a constitutional design favoring the development of a neutral judiciary with broad authority is more likely where at least one opposition party exists whose vote is necessary to pass the reform.

When political actors also implement reform with an eye to the future, a ruling party that expects to remain in power should not be expected to increase the independence and authority of the judicial branch.[21] On the other hand, a ruling party whose probability of reelection is low or decreasing may see such a change as worthwhile. A ruling party with an uncertain future may decide to grant the supreme court independence and the power of judicial review in order to serve as a hedge against possible downturns in the party's future political position. Granting the supreme court the right to declare political acts or national laws null and void reduces the costs a ruling party would face if it were to end up as an opposition party. In particular, a ruling party that has wielded arbitrary power in the past may seek to enable the court to limit the ability of future ruling parties to do likewise. In effect, a ruling party, unsure if it will control political power in the future, may seek to protect the political power of those parties that will not.

Thus judicial reform may operate as a political insurance policy. Much like an insurance policy, moreover, such reform implies up-front costs in exchange for future protection. In the current period, the newly empowered supreme court may challenge the very government that oversaw the increases in judicial power. While these increases imply potential costs to the ruling political leaders in the short run, they may ultimately serve these actors' long-term interests should these leaders eventually lose their position of political dominance.

APPLYING THE ARGUMENT TO MEXICO'S 1994 JUDICIAL REFORM

By the early 1990s, the Mexican president and ruling party had an interest in creating institutional insurance mechanisms to protect themselves, given the likelihood that their power would continue to diminish. Zedillo initiated the reform process, defined the parameters of the debate, and specifically tailored the Supreme Court's two new powers of judicial review to protect the ruling party where it perceived itself to be the most vulnerable. But the PRI did not have the congressional votes necessary to alter the country's constitution unilaterally, and therefore it was forced to seek the support of the PAN. As to be expected of an opposition party, the PAN demanded the establishment of a judiciary stronger than that which Zedillo had originally proposed. The combination of an insecure ruling party seeking insurance and an opposition party pushing for greater judicial empowerment determined the final form of the 1994 judicial reform package.

Domestic Political Uncertainty

As late as the end of Miguel de la Madrid's presidency (1982), guests at a PRI dinner party were discussing their political plans for the PRI's next four *sexenios* in power (Solis 1994, A1). The PRI had dominated Mexican politics since 1929, making Mexico's one of the longest ruling single-party governments in the world. The Mexican president was the leader of both the country and the ruling party. As a result, Mexican presidents enjoyed immense power. The PRI was built on camarillas (networks), with the president's network dominating the party during his term and dictating policy. Thus, Mexican policy during the period of PRI hegemony was both "presidential" and "of the party."

Traditionally, the PRI had used economic growth to legitimize its rule and to obtain votes. Where the PRI could not achieve victory by legitimate means, it resorted to electoral manipulation. By the mid-1990s, both of these strategies were under fire. A debt crisis was undermining PRI hegemony and fundamentally altering Mexico's domestic political arena. Economic stagnation was further weakening the PRI's hold on power, and the presence of international observers to monitor elections reduced the party's ability to retain power through electoral fraud. The opposition, meanwhile, made headway in opening up the country's political playing field. The two most important opposition parties by the mid-1990s were the PAN on the right of the political spectrum and the left-leaning PRD, which began as a coalition of minor parties in the 1988 presidential election.

Mexican electoral trends from 1970 to 1994 are demonstrated in Table 1, which shows the decrease in the (official) vote received by the PRI presidential candidate over the 25 years, from 93.6 percent in 1976 to 48.7 percent in 1994. In the June 1994 presidential election, opposition parties garnered more than 50 percent of the electorate's votes. The PAN chairman, following the party's strong showing, stated that the PAN was establishing as its goals "a majority in Congress in the 1997 elections and then the presidency in the year 2000" (Romero 1995, 12). After the 1994 results, the PRI had to take such election bravado seriously.

Table 1. Mexican Presidential Election Results, 1970–1994 (percent of vote)

	PRI	PAN	PRD/FDN[a]	Other
1970	83.3	13.9	—	1.4
1976	93.6	—	—	1.2
1982	71.0	15.7	—	9.4
1988	50.3	17.0	31.1	1.4
1994	48.7	25.9	16.6	6.0

[a]The National Democratic Front (FDN) was an electoral coalition uniting small left-wing parties behind the PRD's candidate in 1988 and 1994.

"In the new disorder of Mexican politics, the nation's ruling party is no longer the reassuring but undemocratic absolute," wrote the *Wall Street Journal*'s correspondent in Mexico one month after the election that brought President Zedillo to power (Solis 1994, A1). With respect to congressional representation, the opposition made only token advances in membership until 1994, when the proportion of seats held by opposition parties began to have important consequences. In the 1994 congressional election, the PRI received a two-thirds majority in the Senate but retained only a simple majority in the Chamber of Deputies. Thus, for the first time, the PRI no longer possessed the necessary two-thirds majority in the lower house required to approve changes to Mexico's constitution. These electoral changes demonstrate that by 1994, after nearly seven decades in power, the PRI could no longer unequivocally predict that it would win Mexico's presidential election in the year 2000 or continue to maintain its control of Congress.

Paralleling changes at the federal level, political power at the state and local levels in Mexico had also become increasingly diversified by 1994. The PRI was contending with opposition strongholds in the north (the PAN) and the south (the PRD) and with weak electoral support in Mexico City. Members of the opposition had successfully competed against the PRI for governorships and seats in state legislatures, for political offices in the capital city, and for positions at the local level. The first non-PRI governor, a member of the PAN, came to power in Baja California in 1988, and two more PAN governors were elected in 1994. In the 1994 election, "The PRI was seen for the first time as vulnerable to growing voter discontent and a new element, uncertainty, entered the electoral scene" (Serrano 1994, 12).

This trend of increasing opposition control of political office and concomitant loss of the PRI's control over those offices continued with the elections of 1997 and 2000. In the July 1997 congressional election, the PRI lost its majority in the Chamber of Deputies. The mayoralty of Mexico City, decided by popular election rather than appointment for the first time in 1997, was won by the PRD's candidate, Cuauhtémoc Cárdenas. In addition, eight governorships were held by opposition parties, including seven by the PAN and one by the PRD, and the opposition also controlled several state legislatures (see InstitutO Nacional de Geografía e Informática 1999, 623). Opposition parties gained control of one-third of all municipalities (Blum 1997). In 2000, the PRI lost the presidency to the PAN candidate, Vicente Fox, heralding a fundamental change in the Mexican political system. Mexico's 2003 midterm election, in which the PAN was trounced at the polls while both the PRI and PRD gained seats, demonstrates the continued fluidity of political parties in Mexico.

New Judicial Review Powers

The Supreme Court's two new constitutional control clauses operated in the specific areas where the ruling party faced significant threats from its political rivals. Both constitutional controversies and the unconstitutionality of laws provisions would enable the weakened ruling party to challenge laws put in place against the PRT's interests by opposition-controlled state and local governments. Thus, via the use of the court's new constitutional control clauses, the PRI could protect itself against immediate current losses of political power at the state and local levels and against the further deterioration of the ruling party's political position in midterm elections during the Zedillo sexenio and beyond. Furthermore, given the possibility that the PRI could lose the presidential election in 2000, the reformed court could provide a means of challenging Mexico's next ruling party.

Thus, while the decision by the ruling president and party to grant the Supreme Court the attributes of a constitutional court—and thereby check the power of the very government that initiated and approved judicial reform—appears illogical on the surface, it makes sense when regarded as an insurance policy sought by a ruling party that could no longer guarantee its monopoly on political power. With an insurance policy, the ruling party was willing to accept costs in the immediate period (the costs associated with an independent judiciary ruling against the interests of the PRI during the Zedillo administration) as a security hedge against the possibility of paying higher costs later (the costs associated with an opposition party coming to power and wielding unchecked authority contrary to the interests of the PRI in the future). The PRI could have embarked on a reform to grant much more power to the Supreme Court; for example, it could have granted the court expansive judicial review powers or adopted the principle of majority rule for declarations of unconstitutionality to take effect. But the PRI did not choose either of these courses of action. The party was not seeking a more powerful Supreme Court as an end in itself; rather, the PRI's goal was to balance the desire to limit the court's ability to challenge the ruling party in the current period with the desire to protect itself in the future should the opposition dethrone the PRI from its position of political dominance.

It should also be mentioned that the PRI was never a monolithic entity, and indeed, not all factions within the PRI were prepared to tolerate a real democratic opening in Mexico. PRI hardliners opposed relinquishing power, while "softliners" accepted the possible loss of PRI political control. Zedillo's network favored continuing with Mexico's democratic liberalization, even if it meant the loss of political power. As Zedillo and his network within the PRI accepted the potential loss of power, they had a real incentive to seek judicial empowerment, and they had the political power to carry it out.

Additional Players in the Reform Decision

While Mexico's 1994 judicial reform was dictated from within the presidential palace, both domestic and international actors have been involved with certain aspects of it, although in general their role has been limited. Recognizing that judicial changes were imminent, several Supreme Court justices prepared their own judicial reform proposal and submitted it to the executive (Cossío 1998b). According to José Ramón Cossío, a constitutional specialist involved in the drafting of the court's judicial proposal, the court's reform would have emboldened it with extensive powers of judicial review (Cossío 1998b). The president's judicial reform initiative, however, was quite distinct from that of the Supreme Court; for example, firing the entire bench and granting the court much more narrowly defined powers of judicial review than those the court itself suggested. This demonstrates the court's limited influence on the 1994 reform package (Cossío 1998b).

International financial institutions, particularly the World Bank, have encouraged developing countries to engage in judicial reform as a way to promote investor confidence. The World Bank has provided judicial reform loans to several Latin American countries, but Mexico in the 1990s was not among the recipients. The most significant international assistance for judicial reform received by Mexico in the mid-1990s was small-scale funding from the United States Agency for International Development (USAID).[22]

Civil society organizations have also played a role in specific areas of justice reform in Mexico (for example, criminal and penal reforms), but not a major role in the empowerment of the Supreme Court. According to Rafael Harel, vice president of Mexico's

Commission on the Defense and Promotion of Human Rights, neither civil society nor human rights groups were influential or actively involved in the design of the 1994 reform (Harel 1998). Instead, the initiation and development of Mexico's judicial reforms was a presidential prerogative.

While the parameters of Mexico's judicial reform package were defined by the Zedillo administration, the president's party could not single-handedly approve constitutional changes to the judiciary. The Mexican constitution may be changed only with the approval of two-thirds of the representatives from each house of Congress. While the PRI had two-thirds of the seats in the Senate, the party lacked this amount in the Chamber of Deputies, and Zedillo was compelled to court the PAN in order to pass the judicial reform bill. As a result, the PAN was well placed at the bargaining table.

In exchange for its support of the PRI's reform proposal, the PAN was able to extract particular benefits from the PRI with respect to judicial reform and to modify the reform proposal to its advantage. First, the reform established a more conservative Supreme Court, and the sympathies of at least four of the new justices, including the chief justice, lay with the PAN (Begné 1996). Second, the position of attorney general, the individual responsible for the implementation of judicial reform, was given to a member of the PAN. Third, Zedillo's original proposal granted the president the power to appoint two members of the Federal Judicial Council. During the bargaining in Congress, however, the number of appointees the president could name was lowered from two to one, thereby decreasing the executive's (in other words, at that time, the PRI's) weight in the council.

The PAN's position as an opposition party dictated its interest in increasing the Supreme Court's ability to challenge the ruling party. This clearly accords with PAN pressure to modify the PRI proposal in ways that favored the strengthening of the judiciary as a viable check on political power. The most significant modification of Zedillo's original proposal achieved by the PAN was the decrease in the number of legislators required to petition the Supreme Court under the reform's unconstitutionality of laws clause. Zedillo's original proposal had placed this requirement at 45 percent of the members of a legislature, but the reform bill was approved in Congress only after that percentage had been lowered to 33 percent. The reduced percentage greatly enhanced the PAN's ability to challenge decisions made by the PRI. At that time the PAN held one-third of the seats in many northern state legislatures. It could also obtain this amount in Congress and in Mexico City's Legislative Assembly by joining with other opposition parties. Furthermore, with its strong prospects for 1997 congressional elections, the PAN at that time was well placed to capitalize on the potential benefits of this change.

The most prominent political criticism of Mexico's 1994 reform proposal came from the PRD.[23] Given that the PRD was also an opposition party, the argument of this study would predict that the PRD should support changes to increase judicial independence and improve the court's role in the separation of powers. Yet the PRD opposed the PRT-sponsored reform. This apparent paradox can be explained by examining the PRD's perspective more deeply. From the PRD's vantage point, the PRI's provision of limited judicial reform was intended to preserve the PRI's hold on power. This objective, however, undermined the public's perception of the need to engage in a more extensive overhaul of the judicial system, and therefore stymied attempts to undertake more profound political reforms (Penalosa 1996). Thus, as expected of an opposition party, the PRD did not oppose strengthening the judiciary in principle, but it did oppose this particular reform package for not further empowering the Supreme Court. A PRI-PAN congressional coalition was nevertheless able to pass judicial reform without the support of the PRD, and the latter was therefore unable to obstruct or influence Mexico's 1994 judicial reform.

CONCLUSIONS

Mexico's president, leader of the very same ruling party that oversaw the development of a Supreme Court that had refrained from challenging the party's authority over the course of nearly seven decades, willfully undertook institutional reforms in 1994 to establish a judiciary with the potential to constrain the PRI's own political power. Politicians from the ruling party, increasingly unable to control political outcomes at the state and local levels and unsure if they would maintain their dominance of the national government in the future, granted increased independence and the power of judicial review to the Supreme Court. While this appears to contradict the traditional maxim that politicians prefer to increase their political power, the PRI's decision to empower the court makes sense as an "insurance policy" in an uncertain domestic political arena.

Clearly, Zedillo could have granted the Mexican Supreme Court even more extensive judicial review powers but did not, because a more powerful judiciary was not the ultimate goal. Instead, the court's two new constitutional control powers were specifically designed to counter the most salient threats poised by the increasing political power of the PRI's rivals. Specifically, both the constitutional controversies and unconstitutional laws clauses would serve to protect the PRI where it had suffered losses of political power to opposition parties and feared that it would continue to do so. While the PRI might not have been able to prevent decisions and actions taken against its interests by opposition-controlled political offices, at least it could challenge these actions via an autonomous and empowered judiciary.

The constitutional controversies clause enabled the court to serve as an independent arbiter in disputes between government entities, a solution for a ruling party whose loss of power, particularly at the state and local level, had left it no longer capable of quietly and unilaterally resolving issues from behind closed doors. Unconstitutional laws clauses allowed the PRI to use the court to check the arbitrary exercise of authority by executives and legislatures, both in state and national governments, should the PRI become the opposition at either of these levels. Thus, for the PRI, a Supreme Court with the power to invalidate laws and to decide boundary disputes over political power reduced the risks associated with the potential loss of the PRI's dominant political position. For the PAN, the other party that cooperated to enact Mexico's package of judicial changes, the reform increased the number of institutional mechanisms available for challenging the PRI in the current period and the future ruling party, should the PAN have remained the opposition. Because PAN support was necessary to pass the reforms, furthermore, the PAN could extract specific benefits and modify the reform package to augment the viability of the court as a check on current political authority.

Mexico's experience with judicial reform demonstrates that institutional reform in one-party-dominant states may result in the creation of independent and potentially powerful institutions, institutions that can serve as effective counterweights to established political power. Precisely because such reform entails potential costs to the dominant party, however, a ruling party attempts to postpone it for as long as possible, implementing the reform as closely as possible to the time when it might begin to use the reform as protection. This strategy implies that democracy-building institutional reform and the likelihood of retaining office should share an inverse relationship. As the probability of retaining control over political office decreases, motivation for carrying out institutional reform to place constraints on political power increases. In the Mexican case, the result has been a fundamental alteration in the balance of power between the executive and judicial branches. Starting under the Zedillo administration and then under Fox, the Mexican Supreme Court has not only addressed issues that would have remained unexamined by the judiciary in the past but has also begun to exert its authority to resolve disputes over the legitimate use and rightful possession of political power. Clearly, the post-reform Court has proved both willing and able to enter the political fray.

NOTES

1 The broader concept of judicial power is preferred here to the traditional "judicial independence" because the former better defines the concept this study seeks to measure. For an overview of the current definitions of judicial power, see Larkins 1996.

2 Judicial reforms altered the composition of the high court membership (either by a total replacement of justices or by adding new members); the selection process and tenure of justices; the ability of the executive and legislature to change the rules that govern the court; the extent of the court's judicial review powers, if any; the range of court jurisdiction; and the number of votes (a simple or super majority) required for judicial decisions to take effect. With respect to changes in judicial administration, national judicial councils were often established and charged with the naming, promotion, discipline, and removal of judges below the Supreme Court level; with control over the judicial budget; and with the professionalization of the judiciary through the creation of a judicial career path.

3 Cornelius and Craig (1991) describe a semiauthoritarian democracy as characterized by competitive (though not necessarily fair and honest) elections, which install governments more committed to political stability and labor discipline than to expanding democratic freedoms, protecting human rights, or mediating class conflicts.

4 A more favorable historical view of Mexican judicial independence is presented by González Casanova (1966). He writes that of the 3,700 Supreme Court cases between 1917 and 1960 in which the Mexican president was cited as the defendant, the court conceded protection to the plaintiff in one-third of its decisions. "One arrives at the conclusion that the Supreme Court works with certain independence with respect to the executive," but, he concedes, "that it, of course, follows the executive in important political areas and services to provide it with stability" (1996, 56–37, author's translation).

5 For example, judicial councils were recently incorporated into the constitutions of Colombia (1991), Ecuador (1992), Paraguay (1992), and Argentina (1994).

6 The Supreme Court still prepares its own budget, but the CFJ is responsible for the budget for the rest of the judicial branch.

7 For example, the court retains responsibility for compiling and publishing judicial decisions and the list of nominees from which the Chamber of Deputies names members to the Electoral Tribunal.

8 In Spanish, "unconstitutionality of laws" is written as *acciones de inconstitutionalidad* and is usually translated as "unconstitutionality of acts." The term "unconstitutionality of laws" is used in this article because the Supreme Court may use this power to invalidate laws passed by legislative bodies. This power of judicial review does not extend to executive decrees or other government acts or actions.

9 In 1996 the Mexican constitution was modified so that political parties registered with the Federal Electoral Institute also have standing under the "unconstitutionality of laws" clause and enjoy the right to challenge electoral laws, even though they might not be represented in the legislature that passed the law.

10 The reform contains a major technical error. Under both of these constitutional control clauses, the case is not resolved if the agreement of eight justices is not achieved. According to Cossío (1998b), this oversight was unintentional, and it needs to be rectified to allow court decisions that do not achieve supermajority agreement to take effect for the parties involved.

11 It is interesting that "electoral issues" were originally excluded from the purview of the Supreme Court's constitutional control clauses, an indication that the ruling party believed that it would not be able to control the postreform court as it had in the past.

12 Federal and state elections were scheduled for April 1997. The reform stated that those seeking to challenge an electoral law affecting these elections would have only 15 days to petition the Supreme Court from the time the law was enacted, and the court would have only 15 days to respond. The reform's original 30-day limit would be reinstated after that. In addition, the 1996 electoral reform placed the electoral tribunal, the body charged with resolving electoral disputes, under the judicial branch rather than under the executive, as it had been previously. The 1996 electoral reform also granted standing to the directors of officially registered political parties to

challenge electoral laws via the unconstitutional laws clause (in addition to a petition by one-third of the members of a legislature or the attorney general). The court, however, may only examine the validity of the parts of the electoral law challenged and may not extend its ruling to cover constitutional issues that are not formally brought by the petitioners.

13 On average, each justice could appoint two judges per year (Cossío 1998a).

14 Zedillo, however, had more say over the composition of the CFJ than will any future president. According to the rules, the president names only one appointee; but as part of the reform package, Zedillo named all the members of the reconstituted Supreme Court. Because the Supreme Court's chief justice serves as the presiding member of the CFJ, Zedillo indirectly named another member of the council. Zedillo also wielded influence over the two appointees chosen by the PRI-controlled Senate.

15 The opportunity to challenge existing laws, however, presents itself if the law is modified and replaced by the passage of a new law.

16 For example, in reference to the prohibition on examining electoral issues before the 1990 modification, Justice Juan Díaz Romero asked, "what serves a constitutional norm that proclaims and grants a right if the constitutional mechanisms and instruments do not allow the reestablishment of that right if it has been violated?" He added that rights expressed in the constitution come before any other consideration in the interpretation of the constitution. In other words, the protection of natural rights is more important than the sanctity of electoral laws. Quoted in Morgan 1995 (author's translation).

17 For a detailed examination of the 15 Supreme Court decisions addressing the constitutionality of electoral rules filed under the court's two new constitutional control clauses during Zedillo's *sexenio*, see Finkel 2003.

18 The invalidation of the governability clause in Quintana Roo applied only to that state, and governability clauses remained on the books of nearly half of Mexico's state legislatures at that time. Had the Supreme Court invalidated the federal electoral code, the ruling would have applied to all states; but because the court was ruling on a state law, the ruling did not affect the law in other states. Challenges to these clauses will have to wait until a new electoral code is passed in the particular state or until the national congress addresses the issue in a modification of the federal electoral code. According to Corso (2000), the unanimous decision in the Quintana Roo case is a clear signal of way the court will rule on these cases in the future.

19 Opposition Congress members charged that Mexico's Union Bank had contributed millions of pesos to the PRI's campaign coffers in 1994 and, in exchange, had their private debt converted into public liabilities as part of a massive government bailout in 1995.

20 Congress may override a presidential veto of the budget with the vote of two-thirds of those present.

21 The opposition's interests already are to establish a judiciary with greater neutrality and authority; therefore they remain the same in an uncertain environment.

22 The aid, however, addressed judicial training and not the empowerment of the Mexican Supreme Court. For example, USAID's judicial funding for Mexico was targeted for establishing conferences between U.S. and Mexican judges, designing standards for judicial conduct, creating a pilot program to revamp the criminal justice system, and developing a speakers' program (Pérez 1998).

23 The only other party to have representation in Congress, also on the left side of the political spectrum, was the Workers' Party (PT). All eight of the PT's members voted in favor of the reform.

REFERENCES

Begné, Alberto. 1996. Political Consultant. Author interview. Mexico City, July 14.

Blum, Roberto E. 1997. The Weight of the Past. *Journal of Democracy* 8, 4 (October): 28–42.

Bill-Chávez. 2004. *The Rule of Law in Nascent Democracies: Judicial Politics in Argentina*. Stanford: Stanford University Press.

Cornelius, Wayne A., and Ann L. Craig. 1991. *The Mexican Political System in Transition*. San Diego: Center for U.S.-Mexican Studies, University of California.

Corso, Eclgar. 2000. Councilor to the chief justice of the Mexican Supreme Court. Author interview. Mexico City, June 19.

Cossío, José Ramón. 1998a. Constitutional scholar. Author interview. Mexico City, August 27.

———. 1998b. Author interview. Mexico City, September 7.

Domingo, Pilar. 2000. Judicial Independence: The Politics of the Supreme Court in Mexico. *Journal of Latin American Studies* 32, 3 (October): 705–35.

Domingo, Pilar, and Rachel Sieder. 2001. *Rule of Law in Latin America: The International Promotion of Judicial Reform*. London: Institute for Latin American Studies.

Estrada Samano, Rafael. 1995. Administration of Justice in Mexico: What Does the Future Hold? *United States-Mexico Law Journal* 3: 35–48.

Finkel, Jodi. 2003. Supreme Court Decisions on Electoral Rules After Mexico's 1994 Judicial Reform: An Empowered Court. *Journal of Latin American Studies* 35 (November): 1–23.

———. 2004. Judicial Reform in Argentina: How Electoral Incentives Shape Institutional Change. *Latin American Research Review* 39, 3 (October): 56–80.

González Casanova, Pablo. 1966. *La democracia en México*. Mexico City: Editorial RA.

Hammergren, Linn. 1998. *The Politics of Justice and Justice Reform in Latin America: The Peruvian Case in Comparative Perspective*. Boulder: Westview Press.

Harel, Rafael. 1998. Vice President, Mexican Commission on the Defense and Promotion of Human Rights. Telephone interview. Mexico City, September 29.

Helmke, Gretchen. 2002. The Logic of Strategic Defection: Judicial Decision-Making in Argentina Under Dictatorship and Democracy. *American Political Science Review* 96, 2: 291–30.

Hilbrink, Lisa. 2003. An Exception to Chilean Exceptionalism: The Historical Role of Chile's Judiciary and Prospects for Change. In *What Justice? Whose Justice? Fighting for Fairness in Latin America*, ed. Susan Eva Eckstein and Timothy Wickham-Crowley. Berkeley: University of California Press.

Iaryczower, Matias, Pablo Spiller, and Mariano Tomassi. 2002. Judicial Independence in Unstable Environments. Argentina: 1935–1998. *American Journal of Political Science* 46, 4 (October): 699–716.

Instituto Nacional de Geografía e Informática. 1999. *Anuario de estadísticos de los Estados Unidos Mexicanos 1998*. Aguascalientes: Instituto Nacional de Geografía e Informática.

Larkins, Christopher. 1996. Judicial Independence and Democratization: A Theoretical and Conceptual Analysis. *American Journal of Comparative Law* 54, 4 (Fall): 605–26.

Merryman, John. 1985. *The Civil Law Tradition: An Introduction to the Legal Systems of Western Europe and Latin America*. Stanford: Stanford University Press.

Morgan, Raúl. 1995. La Corte Suprema, Antonio Lozano y Oscar Espinosa. *El Proceso* (Mexico City), September 11: 10.

Penalosa, Pedro José. 1996. PRD Legislative Assistant, Mexico City Legislative Assembly. Author interview. Mexico City, July 22.

Pérez, Patty. 1998. USAID Legal Consultant for Mexico. Author interview. Mexico City, September 11.

Popkin, Margaret. 2000. *Peace Without Justice: Obstacles to Building the Rule of Law in Latin America*. University Park: Pennsylvania State University Press.

Romero, Ismael. 1995. Acuerda el PAN fortalecer su llamado redimensionamiento. *La Jornada* (Mexico City), November 19: 12.

Schedler, Andreas, Larry Diamond, and Marc Plattner, eels. 1999. *The Self-Restraining State: Power and Accountability in New Democracies*. Boulder: Lynne Rienner.

Serrano, Mónica. 1994. The End of Hegemonic Rule? Political Parties and the Transformation of the Mexican Party System. In Party Politics in *"An Uncommon Democracy": Political Parties and Elections in Mexico*, ed. Neil Harvey and Serrano. London: Institute of Latin American Studies, University of London. 1–23.

Solis, Dianne. 1994. Weakened Giant: Calls for Reform Check Mexico's Mighty PRI as Elections Loom. *Wall Street Journal*, July 13: Al.

Staton, Jeffrey. 2006. Constitutional Review and the Selective Promotion of Case Results. *American Journal of Political Science* 50, 1 (January): 98–112.

Stotzky, Irwin, ed. 1993. *Transition to Democracy in Latin America: The Role of the Judiciary*. Boulder: Westview Press.

USAID (United States Agency for International Development). 2002. "Achievements in Building and Maintaining the Rule of Law," Occasional Paper, November. Office of Democracy and Governance <http://www.usaid.gov"www.usaid.gov>.

Zedillo, Ernesto. 1995. State of the Union Address. *Informe presidencial*. Mexico City, September 6.

Chapter 11

Indigenous Parties and Democracy in Latin America

Raúl L. Madrid

In recent years, Latin America has witnessed the emergence of important ethnic parties for the first time in its history. In Bolivia, Evo Morales, the leader of a new indigenous party known as Movement to Socialism (MAS), was elected president in 2005 with an astonishing 53 percent of the vote. In Ecuador, the Pachakutik Plurinational Unity Movement has won significant representation in the legislature in every election since 1996 and the party helped elect Lucio Gutiérrez president in 2002. Important ethnic parties have also emerged in the last two decades in Colombia, Nicaragua, and Venezuela.

The indigenous parties differ substantially from the parties that have long dominated Latin American politics in that they have explicitly sought to represent the interests of the long-ignored and subordinated indigenous population. Many people have therefore welcomed the emergence of these parties. Nevertheless, some observers fear that the new parties, and the powerful indigenous organizations that back them, may exacerbate ethnic conflict and destabilize democracy in the region. Critics of the indigenous parties and organizations decry the indigenous movements for rejecting Western culture and for precipitating uprisings that have led to the overthrow of elected presidents in Ecuador and, more recently, Bolivia. These critics are concerned about links between the indigenous movements and radical leftist groups, and they fear that indigenous uprisings in the region could spread (Oppenheimer 2003; *Latin American Andean Group Report 2003; Latin American Weekly Report 2003*).

Are these concerns well founded? What impact will the new indigenous parties have on the consolidation of democracy in the region? This essay argues that indigenous parties in Latin America are unlikely to exacerbate ethnic conflict or create the kinds of problems that have been associated with some ethnic parties in other regions. To the contrary, the emergence of indigenous parties in Latin America may help deepen democracy in the region. This essay focuses primarily on MAS and Pachakutik, the two most important indigenous parties to emerge in Latin America to date. Nevertheless, one would expect the argument developed here to apply to any major indigenous party in the region.

ETHNIC PARTIES AND ETHNIC POLARIZATION

The political science literature on ethnic parties would lead us to view the emergence of indigenous parties in Latin America with some concern. The dominant strain of this literature is highly critical of ethnic parties, which are typically defined as parties that cater primarily to a single ethnic group or cluster of ethnic groups.[1] This literature suggests that ethnic parties will often provoke ethnic polarization and conflict because their leaders have incentives to make incendiary communal appeals (Rabushka and Shepsle 1972; Horowitz 1985; Sisk 1996; Reilly 2002). Horowitz, for example, argues that "by appealing to electorates in ethnic terms, by making ethnic demands on government, and by bolstering the influence of ethnically chauvinistic elements within each group, parties that begin by merely mirroring ethnic divisions help to deepen and extend them" (1985, 291).

Critics of ethnic parties maintain that ethnic parties will not typically be able to attract votes from outside their own ethnic group because of the fixity and sharpness of ethnic group boundaries and the intensity of ethnic group preferences (Horowitz 1985; Rabushka and Shepsle 1972).[2] According to Horowitz, an ethnic party, "recognizing that it cannot count on defections from members of the other ethnic group, has the incentive to solidify the support of its own group" (1985, 318). Leaders of ethnic parties will concentrate on mobilizing voters from their own ethnic group by appealing to ethnic prejudice and resentments and by exaggerating the threat represented by other ethnic groups. Moderate leaders of ethnic parties will quickly be displaced by more extremist leaders in the process that has come to be known as outbidding. As Sisk (1996, 17) portrays it: "Extremist leaders, seeking to capitalize on mass resentment, outbid moderates by decrying acts of accommodation as a sellout of group interests, citing collective betrayal and humiliation." Such appeals typically cause interethnic relations to deteriorate, leading, at times, to outright conflict. Increasing ethnic polarization, in turn, makes it difficult for nonethnic parties to subsist. As a result, Horowitz and others suggest, the emergence of ethnic parties may lead to the disappearance of nonethnic parties.

This doomsday scenario seems unlikely to occur in Latin America, however, in large part because ethnic identities in the region are characterized by a great deal of fluidity and ambiguity. In most Latin American countries, mestizos—that is, people of mixed European and indigenous descent—are the single largest population group, which has helped blur the lines between ethnic categories. Latin America also has a large population that is partly of African descent, which has further clouded the boundaries between different races and ethnicities.

The dominant mestizo population in Latin America has often adopted a contradictory attitude toward its own indigenous ancestry and culture. On the one hand, many mestizos have implicitly accepted their own indigenous roots and have celebrated many of the achievements and legacies of indigenous cultures as part of their national heritage. On the other hand, they have typically not identified themselves as indigenous, and they have frequently looked down on and discriminated against people they do identify as indigenous.

Who has identified themselves as indigenous (or has been identified as indigenous) in Latin America has changed over time and place, depending on numerous factors. In the 1900s, many indigenous people in the countryside in Latin America began to identify themselves as campesinos (peasants), partly because of state efforts to organize them into peasant sectors (Yashar 1999 and 2005). Other indigenous people migrated to the cities, where they frequently shed their indigenous identities. More recently, a process of "reindianization" is taking place in much of Latin America as large numbers of people, including individuals who are only partly of indigenous ancestry, have begun to adopt the indigenous label. Even today, however, many people who are mostly or wholly of indigenous ancestry do not identify as indigenous or will do so only under certain circumstances. In recent surveys and censuses in Bolivia, for example, the percentage of people who are willing to identify themselves as indigenous or with some indigenous category has ranged from 8 to 71 percent, depending in large part on what choices are offered (INE 2001; Seligson et al 2006; PNUD 2004).[3]

The fluidity and ambiguity of ethnic identities in Latin America means that nonethnic or multiethnic parties are likely to retain considerable appeal. Individuals who do not fully identify with a single ethnic group or do so only under certain circumstances may be reluctant to vote for an ethnic party. Even those who do identify with a single ethnic group may be reluctant to cast their votes solely on the basis of their ethnic identity in an environment where ethnic identities are unstable and ambiguous. Therefore, the emergence of indigenous parties in Latin America is unlikely to lead to the disappearance of nonethnic parties. Indeed, nonethnic parties continue to win the vast majority of votes, even in those Latin American countries where important indigenous parties have emerged. Moreover, nonethnic parties continue to do well in indigenous areas in these countries. Nonethnic parties, for example, won almost 60 percent of the vote in majority indigenous provinces in the 2002 Bolivian legislative elections and more than 60 percent of the vote in majority indigenous counties in the 2002 legislative elections in Ecuador.[4]

Nor is the emergence of indigenous parties likely to bring on an ever-worsening spiral of incendiary communal appeals that lead inexorably to ethnic polarization and conflict. The lack of clear boundaries between ethnic groups in Latin America means that leaders of ethnic parties in the region have the potential to attract support from people of diverse racial and ethnic origins. Indigenous parties, for example, might attract votes from people who do not identify as indigenous but may have partial or entirely indigenous ancestry, or they may attract support from people who are not of indigenous descent but identify with indigenous culture and support some of the demands of the indigenous movements. They may also attract support from individuals who do not identify with the indigenous cultures or movements but support the parties' stances on other issues. For this reason, incendiary communal appeals are likely to be counterproductive. Such appeals would not only risk antagonizing potential supporters from other ethnic groups, but might also alienate indigenous voters who do not have strong indigenous identities or who have close ties to people from other ethnic groups.[5]

This does not mean that no indigenous parties will make radical communal appeals. Indeed, some indigenous parties have adopted a radical ethnonationalist discourse. It does mean, however, that the radical ethnonationalist parties are unlikely to win the allegiance of numerous voters, even within their own ethnic group; and as a result, they should have a limited impact on the national political environment. To win large numbers of votes in an environment where ethnic identities are fluid and ambiguous, indigenous parties need to adopt pragmatic and inclusive approaches to politics, which is precisely what the most successful indigenous parties have done.

To date, the indigenous parties that have performed best in elections in Latin America—MAS in Bolivia, Pachakutik in Ecuador, and Alianza Social Indígena (ASI) in Colombia—have largely avoided incendiary rhetoric that could alienate members of other ethnic groups. To the contrary, these parties have actively sought to woo nonindigenous along with indigenous voters. As Dionisio Núñez, a congressional representative of MAS, put it, MAS is "an inclusive not an exclusive party . . . we did not want to go from being excluded to excluding others" (2004). All these parties have recruited nonindigenous as well as indigenous candidates for office, and Pachakutik has formed electoral alliances with important nonindigenous parties. Efforts to woo non-indigenous voters have been largely successful. Data from Bolivia and Ecuador suggest that both MAS and Pachakutik attracted many non-indigenous supporters in the 2002 elections.[6] The same appears to be true in Colombia. Indeed, Van Cott (2004, 292) suggests that indigenous parties in Colombia have received more votes from nonindigenous people than from indigenous people.

Not all indigenous parties have made efforts to attract support from the nonindigenous population, however. Ethnic parties, such as Yapti Tasba Masrika Nani (YATAMA) in Nicaragua and the Pueblo Unido Multitétnico de Amazonas (PUAMA) in Venezuela, have focused largely on attracting support from members of their own ethnic groups (Rizo Zeledón 1990; Van Cott 2004, 292). Even these parties, however, have largely avoided polarizing rhetoric and have sought to work with nonethnic parties and governments. YATAMA, for example, forged alliances with the UNO government in Nicaragua and subsequently with the Sandinistas, while PUAMA has cooperated with the left-wing Patria

Para Todos (PPT) party, as well as with the administration of Hugo Chávez (Hooker 2001; Van Cott 2004, chap. 6).

A few indigenous parties and leaders have expressed hostility to the nonindigenous population, but these parties have traditionally fared extremely poorly in elections in Latin America, even among the indigenous voters they claim to represent. The radical Indianista parties in Bolivia, for example, never obtained more than 2 percent of the vote in national elections. The Movimiento Indígena Pachacuti (MIP), a Bolivian indigenous party whose leader, Felipe Quispe, has at times voiced hostility to nonindigenous people, did win 6 percent of the national vote in the 2002 Bolivian elections, but Quispe's party has fared poorly since then, attracting only 2.2 percent of the vote in 2004 municipal elections and the 2005 general elections. Moreover, even in 2002, the MIP fared poorly outside of the Aymara heartland winning less than 3 percent of the vote in majority Quechua-speaking and majority Spanish-speaking provinces, as opposed to almost 26 percent of the vote in majority Aymara-speaking provinces. The failure of the exclusionary indigenous parties to attract support from most of the indigenous population has meant that even these parties have not significantly worsened interethnic relations in Latin America, although they certainly have not improved matters.

Instead of undermining democracy in the region, the emergence of important indigenous parties in Latin America may actually help bolster it in a number of ways. The indigenous parties will certainly improve the representativeness of the party system in the countries where they arise. The major indigenous parties should also increase political participation and reduce party system fragmentation and electoral volatility in indigenous areas. These parties may even increase the acceptance of democracy among the indigenous population and reduce political violence in areas with large indigenous populations, although whether these latter two benefits are realized will depend largely on the actions of the leaders of the indigenous parties. Each of these potential benefits merits discussion.

IMPROVING POLITICAL REPRESENTATION

The emergence of indigenous parties in Latin America should deepen democracy in the region by providing a voice to a politically and socioeconomically marginalized group that represents a large portion of the population in some Latin American countries. The indigenous population in Latin America ranks well below the nonindigenous population on virtually all major indicators of socioeconomic development, including income, education, health, and housing. Indigenous people, moreover, have traditionally had little political influence. Throughout much of their history, the major parties in Latin America have ignored indigenous voters or have wooed them principally through clientelistic appeals. Some important parties have channeled patronage resources to indigenous leaders, organizations, or communities, but, until recently, they rarely embraced key indigenous demands on issues such as agrarian reform, multicultural education, and regional autonomy.

The major nonethnic parties in Latin America have also traditionally failed to recruit many indigenous people as candidates for electoral office or for leadership positions in the party hierarchy, although they have fielded indigenous candidates for local offices in many instances. Various parties have made some progress in this area in recent years, but the indigenous population is still significantly underrepresented in most countries. In Guatemala, for example, only about 11 percent of legislators in 2000 were indigenous (ASIES 2000, 46). This constitutes a significant increase from earlier periods, but it still represents a very small percentage in a country where indigenous people represent approximately half of the total population.

The indigenous parties, by contrast, have selected large numbers of indigenous people as candidates for important political offices and for leadership positions in the parties themselves. According to one estimate, 85 percent of the MAS's representatives in the 2002–2005 legislature were indigenous, although other estimates are considerably lower (Rivera Pinto 2002, 52). Most of the leaders of Pachakutik, including its representatives in the legislature, are indigenous, although Pachakutik has also supported nonindigenous candidates from other parties in presidential elections. Pachakutik originally intended to run an indigenous candidate in the 2002 presidential elections, but internal divisions made it impossible to agree on a candidate, and the party ultimately decided to support Lucio Gutiérrez of the Patriotic Society Party (PSP), a new nonethnic party. Gutiérrez was an army officer who had come to fame as the leading military supporter of the indigenous uprising that overthrew Ecuadorian president Jamil Mahuad in early 2000.

Both MAS and Pachakutik have styled themselves as the authentic representatives of the indigenous population, and they have maintained close relations with the indigenous organizations from whence they sprang. The Confederation of Indigenous Nationalities of Ecuador (CONAIE) and the unions of coca growers in Bolivia have played an important role in shaping the parties' programs, although tensions have also surfaced from time to time between these organizations and the indigenous parties that they helped create. MAS and Pachakutik have advocated a broad left-wing agenda, including strong opposition to neoliberal reforms. However, they have also placed a great deal of emphasis on issues that have traditionally been important to indigenous movements, such as agrarian reform, local autonomy, and, in the case of MAS, the cultivation of coca. Morales, for example, has argued, "it is necessary to achieve total rights to the land and territory, where the indigenous make decisions and administer natural resources" (Rivero Pinto 2002, 25). Since taking office in early 2006, Morales has sought to jump-start agrarian reform, end some coca eradication programs and expand autonomy in indigenous areas as well as nationalize the country's natural gas industry.

The emergence of indigenous parties in Bolivia and Ecuador thus has placed indigenous demands at the forefront of the policy agenda and has given indigenous people an important voice in policy affairs. Indigenous parties cannot possibly represent all indigenous people, and the more moderate of these parties, such as MAS and Pachakutik, may not represent the more militant members of the indigenous population. Nevertheless, by forcefully advocating the demands of a significant sector of that population, these parties have clearly improved the representation of indigenous people in the political system. Their success has also put pressure on the main nonethnic parties to pay more attention to those demands in order to stem the loss of indigenous votes. Some of these nonethnic parties have therefore recruited more indigenous candidates for political offices and have adopted some indigenous demands in their platforms and programs. Indeed, even in those countries where significant indigenous parties have not yet emerged, nonethnic parties have increasingly embraced indigenous demands in an effort to solidify their support in indigenous areas.

EXPANIND POLITICAL PARTICIPATION

The emergence of indigenous parties should increase voter turnout among the indigenous population in Latin America. Indigenous people have tended to vote at significantly lower rates than nonindigenous people in the region. A recent study found that the proportion of the population that is indigenous had a statistically significant negative impact on voter turnout at the municipal level in the 1990 and 1995 presidential and legislative elections in Guatemala (Lehoucq and Wall 2001).[7] In Mexico, voter turnout has also tended to be lower in indigenous municipalities than in nonindigenous ones (Ruíz Mondragón 1998). In the 2000 elections, for example, only 59.5 percent of the population over 18 years old voted in municipalities that were mostly indigenous, as opposed to 64.4 percent in municipalities where indigenous people represented a minority.[8] Voter turnout has also traditionally been lower in indigenous than in nonindigenous areas in Bolivia and Ecuador.

The lower voting rates have a number of causes. First, a significant percentage of indigenous people do not speak or read Spanish, which can be a substantial impediment to both registration and voting. Second, a disproportionately large number of indigenous people live in rural areas and therefore have to travel longer distances to vote or to register. Third, some Latin American countries have imposed significant financial or bureaucratic hurdles to voter registration, which affect the indigenous population particularly severely because they tend to have limited financial resources. In Bolivia, for example, citizens must obtain identity cards in order to vote, but these cards are costly and not easily obtained in rural areas (Van Cott 2003; Ticona et al. 1995, 181–85).[9]

Fourth, the traditional failure of the major parties to cater to the interests of indigenous people has also probably depressed turnout among this population. Some indigenous people may not vote or even register to vote because they do not have much enthusiasm for any of the parties or the candidates.[10]

The emergence of indigenous parties, however, should boost voter turnout among indigenous people by giving them a greater stake in the elections. More indigenous people will presumably turn out for elections in which candidates or parties specifically seek to represent them. Indigenous parties should also work hard to boost voter registration and turnout in indigenous areas, because the indigenous population typically forms the core of their electoral support. Indigenous parties, for example, may seek to reduce both the financial and bureaucratic obstacles to voter registration through changes in the electoral laws or government policies. In order to facilitate the turnout of indigenous voters, indigenous parties might also push to expand voting centers to more rural areas and to create ballots that are easily understandable to those who do not read Spanish. Indigenous parties will presumably engage in large voter registration and "get out the vote" drives in indigenous areas in order to maximize the number of votes they receive.

The rise of indigenous parties appears to have already increased voter turnout among the indigenous population in Bolivia and Ecuador, although other factors may also be partly responsible. Between 1992 and 2002, the number of votes cast in Ecuadorian counties (*cantones*) where the indigenous population represented the majority rose by 86 percent, as opposed to only 54 percent in counties where indigenous people are in the minority. As a result, turnout in indigenous areas in Ecuador now exceeds turnout in nonindigenous areas. (Turnout is measured here as a percentage of registered voters.) Turnout levels in counties that are majority indigenous have averaged 69 percent since 1996, as opposed to only 67 percent in counties that are less than 50 percent indigenous. Before the emergence of Pachakutik in the mid 1990s, however, turnout was lower in nonindigenous than in indigenous areas. In the 1992 Ecuadorian elections, for example, voter turnout was 65 percent in counties where the indigenous population represented a majority and 69 percent in counties where indigenous people were in the minority.

The emergence of a nationally competitive indigenous party has also significantly increased the number of indigenous voters in Bolivia. Between the 1997 and the 2002 elections, the number of votes cast rose by 35 percent in provinces that are majority indigenous, as opposed to only 21 percent in provinces where indigenous people are in the minority. Turnout, measured as a percentage of the voting-age population, rose from 49.9 percent in 1997 to 55.5 percent in 2002 in majority indigenous provinces, but it actually declined by one percentage point, from 56.7 to 55.7 percent, in minority indigenous areas during this period.[11] MAS and MIP both undertook a variety of efforts to increase turnout in their strongholds in the 2002 elections, as well as to encourage members of these communities to register to vote (Quispe 2004; Peredo 2004; Torrico 2004). Thus, in both Bolivia and Ecuador, the rise of indigenous parties has helped mobilize the indigenous electorate.

REDUCING ELECTORAL VOLATILITY AND PARTY SYSTEM FRAGMENTION

Indigenous parties in Latin America might also help build more stable and cohesive party systems in countries that have large indigenous populations. As Van Cott has shown, the Latin American countries with proportionally large indigenous populations tend to have poorly institutionalized party systems (Van Cott 2000, 155–74). Bolivia, Ecuador, Guatemala, and Peru all have extremely high levels of electoral volatility (the net change in votes, or seats, among parties between elections), which is one commonly used measure of party system institutionalization. All four of these countries also have highly fragmented party systems. Indeed, between 1980 and 2000, Bolivia, Ecuador, and Guatemala had the most fragmented party systems in the entire region, measured in terms of the effective number of parties in presidential elections (Payne et al. 2002, 73). The high levels of electoral fragmentation and volatility have complicated democratic governance in these countries, making it difficult to enact legislation and to sustain policies and programs over time.

This situation has various causes, institutional factors among them; but the voting patterns of the indigenous population in these countries have certainly contributed to the problem (Madrid 2005a and 2005b). In all four countries, electoral volatility and party system fragmentation have typically been higher in municipalities or provinces where indigenous people represent a large proportion of the population. For example, from 1985 to 1997, Bolivian provinces where indigenous people represented less than one-third of the population had an average of 3.3 effective parties, whereas provinces where the indigenous constituted more than two-thirds of the population had an average of 4.7 effective parties. During this same period, electoral volatility averaged 24 percent in the provinces with less than one-third indigenous population and 42 percent in those with more than two-thirds indigenous population.[12]

The problem also stems partly from the failure of the major parties to represent adequately the interests of the indigenous population, especially their low indigenous recruitment levels and their failure to embrace indigenous-supported programs and policies. Partly for this reason, none of these parties has been able to gain the enduring loyalties of a large proportion of the indigenous population. Instead of consistently supporting a single party, indigenous voters have shifted their votes frequently among a variety of different parties.

The emergence of indigenous parties, however, has the potential to remedy this situation. Indigenous parties may be able to gain the enduring allegiances of large numbers of indigenous voters, thereby reducing electoral volatility and party system fragmentation in highly indigenous areas (Birnir 2004; Madrid 2005a and 2005b). Indeed, the emergence of major indigenous parties in Bolivia and Ecuador has already reduced party system fragmentation in such areas. In Bolivia, the effective number of parties in majority indigenous provinces declined after the rise of MAS, dropping from an average of 4.6 in 1985–97 to 4.0 in 2002. The emergence of Pachakutik also led the effective number of parties to decline in majority indigenous counties in Ecuador, from 6.1 in 1992 to 4.8 in the period 1996–2002. In nonindigenous areas in both countries, by contrast, the level of party system fragmentation actually rose during these periods.

INCREASING SUPPORT FOR DEMOCRACY

The emergence of indigenous parties may contribute to democratic consolidation in Latin America by helping to build support for democracy and democratic institutions in the region. Disenchantment with democracy is high throughout Latin America, but it is particularly high in those countries with proportionally large indigenous populations. Surveys conducted in 2005 by Latinobarómetro reveal that only 32 percent of the population in Guatemala, 40 percent in Peru, 43 percent in Ecuador and 46 percent in Bolivia preferred democracy to any other kind of government in 2005, as opposed to 53 percent regionwide (Latinobarómetro 1995: 56).[13] Only 13 percent of the survey respondents in Ecuador, 14 percent in Peru, 24 percent in Bolivia, and 28 percent in Guatemala stated that they were very or fairly satisfied with democracy in 2005, as opposed to 31 percent in Latin America as a whole (Latinobarómetro 1995: 58). Similarly, surveys of democratic values carried out in 2004 by the Latin American Public Opinion Project (LAPOP) at Vanderbilt University found that average support for the political system was lower in Bolivia, Guatemala, and Ecuador than in all but one of the other Latin American countries surveyed (Seligson et al 2006: 129).

Survey data on the political views of the indigenous population in Latin America are relatively scarce, but what material does exist supports the notion that indigenous people are frustrated with the political system and do not feel well represented by the existing parties. In a 1988 survey of the Ecuadorian indigenous population, 46.1 of the respondents said that no party represented their interests (Chiriboga and Rivera 1989, 213). In a 1997 survey in Peru, 48.9 percent of indigenous respondents declared that they had no trust in political institutions, as opposed to only 28.4 of the nonindigenous respondents (Democracy Survey Database 2004). Whereas 34.3 percent of the indigenous respondents in Bolivia said it had no trust at all in political parties in a 1998 survey, less than 29 percent of the nonindigenous population reported similar feelings (Democracy Survey Database 2004). Similarly, a survey carried out in Guatemala in 2001 found that indigenous people expressed significantly less support for the political system, including political parties, than did the nonindigenous (Azpuru 2003).

Public opinion data, however, also indicate that indigenous people continue to prefer democracy to other forms of government. In the 1998 survey in Bolivia, only 27.2 of the indigenous respondents said that a coup would be justified for certain reasons, as opposed to 31.7 of all respondents (Democracy Survey Database 2004). Similarly, in Peru, only 23.1 percent of the respondents who spoke an indigenous language said that a military coup would be justified under some circumstances, as opposed to 26.6 percent of all respondents (Democracy Survey Database 2004). In a 1998 survey in Guatemala, meanwhile, 28.2 percent of indigenous respondents reported that a military coup would not be justified under any circumstances, as opposed to 33.5 perecent of the nonindigenous respondents (Democracy Survey Database 2004). These data suggest that indigenous people continue to believe in the principle of democracy even though they are frustrated with how democratic institutions have functioned to date.

The emergence of indigenous parties might help shore up support for democracy among indigenous people for a number of reasons. Indigenous parties should make elections more meaningful for some indigenous people by enabling them to vote for a party that seeks to represent them. Indeed, the increase in voter participation that has occurred in indigenous areas in Bolivia and Ecuador in recent years suggests that the emergence of indigenous parties has increased interest in the electoral process among indigenous voters in those countries. The rise of indigenous parties will presumably increase the number of indigenous representatives in the legislature, which may, in turn, increase indigenous support for this institution. The electoral success of the MAS and, to a lesser extent, the MIP caused the number of indigenous legislators in Bolivia to grow from 10 in 1997 to 52 (out of 130) in 2002, according to some estimates (Albó 2002, 95; Rivero Pinto 2002, 36). This has given the Bolivian legislature an important indigenous presence.

Indigenous leaders may penetrate other governmental institutions as indigenous parties become more powerful, which should boost indigenous support for these institutions, too. In Ecuador, for example, leaders of Pachakutik took over a number of important governmental ministries after the election of Gutiérrez, although they were obliged to resign these positions after Pachakutik broke with the Gutiérrez administration.

As indigenous parties become increasingly powerful, more indigenous people may come to believe that they can bring about policy change by working through existing political institutions, which should increase support for democracy. Moreover, to the extent that indigenous parties can effect policy changes that benefit the indigenous population, indigenous support for democratic institutions should grow. One of the reasons that so many members of the indigenous population are frustrated with the existing political institutions is that the lives of many indigenous people have not significantly improved since the return to democracy in the region.

Whether the rise of indigenous parties actually does increase support for democracy among the indigenous population will depend partly on the actions of the party leaders. Those leaders must behave democratically and pragmatically themselves. They must not only respect the existing democratic institutions but also work to diffuse democratic practices at the local level. In addition, they must reach out to nonindigenous citizens and parties, practice good governance, and propose realistic solutions to the problems facing their countries and the indigenous population in particular.

REDUCING POLITICAL VIOLENCE

The emergence of indigenous parties may also help reduce political violence involving the indigenous population. Indigenous organizations have participated in many peaceful protests in recent years, but they have also been involved in a significant number of actions that have turned violent, including strikes, demonstrations, roadblocks, and seizures of public or private property. In surveys, indigenous people have also expressed greater support than nonindigenous for these aggressive types of political activities (Seligson 2002, 194–96; Democracy Survey Database 2004).

These protests may have laudable aims, but they have, at times, had destabilizing effects. Many of these activities themselves, such as roadblocks and the seizure of property, are illegal, and the participation of indigenous movements thereby undermines the rule of law. Such actions tend to provoke confrontation with the state and at times have culminated in violence, often initiated by security forces trying to repress the protests. Sometimes these protests have spiraled out of control, directly undermining existing democratic institutions. Indeed, in some cases they have led to the overthrow or resignation of elected presidents.

In Ecuador, indigenous people spearheaded the uprising that led to the removal of President Mahuad in 2000. This revolt began when CONAIE, along with the public sector unions, initiated a series of strikes and marches in late 1999 to protest Mahuad's neoliberal economic and social policies. These protests intensified in January 2000, when Mahuad announced his decision to replace the local currency with the U.S. dollar. CONAIE called for mass protests in Quito, and thousands of its members traveled to the capital to participate. A large number of junior officers in the military, led by Colonel Lucio Gutiérrez, joined in. When the protesters marched on the presidential palace, Mahuad fled, and a junta composed of Gutiérrez; the head of CONAIE, Antonio Vargas; and a former Supreme Court judge took control. The coup lasted less than a day, however. The military forced Gutiérrez to cede his position to an army general, who promptly handed power over to the vice president, Gustavo Noboa. The indigenous movement in Ecuador thus succeeded in helping to topple a president but failed to take power itself. Gutiérrez was subsequently elected president in 2002 with the support of Pachakutik, but he was ousted in the wake of social protests in 2005. Although the indigenous movement had broken with the Gutiérrez by that time and had participated in protests against his administration, it played no role in his 2005 ouster, which was led by middle class groups (Pachano 2005).

Indigenous people also helped to overthrow Bolivian President Gonzalo Sánchez de Lozada. This uprising began in mid-September 2003, when the main indigenous peasant confederation in Bolivia, Confederación Sindical Única de Trabajadores Campesinos de Bolivia (CSUTCB), organized rural roadblocks to protest Sánchez de Lozada's economic and social policies, particularly the decision to export natural gas to the United States. When government troops tried to break a roadblock, four protesters and a soldier were killed. The largest indigenous party, MAS, and the main labor group, the Bolivian Workers' Confederation (COB), then joined in, and with their assistance, protests quickly spread to La Paz and El Alto, the large, mostly indigenous city overlooking La Paz. The government ordered the army to suppress the protests, and in the ensuing clashes, more than 50 people were killed. The repression led Vice President Carlos Mesa and the New Republican Force (NFR), one of the main parties in the ruling coalition, to withdraw their support for the Sánchez de Lozada administration. On October 17, 2003, an increasingly isolated Sánchez de Lozada resigned, leaving Mesa in control.

The participation of indigenous people and movements in certain kinds of protests can thus have destabilizing effects. The emergence of indigenous parties, however, may reduce the appeal of these protests to both indigenous people and their leaders by increasing the costs and reducing the benefits of such activities. Indigenous people and leaders have sometimes supported demonstrations, strikes, roadblocks, and property invasions partly because they believed that such measures were the only available means to exert pressure on the government. The rise of indigenous parties, however, has enabled indigenous people to express their views more fully at the ballot box, and it has given them some degree of influence in the legislature and even in the executive branch. Indigenous people and leaders have thus acquired ways of making their voice heard that are potentially more powerful than protests.

The costs of protests have traditionally been low for indigenous leaders because they did not need to worry about the electoral impact of such measures. Protests bring potentially high costs for leaders of indigenous parties, however, because such protests risk antagonizing moderate indigenous voters, along with nonindigenous people who might otherwise be inclined to vote for the indigenous parties. Indeed, a variety of surveys suggest that the majority of indigenous as well as nonindigenous people oppose such protests. In a recent survey in Bolivia, for example, only one-third of indigenous respondents voiced support for roadblocks, and only 15 percent of them supported property invasions or takeovers of factories or buildings (Seligson 2002, 194–96). The leaders of indigenous parties, particularly major parties with good electoral possibilities, therefore have strong incentives to discourage or moderate such protests, or at least to distance themselves from the protests when they occur.

The electoral successes of MAS and Pachakutik may have had a moderating effect on their leaders, rendering them more cautious than some of the other indigenous leaders in these countries, although it has certainly not led them to foreswear protests altogether. The leadership of Pachakutik did not participate in the overthrow of Mahuad, nor did the party play a role in the recent overthrow of President Gutiérrez. MAS played only a minor and reactive role in the overthrow of Sánchez de Lozada, and may have actually had a moderating effect on the outcome. Antonio Peredo, the leader of MAS's congressional delegation and its 2002 vice presidential candidate, argues, "We are sure of having acted more rationally than others at that time. We were not the organizers of those mobilizations. There wasn't an organizer, there were various. Many of those leaders spoke about installing a revolutionary triumvirate . . . We wanted a constitutional solution" (2004).

In the immediate aftermath of the overthrow of Sánchez de Lozada, moreover, the MAS served as a moderating force in Bolivia. Indeed, it supported the Mesa administration during its first year in power and largely eschewed protests. Gustavo Torrico, a MAS congressional deputy, explains, "when we did not have a legitimate representative we did not have any option other than fighting in the streets and roads. Afterward we gained a significant [legislative] contingent. We decided in Congress to shift from protests to proposals" (2004). Evo Morales similarly emphasizes that MAS has "decided to reach power by means of the vote, not by arms, nor by insurrectional means" (*Economist* 2004, 37).

In early 2005, relations between Morales and Mesa deteriorated, and the MAS and other organizations initiated a series of protests against the government's policies, which ultimately led to the resignation of President Mesa in June 2005. New elections were called for December 2005, and Morales and the MAS won these elections by a large margin. Since Morales took office in January 2006, the indigenous movement has largely eschewed protests. Morales continues to wield a great deal of control over the movement, particularly the coca growers' unions, and he has sought to avoid any protests that might destabilize his government. Most indigenous leaders, meanwhile, have been inclined to assume that Morales is doing his best to respond to their demands, although they have not hesitated from criticizing other members of his administration. Thus, the rise of an indigenous party in Bolivia seems to have dampened indigenous protests to date.

Nevertheless, many people continue to believe that Morales represents a threat to Bolivian democracy. Nonindigenous elites in Santa Cruz and other eastern departments in Bolivia have been particularly suspicious of Morales' intentions and have renewed their push for regional autonomy. The government's efforts to restructure Bolivia's political institutions via a constituent assembly are of particular concern to many people who view this as an attempt by Morales to consolidate his own power. Morales and some members of his administration have also provoked concern by making intemperate statements at times. For example, the Bolivian vice president, Alvaro García Linera, recently had to apologize for a speech he gave in a heavily Aymara province in which he called upon the residents to defend the government's revolutionary policies with their rocks and rifles ("Omasuyos amenaza a Santa Cruz . . ." 2006). This provocative language notwithstanding, the Morales administration has acted somewhat cautiously to date, and it is far too early to tell what impact his government will have on Bolivian democracy.

CONCLUSIONS

This chapter has argued that the emergence of major indigenous parties in Latin America does not pose the serious threat to democracy that some commentators have suggested. Not only are the major indigenous parties unlikely to create more ethnic polarization and conflict, but they actually have the potential to contribute to democratic deepening in a number of significant ways. The major indigenous parties, for example, should improve political representation, expand political participation, and reduce party system fragmentation and electoral volatility in countries with large indigenous populations.

Indigenous parties may even boost support for democracy and reduce political violence in countries with large indigenous populations, but whether they do will depend partly on how indigenous leaders reconcile the conflicting pressures they will face as they attempt to develop competitive indigenous parties. On the one hand, leaders will face pressure from indigenous activists and other members of their traditional constituencies to participate in protests and to demand radical changes in government policy. On the other hand, they will face significant electoral incentives to moderate their views and actions and to form alliances with mainstream political parties in order to attract more voters and gain political influence. If indigenous leaders follow the former path, they risk not only destabilizing democracy but also limiting their own effectiveness, because radical policies and actions are likely to antagonize many voters and marginalize the new indigenous parties from the mainstream, of politics. If they compromise too much, however, they risk alienating their voter base and losing their reason for being.

This, too, could destabilize democracy, because it might ultimately worsen the existing levels of democratic disaffection among the indigenous population and lead to the rise of more radical indigenous leaders and organizations. To succeed, therefore, the leaders of indigenous parties will need to navigate carefully the perilous path between compromise and cooptation.

NOTES

1 A few scholars, however, have suggested that ethnic parties may actually help consolidate democracy, although for very different reasons. See Chandra 2005; Birnir 2004.

2 Constructivists have criticized this primordial approach to understanding ethnicity, arguing that ethnic identities are fluid rather than fixed. For a discussion of what this means for theories of ethnic conflict, see Chandra 2005.

3 Recent surveys suggest that many people who might, under some circumstances, identify as indigenous will self-identify as mestizo if that option is given to them, including people that speak indigenous languages (INE 2001; Seligson 2002; PNUD 2004).

4 All data comparing electoral results in majority and minority indigenous districts in Bolivia and Ecuador are based on the author's analysis of subnational census and electoral data. The Bolivian data come from FUNDEMOS 1998, Bolivia. Corte Nacional Electoral 2002, and INE 2001. The Ecuadorian data were generously made available to the author by Tribunal Supremo Electoral and Sistema Integrado de Indicadores Sociales de Ecuador.

5 The indigenous population is also unlikely to form a uniform voting bloc because it contains considerable internal diversity, which has sometimes led to significant conflicts and divisions. In 2002, the indigenous population in Bolivia split over which indigenous parties to support. Much of the MAS's support came from Quechua areas, whereas the overwhelming majority of the MIP's votes came from Aymara areas.

6 See, for example, the survey data from Bolivia presented in Seligson 2002, 53.

7 Boneo and Torres-Rivas (2001) did not find a correlation between the proportion of the population that is indigenous and voter turnout in general elections in Guatemala, but they did not control for other institutional and socioeconomic factors that affect turnout. They measured turnout as a

percentage of registered voters because they, unlike Lehoucq and Wall (2001), did not have access to data on the voting-age population at the municipal level. However, Boneo and Torres-Rivas present survey results indicating that indigenous people are less likely than ladinos to be registered to vote.

8 Author's findings based on an analysis of municipal-level electoral and census data from Mexico.

9 In a 1998 survey, the most common reason indigenous respondents gave for not voting was that they did not have their identity cards (Democracy Survey Database 2004).

10 Where indigenous people feel that they have a stake in elections, however, they may vote at higher rates than nonindigenous people. For example, voter turnout in indigenous municipalities in Guatemala exceeded voter turnout in nonindigenous municipalities for the 1999 referendum (Consulta Popular), presumably because the ballot contained questions about indigenous rights (Boneo and Torres-Rivas 2001).

11 Survey data from Bolivia also support the notion that the emergence of indigenous parties has boosted voter turnout. In a 1998 survey, only 74 percent of indigenous respondents reported voting in the 1997 elections, as opposed to 77 percent of nonindigenous respondents (Democracy Survey Database 2004). In the 2002 elections, however, 85 percent of indigenous respondents reported voting, the same percentage as nonindigenous respondents.

12 Party system fragmentation is measured here using the Laakso-Taagepera index, which is the inverse of the sum of squares of each party's share of the total vote. Electoral volatility is calculated using the Pederson index, which is half of the sum of the net change in the proportion of votes won by each party from one election to another.

13 These data represent unweighted country averages.

REFERENCES

Albó, Xavier. 2002. Bolivia: From Indian and Campesino Leaders to Councillors and Parliamentary Deputies. In *Multiculturalism in Latin America*, ed. Rachel Seider. New York: Palgrave Macmillan. 74–102.

Asociación de Investigación y Estudios Sociales (ASIES). 2000. *Guatemala: informe analítico del proceso electoral 1999.* Guatemala City: ASIES.

Azpuru, Dinorah. 2003. Indigenous Perceptions of Democracy in Guatemala. Paper prepared for delivery at the 2003 Annual Meeting of the American Political Science Association, Philadelphia, August 28–31.

Birnir, Johanna. 2004. The Ethnic Effect: The Effect of Ethnic Electoral Behavior on the Political Development of New Democracies. Unpublished mss. Bolivia. Corte Nacional Electoral. 2002. Unpublished electoral data supplied to the author.

Bolivia. Instituto Nacional de Estadística (INE). 2001. *Censo de población y vivienda.* <www.ine.gov.bo> (Accessed September 2004)

Boneo, Horacio, and Edelberto Torres-Rivas. 2001. *¿Por qué no votan los guatemaltecos?* Guatemala City: Tribunal Supremo Electoral.

Chandra, Kanchan. 2005. Ethnic Parties and Democratic Stability. *Perspectives on Politics* 3, 2 (June): 235–52.

Chiriboga, Manuel, and Fredy Rivera. 1989. Elecciones de enero 1988 y participación indígena. *Ecuador Debate* 17: 181–21.

Democracy Survey Database. 2004. Sponsored by the U.S. Agency for International Development and the Latin American Public Opinion Project. <www.millennium-int.com/newdsd> (Accessed September 2004).

Economist. 2004. A Political Awakening. February 21: 35–37.

FUNDEMOS. 1998. Datos estadísticos elecciones generales, 1979–1997. *Opiniones y Análisis* 31 (February). (entire issue)

Hooker, Juliet. 2001. The Myth of Inclusion: Mestizo Nationalism, Identity Politics, and Citizenship in Nicaragua. Ph.D. diss., Cornell University.

Horowitz, Donald L. 1985. *Ethnic Groups in Conflict.* Berkeley: University of California Press.

Instituto Nacional de Estadística (INE). 2001. *Censo Nacional de Población y Vivienda: Resultados Nacionales.* La Paz: INE.

Latin American Andean Group Report. 2003. Are Indigenous Uprisings the Latest Domino Theory? November 4: 7–9.

Latin American Weekly Report. 2003. Is "Indigenous Fundamentalism" the New Hemispheric Threat? November 18: 1.

Latinobarómetro. 2005. *1995–2005: A Decade of Public Opinion.* Santiago de Chile: Latinobarómetro.

Lehoucq, Fabrice, and David Wall. 2001. La explicación es institucional o sociológica? In *Construyendo la democracia electoral en Guatemala,* ed. Edelberto Torres-Rivas et al. Guatemala City: FLACSO.

Madrid, Raúl L. 2005a. Ethnic Cleavages and Electoral Volatility in Latin America. *Comparative Politics* 38, 1 (October): 1–20.

———. 2005b. Indigenous Voters and Party System Fragmentation in Latin America. *Electoral Studies* 24: 689–707.

Núñez, Dionisio. 2004. Deputy, MAS. Author interview. La Paz, July 21.

"Omasuyos amenaza a Santa Cruz . . ." 2006. *La Razón,* 21 de septiembre. On-line edition available at <http://www.la-razon.com/>. Accessed: September 22, 2006.

Oppenheimer, Andres. 2003. What Would Latin America Be Without Western Influence? *Miami Herald,* November 6: 16A.

Pachano, Simón. 2005. Ecuador: Cuando la Inestabilidad Se Vuelve Estable. *Íconos.* 23, (septiembre): 37–44.

Payne, Mark J., Daniel Zovatto, Fernando Carrillo Flórez, and Andres Allamand Zavala. 2002. *Democracies in Development: Politics and Reform in Latin America.* Washington, DC: Inter-American Development Bank.

Pedrero, Antonio. 2004. Head of MAS congressional delegation. Author interview. La Paz, July 22.

Programa de las Naciones Unidas para el Desarrollo (PNUD). 2004. *Interculturalismo y globalización: informe nacional de desarrollo humano 2004.* La Paz: PNUD.

Quispe, Felipe. 2004. Founder of MIP, head of the CSUTCB. Author interview. La Paz, July 29.

Rabushka, Alvin, and Kenneth Shepsle. 1972. *Politics in Plural Societies.* Columbus: Merril.

Reilly, Benjamin. 2002. Electoral Systems for Divided Societies. *Journal of Democracy* 13, 2 (April): 156–70.

Rivero Pinto, Wigberto. 2002. Indígenas y campesinos en las elecciones: el poder de la Bolivia emergente. *Opiniones y Análisis* 60: 11–40.

Rizo Zeledón, Mario. 1990. El caso de la RAAN. *Revista de la Costa Caribe Nicaraguense* (July–December): 28–51.

Ruiz Mondragón, Laura. 1998. *Los pueblos indios en los comicios federales de 1997.*Mexico City: Instituto Nacional Indigenista.

Seligson, Mitchell. 2002. *Auditoría de la democracia: Ecuador 2001.* Quito: CEDATOS. 2002. Auditoría de la democracia: Bolivia 2002. La Paz: Universidad Católica Boliviana.

Seligson, Mitchell A., et al. 2006. *Democracy Audit: Bolivia 2006 Report.* Nashville: LAPOP, Vanderbilt University.

Sisk, Timothy. 1996. Power Sharing and International Mediation in Ethnic Conflicts. Washington, DC: U.S. Institute of Peace Press.

Ticona, Esteban, Gonzalo Rojas, and Xavier Albó. 1995. *Votos y wiphalas: campesinos y pueblos originarios en democracia.* La Paz: Fundación Milenio.

Torrico, Gustavo. 2004. MAS Deputy. Author interview. La Paz, July 22.

Van Cott, Donna Lee. 2000. Party System Development and Indigenous Populations in Latin America: The Bolivian Case. *Party Politics* 6, 2: 155–74.

———. 2003. Institutional Change and Ethnic Parties in South America. *Latin American Politics and Society* 45, 2 (Summer): 1–40.

———. 2004. From Movement to Party: The Transformation of Ethnic Politics in Latin America. Unpublished mss.

Yashar, Deborah. 1999. Democracy, Indigenous Movements, and the Postliberal Challenge in Latin America. *World Politics* 52 (October): 76–104.

———. 2005. *Contesting Citizenship in Latin America: The Rise of Indigenous Movements and the Postliberal Challenge.* New York: Cambridge University Press.

Chapter 12

Defining Rights in Democratization: The Argentine Government and Human Rights Organizations, 1983–2003

Michelle D. Bonner

The human rights abuses that occurred in Argentina under the last military dictatorship (1976–1983) were unprecedented in that country. As many as 30,000 people disappeared, thousands were imprisoned for political reasons, and thousands more were killed. Addressing these human rights abuses and confronting a history of differentially applied and often unenforced rights continues to be an important issue in Argentina. Indeed, the current Argentine president, Néstor Kirchner, has stated that human rights are central to the agenda of his new government.

However, the pursuit of human rights by the Argentine government requires a certain level of agreement between political actors in state and society regarding the definition of human rights, the justification for their protection, and their universal enforcement. Since 1983, human rights organizations (HROs) in Argentina have been participating in a public debate regarding the rights that are to be deemed integral to democracy. They have framed this debate by justifying their demands in terms of the need to protect the family. The response of the state to demands framed in this manner suggests a less-than-universal notion of whose rights need protection.

Argentine state actors have been more willing (or able) to respond to demands made by HROs that are presented in a manner that emphasizes the place of the children of the disappeared in the family, rather than the place of the disappeared themselves. In contrast, international courts have increasingly provided HROs that present the family in a manner not supported by the state with an important channel through which to persuade the state of the need to enforce universal rights.

This article argues that the use of international courts by HROs is decreasing their need to tie their demands for the protection of human rights to the protection of particular presentations of the family. The article divides the analysis into the three major presidential periods between 1983 and 2003 in order to illustrate the use of the family frame by different HROs over time, the increased use of international courts, and the corresponding legal responses of the Argentine state.

The idea of social movements framing their demands in order to make them persuasive originates in the literature on collective action frames. In particular, Sidney Tarrow argues that one of the greatest challenges for social movements is framing contention in such a way that the symbols used are both familiar and dynamic (1998, 107). That is, the symbols used by social movement organizations must be rooted in the history of the country but at the same time contain a transformational power. In Argentina, the family is the symbol rooted in history that is used as a reason for the protection of human rights.[1] While Argentina has not had a tradition of rights protection, the justification for the protection of rights based on the family draws on a long history of nationalism that has consistently identified the family as the building block of the nation.[2]

In this article, the persuasive power of HROs' demands is understood as the correlation between the justification of the family as the basis for rights protection and the successful establishment and enforcement of rights by the state. The focus of the analysis, and of most of the HROs, is on the legal recognition and enforcement of human rights as they pertain to the abuses that occurred during the last dictatorship.[3]

The state, in this scenario, is an ambiguous term, especially in Latin America. The literature makes clear that in Latin America there is an important distinction between state institutions and the practices of state actors. On the one hand, state institutions reflect the liberal democratic objectives of nineteenth-century Latin American constitutions. State institutions include the executive, senate, house of representatives, and judiciary. In contrast, state actors and their political practices have been much more heterogeneous (Migdal 2001, 15–16). The impact of state actors on state institutions has consistently kept the liberal democratic state institutions from functioning in the manner for which they were designed. Most important, key decisionmaking has taken place outside of most liberal democratic state institutions, and those alternative groups of state actors and their decisionmaking processes have varied. In Argentina and most of Latin America, key state actors have included the executive, the economic elite, the military, the church, and sometimes organized labor.

Douglas A. Chalmers (1977) refers to this form of state as the "politicized state." Alliances are formed among the elite in order to maintain control of state institutions. These alliances vary as factions emerge within each of the previously identified state actors. What remains consistent is that access to the state has been restricted primarily to the elite, who have often governed with the explicit intention of excluding the masses or including them in a controlled manner (Imaz 1968; Cardoso 1979; Oxhorn 1995).

The striking use of the state to maintain divisions between the elite and the masses leads some authors, such as Diane Davis (1999), to argue that rather than a state–society dichotomy, in Latin America the key division is between the elite and the masses and their relative space from the state. In other words, it is important which political actors from the elite (and sometimes the masses) are included in decisionmaking and how they are included.

While historically, forms of corporatism have been the primary channel for the masses to access decisionmaking, the history of leaders of civil society organizations being coopted by the executive has made HROs cautious about using semicorporatist channels.[4] The noninstitutionalized nature of political parties limits the benefits of using this liberal democratic channel of access to state decisionmaking (Rubio and Goretti 1998, 51–54; Nino 1996, 165–66; Manzetti 1993, chap.3).[5] Because HROs focus on rights, however, and they understand that the definition and enforcement of rights requires the establishment of horizontal accountability, HROs have chosen national courts in combination with international, courts as their key channels of access to state decisionmaking.[6]

Hence, this analysis of debate between HROs and the state will focus on the interaction between the HROs and the courts, national and international. As part of the state, the national courts are subject to the limitations posed by a politicized state, especially excessive executive power and an influential military. In contrast, international courts provide HROs the means and opportunity to challenge the practices of the politicized state.

While the human rights movement in Argentina is very large, this study focuses on a comparative analysis of the ten most prominent HROs, self-identified as the "historical" HROs.[7] The historical HROs consist of five organizations of family members of victims of the last dictatorship (self-identified as the "affected" or *afectados*) and five organizations that have worked in solidarity with the Affected organizations since the disappearances began (self-identified as the Solidarity organizations; see table 1). These organizations are considered by the activist community, media, and government to be the unofficial

Table 1. Historical Human Rights Organizations in Argentina

Affected	Solidarity
Mothers of the Plaza de Mayo—Founding Line (Mothers—Founding Line)[a]	Argentine League for the Rights of Men (Human Rights League)
Association of the Mothers of the Plaza de Mayo (Mothers Association)	Ecumenical Human Rights Movement
Grandmothers of the Plaza de Mayo (Grandmothers)	Permanent Human Rights Assembly
HIJOS (Children of the Disappeared)[b]	Peace and Justice Service
Families of the Disappeared and Imprisoned for Political Reasons (Families)	Center for Legal and Social Studies

[a]The Mothers of the Plaza de Mayo split in 1986 because of internal disputes, especially over leadership and reparations.
[b]Hijos por la Identidad y la Justicia contra el Olvido y el Silencio (Children for Identity and Justice Against Forgetting and Silence).

leadership of the human rights movement.[8] For the sake of simplicity, this study uses the abbreviation HROs to refer to the ten HROs being analyzed, not the human rights movement as a whole.

Not all HROs use the family frame in the same manner, and hence not all receive the same response from state actors. The Affected HROs primarily consist of women who gain significant legitimacy from their traditional role as representatives of the family. Affected HROs generally emphasize their relationship with the "disappeared," with the notable exception of the Grandmothers of the Plaza de Mayo, who emphasize their relationship to their missing grandchildren (children of the disappeared who were adopted into homes the military regime considered "nonsubversive"). Solidarity HROs have primarily male leadership. They provide important legal assistance to Affected HROs and benefit from the latter's emotionally and symbolically powerful family discourse.[9]

STATE-HRO INTERACTIONS IN COURT, 1983–2003

Debates regarding human rights in Argentina take place in the context of democratization. Electoral democracy was restored in Argentina in 1983. Political rights, such as running for office, were extended to all political parties, including the historically controversial Peronist Party. In 1989, Argentina experienced the first peaceful transfer of power from one political party to another since 1916. In 1999, the Peronist Party left office through elections (as opposed to a coup) for the first time ever. But while elections were strengthening, political parties were not institutionalizing. Both Presidents Raúl Alfonsín and Carlos Menem revealed a preference for what Carlos Nino (1996) calls "hyperpresidentialism." This concentration of decisionmaking power in the executive was intensified by increasing economic problems, which provided the executive with a justification for bypassing democratic channels, such as Congress and the judiciary. The concentration of power in the executive and the consequent influence the presidency has had on the pursuit of human rights can be traced over successive presidential periods.

Justice and the Retraction of Justice, 1983–1989

The first democratically elected president, Raúl Alfonsín (1983–89), attempted to build his political party (the Radicals) as a party based on his leadership. He did so by appropriating from the opposition Peronist Party the support of unions, the working class, and the social justice rhetoric (McGuire 1997, 191). However, Alfonsín lacked the charisma and skill to build the support he needed (McGuire 1997, 192), support that was further weakened by military rebellions and economic crisis. At its height in 1989, the economic crisis led inflation to reach 5,000 percent and precipitated the president's early resignation (Frenkel and Rozenwulrcel 1996, 220).

Initially, however, the transition to electoral democracy in 1983 inspired hope for many Argentines. Alfonsín had been active in one of the historical human rights organizations, the Permanent Human Rights Assembly (APDH), during the dictatorship, and many voters thought that he would be committed to seeking justice for human rights violations.

Instead of going to the courts themselves, HROs believed that the new democratic government would take three key actions. First, before 1983 and for a few months after the first presidential election, HRO activists believed that Alfonsín would be able to bring the disappeared back alive. Immediately after his election, Alfonsín met with the Mothers of the Plaza de Mayo; he agreed with them that disappeared people existed who were alive, and he committed himself to finding them (AMPM 1999, 27–28). Unfortunately, however, the disappeared did not return, despite Alfonsín's efforts. It was further expected that the military's self-amnesty would be nullified. On December 13, 1983, Alfonsín passed Decree 158, which called for the trial of human rights crimes committed by all leaders of the military regime and subordinates who went beyond their orders. Decree 158 replaced the self-amnesty law passed by the military government. Third, many Argentines expected that those responsible for the human rights abuses of the dictatorship would be charged. Trials against those who committed human rights abuses began in 1985.

The Mothers of the Plaza de Mayo played a central role in debates with the state regarding human rights during the first few years of democracy. It was initially thought that their children could be brought back alive, and it was expected that those people responsible for the children's disappearance would be brought to justice. The focus was on uniting families (mothers with children) and bringing justice against those who had forced them apart.

Before the trials against the military, Alfonsín established the National Commission on Disappeared People (CONADEP, established December 15, 1983). CONADEP played an important role in collecting the information necessary for the subsequent trials. All the historical HROs, with the exception of the Mothers (and HIJOS, because this group did not exist yet), agreed to provide information to the commission.[10] The CONADEP report, *Nunca más*, published in November 1984, provided an important basis on which to judge the trials that began on April 22, 1985. According to CONADEP, 1,351 people were reported as responsible for human rights violations during the last dictatorship. Almost all of those (1,195) were processed under the Military Justice Code (*Código de Justicia Militar*) in civilian courts. However, only seven of the accused were ever sentenced (although those sentenced included former heads of state) (Familiares 2000).

One of the greatest challenges in debates between the state and society in Latin America, and particularly Argentina, is that of the amorphous nature of the state. While Alfonsín's intention may very well have been to have all those military officers responsible for human rights abuses sentenced by the courts, thereby strengthening institutional democracy and civilian control of the military, the military continued to wield a significant amount of power over the government. Not only did three military rebellions take place during Alfonsín's term in office, but as Patrice McSherry argues, the structural legacy of the Process of National Reorganization—that is, the armed and security forces, intelligence organizations, and the judiciary—remained intact (1997, 2).[11]

Pressure from the military led the government to compromise its initial position on human rights. In December 1986, Alfonsín announced the legislation known as Final Point, which placed a 60-day limit on penal action against those reported to have participated in human rights violations during the dictatorship. Only 450 cases against generals, leaders, officers, subofficers, and police were permitted (García 1995, 263).

Rather than calming the military, Final Point contributed to increased military resistance and rebellion. In response, Alfonsín pushed the Due Obedience law through Congress, gaining its approval on June 5, 1987. Due Obedience made all leaders and officials who had actively participated in the "antisubversive struggle," up to the level of lieutenant colonel, exempt from responsibility and excused them from all charges.

Of the 1,195 military personnel who had been processed for abuses of human rights, 730 benefited from Final Point and 379 were deprocessed as a result of the Due Obedience law. Another 43 people were deprocessed by the Supreme Court. The pardons decreed by President Menem in 1989 deemed another 38 people, who had been processed by the courts, exempt from punishment (in addition to 280 officers involved in issues concerning the Falklands/Malvinas war and the military rebellions in 1987 and 1988. García 1995, 270). In December 1990, Menem decreed further pardons for top-level military officers, freeing six officers, five of whom had fixed sentences (García 1995, 270; see table 2).

The amnesty laws had an important impact on the HROs and the manner in which they pursued justice for human rights abuses. The amnesty laws did not change the way HROs framed their demands, but they did affect the presentations of the family to which the state could legally respond. Consequently, the state placed a priority on interactions with some HROs over others.

Two loopholes in the amnesty laws led to corresponding changes in the priority given to some human rights claims. First, the stealing of babies (allegedly by members of the military dictatorship) was not covered under the amnesty laws. The exemption meant that the courts could still be used to locate and find justice for the grandchildren of the Grandmothers of the Plaza de Mayo. Second, HROs unable to pursue cases of human rights abuses nationally benefited from increased opportunities to do so at the international level.

Table 2. Impact of the Amnesty Laws and Pardons (number of persons)

Human rights violators identified by CONADEP	1,351
Processed in the courts beginning in 1985	1,195
Benefiting from Final Point in 1986	730
Benefiting from Due Obedience in 1987	379
Deprocessed by the Supreme Court	43
Benefiting from 1989 pardon	38
Benefiting from the 1990 pardon	6
Serving full sentences for human rights abuses	0

Sources: García 1995, 263–70; CONADEP 1984; Familiares 2000

The demands of the Mothers of the Plaza de Mayo and Families emphasized the return of the disappeared and justice against those who caused their disappearance. These demands were justified by reference to the destruction of the family the disappearances caused. By the late 1980s, it was clear that the disappeared were not going to return and that justice for those disappearances, at least at the national level, was not going to happen through the courts.

The most significant change in debates on rights between the state and HROs was the new focus taken at the end of the 1980s on the stealing of babies. Since the demands of the Grandmothers focused on uniting the family (grandchildren with grandmothers) and deemphasized justice for the disappeared, the state was best able to continue debates with the Grandmothers. Thus the demands of the Grandmothers and the members of the family they emphasized gained persuasive strength in relation to the state after the amnesty laws were passed.

The Grandmothers met with President Alfonsín for the first time in 1986 (the year of the first amnesty law) and then again in 1988 (Abuelas 1999, 17). Nothing resulted from these meetings. However, the Grandmothers were able to forge alliances with the national Sub-Secretary of Human Rights (SSDH, established out of CONADEP), the Durand Hospital, and the Province of Buenos Aires' Ministry of Social Action to facilitate the development of a proposal for a national bank of genetics data. Alfonsín used the project as the basis for Law 23511 (passed May 11, 1987), which established that bank. The National Genetics Bank has provided important information for the Grandmothers that has helped them locate their grandchildren and pursue court cases against those who stole them.

No military rebellions have been reported as associated with the locating of missing grandchildren or the prosecution of those involved in stealing them. In contrast, military rebellions associated with the prosecution of those involved with the disappearance of "subversives" occurred in 1987, 1988, and 1990. The reason for the military's limited response on the former issue may be the family relationships emphasized by the Grandmothers. The military has always agreed that the children of the disappeared (if under the age of 10 when the parents disappeared) were innocent victims of their parents' subversive behavior. The Grandmothers' presentation of the family emphasizes this innocence. Moreover, the military also supports the link between children's connection with their true family and the maintenance of their religion, which the Grandmothers also advocate.[12]

For those HROs unable to pursue justice for human rights abuses nationally, however, the international arena appeared to be promising. In July 1988, for example, the Inter-American Court of Human Rights charged the State of Honduras with violating its obligation to respect and guarantee the right to personal integrity and the right to life in the disappearance of 100 to 150 people from 1981 to 1984. The court ordered the Honduran state to pay monetary compensation to the family of a student leader, Angel Manfredo Velásquez Rodriguez, one of the disappeared (SERPAJ 1988a). This decision set a precedent, permitting hundreds of cases from Argentina eventually to be heard. The Solidarity HROs assisted the Affected HROs in pursuing court cases at both the national and international levels.

For this reason, in the 1980s, debates between the state and HROs regarding the rights deemed integral to democracy began to exclude all Affected HROs except the Grandmothers, partly because of the state's willingness (or ability) to address the protection of the family primarily as defined and framed by the Grandmothers. That is, it began to be important to the "success" of an HRO at the national level to deemphasize the place of the disappeared in the family and instead emphasize the place of the children of the disappeared. This was the position taken by the Grandmothers and those Solidarity HROs supporting them, particularly the Center for Legal and Social Studies and the Human Rights Assembly. The strength of the military within the state and its understanding of the family were important reasons for this shift.

The Menem Years: 1989–1999

Although President Carlos Menem was able to control hyperinflation through his Convertibility Plan (which included pegging the peso to the U.S. dollar), he also increased the power of the executive, decreased the power of the judiciary, and improved the government's relationship with the military. In response to hyperinflation, in July 1989, Congress delegated its economic powers to the executive (Llanos 2001, 71). Delegated authority was an important means through which Menem was able to increase his power, and where it was lacking, he complemented this delegated authority with extensive use of Need and Urgency Decrees (NUDs) and vetoes (Rubio and Goretti 1998, 38).[13] Menem signed 336 NUDs during his first term in office. When the judiciary questioned Menem's use of decrees, Menem responded by taking control of the Supreme Court, increasing the number of judges from five to nine. In combination with two resignations, Menem was able to appoint six progovernment judges (Llanos 2001, 75). All newly appointed judges were government supporters (Linz and Stepan 1996, 201). On his election in 1989, Menem began aggressively to pursue a radical neoliberal economic plan. Almost all public firms were privatized. Meanwhile, unemployment increased dramatically. In 1989, unemployment in Argentina was at 7 percent; by 1995 it was at 18.4 percent (Teichman 2001, 222; also see INDEC). In 1997, 80 percent of all new jobs were unstable, and 29.3 percent of the economically active population was underemployed or unemployed (Pozzi 2000, 75). The military and police were used increasingly to combat rising crime and quell social protest against the government's economic policies (CELS 1998, 169–173). It is in this context that President Menem extended the pardons, effectively limiting the possibility of pursuing judicial action at the national level against the military for crimes committed during the last military regime.

The amnesty laws of the late 1980s and early 1990s led to a further split between the sites of legal debates between the state and HROs regarding the minimum legal protection of human rights needed in a democracy. At the national level, the rise of the courts as a means for seeking justice for the stealing of babies continued aided by the state's establishment of commissions that worked directly with the Grandmothers. At the international level, those HROs interested in seeking justice for the disappeared and not only the children of the disappeared found international courts increasingly helpful in the 1990s. Not only did the Inter-American Court continue to offer important support for HROs attempting to persuade the Argentine state of the need to enforce rights, but court cases against those responsible for human rights violations during the dictatorship began to be tried in Italy and Spain. These cases put further pressure on the Argentine government.

The Grandmothers of the Plaza de Mayo emphasized the importance of protecting the family while avoiding the issue of whether or not the state recognized the disappeared as subversive. The exemption of the stealing of babies from the amnesty laws provided an important opening for debates with the state. Because the Grandmothers could use this opening best, other HROs rallied behind them, notably the Center for Legal and Social Studies, the Permanent Human Rights Assembly, and the Ecumenical Human Rights Movement. The Center for Legal and Social Studies, an HRO led primarily by lawyers, offered legal expertise, strong financial backing, and significant media and international connections. As the children of the disappeared entered their twenties, some joined together to form the organization HIJOS (established in 1995). HIJOS has also assisted the Grandmothers in court cases.

Initially, court cases were held to permit children and grandparents to have genetic tests done to verify that they were indeed related. To assist in the identification of family members and to side-step legal proceedings, the state established the National Commission on the Right to Identity (CONADI). Created as a direct result of a meeting between the Grandmothers and President Menem in July 1992, CONADI was established in November of that year (Carolotto 2000). CONADI worked directly with the Grandmothers and the National Bank of Genetics Data to identify disappeared children. Its technical director, Claudia Carolotto, is the daughter of the Grandmothers' president, and all the administrative staff has worked in HROs (Carolotto 2000). With the creation of CONADI, the court cases pursued by the Grandmothers and their assisting HROs began to focus on seeking punishment for those who stole children.

As data continue to be collected, it is now thought that five hundred children were stolen (Abuelas 1999, 17; *Página/12* 2000a). Since the establishment of CONADI, approximately 64 new cases have been discovered of women who reportedly were pregnant when they disappeared (CONADI 2001). By September 2001, CONADI had 354 files on youth who were uncertain of their identity or suspected that they might be a child of the disappeared (CONADI 2001). As of June 2006, 83 children of the disappeared have been found (*Clarín* 2006b). Initially military officials, notably General Jorge Rafael Videla and Navy Commandant Admiral Emilio Eduardo Massera (presidents during the last dictatorship), were charged individually for the stealing of children.[14] However, since 1999 the courts have been investigating a systematic plan by the military regime to steal children and have been charging many high-ranking military officials for their participation. By 2001, more than a dozen high-ranking military officers had been accused, including members of the military juntas, such as Alfredo Astiz and Reynaldo Benito Antonio Bignone in addition to Videla and Massera (CELS 1999, 88, 2000, 29, 2001, 34, 2002, 20).

The first international opening for justice in cases of human rights abuses came from the Inter-American Court. The Center for Legal and Social Studies (one of the Solidarity HROs) states that the Inter-American Court is the "mechanism of international protection" most used in Argentina (CELS 1999, 362). By the early 1990s, 270 cases had been brought in the Inter-American Court against the Argentine state for illegal detention alone. In response to these cases, the court's decision was that the Argentine state should be required financially to compensate ex-political prisoners. In 1991, the Argentine government compensated all 270 ex-political prisoners who had pursued international court cases. Recognizing that the selective compensation was not sufficient, the government established a 1992 law of reparation that permitted the compensation of all ex-political prisoners who came forward to claim it. By 2000, approximately 12,800 ex-prisoners had claimed reparation (SSDH 2000b). Ex-prisoners were compensated $76.66 per day in jail (SSDH 2000a). In 1994, financial reparation was extended to families of the disappeared. They could receive $240,000 per loved one who disappeared if the person was recognized by the state as disappeared under Law 24.321, which provided families a certificate of "forced disappearance" (SSDH 2000a).

Reparation was an important "success" in the use of the Inter-American Court. That reparation, however, has been very controversial in the human rights community. The Association of the Mothers of the Plaza de Mayo (Mothers Association) strongly believes that reparation represents the state buying itself out of the responsibility of providing justice for what happened. The state can compensate families without recognizing that the disappeared were not subversives or terrorists. The Mothers Association argues that reparation is like prostitution; that it is equivalent to selling the bodies of their children (AMPM, nd). The other HROs take a more moderate position, arguing that reparation represents some recognition by the state that what happened was wrong. Moreover, some HRO members argue that there are ex-political prisoners and families of the disappeared who need the reparation money because of financial difficulties. However, all HROs agree that reparation is not sufficient justice and does not prevent the abuses from occurring again. That is, reparation is an attempt by the state to compromise with HROs regarding the protection of the family without providing the enforcement of rights.

The Inter-American Court was not the only international court used by HROs in the 1990s. The court cases in Italy and later Spain gave legal support to families in other countries whose loved ones disappeared during the last Argentine dictatorship.

In Italy there were two major proceedings. The first began in 1987 (although it was put on hold until 1990) and involved the families of eight Italian citizens who disappeared. Two of the disappeared were the daughter and grandchild of the president of the Grandmothers of the Plaza de Mayo. The second court case began in 1999 and involved the families of Italians who disappeared during the dictatorship under the Condor Plan.[15] The cases pursued the disappearances of a total of ten Italian citizens (eight from Uruguay who disappeared in Argentina, two from Argentina who disappeared in Paraguay, and two from Argentina who disappeared in Brazil).[16]

The Argentine government's response to the Italian court cases was somewhat mixed. According to a woman involved in the first court case (her husband had disappeared and he was an Italian citizen), the Menem government provided at least her airfare to testify in the trial (Interview 2000). Yet CELS reported that when official support was required, the government was less forthcoming: in 1994, when the Italian judges attempted to obtain evidence, Menem passed an executive decree against collaboration with foreign judges (CELS 2001, 42–43).

Since 1996, Spanish courts have been working to charge Argentine military officers. According to Spanish legislation and its interpretation by Judge Baltazar Garzón, the Spanish courts can charge anyone for crimes against anyone regardless of nationality. On November 2, 1999, the Court of Law began to process 98 Argentine military officers for being involved in crimes of genocide and terrorism. By December 30, 48 officers had been charged, and a call for their extradition was issued (CELS 2001, 46).[17] Although in Italy it is possible to hold trials and sentence people who do not appear in court (allowing for the extradition to take place at a later date), Spanish courts require that the person charged be present at the hearing (Interview 2000).

Possibly because of mounting international pressure to provide legal protection for human rights, the Argentine government incorporated international treaties on human rights into the Argentine Constitution during the 1994 constitutional reforms. The international treaties were given legal superiority over national laws. This provided HROs with a stronger basis for demanding the nullification of the amnesty laws—an issue that achieved significant successes near the end of the 1990s.

The developments of the 1990s gave support to both presentations of the family that HROs favored. At the national level, HROs supporting the Grandmothers and a presentation of the family that glossed over the place of the disappeared achieved important successes. The prosecution of military officers for the stealing of babies during the last dictatorship, in combination with the creation of state commissions supporting these trials, made it clear that both the state and HROs agreed that in a democracy the protection of the civil rights of children under 10 is essential. At the international level, all the HROs were able to find various courts to help them put pressure on the Argentine state to recognize and enforce the civil rights of all people who suffered under the last military regime, regardless of their perceived innocence or lack thereof. These HROs advocated for the protection of the integrity of the family while maintaining an emphasis on the central place of the disappeared in that family. While the international channels provided some "success" (defined as the government's legal response, in this case the provision of reparation), the government avoided punishing those responsible for the violations. Therefore the state did not recognize agreement with HROs that in a democracy the state will legally protect the integrity of the family, regardless of how it is framed; the state did not agree on the enforcement of truly universal rights.

De la Rúa and Beyond, 2000–2003

The most significant characteristic of this most recent political period has been the unprecedented economic crisis. In December 2001, the Argentine economy faced an economic meltdown that led to the resignation of President Fernando De la Rúa and three subsequent presidents in a matter of two weeks. INDEC (Argentine National Institute of Statistics and Census) reported that in 2002, 54.3 percent of the population of Greater Buenos Aires (the wealthiest area of Argentina) was living below the poverty line (up from 35.4 percent in October 2001). Moreover, police violence aimed at combating crime and quelling social unrest increased significantly.[18] It is possible that the rejection of politicians, exemplified in the common protest slogan in 2001–2, "*!Que se vayan todos!*" (get rid of them all), combined with economic instability, may have encouraged President Kirchner to support efforts at further democratization, including an increased commitment to human rights protection. However, the results of Kirchner's policy changes are beyond the scope of this article and, indeed, are still unfolding.

In the context of political and economic change during the first few years of the new millennium, work done by HROs in both national and international courts came together in an important way. Perhaps one of the most significant national court decisions made since the implementation of the amnesty laws was that of March 6, 2001, by Federal Judge Gabriel Cavallo, which declared those laws unconstitutional. An analysis of how this decision was reached and of its consequences reveals how the different sites of debate between HROs and the state converged.

In Argentina, the Grandmothers and the Center for Legal and Social Studies were working on a case involving the stealing of a baby. Claudia Victoria Poblete, 8 months old, was abducted with her mother on November 28, 1978. Her father was taken away the same day, and as a family they were brought to the clandestine detention center known as El Olimpo. Claudia was taken from her parents (who disappeared) and raised by Army Colonel Ceferino Landa. Through the Grandmothers' work, Claudia recovered her identity in 2000 (*Página/12* 2001d). With legal help from the Center for Legal and Social Studies, the HROs charged those responsible with stealing Claudia: military officers Julio Simón (a.k.a. "El Turco Julián") and Juan Antonio Del Cerro (a.k.a. "Colores"). Moreover, the Center added to the case a request that these military officers be charged with the disappearance of Claudia's parents. Because the latter could not be done under the amnesty laws, the Center asked the court to consider international law and find the amnesty laws unconstitutional (*Página/12* 2001d). In particular, the Center cited the superiority of international treaties made effective by the 1994 constitutional reform, including the International Human Rights Pact, the Convention Against Torture, the American Declaration of the Rights of Man, and the American Convention on Human Rights (*Página/12* 2001d).

Of particular importance in this context was the decision, also in March 2001, by the Inter-American Court of Human Rights regarding amnesty laws in Peru. In 1991, a massacre in Barrios Altos, a suburb of Lima, left 15 people dead and 4 injured (*Página/12* 2001e). The Peruvian courts found 5 army officers responsible. In response, the Peruvian Congress passed an amnesty law that prevented the military officers from being sentenced. The victims' families and Peruvian HROs took the case to the Inter-American Human Rights Commission, and it was tried in the Inter-American Court. The court decided, on March 14, 2001, that the Peruvian amnesty laws should be nullified (*Página/12* 2001e), stating, "'the serious violations of human rights such as torture, summary executions (extralegal or arbitrary) and forced disappearance' are not prescribed by the law and are not subject to amnesty" (*Página/12* 2001f).

Judge Cavallo, in his decision, mentioned the hierarchy of the international treaties in Argentine courts and also referred to the court case in Spain regarding Argentine and Chilean military leaders accused of human rights abuses. Using the same legal interpretation as did the Audiencia Nacional de España to confirm Baltazar Garzón's verdict, Cavallo stated that what had occurred were "acts of genocide" (*Página/12* 2001d); he was the first Argentine judge to speak of genocide (*Página/12* 2001d). When Cavallo's verdict went to the Argentine Supreme Court, the Court asked for a copy of the Inter-American Court verdict on the Peruvian amnesty laws. The Supreme Court concluded, "Even before the 1994 reform that gave constitutional hierarchy to the American Convention of Human Rights, the Supreme Court of Justice had stated that its articles had obligatory application in Argentina" (*Página/12* 2001f).

The consequences of the Cavallo decision have been significant both in terms of the military's response and subsequent trials. The immediate response of then-commander-in-chief of the Argentine army, General Ricardo Brinzoni, was to speak with the minister of defense, Ricardo López Murphy, and President De la Rúa. Brinzoni stated on the radio that "the possibility of nullifying the laws of Due Obedience and Final Point appeared to him to be a 'regression' because—he provocatively justified—'they [the amnesty laws] contributed to Argentine society's living in a period of relative calm'" (*Página/12* 2001d). Perhaps because the military did not put adequate pressure on the government, or perhaps because the state became preoccupied with the economic meltdown of December 2001, more judges came out in favor of the decision that the amnesty laws were indeed unconstitutional.

On July 10, 2002, Federal Judge Claudio Bonadio ordered the arrest of the ex-military president Leopoldo Fortunato Galtieri, as well as 41 retired military and police officers, for the disappearance of *Montoneros* (ex-guerrillas) returning from exile in the early 1980s (*Clarín* 2002a). Many of those accused had benefited from the Argentine amnesty laws, which Judge Bonadio had also declared unconstitutional in a previous court case (*Página/12* 2002a ; *Clarín* 2002b). Later, newly elected President Kirchner lent support to the court decisions when he led Congress in August 2003 to vote in favor of nullifying the amnesty laws (*Clarín* 2003a, b). Finally on June 14, 2005, the Argentine Supreme Court voted in favor of nullifying the amnesty laws (*Clarín* 2005). Trials against military officers who allegedly committed human rights abuses during the last dictatorship are currently taking place. The military continues to express its concern about the resumption of trials for human rights abuses from which it was previously exempt (see for example, *Página/12* 2002b). Military opposition has included the organization of a protest in May 2006 commemorating the deaths of military officers by "Marxist terrorists" (using the words of the protesters) during the last military regime (*Clarín* 2006a).

In the 1990s, the state was, in effect, legally restrained in its debates with HROs in the courts. Only the Grandmothers were able to use the national courts because of the

compatibility of their presentation of family relationships with the amnesty laws. The
state celebrated its ability to work with one of the HROs and sought to nominate the
Grandmothers for the Nobel Peace Prize (see, for example, *Página/12* 2000b, 2001a,
b, c). Yet the Cavallo decision opened national courts as a site of debate between all
Affected HROs and the state. Thus Affected HROs that emphasized more controversial
relationships within the family frame gained significant strength from international court
decisions.

Drawing on international law and court cases, the national courts are less influenced
by the presentation of the family used by HROs to justify their demands for the protection
of human rights. Other branches of the state—especially the government and the military
are indeed concerned with how the HROs present the family in their demands. The
development of horizontal accountability—in particular, increasing the relative strength
of the judiciary compared to the military—will have an important impact on the response
of state actors to the demands of HROs. It may be increasingly possible for HROs to
demand the protection of human rights without needing to justify these demands in
terms of the need to protect the family, or a particular presentation of the family. The
current pursuit of military, police, and judicial reform by the Kirchner government is a
promising step in this direction.

CONCLUSIONS

Although it is beginning to undertake some reforms, the Argentine state has yet to make
a clear commitment to the enforcement of human rights. The military pressures the government to place a priority on traditional political practices over liberal democracy (that
is, respecting the independence of the military over the use of liberal democratic state
institutions). Recognizing the need to justify demands for the protection of human rights
in terms that are consistent with traditional politics, human rights organizations have all
drawn to some extent on the concept of the family. However, Argentine state actors
have shown a preference for, or have been better able to, respond to the demands of
HROs that emphasize some family relationships over others. In response, HROs have
used international courts to put increased pressure on Argentine state actors to pursue
the enforcement of human rights, regardless of how the family is presented in their
demands. The increased use of international courts by HROs has yielded important legal
results and poses a potential challenge to the politicized state.

By focusing uniquely on state–society relations at the national level, the concept
of the family clearly has an important impact on debates regarding the protection of
human rights. By framing demands for the protection of human rights in terms of the
family, HROs are drawing on a traditional political discourse. However, the family can
be presented in many ways and some are more encompassing than others. Since the
implementation of the amnesty laws, it appears that the family relationships that state
actors, particularly the government and possibly the military, have been most able to
agree on with HROs is the place of the children of the disappeared. The state's preference for a presentation of the family that glosses over whether or not the disappeared
were subversive has potentially significant consequences.[19]

First, the military's war against "subversion" is implicitly condoned by focusing attention on the stealing of children as the unacceptable excess of an otherwise justifiable "civil
war;" as the military refers to it.[20] Second, the rights deemed necessary to maintain the
integrity of the family could be construed as conditional. In such a case, the family could be
altered from a children–parents–grandparents concept to a grandchildren–grandparents

concept if the parents are deemed by the state to be "subversive."[21] Third, if the family is the building block of the nation and the state is interested in defending the nation or developing a certain type of nation, then the family would be affected. While the Grandmothers, and those Solidarity HROs that support them, would not agree with the first two statements, the state's historical preference for pursuing differential rights suggests that these could be unintended consequences.

Still, an analysis of the impact of international courts on state–society debates over human rights reveals that rights may not always have to be justified in terms of the protection of the family, nor that certain family relationships necessarily need to be emphasized. It is possible that the work of the Grandmothers in national courts, supplemented by the use of international courts by all HROs, may be putting pressure on Argentine state actors to prioritize the protection of human rights without conditions.

NOTES

1 Many authors have written about the use of "motherhood" and "grandmotherhood" by the Mothers and Grandmothers of the Plaza de Mayo to demand the protection of human rights (Navarro 1989; Guzman 1994; Arditti 1999). Other analyses of Argentine HROs have focused on their civil liberty or citizenship demands (Jelin 1995; Peruzzotti 2002). However, few analyses have examined the justification for the protection of human rights in terms of the family across all of the most prominent HROs. Alison Brysk (1994) addresses a range of Argentine human rights organizations that draw on the family, religion, and civil libertarianism, respectively. However, she does not address the role the family plays as a frame for nonfamily-based HROs.

2 Throughout Argentine history, women have been called on to defend the nation and promote public morality through their role as representatives of the family. For example, Juan Perón explained, "I have faith in the women of my *Patria* as a moral reserve of Argentineness [*Argentinidad*]; these women, as actual or potential mothers, are the root of our people" (quoted in Di Liscia 2000, 18). Similarly, the last military regime presented the family as central to the Argentine National Security Doctrine, as both a symbol of the nation and a participant in the realization of the new nation (Laudano 1998, 24). As mothers, women were identified as appendages of the military in the household whose responsibility it was to protect, supervise, and denounce their children (1998, 37).

3 HROs have been pursuing human rights abuses that have occurred since the dictatorship and have been linking socioeconomic issues with that pursuit. While these issues are important, they are beyond the scope of this article.

4 While beyond the time period covered in this article, in 2006 some key Argentine HROs appeared to be more willing to work with the Kirchner government in a manner that suggests cooptation. For example, the Association Mothers of the Plaza de Mayo announced in January 2006 that it would end its yearly March of Resistance because "There is no longer an enemy in the Government House" (*Página/12* 2006a). The Association Madres de Plaza de Mayo and Grandmothers of the Plaza de Mayo also joined President Kirchner on stage to support his unofficial re-election campaign on May 25, 2006 (*Página/12* 2006b). The children of the leaders of both these organizations have been given important positions within the Kirchner government.

5 Noninstitutionalized political parties are those that prefer personalism and strong leaders over democratic internal party practices.

6 Guillermo O'Donnell's definition of horizontal accountability: "the existence of state agencies that are legally empowered—and factually willing and able—to take actions ranging from routine oversight to criminal sanctions or impeachment in relation to possibly unlawful actions or omissions by other agents or agencies of the state" (1998, 117). For horizontal democracy to exist, O'Donnell argues, "the former agencies must have not only legal authority but also sufficient de facto autonomy vis-à-vis the latter" (1998, 119).

7 More than two hundred HROs were involved in the organization of the 2001 demonstration commemorating 25 years since the last military coup.

8 These HROs are the oldest human rights organizations in Argentina (the Human Rights League was established in 1937). On coming to office in June 2003, President Nestor Kirchner set as one of his priorities to address the situation of human rights in Argentina. To this end he gave an audience to eight human rights organizations to discuss what they saw as priorities. The eight HROs were all historical HROs (*Página/12* 2003a). The two HROs excluded from the audience were the two historical HROs that, at the time, refused to work with any government in any way: the Association of the Mothers of the Plaza de Mayo and HIJOS.

9 The analysis provided in this paragraph is drawn from the following sources: SERPAJ 1983, 11; AMPM Nuestra consignas, Carta a nuestro hijos, 1995; MPM-LF 1999; Familiares 1998; *HIJOS* 2000, 12, 2001, 25; HRO interviews.

10 The Mothers did not trust the commission because it was appointed by the government and was not composed of elected officials (AMPM 1999, 30).

11 Some authors argue that the rebellions were attempted coups, others that they were internal disputes in the military. Internal disputes were certainly a component of the issue. The Peace and Justice Service (one of the Solidarity HROs) publication *Paz y Justicia* explained in 1988 that two of the four objectives of the "attempted coups" were to change the leadership of the military and to increase salaries (SERPAJ 1988b, 3). However, the other two common objectives were to have an amnesty law passed and to suspend the judicial processing of human rights violations that had occurred in the past (1998b, 3).

12 The Grandmothers state, "The disappeared children were deprived of their identity, their religion, the right to live with their family" (Abuelas 1999, 19).

13 Mariana Llanos found that Menem used decrees mainly to approve policies that supported his economic plan (2001, 71).

14 Videla, a commander-in-chief of the Argentine army, was found guilty of ordering a systematic plan of stealing children (CELS 1999, 88). Massera was found guilty of stealing 15 babies during the last dictatorship (CELS 1999, 104).

15 The Argentine Federal Court defines the Condor Plan as "the relationship established between governments and intelligence services in various countries [Chile, Argentina, Uruguay, Paraguay, Brazil, and Bolivia] whose principal objective was to share information and cooperate in the illegal persecution of opposition" (*Clarín* 2002b).

16 Information in this paragraph comes from a confidential author interview with a woman involved in the first court case, Buenos Aires, November 1, 2000.

17 In August 2003, Judge Garzón's extradition request was rejected by the Spanish government in response to steps taken by the Argentine government under President Kirchner to annul the amnesty laws and try the military leaders in Argentine courts (*Página/12* 2003b).

18 In the city of Buenos Aires and Greater Buenos Aires combined, the number of civilians killed as a result of police violence was 163 in 1998, 257 in 1999, 232 in 2000, and 261 in 2001 (CELS 2001, 162).

19 The definition of subversive is very broad. Defined by the Argentine military regime, subversives include terrorists identified by General Videla as "not just someone with a gun or a bomb but also someone who spreads ideas that are contrary to Western and Christian civilization" (quoted in Navarro 1989, 244). One military general was reported to have said, "First we will kill all the subversives; then we will kill their collaborators; then their sympathizers; then those who are indifferent; and finally we will kill all those who are timid" (quoted in Snow 1996, 83). The definition of subversive is flexible, and its future meaning could vary.

20 This is the vocabulary used by the Argentine military to refer to what is otherwise known as the Dirty War.

21 Clearly, international human rights rest on the inalienability of human rights. That is, human rights are, by definition, universal. However, this is not the understanding of rights that historically has been practiced by the Argentine state. The issue of the universality of human rights certainly arose during the trials of the former military junta leaders in the 1980s, but current debates within the Argentine state and between the state and society suggest that a state commitment to the universality of rights has not yet been achieved.

REFERENCES

This chapter is based partly on confidential author interviews with members of each of the respective human rights organizations and officials from the Argentine Sub-Secretary of Human Rights, September 2000 to June 2001.

Abuelas (Abuelas de Plaza de Mayo). 1999. *Niños desaparecidos. Jóvenes localizados. En Argentina desde 1976 a 1999.* Buenos Aires: Temas.

Arditti, Rita. 1999. *Searching for Life: The Grandmothers of the Plaza de Mayo and the Disappeared Children of Argentina.* Berkeley: University of California Press.

Argentine National Institute of Statistics and Census (INDEC). n.d. Porcentaje de hogares y personas por debajo de la línea de pobreza en el aglomerado GBA, desde mayo 1988 en adelante. Table. <www.indec.mecon.gov.ar>.

Asociación Madres de Plaza de Mayo (AMPM). 1995. Parir un hijo, parir miles de hijos. Flier. April.

———. 1999. Buenos Aires: AMPM.

AMPM (Associación Madres de la Plaza de Mayo). nd. Nuestras consignas. Flier. *Historia de las Madres de Plaza de Mayo.*

Brysk, Alison. 1994. *The Politics of Human Rights in Argentina. Protest, Change, and Democratization.* Stanford: Stanford University Press.

Cardoso, Fernando Henrique. 1979, On the Characterization of Authoritarian Regimes in Latin America. *In The New Authoritarianism in Latin America,* ed. David Collier. Princeton: Princeton University Press. 33–57.

Carolotto, Claudia. 2000. Technical Director, CONADI. Author interview. Buenos Aires, November 2.

Centro de Estudios Legales y Sociales (CELS). 1998. CELS, *informe sobre la situación de los derechos humanos en Argentina: 1997* Buenos Aires: Eudeba.

———. 1999. *Derechos humanos en la Argentina: informe anual enero-diciembre 1998.* Buenos Aires: Eudeba.

———. 2000. *Derechos humanos en Argentina: informe anual 2000.* Buenos Aires: Eudeba.

———. 2001. *Informe sobre la situación de los derechos humanos en Argentina: enero-diciembre 2000.*Buenos Aires: Siglo XXI.

———. 2002. *Derechos humanos en Argentina, informe 2002: hechos enero-diciembre 2001.* Buenos Aires: Siglo XXI.

Chalmers, Douglas A. 1977. *The Politicized State in Latin America. In Authoritarianism and Corporatism in Latin America,* ed. James M. Malloy. Pittsburgh: University of Pittsburgh Press. 23–45.

Clarín (Buenos Aires). 2002a. Ordenan la detención de Galtieri. July 11.

———. 2002b. Plan Cóndor: podrían unir las causas contra Galtieri y Videla. July 25.

———. 2003a. Afuera, un reclamo masivo que pudo hacerse escuchar. August 13.

———. 2003b. El Senado anuló las leyes de Punto Final y Obediencia Debida. August 21.

———. 2005. En una resolución histórica, la corte anuló las leyes de perdón. June 15.

———. 2006a. Tensión durante un acto con militares en actividad. May 25.

———. 2006b. Las Abuelas identificaron a otra hija de desaparecidos. June 9.

Davis, Diane E. 1999. The Power of Distance: Re-theorizing Social Movements in Latin America. *Theory and Society* 28, 4 (August): 585–638.

Di Liscia, Maria H. B. 2000. Maternidad y discurso maternal en la política sanitaria peronista. In *Mujeres, maternidad y peronismo,* ed. Di Liscia et al. Santa Rosa, Argentina: Fondo Editorial Pampeano. 39–51.

Familiares de Desaparecidos y Detenidos por Razones Políticas (Familiares). 1998. Acerca de la Ley 24.411: llamada de reparación. Pamphlet. December. Buenos Aires: Familiares.

———. 2000. ¿Qué es la impunidad? La impunidad es la falta de castigo. Pamphlet. September. Buenos Aires: Familiares.

Frenkel, Roberto, and Guillermo Rozenwurcel. 1996. The Multiple Roles of Privatization in Argentina. In Institutional Design in *New Democracies: Eastern Europe and Latin America,* ed. Arend J. Lijphardt and Carlos H. Waisman. Boulder: Westview Press. 219–33.

García, Prudencio. 1995. *El drama de la autonomía militar: Argentina bajo las juntas militares.* Madrid: Alianza.

Guzman, Marguerite Bouvard. 1994. *Revolutionizing Motherhood: The Mothers of the Plaza de Mayo.* Wilmington: Scholarly Resources.

Hijos por la Identidad y la Justicia contra el Olvido y el Silencio (HIJOS). 2000. *HIJOS.* Magazine. September.

———. 2001. *HIJOS.* September.

Imaz, José Luís de. 1968. *Los que mandan.* Buenos Aires: Editorial Universitaria de Buenos Aires.

Jelin, Elizabeth. 1995. Building Citizenship: A Balance Between Solidarity and Responsibility. In *The Consolidation of Democracy in Latin America,* ed. Joseph S. Tulchin. Boulder: Lynne Reinner. 83–97.

Laudano, Claudia Nora. 1998. *Las mujeres en los discursos militares.* Buenos Aires: *Página/12.*

Linz, Juan, and Alfred Stepan. 1996. *Problems of Democratic Transitions and Consolidation: Southern Europe, South America, and Post-Communist Europe.* Baltimore: Johns Hopkins University Press.

Llanos, Mariana. 2001. Understanding Presidential Power. in Argentina: A Study of the Policy of Privatisation in the 1990s. *Journal of Latin-American Studies.* 33 (February): 67–99.

Madres de Plaza de Mayo–Linea Fundador (MPM–LF). 1999. Open Letter. Handout. September.

Manzetti, Luigi. 1993. *Institutions, Parties, and Coalitions in Argentine Politics.* Pittsburgh: University of Pittsburgh Press.

McGuire, James W. 1997. *Peronism Without Perón: Unions, Parties, and Democracy in Argentina.* Stanford: Stanford University Press.

McSherry, J. Patrice. 1997. *Incomplete Transition: Military Power and Democracy in Argentina.* New York: St. Martin's Press.

Migdal, Joel S. 2001. *State in Society: Studying How States and Societies and Constitute One Another.* New York: Cambridge University Press.

National Commission on Disappeared People (CONADEP). 1984. *Nunca más.* Buenos Aires: Editorial Universitaria de Buenos Aires.

National Commission on the Right to Identity (CONADI). 2001. CONADI-INFORME (annual report). September. <www.conadi.jus.gov.ar>.

Navarro, Marysa. 1989. The Personal Is Political: Las Madres de Plaza de Mayo. In *Power and Popular Protest: Latin American Social Movements,* ed. Susan Eckstein. Berkeley: University of California Press.

Nino, Carlos S. 1996. Hyperpresidentialism and Constitutional Reform in Argentina. In *Institutional Design in New Democracies: Eastern Europe and Latin America,* ed. Arend J. Lijphardt and Carlos H. Waisman. Boulder: Westview Press.

O'Donnell, Guillermo. 1998. Horizontal Accountability in New Democracies. *Journal of Democracy.* 9, 3 (July): 112–26.

Oxhorn, Philip. 1995. From Controlled Inclusion to Coerced Marginalization: The Struggle for Civil Society in Latin America. In *Civil Society: Theory, History, Comparison,* ed. John Hall. Cambridge: Polity Press. 250–77.

Página/12 (Buenos Aires.) 2000a. 23 anos para hacer un balance de las Abuelas. October 23: 8.

———. 2000b. Ruckauf y los derechos humanos: Nobel para Abuelas. December 27: 13.

———. 2001a. Las Abuelas, el Nobel y Ruckauf. January 3: 8.

———. 2001b. Premio Nobel a las Abuelas. January 10: 8.

———. 2001c. De la Sota con Abuelas. January 11: 5.

———. 2001d. La nulidad de Punto Final y La Obediencia Debida: desarmando la impunidad. March 6: 19.

———. 2001e. La Corte Interamericana anuló la amnistía peruana: fuera de la ley. March 26: 10–11.

———. 2001f. La Corte Suprema pidió el fallo de la Corte Interamericana: notificada. March 28: 13.

———. 2002a. Borrando la impunidad. July 11.

———. 2002b. La pata militar del acuerdo Menem-Duhalde: i guerrieri dall' paddle. October 13,

———. 2003a. Un día lleno de pañuelos blancos en la Rosada. June 4.

————. 2003b. España no impulsará las extradiciones de represores que solicitó Garzón: Argentina puede seguir los juicios. August 30.

————. 2006a. Las Madres nunca retrocedieron, las Madres van a estar siempre. January 26.

————. 2006b. Una demonstración de fuerza a toda plaza. May 26.

Peace and Justice Service (SERPAJ). 1983. Abuelas de Plaza de Mayo: recuperarlos. *Paz y Justicia* 1, 4 (August): 10–12.

————. 1988a. Sentencia de la CIDH. *Paz y justicia* 15, 7 (August–September–October): 14.

————. 1988b. Los milicos siguen avanzando. *Paz y Justicia* 16, 8 (November–December): 2–10.

Peruzzotti, Enrique. 2002. Towards a New Politics: Citizenship and Rights in Contemporary Argentina. *Citizenship Studies* 6, 1 (March): 77–93.

Pozzi, Pablo. 2000. Popular Upheaval and Capitalist Transformation in Argentina. *Latin-American Perspectives* 27, 5 (September): 63–87.

Rubio, Delia Ferreira, and Matteo Goretti. 1998. When the President Governs Alone: The Decretazo in Argentina, 1989–93. In *Executive Decree Authority,* ed. John M. Carey and Matthew Soberg Shugart. Cambridge: Cambridge University Press. 33–61.

Sub-Secretary of Human Rights (SSDH). 2000a. Author interview. Buenos Aires, October 4.

————. 2000b. Author interview. Buenos Aires, December 18.

Snow, Peter G. 1996. Argentina: Politics in a Conflict Society. In *Latin American Politics and Development,* 4th ed., ed. Howard J. Wiarda and Harvey F. Kline. Boulder: Westview Press. 71–108.

Tarrow, Sidney. 1998. *Power in Movement. Social Movements and Contentious Politics.* 2nd ed. Cambridge: Cambridge University Press.

Teichman, Judith. 2001. *The Politics of Freeing Markets in Latin America: Chile, Argentina and Mexico.* Chapel Hill: University of North Carolina Press.

Chapter 13

Sources of Mass Partisanship in Brazil

David Samuels

Partisanship—a psychological attachment to a particular political party—influences voters' policy stances, their evaluation of the economy, attitudes toward democracy, and electoral behavior. The sources of party identification have therefore long motivated political scientists. This chapter explores the evolution and sources of individual-level partisanship in contemporary Brazil. Although many scholars have explored the sources of individual vote choice in Brazil (recent examples include Singer 1999; Baker 2002; Carreirão 2002; Carreirão and Kinzo 2002; Almeida 2004; and Baker et al. 2005), little research exists on the sources of mass partisanship. What does exist includes information that is already ten years old or more (Mainwaring 1999), explores only one slice of Brazil's political spectrum (Mainwaring et al. 2000), or has limited potential generalizability to Brazil's entire electorate (Kinzo 2005). Considering the substantial scholarly debate about the nature of Brazil's political parties, the extent of mass partisanship in Brazil merits further exploration.

Brazil is frequently described as a chronic case of "party underdevelopment." Its party system is highly fragmented; electoral volatility is comparatively high; more than one-third of its sitting legislators change parties during a term; and individualism, clientelism, and personalism, rather than programmatic appeals, dominate electoral campaigns. Mainwaring (1999, 114–19) suggests that mass partisanship in Brazil is both limited and ephemeral, on the basis of immediate political events or personalities; and Power (2000, 28) concludes that "Brazil is an extraordinary case of party weakness." The relative paucity of published research on mass partisanship in Brazil perhaps derives from this view.

Figueiredo and Limongi (2000), however, have challenged this view of partisan weakness. They claim that although the party system is fragmented, Brazil's parties have evolved from an initial and temporary inchoate state and are highly cohesive at present. Yet Figueiredo and Limongi's argument, along with most of the research about the nature of political parties in contemporary Brazil, concentrates on Brazil's legislative parties.[1] This is a critical element in the study of political parties, but not the only (or even the most important) one.

By exploring the status of mass partisanship in contemporary Brazil, this chapter builds on existing research and contributes to ongoing debates. First, it compares the established view of weak mass partisanship in Brazil with survey evidence, both over time and cross-nationally. Somewhat surprisingly for the conventional wisdom, it shows that the aggregate level of mass partisanship in Brazil actually falls only slightly below the world average and exceeds levels found in several other newer democracies. This finding, however, does not turn out to support the "strong parties" thesis, because the distribution of partisan preferences has become increasingly skewed over the last ten years toward only one political party, the Partido dos Trabalhadores (Workers' Party, PT). No other party counts on a large base of partisan identifiers.

Second, exploring the factors associated with this distribution of partisan preferences reveals the sources of partisanship in Brazil more comprehensively than does the existing research. For example, Mainwaring et al. (2000) examine only partisanship for Brazil's conservative parties. Surprisingly, despite the PT's recent rise to power and despite observers' belief that the PT is "different" from other Brazilian parties, no research has explored either the mass bases of *petismo* or the specific factors that differentiate *petistas* from other Brazilians.[2] To accomplish this goal, this research used Brazil's first-ever postelection National Election Study (CESOP 2003).

The results suggest that the differences across parties in terms of mass partisanship derive from the connection between party recruitment activity, individual motivation to acquire political knowledge, and individual engagement in highly politicized social networks. All three appear to be necessary factors, which explain the relative lack of partisanship for parties other than the PT. That is, non-*petista* Brazilians might be both engaged in politics and motivated to learn about politics, but only the PT has developed and maintained an organized web of connections to local, regional, and national political and social organizations, such as church groups, neighborhood associations, and unions. Through such networks, like-minded people are politicized about national issues (Meneguello 1989; Keck 1992; Hochstetler 2008; Samuels 2004). Although partisanship for the PT was initially quite small, by 2002 this activity resulted in the emergence of a relatively deep and wide base of partisan support.

In early 2005, a corruption scandal involving payoffs to allied legislators and the illegal use of campaign funds by the PT damaged the popularity ratings of Brazil's current president, Luis Inácio Lula da Silva.[3] Given the PT's longstanding efforts to paint itself as "different" from Brazil's other parties, moreover, especially in terms of its devotion to the principles of "clean government," the scandal caused much speculation about the future of the PT. However, more recent research (Samuels 2008) reveals that the scandal hardly affected the PT's level of identification in Brazilian society at all.

THE EXTENT OF PARTISANSHIP IN CONTEMPORARY BRAZIL

The conventional wisdom holds that mass partisanship in Brazil is weak; but to what extent does this view reflect reality? Figure 1 reveals the total percentage of Brazilians who declared a party preference for any party from 1989 (when national-level surveys began asking this question) through early 2008.[4] The surveys that provided the information asked for a spontaneous response to the question, "What is your preferred party?" The percentage mostly hovers between 40 and 50 percent, and the average is 45 percent.

The most recent measure in the series reveals that about 42 percent of the electorate currently has a "preferred" party. Does this degree of mass partisanship confirm or refute the conventional wisdom about Brazil? Given the decline of partisanship in many countries around the world (Clarke and Stewart 1998; Dalton and Wattenberg 2000), how does Brazil compare? We now possess a reliable cross-national measure of aggregate mass partisanship from the Comparative Study of Electoral Systems (CSES), a survey module that scholars designed specifically for cross-national application and that has been implemented in dozens of countries' national election studies, including Brazil's (following the 2002 elections).[5] The CSES questions on partisanship first ask respondents, "Do you usually think of yourself as close to any particular political party?" If respondents answer yes, the survey then asks, "What party is that?"

Table 1 compares the level of partisanship in Brazil with the other countries that have implemented the CSES questions. Note that because of the different question format, the BNES survey that included the CSES questions is not included in the series of surveys in Figure 1. As we should expect, the two-question CSES format returns a slightly lower level of aggregate partisanship (35 percent) than the one-question format used in the

Figure 1. Total Expressing Party Preference, Brazil, 1989–2005 (percent)

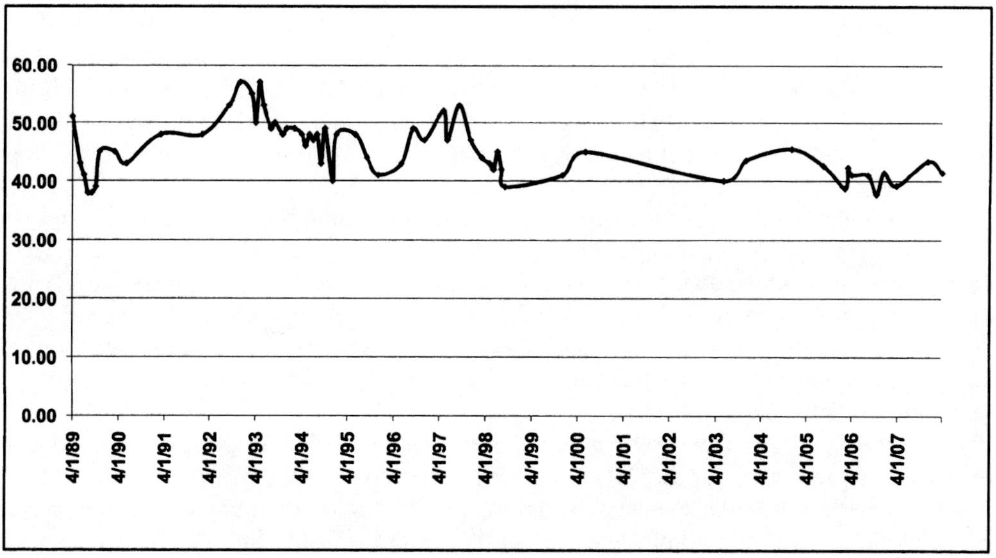

Sources: Carreirão and Kinzo 2002; *Opinião Pública* 2003; Criterium pesquisas 2003; Datafolha 2003, 2004, 2005

Table 1. CSES Party Identification by Country (percent)

Belarus 2001	7.90	Czech Republic 1996	44.43
Thailand 2001	13.88	United Kingdom 1997	45.56
Slovenia 1996	19.01	Sweden 1998	46.24
Chile 1999	19.78	Russia 2000	46.62
Korea 2000	23.18	Portugal 2002	46.74
Peru 2001	26.39	Israel 1999	47.88
Netherlands 1998	27.75	Denmark 1998	48.68
Lithuania 1997	30.62	Poland 1997	48.78
Taiwan 1996	32.33	Canada 1997	49.81
Germany 1998	33.88	Mexico 2000	50.40
Hungary 1998	34.89	Norway 1997	52.31
Brazil 2002	**35.20**	New Zealand 1996	54.98
Switzerland 1999	35.60	United States 1996	56.71
Japan 1996	37.53	Ukraine 1998	59.23
Spain 2000	41.39	Australia 1996	80.76
Romania 1996	44.43	**Average**	**40.06**

Source: CSES.

surveys in Figure 1 (40 percent for the survey taken at the same time as the BNES). Regardless, we can reasonably assume that the CSES format accurately measures cross-national variation in partisanship, which is what interests us at the moment.

The CSES figure for Brazil falls within one standard deviation of the mean for all countries (S.D. = 14.76), and while most established democracies exhibit relatively higher levels of partisanship (all except the Netherlands and Germany), Brazil compares well with many relatively younger democracies. For example, although Mainwaring and Scully (1995, 19–20) declared Peru and Brazil two of the most "inchoate" party systems in Latin America, mass partisanship (one of the elements of party-system "institutionalization") is somewhat more widespread in Brazil than in Peru. More surprisingly, Brazil outperforms Chile, an "institutionalized" party system (Mainwaring and Scully 1995, 17) in which the same parties reemerged in 1990 to compete following a 17-year dictatorship. In Brazil, none of the currently competing parties existed before the onset of a 20-year dictatorship in 1964.

According to Table 1, the aggregate level of mass partisanship in Brazil appears only slightly lower than average. We might thus conclude that the conventional view exaggerates the comparative weakness of partisan attachments in the Brazilian electorate. However, the aggregate level of partisanship is misleading because it obscures the cross-party distribution of partisan identifiers. Figure 2 disaggregates the evolution of partisan preferences by party for three of Brazil's largest parties since 1989, using the same surveys as in Figure 1.

Figure 2 provides three pieces of information. First, the proportion of Brazilians expressing a preference for the PT grew more or less consistently from 6 percent in 1989 to 24 percent in late 2004. However, in mid-2005 a corruption scandal cast a dark cloud over the PT and the Lula administration, and PT partisanship declined to 18.5 percent of the electorate by August of that year. Still, partisanship for the PT seems to have stabilized at about 20 percent of the electorate as of 2008. Second, the PMDB, the party that inherited power in the 1980s from the military regime, has exhibited a steady decline in partisan identifiers, from 15 percent to about 6 percent of the electorate over the same period.[6] Third, no other party has developed a sizable and consistent base of partisans. No other party averages over 5 percent for this time period, and even Fernando Henrique

Figure 2. Evolution of Party Preferences in Brazil, 1989–2005

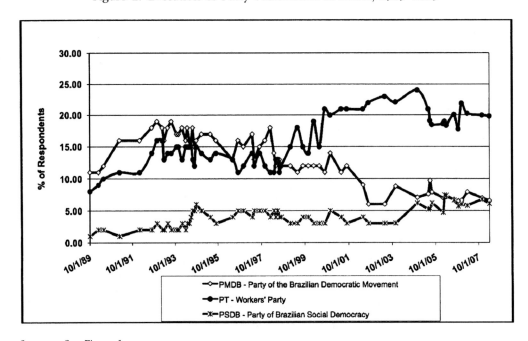

Sources: See Figure 1

Table 2. CSES Party Identification by Party, Brazil 2002

Party	Percent PID in Population	Percent of Valid PID	Percent Vote 2002
PT	23.1	65.6	18.4
PMDB	3.8	10.9	13.4
PSDB	3.7	10.5	14.3
PFL	2.2	6.3	13.4
PDT	0.5	1.5	5.1
PTB	0.5	1.3	4.6
Other (11 parties)	1.4	3.9	30.8
Total	35.2	100.0	100.0

Sources: BNES 2002; TSE 2002.

Cardoso's PSDB, the most prominent governing party from 1995 to 2002, has hovered near or below 5 percent for the entire period.

Because the BNES data are used here for statistical analysis (as a postelection survey and with better sampling methods, BNES has substantial advantages over the commercial surveys used in Figures 1 and 2), the breakdown of partisanship in Brazil in 2002 using the BNES is shown in Table 2, as a proportion of all voters and as a proportion of those expressing a party preference. For reference purposes, Table 2 also includes the percentage of votes each party received in the 2002 Chamber of Deputies elections.

The BNES data confirm that in 2002, almost two-thirds of Brazilians expressed no partisan preference; about one in four Brazilians expressed a party preference for the PT; and about one in ten Brazilians expressed a preference for one of Brazil's many other parties. The distribution of partisan preferences is also clearly skewed relative to the distribution of votes in legislative elections. The PT is the only party that had greater partisan support than vote support in the 2002 legislative elections.[7] The vote totals for all the other parties are several times larger than the number of people who "identify" with those parties. For example, the PFL, PMDB, PTB, and PSDB, four of the larger parties at the center and right of Brazil's political spectrum, obtained 45.7 percent of the votes in the 2002 legislative elections, yet only 10.2 percent of Brazilians express a partisan preference for one of these parties. The numbers drive home a clear message: although Brazil has several electorally strong parties, only the PT can count on a large base of partisan support in its quest for votes.

SOURCES OF PARTISANSHIP

Political scientists define partisanship as self-identification with one party that "structures one's cognitive understanding of politics" (Miller and Klobucar 2000, 675). This identification is separate from vote choice, but partisanship shapes both voting and policy preferences over a relatively long time, even when the political context changes (Green et al. 2002, 39). To what extent are preferences for any party in Brazil an expression of such deeply held notions of political self-identification, as opposed to superficial attachments to various political personalities or to immediate events? To play devil's advocate for a moment, do *petistas* really hold different "cognitive understandings of politics" from other Brazilians? Or does *petismo* echo traditional bases of politics in Brazil and result merely from the personal charisma of the party's longstanding leader, Lula? Likewise, although scholars have suggested that preferences for Brazil's other parties derive from personalism and clientelism, perhaps such expressed preferences are truly partisan but are simply embryonic, reflecting the relative youth of many of Brazil's parties. Perhaps the low levels of partisanship for the PFL, PSDB, and other parties are not superficial but are strongly held despite not (yet) being widespread.

Especially given the recent corruption scandal, which will test the "depth" of partisanship for the PT, these questions merit empirical exploration. This chapter presents hypotheses about the sources of partisanship in Brazil in an effort to provide the first comprehensive picture of the nature of partisanship for parties across the contemporary Brazilian political spectrum. To simplify the discussion, the hypotheses are arranged in five groups, which focus on the potential impact on partisanship of political leaders, group identities, and insertion in social networks, demographic context, and individual attributes. No "comprehensive theory of partisanship" generates these hypotheses; many of them are drawn from the international literature on voter behavior, and some are derived for application specifically to Brazil. The modest goal is to assess how much partisanship for Brazil's parties derives from similar or different bases.

Political Leaders

To what extent does partisanship in Brazil merely reflect voters' personalistic attachments to political leaders? This is an important question in countries like Brazil, where, many scholars argue, political institutions are weakly established and politicians campaign using populist, personalistic appeals (Singer 1990; Von Mettenheim 1995; Mainwaring 1999; Ames 2001). The question is also important because in Brazil, political leaders have often been around just as long as their parties have. This makes partisanship difficult to disentangle from personalism. The "Michigan School" of studying voter behavior assumes that personalistic attachments to politicians follow from partisan attachments, not vice versa. Thus, in the United States, for example, a Republican may have strong positive feelings for George W. Bush. That person's support for the Republican Party, however, most likely predated Bush's arrival on the political stage, and will most likely outlast Bush's political career as well (Green et al. 2002). Of course, citizens' feelings for or against Bush could catalyze an emerging partisan identification, but scholars of voter behavior in established democracies argue that partisanship is better understood as a form of social identity that derives from lived experience rather than as support for or against particular politicians.

However, in countries with relatively young party systems, it is important to question the assumption that partisanship precedes personalistic attachments to politicians. In newer democracies, the opposite is plausible: partisanship may derive precisely from personalism and only subsequently evolve into more complex, deeply held, long-term convictions that outlive any particular politician. An obvious example from one of Brazil's neighbors is Peronism, a form of social identity in Argentina that has long outlived its founder.

Multivariate statistical analysis permits us to study how much partisan attachments are personalistic and whether personalism means different things to different people. Political leaders are not personalistic in the same ways. Some leaders work to develop their party organization so that it will outlive them; others seek to use the party for their own designs; and still others are indifferent to parties or even antipartisan. Support for a political leader may translate into partisanship or not. Using survey data, we may begin to understand whether any observed connection is a function of "personality" or of other factors, such as a politician's policy stances.

Citizens' Group Identities

This approach is inspired by Lipset and Rokkan (1967), who argue that partisanship is rooted in deep societal divisions, such as class, religion, urban or rural location, or race (Campbell et al. 1960; Converse 1969). This hypothesis suggests that partisanship is a sociological reflection of citizens' membership in more or less objectively defined groups. This study includes several variables that scholars have suggested might be connected to the evolution of partisan attitudes. In Brazil, however, scholars generally expect that few such variables will be strongly associated with partisanship, for any party (e.g. Mainwaring et al. 2000).

Citizens' Insertion into Social Networks

For some scholars, the most important elements of partisanship are not individual or even group identities, but the nature and extent of citizens' involvement in politics and social networks. This hypothesis can be taken in two ways: as a test of the notion that "more involved" people are simply more likely to be partisans, or as an indirect test of the notion that recruitment by social activists enhances partisanship (Carmines and Stimson 1989; Rosenstone and Hansen 1993; Dalton and Wattenberg 2000). Both are likely to be true, because although some people may have a greater propensity to participate in politics, it takes some form of recruitment for most people to become involved in politics (Carmines and Stimson 1989).

Demographic Variables

Research on partisanship suggests that "structural" demographic variables can be associated with stronger or weaker tendencies for citizens to acquire partisanship. Such variables cannot be proximate causes of partisanship but can serve as proxies for social context, suggesting that some unmeasured and perhaps unmeasurable variables play a more direct causal role. An optimal variable to proxy for social context (better than region or state, for example) is the Municipal Human Development Index (MHDI). The MHDI was developed by the United Nations Development Program and has been implemented worldwide. The data for Brazil are for the year 2000 (UNDP 2003). The HDI is a composite index based on three indicators of human well-being: life expectancy, which reflects the healthcare conditions available to the population; education level; and per capita income. The HDI scale ranges from 0 to 1, with higher values indicating a tendency toward greater or better human development.

Health, education, and welfare are three key characteristics favorable to the formation of human capital, and municipalities with higher levels of the MHDI can be expected to have denser networks of social and political organizations. As noted, scholars suggest that partisanship is essentially an individual's understanding of how he or she fits into political society, with reference to other social groups (Green et al. 2002, 23). The MHDI is a proxy for a hypothesized relationship between human capital and the formation of partisan preferences. Citizens in municipalities with a greater human capital are not only more likely to be encouraged to participate, but also to have relatively more opportunities to do so. This will lead them to make decisions about whether to get involved, and how (that is, for which party).[8]

Citizens' Individual Attributes

Scholars have posited numerous connections between citizens' individual attributes and partisanship. For example, socialization theories suggest that age is positively associated with partisanship (Jennings and Niemi 1974; Shively 1979). Similarly, scholars have long posited a connection between education and partisanship, often focusing on citizens' political knowledge. Generally, scholars have found that better-informed citizens are more likely to develop a partisan identity (Campbell et al. 1960; Converse 1964; Miller and Shanks 1996). As Brader and Tucker (2001) note, this question is particularly important in new democracies, where information costs are higher because of the newness of open politics and citizens' comparative lack of experience with democratic politics. In newer democracies, we have an even stronger expectation that partisanship for any party will develop among educated citizens or those with a high degree of interest in and knowledge about politics.

Scholars have also hypothesized that individual beliefs about democracy are important components of partisanship (Almond and Verba 1963). Citizens who hold positive attitudes about democracy and who believe in the efficacy of political participation are more likely to develop partisan attachments. Along similar lines, we should explore whether certain cultural attitudes are associated with partisanship. The key question at hand is whether Brazilians who hold what might be called "traditional" versus "modern" cultural beliefs are more or less likely to develop a partisan identity for particular parties (Soares 1961; Reis 1978).

DATA AND MEASURES

The five sets of hypotheses are not mutually exclusive and do not describe all possible factors associated with the evolution of partisanship, but are longstanding arguments in the theoretical literature and are relevant to the Brazilian context. These hypotheses were tested using data from the 2002 BNES survey.[9]

Brazil's 2002 presidential election was significant. After winning reelection in 1998, president Fernando Henrique Cardoso saw his popularity ratings sag during his second term as Brazil's economy remained stuck in the doldrums. Lula, who had run and lost the presidential race in 1989, 1994, and 1998 (against Cardoso the last two times), mounted a successful campaign in 2002, which capitalized on Brazilians' displeasure with Cardoso and their desire for a change of direction. Lula easily beat José Serra, the candidate Cardoso's party nominated, and four other candidates.

The dependent variable explored here is self-reported party identification, derived from the CSES format as described above, for the four parties with the largest partisan bases: the PT, PSDB, PMDB, and PFL. Even with the BNES's large national sample, too few people reported a partisan preference for any of Brazil's other parties to permit statistical analysis for those parties. To reveal the relationships underlying the sources of partisanship, the statistical method of multinomial logit is used, with robust standard errors.[10] This procedure estimates the impact of explanatory variables on a dependent variable that can take more than one categorical value. In this case there are six categories: partisanship for the PT, PMDB, PSDB, or PFL, other partisan identification, and no partisan identification. No identification is the reference category.

The following independent variables were explored, each of which fits into one of the three groups. Several of these variables are composite indexes.[11]

- Political leaders: thermometer scores measuring respondents' like or dislike of the leaders of the four main parties.
- Group identity: gender, age in years, race (white or nonwhite), religion (Catholic or not, and Evangelical Christian or not), and family income.[12]
- Social networks: index variables that measure respondents' degree of participation in electoral politics and in nonelectoral politics.
- Demographic context: the Municipal Human Development Index (a continuous variable that ranges from 0–1).
- Individual attributes: retrospective evaluation of the Cardoso administration, belief in the efficacy of the vote, extent of political knowledge (index), support for clientelism (index), tolerance of corruption (index), degree to which citizens see the world in terms of social hierarchies (index), years of education, and support for suppression of political protest (called political liberalism, also an index variable).

Multinomial logit generates regression coefficients for each category of the dependent variable; in this case, thus, for each of the four parties. Each coefficient tells whether a particular independent variable distinguishes partisans for that party from Brazilians who have "no" partisan identification.[13] Table 3 presents the results (results for "Other" identification are not shown).

For the political leaders variable, the model generates clear and intuitive results for all parties. The survey asked all respondents for thermometer rankings of the following political leaders: Antônio Carlos Magalhães, a longtime political boss from the northeastern state of Bahia who is known by his initials, ACM, and who is the most widely

Table 3. Factors Associated with Partisan Identification with the Largest Parties in Brazil, 2002

	PFL	PT	PMDB	PSDB
Lula opinion	−.050 (.043)	.367 (.039)***	**−.081 (.031)****	**−.158 (.037)*****
Cardoso opinion	.021 (.058)	**−.067 (.022)****	.059 (.039)	**.177 (.046)*****
Jader opinion	−.076 (.064)	.008 (.030)	**.143 (.048)****	−.003 (.059)
ACM opinion	.175 (.049)***	−.030 (.023)	−.094 (.047)	−.092 (.049)
Gender	−.117 (.316)	−.179 (.117)	**−.461 (.225)***	−.032 (.252)
Age	.003 (.011)	−.008 (.004)	.001 (.007)	−.012 (.009)
White	−.386 (.355)	.027 (.119)	.238 (.229)	−.159 (.255)
Evangelical	−.283 (.625)	−.035 (.211)	.274 (.606)	−.294 (.453)
Catholic	−.011 (.486)	.060 (.172)	1.006 (.542)	.184 (.393)
Income	−.001 (.001)	−.001 (.001)	**−.0006 (.0002)***	.0001 (.0001)
Electoral participation	.087 (.127)	**.209 (.046)*****	**.385 (.078)*****	.172 (.093)
Nonelectoral participation	**.315 (.102)****	**.177 (.041)*****	.085 (.080)	.101 (.090)
MHDI	**−5.154 (1.712)****	3.020 (.908)***	−2.033 (1.511)	−2.572 (1.854)
Political knowledge	**.156 (.080)***	**.127 (.033)*****	.024 (.059)	**.263 (.063)*****
Retrospective evaluation	.186 (.109)	−.079 (.044)	−.029 (.086)	.042 (.086)
Left-Right placement	.027 (.055)	**−.072 (.019)*****	**.089 (.039)***	−.033 (.043)
Protest suppression	.035 (.040)	−.020 (.015)	**.065 (.028)***	**.074 (.037)***
Efficacy	.188 (.142)	**.190 (.057)****	.025 (.089)	.016 (.091)

*p < .05, **p < .01, ***p < .001.

recognized leader of the PFL; Lula; Cardoso; and Jader Barbalho, a political boss from
the northern state of Pará, known by his first name. The PMDB had no clear national
leader at this time, but Jader had been in the news frequently as the target of corruption
investigations and as a prominent senator from the PMDB. (The BNES did not include
another PMDB leader.)

For each party, partisanship is associated with positive sentiment for the party's
leader. In every case except the PFL, partisanship is also associated with a clear dislike
for at least one rival party leader. These results support the hypothesis that partisanship
in Brazil is partly driven by personalism, yet they beg two further questions: To what
extent do attachments to political leaders shape partisanship? To what degree can we
predict partisanship without including the thermometer scores for political leaders?

Using the CLARIFY statistical software package (Tomz et al. 2003), a thought experiment can be conducted to answer these questions. Using the survey data, CLARIFY lets
the researcher set the values of the independent variables and then predict the probability
that a survey respondent with those values would "choose" categories of the dependent
variable. To understand how much personalism is associated with partisanship, we can
contrast the predictions CLARIFY generates from two simulations for each party. These
simulations do not predict the probability that an "average Brazilian" will identify with a
particular party; they predict the probability that a Brazilian with certain characteristics,
which the researcher chooses, will identify with a particular party, relative to the probability he or she would identify with another party or with no party. Obviously, very
few Brazilians actually have these characteristics, but we can learn a great deal about the
relative impact of different independent variables by running the simulations.

For each party, the first simulation takes the variables that were significantly associated with partisanship for that party in Table 3 and sets them at their "most likely to be
a partisan" value for that party, except for the leadership opinion variable, which is set
at its mean value. The second simulation changes only the leadership opinion variable,
to its maximum value.[14] Thus the first simulation predicts the probability that a Brazilian will express a partisan preference for a particular party given certain characteristics
and given relative indifference to that party's leader. The second simulation reveals the
extent to which partisanship for that party increases when we add in a highly positive
leadership assessment. Table 4 provides the predicted probabilities for each party for
each simulation.

The second column of the table reveals substantial differences in the ability to
predict partisans for each of Brazil's major parties, assuming indifference to the political
leader of that party. For example, even assuming relative indifference to Lula, we can
predict PT partisanship 87 percent of the time using the "likely *petista*" variables. There
is not much room for improvement here, but changing "Lula opinion" in Table 3 to its
maximum value and rerunning the simulation does increase the predicted probability
to 95 percent. In short, with just a few variables, we can confidently predict which

Table 4. Predicted Probabilities of Identifying with a Party

Party	Without Leader	Including Leader
PT	.868 (.095)	.953 (.042)
PFL	.160 (.193)	.334 (.275)
PMDB	.373 (.291)	.557 (.313)
PSDB	.451 (.120)	.666 (.119)

Standard errors in parentheses.

Brazilians are likely to be *petistas*; PT partisanship is not simply or even largely a function of Brazilians' sentiments about Lula.

We already know that far more Brazilians identify as *petistas* than identify with all other Brazilian parties combined. Yet we can only confirm that *petismo* is "less personalistic" than partisanship for other parties by comparing the results for the PT in Table 4 with similar simulations for the other parties. Doing so reveals a sharp contrast between *petismo* and partisanship for other parties, supporting the conclusion that *petismo* is (at least as of 2002) a sentiment not only more widely held among Brazilian voters but also more deeply held than the infrequent and relatively more personalistic attachments Brazilians hold for other parties.

When we run similar simulations for the PFL, the results in column 2, not surprisingly, generate a far weaker (and less confident) prediction. Without including the evaluation of ACM, we can predict PFL partisanship only about 16 percent of the time with the three other significant variables. When we set the opinion of ACM at its maximum value, the probability of identifying a *pefelista* increases to 33 percent. Given that we could predict a *petista* 87 percent of the time even without including Lula, it is clear that PFL partisanship is not only weaker than PT partisanship, but it depends relatively more heavily on a positive leadership assessment.

Slightly better results obtain for the PMDB. Using the variables associated with PMDB partisanship except for the respondent's opinion of Jader Barbalho, we can predict a PMDB partisan about 37 percent of the time. Yet, similar to the PFL, PMDB partisanship depends a great deal on personalistic sympathies: our ability to predict a PMDB partisan improves considerably when we include respondents' evaluations of Jader, to nearly 56 percent.

The results for the PSDB are similar to those for the PMDB. Initially we predict PSDB partisanship about 45 percent of the time, again relatively weak compared to our ability to predict a *petista*. When we include the evaluation of Cardoso, the probability of identifying a PSDB partisan increases to 67 percent. Thus PSDB partisanship is similar to partisanship for the PFL and PMDB in that it is weaker than *petismo* and depends relatively heavily on personalistic sentiment for the party leader.

These simulations reveal that it is relatively easy to predict a *petista* using the BNES data, but relatively difficult to confidently predict partisans for the PFL, PMDB, or PSDB. Moreover, only for the PT can we predict partisanship well without taking into account Brazilians' sentiments about political leaders.

The findings about personalism's impact on even the limited degree of partisanship for several of Brazil's major parties motivates a second question about the relationship between personalism and partisanship in Brazil: does personalism mean the same thing for partisans of different parties and different leaders (Miller et al. 1986, 1998)? While there is no direct way to test this proposition in the BNES, an indirect way is to correlate respondents' leadership thermometer scores with their responses to batteries of questions about certain cultural values. This reveals what values are associated with positive assessments of each leader.

Brazilians' sentiments about each political leader can be correlated with four index variables also used in the regression analysis: clientelism support, corruption support; support for suppression of protest; and hierarchical values. If personalism means different things to supporters of different political leaders, the cultural values ought to reveal different correlations with each leader. Table 5 provides results that support the idea that personalism means different things for supporters of different leaders.

Brazilians with positive sentiments toward Lula are neither more nor less supportive of clientelism than other Brazilians, but support for clientelism is correlated with positive

Table 5. Correlations Between Personality Thermometer Scores and Cultural Values

Values	Lula	Cardoso	Jader	ACM
Clientelism	.00	.05*	.12**	.15**
Corruption	−.01	−.03	.19**	.23**
Protest suppression	−.15**	.06**	.05*	.09**
Hierarchical values	.03	−.07**	.17**	.21**

*p ≤ .05, **p ≤ .01.

feelings for the other three political leaders. Attitudes about political corruption are not associated with sentiment for Lula or Cardoso, but supporters of Jader and ACM tend to have slightly positive sentiments about corruption. The clearest distinction between Lula supporters and supporters of other leaders is that those who like Lula oppose the suppression of political protest, while supporters of the other leaders all favor some degree of suppression of protest. Supporters of Cardoso, moreover, hold the least "hierarchical" visions of Brazilian society. Lula supporters are indifferent in this regard, while Jader and ACM supporters hold highly hierarchical views. These findings indirectly suggest that personalism means different things to different Brazilians; future research should investigate this question further.

At this point let us return to Table 3, to discuss further the results beyond "political leaders." Turning to the group identity variables, we see very few strong relationships for any party—only 2 of the 24 coefficients reach the .05 level of statistical significance. The results for age merit comment because the literature on partisanship in older democracies associates age with partisanship through a life cycle perspective, meaning that scholars expect older voters to be more partisan (Converse 1969; Jennings and Niemi 1981). We cannot generalize this hypothesis to newer democracies, however, because many voters have not participated in democratic politics for their entire "life cycles." In Brazil, age is not strongly associated with partisanship for any party (youth is only slightly associated with *petismo*).

Race, despite its critical importance in Brazilians' lives and despite the prominent role that some Afro-Brazilians have come to play in national politics, also appears wholly unrelated to partisanship for these parties, and gender matters only for the PMDB, whose supporters are more likely to be men. PMDB supporters are also more likely to be slightly less well off, as defined by family income. What's more, despite the growth of Evangelical Christianity in Brazil in recent decades, religious affiliation is not associated either positively or negatively with partisanship for any of these four parties.

Given the general absence of strong effects across parties, more or less objectively defined group identities therefore seem relatively unimportant for shaping partisanship in Brazil. These results echo the findings of Mainwaring et al. (2000), who argue that these sorts of weak results appear because parties have never politicized any of these (or other) potential cleavages.

Stronger results emerge from the third group of variables, which associate citizens' insertion into social and political networks with partisanship. The regression tested for relationships between partisanship and respondents' degree of electoral or nonelectoral participation. The former measures citizens' participation in campaigns, and the latter measures their participation in such activities as neighborhood associations and social movements. At least one of these variables is associated with partisanship for three of the four parties, indicating that political or social engagement is frequently associated with partisanship in Brazil. However, the result for the PSDB is distinctive in that electoral participation is only weakly associated (at the .10 level of statistical significance) with partisanship.

Both of the participation variables are strongly associated with PT partisanship. The PT emerged out of activism associated with Brazil's independent union movement, Catholic base communities, and other social movements (Meneguello 1989; Keck 1992). This finding confirms that *petismo* remains linked to social and political activism. However, the precise nature and influence of these networks require additional investigation, given the changes in the PT and in Brazil's social movements since redemocratization (Hochstetler 2008; Samuels 2004), and especially given the divisions within the PT and the impact of the ongoing corruption scandal.

Partisans of the PMDB and PFL are also politically engaged in different ways. For example, nonelectoral participation is associated with PFL partisanship. Analysis of the eight components of the index of nonelectoral participation reveals that "participation in a neighborhood association" and "working together with similar-minded people" correlate with PFL partisanship. In contrast, all eight components of the nonelectoral participation index are positively correlated with PT partisanship, and all to a greater degree than for PFL partisanship. Future research could attempt to distinguish the ways in which different forms of sociopolitical action are associated with partisanship for different parties in Brazil.

In terms of the impact of sociodemographic context, the Municipal Human Development Index is positively associated with *petismo* and negatively associated with PFL partisanship. The MHDI is likely to be positively correlated with the density of local social and political organizations. Personalism and clientelism are therefore likely to be negatively correlated with the MHDI. *Petismo* is the only partisan sentiment associated with individuals living in more modern and highly developed localities, while *pefelismo* is a puzzling case of partisanship that emerges in a context of low social capital (Mainwaring et al. 2000). This finding certainly contradicts the main hypotheses that link social context to the emergence of partisan attachments.[15]

The final category in Table 3 is individuals' particular attributes or dispositions. For the PFL, only political knowledge is associated with partisanship. Partisanship for the PFL is relatively uncommon and relatively weak, associated with socially active, politically aware people who like ACM but who live in relatively underdeveloped locales.

In contrast, several variables are associated with *petismo*. *Petistas* have a high degree of political knowledge, and they also self-identify as leftists. *Petismo* also embodies several political-culture factors. PT identifiers tend to believe in the efficacy of the vote, in contrast to supporters of other parties, and they tend to affirm less support for clientelistic behavior than other Brazilians. In short, the average *petista* likes Lula and dislikes Cardoso, participates actively in politics, is highly knowledgeable about politics, identifies as left of center, supports clean government, and believes that his or her vote can make a political difference. Note, however, that "corruption support" is not significantly associated with *petismo*. This lack of a strong connection between attitudes about corruption and *petismo* may prove important in how the PT survives the current scandal.

In contrast, PMDB supporters are found among lower-middle-class, conservative males who self-identify as right-of-center and support some degree of suppression of social protest. This image of the average PMDB supporter suggests that the party's support base has changed a great deal since the party fought against the military regime and led the struggle for redemocratization in Brazil in the 1970s and 1980s. Today, the remaining PMDB partisans represent a conservative political force in Brazil.

As for the PSDB, although we can predict its supporters with only about as much confidence as PMDB supporters, we see that PSDB supporters strongly dislike Lula but like Cardoso, and are highly knowledgeable about politics. They appear to be centrists who favor "law and order" because, although they identify as neither right nor left, they oppose corruption but support suppression of some degree of social protest. As noted, partisanship for the PSDB seems relatively "passive" compared to partisanship for the other parties, in that participation in politics does not seem to shape partisanship for the PSDB.

In sum, the findings from Table 2 and the results of the regression analysis indicate that partisanship for the PT is more widespread than for any other Brazilian party and is also a more deeply held substantive attachment. In contrast, partisanship for other parties is not widespread and rests relatively more heavily on personalism.

CONCLUSION

The conventional view that few Brazilians have strong attachments to political parties and that personalism rather than programmatic attachments shapes partisan identification is partly true. On the one hand, as of 2002, about one in four Brazilians had developed a partisan attachment to the Workers' Party, and PT partisanship differs substantially from traditional political attachments in Brazil. On the other hand, after nearly two decades of democracy, two-thirds of Brazilians still express no partisan identity. About one in ten Brazilians expresses a partisan preference for some party other than the PT. However, these partisan preferences are relatively weakly held and considerably driven by personalism. That is, partisanship for parties other than the PT continues to reflect the traditional bases of Brazilian politics and only partly reflects partisanship in the way that political scientists typically employ the term. Although this study does not explore the factors associated with the vote, we can certainly conclude that partisanship does not drive the vote for most Brazilians.

The results presented here should be incorporated into ongoing debates about the status of Brazil's political parties and used to inform future research. Clearly, mass partisanship, associated with voters' ideologically driven demands for legislators' policy unity, cannot be driving the relatively high levels of legislative cohesion exhibited by all of Brazil's parties (Figueiredo and Limongi 2000). This generates a puzzle for understanding Brazil's major parties: if most voters have little interest in parties per se as collective entities, then it is unclear why politicians should care either. An argument for "party strength" rings hollow when voter sentiments remain absent.

For explaining the evolution of this distribution of partisan preferences, the growth of partisanship for the PT and the weakness of partisanship for Brazil's other parties supports the general hypothesis that partisanship emerges as a function of both individual motivation to acquire knowledge and become involved in politicized social networks (Shively 1979) and parties' organizational and recruitment efforts (Carmines and Stimson 1989). This conclusion rules out the hypothesis that education is associated with partisanship, even though scholars have long suggested that the most knowledgeable citizens are the most partisan (Campbell et al. 1960; Miller and Shanks 1996). In Brazil, education itself is unimportant for the acquisition of partisanship. (The coefficient on education is significant only at the .10 level for the PT.) Some Brazilian scholars (e.g., Moisés 1992; Balbachevsky 1992; Carreirão and Kinzo 2002) have associated education with partisanship in Brazil, but this conclusion is mistaken. Education and partisanship are positively correlated, but the relationship vanishes when multiple regression techniques are used.

According to the BNES, the average Brazilian stays in school 9.4 years, which means that it does not even take a high school diploma to develop a partisan attachment in Brazil.[16] Political knowledge—associated with the emergence of partisanship for three of Brazil's four largest parties—plays a more important role. It is not education per se that shapes partisan attachments, but rather whether Brazilians with even relatively limited degrees of education have the motivation to obtain political information, which requires actively paying close attention to politics or getting involved. This follows scholarship that holds that partisanship is a function of rational information seeking (e.g. Shively 1979) rather than of rational ignorance.

What motivates individuals to obtain political knowledge and get involved? As Carmines and Stimson (1989, 109–14) cogently argue, both politicians and voters are fundamentally inertial and prefer the status quo to any sort of change. Explaining change—for example, the growth of partisanship—requires the introduction of a dynamic, noninertial set of actors: political activists. Most citizens prefer to pay little attention to politics and to gather information from more politically attentive people around them, people whose views they know and trust. Political activists therefore can play a critical role in the formation of mass partisanship because they mediate complex political information about policy positions into relatively simple partisan cues. Thus mobilization, conversion, and recruitment start the process of political change, which can lead to the emergence of mass partisanship (Carmines and Stimson 1989, 145). That is, individual motivation to acquire knowledge appears sufficient to encourage a limited sort of partisanship, but the emergence of a full-blown partisan identity probably requires active participation in politics in some way, which highlights the role of party activists.

In terms of mobilization and recruitment, the PT remains the only Brazilian party with an extensive, institutionalized national organization (Keck 1992; Samuels 2004). The growth of partisanship for the PT up through 2004 was not exclusively or even mainly linked to the party's leftism, which it moderated over time (and refused to define), nor to its policy positions, which it also moderated, but rather to its ongoing recruitment efforts, its links to various social movements, the ability of rank-and-file members to participate actively in party politics, and the party's emphasis on gradual political change through the ballot box. Quantitatively and qualitatively, Brazil's other parties differ substantially from the PT in terms of their limited membership, grassroots connections, and recruitment efforts. The PT, despite its moderation and accession to power in recent years, remains the only Brazilian party with extensive roots in civil society (see, e.g., Baiocchi 2003; Hochstetler 2008) and the only party with relatively widespread member involvement in its governance (Samuels 2004).

The PT's ascension to power following Lula's victory in the 2002 presidential election, and the impact of the 2005 corruption scandal, raise pertinent questions about the future of PT partisan support. Both Lula and the PT moved to the center over the past decade or so (Samuels 2004; Hunter 2008), yet partisan identification with the PT grew throughout the 1990s and up through 2004, suggesting that PT "pragmatism" went hand-in-hand with growth in PT partisanship.

In government, Lula has adopted policies that have alienated some PT supporters. The corruption scandal tarnished the PT's reputation as a standard-bearer for clean government. However, the PT apparently suffered relatively little long-term damage as a result of these scandals, perhaps because—as the regression results suggest—sentiment about corruption is (somewhat surprisingly, perhaps) not among the most important determinants of partisanship for the PT. Moreover, the party's ongoing efforts further to expand and consolidate its organizational reach and to recruit new members (Genoino 2003; *Primeira Leitura On-Line* 2004) may have compensate for any losses; newly recruited supporters may care relatively little whether the PT has or has not abandoned its historical "mission" (Samuels 2008).[17]

This chapter has explored the nature and extent of partisanship in contemporary Brazil. The PT is not simply the only party that devotes substantial resources to recruitment of partisan support; clearly, something about its message resonates with a growing cohort of Brazilians. Additional survey research and especially interviews in smaller focus groups should attempt to probe more deeply the sources of *petismo*—the link between individual motivation to acquire knowledge and to participate in political life and the party's deliberate strategy to recruit supporters. Future research could also explore more extensively the meaning of "personalistic partisanship," could connect partisanship to vote choices in executive and legislative elections, and could seek to discover what sorts of people have recently declared an attachment to the PT and what sorts have decided that they no longer identify with the PT, given the party's recent pragmatism and the tarnish from political scandal.

NOTES

1 For a review of the main debates, see Amorim Neto 2002; an excellent example of recent research is Amorim Neto et al. 2003.

2 Meneguello (1989) and Keck (1992) focus on the origins of the PT. Neither explores the sources of mass partisanship. Note that Mainwaring (1999, 115) even hedges on whether mass partisanship for the PT partisanship is strong. Kinzo (2005) draws conclusions about partisanship in Brazil, and about *petismo*, from a study of the Saõ Paulo metropolitan area.

3 One can check updates on the scandal at <www.primeiraleitura.com.br> (which takes an explicitly anti-Lula tack), <http://noblat1.estadao.com.br/noblat> (a journalistic blog), <www.infobrazil.com> (a wide-ranging political analysis website), or <www.brazilnetwork.org> (a self-proclaimed "alternative" website).

4 All the surveys used in Figure 1 are publicly available from the Center for the Study of Public Opinion (CESOP) at the State University of Campinas, São Paulo (UNICAMP). See <www.unicamp.br/cesop>. The BNES is also available through CESOP.

5 The BNES will also be made available (with an English translation) on the CSES website.

6 The levels of partisan identification for the PT and PMDB do exhibit short-term fluctuations, but this study is more interested in the long-term trend, which is clearly upward for the PT and downward for the PMDB, than in any particular "blip" in the pattern.

7 This is not entirely counterintuitive. In the United States, for example, a voter may prefer one party generally but may vote to reelect the other party's candidate because the voter values the incumbent's personal qualities or particular policy positions more than voting a straight ticket.

8 The MHDI is also superior to population density, which is a proxy for urbanization, which is itself a proxy for the density of social organization and human capital.

9 Face-to-face interviews were conducted with 2,513 respondents, who were selected using a three-stage probabilistic method. The survey was implemented under the direction of Alberto C. Almeida, Zairo Cheibub, Andreia Schroeder, Rachel Meneguello, and Fernando Lourenço.

10 This study used the AMELIA software package (Honaker et al. 2001) to impute missing values. Values could be imputed for 2,491 cases of the 2,513 total.

11 Please consult the author's web site <www.polisci.umn.edu/faculty/dsamuels> for a version of this article that contains the question wordings in English. The original BNES survey instruments and data are available through CESOP <www.unicamp.br/cesop>.

12 The results do not change using personal income. The BNES did not include an urban–rural location variable.

13 To be clear, therefore, the statistical results do not distinguish partisans of one party from partisans of other parties. The coefficients detail the degree to which partisans for each party differ from Brazilians who express no partisan preference. Other statistical models could specify

the extent to which partisans for each party differ from each other on certain questions, a topic beyond the scope of this paper.

14 The values chosen for the simulations are relatively unimportant. Using different values (e.g. 20th and 80th percentile instead of the mean and the maximum) would not change the substantive interpretation of the results.

15 In 2006, *petismo* was again positively correlated with HDI, even though a vote for Lula was *negatively* correlated with HDI. See Hunter and Power (2007).

16 This is self-declared number of years in school, and is not necessarily equal to finishing the ninth grade. Other government agencies provide different statistics on schooling.

17 I thank Fábio Wanderley Reis for thoughts incorporated into this paragraph.

REFERENCES

Almeida, Alberto C. 2004. A Explicação do Voto nas Eleições Presidenciais de 2002. Unpublished, Fundação Getúlio Vargas, Rio de Janeiro.

Almond, Gabriel and Sidney Verba. 1963. *The Civic Culture*. Boston: Little Brown.

Ames, Barry. 2001. *The Deadlock of Democracy in Brazil*. Ann Arbor: University of Michigan.

Amorim Neto, Octavio. 2002. The Puzzle of Party Discipline in Brazil. *Latin American Politics and Society*. 44(1) (Spring), 127–144.

Amorim Neto, Octavio, Gary Cox and Mathew McCubbins 2003. Agenda Power in Brazil's Câmara dos Deputados, 1989–98. *World Politics* (55)4, 550–578.

Baiocchi, Gianpaulo (ed.) 2003. *Radicals in Power: The Workers Party and Experiments in Urban Democracy in Brazil*. London: Zed Books.

Baker, Andy. 2002. Free-Market Reform and Presidential Approval: The Politicization of Economic Policy Debates in Brazil. *Dados* 45(1), 39–76.

Baker, Andy, Barry Ames and Lúcio Rennó. 2005. Social Context and Voter Volatility in Weak-Party Systems: Networks and Neighborhoods in Brazil's 2002 Elections. Unpublished, Northeastern University.

Balbachevsky, Elizabeth. 1992. Identidade Partidária e Instituições Políticas no Brasil. *Lua Nova* 26.

Brader, Ted, and Joshua Tucker. 2001. Pathways to Partisanship in New Democracies: Evidence from Russia. Unpublished, University of Michigan.

Campbell, Angus et al. 1960. *The American Voter*. New York: Wiley.

Carmines, Edward and James Stimson. 1989. *Issue Evolution: Race and the Transformation of American Politics*. Princeton: Princeton University Press.

Carreirão, Yan de Souza. 2002. *A Decisão do Voto nas Eleições Presidencias Brasileiras*. Florianó-polis/Rio de Janeiro: Editora da UFSC/Editora FGV.

Carreirão, Yan de Souza, and Maria d'Alva Gil Kinzo. 2002. Os Partidos Políticos e a Decisão de Voto no Brasil. Paper presented at the meeting of the Brazilian Political Science Association, Niterói.

CESOP. 2003. Estudo Eleitoral Brasileiro. SPSS database. Campinas: Centro de Estudos de Opinião Pública.

Clarke, Harold and Marianne Stewart. 1998. The Decline of Parties in the Minds of Citizens. *Annual Review of Political Science* 1, 357–378.

Converse, Phillip. 1964. The Nature of Belief Systems in Mass Publics. In *Ideology and Discontent*, ed. David Apter. New York: Free Press.

———. 1969. Of Time and Partisan Stability. *Comparative Political Studies* 2, 139–71.

Criterium Pesquisas de Opinião e Avaliação de Políticas Públicas, 2003. Expectativa Governo Lula. São Paulo: Criterium.

Dalton, Russell J. and Martin Wattenberg, eds. 2000, *Parties Without Partisans: Political Changes in Advanced Industrial Democracies*. Oxford: Oxford University Press.

Datafolha. 2003. Avaliação Lula—1 Ano (December 21, 2003). São Paulo: Datafolha Instituto de Pesquisas. Download from http://www1.folha.uol.com.br/folha/datafolha/, accessed April 12, 2005.

———. 2004. Avaliação Presidente Luiz Inácio Lula da Silva—14 a 17 Dezembro 2004. São Paulo: Datafolha Instituto de Pesquisas. Download from http://www1.folha.uol.com.br/folha/datafolha/, accessed April 12, 2005.

———. 2005. Avaliação Presidente Luiz Inácio Lula da Silva—10 de Agosto 2005. São Paulo: Datafolha Instituto de Pesquisas. Download from http://www1.folha.uol.com.br/folha/datafolha/, accessed October 24, 2005.

Figueiredo, Argelina, and Fernando Limongi. 2000. Presidential Power, Legislative Organization, and Party Behavior in Brazil. *Comparative Politics* (January): 151–170.

Genoino, José. 2003. A campanha de filiação do PT. http://www.pt.org.br/site/artigos/artigos_int.asp?cod=571. Accessed April 11, 2005.

Green, Donald, Bradley Palmquist, and Eric Schickler. 2002. *Partisan Hearts and Minds: Political Parties and the Social Identities of Voters*. New Haven: Yale University Press.

Hochstetler, Kathy. 2008. Civil Society in Lula's Brazil. In *Democratic Brazil Revisited*, eds., Peter R. Kingstone and Timothy J. Power. Pittsburgh: University of Pittsburg Press: 33–56.

Honaker, James et al. 2001. Amelia: A Program for Missing Data (Windows version). Cambridge, MA: Harvard University. Available at http://gking.harvard.edu.

Hunter, Wendy, and Timothy J. Power. 2007. Rewarding Lula: Executive Power, Social Policy, and the Brazilian Elections of 2006. *Latin American Politics and Society* 49(1): 1–30.

Hunter, Wendy. 2008. The Partido dos Trabalhadores: Still a Party of the Left? In *Democratic Brazil Revisited*, eds. Peter Kingstone and Timothy Power. Pittsburgh: University of Pittsburgh Press: 15–32.

Jennings, M. Kent and Richard Niemi. 1974. *The Political Character of Adolescence: The Influence of Families and Schools*. Princeton: Princeton University Press.

Jennings, M. Kent and Richard Niemi. 1981. *Generations and Politics: A Panel Study of Young Adults and Their Parents*. Princeton: Princeton University Press.

Keck, Margaret. 1992. *The Workers' Party and Democratization in Brazil*. New Haven: Yale University Press.

King, Gary, Michael Tomz, and Jason Wittenberg. 2000. Making the Most of Statistical Analyses: Improving Interpretation and Presentation. *American Journal of Political Science* 44(2), 347–61.

Kinzo, Maria d'Alva. 2005. Os Partidos no Eleitorado: Percepções Públicas e Laços Partidários no Brasil. *Revista Brasileira de Ciências Sociais* 20(57): 65–81.

Lipset, Seymour M. and Stein Rokkan. 1967. *Party Systems and Voter Alignments*. New York, Free Press.

Mainwaring, Scott. 1999. *Rethinking Party Systems in the Third Wave of Democratization: the Case of Brazil*. Stanford: Stanford University Press.

Mainwaring, Scott and Timothy Scully, eds. 1995. *Building Democratic Institutions: Party Systms in Latin America*. Stanford: Stanford University Press.

Mainwaring, Scott, Rachel Meneguello, and Timothy Power. 2000. Conservative Parties, Democracy, and Economic Reform in Contemporary Brazil. In *Conservative Parties, the Right, and Democracy in Latin America*, eds., Kevin J. Middlebrook. Baltimore: The Johns Hopkins University Press: 164–222.

Meneguello, Rachel. 1989. *PT: A formação de um partido, 1979–1982*. São Paulo: Paz e Terra.

Miller, Arthur H. and Thomas F. Klobucar. 2000. The Development of Party Identification in Post-Soviet Societies. *American Journal of Political Science* 44(4), 667–685.

Miller, Arthur, Willian Reisinger and Vicki Hesli. 1998. Leader Popularity and Party Development in Post-Soviet Russia. In *Elections and Voters in Post-Communist Russia*, ed. Matthew Wyman, Stephen White, and Sarah Oates. Cheltenham: Edward Elgar 100–135.

Miller, Arthur H., Martin Wattenberg, and Oksana Malanchuk. 1986. Schematic Assessments of Presidential Candidates. *American Political Science Review* 80(2), 521–40.

Miller, Warren and J. Merrill Shanks. 1996. *The New American Voter*. Cambridge: Harvard University Press.

Moisés, José Álvaro. 1992. *Os Brasileiros e a Democracia*. São Paulo: Paz e Terra.

Opinião Pública. 2003. Encarte Tendências. *Opinião Pública* 9(2), 119–167.

Power, Timothy. 2000. Political Institutions in Democratic Brazil: Politics as a Permanent Consitutional Convention. In *Democratic Brazil*, eds. Timothy Power and Peter Kingstone. Pittsburgh: University of Pittsburgh Press, 17–35.

Primeira Leitura On-Line. 2004. PT-empresa se prepara para eleições municipais. Number 1061, January 30 2004. www.primeiraleitura.com.br, Accessed April 11, 2005.

———. 2005. Cem filiados se desligam do PT. Number 1367, January 31 2005. www.primeiraleitura.com.br. Accessed April 11, 2005.

Reis, Fábio W. (ed.). 1978. *Os Partidos e o Regime*. São Paulo, Símbolo.

Rosenstone, Steven and John Mark Hansen. 1993. *Mobilization, Participation and Democracy in America*. New York: Macmillan.

Samuels, David. 2004. From Socialism to Social Democracy? Party Organization and the Transformation of the Workers' Party in Brazil. *Comparative Political Studies* 37(9), 999–1024.

———. 2008. The Evolution of *Petismo* (2002–2008). Forthcoming, *Opinião Pública* (São Paulo).

Shively, W. Phillips. 1979. The Development of Party Identification among Adults: Exploration of a Functional Model. *American Political Science Review* 73(4), 1039–54.

Singer, André. 1990. Collor na Periferia: a Volta por cima do Populismo? in Bolivar Lamounier (ed.) *De Geisel a Collor: o Balanço da Transição*, Sumaré/IDESP.

———. 1999. *Esquerda e Direita no Eleitorado Brasileiro*. São Paulo: EdUSP/FAPESP.

Soares, Gláucio Ary Dillon. 1961. As Bases Ideológicas do Lacerdismo. *Revista Civilização Brasileira* 1(4), 49–70.

Tomz, Michael, Jason Wittenberg, and Gary King. 2003. CLARIFY: Software for Interpreting and Presenting Statistical Results. Version 2.1 Stanford University, University of Wisconsin, and Harvard University. January 5. Available at http://gking.harvard.edu.

TSE (Tribunal Superior Eleitoral). 2002. Resultados das Eleições de 2002. Brasília: TSE. Microsoft Access computer files.

United Nations Development Program. 2003. Atlas do Desenvolvimento Humano no Brasil. Version 1.0.0. Brasília: United Nations Development Program for Brazil. CD-ROM.

Von Mettenheim, Kurt. 1995. *The Brazilian Voter: Mass Politics in Democratic Transition (1974–1986)*. Pittsburgh: The University of Pittsburgh Press.

Chapter 14

Brazil's Agrarian Reform: Democratic Innovation or Oligarchic Exclusion Redux?

Anthony W. Pereira

The prominence of agrarian reform as a political issue has been one of the great surprises of Brazilian politics since 1995. The mobilization for reform has been widespread and intense. The topic occupied a prominent place in the rhetoric of both the Fernando Henrique Cardoso (1995–2002) and Lula governments (2003–2010). Land redistribution under both of these governments extended farther than similar programs under their predecessors, and went beyond what most political observers anticipated. Agrarian reform also became a symbol of and a focal point in the battle between supporters and opponents of the government's macroeconomic policies.

How to explain and interpret this surprising outcome? What does the Federal government's agrarian reform represent for Brazil's politics and economy? One answer to the latter question is that the increase in land redistribution represents a major economic and political reform. In this view, the Cardoso and Lula governments, reflecting both presidents' progressive backgrounds, broke with past policies. By granting small producers a more secure place in the agricultural sector and by recognizing, negotiating with, and partly accommodating the landless, the Cardoso and Lula governments democratized economic and social policy in the countryside.

An alternative interpretation, however, would stress the continuity of the governments' policies with the past. In this interpretation, a look behind and beyond land redistribution reveals policies that disproportionately benefit a small number of politically powerful, large producers, and a series of missed opportunities to benefit the rural poor.

This chapter argues that the second interpretation is more accurate than the first. It begins by examining some claims about past policies and the Federal government's impact on them. Then it looks at the situation the Cardoso government inherited, and the trends in agriculture and land use that preceded the government's ascension to power. Tracing the course of agrarian reform since 1995, this chapter looks beyond the statistics on land redistribution to examine the issues of land titling, agricultural credit, taxation, payments for expropriated land, and rural violence. Finally, it suggests that the Cardoso and Lula governments did not fundamentally alter the development model or the pattern of policies in agriculture.

Such an analysis of Brazil's agrarian reform as offered here might be seen as misleading, by treating as a single phenomenon a whole series of complicated processes that vary enormously by region and over time. It is possible, however, to recognize the complexity and variability of the reform process, as this study does, and at the same time seek some preliminary generalizations about its overall trends and consequences. Reasonable people can, of course, differ as to what those generalizations should be.

PRIOR POLICIES OF CONSERVATIVE "MODERNIZATION"

Brazil's state policies have traditionally followed a pattern well summarized by Sorj: "the state takes responsibility for the onus, the bonus is distributed among the dominant classes, and the crumbs [*migalhas*] are left over for the subaltern groups" (Sorj 1998, 28).

The oligarchic and patronage-based features of these policies are rooted in the agrarian past. Land in Brazil has traditionally been not merely a factor of production but a reward for service and proximity to power, as well as a foundation for the accumulation and maintenance of more power and privilege. This power includes the ability of large landowners to direct the legal and coercive apparatus of the state in their region. It also entails landlord control over and obligations to subaltern populations.

The original division of the colonial land grants or *capitanias* among a handful of amigos do rei (friends of the king) reflects this reality (Gonçalo 2001, 23). In Brazil, unlike the United States, the state's exclusionary tendencies were not substantially mitigated in later stages of development by frontier policies that granted land to the landless. Whereas the U.S. Homestead Act of 1862 granted frontier land to anyone willing to settle it, Brazil's 1850 Land Law (*Lei da Terra*) prohibited the acquisition of public land by any means other than purchase, thus putting an end to previous rights to gain land through occupancy (*posse*) (Viotti da Costa 2000, 78–79).

Brazilian policies in agriculture in more recent years can best be characterized as the promotion of conservative "modernization." Unlike Latin American countries such as Mexico and Bolivia, Brazil has never had a political rupture that weakened the landed oligarchy and allowed large-scale redistribution of land to those who cultivate it. In addition, Brazil's rural workers have never fully enjoyed the benefits of the Vargas-era Consolidated Labor Laws (*Consolidação das Leis do Trabalho*), unlike urban workers.

The brief period of mobilization around land and rural labor issues in the late 1950s and early 1960s, which saw the emergence of the Peasant Leagues and rural trade unions, was ended forcefully by the military coup in 1964. The military regime of 1964–85 subsequently imposed policies that essentially took land redistribution in already settled areas off the political agenda. Government policies of subsidized credit (mainly for large producers), tax breaks, price supports, and other incentives promoted the development of large, highly capitalized, mechanized farms and ranches, many of them producing for export. This conservative "modernization" created an exodus from the countryside, as sharecroppers, tenants, and small farmers lost access to land, and rural workers lost jobs (Pereira 1997).

At the same time that land concentration was taking place, new, previously unused lands were also passing into private hands. Leite calculates that the private sector acquired, by purchase and government grants, some 31.8 million hectares of previously public land in the 1970s alone (Leite 1999, 173). This phenomenon was especially marked in the west and north of the country. To minimize potential social unrest in the face of these policies, the military regime initiated programs of rural social assistance (pensions and health), as well as colonization (mostly in the Amazon region).

The Cardoso government, some observers believe, made a historic break with those policies. This view places Cardoso in the mold of previous presidents, such as Getúlio Vargas (1930–45, 1950–54) and Juscelino Kubitschek (1955–60), who were credited with creating a new order in Brazilian politics (see, for example, Roett 1999; Sorj 1998; Gordon 2001, 125–30). The prominent Brazilian rural sociologist José de Souza Martins is probably the best-known proponent of this view (Martins 1999, 2000). Martins sees the Cardoso government's agrarian reform as the culmination of one process and a dramatic break with another. It is the capstone of a process that began under Getúlio Vargas, to undo the absolute dominion given to private property in land by the 1850 *Lei da Terra*, and to reassert the public and social character of landholding.[1] On the other hand, it also represents a long-awaited supersedence of the oligarchic, personalistic, and patronage-based pattern of Brazilian politics in the countryside that prevailed even under democratic regimes. Martins sees President Cardoso's Brazilian Social Democratic Party (PSDB), and the Workers' Party (PT) as antioligarchical political parties with enough force to push Brazil toward political modernity in the rural areas (Martins 1999, 117).[2]

Martins sees in land reform four fundamental changes in Brazil's society and state. First, unproductive or underproductive large estates (*latifúndios*) have become capitalized and "empresarialized," submitting themselves to the logic of capitalist reproduction and integrating with financial and industrial capital. Second, family farmers have finally won guarantees to a place in the economy and society. Third, the state has become more representative, institutionalized, pluralized, and democratic. Finally, the state has replaced repression with law and negotiation in the countryside, submitting erstwhile *latifundiários* to the rational-legal control of public authority (Martins 1999, 119, 121, 125). In his enthusiasm, Martins redefines the Federal government's most active critics on the land reform issue—the Landless Workers' Movement (*Movimento dos Sem Terra*, or MST) and the Catholic Church's Pastoral Land Commission (*Comissão Pastoral da Terra*, or CPT)—as its real allies in this historic transformation (Martins 1999, 120).

There is some wishful thinking in this portrait; most specialists on agrarian reform do not share Martins' views (see Ondetti 2008, 200–219). While certain of the trends that Martins points to have occurred, policies in land and agriculture did not, across the board, reflect the kind of wholesale innovation he describes. Before considering the evidence for this, however, it is necessary to examine the general tendencies in land and agricultural policies before 1995, and how the subsequent agrarian reform related to them.

Trends in Agriculture and Land Use

With the election of a civilian president in 1985, land redistribution returned to the political agenda, mainly because of pressure from below. José Sarney (1985–90) promised a massive land redistribution program through the expropriation of unproductive estates. Yet very little of this reform was actually carried out, either by Sarney's government or those of his successors, Fernando Collor de Mello (1990–92) and Itamar Franco (1992–94) (see Table 1). At the same time, partly as a result of the debt crisis, government subsidies to agriculture dropped precipitously. Agricultural credit, for example, declined from $27 billion in 1986 to only $6 billion in 1996, as measured in 1996 U.S. dollars (Leite 1999, 162). Price supports were also reduced (Leite 1999, 164).

This sharp cut in government support reflects a more market-driven approach to agriculture, enacted at first through sheer necessity and later as a conscious strategy. This "sink-or-swim" strategy led to the demise of many small farms and contributed to the dismissal of many farm workers. To offset the potential for conflict and resistance generated by such policies, the government began to increase its spending on rural social

Table 1. Beneficiaries of Land Reform Claimed by Civilian Governments in Brazil, 1985–2006 (number of families)

Government	Beneficiaries Claimed	Beneficiaries Promised	Average Per Year
Sarney (1985–90)	89,950	1,400,000	17,990
Collor (1990–92)	38,425		12,808
Franco (1992–94)	21,763		10,881
Cardoso I (1995–98)	287,994	280,000	71,998
Cardoso II (1999–02)	252,710		63,178
Lula I (2003–06)	381,419	400,000	95,355

Source: Rows 1–3: Ondetti, 2008, 148; Rows 4–6 (Cardoso I and II and Lula I): Arruda 2007, p. A10.

security and welfare (*previdência social*) (Leite 1999, 169), as it did on social programs in general.

On one level, government policy in agriculture was successful. By the mid-1990s, Brazil's agricultural sector was clearly one of the most dynamic and productive in the developing world. Its productivity (value added per agricultural worker) doubled between the periods 1979–81 and 1996–98, becoming almost twice that of Mexico in the latter period (World Bank 2001). Still the world's leading producer and exporter of coffee and sugar, Brazil has expanded into new agricultural markets, acquiring the largest herd of cattle in the world and becoming the world's second-largest producer of soybeans. The country supplies 85 percent of the world market for orange juice concentrate and exports tobacco, chicken, cocoa, cotton, butter, beef, and corn (Brogan 2000, 185; Rohter 2004, 2). Between 1996 and 2006, the cultivated area in Brazil grew 83.5 percent, with the biggest increase occurring in the north of the country (Soares and Lobato 2007: 1). Brazil's potential for even greater agricultural production is high. It still has a land frontier, and analysts estimate that the area devoted to crops in 1999—around 112.5 million acres—could easily be doubled (Economist Intelligence Unit 1999, 1).

Agriculture is still experiencing growth in capital intensivity and mechanization, and its importance to the Brazilian economy is higher than agriculture is to the economies of the richest countries. While agriculture accounts for only about 9 percent of Brazil's gross domestic product, it is responsible for around 40 percent of exports and 23 percent of the economically active population (Brogan 2000, 185; Rohter 2004, 2).[3] Agriculture, furthermore, is internationally competitive and highly "globalized": 16.4 percent of all agricultural production was exported in 1995 (Leite 1999, 160), almost twice the rate of the economy as a whole. These exports generate the largest positive trade balance of any sector of the Brazilian economy (Graziano Neto 1998, 168–69), amounting to US$19 billion in 2001.[4] Overall, the Brazilian agricultural sector produced goods worth $150 billion in 2004, and is sometimes called the "green anchor" of the economy (Rohter 2004: 2). Furthermore, the growing U.S. demand for biofuels is likely to increase Brazilian exports of alcohol, made from sugar, to the United States. This strong performance, moreover, has been achieved with far fewer subsidies than those that prevail in the United States and the European Union. According to scholar Marcus Sawaya Jank, Brazilian agricultural subsidies, which benefit about two million farmers, are only one-third of what the U.S. government spends on only 250,000 farmers (Jank 2001).[5]

Brazilian agriculture is also successful at home. Brazil's food production index has risen from 69.5 in 1979–81 to 125.7 in 1996–98. (The period 1989–91 = 100. World Bank 2001, 288). In 2001 the Brazilian government forecast a record grain crop of 91.6 million tons, a 10 percent increase over the 83 million tons produced in 2000 (Rinelli 2001, 4). The continuing problem of hunger in Brazil is thus the consequence of lack of sufficient income on the part of the poor, not an inadequate supply of food from Brazil's farms and ranches.

Behind the glittering trajectory of Brazilian agriculture, however, lies what historian Kenneth Maxwell calls "the other Brazil" (Maxwell 1999–2000). According to the International Fund for Agricultural Development (IFAD), about one half of Brazil's rural population was poor in 1998, living on less than two dollars per day.[6] With one of the most unequal distributions of land in the world, the Brazilian countryside has been the site not only of the creation of great fortunes, but of social devastation reminiscent of the enclosure of common lands in early modern Europe or the outmigration of displaced smallholders in the U.S. Dust Bowl during the Great Depression. This devastation has been created partly because the policies promoting the "modernization" of agriculture have placed a premium on narrow criteria: the creation of a large, exportable surplus of agricultural goods. Other considerations, such as maximizing rural employment, intensify-ing the cultivation of the land, and accommodating the desire of small farmers to remain independent small producers, have been neglected.[7]

Furthermore, social relations have changed in the countryside. Large landowners have jettisoned traditional bonds of obligation to the rural poor, who used to be their tenants, sharecroppers, dependents, or clients. That sense of *noblesse oblige* was, at one time, a key component of the rural social order, but it has eroded as large landowners have used their privileged connection to the state to transform themselves into entrepre-neurs of the new agribusiness. Indeed, in many regions, face-to-face contacts between large landowners and the rural poor have become a thing of the past.

A major survey of 159,778 people resettled on land under the federal government's agrarian reform program from the period before 1960 until 1996, conducted in December and January 1996–97, reveals the extent of deprivation that many rural dwellers face. Thirty percent of those surveyed were illiterate, while less than 14 percent had received more than four years of primary school education (Schmidt et al. 1998, 24, 65). Sixty-four percent of those surveyed had no training or skills in the labor market other than their knowledge of farming (the survey used the terms *agricultor* and *campones*); and 87 percent farmed their land themselves, without being in a cooperative or part of a larger enterprise.

Well over half these farmers said that they received "no" or "precarious" technical assistance from the government. The average household income of these smallholders was 722 reais per year, or about the same amount in U.S. dollars at the then-prevailing exchange rate. But only a small minority lived in houses with running water or sewer-age. Only 5 percent of these struggling farmers, growing mainly basic staples, such as corn, manioc, beans, sweet potatoes, and rice, had the benefit of irrigation, while in most regions even fewer had access to farm machinery or motorized vehicles. Their access to education and health services was tenuous or nonexistent, and many of them reported serious health problems, such as intestinal parasites (15 percent) and malaria (8 percent) (Schmidt et al. 1998, 55–112).[8]

The conditions described in this report have improved since the mid-1990s due in part to the expansion of social programs.[9] The *Bolsa Família* (Family Allowance) program, initiated by the Cardoso government and expanded under President Lula, reached 11.2 million families in 2006, providing them with a small income supplement (Mercadante 2006: 123). However, this income supplement, as positive a development as it is, has not really altered the location of the poor in the rural social structure.

Brazil's poorest farmers thus still have a precarious toehold in the new agrarian order. Below them in the rural social order are the landless. These former small farmers, rural workers, and even urban workers face dim prospects in urban labor markets, where unemployment has risen in recent years. While the new rural Brazil boasts of vast farms and ranches run by prosperous owners with cell phones and pickup trucks, small armies of the dispossessed move, sometimes unseen, within it, migrating in search of seasonal jobs, shelter, and—the biggest hope of many—land. Despite the difficult conditions of life for small farmers, many of the landless seem to prefer this option to any existing alternatives.

The official system of representation in Brazilian agriculture has not been fully able to accommodate those losing access to land in the new agrarian economy. The National Agrarian Confederation is the official, state-recognized entity representing agricultural employers, while the National Confederation of Workers in Agriculture (CONTAG) is its counterpart on the labor side. While CONTAG does speak out on the issue of landlessness and agrarian reform and its member unions do sometimes organize land occupations (Sigaud 2000), its organizational structure makes it a more effective representative of small family farmers and wageworkers than of the landless.

This shortcoming was a factor in the emergence of the MST, the government's principal critic on land reform (Pereira 1999). The MST, which began its activity in the early 1980s, claims to speak for the estimated 4.8 million landless families in the country and organizes marches, occupations (or, as others say, invasions) of unused public and private land, and more recently, occupations of government offices. It demands the radical deconcentration of land ownership via widespread redistribution of land from large landowners to the dispossessed. It has attempted to prod the national conscience and to speak for those excluded from the benefits of the modern economy (Carter 2005; Comparato 2001; Hammond 2004; Hochstetler 2006, 18, 24; Navarro 2005; Ondetti 2008; Pereira 1999, 115, 119; Stédile 2007; Wright and Wolford 2003).

The MST and its demand for agrarian reform, in turn, were opposed by the Democratic Rural Union (UDR), an organization of large landowners opposed to land reform that emerged after 1985 (Sorj 1998, 29; Payne 2000). These last two organizations, both of which lie outside the official system of representation, garnered most of the early headlines in the struggle over agrarian reform in Brazil. While the UDR has become much less visible in recent years (Carter 2005, 18–19) the power of the agribusiness lobby has remained formidable, exercised through informal channels and the large *bancada ruralista* (rural bloc) in Congress.

The Cardoso government therefore inherited an agricultural sector that was generating both enormous wealth and misery, a dualistic process that in turn was creating a crisis of representation in the countryside. Despite the market-oriented reforms of the 1980s and 1990s, Brazilian agriculture, like agriculture everywhere, was still strongly dependent on the state. At its inauguration, the Cardoso government faced basic choices about what kinds of policies to enact and what groups to negotiate with.

STATE POLICIES UNDER CARDOSO AND LULA: THE MST VS. THE FEDERAL GOVERNMENT

Both supporters and opponents of the Cardoso government's land reform policies saw the struggle over land in epochal terms. For the government, the reforms reflected Cardoso's observation during his campaign that "Brazil is not anymore an underdeveloped country. It is an unjust country" (Cardoso 1994, 9). In this view, the state's responsibility was to maintain and stimulate a modern agricultural sector that finally produced for the best interests of the larger society, while using welfare programs, including land reform, to ameliorate the worst social effects of agricultural modernization and provide some relief to a conflict-ridden countryside. Then—Minister of Agrarian Development Raúl Jungmann declared in 2002 that Brazil's land reform was "perhaps the biggest ever realized in an atmosphere of democratic stability and respect for institutions" (*Folha de São Paulo* 2002); and President Cardoso equated it with "a veritable peaceful revolution in the countryside" (quoted in Margolis 2002, 1).

For opponents of the reforms, however, the Cardoso government perpetuated a fraud about its accomplishments while colluding with retrograde elements of the old social order, thus perpetuating oligarchic domination in the guise of "modernization." In the words of Dom Tomás Balduíno, president of the CPT in 2002, "From the point of view of propaganda, it [the government] has achieved success. There is no lack of numbers, which are presented in accordance with their own criteria. The reality is totally different" (*Folha de São Paulo* 2002).

Candidate Cardoso promised to settle 280,000 landless families on land by the end of his four-year term (Cardoso 1994, 103). Once elected, however, Cardoso did not seem to make agrarian reform a priority. The government's overriding concern was to ensure the success of the anti-inflation Real Plan, initiated before the election in July 1994. The government's basic attitude toward agriculture seemed to be that, regardless of the dubious conditions under which many large landowners had obtained their lands and the benighted history of the *latifundio* in general, the sector had been professionalized and modernized to such an extent that it would be counterproductive to threaten it with too heavy an emphasis on land reform (Graziano Neto 1998, 108). Agriculture was one of Brazil's most competitive sectors; it could generate exports, anchor the Real Plan, provide cheap food to the cities, and survive any process of deepening regional trade integration that the government decided to undertake.

At the same time, the Cardoso government tended to regard groups pressing for land reform with skepticism and sometimes alarm. It saw the demand for land reform as an archaic and primitive "agrarian redistributivism" that advocated land expropriation and redistribution as a solution to Brazil's past and present problems (de Souza 1997, 80; Martins 1999), based on an outdated ideology that criticized a system of unproductive *latifundios* that no longer existed. That ideology mistakenly assumed that only the ownership of the means of production (rather than the training, skills, and human capital of individuals) determined the distribution of income, and reflected a romantic reification of a traditional peasantry that was largely passing out of history (Sorj 1998).[10]

In the government's view, land reform programs would primarily be for purposes of social welfare rather than agricultural production. Programs designed to alter fundamentally the structure of production and to include in it more small farmers were foolhardy and pushed against the global trend toward the concentration of land and increasing capital intensivity in agriculture. For this reason, President Cardoso dismissed advocates of land reform for making a "nineteenth-century demand."

In making this remark, the president seemed to assume that the landless, or at least their leaders, were fighting for land out of some romantic, mystical attachment to the soil, or mere ideological bias. It seems more plausible, however, that the landless are quite pragmatic, and that they struggle for land because of a lack of viable alternatives. Many of them are relatively unschooled, unskilled, older workers, whose employment prospects in the Brazilian economy are bleak. A study of land occupiers by the Brazilian Intelligence Agency revealed that some 40 percent had at one time worked in cities (cited in Gonçalo 2000, 5), which indicates that at one time they were willing at least to try to find a place in urban labor markets. In the advanced capitalist countries, many rural dwellers welcomed the opportunities created by industrialization, and there is no reason to believe that Brazilians are fundamentally different from Europeans and North Americans in this regard. The Brazilian economy, however, is not creating enough industrial jobs to absorb the landless.

President Cardoso's stance also ignored the possibility that small-holder agriculture could be more fully integrated into the productive structure of the country. Policies to redirect subsidies from larger to smaller farmers and to increase infrastructural, technical, marketing, and financial support to labor-intensive small farms could be appropriate, and not "backward," in an emerging market economy such as Brazil's. Such policies could also have dynamic effects on the domestic market, as their redistributive effects would increase demand in the countryside. Yet the government did not seem to seriously contemplate such a strategy, and kept the old model of agricultural modernization largely intact. This was largely for political rather than economic reasons.

The Achilles' heel of the Cardoso strategy, at least in political terms, was that it could not offer a significant portion of the rural population a place in the new, "globalized" economic order. (In this sense, Cardoso's social democracy differs markedly from European social democracy of the early twentieth century, which did have a project for the rural poor). The Cardoso government's early policy position seemed to consign several generations of the rural poor to social, economic, and political oblivion.

The president frankly admitted that his policies could not include everyone in a lengthy interview with a journalist from *Folha de São Paulo* conducted in 1996. Declaring that his government favored the most advanced capitalist sectors of the economy rather than the traditional "monopolistic and bureaucratic capitalism" or the "corporatists" [corporativistas] of the old patrimonial state, he added,

> I am also not going to say that it [my government] is of the excluded, because it cannot be. . . . Certain sectors are not part of this dynamic segment of the economy. And then what? [E daí?] . . . I don't know how many excluded there will be (Cardoso 1996, 6).

After reflecting, he added that the excluded might number somewhere around 16 million people!

Under these conditions, the organizing efforts of the MST and its multiple offshoots bore rapid fruit, partly filling the void left by the decline of the organized labor movement under the Cardoso government. Tens of thousands of landless occupied unused private and sometimes public land (mostly in already settled areas rather than frontier, previously unfarmed land) in hundreds of encampments around the country, which peaked at 502 separate land occupations in 1997 (INCRA 2001). An estimated 65,000 people were in such encampments in 2000 (Ondetti 2008, 190).

The pressure on the government from these encampments was considerable; however, what seemed to trigger a change in the administration's attitude to agrarian reform were massacres of the landless in 1995 and especially 1996. Ondetti argues persuasively that the rhythm of land expropriations closely follows the outcry that accompanied the killing of 10 landless people in Corumbiara in Rondônia on August 9, 1995, and 19 landless (and the wounding of 69) in Eldorado de Carajás in the state of Pará on April 17, 1996 (Hammond 2004; Ondetti 2008). In the wake of these atrocities, committed by military police forces ostensibly controlled by state governments, the federal government accelerated land expropriations and increased the number of people resettled on land. The MST, in turn, utilized its newfound media spotlight to organize more land occupations and other actions, including a highly publicized march to Brasília in April 1997.

According to the government's figures from 1995 to 1998, roughly 287,000 landless families received land under the land reform program (Ondetti 2008, 148). This exceeds the 280,000 families to whom Cardoso, in his 1994 presidential campaign, promised to give land. According to the official data, in eight years, the Cardoso government benefited 540,704 landless families, or more than three times as many as the 150,138 families listed as beneficiaries under its three predecessors combined. This trend continued under Lula, with the Lula government's data on families settled on land exceeding that of his predecessor (see Table1). According to government data, roughly 50 million hectares, mostly in unused private holdings, were acquired for redistribution under the land reform program, with almost two thirds of that land being acquired under the first Lula government of 2003–2006. In the latter period, over 30 million hectares were acquired, compared to an average of 10 million hectares in each of Cardoso's two terms (1995–1998 and 1999–2003; from Arruda 2007, A10).

The MST and the CPT dispute the Federal government's claims made during both the Cardoso and Lula presidencies. This discrepancy occurs partly because the MST and CPT do not count squatters who were already on land before receiving legal title from the government, or beneficiaries who entered the land redistribution system before the advent of a particular government (*Sem Terra* 2000, Marreiro 2007, A7).[11] The MST also referred to data from the Escola de Economia da Universidade de São Paulo showing that from 1995 to 2000, 400,000 small farmers lost land and 1.2 million rural workers lost jobs (cited in Gonçalo 2001, 4). The MST newspaper asserted that some 900,000 small-holders lost access to land in this period (*Sem Terra* 2000). More recently, MST leader João Pedro Stédile has claimed that almost 300,000 rural workers lost their jobs and moved to cities in 2005 (Stédile 2007, 2). Other data show that overall rural employment fell by 1.5 million jobs between 1996 and 2006.[12] Critics of the agrarian reform further cite partial surveys that found that within two years of receiving their land, approximately a quarter of the beneficiaries of land reform abandoned their plots because they were unable to service loans, among several reasons (Margolis 2002).

The MST also argued that despite the Federal government's policies, unproductive lands were still plentiful. The agrarian atlas (*Atlas fundiário brasileiro*) put out by the Ministry of Agrarian Policy, for example, shows that only 28 percent of Brazil's cultivable land is being used in some productive activity, while 62 percent of it remains unproductive (cited in Borin 1997, 25). The MST even disputed the Federal government's right to call its policies agrarian reform, because, in the MST's view, the reform did not change the productive structure of agriculture, and was therefore merely *assistencialismo* (welfarism, or a form of social assistance, rather than inserting the landless into the productive system). This criticism was echoed by José Juliano de Carvalho Filho, a disaffected architect of the Lula government's agrarian reform plan who denounced the latter's "emptying" of agrarian reform in early 2007 (Carvalho Filho 2007).

Federal government leaders have sometimes rebutted such attacks by asserting that widespread public support for agrarian reform, if not for the MST's methods, came largely out of the urban population's stereotypical attitude to landowners as semifeudal latifundiarios (Graziano Neto 1998, 168). For example, President Cardoso complained that TV Globo's 1996 telenovela *O rei do gado* (Cattle King), which portrayed grassroots members of the MST, if not the movement's leaders, in a sympathetic light, put pressure on his government to redistribute more land (Pompeu de Toledo 1998, 324), even though such policies had questionable economic value. The government's position was that land reform was unlikely to increase output or raise rural incomes in what was a highly productive agricultural economy. Land redistribution should therefore not be a priority; it was better to tax unproductive land and encourage tenancy and crop-sharing arrangements to increase employment and alleviate poverty (de Souza 1997, 80).

In its conflict with the MST, the Cardoso government emphasized the occasional violence of the landless themselves and the apparent lack of commitment of some of the MST leaders to Brazil's currently existing version of democracy. The government and its supporters sometimes characterized the MST as a political party rather than a social movement. They alleged that the MST's broad attacks on the government's economic policies proved that it used land reform as a means to demoralize the government rather than as an end in itself. They further charged that the MST's opposition to the government's measures to decentralize land reform and create a "market-assisted" land reform program with the help of the World Bank—which would complement land expropriation by the National Institute for Colonization and Agrarian Reform (INCRA) through the purchase of unproductive land—was based on purely ideological grounds.

The MST's leader, Joao Pedro Stédile, responded in pragmatic terms. He claimed that, given the government's budget of R$1 billion for the market-assisted land reform program and an average cost of R$20,000 for each family settled, the program would be able to settle about only another 50,000 families on the land (Stédile and Fernandes 1999, 141). The MST also complained that the program was more generous to landowners and banks than to the landless.[13] (For a good analysis of the market-assisted land reform, see Sauer 2006, 285–311.)

The first Lula government, for its part, has been less confrontational with the MST than its predecessor. Its ministers for agrarian reform have been close to the land-less movement. It increased loans to small farmers, accelerated land settlements, and increased the budget for and the number of personnel at INCRA (Stédile 2007, 2 and Arruda 2006, A4).[14] But it has also not abandoned the Federal government's long-standing commitment to the conservative modernization of agriculture, and the resulting large-scale, capital-intensive, export-oriented agribusinesses that dominate the sector in Brazil. Under President Lula, the dispute between the government and rural social movements over the data on the number of beneficiaries of land reform has continued. The MST, for example, only counts as beneficiaries families that were taken to new settlements, where land was expropriated or purchased expressly for agrarian reform. At the beginning of 2007 the MST accused the Lula government of "inflating" the numbers about the number of beneficiaries of land reform. Along with the CPT, it also demanded the abolition of the Land Reform Ministry (Ministério de Reforma Agrária e Desenvolvimento, or MIRAD), created in 1996, because it was allegedly too bureaucratic and powerless, and slowed down the land reform process. According to the MST and CPT, INCRA was more capable of continuing the land reform process without MIRAD (Arrruda 2006).

As an actor in a democracy, the MST poses uncomfortable challenges to the status quo. The attitude of some of its leaders toward the agrarian structure seem quixotic, in that they appear to regard any landholder with property above a certain size as a *lati-fundiário*, regardless of whether that property was productive or unproductive. Stédile, for example, said in an interview that the maximum size of rural properties should be one thousand hectares (Stédile and Fernandes 1999). It is not clear how such a radical deconcentration of landholding can take place under conditions of democracy and legal continuity; that is, a nonrevolutionary situation. Such a declaration, however, should not be interpreted as representing the view of all members of the movement. Furthermore, the MST (and not just it; about half of all land occupations were led by other groups) has consistently pushed for an expansion of the beneficiaries of economic development. The movement raised serious questions about the direction of Brazilian society in general, and not just the fate of agrarian reform.[15]

The debate between the Federal government and the MST exposes the cruel dilem-mas that all of Brazil's national leaders face. The government bases its agricultural policies on agribusiness, but can not adequately address the needs of the rural dispossessed. It redistributes land, but accelerating land redistribution seems to lead to more occupations; at the same time, almost as many people appear to leave the land as were resettled on it. The government might question the economic viability of land redistribution, but the public continues to support it. This public support is likely to be been based in part on personal or familial acquaintance with the injustice and violence of the social order in the countryside.[16] After all, the great waves of migration that transformed Brazil into an urban country occurred only in the last three decades, and many urban Brazilians retain links to the land. It is all the more impressive because, despite the popularity of telenovelas such as *O rei do gado*, analysis of the Brazilian media suggests that television news coverage of the landless movement's leadership has been generally negative (Porto 2001, 21–24).

The essential aspect of agrarian reform being explored here, however, is the extent to which it represents a major reform of preexisting policies. In this regard, land redistribution itself is less important than a series of other, related measures. These include price stability brought by the 1994 Real Plan, which has reduced speculation in land as a hedge against inflation, thus lowering land prices and leading to rationalization of the use of land as a factor of production. A gun control law was passed in 1997 to curb rural violence, especially by landowners wishing to evict land occupiers. In 1996, the government enacted a judicial reform to send members of the military police who commit intentional homicide to jury trials held in civilian courts. Policies have also been created to decentralize land reform and to supplement land expropriation with "market-assisted" initiatives that buy unused land from owners. The most important reforms, however, were the increase in the rate of progressive taxation on unproductive land, and laws facilitating land expropriation and defending the rights of land occupiers.

In December 1996 the Brazilian National Congress approved legislation concerning the rural tax (*imposto territorial rural*, or ITR) and the procedure for land expropriation (*rito sumário de desapropriação de terras*). The landowners' lobby in Congress succeeded in reducing the tax rate on productive land, but the government increased it on unproductive land; the top rate for the largest estates rose from 4.5 percent to 20 percent (Cardoso 1997, 83). The modification of the land expropriation procedure allows the rapid expropriation and distribution of unproductive land and the subsequent negotiation of its price. At the same time, Congress also passed a law that brings in the Public Ministry (*Ministério Público*) in situations of land conflict (Sorj 1998, 38). This legislation was introduced by the *núcleo agrário* of the PT (the party's caucus on agrarian issues), and states that any expulsion order (*processo de despejo*) entails following a procedure in which the Public Ministry must be present and a judge must hear both sides before making a decision (Stédile and Fernandes 1999, 116).

These legal changes, for many analysts, represent "another step in the integration and disciplining of the rural areas within the political-administrative structures of the Brazilian state" (Sorj 1998, 38). President Cardoso described them as a fundamental restructuring of the legal framework governing land (*arcabouço jurídico da terra*) that signified the definitive political defeat of *latifundiários*, who were now "paper tigers" that no longer controlled Congress (Pompeu de Toledo 1998, 321–22). Yet is such a conclusion warranted?

THE MODEST IMPACT OF OTHER REFORMS

Despite the relatively large scale of land redistribution and the important legal changes under the Cardoso government, there is considerable evidence that other policy changes have had relatively little impact on the countryside. Furthermore, important initiatives that could have been taken were not.

MST leader Stédile complained, for example, that the law requiring the Public Ministry to be involved in land conflicts was poorly enforced. He asserted that judges tied to large landowners did not respect the law, but instead continued to grant evictions (*dar liminar para despejos*), failed to follow the procedures laid down for them, and failed to listen to the Public Ministry (Stédile and Fernandes 1999, 116). The known autonomy of the Brazilian judiciary certainly lends plausibility to this account (Prillaman 2000). Enforcement of the other legal changes should also not be taken for granted. An example is the 1997 arms control law. There has been an important decline in violence over land and rural labor conflicts since 1985 in Brazil; the average number of rural workers assassinated per year in the period 1985–94 was 91, whereas this dropped to 40 per year for the period 1995–2005.[17] Rural violence of this magnitude, however, is still a major impediment to the full enjoyment of civil and political rights by the poor in the countryside, especially in southern Para and Maranhão.

Another area in which policies have not had a major impact is the system of land titling. Formal, enforceable claims to property are unevenly distributed in the countryside. Small farmers, and the rural poor in general, face a double-edged sword in the property rights regime. Barriers to obtaining formal legal title to the land they occupy make them vulnerable to removal by large landowners and their gunmen, while large landowners can sometimes obtain, through de facto possession, huge tracts of land to which they do not have legal title, thus "crowding out" the rural poor (Sorj 1998, 38). In the words of one squatter in the county (*município*) of Conceição de Araguaina in Pará, "Here the best title is the biggest ax" (quoted in Alston et al. 2000, 165).

A major reason for this state of affairs is a lack of efficiency in the demarcation of lands and their documentation and titling (*cadastramento*). Because of a costly, confusing, slow, and often politically manipulated and corrupt process of land registration, many farmers do not hold titles to their properties. Small farmers are much less likely to be able to obtain legal title than large farmers.[18] They are then usually unable to obtain credit with which to boost productivity through the purchase of new inputs or the adoption of more efficient techniques (Bryant 1998, 39, Table 8).[19] Small farmers thus cannot fully enjoy private property rights to the land they cultivate. This has a big impact on rural poverty, because studies show that small and medium-sized farms in Brazil produce far more employment per acre, on average, than large ones.

Furthermore, many rural properties were simply taken from the public domain. This process is not limited to remote regions, but happens also in the more prosperous Southeast. In the disputed area of São Paulo's Pontal do Paranapanema, for example, of the roughly 1 million hectares, only 20 percent were legally titled; the rest were *terras devolutas do estado* or irregularly occupied by large landowners (Gonçalo 2001, 22–23). There are also cases of large landowners receiving lands from the state without paying for them, then receiving fiscal incentives to produce, but not producing anything and simply holding on to the land (Gonçalo 2001, 23). The illegal acquisition of lands, or claim jumping (*grilagem*), is often associated with violence, because *grileiros* are often heavily armed hired hands committed to defending their employers' land.

Improvements in the operations of the *cartórios*, the land registration agencies located in almost every *município*, have been reported; many have computers now, for example (Fleischer 2001). In 2001 the government also passed a law to create a single land registry of all rural properties in the country under the control of the MIRAD. The government hopes that the registration project will be complete by 2003 (*Economist* 2001). This could improve the situation, but there is now evidence that the reform has yet been implemented.

Smallholders are also marginalized by the prevailing system of agricultural credit. The state still dominates the provision of this credit, and large landowners obtain a disproportionate share of these funds. Large landowners, furthermore, have used their political power to default on loans at a high rate, resist foreclosure, and renegotiate loans to their advantage.[20]

A striking example of this occurred in 1995–96, when large landowners used their political influence to persuade Congress to cancel indexation for inflation on outstanding agricultural loans—a move that cost the Bank of Brazil between R$1.8 to R$2.5 billion (Bryant 1998, 16). Large landowners also successfully lobbied Congress for another break on agricultural loans in 1999 (Martins 1999, 117). These rural credit renegotiations, in effect, punished small and medium-sized producers, who generally repaid their loans on time. (Some small producers have benefited, but large producers have been the major beneficiaries.) Rural debt renegotiation is also one of the causes of the fiscal deficits that contributed to Brazil's economic instability during President Cardoso's second term.

Large landowners are also notorious for evading taxes. The ITR has a high rate of avoidance (Leite 1999, 158); and a study carried out as recently as 1999 showed that 98.7 percent of the two hundred largest rural properties simply did not pay the ITR at all (Gonçalo 2001, 22). The 1997 change in the ITR was potentially a significant step in curbing landowners' traditional free ride in taxation. The new law also reduced the size of property subject to the top tax rate from more than 15,000 hectares to more than 5,000 hectares. A number of potential loopholes in the law remain nevertheless. For the government to charge a rate of 20 percent, it has to determine that 30 percent or less of the rural property is being productively used. But Brazilian landowners have shown great ingenuity in demonstrating land use and in cultivating favorable rulings from local administrators.

Furthermore, greater utilization rates significantly diminish the tax rate for the largest farms (Cardoso 1997, 83). Considering that Brazil's top corporate tax rate is reportedly 15 percent (World Bank 2001, 306), these numbers suggest that rural properties are still relatively lightly taxed. Furthermore, despite the 1997 law, the real value of the revenue obtained from collecting the ITR declined from 1998 to 2001 and also declined as a percentage of total federal revenue, from 0.106 percent in 1998 to 0.071 percent in 2001. In 2005, under the Lula government, the Brazilian Congress municipalized the ITR, transferring the responsibility for collecting it to municipal governments, who can now spend the revenues as they choose. This reform removed the ITR as a potential tool for agrarian reform. It also is a potential boon to large landowners, who might be able to use their political influence with mayors to keep their tax low.[21]

The system by which land was expropriated under the Cardoso and Lula agrarian reforms also reveals evidence that policies disproportionately benefit those already privileged by the agrarian political economy. Although the success of the Real Plan brought about a marked reduction in the price of land, critics allege that the government continued to buy land at prices equal to or higher than those in effect before 1994 (Borin 1997, 25). This appears to have been caused both by judicial decisions and by collusion between INCRA officials and landowners (Sorj 1998, 29). In a September 1999 study of more than 70 cases in which owners of expropriated land had brought judicial actions against INCRA, the Extraordinary Ministry of Agrarian Policy (*Ministério Extraordinário de Política Fundiária*) estimated that the government had overpaid for land on the order of R$7 billion, or enough to place three hundred thousand families on the land (cited in Martins 2000, 125).

The compensation paid to landowners is thus often far higher than the estimated value of land calculated by the government (Martins 1999, 124). This policy has amounted to a veritable giveaway to large landowners, some of them the very idle and unproductive *latifundiarios* whom modern agricultural markets were supposed to punish (Leite 1999, 172). Because the cost of the land is part of the debt contracted by those resettled in the land reform program, the former landless "run the risk of paying for the poor management [and corruption] of INCRA for the rest of their lives" (Borin 1997, 25). This is a striking example of the maxim offered by Sorj—the state takes the onus, the dominant classes get the bonus, and the subordinate groups are left with the crumbs—and indicates that some of the major beneficiaries of land reform have been landowners rather than the landless.

Some observers disagree strongly with the interpretation offered here. Alston et al. (2000, 167) write that "land owners historically have received less than the market value of their land in an expropriation," partly because INCRA pays for expropriated land in *títulos de divida agrária* (TDAs), which are heavily discounted, and pays cash only for improvements to the property. In the same passage, they also write, "The landowner could also scheme with local INCRA officials or use the courts to set the compensation for expropriated land above its market value. Such actions, however, appear to be very isolated events." Such an interpretation, however, is belied by the Cardoso government's own rhetoric, actions, and data. The data about overpayment described above come from government sources. And in justifying the "market-assisted" land reform program administered by the Ministry of Agrarian Policy President Cardoso decried INCRA's "corruption." Government policy reforms therefore seem to be based on an assumption that overpayments for expropriated land were not "isolated events."

Finally, the Cardoso administration missed an opportunity for significant policy reform regarding rural violence. Although rural violence appears to have diminished under Cardoso, killings of rural workers and the landless by the military police and landlords' gunmen are still common in some regions, and usually go uninvestigated and unpunished. In the wake of the massacres in Corumbiara and Eldorado de Carajás, human rights activists called on Cardoso to push for a constitutional amendment allowing the federal government to intervene in the investigation and prosecution of human rights violations when officials at the state level fail to carry out unbiased investigations. This "federalization" amendment, introduced in Congress in 1996, has not been passed, even under the Lula government elected in 2002 and re-elected in 2006. It could represent a major step toward ending the impunity of perpetrators of violence against the rural poor, but the federal government has not prioritized it (Amnesty International 1998, 32–33).

CONCLUSIONS

Moving beyond land redistribution figures to examine other, less-noted aspects of the Federal government's policies in land and agriculture, therefore, we can conclude that the government has largely maintained the general policy tilt in favor of conservative modernization. This policy orientation gives little opportunity to the landless and the poor, punishes small and medium-sized farmers, and generously rewards politically influential large landowners. Brazil may have a capitalist democracy, but its form of capitalism in the countryside is not very democratic. In agriculture, as elsewhere in the economy, markets are still strongly shaped by political manipulation. For the poor, this results in a system in which access to land is limited, land distribution is highly unequal, property rights to land are precarious, land markets are underdeveloped, access to credit is dominated by large landowners who use their political influence to renege on their loan repayments and tax obligations; and the poor are subject to the possibility of violence at the hands of the military police or landlords' gunmen, with little protection from the state. Such a conclusion fits with the assessment of many observers that the Cardoso and Lula governments' accomplishments in the area of political and institutional reforms were limited.

The Cardoso and Lula governments faced daunting social problems and enacted some significant reforms. The extent of land redistribution carried out from 1995 to 2006 was impressive and surprising, whether measured by the official government data or those of the opposition. The acquisition of land by previously landless rural people, as well as the securing of legal title to land by squatters previously without secure property rights, is an important achievement, because it means that marginalized Brazilians have, largely through their own tenacious efforts, obtained at least the possibility of inclusion in the economy and recognition as citizens in the political sphere. There was also an important decrease in rural violence in recent years. The land reform thus represents small victories for hundreds of thousands of people.

As the government redistributed some unproductive land to those people, however, a roughly equal number of small farmers, tenants, and squatters left the land because of prevailing policies of conservative modernization in agriculture. This economic model in itself would not necessarily be undesirable for Brazil as a whole; but without employment opportunities for the unschooled, the process represents the marginalization of a significant proportion of those Brazilians unlucky enough to stand at the bottom of the rural social hierarchy.

In addition to redistributing land, the Cardoso and Lula administrations enacted a number of related reforms. They facilitated land expropriation, centralized the land-titling system, and controlled unregistered guns. This study suggests that these measures did not have a major impact on Brazil's agrarian political economy. Not all of them were actively enforced, a historical problem of the Brazilian state. Others were implemented late or halfheartedly applied. Furthermore, an opportunity to federalize human rights abuses, thus diminishing impunity for rural violence, was missed. It is therefore inaccurate to declare the Federal government's agrarian reform a "revolution" in the countryside.

This is not to argue that none of Cardoso's or Lula's policies resulted in major reforms. The achievement of price stability for twelve years, for example, was a notable success. At the same time, it is not unreasonable to judge the government's performance at least partly by how it affected the most vulnerable segments of the population, including the rural poor. This chapter suggests that policies of conservative modernization—marked by the use of state personnel and resources primarily to serve a small but powerful set of large agricultural producers—largely continued in the Brazilian countryside. While these policies have gradually become more market and export oriented since the early 1980s, the Cardoso and Lula governments did not represent a fundamental break with them. The resulting model is still a highly politicized one, in that access to and repayment of credit depend on political as much as on market criteria. While the Cardoso and Lula administrations bolstered the state's commitment to compensatory social programs for the rural poor, the productive structure is still dominated by the large producers most favored by government policies. In this sense, the agrarian reform has been limited, and will probably eventually be seen as a modest but not fundamental modification of government policies in agriculture.

NOTES

1 This process includes the constitutional allocation of subsoil mineral rights to the national state rather than to individual landowners, and the right of the state to expropriate land not fulfilling a "social function." From an Anglo-American liberal perspective, of course, such assertions of the state over individual rights are anathema.

2 Martins admits that the PSDB allied itself with an oligarchical party, the Liberal Front (PFL), and that the decentralization of land reform discussed here might well lead to the reform's domination by large landowners in some regions. I have extrapolated his views about the PSDB's fundamentally anti-oligarchic nature to the PT by inference. For example, Martins argues that rural social movements have found expression in various parties, including the PSDB, PT, PDT, PSB, PPS, and others; see Martins 2000: 83.

3 Agriculture accounts for 28 percent of male and 14 percent of female employment (Brogan 2000, 184). The figure for the share of agriculture in GDP is value added as a percentage of GDP in 1999 and comes from World Bank 2001, 296.

4 Fleischer (2002, 7) reports, "Brazil's agribusiness sector posted a US$19 billion trade surplus in 2001, with exports of US$23.9 billion and imports of US$4.9 billion. This was a 28 percent increase from the US$14.8 surplus posted in 2000."

5 The U.S. government's protection of agriculture increased in May 2002 when President George W. Bush signed a bill authorizing a 70 percent increase in subsidies to the sector over the next ten years. See Hook 2002; Sanger 2002.

6 From "Rural Poverty in Brazil" at IFAD's web site: http://www.ruralpovertyportal.org/English/regions/Americas/bra/index.htm accessed on January 6, 2008.

7 Contrary to the common prejudice, large farms are not necessarily more efficient than small and medium-sized ones. In terms of economic efficiency, measured by comparing output to inputs of land, labor, and capital, small and medium-sized farms often outperform large ones; in pecuniary efficiency, measured by the advantages of vertical integration, tax breaks, and subsidies, large farms do better. In Angus Wright's words, "This then explains why less 'economically efficient' large farms prevail over small ones. And, of course, what this means is that their advantages are preeminently political and at least subject to policy reform." Wright 2002.

8 These data are a snapshot intended to illustrate the prevalence of rural poverty that existed at the beginning of Cardoso's presidency. They are not intended to establish a relationship between Cardoso's policies and trends in rural poverty. For such an analysis, time-series data from the period 1995–2002 would have to be examined.

9 For more on the decrease in rural poverty in Brazil, see Helfand and Levine 2005.

10 Sorj makes the valuable point that unlike the Peasant Leagues and other "peasant" social movements of the late 1950s and early 1960s, the MST and its offshoots do not defend rural cultivators' traditional use rights to land, but instead organize the rural and often the urban poor from all over the country, leading them in land occupations on carefully selected properties in areas where many occupiers have never lived before. Thus, while MST leaders see themselves as the inheritors of the Peasant Leagues' mantle, they lead a very different kind of organization. See Sorj 1998.

11 Official government data lists beneficiaries as 30,700 families in 1995, then 41,700 in 1996; 66,800 in 1997; and 98,700 in 1998. There were 99,200 families listed as beneficiaries in 1999; 69,900 families in 2000; 73,700 in 2001; 43,400 in 2002; 36,300 in 2003; 81,300 in 2004; 127,500 in 2005; and 154,000 families in 2006. From Arruda 2007.

12 From "1.5 milhão de trabalhadores deixam campo" in Folha de São Paulo, Dinheiro section, 22 December 2007. I am grateful to William Smith for sending me this article.

13 For an initial assessment of the possibilities of market-assisted land reform, see Pereira 1999.

14 Arruda 2006, A4 notes that under President Lula, the INCRA budget was increased from R$1.5 billion in 2003 to R$ 3.7 billion in 2006, with R$ 1.4 of the latter earmarked for the purchase of expropriated land for the landless. Also, in Lula's first term 1,700 new employees were hired at INCRA, bringing the total number of functionaries to 6,590, with plans to hire another 3,200 in Lula's second term.

15 For support for the MST from an unlikely source—a retired Air Force brigadier-lieutenant—see Xavier Ferolla 2006. Xavier Ferolla extols the MST's work in favor of social justice and national interests, and compares them favorably to the alienated and denationalized middle and upper classes. I thank Tim Power for bringing this article to my attention.

16 Barreira records the words of a poem about a *pistoleiro* from the *literatura de cordel* (popular ballads) that reflects popular conceptions about the rule of large landowners: "One feels sorry for Miranda [the *pistoleiro*]/because he is the product/of a violent world/and a corrupt system." [*De Miranda tem se e pena/porque ele e um produto/de um mundo violento/de um sistema corrupto*] Otavio Menezes, *A prisão de pistoleiro Miranda*, quoted in Barreira 1999, 124.

17 The source for these data is the Comissão Pastoral da Terra (CPT), as reported in the Folha de São Paulo 2002 (for the years 1985–2001) and the CPT National Secretariat web site at http://www.cptnac.com.br, accessed on January 6, 2008 for the years 2002–2005.

18 In a recent survey, of the total land area on farms of less than 10 hectares in size, only 65 percent of the land was registered. For land on farms of between 1,000 and 10,000 hectares, the corresponding figure was 83 percent; and for farms larger than 10,000 acres, 91 percent. Bryant 1998, 39, Table 8; data from INCRA 1992. A hectare is roughly 2.5 acres.

19 The lack of land titles is a larger problem in the Northeast, where 64 percent of the farms smaller than 25 acres are located; only 41 percent of the land on such farms is registered. See Pereira 1999, 117–18.

20 In 1995, for example, more than half of all outstanding agricultural loans made by the federally owned Bank of Brazil were for more than R$500,000 (at that time, roughly the equivalent in U.S. dollars). Default rates on these large loans averaged 33 percent nationally. The debt was owed by 1,477 large landowners (less than one-half of one percent of the total of 297,827 borrowers), whose default represented 73 percent of the value of all agricultural loans made by the Bank of Brazil that were delinquent at that time. Owners of small and medium-sized farms, in contrast, generally repaid their debts. The default rate for loans up to R$30,000 was only 6 percent of the total loan value, while the rate for loans up to R$150,000 was 8 percent. The state bank, in effect, subsidized the very largest landowners by refusing to subject them to a "hard budget constraint." Bryant 1998, 43, Table 11. Data refer to outstanding loans as of May 31, 1995.

21 From João Pedro Stédile (2007) "Imposto Territorial Rural: Os Latifundiários Agradecem, Presidente" on the web site of DesempregoZero.org at http://www.desempregozero.org.br/artigos/imposto_territorial_rural.php, accessed on January 6, 2008.

REFERENCES

Alston, Lee, Gary Libecap, and Bernardo Mueller. 2000. Land Reform Policies, The Sources of Violent Conflict, and Implications for Deforestation in the Brazilian Amazon. *Journal of Environmental Economics and Management* 39: 162–88.

Amnesty International. 1998. Brazil: *Corumbiara and Eldorado de Carajás: Rural Violence, Police Brutality, and Impunity.* New York: AI. Index: AMR 19/01/98, January.

Arruda, Roldão. 2006. MST e Igreja Pedem Extinção do Ministério da Reforma Agrária. *O Estado de São Paulo* (December 29): A4.

———. 2007. Total de Assentados Atinge 95% da Meta." *O Estado de São Paulo*, (January 31): A10.

Barreira, César. 1999. *Crimes por encomenda: violência e pistolagem no cenário brasileiro.* Rio de Janeiro: Relume Dumará.

Borin, Jair. 1997. Reforma agrária no governo FHC. In *A crise brasileira e o governo FHC*, ed. Alvaro Bianchi. São Paulo: Xama Editora.

Brogan, Chris. 2000. Brazil. In *Nations of the World: A Political, Economic and Business Handbook.* Millerton, NY: Grey House. 181–86.

Bryant, Coralie. 1998. Northeast Brazil: Market Assisted Land Reform: Private Property Rights for the Rural Poor. Unpublished mss. Washington, DC, April.

Cardoso, Fernando Henrique. 1994. *Mãos à obra Brasil: proposta de governo.* Brasília: Instituto Brasileiro de Analises Sociais e Econômicas/Banco Arbi.

———. 1996. O regime não é dos excluídos. Interview. *Folha de São Paulo*, October 13: caderno 5, 6.

———. 1997. *Reforma agrária: compromisso de todos.* Brasília: Presidência da República/Secretaria de Comunicação Social.

Carter, Miguel. 2005. The Landless Rural Workers' Movement (MST) and Democracy in Brazil. Oxford: Oxford University Center for Brazilian Studies Working Paper Number CBS-60-05.

Carvalho Filho, José Juliano de. 2007. O Esvaziamento da Reforma Agrária sob Lula." *Folha de São Paulo*, February 1, at folha.com.

Comparato, Bruno Konder (2001) A Ação Política do MST. *São Paulo em Perspectiva* 15, 4: 105–118.

De Souza, Amaury. 1997. Redressing Inequalities: Brazil's Social Agenda at Century's End. In *Brazil Under Cardoso*, ed. Susan Kaufman Purcell and Riordan Roett. Boulder: Lynne Rienner. 63–88.

Economist. 2001. Managing the Rainforests. May 12: 84.

Economist Intelligence Unit. 1999. Country Report: Brazil. November 8: 1. <www.eiu.com>
Fleischer, David. 2001. Professor of Political Science, University of Brasília; author of *Brazil Focus Weekly Report*. Personal communication. May 18.
————. 2002. *Brazil Focus Weekly Report*. January 5–11.
Folha de São Paulo. 2002. Credito ainda desafia reforma, diz governo. January 6: A-8.
Gonçalo, José Evaldo. 2000. Violência no campo–Ação orquestrada pelas elites rurais com o apoio de setores do estado. Partido dos Trabalhadores, Secretaria Agrária Nacional. December. <www.pt.org.br/assessor/agrario>.
————. 2001. Globalização e reforma agrária. PT, Secretaria Agrária Nacional. January. <www.pt.org.br/assessor/agrario>.
Gordon, Lincoln. 2001. *Brazil's Second Chance: En Route Toward the First World*. Washington, DC: Brookings Institution Press.
Graziano Neto, Francisco. 1998. *A difícil interpretação da realidade agrária*. In Schmidt et al. 1998. 153–69.
Hammond, John L. 2004. The MST and the Media: Competing Images of the Landless Farmworkers' Movement." *Latin American Politics and Society*, 46, 4 (Winter): 61–90.
Helfand, Steven M. and Edward S. Levine. 2005. The Impact of Policy Reforms on Rural Poverty in Brazil: Evidence from Three States in the 1990s." Accessed online at www.economics.ucr.edu/papers/papers05–06.pdf on 6 January 2008.
Hochstetler, Kathryn. 2006. Organized Civil Society in Lula's Brazil. San Juan, Puerto Rico: Paper prepared for presentation at the Latin American Studies Association, March 15–18.
Hook, Janet. 2002. Congress Unites on Federal Farm Policy. *Times-Picayune* (New Orleans), April 27: A-15.
Instituto Nacional de Colonização e Reforma Agrária (INCRA). 1992. *Estatísticas cadastrais anuais*. Brasília: INCRA.
————. 2001. Balanço da reforma agrária e da agricultura familiar 2001. <www.incra.gov.br>.
Jank, Marcus Sawaya. 2001. Professor, Department of Agricultural Economics and Rural Sociology, University of São Paulo. Comments in the panel discussion "Sustainable Development and Rural Poverty: A Brazilian Perspective," Woodrow Wilson Center, Washington, DC, May 24.
Leite, Sérgio. 1999. Políticas públicas e agricultura no Brasil: comentários sobre o cenário recente. In *O desmonte da nação: balanço do governo FHC*, ed. Ivo Lesbaupin. Petrópolis: Vozes. 153–80.
Margolis, Marc. 2002. A Plot of Their Own. *Newsweek International Online*. <www.msnbc.com/news> Accessed February 6.
Marreiro, Flávia. 2007. Governo Diz Ter Atingido 95% da Meta de Assentamentos. *Folha de São Paulo*, January 31: A7.
Martins, José de Souza. 1999. Reforma agrária: o impossível diálogo sobre a historia possível. *Tempo Social*, 11, 2 (October): 97–128.
————. 2000. *Reforma agrária: o impossível diálogo*. São Paulo: Editora da Universidade de São Paulo.
Maxwell, Kenneth. 1999–2000. The Two Brazils. *Wilson Quarterly* (Winter): 50–60.
Mercadante, Aloízio. 2006. *Brasil: Primeiro Tempo*. São Paulo: Planeta.
Navarro, Zander. 2005. The Landless Movement and Land Reform in Brazil." *IDS Bulletin*, 36, 1, January.
Ondetti, Gabriel. 2008. *Land, Protest and Politics: The Landless Movement and the Struggle for Agrarian Reform in Brazil*. University Park: Penn State University Press.
Payne, Leigh. 2000. *Uncivil Movements: The Armed Right Wing and Democracy in Latin America*. Baltimore: Johns Hopkins University Press.
Pereira, Anthony. 1997. *The End of the Peasantry: The Rural Labor Movement in Northeast Brazil, 1961–1988*. Pittsburgh: University of Pittsburgh Press.
————. 1999. God, the Devil, and Development in Northeast Brazil. *Praxis* 15: 113–36.
Pompeu de Toledo, Roberto. 1998. *O presidente segundo o sociólogo: entrevista de Fernando Henrique Cardoso a Roberto Pompeu de Toledo*. São Paulo: Companhia das Letras.
Porto, Mauro. 2001. Mass Media and Politics in Democratic Brazil. Paper presented at the conference "15 Years of Democracy in Brazil," Institute of Latin American Studies, University of London, February 15–16.

Prillaman, William C. 2000. *The Judiciary and Democratic Decay in Latin America: Declining Confidence in the Rule of Law*. Westport: Praeger.

Rinelli, Michael. 2001. Brazil Economic Briefing (BEB). 01/2001. 7th ed. Washington, DC: Brazilian Embassy. April 12.

Roett, Riordan. 1999. *Brazil: Politics in a Patrimonial Society*. 5th ed. Westport: Praeger.

Rohter, Larry. 2004. "South America Seeks to Fill the World's Table" in *The New York Times*, December 12, at nytimes.com.

Sanger, David. 2002. Bush Signs Farm Subsidies Increase. *Times-Picayune* (New Orleans), May 14: A-3.

Sauer, Sérgio. 2006. "Estado, Banco Mundial, e Protagonismo Popular: O Caso da Reforma Agrária de Mercado no Brasil" in Sérgio Sauer and João Mendes Pereira, eds. *Capturando a Terra: Banco Mundial, Políticas Fundiárias Neoliberais e Reforma Agrária de Mercado*. São Paulo: Editora Expressão Popular. 285–311.

Schmidt, Benício Viero, Danilo Nolasco C. Marinho, and Sueli L. Couto Rosa, eds. 1998. *Os assentamentos de reforma agrária no Brasil*. Brasília: Editora UnB.

Sem Terra (Brasília). 2000. Por que a reforma agrária no Brasil. No. 1 (July): 2.

Sigaud, Lygia. 2000. A forma acampamento: notas a partir da versão pernambucana. *Novos Estudos CEBRAP* 58 (November): 73–92.

Soares, Pedro and Elvira Lobato (2007) "Área de lavoura cresce 83% em dez anos" in *Folha de São Paulo* 22 December 2007, Dinheiro section.

Sorj, Bernardo. 1998. A reforma agrária em tempos de democracia e globalização. *Novos Estudos CEBRAP* 50 (March): 23–40.

Stédile, João Pedro. 2007. "The Neoliberal Agrarian Model in Brazil" in *Monthly Review*, Volume 58, Number 8, February, at http://www.monthlyreview.org/0207stedile.htm accessed on 2/16/07.

Stédile, João Pedro, and Bernardo Mancano Fernandes. 1999. *Brava gente: a trajetória do MST e a luta pela terra no Brasil*. São Paulo: Fundação Perseu Abramo.

Viotti da Costa, Emília. 2000 [1985]. *The Brazilian Empire: Myths and Histories*. Revised ed. Chapel Hill: University of North Carolina Press.

World Bank. 2001. *World Development Report 2000/2001*. New York: Oxford University Press.

Wright, Angus. 2002. Professor of Environmental Studies, California State University at Sacramento. Personal communication. April 11.

Wright, Angus and Wendy Wolford. 2003. *To Inherit the Earth: The Landless Movement and the Struggle for a New Brazil*. Oakland: Food First Books.

Xavier Ferolla, Sérgio. 2006. "O Grito dos Necessitados" in *Folha de São Paulo*, November 5, Tendencies/Debates.

Chapter 15

The Indian Movement and Political Democracy in Ecuador

León Zamosc

This work investigates the implications of the Ecuadorian Indian movement for democratic politics. While its empirical questions focus on Ecuador's political processes, a key purpose is to offer a Latin American perspective on the broader debate on the "civil society argument"; namely, the proposition that civil association has intrinsically positive effects on democracy.

The assumption herein is that particularization is essential for appraising this wide-ranging claim. Civil society and democracy are knotty concepts because they refer to complex realities that can be approached from different points of view. To cut through the complexity, this study follows a strategy of double specification, concentrating on social movements as a distinct type of civil association and demarcating discrete functional terrains to observe their bearing on democracy. Applied to the case at hand, this strategy provides a basis for a contextualized assessment of the putative democratic benefits of civil association and offers insights on the conditions of political engagement that social movements share with other kinds of civil society groups.

The pivotal claim of this study is that civil society actors may or may not contribute to democracy and that, in the particular case of social movements, the underlying tension between the participatory and institutional dimensions of democracy may be expressed through a mixed bag of favorable and unfavorable effects on the different components of political democracy. The analysis of the Ecuadorian Indian movement demonstrates that to understand the varying impact of civil activism on democracy, scholars must adopt a nuanced, context-specific approach that does not lose sight of the particularistic orientations of civil associations and that pays close attention to their definition of means and ends, the institutional responses evoked by their initiatives, and the unintended consequences of their actions.

The relevance of the case cannot be overstated. The Ecuadorian Indian movement is often cited as the best-organized and most influential indigenous movement in Latin America (Lucero 2001, 61; Andolina 2003, 721). Its origins date back to the rise of local and regional organizations that, in the 1980s, came together in CONAIE, the Confederation of Indigenous Nationalities of Ecuador. The spectacular battles of the 1990s transformed the movement into a powerful force that, in addition to pressing indigenous demands, took up a leadership role in the wider resistance to the imposition of neoliberal reforms. By 1997 CONAIE had launched the Pachakutik party to take part in elections, and its political clout had been boosted by its role in the developments that led to the fall of President Abdalá Bucaram and the convening of a constitutional assembly. In January 2000, amid an economic and political crisis of unprecedented proportions, CONAIE joined a group of military officers led by Colonel Lucio Gutiérrez in a nonviolent coup that toppled President Jamil Mahuad but failed to hold on to power. Three years later, the same actors made another bid for power as an electoral coalition, which succeeded in winning the presidential elections. The presence of Indian leaders in the government was a high point for the movement, but it did not last long. After six months of conflicts over President Gutierrez's neoliberal turn, CONAIE withdrew its support and Pachakutik's ministers abandoned the cabinet.

Clearly, this is a movement that has reached well beyond the bounds of a bid for indigenous rights. Much more has been at stake, including matters of national economic and social policy and issues that are directly related to the struggle for political power and the fate of Ecuadorian democracy[1]. In the context of contemporary Latin America, then, this case is highly relevant to the discussion of the various types of impact that social movements can have on democracy.

This article lays the groundwork for the analysis with a conceptual discussion elucidating the notion of civil society, the specificity of social movements as a variant of civil association, and the paradoxical relationship between social movements and democracy. The factors behind the rise of Ecuador's Indian movement, the broadening of its struggles, and the saliency of its political protagonism are then reviewed. The inquiry is framed as a scrutiny of the movement's consequences for the participatory and institutional dimensions of democracy. After exploring the bases of CONAIE's support, the study examines the movement's two main modalities of political engagement: its efforts to influence government policies and its struggles to conquer positions of power.

The appraisal of the effects on the democratic regime covers four areas: interest representation, control of state power, legitimacy, and political socialization. The conclusions assess the significance of the Indian movement for democracy, briefly rejoining the debate on the "civil society argument" and commenting on the present challenges for Ecuadorian indigenous activists.

CIVIL SOCIETY, SOCIAL MOVEMENTS, AND DEMOCRACY

This work adopts a modified version of Michael Walzer's definition of civil society (2002, 36), taking it to refer to the ensemble of social practices that generate a space of voluntary association and the sets of relational networks, or social actors, that occupy that space. Within this scope, the cast of civil society actors includes all voluntary groups formed for the sake of the common aspirations and concerns of its members. This formula is useful because it grasps civil society on its own terms, avoiding the pitfalls of definitions that imply assumptions about its relationships with the political institutions, such as the idea that civil society is necessarily autonomous from the state, necessarily opposed to the state, or necessarily good for democracy.

A good antidote to the mystifying sway of prescriptive definitions of civil society is to keep in mind that the realm of voluntary association is thoroughly marked by pluralism, particularism, and inequality. Civil society is pluralistic because its practices are based on multiple forms of participation, express many social identities, and pursue a wide variety of goals (Rosenblum and Post 2002). Civil society is particularistic because its groups have their own norms and because, with rare exceptions, they restrict benefits to members and pursue goals that reflect their own priorities-even when, as often is the case, they claim to represent the public interest (Carothers 1999). Moreover, civil society is tied up with inequality not only because different groups have different levels of opportunity to associate and further their ends, but also because a great deal of what associations do has consequences in terms of widening, maintaining, or narrowing existing social gaps (Oxhorn 2003).

Social movements are a particular form of civil association. They can be defined as organized drives to promote or resist change through collective practices that are embedded in a structure of conflict, involve episodes of mass participation, and challenge existing institutions.[2] The reference to conflict implies that social movements confront opponents in struggles over values and claims to resources, status, or power (Coser 1956, 8), a feature that sets them apart from civil associations that are not involved in such confrontations (e.g., social clubs, churches, and charitable foundations). On the other hand, the emphasis on events in which large numbers of people engage in noninstitutional forms of action foregrounds popular participation and defiance of prescribed rules, two elements that are absent in the case of associations whose activities are carried out by small circles of activists or professionals who follow "the proper institutional channels" (e.g., interest groups and advocacy organizations).

To understand movements, one must ascertain what is at stake in the conflicts in which they are involved (Touraine 1981). In empirical studies, the stakes can be inferred from their goals, their actions, and the context of their struggles. The conceptual distinction between civil and political engagement is a useful tool for initiating that inquiry. In civil engagement, the conflict is located in civil society itself. There are two variants of this kind of engagement: construction of collective identity, in which movements seek to alter the self-consciousness of actual or potential followers (Touraine 1988, 75–82; Cohen and Arato 1992, 526); and cultural crusades, in which movements act on the general public to change dominant values or attitudes (Melucci 1994, 123–25). In political engagement, the conflict is played out through interactions with state actors or other agents from political society; that is, the arena of competition for control over the state apparatus and public policy (Stepan 1988, 4). Here, the actions of movements are usually aimed at inducing policy changes. Sometimes, however, their struggles may turn into attempts to control the positions of power themselves.

Social movements are a modern form of participation that emerged with the changes related to the consolidation of capitalism, the national state, and liberal democracy (Tilly 1998). As a rule, movements have served as a medium for the participation of excluded groups and for the politicization of issues that the institutions are unwilling or unable to address. By engaging in confrontational practices like marches, boycotts, and demonstrations, movements have shown that ordinary people can capitalize on numbers, unity, and determination to achieve goals against the will of the most adamant opponents or rulers. Movement practices, then, must be seen as practices of noninstitutional power. Lacking other resources, excluded and powerless people use disruption. They generate might by withdrawing the tacit support that power holders derive from "business as usual," thus creating a political market in which they can trade the lifting of their sanctions for the changes they seek (Piven and Cloward 1977, 24–27; Pizzorno 1978, 279).

Some authors have argued that movements and revolutions are variants of contentious politics; namely, a particular kind of political activity in which challengers use noninstitutional means in their interactions with elites and the state (McAdam et al. 1996; Goldstone 2003). By itself, though, the opposition of institutional and noninstitutional means cannot capture the diversity that exists in civil society's political practices. In the view of this study, it should be combined with another distinction that, considering the actors' ends, marks the contrast between the politics of influence, which focus on swaying public policy decisions; and the politics of power, which are played as attempts to seize the positions from which the decisions are made. On the basis of the combinations of means and ends, table 1 identifies four alternative forms of civil society's political engagement.

As a static categorization, this matrix marks out the specificity of movements in regard to other forms of civil political involvement. But the framework can also serve as a dynamic referent for variants and transformations. Variants are relevant because movements often combine the use of noninstitutional means with conventional

Table 1. Civil Society's Alternative Forms of Political Engagement

	Means	
Ends	Institutional	Noninstitutional
Politics of Influence	Interest Groups	Social Movements
Politics of Power	Political Parties	Revolutions

modalities of action. Transformations are also relevant because movements develop over time in a sequence of events that at some point is completed. At the peak of its cycle, a movement that initially focused on reforms may blend into a revolution, a sweeping challenge to the structure of power, which is usually violent and, if successful, involves dramatic changes in the organization and policies of the state (Tarrow 1994, 25). Far more frequent, however, is institutionalization, which takes partial forms when movements spawn lobbying agencies or political arms and final forms when they abandon the unconventional forms of action and reorganize themselves as interest groups or political parties (Goldstone 2003).

What is the relationship between movements and democracy? To elucidate this, we must first dispel the myth that civil society activities are always beneficial to democracy. It is true that civil associations can assist democracy by disseminating its values, representing social interests, resisting state arbitrariness, and educating people for democratic participation. But although associations can fulfill these positive functions, they may not always do so. Indeed, they may also harm democracy in various ways, such as upholding antidemocratic ideologies, using corruption to get privileges, and seeking co-optation as state clienteles. The key point is that civil society actors may or may not contribute to democracy; and in both cases, what they actually do may vary greatly. The groups that are not helpful run the gamut from associations whose activities are devoid of political consequence to organizations that may be conspiring to subvert a democratic regime. When associations contribute to democracy, by contrast, they rarely do it by design, but as a byproduct or contingent result of their efforts to attain their own particularistic goals.

All the foregoing holds true for social movements, but with a special twist: their status in democratic polities is haunted by an intrinsic ambivalence. Definitions of democracy can be broadly divided into procedural definitions, which view democracy as a regime based on electoral representation and guaranteed civil and political rights; and substantive definitions, which see it as a principle of participation that guides all political practices (Held 1996, 6). This counterpoint highlights a fundamental tension between two ingredients of democracy: the principle that "the people rule" and the institutional procedures that, at any given time, embody that principle (Markoff 2004). Generally speaking, institutions produce social order by imparting stability and meaning to behavior (Scott 1995, 33). In their domain, democratic institutions contribute to that order by protecting citizens' rights and providing means for their participation in politics. But institutions have a downside, aptly captured in Jean-Paul Sartre's assertion that they amount to "the systematic self-domestication of man by man" (1976, 606). In dictating the acceptable ways of doing things, institutions foreclose alternatives, generating an effect of suppression that is magnified by their tendency to get entrenched in their own inertia. The case of representative democracy is especially poignant because, for most citizens, the same institutions that enable them to choose their rulers also imply their exclusion from further participation.

This tension underlies the paradox of social movements in democracies. As a form of political engagement that involves large numbers of normally excluded people, movements fulfill the principle of citizen participation. But their reliance on noninstitutional means implies that they are often in breach of the rules that define how the polity works. What turns the inconsistency into a paradox is that it has not prevented the emergence of movements as a regular feature of political life. To the contrary, viewed from the side of democracy, the key element in the relationship is that political democracy is an open invitation to social movements. Democracy offers fertile ground because it guarantees the rights of expression and assembly and, perhaps more important, because its own claim to legitimacy, grounded as it is in a discourse of popular sovereignty, citizenship rights, and inclusion, lends legitimacy to the claims of those who do not feel represented and want changes in public policies, in the definition of rights, or in the democratic institutions themselves.

Viewed from the side of movements, however, the relationship cuts both ways. In positive outcomes, the paradox is resolved in the deepening of democracy; that is, in situations in which a movement helps make a polity more democratic by winning reforms that broaden citizenship rights and provide for greater citizen participation in politics. Europe and the United States offer many examples of movements that advanced democracy through struggles against slavery, for labor's freedom of association, for the enfranchisement of women and the poor, and for the civil rights of racial, ethnic, and religious minorities. But there have been negative outcomes, too, including the Nazi and Fascist movements, which ushered in a catastrophic period when democratic institutions were wiped out, the political and civil rights of entire populations were revoked, slavery was reinstated, and genocide became state policy. Finally, there may also be cases in which a movement's impact is a mixed bag of favorable and unfavorable effects on different components of political democracy.

The paradox of social movements should give us pause. We cannot assume that movements always contribute to political democracy just because they involve popular participation. But it is also a mistake to think that movements automatically detract from democracy because they infringe on institutional rules. Mindful of the complexities, political philosophers have long been engaged in discussing the circumstances in which civil disobedience may be justified in democratic polities (Rawls 1971, chap. 6; Dworkin 1978, chap. 8; Habermas 1985; Cohen and Arato 1992, chap. 11). For social analysts, the challenge is different. We must use the complications as pointers for trying to provide more nuanced answers to empirical questions about the origins of social movements, the sources of their power, and their consequences for democracy. These are the questions addressed in this work on the Ecuadorian Indian movement.

THE CONTENTIOUS CYCLE OF THE 1990S

In 1979, Ecuador turned from military to civilian rule. By way of background, it is worth calling attention to three aspects of that transition. First, the Ecuadorian generals did not display the repressive and pro-business zeal that typified military rule elsewhere in Latin America. Instead, they pursued a nationalistic agenda focused on the development of oil exports, agrarian reform, and "inward-oriented" industrialization (Isaacs 1993, 35–65). During the 1970s, the economy expanded, and there were ostensible improvements in the living standards of the popular sectors. This, and the absence of severe repression, fostered attitudes of support for the military regime.

Second, the democratic transition was initiated and tightly controlled by the armed forces (Isaacs 1993, 113–15). The "handed down" democracy did not inspire the sense of commitment that could have existed if the political parties and civil society had played a greater role in wresting it from the military (Pachano 1996, 32–34). Because they had not been crafted through political compromises, moreover, the new institutions proved ill-suited for the resolution of conflict, which set the stage for relentless strife between the executive and congress, constitutional tampering in all branches of government, and a chronic exacerbation of party fragmentation, regionalism, and personalistic politics (Conaghan 1989).

Third, the transition to democracy offered opportunities for the political involvement of the indigenous population. The 1979 Constitution eliminated the literacy requirement, which had excluded most Indians from the vote. The process was boosted by the first civilian president, populist politician Jaime Roldós (1979–81), who promoted the participation of Indian organizations in rural development and literacy programs (Ibarra 1987, 169–233). The downsizing of these initiatives under President Osvaldo Hurtado (from the centrist Christian Democratic party, 1981–84) and their elimination altogether by León Febres Cordero (from the conservative Social Christian party, 1984–88) provided an early rallying point for criticism and contentiousness among the Indian activists.

These elements must be kept in mind to understand the developments of the 1990s. On the one hand, they draw a connection between the tumultuous nature of Ecuadorian politics and the reality that after a decade of civilian rule, Ecuador was still plagued by the flaws of its democratic institutions, the dubiousness of its politicians' allegiance to the rules of democracy, and the shallowness of its citizens' democratic political culture. On the other hand they indicate that, by the late 1980s, favorable conditions for an Indian movement had appeared. The extension of political rights and the openings in government policy had stimulated indigenous organization. The subsequent withdrawal of state support, the policies of adjustment, and the downturn of the economy would provide strong motives for the Indian insurgency of the 1990s.

Rise of the Indian Movement

In the 2001 census, only 6.6 percent of all Ecuadorians identified themselves as Indians (INEC 2001). Including those who declared that they or their parents spoke indigenous languages, the proportion rises to 14.3 percent, which is the best available approximation of the size of the indigenous population (León Guzmán 2003). The Quichuas of the Sierra account for about three-quarters of that population, with most of the rest distributed among smaller groups in the Amazon. Throughout Ecuador, the basic unit of Indian settlement is the community, which, despite variations, presents generic characteristics that will be discussed later.

The process of Indian organization was a classic example of bottom-up networking based on local and regional associations of communities. In the Amazon, it came in response to the arrival of peasant colonists, oil companies, and state agencies. In the Sierra, the stimulus was the fight for the land, which peaked with the military's agrarian reform of the 1970s (Zamosc 1994, 46–48). With the return to democracy, the indigenous organizations continued to work for development and the defense of their culture and lands, coming together under umbrella federations in the Sierra and the Amazon and eventually under CONAIE, the Confederation of Indian Nationalities, in 1986. Since its inception, CONAIE has combined livelihood goals and citizenship aspirations. The former have focused on economic improvements, education, health, and the protection of Indian lands; the latter on the redefinition of Ecuador as a plurinational state, the end of discrimination, territorial autonomy, representation in state institutions, control over education and development programs, and official recognition and funding for the indigenous organizations (CONAIE 1988).

CONAIE's first achievement came in 1988, when it negotiated with President Rodrigo Borja (from the Democratic Left party, 1988–92) the creation of a national program of bilingual education, funded by the state and run by indigenous personnel connected with the Indian organizations (Moya 1990). But the presentation of CONAIE's contentious credentials was the 1990 levantamiento (uprising), a huge mobilization that vented the frustrations of a rural population that had been severely punished by the adjustment policies and the long recession of the 1980s (Zamosc 1994, 50–53). The uprising was a peaceful civic strike in which tens of thousands of highland Indians blocked highways and marched into cities to seize public offices (León 1994, 17–59). The protest continued for several days, until the government agreed to discuss the demands. There were measures to alleviate the situation in the rural areas and settle some pending land conflicts, but an issue that remained unsolved was the status of the ancestral lands in the lowlands. Two years later, CONAIE sponsored a large march from the Amazon. Once again, President Borja was forced to negotiate with the Indians, who stayed put in the capital until he agreed to demarcate and title their lands (Sawyer 1997).

The Sierra uprising and the Amazon march revealed the depth of the Indians' discontent and opened the eyes of all Ecuadorians to their return as actors who could exert influence in national politics. The uprising, in particular, was a real shake-up. As a rural protest on a national scale, it had no precedent in the country's history. In most respects, it was a feat of collective creativity, the spontaneous invention of a new form of contention that turned into a blueprint for the string of mobilizations that would follow in the 1990s.

The Indian–Peasant Front

The 1992 election gave the presidency to Sixto Durán, a conservative independent candidate. His economic plan focused on deregulating trade and capital flows, reducing social spending, eliminating subsidies, and privatizing state enterprises and social security (Viteri Díaz 1998, 89–95). But Durán lacked reliable support in the legislature, and his privatization initiative was also opposed by the military, which saw the state enterprises as an important legacy of the military regime (NotiSur 1994; Lucero 2001). In addition, Durán encountered resistance in civil society. The main challenges came from the Indian movement, which, buoyed by its initial successes, was displacing the labor federations as the beacon of popular opposition (Zamosc 2004, 134).

The first confrontation took place in 1993, over the plan to cut the social security budget and liquidate the health service for rural areas. CONAIE and other peasant organizations supported the strike of the social security employees and a massive protest of the beneficiaries of the rural health service. After two days of blockades and demonstrations, Durán was compelled to restore the budget and reaffirm the continuity of the health service (Kipu 1993). The success of this struggle proved that well-organized protests could thwart an antipopular policy. In addition, it was an important precedent of collaboration between the Indian movement, other peasant organizations, and the unions from the public sector.

Next came the battle over the government's Law of Agrarian Modernization. The bill sought to abolish the legal basis for land expropriation, concentrate state support on capitalist agriculture, eliminate communal property, and privatize irrigation water. CONAIE sponsored the formation of the Coordinadora Agraria Nacional (CAN), a coalition that included smaller Indian and peasant organizations, such as FEINE (Indigenous Evan-gelical Federation) and FENOCIN (Federation of Peasant and Indigenous Organizations, influenced by the Socialist Party). CAN proposed its own bill and staged public debates on the issue (CAN 1993a, b). In June 1994, the Coordinadora Agraria called an uprising that, once again, paralyzed the country for several days. Eventually, President Durán was forced to negotiate the bill. In its final version, the law defined peasant agriculture as deserving full state support, reaffirmed that water was a public resource, and recognized the legality of communal and cooperative forms of ownership (Kipu 1994).

The Popular Front

By 1995, CONAIE and its allies had participated in the formation of the Coordinadora de Movimientos Sociales, a broad coalition that included Indian and peasant organiza-tions, unions from the public sector, and a large number of neighborhood associations, feminist groups, and human rights activists (Tamayo 1996). Meanwhile, President Durán had called for a referendum that proposed constitutional reforms to strengthen the execu-tive, weaken the unions, and allow the privatization of the state enterprises and social security. While the business sector generously financed the "yes" advertising campaign, the Coordinadora de Movimientos Sociales and the labor federations mounted an intense grassroots effort to bring out the "no" vote. On the day of the referendum, the voters rejected all the reforms (NotiSur 1995). The defeat closed the books on Durán's initia-tives, leaving in place an empowered popular coalition.

The success of the "no" campaign reinforced the position of the activists who had been calling for electoral participation. In its December 1995 assembly, CONAIE launched a political party that was intended to be based on the Indian movement and its allies (CONAIE 1995). The Pachakutik Movement of Plurinational Unity (Pachakutik means "time of resurgence" in Quichua) entered the scene in the elections of 1996, in alliance with an independent group led by television commentator Freddy Ehlers (Beck and Mijeski 2001). Ehlers did not qualify for the second presidential round, but Pachakutik won 10 percent of the congressional seats and significant representation in provincial legislatures, local councils, and mayoralties (Kipu 1996).

The victory of Abdalá Bucaram in the 1996 election opened a period of enhanced turbulence in Ecuador. This clownish politician led the Roldocista Party, a populist force with its main base of support in the suburbs of Guayaquil. As mayor of that city, Bucaram had earned a reputation for corruption, but he had also extended his clientelist net-works (de la Torre 1997). During the campaign he attacked "the oligarchy" and Durán's aborted reforms. As president, however, he focused on dividing the Indian movement, creating a Ministry of Indigenous Affairs and trying to buy the support of some Indian leaders (Kipu 1996). At the same time, Bucaram stuffed the government with relatives and friends, and it soon became evident that the country was sinking to new depths of corruption. Bucaram's discourse had also changed. Now he spoke about pro-market reforms, trying to ingratiate himself with the International Monetary Fund and inviting Domingo Cavallo, the architect of Argentina's neoliberal program, to be the consultant for his economic plan (NotiSur 1996).

Bucaram announced that plan at the beginning of 1997, when the labor unions and CONAIE were preparing a rally opposing neoliberal policies, corruption, and the Ministry of Indigenous Affairs. The measures included stiff budget cuts, higher electricity and gas rates, labor reforms, and a timetable to tie the currency to the dollar (NotiSur 1997a). The rally turned into a mobilization for the president's removal, and was supported by the main political parties. As Quito swarmed with Indian demonstrators, Congress removed Bucaram on grounds of mental incompetence and named its speaker, Fabian Alarcón, as acting president (NotiSur 1997b). In the process, CONAIE and the other organizations extracted the promise that an assembly would be convened to reform the constitution. The 1997 elections for that assembly gave Pachakutik 10 percent of the seats. Its delegates pushed through several reforms, including sections that defined Ecuador as a multicultural state and recognized social, cultural, and political rights for the indigenous peoples (Andolina 2003).

The next presidential election was won by Jamil Mahuad, from the Christian Democratic Party. The new president faced strong pressure from the IMF, which was vexed by the stagnation of Ecuador's reforms. At the same time, he confronted a popular coalition that rejected those reforms and had proven its oppositional power. To top it off, the economy sank into its worst recession since the 1930s (NotiSur 1998a). The economic collapse of 1998–99 was triggered by the fall of oil prices and the devastation of the coast by the climatic phenomenon of El Niño. When the banana and shrimp exporters stopped repaying their loans, the banks plunged into crisis and, despite Mahuad's billion-dollar bailout program, the financial system collapsed. A massive flight of capital ensued, the gross domestic product shrank by 7.1 percent, and it became obvious that the country would not be able to pay its external debt (NotiSur 1998b, 1999a).

Mahuad devalued the currency, froze bank accounts, and focused on securing the support of the Social Christian Party, traditional advocate of the coastal exporters and banks (NotiSur 1999b, c). But the IMF's conditions for a stabilization loan were tough: eliminate all subsidies, privatize public enterprises, raise taxes on income and rent, and refrain from saving the banks (NotiSur 1999e). Mahuad's situation became untenable. On the one hand, the popular opposition fought back against the cuts and privatization. In 1998 and 1999, Mahuad had to deal with three large mobilizations in which the popular front led by CONAIE broadened to include middle-class sectors, such as truckers, bus operators, and small and medium-sized entrepreneurs (Zamosc 2004, 138–40). On the other hand, the IMF's insistence on tax reform and forsaking the banks alienated the business sectors. When the Social Christian Party pulled out of the negotiations, it became clear that Mahuad's presidency would not last long (NotiSur 1999d, f).

In the last days of 1999, Mahuad announced a plan to dollarize the economy and implement the IMF measures. Assisted by soldiers, Indian crowds flocked to Quito demanding his dismissal and occupying Congress and the Supreme Court (NotiSur 2000a). On January 21, 2000, indigenous activists and young military officers cheered in Congress as Colonel Lucio Gutiérrez and CONAIE's president, Antonio Vargas, proclaimed a "government of national salvation." After frantic consultations among generals, politicians, and U.S. diplomats, however, the armed forces announced that they were restoring constitutional order by installing Vice President Gustavo Noboa as the new president. Gutiérrez and the other officers involved in the coup were arrested, and the Indian leaders were forced to order the protestors to retreat.[3] In the ensuing months, the detainees were granted amnesty and discharged from the army. While dollarization was maintained, the IMF negotiations were eventually abandoned without an agreement (NotiSur 2002a).

Much speculation has been offered about who manipulated whom in the military-Indian coup. In some versions, the conspirators appear as victims of a plot to get rid of a weakened president and proceed with dollarization (Lucas 2000, 170; Dávila Loor 2000). But the truth is that the colonels had been pressing their superiors for decisive action against Mahuad (Dieterich 2001, 153–54) and that their contacts with the Indian leaders intensified after the Parlamento Popular, an assembly in which more that three hundred delegates of CONAIE and other groups called for Mahuad's removal and the formation of a popular government (Lucas 2000, 89–93; Hernández et al. 2000, 221–22). Thus it is unquestionable that the coup's organizers were acting on their own initiative.[4] Their inability to hold on to power, however, proved that the whole enterprise had been utterly misguided.

Disillusionment and Demobilization

In preparation for the 2002 elections, Colonel Gutiérrez founded the Patriotic Society Party, PSP, which put forward his candidacy for president. After failed attempts to forge a center-left coalition, CONAIE and Pachakutik decided to form an alliance with the PSP (*El Comercio* 2002a, b, c). Benefiting from the Indian vote and a fragmented field of 11 candidates, Gutiérrez won the first round with 20.4 percent of the total (NotiSur 2002b). In the second round he defeated banana tycoon Alvaro Noboa, an independent conservative, by 9.6 percent. Like previous presidents, Gutiérrez lacked majority support in Congress, where the PSP–Pachakutik alliance had won only 17 of the 100 seats (NotiSur 2002c).

After the coup, Gutiérrez had cultivated the image of a progressive populist. As the elections approached, however, he toned down his discourse and included business leaders among his advisers. He visited Washington to meet with IMF and U.S. officials and, immediately after his election, started to talk about austerity measures (*El Comercio* 2002d). The new attitude was reflected by the make-up of his cabinet. Although Gutiérrez appointed some Pachakutik ministers, the posts responsible for economic policy were assigned to the advisers who had been functioning as links with the business sectors and the IMF (NotiSur 2003a).

Gutiérrez's priority task was a deal with the IMF, which wanted the fiscal deficit elminated. Knowing that an agreement would open the door to loans for social investment and development, Pachakutik's cabinet ministers went along with the austerity measures, doing their best to moderate them. The result was a salary freeze in the public sector and higher prices for fuel, transportation, and electricity (NotiSur 2003b). Many activists saw this as a betrayal. The Indian federation of the Sierra, Ecuarunari, demanded the resignation of the responsible ministers (Ecuarunari 2003). CONAIE echoed Ecuarunari's reproofs, calling for a rectification of the government's economic policies (CONAIE 2003).

By mid-2003, disagreements over several issues, including the government's handling of strikes by teachers and oil workers, had aggravated the tensions in the coalition (NotiSur 2003c). Gutiérrez's intense proselytizing in rural areas irritated the indigenous activists, who decried it as a scheme to bypass CONAIE and form clientelist networks. While the cabinet was torn by mutual accusations, the "allies" maneuvered in opposite directions in Congress, where Pachakutik tried to form a center-left block and the PSP courted the Social Christian Party. The alliance collapsed in August 2003, when Pachakutik refused to support a bill that modified labor contracts in the public sector and Gutiérrez dismissed its ministers (*El Comercio* 2003a, b).

With the end of the alliance, CONAIE's internal divisions rose to the surface. Amazon groups criticized the leaders for leaving the government, and radical sectors of the Sierra reproached their delay in breaking with Gutiérrez (*El Comercio* 2003c, d). Meanwhile, Gutiérrez went on the offensive to weaken CONAIE further, issuing a decree that allowed him unilaterally to appoint the personnel of the state agencies that dealt with indigenous issues (*El Comercio* 2003e). This ended the practice by which the officials were nominated by CONAIE and ratified by the president. The next step was the replacement of the agencies' staff with activists who had signed up with the PSP and leaders from FEINE and FENOCIN.

By the end of his first year in office, Gutiérrez was facing accusations of nepotism and corruption. He had not succeeded in winning support from the Social Christian Party (NotiSur 2003d). CONAIE proposed a rally to demand his dismissal, but the Amazon groups opposed it, and the other organizations ignored the call (*El Comercio* 2004a). FEINE had chosen to back Gutiérrez in exchange for programs for the Protestant indigenous communities, and some of CONAIE's own groups, particularly in the Amazon, were involved in similar dealings (*El Comercio* 2004b, c). Despite the warning signs, CONAIE staged a protest in February 2004. The Indian federation of the Amazon and the other organizations refused to participate; the grassroots response was decidedly weak; and by the end of the first day, the mobilization was called off (*El Comercio* 2004d, e). Four months later, CONAIE organized another protest. The outcome was the same, aggravated by the Amazon groups' public support of Gutiérrez, who had just appointed his former fellow coup leader, Antonio Vargas, minister of social welfare. Vargas, himself a Quichua from the Amazon, had left CONAIE in 2002, eventually joining FEINE and becoming a staunch supporter of Gutiérrez (NotiSur 2004a; *El Comercio* 2004f, g, h).

The failure of the 2004 protests exposed CONAIE's crisis. But Gutiérrez's success in neutralizing the movement did not solve his problems in Congress. In November he barely survived an impeachment vote amid charges that he had bribed legislators and had secured the Roldocistas' support by promising the return of their exiled leader, Bucaram (NotiSur 2004b). Then Gutiérrez dismissed 27 of the 31 Supreme Court justices, installing docile judges who overturned Bucaram's corruption convictions (NotiSur 2005a). On April 15, 2005, after three months of constitutional upheaval, Gutiérrez declared a state of emergency and ordered the police to repress protesters in Quito. The move backfired when the radio stations opened their microphones to an outpouring of indignation against his attempts to assume dictatorial powers. Following a week of demonstrations, the military withdrew its support, Gutiérrez abandoned the presidential palace, and Congress replaced him with Vice President Alfredo Palacio (NotiSur 2005b).

Once again, an Ecuadorian president had been ousted on the crest of street protests. This time, however, the main protagonists had been the urban crowds of Quito. CONAIE's leaders were slow in deciding to join in the protests, and when they finally did, their calls brought few Indians to the capital. Ironically, the fall of Gutiérrez offered further evidence of the prostration of the indigenous movement.

THE INDIAN MOVEMENT AND DEMOCRACY

This section elucidates the implications of the Indian struggles from the point of view of democracy. First, it looks at participation as a source of power for the Indian movement. Next, it assesses the consequences, through separate inquiries into the politics of influence and the politics of power. The last part examines the various impacts on Ecuador's democratic institutions.

The Secret of the Indians' Power

The Indian movement became a significant force because it was able to compel governments to pay heed to its demands. It was a classic expression of the power that grows out of the effective use of disruption. To determine the sources of that power would entail exploring many factors, including the geopolitical assets of the Indian groups (strategic location in places where they could block the main national highways), the functional capabilities of their activists and organizations, and the financial and logistical assistance of external allies, such as progressive sectors of the Catholic Church and a variety of domestic and foreign NGOs. Some of these elements were addressed in a previous study (Zamosc 1994); therefore the focus here is on what can be considered the main source of the effectiveness of the mobilizations: at the grassroots level, people were willing and ready to participate in them.

Throughout Ecuador, the decisions to respond to CONAIE's mobilization calls were taken by the Indian communities. Legally recognized as rural neighborhood associations, these communities have roots that go back to the colonial system of resguardos, or reservations (Ramón 1981). Their revitalization was boosted by the land struggles of the 1960s and 1970s, which, insofar as they involved appeals to primordial loyalties of extended kinship and reciprocity, reinforced the old community as the natural framework for these relationships (Zamosc 1994). At the same time, the agrarian reforms diluted the landowners' power, creating spaces in which the communities, by taking up the representation of the Indian peasants, gained prominence as relevant actors in local and regional politics (Carrasco 1993; Zamosc 1994).

Today, Ecuador has about 2,100 Indian communities, functioning as self-regulated entities based on the authority of their asambleas (in which everybody participates) and *cabildos* (executive committees of five members). All important issues are discussed in the asambleas, where agreement is usually reached by consensus rather than by voting. The decisions are binding for all members, with formal and informal mechanisms to ensure compliance (Sánchez Parga 1986, 1–176; Korovkin 2001, 52–58). Thus, joining in a mobilization is always the result of a decision of the community, which exerts its influence to make sure that the members join in the roadblocks and rallies.

The secret of CONAIE's power, then, lies in its ability to harness the resources for collective action that exist in the Indian communities. Pierre Bourdieu's concept of social capital helps elucidate this process. Bourdieu sees social capital as the aggregate of resources linked to the possession of a network of relationships of mutual acquaintance or recognition (1985, 248). Members of a group that, like the Indian community, is based on reciprocity and solidarity can claim access to the resources of their peers by virtue of belonging to the group. But the group as such can also use the resources embedded in the network. Indeed, the accumulation and use of social capital are always guided by contextual norms and institutions (Roña Tas 1998). This is particularly visible in communal groups, whose formal and informal rules define the available resources, the ways they can be claimed, and the sanctions that enforce delivery. The rules circumscribe and aggregate social capital, ensuring that its use is restricted to members and taking advantage of the effect of concentration to maximize benefits (Bourdieu 1985, 249). In such circumstances, social capital is an asset that belongs to the group, which can institute itself as collective beneficiary in activities that benefit the group as a whole.

In practical terms, this means that a community that joins a mobilization is making a claim on its social capital, and that the members' readiness to participate is a resource that they owe to the community. As Alejandro Portes (1998, 7–9) has shown, different motives may be at play when members contribute resources, including feelings of obligation (internalized norms), expectations of future repayment (norm of reciprocity), identification with the group (bounded solidarity), and fear of sanctions (enforceable trust). The same motives can explain the behavior of each individual community within the networks of communities that make up the Indian movement. The general point is that the Ecuadorian Indian movement operates as a network of networks, whose activities can be analyzed as a process of accumulation, concentration, and deployment of the social capital embedded in its grassroots community structures. By bringing that social capital to bear on the political system, CONAIE has been effecting its conversion into political capital; that is, into leverage that can be used to wrest concessions from governments or to compete for direct access to power.

The Politics of Influence

In the politics of influence, social movements seek changes in public policy decisions. We are interested, then, in these questions: On which issues did the Indian movement try to influence government policy? What was at stake in those issues? How effective were the mobilizations in achieving their goals? Here, we should keep in mind that the issues changed with the evolution of the struggles. Initially, when the Indians were fighting alone, they focused on their own demands. Later on, CONAIE's coalition-building initiatives broadened the confrontation, incorporating issues that were relevant to the other rural groups and, eventually, to the popular sectors at large.

Through the issues we can discern the stakes. The Indians' demands focused on achieving the status of recognized ethnic groups with territorial rights and some degree of autonomy. This challenged the existing notions of nationhood and citizenship; the former by defying the assumption that white-mestizo identity was the foundation of Ecuadorian identity, and the latter by questioning the liberal axiom that citizen rights could only be individual, not collective rights. The Indian claims, then, sought changes in the existing conditions. By contrast, the struggles over agrarian and national economic policy matters were attempts to resist changes. The fights over the Seguro Campesino and the Agrarian Modernization Law focused on thwarting initiatives that would have worsened the situation of the rural population. Similarly, the national protests against neoliberalism were defensive responses to attempts to unload the burdens of reform onto the shoulders of the popular sectors. The stakes, then, had to do with the distribution of the costs of adjusting the economy to the new conditions of global capitalist development.

Did the struggles achieve their goals? We may start with the opposition to the neoliberal agenda, the results of which are trickier to appraise. Studies have shown that Ecuador ranks among the least effective reformers in Latin America (Morley et al. 1999; Lora 1997). Clearly, the popular struggles played a role in this outcome, but their influence cannot be disentangled from the effects of the lack of political support and the hostility of the business sector to some reforms. Besides, we should not forget that neoliberalism was never really defeated in Ecuador, as its setbacks were always followed by renewed attempts to enact its reforms. We can conclude, then, that in this area the struggles had limited success. Interacting with other factors, they delayed the reforms and, in some cases, mitigated their impact on the popular sectors; but they were unable decisively to vanquish the neoliberal agenda.

On the rural-agrarian front, CONAIE and its peasant allies were much more effective. After soundly defeating the attempt to scrap the rural health service, they succeeded in influencing the new agrarian legislation to keep water in the public domain, secure the status of communal property, and restore the state's support to the peasant economy. Eventually, the 1998 constitutional reform enshrined all these attainments in the Ecuadorian charter (República del Ecuador 1998, articles 60, 84, 247, 269).

Concerning Indian ethnic demands, the initial fights established CONAIE's contentious credentials and led to significant gains on the land rights front, particularly in the Amazon. Later, the confrontations over broader national policy issues became an effective means for attaining the particularistic goals of the Indian movement (Zamosc 2004, 146). In the give and take after the fall of Bucaram, for example, CONAIE won one of its most important achievements: the creation of CODENPE (Ecuadorian Council of Indian Nations and Peoples), the agency that now coordinates all support programs for indigenous groups with participation of their own organizations (Zamosc 2004, 146). Further concessions were wrested from Mahuad in the battles of the late 1990s, including an investment fund for Indian areas, the legalization of traditional medicine, and budget increases for the state's indigenous agencies (Kipu 1998, 1999a, b).

On the whole, the movement was able to accumulate an uneven but substantial record of success in influencing government policies. One upshot was that CONAIE could reinvest political capital earned through the mobilizations in other forms of action and more ambitious goals. On the one hand, its lobbying drives yielded significant gains without having to resort to protests, including the creation of PRODEPINE (Development Program for Indian and Black Populations, initiated in 1997 with World Bank funding), the establishment of a health program for Indian communities, and the launching of CODENPE projects of infrastructural works, water and irrigation, soil improvement, rural housing, and organizational capacity building (Kipu 1998, 1999a, b). On the other hand, the Indian movement took steps to establish itself as a contender in the struggle for political power.

The Politics of Power

In the politics of power, agents participate in contests to occupy the positions that control and direct public policymaking. The three main manifestations of the Indian movement's struggles for power were the fight for control over the state's agencies of indigenous affairs, Pachakutik's engagement in electoral politics, and CONAIE's involvement in the coup against Jamil Mahuad.

For the Indian movement, the agencies in charge of bilingual education and indigenous health; the council of indigenous peoples, CODENPE; the development program PRODEPINE; and the indigenous investment fund constituted a first major arena of power contestation. Steered by the movement, the agencies of indigenous affairs could serve as a means to attain objectives while fulfilling the programmatic ambition of exercising autonomy. Controlled by governments, they could be turned into tools of clientelistic domination. In the heat of the struggles, CONAIE wrested from the government an informal deal whereby the officials were appointed on the basis of its nominations. Later, however, President Gutiérrez's actions showed that, in a less favorable climate, CONAIE's grip could be easily broken. The situation was complicated by the rivalry among indigenous-peasant organizations. Under the initial arrangement, CONAIE monopolized the representation of the Indians; this had always been resented by smaller groups like FEINE and FENOCIN. Thus, Gutiérrez's repeal of CONAIE's privileges was more than a step to exclude it from the agencies' resources. It was also a gambit aimed at luring the other organizations into a network of patronage and using their example to entice CONAIE's local and regional chapters onto the clientelistic bandwagon.

The second front in the struggle for power was electoral competition. Pachakutik was launched in 1996 as a party based on CONAIE and its closest allies. In practice, however, it has been the political arm of the Indian movement, which provides most of its candidates for office. The best indicator of Pachakutik's overall strength is the congressional elections, in which its candidates have won, on average, 7.5 percent of the seats.[5] While this falls short of the estimated size of the indigenous population, it can still be seen as a fair result for a new party. Moreover, the 2002 presidential election proved that Pachakutik's vote can be decisive, since Gutiérrez qualified for the second round by a margin of less than 5 percent. But it is at local and regional levels where

Pachakutik's results have been especially significant. In the 2000 elections it won 4 governorships, 17 mayorships, and substantial representation in the provincial, municipal, and parish councils of the Highlands and the Amazon. The party's performance was similar in 2004, with 3 governors and 20 majors elected. Thus, while Pachakutik has not yet fulfilled its potential, it is clear that it is serving as a vehicle for self-government in the main indigenous areas.

We do not have enough studies to draw a panoptic picture of Pachakutik's perform-ance at the different levels of government. One area in which the outcome can be readily recognized is the country's charter. In the 1997 constitutional assembly, Pachakutik nego-tiated important provisions, including the definition of Ecuador as a multicultural state, the designation of the indigenous groups as peoples, and the recognition of their rights to preserve their culture and their forms of political organization and administration of justice (CODENPE 2000). Together with other clauses about the creation of indigenous territorial entities, these rights offer a framework for some degree of autonomy. But implementation depends on further legislation by Congress, where Pachakutik's moves have been conditioned by its minority status and its role as an opposition party focused on undercutting initiatives coming from the executive.

In contrast to its adversarial role in Congress, Pachakutik's gains in local elections created real opportunities for exercising power. The initial research on these experiences has focused on counties with dense Indian populations or visibility as tourist or artisan centers, including Guamote, Otavalo, Cotacachi, Saquisili, and Bolívar (Larrea and Larrea 1998; Cameron 2005; Radcliffe et al. 2002; Almeida and Arrobo 2002, 37–44; Barreda et al. 2005, 78–79). The studies cast light on innovative efforts to encourage grassroots participation, establish practices that are free of corruption and clientelism, foster fairness in the distribution of resources, and promote multiculturalism by adapting traditional indigenous institutions. But they also show that the progress has been uneven and that, in some cases, Pachakutik's local authorities have been disappointing.

The third and by far the most dramatic incursion of the Indian movement into the politics of power was the January 2000 coup against Mahuad. In that episode, CONAIE conspired with military officers to overthrow the government and assume the powers of the state. One way of coming to terms with the outcome is to look into the reasons for the coup's failure. In retrospective accounts, the Indian leaders have mentioned the generals' betrayal, the machinations of the elites and the U.S. embassy, the hostility of the press, the lack of popular response in the cities, and their own unpreparedness to take power (Lucas 2000, 146–50, 158–66; Dieterich 2001, 100–126). From this, one can conclude that the coup failed because it was marked by improvisation and, ultimately, because it reflected a gross misreading of the political scene.

Another way of assessing the coup's significance is to consider its repercussions for the Indian movement itself. The evidence indicates that there was public support for the removal of Mahuad but not for a military-Indian takeover. In the polls taken on the day of the coup, only 6 percent believed that Mahuad could continue, 71 percent approved the protests, and 79 percent thought that Mahuad had to be replaced without breaking the constitutional order (Cedatos 2000a, 6). Two days later, the polls showed that 80 percent were pleased that democracy had been maintained, 77 percent supported the investiture of Vice President Noboa, and only 13 percent would have preferred to keep the military-Indian junta (Cedatos 2000b, 7).

The overall pattern is clear. While CONAIE fulfilled a well-regarded role in express-ing public discontent, its attempt to take power by force was rejected. The payoff for the Indian movement was also ambivalent. At the time, its image as a powerful player may have been boosted and its undemocratic behavior may have been glossed over amid the general complacency with Mahuad's removal. But in the long run, CONAIE's collusion with the colonels put it on track for further blunders whose consequences would be far more damaging.

Recapitulating, what can we make of the Indian movement's involvement in these diverse forms of the politics of power? As we saw in the conceptual section, it is not rare for a movement to launch a party and combine protest with electoral participation. The juxtaposition of CONAIE's struggles over the indigenous agencies and Pachakutik's electoral ventures, then, are an example of what a movement undergoing institutionalization typically does. The coup, though, was a very different matter. If we were dealing with a revolutionary group, we might think about the use of force as part of the strategy of "combining all forms of struggle." But CONAIE and Pachakutik have never claimed to be revolutionary organizations. We are left, then, with the sense that the coup was an anomalous deviation from the path that the movement had been following. To account for it, one could make allowances for the magnitude of the crisis, the intensity of the public's outrage, and the leaders' rashness and lack of vision. What is difficult to fathom is why, to this day, the activists have not conducted a real evaluation of those events and their fallout.

In the absence of soul searching, the naive opportunism that transpired in the coup kept haunting the Indian movement. Indeed, the leaders' decision to support Gutiérrez in the 2002 elections can only be seen as an attempt to cash in on whatever political capital they believed they had gained from the January 2000 adventure. Gutiérrez won the election, but the quick unraveling of the alliance showed that the move had been another serious mistake. The Indian movement could not stop Gutiérrez's neoliberal turn, Pachakutik was forced to leave the government, and CONAIE was weakened by divisions. But the worst damage came from the disappointment at the grassroots, where Pachakutik's presence in the government had been hailed as an opportunity to access the resources that had been always denied to the Indians. Combined with the effects of Gutiérrez's clientelist strategy, the loss of trust at base level became a major factor in the failure of CONAIE's latest mobilizations.

Impact on Democracy as a Political Regime

This assessment of the Indian movement's impact on the regime is grounded on elaborations of four ways that civil associations may impinge on democratic institutions. The first of these is interest representation. In democratic regimes, political parties are the prescribed medium for representing citizen interests. Very often, however, party systems cannot express the diversity that exists in society (Heberle 1951, 52–55; Forbrig 2002). Civil associations can compensate for this deficit by conveying the interests of specific sectors to the political system. The Ecuadorian Indian movement exemplifies this function. It gave voice to excluded groups, projected their concerns into the public agenda, and opened new areas for policymaking. Furthermore, its strategy of alliances was instrumental in aggregating and expressing the demands of all the rural groups and, eventually, the popular sectors at large. To this we can add the creation of a party that incorporated marginalized interests into the system and spurred indigenous participation in elections.

Interest representation by civil associations can help fulfill three principles of democratic governance: responsiveness (serving all sectors), consensus orientation (mediating among different interests), and equity (treating everyone equally). Realizing this potential, however, does not depend on the civil groups alone. It also depends on the institutional actors' willingness to consider their views and adhere to democratic principles (Schölte

2004). In Ecuador, incumbent governments had many opportunities to hear what the indigenous and popular sectors wanted and to fulfill their side of the democratic governance bargain. But those governments chose to ignore the input that came from below. Insisting on the imposition of unpopular reforms, they wasted the opportunities for building the kind of consensus that would have strengthened democratic governance.

This calls attention to a second function of civil associations: the control of state power. Liberal formulations emphasize the notion that citizens should protect themselves from state intrusion in private affairs and from violations of civil and political rights. Broader interpretations, however, include additional issues related to transparency and accountability (Schölte 2004; Forbrig 2002). Once again, we find a connection with the principles of democratic governance, since the contribution of civil associations consists in holding governments responsible for fulfilling those principles. In Ecuador, the popular opposition to neoliberal governments repudiated the governments' insensitivity to the concerns of the majority, unwillingness to compromise, and unilateral commitment to the priorities of the business elites and the IMF. Thus, in the process of defending the interests of the popular sectors, the Indian movement and its allies were also fulfilling the watchdog role of trying to counterbalance what was widely seen as an unfair use of authority.

The foregoing interpretation leads to a third function: legitimation. In democratic polities, governments are acutely dependent on legitimacy because it is the people's support that justifies the right to exercise authority. Citizen groups can reaffirm legitimacy in two ways: explicitly, through actions that convey support; or tacitly, by doing nothing that might be construed as opposition. The denial of support, however, must take the form of explicit oppositional action if it is to be understood as such. It is also worth noting that, in democracies, legitimation is rarely an all-or-nothing matter. The reason is that civil associations can legitimate or delegitimate authority at different levels. Opposition to a policy does not necessarily imply disaffection with a government, and disaffection with a government does not necessarily entail rejection of the regime. Indeed, a common result of challenges at lower levels is the reinforcement of legitimacy at higher levels, as illustrated by cases in which a negotiated solution of a policy conflict boosts the image of a government, and situations in which the constitutional replacement of an unpopular government reaffirms the credibility of a democratic regime.

The legitimacy issue is particularly sensitive in the case of social movements because their motives are oppositional and their activities assume noninstitutional forms. Still, taking into account the nuances of legitimation, there is much room for their fulfillment of this function. The Ecuadorian Indian movement was certainly shoring up the political institutions when it created a party and urged its base to go to the polls. Beyond that, the routine challenges of the movement focused on policy matters that did not question the legitimacy of the governments or the regime as such. Through a different route we return to the point that, if the Ecuadorian governments had been more open to negotiation, the results could have enhanced their standing. Instead, their inflexibility became a factor in the escalation of conflict that led to their delegitimation.

It was against this background that the Indian movement played an active role in the demise of two presidents. In the fall of Bucaram, the legitimacy of the regime was not at stake. The ousting of Mahuad was different because it involved a conspiracy to usurp power, which, had it succeeded, would have implied the breakdown of democracy. But the coup failed, and as a result, its actual impact on regime legitimacy is difficult to assess. Intuitively, one would think that, by exposing the frailty of the institutions, the affair may have eroded their credibility. This inference, though, is not supported by the evidence. Over the last decade, the Latinobarómetro polls have shown a general softening of support for democracy, but the trend has been much less pronounced in Ecuador than in the rest of the Latin America. Comparing the periods 1996–99 and 2000–2004 (before and after Ecuador's January 2000 coup), support for democracy declined by 12 percent in the region as a whole but only by 6 percent in Ecuador (Latinobarómetro 2004, 5). One can speculate that, to some extent, Ecuadorians felt reassured that their democracy had survived the crisis.

Speculations aside, the movement's attempt to subvert the regime raises questions about a fourth function attributed to civil society: political socialization. In one of the most prominent formulations of the "civil society argument," associations are presented as frameworks in which citizens acquire the values and dispositions that are needed for a workable democratic polity (Putnam 2000, 339). This claim relies on two basic assumptions about political socialization: that it is a matter of the formation of individuals, and that its results can somehow "free-float" into the public sphere as a resource that can be readily harnessed for the benefit of democracy. What these assumptions miss is the significance of the mediation of the group, which becomes a collective subject of its own socialization process, inculcates its particularistic norms along with the more general dispositions, and regulates the use of the resources that make up the network's social capital. In so doing, civil society groups invariably condition the impact their socialization may have on the political system.

Taking this into account, we can tackle what appears to be one of the most puzzling questions about the Ecuadorian Indian movement. This study has demonstrated that the movement's struggles have induced vast changes in the behavior of the indigenous groups. Because those changes would not have been possible without processes of socialization, it is clear that the movement has been doing a massive job teaching people to work together, cultivating interest in policy issues, and providing knowledge and skills for participating in public activities, such as mobilizations and elections. The seemingly puzzling question is how these contributions to political socialization, which, according to the celebrated claim, should be functional to democracy, square with the attempt to take power by force. The matter is less baffling if we keep in mind that movements do not socialize people to help the workings of democratic regimes; they do it to attain their goals. The real question, then, concerns the movement's lack of commitment to Ecuadorian democracy.

This lack of commitment can be traced to three sources. One is the conviction that Ecuador's democracy is a fraud. Time and again the Indian militants have decried what they view as a corrupt democracy, with institutions that are discriminatory and governments that benefit the elites at the expense of the common people (Lluco 2000; Zhingri 2002). Another source is the disrespect of all the political players for the rules of democracy. Willy-nilly, the indigenous activists have "learned the ropes" of practical politics within a system of interactions in which the prevailing attitudes are not distinguished by reverence for constitutional conventions.

The third source is the tension between the principles that inspire the indigenous internal practices and the liberal notions of democracy. At one level, it is a matter of the contrast between direct and indirect democracy; the former embodied in the participation of all in communal decisionmaking, and the latter in the elected officials who decide for all citizens in the broader Ecuadorian polity. At another level, it is a contrast between two canons of representation. When the communities elect representatives to the associations, and when the associations elect representatives to the next-level federations, the elected persons function as delegates, whose powers are limited to specific mandates and whose authority can be revoked at will by those who elected them. In a liberal democracy, by contrast, elected officials operate as fiduciaries who use their discretion to interpret the interests of the represented and act on their behalf.[6]

This raises the question of what the Indian movement's democratic ideals are, and whether these ideals and the standards of Ecuador's democracy are so incompatible as to justify the repudiation of the latter by the activists. In a political declaration approved in 1993, CONAIE called for a "plurinational communitarian democracy" based on equality, liberty, fraternity, and social peace. This goal would be achieved through a political reorganization aimed at guaranteeing the full participation of the Indian peoples and the other social sectors (CONAIE 1993). The platform adopted by the first congress of Pachakutik in 1999 was more specific, proposing a "radical democracy" based on a semi-parliamentary system, decentralization, civil society representation in some state agencies, and direct participation through citizen initiatives, referenda, and recall of elected officials (Pachakutik 1999). These proposals could be easily integrated into an agenda to "deepen" the democratic character of existing institutions. The activists' lack of commitment, then, is not rooted in an unbridgeable programmatic rift. Rather, it seems to result from a double ideological distortion: a view of Ecuadorian democracy that chooses to dwell on its deficiencies (ignoring that the conquest of indigenous rights and the Indian movement itself would hardly have been possible without it), and an exaggerated sense of the contradiction between the indigenous principles and those of the existing institutions.

CONCLUSIONS

This work has investigated the consequences of the Ecuadorian Indian movement for democracy. Its inquiry was based on conceptualizations that defined the specificity of movements as a form of civil society's political engagement and offered guidelines for studying their effects on the participatory and institutional dimensions of democracy. The analysis showed that the Indian movement had roots in communal mechanisms of direct democracy, that its multilayered structure had been built through bottom-up networking based on delegative representation, and that its protagonism in the contentious cycle of the 1990s marked a historic milestone for the involvement of the indigenous groups in Ecuador's public life.

The participatory breakthrough came on two fronts. Practicing the politics of influence, the movement forced new issues onto the public agenda, wrested concessions from governments, and led alliances that repeatedly hindered the imposition of neoliberal reforms. Engaging in the politics of power, it contested the control of the state's indigenous agencies and spawned a party that made strides in the electoral representation of the Indian groups, the procurement of their collective rights, and their progress toward self-government. These initiatives fulfilled important functions for Ecuador's democratic institutions. In the areas of interest representation and control of state power, the demands and protests provided ideas and contributions for improving the quality of democratic governance and imposed restraints on policies that were widely rejected by civil society. The launching of a new party was also significant as a development that upheld the legitimacy of the democratic regime.

It is unquestionable, then, that the Indian movement has made remarkable contributions to Ecuadorian democracy. Yet we have also seen that the swell of activism was not an unmitigated blessing for democratic politics. The critical drawback was the January 2000 attempt to subvert the constitutional order. At that point, CONAIE transgressed the threshold beyond which, in a democracy, an opposition becomes disloyal (Linz 1978, 27–38). The analysis here showed that the coup was inconsistent with the behavioral pattern of the Indian movement and that its negative impact was mitigated by its own failure and by the special conditions under which it happened. But the extenuating circumstances cannot absolve the movement of responsibility for threatening the democratic regime. Further scrutiny emphasized the reality that political socialization within the Indian movement had not fostered a sense of commitment to Ecuadorian democracy.

This evidence of contradictory consequences is consistent with the critique that the "civil society argument" plays up beneficial effects and ignores the possible downside. It also underscores that in Latin America, the study of the impact of civil associations on democracy cannot overlook three crucial points. The first is that the realization of the democratic potential of any civil society initiative depends on how the political institutions process it. Democratic governance is enhanced when decisionmakers take the concerns of civil associations into account. Conversely, democracy suffers when governments ignore citizen feedback, treat it perfunctorily, or demonstrate biases in their reactions to the bidding of different sectors.

The second point is that when civil associations mobilize broad support, the institutional responses to their functions of interest representation and control of state power can be highly consequential for regime legitimation. The legitimacy of democratic politics is strengthened when governments take notice of popular sentiment; but democratic regimes may fall into a tailspin of delegitimation when the inputs from below are repeatedly rebuffed.

The third point is that it is a mistake to view civil society groups as neutral purveyors of citizens trained for democracy. Like other social capital resources, the results of political socialization remain embedded in the networks of interaction that produce them (Edwards and Foley 1998). As collective structures that constitute the primordial source of social capital, regulate its uses, and mediate between individuals and society, civil associations impart their particularistic slant to socialization and influence its fallout in the political system.

For Ecuador's indigenous activists, the stark contrast between the successes of the 1990s and the more recent frustrations underscores the urgency of rethinking their bearings. To a large extent, their present predicament is a result of their own inability to respond to the complexities of the movement's institutionalization process. Two tasks in particular were sorely neglected. One was in the area of strategic development. To maintain coherence in situations of partial institutionalization, social movements must define a roadmap for combining protest with the use of prescribed means, and they must do it in such a manner that the two forms of action reinforce rather than interfere with each other.

The other neglected task was ideological elaboration. In the politics of influence, social movements can afford to condemn unstintingly the poverty of democracy. But in a democratic system, whatever its shortcomings, a movement that acts in the name of democracy cannot make the transition to the politics of power without taking a more constructive stance toward the existing institutions. Essentially, it is a matter of reframing the movement's ideology by shifting the emphasis from antisystem representations to imageries of democratic renovation from within (Della Porta and Diani 1999, 80–82). In Ecuador, the lack of strategic guidelines and the shortsighted attitude toward the democratic institutions jumbled the responsibilities of CONAIE and Pachakutik, muddled their priorities, and paved the way for the missteps that weakened the Indian movement.

It may be a commonplace to say that a crisis can be turned into an opportunity, but that is precisely the challenge that the Ecuadorian indigenous activists face today. Whether or not they succeed will depend on their willingness to recognize that the time for reckoning and self-criticism is long overdue.

NOTES

I am indebted to Susan Eckstein, Richard Madsen, and four anonymous reviewers of LAPS for their useful comments on the original manuscript.

1 The ongoing indigenous struggles in Latin America falsify the basic tenets of the "new social movements" approach. Proponents of this approach emphasize identities and the cultural significance of social mobilization, disdaining class conflicts and openly political battles (Escobar and Alvarez 1992a, b). Because of their specificities of identity and culture, indigenous movements could have emerged as archetypes of the "new social movements." Instead, what we are seeing in countries like Ecuador, Bolivia, and Mexico is that their struggles have not been limited to cultural affirmation or ethnic rights. While these goals have been important, the indigenous movements have transcended them, getting involved in broader battles over social issues and political power.

2 This definition articulates three elements that have been consistently emphasized in classic works on social movements: their nature as enterprises of change (Blumer 1951; Heberle 1951, 447–59), their embeddedness in conflict (Touraine 1981; Tarrow 1994; Della Porta and Diani 1999), and the use of noninstitutional forms of action (Piven and Cloward 1977; Tilly 1978; Marx and McAdam 1994).

3 For journalistic accounts of these events, see NotiSur 2000b; Ponce 2000; Hernández et al. 2000; Lucas 2000.

4 Lucero (2001, 64–66) offers a perceptive analysis of the factors behind the military–indigenous alliance.

5 The 7.5 percent average reflects Pachakutik's results in the 1997 election to the constitutional assembly and the congressional elections of 1996, 1998, and 2002. The source of all the electoral data referenced in this paragraph is from Ecuador's Supreme Electoral Court.

6 This distinction between delegation and fiduciary representation is based on Bobbio 1987, 43–62. On the contrast between indigenous and liberal concepts of democracy, see also Macas 2004; León 1991; and the views of Fernando Bustamante as quoted by Ponce 2000, 113–14.

REFERENCES

Almeida, Ileana, and Nidia Arrobo. 2002. Ecuador: Informe final. Report of the LatAutonomy project. Vienna: Ludwig Boltzmann Institute for Contemporary Research on Latin America.

Andolina, Robert. 2003. The Sovereign and Its Shadow: Constituent Assembly and Indigenous Movement in Ecuador. *Journal of Latin American Studies* 35, 4: 721–51.

Barreda, Mikel, Marc Bou, Oscar del Alamo, Inigo Marías, Marc Navarro, and Pere Torres. 2005. *Perfil de gobernabilidad de Ecuador*. Barcelona: Institut Internacional de Governabilitat de Catalunya.

Beck, Scott. H., and Kenneth J. Mijeski. 2001. Barricades and Ballots: Ecuador's Indians and the Pachakutik Political Movement. *Ecuadorian Studies* 1. <www.yachana.Org/ecuatorianistas/journal/l/beck/beck.htm>.

Blumer, Herbert. 1951. Social Movements. *In New Outline of the Principles of Sociology*, 2nd ed. rev., ed. A. M. Lee. New York: Barnes and Noble. 199–220.

Bobbio, Norberto. 1987. *The Future of Democracy*. Minneapolis: University of Minnesota Press.

Bourdieu, Pierre. 1985. The Forms of Capital. In *Handbook of Theory and Research for the Sociology of Education*, ed. J. G. Richardson. New York: Greenwood Press. 241–58.

Cameron, John D. 2005. Municipal Democratization in Rural Latin America: Methodological Insights from Ecuador. *Bulletin of Latin American Research* 24, 3: 367–90.

Carothers, Thomas. 1999. Civil Society. *Foreign Policy* (Winter): 18–29.

Carrasco, Hernán. 1993. Democratización de los poderes locales y levantamiento indígena. *In Sismo étnico en el Ecuador: varias perspectivas*, ed. José Almeida et al. Quito: Abya-Yala. 29–69.

Centro de Estudios y Datos (Cedatos). 2000a. Los acontecimientos nacionales del 21 de enero. *Estudios y Datos* 25: 173.

———. 2000b. Reacciones frente al cambio de gobierno. *Estudios y Datos* 25: 173.

Cohen, Jean L., and Andrew Arato. 1992. *Civil Society and Political Theory*. Cambridge: MIT Press.

Conaghan, Catherine. 1989. Ecuador: The Politics of Locos. *Hemisphere* 1, 1: 13–15.

Confederación de Nacionalidades Indígenas del Ecuador (CONAIE). 1988. Memorias del segundo congreso de la CONAIE.

———. 1993. Proyecto político de las nacionalidades y pueblos del Ecuador.

———. 1995. Resoluciones de la asamblea extraordinaria. December 3·

———. 2003. Resoluciones de la asamblea. February 18.

Consejo de Nacionalidades y Pueblos Indígenas del Ecuador (CODENPE). 2000. *Nuestros derechos en la constitución*. Quito: Génesis.

Coordinadora Agraria Nacional (CAN). 1993a. Por la tierra, la paz y el desarrollo. March 10.

———. 1993b. Proyecto de ley agraria integral. July 5.

Coser, Lewis A. 1956. The *Functions of Social Conflict*. New York: Free Press.

Dávila Loor, Jorge. 2000. El salto al vacío y el asalto al cielo: reflexión sobre los acontecimientos del viernes 21 y sábado 22 de enero del 2000. *Ecuador Debate* 49.

De la Torre, Carlos. 1997. Populism and Democracy: Political Discourses and Cultures in Contemporary Ecuador. *Latin American Perspectives* 24, 3: 12–25.

Della Porta, Donatella, and Mario Diani. 1999. *Social Movements: An Introduction*. Oxford: Blackwell.

Dieterich, Heinz. 2001. *La cuarta vía al poder*. Bogotá: Desde Abajo.

Dworkin, Ronald M. 1978. *Taking Rights Seriously*. Cambridge: Harvard University Press.

Ecuarunari—Confederación de Pueblos de la Nacionalidad Quichua. 2003. Resoluciones de la asamblea extraordinaria. February 14.

Edwards, Bob, and Michael W. Foley. 1998. Civil Society and Social Capital Beyond Putnam. *American Behavioral Scientist* 42, 1: 124–40.

El Comercio (Quito). 2002a. La centro-izquierda lucha por su unidad. May 30.

———. 2002b. Sin mayores resultados la cita de centro-izquierda. February 27.

———. 2002c. Tres factores jugaron en favor de Lucio Gutiérrez. July 10.

———. 2002d. Gutiérrez: el pinchazo va. December 13.

———. 2003a. Pachakutik se quedó fuera del poder. August 7.

———. 2003b. La alianza de Gobierno cayó por su propio peso en 6 meses. August 10.

———. 2003c. La Conaie y Pachakutik con una táctica defensiva. August 16.

———. 2003d. La relación Conaie-Pachakutik está en crisis. September 3.

———. 2003e. Lucio Gutiérrez gana un "round" a la Conaie. October 18.

———. 2004a. La Conaie pone pausa a su protesta contra el gobierno. January 12.

———. 2004b. Los amazónicos en paz. January 20.

———. 2004c. La Feine hace la paz con Gutiérrez. February 1.

———. 2004d. Indígenas suspenden las protestas. February 17.

———. 2004e. En las movilizaciones se evidenció la crisis de la Conaie. February 21.

———. 2004f. Presidente Gutiérrez posesionó a Vargas. May 31.

———. 2004g. Dirigencia de la Conaie prepara levantamiento. June 6.

———. 2004h. La Conaie y Pachakutik se critican por el fracaso del levantamiento. June 11.

Escobar, Arturo, and Sonia E. Alvarez. 1992a. Introduction: Theory and Protest in Latin America Today. In *The Making of Social Movements in Latin America: Identity, Strategy, and Democracy*, ed. Escobar and Alvarez. Boulder: Westview Press. 1–15.

———. 1992b. Conclusion: Theoretical and Political Horizons of Change in Contemporary Latin American Social Movements. In *The Making of Social Movements in Latin America: Identity, Strategy, and Democracy*, ed. Escobar and Alvarez. Boulder: Westview Press. 317–29.

Forbrig, Joerg. 2002. The Nexus Between Civil Society and Democracy. In *Political Priorities Between East and West: Europe's Rediscovered Wealth*, ed. W. Reichel. Vienna: Institut für den Donauraum und Mitteleuropa. 79–103.

Goldstone, Jack A. 2003. Bridging Institutionalized and Noninstitutionalized Politics. In *States, Parties, and Social Movements*, ed. Jack. A. Goldstone. New York: Cambridge University Press. 1–24.

Habermas, Jürgen. 1985. Civil Disobedience: Litmus Test for the Democratic Constitutional State. *Berkeley Journal of Sociology* 30: 96–116.

Heberle, Rudolf. 1951. *Social Movements: An Introduction to Political Sociology.* New York: Appleton-Century-Crofts.

Held, David. 1996. *Models of Democracy.* Stanford, CA: Stanford University Press.

Hernández, José, Marco Aráuz, Byron Rodríguez, and Leonel Bejarano. 2000. *21 de enero: la vorágine que acabo con Mahuad.* Quito: El Comercio.

Ibarra, A. 1987. *Los indígenas y el estado en el Ecuador.* Quito: Abya-Yala.

Instituto Nacional de Estadística y Censos. (INEC). 2001. Sexto censo nacional de población, 2001. Quito: INEC.

Isaacs, Anita. 1993. *Military Rule and Transition in Ecuador, 1972–92.* Pittsburgh: University of Pittsburgh Press.

Kipu—el mundo indígena en la prensa ecuatoriana. Press reports. 1993. Press reports on the mobilization to defend the rural health service. January 9–18.

———. 1994. Press reports on protest mobilizations. May 7–July 16.

———. 1996. Press reports on Pachakutik's electoral results. May 20–30.

———. 1998. Press reports on protest mobilizations. September 9–October 21.

———. 1999a. Press reports on protest mobilizations. March 11–25.

———. 1999b. Press reports on protest mobilizations. July 7–August 3.

Korovkin, Tanya. 2001. Reinventing the Communal Tradition: Indigenous Peoples, Civil Society, and Democratization in Andean Ecuador. *Latin American Research Review* 36, 3: 37–77.

Larrea, Fernando, and Ana M. Larrea. 1998. Participación ciudadana, relaciones interétnicas y construcción del poder local en Saquisilí. Paper presented at the conference "Gobiernos Locales y Desarrollo Rural en los Andes," Lima, September 14.

Latinobarómetro. 2004. Informe resumen: una década de mediciones, 1996–2004. Santiago de Chile: Corporación Latinobarómetro.

León, Jorge. 1991. Las organizaciones indígenas: igualdad y diferencia. In *Indios: una reflexión sobre el levantamiento indígena de 1990*, ed. D. Cornejo Menacho. Quito: Abya-Yala, 373–418.

———. 1994. De *campesinos a ciudadanos diferentes: el levantamiento indígena.* Quito: Abya-Yala.

León Guzmán, Mauricio. 2003. Etnicidad y exclusión en el Ecuador: una mirada a partir del censo de población de 2001. Internal memo. Quito: Sistema Integrado de Indicadores Sociales del Ecuador.

Linz, Juan J. 1978. *The Breakdown of Democratic Regimes: Crisis, Breakdown, and Reequilibration.* Baltimore: Johns Hopkins University Press.

Lluco, Miguel. 2000. El movimiento indígena y la construcción de una democracia radical. *Boletín del Instituto Científico de Culturas Indígenas* 10.

Lora, Eduardo. 1997. A Decade of Structural Reforms in Latin America. Working Paper Green Series 348. Washington, DC: Inter-American Development Bank.

Lucas, Kintto. 2000. *La rebelión de los indios.* Quito: Abya-Yala.

Lucero, José A. 2001. Crisis and Contention in Ecuador. *Journal of Democracy* 12, 2: 59–73.

Macas, Luis. A. 2004. Democracia e interculturalidad. *Boletín del Instituto Científico de Culturas Indígenas* 63.

Markoff, John. 2004. Contention and the Troubled History of Democracy. Paper presented at the Workshop on Contentious Politics, Binghamton University, April 18.

Marx, Gary T, and Douglas McAdam. 1994. *Collective Behavior and Social Movements: Process and Structure.* Englewood Cliffs: Prentice Hall.

McAdam, Douglas, Sidney Tarrow, and Charles Tilly. 1996. To Map Contentious Politics. *Mobilization* 1, 1: 17–34.

Melucci, Alberto. 1994. A Strange Kind of Newness: What's "New" in New Social Movements? In *New Social Movements: From Ideology to Identity*, ed. Enrique Larafta, Hank Johnston, and Joseph R. Gusfield. Philadelphia: Temple University Press. 101–30.

Morley, Samuel A., Roberto Machado, and Stefano Pettinato. 1999. Indexes of Structural Reform in Latin America. Economic Reform Series 12. Santiago: Economic Commission for Latin America and the Caribbean.

Moya, Ruth A. 1990. A Decade of Bilingual Education and Indigenous Participation in Ecuador. *Prospects* 20, 3: 331–43.

NotiSur—*South American Political and Economic Affairs* (newsletter). 1994. President Durán Battles Congress over Constitutional Reforms. October 21.

———. 1995. President Sixto Duran Suffers Defeat in Referendum on Constitutional Reforms. December 1.

———. 1996. Controversy Permeates President Abdalá Bucaram's Tumultuous First Three Months in Office. November 15.

———. 1997a. Government Economic Plan Continues to Generate Broad Opposition. January 10.

———. 1997b. Congress Votes to Oust President Abdalá Bucaram, February 7.

———. 1998a. President-Elect Jamil Mahuad Must Walk Political and Economic Tightrope. July 24.

———. 1998b. President Jamil Mahuad Introduces Unpopular Economic Measures. September 18.

———. 1999a. President Jamil Mahuad Says Country Is in Financial Crisis. January 22.

———. 1999b. Ecuador Devalues Its Currency as Crisis Continues, February 26.

———. 1999c. Congress Approves President Jamil Mahuad's Economic Package. April 30.

———. 1999d. President Jamil Mahuad Battered by Protests. July 16.

———. 1999e. International Monetary Fund Approves Standby Loan. September 3.

———. 1999f. Crises Plague Administration. November 5.

———. 2000a. Cabinet Resigns After President Jamil Mahuad Adopts Dollar as Local Currency Amid Protests. January 14.

———. 2000b. Indian Protests Topple Presidency of Jamil Mahuad, Vice President Gustavo Noboa Takes Over. January 28.

———. 2002a. Economy Minister Resigns amid Scandal. June 28.

———. 2002b. Presidential Elections Go to Runoff. October 25.

———. 2002c. Lucio Gutiérrez Wins Presidency in Runnoff. December 6.

———. 2003a. Lucio Gutiérrez Takes Office as President. January 17.

———. 2003b. Indigenous Cabinet Members Walk Tightrope Between Administration and Communities. February 14.

———. 2003c. President Lucio Gutiérrez Hit by More Strikes, Dissention Within Coalition Government. June 20.

———. 2003d. Narco-Scandal Threatens Government of President Lucio Gutiérrez. December 5.

———. 2004a. Miss Universe Contest, OAS Summit Draw Protests to Quito. June 11.

———. 2004b. President Lucio Gutiérrez Overcomes Impeachment Effort. November 19.

———. 2005a. Constitutional Crisis Erupts After President Lucio Gutiérrez and Parliament Remove Supreme Court. January 7.

———. 2005b. Congress Removes President Lucio Gutiérrez. April 22.

Oxhorn, Philip. 2003. Social Inequality, Civil Society, and the Limits of Citizenship in Latin America. In *What Justice? Whose Justice? Fighting for Fairness in Latin America*, ed. Susan Eckstein and Timothy Wickham-Crowley. Berkeley: University of California Press. 35–63.

Pachakutik—Movimiento de Unidad Plurinacional Pachakutik. 1999. Hacia el nuevo milenio: base ideológica y programática. *Boletín El Churo* MUPP 2.

Pachano, Simón. 1996. *Democracia sin sociedad*. Quito: ILDIS.

Piven, Francis F., and Richard A. Cloward. 1977. *Poor People's Movements: Why They Succeed, How They Fail*. New York: Pantheon.

Pizzorno, Alessandro. 1978. Political Exchange and Collective Identity in Industrial Conflict. In *The Resurgence of Class Conflict in Western Europe since 1968*, ed. Colin Crouch and Alessandro Pizzorno. London: Macmillan. 277–98.

Ponce, Javier. 2000. La *madrugada los sorprendió en el poder*. Quito: Planeta.

Portes, Alejandro. 1998. Social Capital: Its Origins and Applications in Modern Sociology. *Annual Review of Sociology* 24, 1: 1–25.

Putnam, Robert D. 2000. *Bowling Alone: The Collapse and Revival of American Community*. New York: Simon and Schuster.

Radcliffe, Sarah A., Nina Laurie, and Robert Andolina. 2002. Re-territorialised Space and Ethnic Political Participation: Indigenous Municipalities in Ecuador. *Space and Polity* 6, 3: 289–305.

Ramón, Galo. 1981. La comunidad indígena ecuatoriana. In *Comunidad andina: alternativas políticas de desarrollo*, ed. A. Guerrero et al. Quito: CAAP. 65–86.

Rawls, John. 1971. *A Theory of Justice*. Cambridge: Harvard University Press.

República del Ecuador. 1998. *Constitución política de la República del Ecuador*. Quito: República del Ecuador.

Roña Tas, Akos. 1998. Path Dependence and Capital Theory: Sociology of the Post-Communist Economic Transformation. *East European Politics and Societies* 12, 1: 107–32.

Rosenblum, Nancy L., and Robert C. Post. 2002. Introduction. In *Civil Society and Government*, ed. Rosenblum and Post. Princeton: Princeton University Press. 1–26.

Sánchez Parga, José. 1986. *La trama del poder en la comunidad andina*. Quito: CAAP.

Sartre, Jean-Paul. 1976. *Critique of Dialectical Reason*. London: New Left Books.

Sawyer, Suzana. 1997. The 1992 Indian Mobilization in Lowland Ecuador. *Latin American Perspectives* 24, 3: 65–83.

Schölte, Jan A. 2004. Civil Society and Democratically Accountable Global Governance. *Government and Opposition* 39, 2: 211–33.

Scott, Richard. 1995. *Institutions and Organizations*. Thousand Oaks: Sage.

Stepan, Alfred. 1988. *Rethinking Military Politics: Brazil and the Southern Cone*. Princeton: Princeton University Press.

Tamayo, Eduardo. 1996. *Movimientos sociales: la riqueza de la diversidad*. Quito: ALAI.

Tarrow, Sidney G. 1994. *Power in Movement: Social Movements and Contentious Politics*. New York: Cambridge University Press.

Tilly, Charles. 1978. From *Mobilization to Revolution*. New York: McGraw Hill.

———. 1998. Social Movements and (All Sorts of Other Political Interactions. *Theory and Society* 27, 4: 453–80.

Touraine, Alain. 1981. *The Voice and the Eye: An Analysis of Social Movements*. New York: Cambridge University Press.

———. 1988. *Return of the Actor: Social Theory in Postindustrial Society*. Minneapolis: University of Minnesota Press.

Viteri Díaz, Galo. 1998. *Las políticas de ajuste: Ecuador 1982–1996*. Quito: Corporación Editora Nacional.

Walzer, Michael. 2002. Equality and Civil Society. In *Alternative Conceptions of Civil Society*, ed. S. Chambers and W. Kymlicka. Princeton: Princeton University Press. 35–49.

Zamosc, Leon. 1994. Agrarian Protest and the Indian Movement in the Ecuadorian Highlands. *Latin American Research Review* 29, 3: 37–68.

———. 2004. The Indian Movement in Ecuador: From Politics of Influence to Politics of Power. In *The Struggle for Indigenous Rights in Latin America*, ed. N. G. Postero and Zamosc. Brighton: Sussex Academic Press. 131–57.

Zhingri, Patricio. 2002. *Democracia y pueblos indígenas*. Boletín del Instituto Científico de Culturas Indígenas 35.

Chapter 16

Local Democracy and the Transformation of Popular Participation in Chile

Paul W. Posner

From the late sixties until the 1973 overthrow of Salvador Allende, Chile convulsed with grassroots political activity. Rallies, demonstrations, and land seizures were increasingly common in shantytowns surrounding Santiago and other major urban centers. Perhaps unwittingly, the Christian Democratic Party, under President Eduardo Frei Montalva (1964–70), facilitated this intense grassroots mobilization. The centrist party established a corporatist program through municipal government, *Promoción Popular* (Popular Promotion), which it hoped would provide a monopoly of influence over previously marginalized and unincorporated segments of the population. In this manner, the Christian Democratic Party (*Partido Demócrata Cristiano*, PDC) intended to broaden its base of support and establish itself as the ultimate arbiter of Chile's political destiny. Instead, it alienated the right and provoked intense competition from the left.

Like the Christian Democrats, the Socialists and Communists aggressively organized, mobilized, and encouraged previously marginalized segments of the population to demand greater responsiveness and resources from the state. This dynamic intensified under President Salvador Allende, threatening the Chilean state's fiscal and political stability and ultimately contributing to the democratic breakdown of 1973. It was not surprising, therefore, that soon after taking power the military regime initiated forceful steps to suppress local collective action and to break the nexus between political parties and their grassroots constituents. Despite this repression, popular resistance and mass demonstrations emanating from the shantytowns challenged the Pinochet regime's legitimacy and prompted the liberalization process that concluded with the return to democracy in 1990.

Since that time, Chile's economic and political stability have been the envy of Latin America. The country is widely viewed as the region's most successful case of transition from state-led to market-driven economy and from authoritarianism to democracy. Yet now that the difficult hurdle of democratization has been largely overcome throughout the region, Chile and its neighbors are being judged increasingly by a new standard. The preoccupation of policymakers and researchers has shifted from the establishment or stabilization of new democratic regimes to their improvement (Hagopian 1998, 99). One of the essential questions in this regard is how to facilitate organization and political participation for segments of the population who have benefited little, if at all, from the region's recent wave of economic and political reform.

For a variety of reasons, examination of local politics in Chile promises substantial insight into this question. For one, the significant role local politics has played in Chile's recent political history provides a useful basis of comparison by which to assess popular participation and local government under different regime types and development models. In addition, as in many other Latin American countries, radical transformations in Chile's social structure brought about through authoritarian repression, structural reform, and economic liberalization have tended to shift the relative importance within the popular sectors "from the classes to the masses"—that is, from the organized labor movement to the more heterogeneous, less well organized agglomeration of the popular sectors in the shantytowns surrounding major urban centers.[1] For many in the popular sectors, moreover, the institutions of local government provide the primary, if not the only, point of contact with the political system and the state. These conditions make examination of popular sector participation in local government all the more relevant to any qualitative assessment of new democracies such as Chile's.

To what extent, then, does municipal government in Chile facilitate the participation in local politics of groups which historically have been marginalized? The argument presented here provides a disappointing answer to this question. Structural reforms, institutional arrangements, and the dominant mode of political party-base linkage all militate against effective popular sector participation in local democracy. Structural reforms have severely constrained local leaders' resources as well as their policymaking prerogatives, thereby undermining incentives for popular participation. Meanwhile, institutional arrangements limit public officials' accountability to their constituents and severely circumscribe opportunities for citizens' input in decisionmaking, creating a vicious cycle of low levels of popular participation and limited accountability. The parties of the governing center-left coalition, the Concertación, have reinforced this vicious cycle by pursuing a mode of linkage with civil society designed to promote their electoral success with only minimal organization and participation of their grassroots constituents.[2] Such conditions fit well with the desire of elites of both the right and the Concertación to depoliticize civil society in order to preserve macroeconomic and political stability. Yet they leave in doubt the efficacy of popular participation and the strength of local democracy in Chile. To develop this argument, the following section delineates essential conditions for facilitating popular participation in local democracy. Subsequently, the analysis examines popular participation in local government in the precoup, military regime, and posttransition periods.

LOCAL DEMOCRACY AND POPULAR PARTICIPATION

Strong local democracy requires accountability of public officials and institutional access that facilitates the active political participation of local constituencies. If citizens are to hold their local officials accountable and if the officials are to be responsive, then the citizens must participate through established local institutional channels. Institutional arrangements that facilitate accountability and access include direct election of mayors and other public officials and institutional channels that allow citizens to participate in decisionmaking in their jurisdictions.

Direct election of mayors is desirable because indirect elections have "tended to perpetuate the strength of political insiders, who are often more accountable to their party hierarchy than to the public at large" (Peterson 1997, 14). Institutional channels must facilitate participation beyond the mere act of voting, because elections occur infrequently and allow for only limited citizen input or feedback regarding specific local concerns or policy options. Therefore, "direct citizen participation requires that citizens have clear information regarding the municipal budget and service costs and that they participate in actual budget choices" (Peterson 1997, 20). Moreover, there should be formal structures that clearly spell out the roles that citizens and community organizations should play in collaborating with municipal government. In this regard, "advisory committees" are not highly valued by the population. Instead, "effective participation with local government has been organized mostly around public works projects that bring immediate benefits, and around a process that allows participation in budget allocation" (Peterson 1997, 16–17).

The foregoing assessment suggests that popular sector participation in local government is highly sensitive to the prevailing opportunity structure. A wide range of research supports this conclusion. Such research indicates that state structures and institutions, along with the kinds of linkages political parties develop with civil society, are the primary determinants of the level and form of popular sector political participation. Recent comparative work by Portes and Itzigsohn (1997) and Houtzager and Kurtz (2000), as well as earlier studies by Goldrich (1970), Cornelius (1974), Eckstein (1977), and Castells (1983), among others, concludes that popular sector constituencies structure their participation in accordance with the political opportunities and resources that are available to them. Accordingly, structural arrangements that severely limit local officials' revenue base and their ability to shape policies in accordance with constituent demands will, all things being equal, act as disincentives to popular participation. Without the ability to address constituents' demands, local officials will have little incentive to encourage, and constituents little incentive to engage in, political participation and collective action.

Whether parties facilitate popular sector access and participation depends on the kinds of relationships they assume with civil society. Parties that adopt a participatory form of linkage, for example, attempt to serve as an agency through which citizens can themselves participate in government, and tend to be closely linked with organizations in civil society; they have strong grassroots organizations and are internally democratic. In contrast, electoralist parties are primarily concerned with mobilizing an electoral constituency rather than organizing and mobilizing groups in civil society. Their primary objective is to develop the broadest possible base of electoral support, which requires attracting unorganized and often independent voters and developing a multiclass electoral constituency. To the extent that grassroots party structures exist, party leaders typically control them and mobilize party activists only for electoral purposes (such as registering new voters, canvassing, getting out the vote, and so on). Without high levels of autonomous organization in civil society, this form of linkage will not be an effective means for grassroots constituents to promote their interests. Similarly, in parties that adopt clientelistic linkages to civil society, grassroots structures are boss-ruled or nonexistent and therefore do not facilitate effective collective action; such parties act as vehicles for the exchange of votes for favors. Finally, parties that adopt a directive form of linkage act as agents of political education or coercion. Such parties attempt to maintain control over their constituents (Lawson 1988, 16–17). They typically have strong roots in social organizations (labor unions, peasant associations, urban neighborhood organizations, and so on), but their work with these groups is an extension of party organizing and reflects an effort to build social bases for the party's political project rather than for the purpose of strengthening civil society in its own right (Roberts 1998, 75).

As the following analysis demonstrates, center and left parties in Chile have adapted their mode of party-base linkage in accordance with changing political and structural conditions and related changes in their agendas and their perceptions of democracy. Under state-led development before the 1973 coup, center and left parties were driven by the desire to control the state and its resources in order to realize their distinct ideological objectives. To achieve those objectives, they pursued primarily directive and clientelistic linkages with constituents in the local political arena. By the mid- to late 1980s, however, conditions had changed dramatically. State resources on which to build and maintain grassroots constituencies had been severely curtailed, and the left's primary base of support, the labor movement, had been decimated. Most parties of the center and left, moreover, had concluded that their ideological zeal and inflexibility had contributed to the collapse of democracy. Their new focus became the achievement of elite consensus and the establishment of an electoral democracy in which the market, not the state, predominated and parties mobilized constituents to win elections rather than to transform society or to promote participation.

This strategy, and the structural and institutional reforms that have supported it, has served to perpetuate the military regime's project of depoliticizing civil society in order to maintain political and macroeconomic stability. Yet it has done little to facilitate the participation and collective action of those segments of society that, after years of authoritarian repression and radical economic reform, are most in need of political representation. Comparison of contemporary local politics in Chile with local politics during the precoup and military regime eras substantiates this conclusion.

LOCAL GOVERNMENT AND POPULAR PARTICIPATION DURING THE PRECOUP PERIOD

From the 1940s until the 1973 military coup, a number of forces interacted to expand popular participation in Chilean local government. Unfortunately, the same forces that propelled increased popular participation also provoked political and fiscal instability and contributed to the collapse of democracy. These forces were related to Chile's state-led development model and to the prevailing form of party competition and party-base linkage.

Consistent with the logic of state-led development, fiscal resources in the Chilean state were increasingly centralized. As a result, the fiscal dependence of local governments and the fiscal pressure on the central government intensified. The manner in which increasing party competition and ideological polarization expressed themselves exacerbated these fiscal pressures. Driven by the desire to realize their distinct ideological objectives, center and left parties (primarily the Christian Democratic, Socialist, and Communist parties) competed for political dominance through both clientelistic and directive linkages, particularly with previously politically excluded segments of the population, such as urban shantytown dwellers.

Through clientelistic ties, local leaders exchanged votes they could deliver on behalf of congressional members for patronage these national politicians could distribute through party networks. Under directive linkage, "political action consisted of organizing a social base in order to bind it to party structures and thus exert pressure on the state, at times demanding fulfillment of claims and at other times seeking to take control of the state itself" (Garretón 1989a, 12). On one hand, party efforts at cooptation either treated the popular sectors as political pawns in the ideological competition. On the other, it made the parties victims of their own strategies by unleashing popular demands they could not satisfy and popular protests they could not contain. Ultimately, increasing popular sector political activity and demands threatened the economic privileges of conservative elements in Chilean society, who consequently allied themselves with the armed forces to carry out a military coup. A brief historical overview will clarify these interrelationships and their repercussions.

Since the 1940s, the center and left political parties that dominated the Chilean state had resisted attempts by oligarchic elements in the provinces to decentralize resources or political power (Cleaves 1969, 10). As a result, power, and the responsibility for addressing social and political demands, was increasingly concentrated in the hands of the central government. In order to meet the increased obligations that centralization brought, the central government routinely channeled funds collected from municipalities to the *Tesorería General* (General Treasury) and delayed repayment of its debt to local governments for long periods. Thus the percentage of state funds allocated to the municipalities steadily declined after World War II, while the lion's share of local budgets, instead of being devoted to social investment, was consumed by basic operating expenses (Cleaves 1969, 25–26; Valenzuela 1977, 52). The growing disparity between local needs and local governments' ability to meet them forced local leaders to rely on their political and bureaucratic contacts at the national level to gain access to scarce resources. Linkages between local officials and their national political party brokers therefore provided key channels for mediating local political interests. Local political leaders extracted resources from the central government through their contacts with these national political brokers (Valenzuela 1977, 154–56). In return, local leaders turned out the vote for congressional representatives, who delivered patronage through party networks. Particularly in the emerging urban shantytowns, center and left parties complemented these essentially clientelistic practices by operating in a more ideological and collective fashion (Valenzuela 1977, 161). They organized and controlled squatter settlements, helping residents place resource demands directly on the state (Castells 1983, 207).

Although these modes of interest mediation gave the central government and the political parties that controlled it considerable control over local politics, they also placed enormous political and fiscal pressures on the Chilean state. This pressure, and the popular sector mobilization that helped to fuel it, increased exponentially with the rise of the PDC in the 1950s. Unlike the previously dominant centrist party, the Radicals, the PDC was programmatic and highly ideological; it was much more interested in pursuing its own agenda than in finding compromise positions between extremes on the left and the right (Scully 1992, 11). Thus, ideological division and party competition, already a significant feature of the Chilean political system, increased substantially with the PDC's ascendance.

At the local level, such ideological polarization and competition were the impetus behind reforms that the Frei government instituted in 1968. Frei's program of *Promoción Popular* involved, among other things, the establishment of *juntas de vecinos*, or neighborhood associations, which were to form a network of community organizations coordinated at the national level by a *Consejería de la Promoción Popular* (Council of Popular Promotion). In establishing this corporatist institutional framework, the PDC hoped to increase dramatically its political support, which would, in turn, facilitate the realization of its ideological project. The PDC's corporatist reform measures failed, however, primarily because the legal sanctioning of the *juntas* greatly intensified local political participation and demandmaking beyond a level the central government had the capacity to satisfy (Portes and Walton 1981, 125–26). The various parties and factions of the center and left fueled this demandmaking from below through their competitive efforts to organize and mobilize rural peasants and urban shantytown dwellers, previously dormant segments of the popular sectors (Castells 1983, 207).[3]

Thus the inauguration of *Promoción Popular* helped unleash material demands from sectors of Chilean society that had never before played an active role in politics. The increase in land seizures—8 in 1968, 73 in 1969, and 220 in 1970—exemplified this upsurge in material demands at the local level (figures are taken from Castells 1983, 200; and Stallings 1978, 115). It also underscored the government's inability to satisfy popular demands—or to assuage the business community's concerns about the increasing spread of leftist radicalism. Under these circumstances, the Chilean right had little reason to lend its electoral support to the Christian Democrats, as it had done in 1964. This condition made it possible for Allende's leftist *Unidad Popular* (Popular Unity) coalition to win the 1970 presidential election.

With Allende's ascension to power, the polarizing dynamics put in play under the Frei administration continued unabated. In an effort to respond to popular demands, the

Popular Unity government increased fiscal spending by more than 70 percent (Ascher 1984, 243). Under such circumstances, inflationary pressures accelerated, and Allende's already meager support from the business community evaporated. As the newly mobilized segments of the popular sectors joined organized labor to press for greater concessions, business and other right-wing elements sought to derail the socialist government. Such political polarization precipitated the 1975 military coup.

LOCAL GOVERNMENT AND POPULAR PARTICIPATION UNDER THE MILITARY REGIME

Once the Chilean military had toppled the Allende government, it embarked on a radical overhaul of the Chilean state, including a fundamental restructuring of local government. The objective of the military regime's state reform project was to guarantee the order and political stability needed to carry out neoliberal economic restructuring. To achieve this goal required the political, economic, and social exclusion of the previously mobilized popular masses (Garretón 1989a, 81–83). Thus the military regime's decentralization reforms were designed to limit the democratic freedoms and demandmaking capacity of the popular sectors in order to protect the fiscal stability of the Chilean state and the macroeconomic performance of the Chilean economy. As such, decentralization under the military regime transferred significant administrative responsibilities to lower levels of government while further centralizing political power and control over resources. From a system of governance that facilitated the representation of local interests at the national level (Valenzuela 1977), the military regime sought to transform the Chilean political system into an institutional vehicle for promoting the interests of the national government at the local level (Marcel 1994, 104).

Almost as soon as it assumed power, the military regime took steps to achieve its objective. On September 25, 1973, just 14 days after its violent overthrow of President Allende, the military regime enacted Ley 25, which mandated that the municipal councils and their democratically elected representatives cease their functions and established a mayor designated by the military junta as the sole political authority in each municipality. In place of the municipal councils, the military regime established the *Consejos de Desarrollo Comunal y Social* (CODECOS, Communal Social Development Councils) to advise mayors on issues of concern to their communities. The regime attempted to portray the CODECOS as legitimate institutions for popular participation. Yet with members appointed by the central government and with no decisionmaking authority, there appeared to be no legitimate basis for this claim (Pozo 1981, 29, 1986, 21).

In conjunction with these reforms, the military government forced the resignation of all community leaders and designated their replacements, outlawed Marxist political parties, and prohibited unions, trade associations (*gremios*), and public administration organizations from participating in the CODECOS. To prevent the autonomous action of community organizations, the Interior Ministry mandated that such organizations must receive prior governmental permission before holding meetings (Pozo 1981, 27–30, 1986, 15–21; Gallardo 1989, 22–25). Consequently, the authoritarian regime's program of administrative decentralization and limited "democratic participation," coupled with armed repression, enabled it to subvert the brokerage and directive roles played historically by Chilean political parties. The regime destroyed the institutional nexus through which parties could represent the interests of their constituents before the state.

The military regime did not stop there. It reorganized the provision of social welfare services in a manner that shifted fiscal responsibility onto municipal governments at the

same time that it severely limited their decisionmaking and revenue-generating autonomy. The dictatorship's neoliberal social welfare scheme neutralized the significance
of political participation characteristic of the previous welfare system, in which social
policy originated in response to citizens' demands mediated through the party system.
Now the design and implementation of social policy would be handled by government
technocrats insulated from the pressures of popular demands, the intended result being
the depoliticization of social policy.[4]

The military regime attempted to justify its policy of municipalization on the grounds
that it would increase administrative efficiency and augment opportunities for constituent populations to participate in the shaping of policies directly affecting them. Yet
the institutional arrangements the military regime established for popular participation
were patently undemocratic. The regime consulted none of the relevant populations on
whose behalf it allegedly designed and implemented social policies. Moreover, its claims
concerning the gains in administrative and economic efficiency to be achieved through
municipalization were contradicted by the objective outcomes of such reforms. Indeed,
instead of improving economic efficiency, the transfer of responsibility to municipal
governments for the provision of education and health care generated municipal deficits
(Raczynski 1994, 58).

The causes and consequences of such deficits were similar for both educational and
health care reforms. In each case, municipal deficits were precipitated by two factors:
the privatization of services, which allowed the diversion of substantial resources away
from the public sector, and the central government's setting of fee-for-service payments
(that is, conditional transfer payments) significantly below the rate of inflation (Castañeda
1992, 20). The regime's policy of allowing private schools to compete for students, and
therefore for funds typically allocated to public schools, only exacerbated the fiscal
problems confronted by the municipal school systems. The increase in numbers of students attending private schools, coupled with a sizable decrease in overall government
expenditures, resulted in a significant decrease in funds for public education.[5] Similarly,
the creation of private alternatives to services previously provided almost exclusively
by the public sector produced a demonstrable decline in the public health care sector's
revenues and expenditures (Raczynski 1994, 69).

In general, instead of granting local governments greater freedom to borrow funds
or collect revenues to meet their increased fiscal obligations, the dictatorship insisted on
increasing their dependence on funds transferred from the central government through
the *Fondo Comunal Municipal* (Municipal Common Fund). This was evident in its
municipal tax policy. This policy prevented municipal governments from borrowing
funds to meet their fiscal needs.[6] Instead, they were expected to derive their operating
revenues from vehicle and property taxes, taxes on productive and business activities,
and user fees for municipal services (Ley Orgánica Constitucional de Municipalidades,
Artículos 11, 12; Dockendorf 1990, 188). Because under this system tax rates were (and
continue to be) set by the central government, municipal governments had limited ability
to structure revenue collections in accordance with local needs (Marcel 1994, 107, 108).

Thus the Pinochet regime very effectively restructured government in Chile in a
manner that shifted the fiscal burden from the national to the local level, and thereby
protected the national budget and economy from inflationary pressures generated from
below. It achieved this objective first by severing the institutional linkage between political parties and grassroots constituents, and second by making local officials accountable
to regime leaders rather than to the constituents residing in their municipalities. Accordingly, groups organized at the local level lost the demandmaking capacity that they had
used so effectively before the democratic breakdown. Moreover, even if local leaders

wanted to be more responsive to the needs and concerns of the citizens over whom they ruled, they had virtually no autonomy to generate revenue or to design or implement policy, given the restrictive fiscal and administrative reforms imposed by the dictatorship.

Many *pobladores* reacted to the economic, political, and social exclusion the military regime's policies imposed on them by organizing in the shantytowns to promote and protect their interests. Ironically, the military regime's political repression and constriction of resources and local institutional channels for demandmaking provided the impetus for the emergence of a plethora of popular sector groups. When the regime dismantled the populist state and banned political parties, these groups—community soup kitchens, self-defense organizations, youth and religious groups, among many others—developed in isolation from traditional forms of state and party control. They played a key role in the mass mobilizations and public protests that, from May 1983 through July 1986, put increasing pressure on Pinochet to loosen his authoritarian grip. They also provided fertile opportunities for the many intermediate and lower-level party leaders who went into hiding in the shantytowns to develop direct ties to the *pobladores*. Yet once the popular protests had created sufficient space in civil society for party elites to resurface, these elites reasserted their dominance over the popular sectors and took control of the opposition movement.

Ultimately, the reemergent party elites transformed the popular struggle from one of mass mobilization and violent opposition to electoral contestation. Several reasons lay behind this fundamental shift in strategy. First, though many (if not most) shantytown dwellers believed that Pinochet could be forcibly ousted from power, party leaders viewed such a victory as implausible, as evidenced by the military regime's ability to withstand and contain popular resistance. Accordingly, they began to contemplate a negotiated return to democracy. Some party leaders, however, were quicker than others to accept, and therefore adapt to, the new strategic calculus a negotiated transition implied. The Christian Democratic leadership, afraid that continued violent protests would alienate its primary base of support among the middle class, was quickest to make the switch from mass opposition to elite negotiation. Similarly, the Socialist Party faction with the strongest ties to the middle class (led by Ricardo Nuñez, hence referred to as the PS-Nuñez) had similar concerns. It recognized that with the military regime's decimation of the labor movement, the party needed to increase its middle-class support in order to continue as a viable political force. With these considerations in mind, it was quick to realize that the leftist party that first established an alliance with the PDC would have the best opportunity to shape the terms of the transition. The opposing Socialist Party faction, the PS-Almeyda (led by former Allende foreign minister Clodomiro Almeyda), had much deeper roots in the shantytowns than did the PS-Nuñez and therefore was slower to abandon its emphasis on popular resistance. (see Roberts 1998; Walker 1990 for a more detailed account of this history.)

Eventually, however, the PS-Almeyda accepted the need to join the alliance led by the PDC, called the *Alianza Demócrata* (Democratic Alliance, AD, precursor to the present Concertación), if only to prevent its own political irrelevance. The PS-Almeyda's abandonment of the popular struggle left the Communist Party, the party most deeply entrenched in the shantytowns and most strongly committed to popular insurrection, isolated and without allies. Though the PC eventually abandoned the *via armada* and supported an electoral exit from authoritarianism, it never overcame its political isolation. Thus, with the PS-Almeyda joining and the PC excluded from the dominant AD, those political elements most strongly committed to promoting popular sector organization and participation were destined to have virtually no influence in shaping the terms of the transition.

This lack of influence would persist through the transition and would be reinforced by the "renovation" of the dominant parties that composed the AD. Between the Chilean military's overthrow of the Popular Unity government and when the democratic opposition entered transition negotiations with the military, the elites and parties leading the opposition movement underwent a process of political renovation (Roberts 1998; Walker 1990). This renovation facilitated a convergence between the constraints that the military regime wished to impose on Chile's new democracy and the steps the democratic opposition was willing to take to ensure the stability of the new regime.

The leaders of the democratic opposition parties reasoned that if ideological polarization and overpoliticization of the state and civil society had precipitated the breakdown of Chilean democracy, then only depoliticization could assure future democratic stability. Practically speaking, this meant significantly increasing the role of the market and proportionally decreasing the state's role in running the economy and organizing civil society. It also meant reducing the role of political parties in organizing and mobilizing groups in civil society. Consequently, the renovated democratic opposition demobilized its mass opposition movement and accepted the military regime's neoliberal economic model and 1980 Constitution, along with the demobilization of its mass opposition movement, as preconditions to democratization.[7] Party leaders dissolved the umbrella organizations they had constructed to shape the disparate opposition groups in the shantytowns into a broad-based, unified opposition. Without the parties' overarching political leadership, these groups atomized and lost their ability to influence the democratic transition (Oxhorn 1995, 258). Under these conditions, the Concertación shifted the opposition's focus to electoral contestation, orchestrated the defeat of Pinochet in the 1988 plebiscite, and restored civilian rule under the leadership of Christian Democratic president Patricio Aylwin in 1990.

Local Government and Popular Participation after Redemocratization

The opposition's acceptance both of the military regime's preconditions and its commitment to depoliticizing civil society determined that many of the essential elements which defined local government under the dictatorship would remain intact after the democratic transition. It also signaled that once in power, the Concertación would take steps to ensure elite control over local politics. Thus, while redemocratization has brought important reforms of municipal government, significant impediments to effective accountability and local political participation persist.

To be sure, residents of municipalities no longer live under the constant threat of authoritarian repression and can once again elect their local officials. Yet they do not enjoy the connection or influence with political parties that they possessed before the coup or even during the dictatorship.[8] Instead, the parties of the center and left have distanced themselves from their followers at the base.[9] Moreover, local institutional arrangements do not hold leaders fully accountable to their constituents or give citizens a meaningful voice in municipal decisionmaking and budgeting. The administrative and financing structures of local government remain essentially the same as they were under the dictatorship, giving local leaders little discretionary control over resources or policy design and implementation. Therefore, municipal residents have little incentive to participate in local government, levels of participation are quite low, and local democracy remains weak. At the same time, municipal governments in Chile continue to bear a fiscal burden that generally exceeds their capacity to generate revenue, while the national government puts significant restrictions on transfer payments and thereby can maintain limits on local-level fiscal demands and expenditures.[10]

Examination of the institutional, fiscal, and administrative structures of local government in Chile substantiates this argument. With respect to institutional structures, while Chilean municipal government has made important strides toward greater democratic accountability in recent years significant constraints remain. For example, existing municipal electoral arrangements do not allow the direct election of municipal council members (*concejales*). Instead, municipal election outcomes are largely determined by electoral pacts and subpacts among allied political parties, an arrangement that means, in many instances, that the candidates receiving the highest number of votes are not the same candidates who actually assume office.[11] In fact, on average, 43 percent of council members elected in metropolitan Santiago in 1996 received a lower percentage of the vote than the highest vote getters among losing candidates (Posner 1999, 76–77).

The pact arrangements that characterize the municipal electoral system, moreover, diminish its proportionality. This is because only parties or candidates who have pacted with either the major right-wing pact (which includes the RN and the UDI) or the center-left Concertación (which includes the PDC, PPD, PS, and PRSD) have a reasonable chance of winning a significant number of municipal council seats. Results from the 2004 municipal elections illustrate this point well. Out of a total of 2,144 seats, these two pacts won 2,012. Three other pacts along with a number of independent candidates gained the remaining 132 seats. The poor showing by the pact headed by the PC illustrates another significant consequence of this electoral system. Without the benefit of an alliance with the PS, which it enjoyed before the coup, the PC won only 4 mayoralty and 38 council seats in the entire country. The comparable numbers for the PS were 45 and 255 (see table 1 for these data).

Table 1. Municipal Election Results 1996, 2000, and 2004

Electoral Pact	Mayors 1996	Mayors 2000	Mayors 2004	Council Members 1996	Council Members 2000	Council Members 2004
CONCERTACIÓN PACT						
PDC	102	85	99	456	424	456
PRSD	16	15	12	173	102	119
PPD	34	28	34	201	215	231
PS	38	32	45	171	207	255
INDEPENDENT	7	9	13	53	87	65
TOTAL	197	169	203	1054	1036	1126
ALLIANCE FOR CHILE PACT						
RN	67	72	38	288	292	386
UDI	5	45	51	35	184	404
INDEPENDENT	60	48	15	315	208	96
TOTAL	132	165	104	638	684	886
LEFT PACT						
PC	2	1	4	28	21	38
PH	0		0			27
INDEPENDENT	0	0		5	2	24
TOTAL	2		4			89

Note: The remaining seats were divided among several pacts and independent candidates.
Source: República de Chile, Servicio Electoral 1997, 2001 and Gobierno de Chile, Ministerio Interior, Sitio Histórico Electoral (http://www.eleciones.gov.cl).

Thus Chile's municipal electoral system, in theory proportionally representative, in practice functions like a majoritarian or plurality system in that it favors larger parties or pacts. As a result, the right and center-left pacts have managed to thwart challenges to their dominance and to maintain their elitist manner of governing.

Recent municipal electoral reforms, which mandate the direct election of mayors and allow their reelection, provide an important, though only partial, antidote to this problem. In its original form, the Ley Orgánica Constitucional de Municipalidades did not allow the direct election of mayors. Instead, it stipulated that the municipal council candidate that received the greatest number of votes and who also received at least 35 percent of the vote would become mayor. However, due to the large number of parties that typically field candidates[12] and because even the party with the largest following, the PDC, can claim on average the allegiance of less than 20 percent of the electorate, it was not uncommon for no candidate to reach the 35 percent threshold to become mayor. Under the electoral arrangement in operation before the 2004 municipal elections, when no candidate received the necessary quota of votes to become mayor, the municipal council selected the mayor from among its members.[13] Naturally, the council members who united in electoral pacts negotiated to elect one of their own. Under these circumstances, mayors—like the municipal council members who elected them—were beholden to party elites as much as or more than they were to the constituents of their communities.

By establishing the direct election of mayors and by allowing for reelection, Ley 19.737 helps to diminish the elitist nature of municipal electoral arrangements and to increase the accountability of local elected officials to their constituents. However, as table 2 illustrates, party elites in all the major parties maintain a significant degree of control over candidate selection for municipal elections, thereby limiting the positive impact of this reform in terms of democratic accountability.[14]

The institutional channels established to allow grassroots constituents input on local policy issues, the CESCO (Community Economic and Social Councils) and the *juntas de vecinos*, are equally unrepresentative. These institutions are strictly advisory in nature and therefore largely ineffective at encouraging popular participation or transmitting community demands to local leaders. For example, as an advisory board to the mayor, the CESCO (like its precursor under the military regime, the CODECO) has no power to ensure mayoral accountability; it cannot make binding resolutions, create or implement policy, or impose sanctions. Its sole function is to offer advice on community concerns, which the mayor is free to heed or ignore. As one leader and CESCO member in the municipality of La Granja in metropolitan Santiago observed,

> CESCO is merely a consultative body with no real power. Those of us who belong to CESCO are like an umbrella that protects the mayor. He asks our opinion and we can say either yes or no to his projects, but that's it. . . . A law needs to be passed to make this organization more pluralistic (Robles 2001).

Grassroots leaders are not alone in holding this critical view of the CESCO. Indeed, *concejales* (council members) from the three primary municipalities in metropolitan Santiago investigated in this study all share the view that these community councils function poorly as representative institutions.[15] For example, Carmen Gloria Allende, Socialist *concejal* in the Santiago municipality of Huechuraba, noted that because of extremely low community participation in the neighborhood associations, from which a large percentage of CESCO representatives are elected, the CESCO themselves are unrepresentative of popular interests.

Table 2. Political Parties' Methods of Selecting Candidates—Municipal Elections[16]

Political Party	Method of Candidate Selection
Partido Comunista—PC	Cells produce a list of recommended candidates which they present to the 80 member Central Committee. The Central Committee makes the final selection of candidates.
Partido Socialista—PS	Every 4 years the party's Central Council establishes the criteria necessary to become a candidate. Party members who meet these criteria compete in preelections in the municipalities where they want to run for office. If the aspiring candidates do not meet the party's criteria, party leaders in the community submit a proposed list of candidates to the 90 member Central Committee, which then makes the final selection.
Partido Por Democracia —PPD	The party holds a municipal level vote to choose pre-candidates. Local leaders order the list of pre-candidates according to their respective vote percentages and sends the list to the National Council (*Consejo Nacional*). The Council then picks the candidates it wants, irrespective of the order of the list sent by the community.
Partido Demócrata Cristiano—PDC	Any party member in good standing is eligible to be considered as a candidate. The list of interested candidates is passed on to a selection committee, made up of ex-party presidents and party luminaries, which picks the local government candidates.
Renovación Nacional—RN	Interested party members in good standing present themselves to the party. The General Council (*Consejo General*) chooses those candidates which it feels have the best possibility of winning.
Unión Demócrata Independiente—UDI	Party members interested in being candidates for office in municipal government present themselves to the local party office. In turn, this office sends the names of all prospective candidates to the National Directive (*Directiva Nacional*), which is comprised of 9 people (1 president, 5 vice-presidents, 1 secretary general, 1 treasurer, and 1 pro secretary). The directive chooses the candidates.

This organization [CESCO] functions as an advisory board. You can either take or ignore what CESCO says. People are really skeptical about politicians. This can be illustrated by the fact that only one hundred neighbors from the *juntas de vecinos* are registered. [Being formally registered with the *juntas* entitles them to vote for members of the CESCO.] And they register because they feel that they have to do it. So, I have the impression that the communal organizations are not well represented by CESCO. With municipal councils, people are legally compelled to vote. But this is not the case with CESCO. Thus, the leaders are not chosen by the *pobladores* (Allende 2001).

For many grassroots leaders, the low levels of membership and citizen participation in the neighborhood associations have common origins in the institutional legacy of the dictatorship. As grassroots leaders involved with the neighborhood associations were quick to point out, the existing law governing neighborhood associations is the same law implemented by the military regime. To ensure that the neighborhood associations would not recapture their former political power when democracy was restored, the military government instituted its new *Ley de Junta de Vecinos* on December 30, 1989, just months before President Aylwin took office.

With the military's law still in force, it is widely perceived among grassroots leaders that the neighborhood associations have not regained the legitimacy and influence they held before the military takeover. The original law governing *juntas de vecinos*, Ley 16.880, passed on August 7, 1968, granted the neighborhood associations substantial powers and responsibilities. These included

> the preparation of both an annual plan for urban betterment and a budget for the execution of the plan . . . the organization, promotion, and participation in the formation of cooperatives, especially consumer goods, handicrafts, and housing . . . with the object of bettering the socioeconomic conditions of the inhabitants of the respective neighborhood units . . . to collaborate in the control of prices, as well as the distribution and sale of necessities . . . ; to contribute to the removal of trash, the management of collective transit, to render an opinion before granting licenses for the sale of alcoholic beverages . . . ; to collaborate in the protection of persons and property in the neighborhood . . . ; to assets in finding work for the unemployed. . . . (Gonzáles Moya 1993, 7–8).

In contrast, the military government's 1989 law, Ley 18.899, says virtually nothing in regard to the objectives and functions of the neighborhood associations or community organizations and, in essence, grants them no substantive powers or responsibilities.

In addition, the military regime's neighborhood association law encourages the formation of several neighborhood associations within the boundaries of one territorial unit, a provision which reinforces partisan divisions and limits popular unity. Given these circumstances, it is not surprising that grassroots leaders characterize the neighborhood associations as lacking resources and decisionmaking authority and incapable of overcoming factional divisions or motivating *pobladores* to participate, Indeed, the grassroots leaders interviewed for this study estimated that one percent or less of their respective communities' populations participate in the neighborhood associations.[17] When compared with the estimated 15 to 20 percent of *pobladores* who actively participated in local organization and mobilization during the dictatorship, and an even higher percentage who participated in the neighborhood associations and other popular organizations before the coup, these figures appear abysmally low.[18]

The vast majority of the grassroots leaders interviewed attributed such low levels of popular participation to the Concertación leaders' failure to give the juntas more resources and greater capacity to encourage grassroots unity, As one social leader summarized it,

> After the transition, the juntas de vecinos did not organize. The people of the *población* did not see them as presenting solutions to their problems, The communities have no money and the political leaders are not preoccupied with the people's concerns, The connection with people at the base does not exist—the *juntas de vecinos* do not represent anyone! This is part of the overall process of depoliticization and disarticulation, The lenders of the Concertación realized that the powerful popular organizations that helped to oust Pinochet could be used against them. So they tried to weaken and disarticulate the popular organizations. They come to the *poblaciones* only when they need votes (Molina 2001).

The frustration and cynicism expressed in such comments reflect grassroots leaders' disenchantment with both the institutions of municipal government and the political parties that control them. The basis of this disenchantment lies in the renovation of parties historically most closely associated with the popular sectors in Chile, particularly the PS and the PDC, as well as the more recently established (1987) center-left PPD. In theory, this renovated, *laissez-faire* posture of political parties toward civil society was to prevent the kind of ideologically charged, politically divisive manipulation of the popular sectors that party leaders understood as a primary cause of the 1973 democratic breakdown. It would, in the words of former Socialist Party secretary-general and labor minister Jorge Arrate, make "politics less elitist and gradually more popular" (Arrate and Hidalgo 1989, 107). In practice, however, this new posture only widened the breach between grassroots activists and party elites that evolved over the course of Chile's transition to democracy.

This breach has persisted since the transition, perpetuated partly as a result of the military regime's binomial electoral system. According to this system, a party or political pact is guaranteed a seat in any electoral district in which it receives a minimum of 33.4 percent of the vote. This percentage unduly rewards second-place finishers and, not coincidentally, is roughly equivalent to the percentage received by the Chilean right. With the undue advantage this arrangement gives to the right, the center and left have been encouraged to subordinate their programmatic differences and maintain their electoral alliance, the Concertación, to prevent an even greater overrepresentation of the right. Thus, by imposing a bipolar pattern of competition on parties that historically have divided themselves according to three ideological blocs—right, center, and left—the binomial electoral regime seriously distorts the extent to which societal interests are fairly represented in the political arena (Munck and Bosworth 1998, 486–87). In short, the electoral regime has increased the incentives for party cooperation and alliances, reduced the incentives for competition, and reinforced the tendency already prominent among the center-left parties of the Concertación to deemphasize ideological differences and focus on elite consensus to the exclusion of popular sector input.

Consequently, the posttransition period has witnessed a significant decline in party identification among the Chilean electorate.[19] Apathy has increased among grassroots leaders and their followers. (For an account of the nature and extent of this apathy, see Posner 1999.) Municipal elections have seen significant voting abstention and nullification.[20] One of the primary causes behind these negative trends appears to be the public's perception that local leaders are not in touch with their communities. When asked in a 1996 *Centros de Estudios Públicos* survey to identify the primary problem affecting their communities, low- and middle-income respondents most frequently named local politicians' "lack of contact with the community" (CEP 1996, 32).[21] More recent survey data suggest that this feeling of disenchantment with political parties is widespread among the Chilean public. In a 2002 CERC survey, for example, 92 percent of respondents agreed with the statement that "the majority of politicians remember the people ONLY during elections after which they forget them" (CERC 2002:6; author's translation).

The detachment of center-left parties from their constituencies at the municipal level has created a space for political influence which the far-right UDI, the party most closely linked with the Pinochet legacy, has effectively exploited. The rise in the UDI's influence in local government is evident in recent electoral trends. While the UDI was only able to elect 5 mayors and 35 council members in 1996, by 2004 it had elected 51 mayors and 404 council members (see table 1).When asked to explain this relative shift in local government influence, representatives from the dominant parties of the Concertación acknowledged their parties' failure to get sufficiently involved in building and maintaining grassroots constituencies. Most striking in this regard was the admission by Luciano Valle, National secretary of Social Organization of the Chilean Socialist Party, that the party currently has no formal organization devoted to popular sector political education or organizing and has essentially abandoned its tradition of grassroots organizing (Valle 2001). However, both party leaders and grassroots activists from the Concertación are quick to identify other significant factors in the local rightward shift: the UDI's superior resources and clientelistic practices. In this regard, the comments of Anastasio Castillo, a community leader affiliated with the PDC in Huechuraba, were typical: "People here are poor. The UDI takes advantage of them to gain political support by distributing food . . . and money . . . to win votes" (Castillo 2001).

Alfredo Galdames, national director of UDI's project to build support among *pobladores* and chief of staff for UDI mayor Pilar Urrutia in the municipality of Conchali, cast the situation in a different light. He ascribed the Concertación's declining support and the lack of local participation to the center-left alliance's focus on politics rather than on good management and solutions to local problems, a criticism not unlike those lodged by the Concertación's own grassroots constituents.

Conversely, he attributes the UDI's success to its leaders' effective management, as well as their high ethical standards. When asked to identify the differences between the manner in which leftists have governed and the UDI's governing style, he noted the party's willingness to draw on private sector assistance. This willingness was evidenced in his discussion of local education. "The schools in this community, the preparation of the teachers and the students, is very poor. We cannot compete with the private schools—the state does not have sufficient resources. So we seek assistance from the private sector. We have very good relations with the business community here" (Galdames 2001).[22]

To illustrate how this strategy has been effective, Galdames noted that under Mayor Urrutia the local government had succeeded in acquiring funds to establish and maintain a school for young pregnant girls. He was particularly proud that the mayor had recently signed an agreement in New York for an annual twenty-thousand-dollar grant from the conservative Manhattan Institute to help operate the school and to evaluate its success. He also noted the local government's success in securing private sector support for the construction of low-cost housing in the community (Galdames 2001). UDI grassroots supporters reinforce this image of the party drawing on private resources with much more modest examples, such as the provision of food or resources for local organizations, such as sports clubs and youth groups.

These examples suggest not that the UDI is alone in its use of traditional patronage strategies but that the party has superior access to private sector resources, which enable it to employ such strategies with greater effect. The party's success in utilizing private sector resources to cultivate popular sector support provides vindication for the architects of Chile's neoliberal revolution, particularly Jaime Guzmán, the UDI's founder and principal author of the military regime's 1980 Constitution. One of the fundamental principles Guzmán and his fellow neoliberal architects espoused, and which is deeply embedded in the 1980 Constitution, is the notion of the subsidiary role of the state. Instead of trying to supplant or control the market, as was the case under import substitution industrialization (ISI), proponents of neoliberalism asserted that the state should play a subordinate and supportive role in relation to the market. The scaling back of the state that followed from this ideological precept cut off the lifeblood of center and left parties, which had depended on access to state resources to build and mobilize their constituencies. The Concertación's abandonment of traditional mobilization strategies and commitment to preserve the primacy of the market has reinforced the impact of these neoliberal reforms. As a result, local politicians who lack outside support for their community projects are hamstrung in a number of ways.

First, taxes are both set and collected by the central government (Yáñez and Letelier 1995, 143). Consequently, local governments have a severely limited capacity to structure taxes, including the creation of new taxes or the setting of tax rates, in line with local needs (154). Because the Treasury Department sends the property taxes it collects to the municipalities, moreover, it has no incentive to deal rapidly with delinquent taxpayers, and consequently local governments lose significant amounts of money (169).[23] second, the central government's strategy for helping municipalities deal with their fiscal short-falls—namely, financial transfers—puts substantial constraints on how municipalities can spend their resources while simultaneously underfunding them (Nickson 1995, 139–40).

The central government's method of funding and regulating education and health care services provided at the municipal level epitomizes each of these problems. Because the fixed rate at which the central government subsidizes local governments for each enrolled student or each clinic visit is insufficient to cover the real cost of providing these services, the municipalities' financial situation has deteriorated. To cover the short-fall caused by inadequate funding from the central government, the municipalities have had to use their own income, thereby reducing the funds they have available for social investment and producing a transfer to the central government (Nickson 1995; Yáñez and Letelier 1995, 149, 154).

Third, while some municipalities might be tempted to borrow to compensate for the central government's insufficient funding or to circumvent its tight regulatory control, statute prohibits them from doing so (Nickson 1995,140; Yáñez and Letelier 1995, 170).[24]

These policies exacerbate the dire fiscal straits of Chile's poor municipalities, constrain the ability of local leaders to respond to constituent needs and concerns, and undermine incentives for popular participation.

CONCLUSIONS

In response to the UDI's ascension and the collapse of their historical monopoly of influence in the shantytowns, the Socialist and the Christian Democratic parties have begun to rethink their relationship with their constituents at the grassroots. Julio Pérez, national secretary of the Christian Democrats' Community and Neighborhood Action Front (formerly the Department of Pobladores), said that the party has begun a new, grassroots effort to rebuild support in the shantytowns and to encourage political partici-pation (Pérez 2001). Similarly, Luciano Valle of the PS confided that although his party has no formal organization devoted to political education or popular organization, there is recognition in the party that strategies need to be developed to encourage popular participation (Valle 2001).

This shift in thinking is no doubt a positive sign for the strengthening of local democ-racy in Chile. In contrast to the PS and the PDC, however, the PPD has no plans to step up its organizational activities in regard to the popular sectors, according to Juan Reyes, the PPD's national secretary for unions (Reyes 2001). Moreover, structural reforms and local institutional arrangements still stand in the way of more meaningful and effective political participation in local government. Institutionally, indirect election of mayors weakens the nexus between constituents and elected leaders; the Community Economic and Social Councils (CESCO) remain unrepresentative and ineffective; and neighborhood associations have little formal power or influence, and therefore very few citizens are motivated to get actively involved in them.

These institutional impediments to strong local democracy in Chile exist in a structural context equally stultifying to local accountability, control, and participation. The mili-tary government implemented decentralizing reforms that increased local governments' responsibilities while seriously constraining their fiscal and policymaking autonomy. The Concertación has essentially maintained those reforms. Thus, while local governments are responsible for administering primary education and health care services, they have virtually no policymaking autonomy in these areas. They are also greatly restricted in their ability to raise revenue and to utilize central government transfer payments. Such reforms enable the central government to maintain its control over local governments while providing local officials little capacity to construct policies or provide resources in response to their constituents' demands or concerns.

Under these circumstances, it is little wonder that disenchantment with local government in Chile is on the rise while local political participation is on the decline. The UDI has been able to take advantage of this disenchantment through its capacity to distribute private sector resources to popular sector clients. If the parties of the Concertación wish to confront this challenge from the right and enhance participation in local government, adopting a more participatory form of linkage with their grassroots constituents may be the answer. Facilitating the organization of grassroots constituents will make them less susceptible to the divisive appeals of clientelism and better able to demand public solutions to common problems. Compelling the state to address community concerns through broad-based popular pressure has the potential to produce more encompassing remedies than appear feasible under the status quo. Reinvigorating the linkage between the popular sectors and their traditional party allies may provide at least a partial antidote to the sweeping social disarticulation that neoliberal reforms and authoritarian repression have produced. In the end, such a radical shift of party-base linkage may both improve electoral outcomes for the Concertación and strengthen Chilean democracy from the ground up.

NOTES

1 I borrow this apt phrase from Garretón 1989b, 274.

2 The members of the center-left Concertación include the Christian Democrats, the Socialists, the Party for Democracy, and the Social Democratic Radical Party.

3 According to Castells, each *campamento* (squatter settlement) was dominated by one political party, which determined the *campamenio's* political direction (1983, 207). Such partisan divisions at the grassroots both reflected and reinforced the ideological polarization among Chile's center and left political parties. (Right-wing parties were equally polarized, if not more so, but were not engaged in grassroots organization at this time.)

4 See Posner 2002 for a detailed discussion of the military regime's social welfare policy reforms and their impact on the popular sectors in terms of the propensity and capacity for collective action.

5 By 1988, fiscal spending devoted to education calculated as a percentage of GDP was 2.73 percent, little more than half the average percentage of GDP devoted to education between 1970 and 1973 (Cox 1989, 6–8). In Santiago, the burden of sacrifice caused by the drop in fiscal expenditure on education appears to have been experienced almost exclusively by the poorer municipalities (Dockendorf 1990, 101).

6 Instead of strictly forbidding municipal borrowing, the statute required a special law to authorize each loan. In the face of such a stringent requirement, only two such borrowing operations were recorded between 1979 and 1994 (Marcel 1994, 111).

7 The democratic opposition accepted the 1980 Constitution not because it shared the military's vision of a restricted or tutelary democracy, but for several strategic reasons. First, recognizing that they could not remove the Pinochet regime from power through force, opposition leaders were obliged to negotiate a transition to democracy on the military regime's terms, which included acceptance of its 1980 Constitution. Second, the democratic opposition wanted to create a new democratic regime that was based on the rule of law. Attempting to transform the political system through existing constitutional principles was an important means of accomplishing this objective, even if the legitimacy of that constitution was questionable. Third, the democratic opposition attempted through negotiations to remove the most egregiously antidemocratic elements of the

1980 Constitution and viewed constitutional reform as part of the process of democratic transition. It therefore saw its acceptance of the military regime's constitution as the beginning, not the end, of the establishment of a new democratic order in Chile. See Ensalaco 1994 for a detailed discussion of constitutional reform in Chile.

8 See Campero 1987; Oxhorn 1995; Roberts 1998; and Schneider 1995 for a description and analysis of party-base relations during the dictatorship.

9 The Chilean Communist Party remains an exception to this rule, but its exclusion from the ruling Concertación and its low level of electoral support substantially weakens the significance of its more aggressive grassroots organizational efforts.

10 Because Chilean municipalities differ significantly in their class composition, this lack of fiscal sufficiency and autonomy weighs most heavily on the Chilean underclass. The Pinochet regime's policies of spatial segregation and its forced relocations of poorer citizens from wealthier neighborhoods greatly exacerbated this tendency (Morales and Rojas 1987; Portes 1989, 21–22).

11 The municipal electoral system implemented after the transition, a modified D'Hondt, is a proportional representation system. Citizens vote for individual candidates belonging to pacts rather than closed party or pact lists. To determine the number of candidates elected by each list, the Tribunal Electoral Regional totals the number of votes cast in favor of each candidate of the same list and uses the sums to determine the electoral quotient according to the formula standard to D'Hondt electoral systems. The electoral quotient is then used to determine the number of seats to which each pact or party is entitled. In the event that a pact has more candidates than council seats, the candidates receiving the highest number of votes in the pact are entitled to the council seat(s) awarded to the pact. See Articles 109 through 114 of the Ley Orgánica Constitucional de Municipalidades for a detailed explanation of these procedures and stipulations (González Moya 1992).

12 There are seven primary political parties—the PDC, PRSD, PPD, PS, PC, RN, and UDI—which typically field candidates in municipal elections as well as a number of smaller parties. In addition, a significant number of independents run for office.

13 See Article 115 of the Ley Orgánica Constitucional de Muncipalidades for a detailed explanation of these stipulations.

14 See Eaton (2004, 227) for discussion of national party leaders' control over candidate selection for subnational elections.

15 I am grateful to Liesl Haas for providing me with this information based on her interviews with party officials.

16 The majority of grassroots leaders were interviewed in La Pincoya, Lo Hermida, and Yungay, three shantytowns in Greater Santiago, which, according to Schneider (1989, 218, 222), demonstrated during the dictatorship respectively high, medium, and low levels of organization and mobilization. These three types of communities provided a comparative basis on which to gauge the change in grassroots organization and mobilization since the democratic transition. Additional grassroots leaders were interviewed in Huechuraba and Santiago. The interviews revealed no significant distinction among the *poblaciones* in the levels of popular participation since that time. Despite their past differences, all these communities can now be characterized as having equally low levels of grassroots involvement in politics.

17 An anecdotal account will illustrate these circumstances. During a meeting of Neighborhood Association number 11 in Santiago on June 14, 2001, I inquired how many potential, as well as actual, members this association had. The group's president informed me that there were 40,000 potential members but only 150 actual members. Eight members were present at the meeting, which, they said, was the norm.

18 For these figures and an excellent historical analysis of popular organization and mobilization in Santiago, see Campero 1987.

19 Between 1993 and 2004, those identifying with the right or center-right of the political spectrum declined from 28 to 21 percent, those identifying with the center declined from 18 to 12 percent, and those identifying with the left or center declined from 37 to 24 percent. During this same period, the number of voters identifying themselves as independents increased from 14 to 36 percent. See Centro de Estudios Públicos (1997) for these data.

20 The combined percentage of null and blank votes along with abstentions was 23.14 percent in 1996 and 20.46 in 2000 (Servicio Electoral República de Chile 1997, 2001). While these numbers may not seem significant in comparison with rates of voter turnout for local elections in the United States, it is important to recognize that voting in municipal elections in Chile is legally mandatory, and failure to do so is punishable by a substantial fine, nearly half the monthly minimum wage.

21 Forty-eight percent of low- and middle-income respondents gave this response. The figure for low-income respondents alone was 54.3 percent. The second most frequent response among low- and middle-income respondents to the question, "What do you think is the primary problem affecting your community?" was "too much bureaucracy." Less than 17 percent of low- and middle-income respondents indicated that too much bureaucracy was the primary problem in their municipalities. Thus local political leaders' failure to maintain contact with their communities was far and away the most significant problem these respondents identified.

22 Of course, the irony that did not occur to Galdames when making these statements is that it was key figures from his own party who, under the military regime, pressed for structural reforms that severely reduced state funding in education, health care, and other social programs on which poor communities like Conchali are so dependent.

23 This is essentially the same fiscal arrangement that existed before the coup, with similar negative repercussions for local government. In the precoup period, however, intense party competition and substantial state involvement in the economy gave local communities significant leverage in translating their demands into resources from the central government. Today, competition among center-left parties and state involvement in the economy have both declined, leaving local communities with significantly diminished capacity for extracting state resources to meet their needs.

24 Chilean local government possesses the lowest borrowing autonomy among the 18 countries evaluated by the Inter-American Development Bank (1997, 176).

REFERENCES

Allende, Carmen Gloria. 2001. Socialist Party council member, Huechuraba municipality, Santiago. Author interview. June 12.

Arrate, Jorge, and Paulo Hidalgo. 1989. *Pasión y razón del socialismo Chileno.* Santiago: Ediciones del Ornitorrinco.

Ascher, William. 1984. *Scheming for the Poor: The Politics of Redistribution in Latin America.* Cambridge: Harvard University Press.

Campero, Guillermo. 1987. *Entre la sobrevivencia y la acción política: las organizaciones de pobladores en Santiago.* Santiago: Ediciones ILET.

Castañeda, Tarsicio. 1992. *Combating Poverty: Innovative Social Reforms in Chile During the 1980s.* San Francisco: ICS Press.

Castells, Manuel. 1983. *The City and the Grassroots: A Cross-Cultural Theory of Urban Social Movements.* Berkeley: University of California Press.

Castillo, Anastasio. 2001. Grassroots community leader, Huechuraba municipality, affiliated with the PDC. Author interview. June 14.

Centro de Estudios Públicos (CEP). 1996. *Percepciones del municipio de hoy: continuidad y cambios.* Documente) de Trabajo no. 251. July. Santiago: CEP.

———. 1997. Estudio nacional de opinión pública 6, tercera serie. Documento de Trabajo 271. August. Santiago: CEP.

Centro de Estudios de la Realidad Contemporánea (CERC). 2002. Informe de prensa sobre temas económicos y políticos. September. Santiago: CEP.

Cleaves, Peter S. 1969. Development Processes in Chilean Local Government. Politics of Modernization series, no. 8. Berkeley: University of California.

Cornelius, Wayne. 1974. Urbanization and Political Demand Making: Political Participation Among the Migrant Poor in Latin American Cities. *American Political Science Review* 68, 3: 1125–46.

Cox, Cristián, and Cecilia Jara. 1989. *Datos básicos para la discusión de políticas en educación,* 1979–1988. Santiago: CIDE/FLACSO.

Dockendorf, Eduardo, ed. 1990. *Santiago dos ciudades: análisis de la estructura socio-económico espacial del Gran Santiago*. Santiago: Centro de Estudios del Desarrollo.

Eaton, Kent. 2004. Designing Subnational Institutions: Regional and Municipal Reforms in Postauthoritarian Chile. *Comparative Political Studies* 37:2, 218–44.

Eckstein, Susan. 1977. *The Poverty of Revolution: The State and the Urban Poor in Mexico*. Princeton: Princeton University Press.

Ensalaco, Mark. 1994. "In with the New, Out with the Old? The Democratising Impact of Constitutional Reform in Chile." *Journal of Latin American Studies* 26: 409–29.

Galdames, Alfredo. 2001. National director of UDI's project to build support among *pobladores*; chief of staff for UDI mayor Pilar Urrutia in Conchali municipality, Santiago. Author interview. June 8.

Gallardo, Bernardo. 1989. De la municipalidad, el autoritarismo y la democracia: una reflexión. Documento de Trabajo no. 423. Santiago: FLACSO.

Garretón, Manuel Antonio. 1989a. *The Chilean Political Process*. Boston: Unwin Hyman.

——. 1989b. Popular Mobilization and the Military Regime in Chile: The Complexities of the Invisible Transition. In *Power and Popular Protest: Latin American Social Movements*, ed. Susan Eckstein. Berkeley: University of California Press. 259–77.

Goldrich, Daniel. 1970. Political Organization and the Politization of the Poblador. *Comparative Political Studies* 3, 2: 176–202.

González Moya, Carlos A., ed. 1992. [1996.] *Ley orgánica constitucional de municipalidades*. Santiago: Editora Jurídica Manuel Montt S.A.

——. 1993. *Ley de juntas de vecinos*. Santiago: Editora Jurídica Manuel Montt S.A.

Hagopian, Frances. 1998. Democracy and Political Representation in Latin America in the 1990s: Pause, Reorganization, or Decline? In *Fault Lines of Democracy in Post-Transition Latin America*, ed. Felipe Agüero and Jeffrey Stark. Coral Gables: North-South Center Press. 99–143.

Houtzager, Peter P., and Marcus J. Kurtz. 2000. The Institutional Roots of Popular Mobilization: State Transformation and Rural Politics in Brazil and Chile, 1960–1995. *Comparative Studies in Society and History* 42, 2: 394–424.

Inter-American Development Bank (IADB). 1997. *Latin America After a Decade of Reforms: Economic and Social Progress in Latin America*. Washington, DC: IADB.

Lawson, Kay. 1988. When Linkage Fails. In *When Parties Fail: Emerging Alternative Organizations*, ed. Lawson and Peter H. Merkl. Princeton: Princeton University Press. 13–38.

Marcel, Mario. 1994. Decentralization and Development. In *En Route to Modern Growth: Latin America in the 1990s*, ed. Gustav Ranis. Washington, DC: IADB.

Molina, Jorge. 2001. Social leader in Población La Pincoya. Author interview. Santiago, June 14.

Morales, Eduardo, and Sergio Rojas. 1987. Relocalización socioespacial de la pobreza, política estatal y presión popular, 1979–85. In *Espacio y poder: los pobladores*, ed. Hernán Pozo. Santiago: FLACSO.

Munck, Gerardo L., and Jeffrey A. Bosworth. 1998. Parties and Democracy in Post-Pinochet Chile. *Party Politics* 4, 4: 471–93.

Nickson, R. Andrew. 1995. *Local Government in Latin America*. Boulder: Lynne Rienner.

Oxhorn, Philip D. 1995. *Organizing Civil Society: The Popular Sectors and the Struggle for Democracy in Chile*. University Park: Penn State University Press.

Pérez, Julio. 2001. National Secretary, Community and Neighborhood Action Front of the Chilean Christian Democratic Party (formerly Departmento de Pobladores). Author interview. Santiago, June 15.

Peterson, George E. 1997. *Decentralization in Latin America: Learning Through Experience*. Washington, DC: World Bank.

Portes, Alejandro. 1989. "Latin American Urbanization in the Years of the Crisis." *Latin American Research Review* 24, 3: 7–44.

Portes, Alejandro, and John Walton. 1981. *Labor, Class, and the International System*. New York: Academic Press.

Portes, Alejandro, and José Itzigsohn. 1997. The Party or the Grassroots: A Comparative Analysis of Urban Political Participation in the Caribbean Basin. In *Politics, Social Change, and Economic*

Restructuring in Latin America, ed. William C. Smith and Roberto Patricio Korzeniewicz. Coral Gables: North-South Center Press.

Posner, Paul. 1999. "Popular Representation and Political Dissatisfaction in Chile's New Democracy." *Journal of Interamerican Studies and World Affairs* 41, 1 (Spring): 59–85.

———. 2002. "Development and Collective Action in Chile's Neoliberal Democracy." Paper presented at the annual conference of the American Political Science Association, Boston, August 29.

Pozo, Hernán. 1981. La situación actual del municipio chileno y el problema de la municipalizacion. Contribuciones Programa FLACSO no. 7. Santiago: FLACSO.

———. 1986. La participación en la gestión local para el régimen autoritario Chileno. Documento de Trabajo no. 287. Santiago: FLACSO.

Raczynski, Dagmar. 1994. Social Policies in Chile: Origin, Transformations, and Perspectives. Democracy and Social Policy series, Working Paper no. 4. Notre Dame: Kellogg Institute for International Studies, University of Notre Dame.

Reyes, Juan. 2001. National Secretary for Unions for the PPD. Author interview. Santiago, June 6.

Roberts, Kenneth M. 1998. *Deepening Democracy? The Modern Left and Social Movements in Chile and Peru.* Stanford: Stanford University Press.

Robles, Juan. 2001. PS member, CESCO representative, neighborhood association vice president in Población Yungay, La Granja municipality, Santiago. Author interview. June 11.

Schneider, Cathy Lisa. 1989. *The Mobilization at the Grassroots: Shantytowns and Resistance in Authoritarian Chile.* Ph.D. diss., Cornell University.

———. 1995. *Shantytown Protest in Pinochet's Chile.* Philadelphia: Temple University Press.

Scully, Timothy R. 1992. *Rethinking the Center: Party Politics in Nineteenth and Twentieth Century Chile.* Stanford: Stanford University Press.

Servicio Electoral República de Chile. 1997. *Escrutinos elecciones municipales 1996.* October 27. Santiago.

———. 2001. *Escrutinos elecciones municipales 2000.* October 29. Santiago.

Stallings, Barbara. 1978. *Class Conflict and Economic Development in Chile, 1958–1973.* Stanford: Stanford University Press.

Valenzuela, Arturo. 1977. *Political Brokers in Chile: Local Government in a Centralized Polity.* Durham: Duke University Press.

Valle, Luciano. 2001. Chilean Socialist Party National Secretary of Social Organization. Author interview. Santiago, June 19.

Walker, Ignacio. 1990. *Socialismo y democracia: Chile y Europa en perspectiva comparada.* Santiago: Cieplan-Hachette.

Yáñez, José H., and Leonardo Letelier S. 1995. Chile. In *Fiscal Decentralization in Latin America*, ed. Ricardo Lopéz Murphy. Washington, DC: Inter-American Development Bank.

Chapter 17

Indictments, Myths, and Citizen Mobilization in Argentina: A Discourse Analysis

Ariel C. Armony
Víctor Armony

The recent economic and political crisis in Argentina has raised many questions regarding its causes, its distinctive characteristics, and its consequences. One of its most interesting aspects is that it exposed a profound gap between the citizenry and the "ruling class." Not surprisingly, most economists, political scientists, and media pundits have explained Argentina's crisis and the ensuing "social explosion" by referring to adverse macroeconomic factors, ill-advised policymaking, and institutional dysfunction. Less attention has been given to culturally framed explanations that explore how cognitive patterns influence people's behavior.

This analysis argues that the Argentine crisis of 2001–02 cannot be fully understood without considering how citizen mobilization and the "indictment" of the political class are connected to longstanding conceptions of national identity, particularly to national myths. The Argentine case offers a valuable opportunity to explore the ways that citizens react to definitional questions of national purpose—what kind of country citizens believe they can, should, and want to have—in the midst of an economic and political crisis.

This exploration employs cultural and discursive analysis and, in doing so, represents a different perspective with respect to traditional explanations based on the weakness of a "civic culture"—still an account even for those claiming to conduct a "scientific" study of Latin America. The chapter will analyze, quantitatively and qualitatively, nearly a thousand contributions to Internet forums and a large collection of presidential discourses, which are untapped sources of information and rich data for understanding the complex meanings of the "people's indictment" in Argentina. In this respect the article proposes, methodologically speaking, to go beyond the useful but limited world of survey research and elite interviewing.

As we will see, the "indictment" has valid explanations, focused on economic and political factors. This study does not intend to underestimate the impact of socioeconomic structures and political institutions on social behavior. If one agrees that protest movements are not fundamentally irrational—in the sense of an angry or desperate crowd resorting to random acts of disruption—but rather based on the actors' shared subjective assessment of the situation, then it is worthwhile to search for other factors that could complement economic and political approaches. Accordingly, the main objective here is to look inside the "black box" of participants in order to understand the perceptions that structure the behavior of these actors. This has been a missing piece in the Argentine puzzle.

From this perspective, cultural traditions, collective memories, values, and symbols play a significant role in determining how actors represent themselves in society. More important, the phenomenon of actors collectively crossing the threshold of social conventions openly to defy the established authorities is mainly explained by their shared anticipation of certain or probable gains and losses compared to real or idealized, past or current conditions. In other words, people act rationally, but their points of reference are strongly influenced by cognitive patterns that are psychologically and cultur-ally framed. Therefore, we must keep in mind that the Argentines' embittered mobilization was linked not only to deficits of political representation, weak institutionalization, or a dramatic economic downturn, but also to a crisis of national conceptions of identity that preceded—and will surely outlast—the events of December 2001.

ECONOMIC AND POLITICAL EXPLANATIONS

The economic argument dominated most foreign media accounts of Argentina's col-lapse. While many economists agreed that politicians should bear some responsibility for Argentina's meltdown, most tended to stress—not surprisingly—the macroeconomic factors at play (see, for example, Mahon and Corrales 2002). Although he concedes that the corruption of public officials was a pernicious trend in Argentina, Joseph Stiglitz (2002) proposes that the fixed exchange rate led to a vicious circle of heightened risks of devaluation and debt default. He specifically blames the International Monetary Fund for supporting the dollar peg and imposing contractionary fiscal policies during an eco-nomic downturn. Anne Krueger (2002), the former IMF's first deputy managing director, obviously disagrees with this analysis; but she shares the notion that "Argentina became caught in a vicious cycle of weak activity, overvaluation, and mounting debt."

Most political analysts have concurred with this type of explanation. Indeed, they are reluctant to see the local political class as the sole or main culprit. These analysts argue that the Argentine crisis was triggered by at least one of the following factors: the vulnerability of Argentina's economy in a context of global recession, the role played by the IMF technocrats, and the economic policies implemented by the Carlos Menem administration and continued by Fernando De la Rúa. According to this perspective, the crisis unfolded from the economic realm: economic instability created social turbulence, which provoked a political implosion.

Through the prism of this analysis, the crisis is seen as the result of "impersonal" forces (such as volatile financial markets) and poor decisionmaking (by IMF experts, global investors, or Argentina's economic planners). In the accounts that give preemi-nence to the role of the IMF, the "toughen as you sink" approach is deemed central to the worsening of Argentina's 1999 recession and the outbreak of the depression in 2001–02 (Corrales 2002). Some analysts view the crisis as the result of a cycle of "debt-boom-bust" that had a particularly negative impact on emerging economies because of their high vulnerability to capital flight. According to this perspective, Argentina's economy was too closed and dollarized to weather the effects of the Russian recession of the late 1990s (see Armony and Schamis 2003). Thus a highly volatile international financial context intensified the harmful effects of the convertibility regime and the bloated foreign debt burden on the Argentine economy (Levitsky and Murillo 2003; Hanke 2002). The De la Rúa government's failure to abandon the fixed exchange rate and monetary regime of the Menem administration were seen as key pieces of the puzzle.

Ironically, many analysts from the Marxist left share this structuralist approach, although in this perspective, the impersonal forces were not "innocent"—they responded to capitalist constraints—and the powerful did not make "bad" decisions but rather "good" decisions that were coherent with their agenda (of economic and political domination). As a vocal opponent of the so-called Washington Consensus puts it, the crisis in Argentina expressed a "structural weakening of neoliberalism" on the global stage (Taddei 2002).

In spite of its obvious economic aspects, Argentina's crisis was also political. This perspective focuses on the question of governance; taking into account factors such as the role played by a corrupt, unresponsive, and undisciplined political class and the preeminence of informal rules in the realm of policymaking. Political accounts of the crisis center primarily on three dimensions: the party system, democratic institutions (their strength, legitimacy, and capacity to represent the interests of the electorate), and the executive's style of rule.

Some accounts point to the crisis in the political parties as a fundamental explanation for the events of December 2001; they emphasize the fragmentation and polarization in the political system (Ollier 2003a). The atomization of political groups helped to shape a landscape of political competition marked by bitter animosity, lack of cooperation, and inability to cater to the demands of the electorate. This level of fragmentation also affected the internal politics of the ruling coalition. The weakness of the Alianza was manifest in its inability to evolve from a purely electoral coalition to an organization responsible for managing the state apparatus, its fragile power at the federal level, and its lack of a cohesive and supportive congressional wing (Ollier 2003a). Attention is also given to the unending conflict between the president, his own party, and the rest of the ruling coalition; his dissociation from political society in general; and his decision to seek inexperienced advisers (such as relatives and friends), who contributed to his political isolation (Corrales 2002; Schamis 2002). While the coalition that brought De la Rúa to office demonstrated a weak capacity to rule, the excessive rapaciousness of the Peronist opposition intensified political instability. Both the Alianza and the Peronists are viewed as decisive forces in the making of the crisis (Ollier 2003b).

Some political explanations place most of the weight on the "crisis of political representation" in Argentina. There are at least two ways to explain the character of this crisis. One stresses that political authorities failed to respond to a key dimension of the democratic contract: the accountability of public officials. The crisis of representation occurred when the demands for accountability advanced by a highly mobilized sector of civil society clashed with an unresponsive political class that clung to Argentina's longstanding populist tradition, according to which the electorate was expected to subordinate itself to the leader's decisions until the next election (Peruzzotti 2002). In this sense, the links that traditionally legitimated the connection between civil society and political society were severed, which triggered a political crisis.

Other political explanations highlight the need to consider the impact of *Menemismo*— as a way of doing politics—in Argentina (Jozami 2003; Schamis 2002). *Menemismo* entailed a set of political practices that simultaneously called for reform of the country's economy, constitution, and institutions (in order to update them to the new national and international conditions) and bolstered subnational authoritarianism (provincial caudillos financed by the federal government) and all-encompassing nepotism, corruption, and frivolity. This type of presidential rule (which defined a form of "delegative" democracy, according to Guillermo O'Donnell 1994) was marked by a strong reliance on executive decrees, an autocratic style of policymaking, and general disregard for Congress, the judiciary, and civil society. To practice *Menemismo* became synonymous with a drive to monopolize power at any cost (Mocca 2002).

For some scholars, however, President Carlos Menem only deepened a process of "deinstitutionalization of politics" that had shaped Argentina since the return to democracy (Tedesco 2002). Therefore, De la Rúa's decision to continue practicing *Menemismo* represented a major blow to the functioning of institutions. In a context of widespread citizen disaffection and lack of trust in political institutions, De la Rúa's embrace of Menem's "delegative" legacy carried the political crisis to a point of no return (Corrales 2002). At that point, the time was ripe to change the players. Indeed, some analysts argue, this pattern was not new for a country that had failed to develop clear and sound rules to institutionalize the democratic political game (Levitsky and Murillo 2003). The Argentine case conforms in an interesting way to a broader regional pattern (Brazil, Venezuela, Guatemala, Ecuador, Paraguay, and Peru) in which political instability and mass popular protests resulted in presidential crises but not in the breakdown of the democratic regimes (Pérez-Liñán 2003).

SOCIAL EXPLANATIONS

The social roots of the crisis have received comparatively less attention. Indeed, most explanations assume that the actors' interests and identities were defined by economic and institutional structures. Therefore it is important to explore in more detail voluntarist approaches that emphasize the choices and subjective goals of actors. The few analyses that do look at the crisis from this perspective yield three types of explanations.

First is the notion that the upsurge of popular protest constituted a reaction to social exclusion and a defensive behavior in the context of a severe economic crisis. Indeed, some of these accounts view the rise in mass mobilization as a popular response to the social problems caused by the neoliberal economic reforms of the 1990s. A second perspective places the emphasis on the general decline in trust in political institutions and frustration with politics among the population. Third, some accounts of the crisis view the events of December 2001 as a climax in a broader cycle of contentious mobilization.

Following the first approach, a number of analyses give popular protest a central role in the political events that led to the collapse of the De la Rúa government. Some accounts describe the rise of middle-class mobilization as a form of defensive action in a context of a rapidly decreasing social distance between this sector and the working class. This explanation considers the mobilization of middle-class citizens an effort "to protect themselves as individuals as opposed to acting in solidarity with each other" (Ollier 2003a, 182). To explain why the upsurge of protest did not occur earlier, analysts argue that the worsening economic conditions eliminated the possibility for the middle class to benefit from the "politics of informality" that had spread to everyday life interactions, thereby severing ties between this sector of society and the government (Tedesco 2002, 479–80). For some scholars, a similar logic applies to the working class, which finally reacted to economic policies that had brought far-flung social exclusion (Levitsky and Murillo 2003).

In terms of the second approach, although public trust had been low since the onset of democracy, successive corruption scandals, political mischief, and the general lack of accountability in the 1990s brought the state–society tension to a critical point at the turn of the century. Furthermore, some social scientists interpret the lack of trust as rooted in a general frustration with politics in Argentina. These accounts see the rebellion of the middle class as an emotional response to the gap between what this societal sector demanded from politics and what politics actually delivered (Portantiero 2002). The expansion of an independent citizenry progressively disengaged from the political system is viewed as a critical development of the 1990s. Unlike previous social movements in Argentina, some analysts argue, the new wave of mobilization emphasized the autonomy of participants from traditional forms of leadership (Cheresky 2002).

A different reading emphasizes the role of social movements as key forces in provoking the presidential crisis of late 2001. One perspective focuses on the middle class, viewing the upsurge of protest not as a sudden social uproar but as a third wave of a broader cycle of citizen participation. This cycle of mobilization, initiated with Argentina's return to democracy, sought to improve the mechanisms of representation and accountability (Cheresky 2003). It began with the human rights movement, followed by the emergence of citizen organizations and a new "journalism of exposé" oriented to respond to police violence, government corruption, and social exclusion in the 1990s. The third wave took shape as a reaction to the crisis in the Senate in 2000 (when it was revealed that a number of legislators had been bribed to vote for a labor reform promoted by the De la Rúa administration). It deepened with the massive denunciation of political parties and "politics as usual" in the legislative elections of October 2001, and it exploded with the "pots and pans" mobilization of thousands of middle-class citizens (the *cacerolazos*) at the end of 2001 and beginning of 2002 (Peruzzotti 2002).[1]

A similar analysis centers on the contentious mobilization that had mounted since the end of the 1980s, but it assigns a primary role to the working class (both employed and unemployed workers). According to this perspective, the events of December 2001 represented a culmination in a process of social struggles against the socially regressive policies of neoliberalism. The so-called *Santiagüeñazo*, the riots in Santiago del Estero in December 1993, marked the end of the "social isolation of the working class" and the beginning of a new wave of mobilization against neoliberal policies (Iñigo Carrera and Cotarelo 2003, 205). These observers trace the rejection of politicians, political parties, and traditional political mediations to the grassroots practices (such as popular assemblies) developed in the flourish of strikes and protests in Jujuy, Santiago del Estero, Neuquén (the *Cutralcazo*)., Tierra del Fuego, Córdoba (Cruz del Eje), Santa Fe (Capitán Bermúdez), Río Negro (Catriel), Greater Buenos Aires (La Matanza, Florencio Varela, and Quilmes), Salta (Tartagal-General Mosconi), and other parts of the country (Oviedo 2001; Auyero 2002). These protests set the grounds for the emergence of the Piquetero movement, which became a major player at the national level in 1998, when thousands of protesters set roadblocks on the bridges and highways connecting Buenos Aires to its depressed industrial belt. This movement soon became the symbol of resistance to the structural adjustment program.

Some explanations reject the idea that the December 2001 social protest resulted either from a working-class rebellion against unemployment and poverty or from the reaction of an alienated middle class. Focusing on the repertoires of contention and the participants in the protests, this approach highlights a shared culture of protest across the working and middle classes. This culture was shaped by structural changes that had an impact across society: the dramatic increase in unemployment, the withdrawal of the welfare state, and the decentralization of health care and education. The resulting interests, opportunities for mobilization, and organizational patterns cut across classes. In this context, the mobilization of teachers, students, and municipal employees along with union leaders, retirees, unemployed industrial workers, and other groups, all under the rubric of *autoconvocados* (self-assembled), gradually defined a form of protest based on the notion of "the people against the political class" (Auyero 2002).

In sharp contrast to these accounts, some analysts react against the idea of a "victimized" society. They argue that Argentine society itself was responsible for the deterioration of democracy and the worsening of socioeconomic conditions. For a large number of Argentines, they claim, the tendency to project an image of a society oppressed by a minority (for example, the military, the "financial oligarchy," the political class) produced a collective self-representation much more positive than what the country's actual history reveals. Thus, they argue, Argentine society has been predisposed to believe that the responsibility for the deficits of democracy or even its collapse "always rests in somebody else" (de Ipola 2002; Altamirano 2002).

Social explanations of the crisis have an underlying common denominator: they all imply the existence of a crisis of social cohesion. While the political crisis in Argentina was, at least in part, a result of a gridlocked political system without the ability to mediate between society's demands and policy outputs, we have to take into consideration that at a more fundamental level, Argentina's social fabric was facing a steady corrosion (see A. Armony 2004). A society that is breaking down seems unable to "get its act together" and "restart the engine," to use Stiglitz's telling metaphors about Argentina. The 1990s were a decade of deep transformation in Argentina, one that bred a "winner take all" economic logic; generated, in a short period, inordinate numbers of losers (in terms of downward mobility for some and deprivation of minimal resources for others); and furthered a dramatic wave of "interindividual competitiveness" in a context in which the spectacle of the *farándula* (a mix of politics, money, sports, and show business) helped to disconnect even more the elites from the average citizen (Svampa 2002; de Ipola 2002; V. Armony 2001a).

Simultaneously, as democracy gained in experience, the rule of law—at the level of institutions, state–society relations, and interactions among citizens—seriously weakened. Increased levels of criminal activity, fueled by economic and social problems, as well as by an emerging world of organized crime with significant ties to corrupt police forces and local politicians, led to the rise of *inseguridad*, a combination of real-life criminality, media-driven hyperrealism, and middle-class fears in a context of diminishing social distances (Guemureman 2002). These factors contributed to a deepening social fragmentation, in which vast numbers of people withdrew into their private lives (Gayol and Kessler 2002). The combination of fragmentation in society with increased cynicism about the virtues of politics and the role of the law reinforced a sense of anomie and disorientation, captured in a number of studies and polls (see, for example, Filmus 1999).

To put it bluntly, society itself became nearly "unrepresentable." The question of representation brings us to a key aspect of the crisis that has been neglected by most scholarly analyses: the specific ways that people construed the reality of Argentina's "crisis of political representation" and the ways that citizens responded to widely shared conceptions of national identity in the midst of an economic and political crisis. These two issues are related because the "indictment" of the political class is defined in reference to a given conception of the national essence—grounded in an "Argentine Dream" of greatness—while the problem of identity, which we read in terms of national myths, pertains to that very essence; that is, definitional questions that refer to the kind of country Argentines believe they can, should, and want to have.

THE PEOPLE'S INDICTMENT

By people's indictment, we mean the manner in which the actors themselves frame their actions in a meaningful way. We have seen that the latest protest wave that shook Argentina was clearly fueled by anger and frustration, and all its expressions shared a negativity toward a perceived common enemy: the "political class," and in a larger perspective, the "ruling class," which includes business leaders, union bosses, and other "privileged groups."

Indeed, when it came to pinpointing the main cause of their country's economic downturn, most Argentines reached the same conclusion: it was the politicians' fault, not a particular leader or specific party or ideology. The people's indictment was rendered in the now internationally famous slogan ¡*Qué se vayan todos!* (Let's get rid of them all!), sometimes coupled, as if to make sure the point was clear, with ¡*Que no quede ninguno!* (Don't let a single one stay!). The political parties, and particularly the politicians, were perceived as having blatantly failed to respond to society's needs and demands. In this sense, the people's indictment of the "ruling class" was not a misguided or delusional sentiment, even if it was based, as we will see, on exculpatory self-victimization.

The forms of contention that characterized the public sphere in the late 1990s—from the *puebladas* (townwide riots) and the *piquetes* to the *escraches* (public shaming) and the teachers' "white tent" in front of the National Congress—conveyed a highly critical discourse of government officials, "old-style politics," and established authorities in general (see Laufer and Spiguel 1999; Kaiser 2002; Giarracca and Bidaseca 2001).[2] In this context, mobilized groups performed a social "reappropriation" of public spaces, institutions, and even symbols, claiming a preeminence of legitimacy over legality when, in their view, the bond of trust between the citizenry and those who hold power had been broken. As a Piquetero leader argued in the midst of the looting that shook the city of Rosario in December 2001, those who broke the law were not the desperate citizens who ransacked several supermarkets but the elected politicians who plundered the country (Armony and Bessa 2002).

In contrast with the social mobilization in the 1960s and 1970s, the actors of the 1990s rarely categorized themselves as members of a particular class, political group, or ideological tendency. Indeed, the most recent cycle of social mobilization was characterized by a relative blurring of class frontiers, not in terms of a multiclass alliance but through ad hoc convergence and mutual reinforcement. For example, the tactics of the Piqueteros and, in some ways, even their identity markers were adopted by other groups, such as shopkeepers, pensioners, health workers, schoolteachers, public servants, university students, street venders, day laborers, and household workers. Most protesters, regardless of social origin, used universalistic notions such as "citizen," "person," or even "human being," and they demanded to be "seen," to be "heard," and to be "recognized." The emphasis was on pressure tactics—sometimes including civil disobedience—rather than political violence; on gaining public sympathy—particularly through the deliberate use of the media—rather than deepening social conflict; and on a more pragmatic and individualistic stance rather than an ideological, class warfare perspective. Interviews consistently revealed the protesters' aim to force the authorities to look at them "in a different way" and to "make the authorities listen" (Armony and Bessa 2002).

Some analysts have pondered the real meaning of the phrase *Let's get rid of them all.* Were Argentines calling for the ousting of every "old-school" politician in order to make room for new, unspoiled leaders? Or were they expressing their out-and-out dismissal of all figures of authority, from elected representatives to judges, union bosses to clergy? The ambiguity of the charge bred different interpretations. A few observers acknowledged the slogan's relevance as a legitimate expression of the citizens' rage and desperation but maintained that it could not be understood at face value (Aguinis 2003). Others interpreted the wave of mobilization that spread out in late 2001 as an attempt to broaden the public space in order to "fill in" for the unresponsive and unrepresentative political parties by creating new forms of citizen engagement (Cheresky 2002). The intensity of the social upheaval, however, made many Argentines take the slogan rather seriously. As some social commentators suggested, the apparent call for anarchy could also be construed as an invitation to authoritarian responses (see Feinman 2003). Some voices among the radical left saw the slogan as a first step in the creation of innovative forms of direct democracy that would replace traditional mechanisms of political representation.

Still, most of these interpretations were based on purely impressionistic accounts rather than on systematic analysis of data. Public opinion polls have provided ample evidence of the growing political alienation and cynicism in Argentina. They have shown that confidence in political institutions reached record lows during this period. But surveys—though based on representative samples—are thin when it comes to understanding the nuances of people's discourse. An untapped source of information is Internet forums; they are a rich data source because they attract actors with some level of civic engagement, ask meaningful questions (in the sense that they provoke complex reactions in the subjects), and provide enough information for multilevel analysis.

Obviously, this source has important limitations: these actors are self-selected; they belong to a specific social sector; they are, by definition, computer literate; and they tend to hold what could be called middle-class values.[3] In spite of these restrictions, the discourse collected in Internet forums is particularly interesting, in that it usually conveys ideas and clichés that stem from a "common wisdom." Like call-in radio talk shows, Internet forums pull in contradictory perspectives and socially dominant narratives. Unlike talk shows, however, no outspoken, opinionated hosts regulate the flow of discourse. An Internet forum allows a more diverse, unrestricted, and spontaneous interaction between participants.

This discourse analysis focuses on the middle class, a social stratum that played a decisive role in triggering the crisis. Even though the middle class is quantitatively a minority in Argentina, it is by no means an elite cut from the lower strata in terms of identity and aspirations. Regardless of objective indicators, most Argentines (about 70 percent of them in the 1970s; see Minujin and Kessler 1995) feel that they belong—or should belong—to the middle class. The upward mobility of immigrants in the first decades of the twentieth century and the redistributive policies of populism in the 1940s and 1950s created a widespread sense of entitlement that persisted well into the 1980s and 1990s. This aspiration to lead a "normal life" appears clearly in the Piquetero movement's discourse—for instance, the emphasis on the right to earn a salary, to receive decent pay, and to "live like any other citizen" (Armony and Bessa 2002). Therefore the kind of analysis proposed in this study has implications for a broader segment of society.

A PUBLIC FORUM

A discourse analysis of nearly a thousand messages sent to an Internet forum in May 2002 reveals the extent to which the "bad politicians" argument framed the perception of the crisis, particularly by middle-class Argentines. The forum was held by Argentina's most widely read newspaper, *Clarín*, a mainstream voice in the public arena.[4] *Clarín* readers were asked for their reactions to the following question: *Usted, a pesar de todo, ¿se siente orgulloso de ser argentino? ¿Por qué?* (In spite of the current situation, do you feel proud to be Argentine? Why?). This question itself is quite revealing: readers were invited to assess their attachment to the country rather than, for example, to evaluate their own responsibility as citizens in the country's decline. Ironically, one can infer that many of those who responded to *Clarín's* call were among the direct beneficiaries of the convertibility model: the middle class sector that traveled around the world, consumed imported goods, and obtained improved services, including computer and telecommunications technology, thanks to the dollar-to-peso parity.

While some participants sent straightforward responses (Yes, I'm proud; No, I'm not proud—the kind of response obtained in public opinion surveys), many others used different expressions or chose alternative wordings. The analysis began by estimating the overall distribution of responses, with four main options: Very proud (10 percent); Proud (59 percent); Not proud (20 percent); Ashamed (11 percent).[5] Seven out of 10 of those who sent messages to the *Clarín* forum remained attached to their national identity, stating in one way or another that they felt proud of their country. These results

Table 1. Keyword Frequency Index

Word	Frequency
argentino-s / argentina-s	1,722
orgullo / orgulloso-s / orgullosa -s	1,599
país	1,510
Argentina	538
gente	501
político-s / política-s	491
vida / vivir /viviendo	384
sentir / sentirse /sentirme / sentirnos / sentimiento-s	360
mundo	302
trabajo / trabajar	240
pueblo	224
patria	217
dirigente-s / dirigencia	215
tierra	206
hijo-s	177
nacional / nación /nacionalidad	168
amo / amor	165
culpa / culpables	152
corrupto-s / corrupción	151
nacido / nací / nacer	150

coincide with public opinion data. For example, in a poll conducted in March 2002, 82 percent of the individuals said that they were proud to be Argentine.[6]

The next step in the analysis involved a description of the "average" person's discourse. For this, the study looked at the most frequently used words (or sets of words having a common root) that are semantically "full" (nouns, adjectives, or nonauxiliary verbs that denote entities, ideas, qualities, or actions). Table 1 shows the keyword frequency index for the 20 most frequent words in the messages. This list portrays the average person's discourse, which was likely to express a personal bond with the country by means of terms such as life, soil, children, love, and born. Examples reveal this tendency to relate to the national identity mainly through the subjective experience, rather than by a reference to shared values or a common destiny: "*adoro y adoraré toda mi vida mi país*" (I adore and will adore my country all my life); "*nací, me crié y moriré en mi país*" (I was born, raised, and will die in my country); "*aquí nacimos y vivimos nuestra infancia, nuestra adolescencia, aquí tuvimos nuestros hijos*" (we were born and spent our childhood and teenage years here, we had our children here); "*a pesar de todo, amo mi tierra, tengo acá mis afectos, el aire que respiro*" (no matter what, I love my country, my loved ones are here, this is the air I breathe). Some participants even made an analogy with filial love, thereby stressing their emotional, unquestionable commitment to the country: "*luchemos por nuestra patria como lo haríamos por nuestra madre*" (let's fight for our fatherland as we would fight for our mother); "*patria, así como madre, ¡hay una sola!*" (as there is only one mother, there is only one fatherland!).

To examine the concrete way that keywords are used, the analysis applied a statistical procedure that retrieves their significant collocates (i.e. words that have a strong tendency to co-occur in the same sentence). This technique allowed us to observe patterns of word association, along with "semantic networks"; that is, some recurrent word combinations that sustain relatively structured representations. Table 2 shows the main

Table 2. Keyword Collocations

Keyword	Main Collocates
argentinos+	orgullo, siento, vergüenza, muerte, pueblo, nacido, Dios
orgullo+	siento, argentinos, pertenecer, arrogancia, nacido, país
país	hermoso, rico, bendito, querido, amor, pertenecer, salga, nacido
Argentina	nueva, aguante, viva, querida, ayuda, nacido, hermosa, amo, quiero
gente	honesta, costumbres, buenas, capaz, inteligente, ayudar, merece, trabaja
políticos+	sindicalistas, sindical-es, dirigentes, corruptos, empresarios, culpa
vida	dignamente, digna, extranjero, casa, dignidad, trabajo, mejor, afuera
sentir+	orgullo, argentinos, vergüenza, nacional, tierra
mundo	primer, tercer, resto, ante, mejor, todo, parte, mejores, único, país
trabajo+	dignamente, cultura, vida, tener
pueblo	solidario, gran, hambre, parte, argentino
patria	viva, defendido, traidores, amo, grande, única, futuro
dirigentes+	clase, empresarios, sindicalistas, políticos, corrupta, nuevos, culpa
tierra	bendita, nacido, amar, hermosa, amo, propia, orgulloso, patria, siento
hijos+	criar, futuro, padres, espero, nacido
nacional+	himno, sentido, sentir, orgullo
amo	patria, libertad, tierra, país, Argentina, argentinos, orgullosos
culpa+	echarle, políticos, todos, nosotros, toda, otros
corruptos+	ladrones, ineptos, política, jueces, justicia, dirigentes, grandes, clase
nacido+	tierra, país, orgullo, Argentina, siento, argentinos, hijos, siempre

+Includes word variations.

Table 3. Representations of Argentina: People and Politicians

Representations	Word Association
1. Argentina as a dearly loved, beautiful, richly endowed country	*Argentina*: nueva, aguante, viva, querida, ayuda, nacido, hermosa, amo, quiero
2. The "ordinary people," who are honest, hardworking, and generous	*gente*: honesta, costumbres, buena, capaz, inteligente, ayudar, merece, trabaja
3. The "ruling class," which includes politicians, union bosses, judges	*políticos*: sindicalistas, sindical-es, dirigentes, corruptos, empresarios, culpa

results of this procedure. The objective of this analysis was to trace the main types of representations contained in the messages sent to the forum.

The analysis of the data reveals that the participants' discourse essentially conveyed three distinct representations: Argentina as a dearly loved, beautiful, richly endowed country; the "ordinary people," who are honest, hard-working, and generous; and the "ruling class," which includes all those who hold power in political, labor, judicial, and corporate matters. The sets of representations are summarized in table 3. The first category results from a strong correlation between Argentina and words conveying positive attributes. In this respect, we found that the crisis did not affect the general perception of Argentina as a "great country." This correlation shows the endurance of the idea that Argentina is meant to become a successful nation. As one participant in the forum explained, "Having had the opportunity to travel abroad, I can assure you that Argentina is the best country in the world because of its climate, landscapes, soil, fauna, forests, deserts, and anything else you could think of."

If Argentines believed that their country was destined to fulfill an original promise of greatness, then the bursting of that bubble could easily lead to high levels of frustration. The target of this frustration was the political class. A statistical analysis of word associations confirms a strikingly coherent and utterly negative perception of the "ruling class." Words such as corrupt, thieves, guilty, inept, and caste were recurrent in the participants' discourse. Some granted, though, that all Argentines shared the blame, "because we all voted for these politicians," or because they "are the reflection of who we are as a people." For these individuals, the main concern was about the contradiction between an idealized nation and a people that did not deserve it.[7] However, most participants drew a clear opposition between a victimized society and a culpable minority—as the last two categories (the "ordinary people" and the "ruling class") show.[8]

A PRESIDENT'S STATEMENTS

Paradoxically, President Carlos Menem himself advocated a harshly critical attitude toward the "political class" in the 1990s. His discourse, crafted as an indictment of the state, was actually oriented against the political class, which he constantly denounced as an obstacle for a country that, in his words, "deserves a future of happiness and glory."

Anti-political discourse was, of course, not without precedent in Argentina. Populists, revolutionaries, and nationalists had strongly criticized representative democracy, particularly from the 1920s to the 1970s. The return to constitutional rule under Raúl Alfonsín in the 1980s attenuated this ideological strain. But Menem's rhetoric—though nurtured by the neoliberal assault on "big spending" and "white elephant" government—undoubtedly contributed to the rise of an antipolitical mood. His representation of a nation choked by the state did not differ much from that of the infuriated Argentines who joined *Clarín's* forum.

Soon after taking office, Menem promised to build a different type of capitalism, "a capitalism that is no longer tied to a welfare state (welfare for a privileged few), the occasional prebend, the artificial manipulation of economic variables, bureaucratic obstacles, the spurious relationship between politicians and businessmen, [and] the lobby that always creates pressure to obtain a privilege" (1990b). He promised to transform a state from which only a few extracted benefits into one that would serve the entire Argentine community. His goal was to see Argentina become "a nation that its people could be proud of." To do so, it was necessary to dismantle the political class: "It is time to free the political system from *caciquismos*, oligarchies, and bureaucracies that preserve privileges and prebends and restrain the popular will at the same time" (April 19, 1993; quoted in V. Armony 2001b). Responding to increased public cynicism toward the capacity of politicians to solve the major political problems confronting society, Menem echoed the anger and frustration of the average citizen with a discourse centered on a "common sense" (rather than ideological or bureaucratic) approach to problem solving.

For decades now, each president, constitutional or military, has promised to put Argentina back on track "the way it was supposed to be." Menem masterfully played on this collective belief by placing the blame for all Argentina's woes on the state ("The Argentine state buried us. It went bankrupt and bankrupted all Argentines." 1990a) and by using the sudden and far-reaching effects of the Convertibility Plan as proof of the revival of the Great Argentina.

> Our country is the leader of a new order. A new, home-grown Argentina will join the First World as a number-one country. The leader of new changes. The leader of a leap toward the future. We have joined the Brady Plan, which shows the world that it is possible to invest in our country today. Because our currency has the weight of stability, because investors enjoy all possible guarantees, and because there is more employment and well-being for all Argentines (1992).

The psychological impact of the economic stability brought by the pegged peso cannot be exaggerated. The "engine" actually started, and Argentina seemed to be moving again in the right direction. The country was praised by the powers that be (the *Wall Street Journal* hailed the "Argentine Miracle" on its front page).[9] It was portrayed as a close friend of the U.S. government (the so-called "carnal relations" with the superpower; Rock 2002). Shaken by the rapid modernization and Americanization of infrastructures (airports, toll highways, five-star hotels, shopping malls) and services (telephones, banking, cable TV, and others), Argentina did seem to be waking up after a long sleep. The country's strong currency, the access to foreign consumer goods, and the ability to travel abroad gave the middle classes a taste of a First World lifestyle.

The mythic narrative appeared to be validated: the obstacle had been *estatismo*, and once it was removed, Argentina could join the ranks of the "best countries in the world." Although we can smile now at this preposterous claim, we must remember that in the mid-1990s, it might have been considered a bit immoderate but not completely unfounded. As the most elementary psychology tells us, however, the higher that hopes are raised, the harder frustration will hit. The end of convertibility and the rebound of Argentina back to the reality of the Third World brought about—once again—the crisis of the myth. In brief, middle-class citizens who took to the streets to demand the resignation of all political representatives under the slogan "Let's get rid of them all," who flooded virtual forums to express their anger at politicians, and who fled the country en masse were reacting not only to the deficits of democracy but also to the end of a dream that, for almost a decade, appeared to have become reality.

"A GREAT ARGENTINA"

The other contextual element that should be considered regarding the crisis of social cohesion is a cognitive dimension that underlies and determines to some extent the actors' perceptions and behavior. Current events in Argentina cannot be fully apprehended outside the paradigm of national identity and the collective representations that sustain it. This approach emphasizes the role of ideological narratives in the analysis of social and political phenomena. While individuals are capable of rational judgments based on their own interests, they are also open to emotional appeals and exalting images. Evidence can be summoned to suggest the idea that the Argentine Dream was suddenly shattered (but not for good) by the crisis of 2001 and that the wave of extensive and vehement mobilization was, at least partly, a sign of this disillusion.

To speak of an Argentine Dream might seem odd to a U.S. citizen, who associates this kind of expression with the promise of freedom and prosperity embodied in the United States and its Manifest Destiny. However, the American Dream—understood more broadly as the New World dream—is a constitutive element of many Latin American national identities, particularly among those countries that received a significant influx of immigrants during the late nineteenth and early twentieth centuries (such as Argentina, Brazil, Chile, and Uruguay). It goes without saying that this "dream" is framed in a larger cultural matrix. Latin American national identities are embedded in the Catholic worldview of Mediterranean Europe, coupled with a strong positivistic and republican influence from the French Enlightenment. The propensity to establish centralized government, or to link patriotism to both religion and civic education (creating a sort of "civic religion"; Devoto 1992), can be traced to these origins.

In Argentina, however, this cultural background encountered a very particular geographic and demographic setting: immense fertile farmlands, extremely low population density, very small and scattered indigenous and black minorities, early and intense financial linkages to Great Britain, and a powerful elite with a penchant for liberal ideas. Rather than thinking of itself as a peripheral enclave, as Polish writer Witold Gombrowicz observed in the 1940s, this frontier society had much bigger dreams.

> There is a nebulous premonition of empire in the Argentine, the premonition that one day he will be powerful, that the weight of power, struggle, and responsibility will fall onto his shoulders; and each of them, despite their provincial amiability, cherishes that imperialist dream (Quoted in Lanata 2002, 440).

Millions of European immigrants settled in Argentina, then seen as a young, rich, and progressive "American" country, one that many compared to Canada. These immigrants and their descendants would form the core of the middle classes, but they would also join the ranks of a nascent working class that soon adhered—through Peronist redistribution policies—to middle-class values, lifestyle, and aspirations. Along with Argentina's decadence during the second half of the twentieth century, a myth of past and future national grandeur definitely shaped public discourse. The relentless failure to achieve such grandeur engendered a narrative of victimization, which became the staple of almost every political point of view: there is someone who is liable for robbing Argentina's wealth, and worse, for steering the country away from its glorious destiny.

To be sure, the belief that one's country is somehow unique is not exclusive to Argentina. Even the notion of greatness is quite widespread in Latin America; Brazil and Mexico are clear illustrations of this pattern. However, the Argentine idea of exceptionality has been built on the idea of potential. In this sense, Argentina illustrates, perhaps as no other country in the region does, the tension between the New World promise of recreating the positive and rational potentials of human society and the reality that this promise remains continually unfulfilled (V. Armony 2004).

If there is an "exceptionality" in the case of Argentina, it has been the capacity to preserve—over coups, economic debacles, genocide, and outlandish government corruption—the belief in the country's potential to achieve a superior destiny. This type of nationalistic stance entailed the promotion of "the vision [of] the Argentine nation as a unique ethnocultural community" and the legitimation of the "concept of Argentina's unique historical destiny" (DeLaney 2002). Argentine political discourse and popular perceptions consistently assigned the blame for the country's failure to achieve its potential to specific social groups, successively construed as "the other." These included, at different points in time, the intemperate immigrants, the "oligarchy," the leftist "subversives," the *patria financiera* (financial elite), the armed forces, the state bureaucracy, and more recently, the "political class."

The myth of a Great Argentina has deep roots. In the nineteenth century, Argentina perceived itself as an aspiring power in the hemisphere. As the Buenos Aires newspaper *La Prensa* asserted in the early 1890s, Argentina was destined to play "a great civilizing mission in the New World" (quoted in Smith 2000, 99). Domingo F. Sarmiento, one of Argentina's leading political figures of the nineteenth century, imagined a future of greatness for his country. As he wrote in 1888, "We shall reach the level of the United States.

We shall be America as the sea is the ocean. We shall be the United States" (quoted in Smith 2000, 98). "Argentines refuse to accept any truth which makes them inferior to anyone else," commented President Marcelo T. de Alvear in the 1920s. "Theirs is the greatest city in the world, their frontier mountains the highest and their pampas the widest; theirs the most beautiful lakes, the best cattle, the richest vineyards, and the loveliest women." Pointing out a view of their own country that has permeated the Argentine experience, even to the very forum analyzed above, Alvear stressed, "They accept no qualifications nor the fact that there might be some other country which surpasses them in anything" (quoted in Bruce 1953, 7).

At the end of World War II, the perception was that Argentina, once again, could achieve its destiny. As Juan Perón said on October 10, 1945, "These achievements are the goals that will place our nation at the lead of all nations in the world." Five years later, Perón reasserted the idea of Argentina's manifest destiny when he claimed, "Today the Argentine people, having now recovered their dignity, march toward a destiny whose greatness they recognize" (Frondizi 1950, both quoted in Perón 1973). And almost a decade later, during which Argentina experienced high levels of political and social instability, civilian president Arturo Frondizi referred to the myth of the Great Argentina: "The second, fundamental objective was to overcome recession and economic backwardness, defeat the impediments that had slowed down national development, and unleash all the country's creative forces to turn Argentina into the great nation it deserves to be, because of its people and natural wealth" (Frondizi, 1959). This trend would continue throughout the twentieth century, keeping alive the idea of a country destined to join the club of the world's most powerful nations.

It is interesting to note that for the United States, "the charm of anticipated success" (using the words of Alexis de Tocqueville in *Democracy in America*) became, in spite of periods of trouble and uncertainty, a palpable reality (Cullen 2003). In contrast, an intriguing dimension of Argentina's sense of manifest destiny is that the promise of success failed, systematically, to materialize. Indeed, Argentina's greatness can be found only in the future or in a mythical past. Accordingly, the question is not why such a myth exists but why it has lasted so long. It is interesting that the same question can be asked about the Convertibility Plan. Why was it maintained in light of abundant signs that it had run out of steam? One may point out the discretionary nature of the policymaking process, which translated into low capacity to absorb information, assess alternative scenarios, and make timely decisions in response to changes in global markets and domestic conditions (Armony and Schamis 2003).

A different answer, however, can be found in political discourse. The idea that the country's greatness was intimately tied to convertibility was sustained primarily by Menem's discourse, which was built "around constant but unexamined invocations of the need for 'stability'" (Schamis 2002: 84)—especially as the president worked on his reelection campaign. Menem's discourse concurred with the voters' demand for stability. In the presidential discourse, however, this stability was tied—by necessity—to the fixed exchange rate. In this way, Menem's discourse contributed to the process of redefining people's perceptions about their country and reconstituting the conceptual universe that sustained the myth of Argentina's manifest destiny.

A statistical analysis of 310 speeches Menem delivered during his presidency reveals a depiction of Argentina in terms of "spiritual grandeur" and glory (data and analysis from V. Armony 2001b). This success was presented as intimately linked to economic liberalization and a particular type of insertion into a "new world being born." Statistically significant collocations associated with the term *Argentina* in Menem's discourse included words such as *change, great, greatness, history, new,* and *transformation.* The presidential discourse systematically suggested a dichotomy between the Argentina of the future—"coherent," "powerful," "glorious," "transcendent"—and the Argentina of the past—"chaotic," "closed," "sleeping," "isolated." Menem's pronouncements advanced especially the idea of an Argentina capable of realizing its potential: "I want to tell you once again that Argentina and its people were born to triumph, they were born to win, they were born to become a great nation, a powerful state" (1989). This promise became intertwined with the stability of an economic plan that allowed Argentina, in Menem's words before his reelection in 1994, to become "the most powerful country in Latin America and in some parts of the world" (1993). On March 1, 1999, Menem said, "the global prestige that our country enjoys today lies in our transformation into a nation that rises to the face of the earth proud of its predictability and credibility" (1999). As this quotation illustrates, Menem, at the end of his second term, reasserted his legacy in terms of a core value: stability.

But national myths, like all collective representations, do not simply vanish. The "original promise" of success appeared to persist even after the dramatic collapse of the economy at the turn of the twenty-first century, when Argentina's cumulative fall in output (1998–2002) was nearly twice the fall experienced by the United States in the Great Depression of the 1930s (according to IMF 2002). In the midst of the most serious crisis to hit the country, caretaker president Eduardo Duhalde declared, "Argentina is doomed to succeed." This kind of talk should not be dismissed as mere political bravado or as masterful Peronist rhetoric.

The promise of a destiny of greatness was conveyed even by the center-right candidate in the 2003 presidential elections, Ricardo López Murphy, a technocrat running on an unpretentious, "common sense" platform. His full-page advertisement in one of the country's leading newspapers, La Nación, listed many of Argentina's shortcomings and acknowledged the need to accept a more modest, normal, even peripheral future for the country. But that was not his real message. At the bottom of the page, in small print, the candidate alerted readers that to unveil his actual message, the ad had to be read from bottom to top. The "real" message stated that Argentina had an unequivocal path to follow; namely, the destiny to unleash its true potential to become one of the greatest countries in the world. In other words, the solution to the crisis was entwined with the pursuit of the dream.

CONCLUSIONS

Many new, unconventional forms of protest emerged in the 1990s and the early twenty-first century, and the events of 2001 therefore must be seen as the climax of a relatively long process of social mobilization in Argentina. While it is obvious that an acute economic downturn provoked the popular protests of December 2001 that deposed President De la Rúa, this study has shown that an analysis with a broader focus offers a much more comprehensive picture. The citizens' rage has been seen by a number of economists and political scientists as either purely emotional and defensive (Argentines were understandably outraged) or misguided (they sought to "personalize" the blame), or as the result of a crisis of political representation involving a lack of correspondence between the public demand for accountability and the elected authorities' unresponsiveness, along with the political practices stemming from a powerful executive (Menemismo). These are, however, incomplete explanations. Situating its analysis among those that look at actors' choices and subjective goals, this study has asserted that the crisis should be explained in the context of enduring conceptions of national identity and their interaction with political and economic factors.

This analysis considered the apparent demise of the Argentine Dream a key factor in the way Argentines frame their national identity and conceive social bonds. This is a controversial issue, and this chapter puts it forward to provoke a twofold debate. On one hand, the myth of Great Argentina arguably has played a significant role throughout the country's history, and the middle classes have been particularly attached to it. To understand why they took to the streets, we have to understand what made them tick. On the other hand, the study of social mobilization must focus on perceptions and beliefs, seen as both subjectively construed and objectively shaped by public discourse and institutions. Both leaders and citizens held on to an ideal of Argentina that hardly corresponded to the reality of most citizens' everyday lives. Nor did it fit a country that continued to undergo sharp cycles of boom and bust in both politics and economics. When citizens challenge an existing social and political situation, their demands respond, at least in part, to collective notions of their potential as a nation. Shared myths, memories, and dreams are vital components of this cultural framework.

The caretaker presidents who followed De la Rúa continued to express a discourse based on the myth of a Great Argentina (in his inauguration speech, Adolfo Rodríguez Saá expressed his wish to give Argentina back its *grandeza*). Elected President Néstor Kirchner, however, surprised most analysts by breaking with this longstanding tradition. For instance, in his speech before the Legislative Assembly, he made no references to the nation's or its people's greatness. In contrast, he spoke about a "dream" of an "ordinary" Argentina: "I want a normal Argentina. I want a serious country. But also a more just country" (Kirchner 2003). These words sound distant from the traditional Argentine aspiration of becoming a new United States, a regional power, or a First World country.

It is interesting that once the "normalcy" of the crisis becomes part of everyday life, the maintenance of the myth can rapidly steer people toward blind optimism. This could explain why Kirchner's election expressed an apparent "reconciliation" between citizens and (at least, parts of) the political establishment. The sense of a quick economic improvement during the first months of Kirchner's tenure—still a very modest improvement in relation to the downfall of previous years—fueled an incredible 88 percent rate of approval (see *Clarín* 2003). How to explain this dramatic reversal in public opinion? If the surge of social mobilization was mainly a reaction to worsening economic conditions, the slightly better current situation hardly justifies so sheer a turnaround in the collective mood. There is no doubt that the sustained growth of the economy in 2004, 2005, and 2006 at what some observers call "Chinese rates"—8 percent annually—plays a factor in upholding Kirchner's impressive levels of popularity. But if the main reason for the citizens' revolt was a deep crisis of political representation, it remains difficult to explain the strong support for old-school politicians, including Kirchner himself, a long-time Peronist chieftain; or the turnaround that some spontaneous leaders of the social rebellion later ran as candidates for traditional parties. The October 2005 legislative election, in which voters supported Kirchner's candidates all over the country, showed that Argentines were largely comfortable with the political status quo.

The people's indictment of the political class in 2001 was not simply the expression of a divide between citizens and their representatives. That phenomenon is by no means exclusive to Argentina; not even to Latin America. In fact, citizens in almost every Western democracy have denounced the political class as being concerned only with advancing particular interests (especially those of the rich and powerful) rather than the common good and as generally corrupt and morally decadent (Schnapper 2002). It has been suggested that the growing use of references such as "political class" implies an alienation of people from their political institutions and the perception of politicians "as a distinct category of beings" (Cox 1996). Public cynicism toward political leaders and politicians in well-established democracies steadily increased in the last quarter of the twentieth century. In Austria, Britain, Canada, Denmark, Finland, Germany, Italy, Japan, the Netherlands, Norway, Sweden, and the United States, disillusionment with politicians became a key aspect of the political landscape (Pharr and Putnam 2000; Pharr et al. 2000).

In the case of Argentina, the revolt against the "political class" reflected the mutual reinforcement between an antipolitical attitude—strongly encouraged by *Menemismo*—and the belief that Argentina had once again been steered away from its destiny. If Menem succeeded in placing the blame for the country's decadence on the state bureaucracy and entrenched interests, *Menemismo* (viewed as a paradigm of dishonesty, pretension, excess, and frivolity) itself became the main culprit in the eyes of most Argentines once the convertibility model collapsed. Kirchner embodied the anti-Menem sentiment by stressing the opposite values: honesty, humility, moderation, dignity. Kirchner has been careful to emphasize his willingness to listen to the people (as if he were responding to the last wave of civic mobilization). He also has built a discourse with few references to the legacy of Perón (usually read as a mark of populism) but with repeated allusions to a new generation of political leaders (as if he were stressing his distance from the political class "indicted" by the people).

Even though Kirchner has generally played down the myth of Great Argentina, he became, ironically, the focus of a revived hope in the country's future. Recently, some observers have wondered whether Argentines are "living a fantasy" because of their belief, fueled by Kirchner's rhetoric, that their country is on a fast track to recovery "from domestic despair and international disgrace" (Alan Stoga, vice chairman of the Americas Society, quoted in *Miami Herald* 2003). During his second and third years in office, Kirchner increasingly asserted his authority—by further strengthening presidential supremacy in the political system and even resorting to some controversial gestures to curb criticism in the media—and his public discourse acquired some distinctive nationalist overtones, albeit focused on patriotic sentiment rather than on militant nationalism: "I want us to feel fanatically Argentine" (*Clarín* 2005). In his 2006 Address to the Congress, Kirchner referred for the first time to Argentina's "destiny." Some days before, during the ceremony that marks the opening of the school year across the country, he had declared: "We are ready to tell the world that Argentina is a great and a glorious nation" (Kirchner 2006).

Does this mean that Argentina has returned to politics as usual, with its accustomed penchant for charismatic leaders and dreams of salvation? Not necessarily. There are many indications that although social mobilization has clearly subsided, a heightened citizen awareness still permeates Argentine society. Moreover, the residue of the recent wave of mobilization (such as the decision of grassroots movements to create new political coalitions that challenge traditional forms of leadership) may have a favorable impact on Argentina's democracy.

Myths, though, are hard to kill. It might be argued that, embedded as they are in the national identity, they are subject to cyclical revivals and periods of latency, correlated to economic, political, and social trends. The ostensible reconciliation between citizens and the political establishment (which is difficult to understand from traditional economic and institutional perspectives) gives support to this analysis. The indictment of politics as usual was more a response to a shock of reality than a firmly rooted desire to renew the nature of the political game in Argentina. With the myth of national success in the background—a myth that experiences surges and decays—it is possible to understand why Argentines were ready to trust politicians again as the unprecedented crisis subsided. Indeed, it would seem that many Argentines still expect—perhaps now more than ever—that the promise of a Great Argentina will finally come true.

NOTES

1 On October 14, 2001, Argentines voted to renew half the seats in the Cámara de Diputados and the whole Senate. The *voto bronca* (rage vote), cast by inscribing a protest legend on the ballot or by including a foreign object in the ballot envelope (for example, an image of the popular cartoon character Clemente or a picture of Che Guevara), finished second, receiving almost 4 million votes (more than 20 percent of the national total). Moreover, 90.8 percent of those who cast the *voto bronca* said they wanted to express their anger at the "political class." See *Clarín* 2001.

2 The white tent was set up on April 2, 1997, by the teachers' union CTERA (Confederación de Trabajadores de la Educación de la República Argentina) on a public square in front of the National Congress in Buenos Aires. The huge tent stood there for almost three years as a means of pressuring the federal government to enact a new law on education funding. Different groups of teachers would go on a hunger strike for a week inside the tent. This form of citizen protest attracted much media attention and was later used by other actors elsewhere in the country (Giarracca and Bidaseca 2001).

3 Even though they do not belong exclusively to the upper strata. Indeed, 13 percent of lower-middle-class households in Argentina have an Internet connection. Data from Carrier y Asociados 2002.

4 A computer-assisted analysis was performed on 1,078 messages (totaling 146,792 words) sent to *Clarín's* website from May 12 to 19, 2002, by 651 different individuals.

5 The procedure entailed detecting all instances of these phrases: *estoy muy orgulloso-a, me siento muy orgulloso-a, me siento orgulloso-a, estoy orgulloso-a, siento orgullo, podemos estar orgullosos, cómo no estar orgulloso-a, no me siento orgulloso-a, no estoy orgulloso-a, no me puedo sentir orgulloso-a, me da vergüenza, me avergüenza, siento vergüenza, como no sentir vergüenza, me avergüenzo.*

6 The survey was conducted by Cuore Consumer Research (CCR 2002) (N = 4,500).

7 As one message noted, "The problem here is another one: this poor country has nothing to do with the garbage that walks on it."

8 The following message illustrates this pattern: "The current chaos is not the responsibility of . . . 37 million Argentines, but of a few crooks in the ruling and political class."

9 "That is what is being called the Argentine Miracle. Under President Carlos Menem and his economy minister, Domingo Cavallo, Argentina is experiencing a spectacular revival. [. . .] Argentina—mired during 'the lost decade' of the 1980s in inflation, stagnation, debt and deficits—is becoming something of a showcase of Latin America's free-market revolution" (*Wall Street Journal* 1992).

REFERENCES

Aguinis, Marcos. 2003. En busca del enemigo que es preciso vencer. *La Nación* (Buenos Aires), January 12.

Altamirano, Carlos. 2002. ¡Que se vayan todos! *La Ciudad Futura* 51 (August): 8–10.

Armony, Ariel C. 2004. *The Dubious Link: Civic Engagement and Democratization*. Stanford: Stanford University Press.

Armony, Ariel C., and Hector E. Schamis. 2003. *Repensando la Argentina: antes de diciembre de 2001 y más allá de mayo de 2003*. Washington, DC: Woodrow Wilson International Center for Scholars.

Armony, Victor. 2001a. Is There an Ideological Link Between Neopopulism and Neoliberalism? *Brazilian Journal of Political Economy* 21, 2: 62–77.

———. 2001b. National Identity and State Ideology in Argentina. In *National Identities and Sociopolitical Changes in Latin America*, ed. Mercedes F. Durán-Cogan and Antonio Gómez-Moriana. New York: Routledge. 293–319.

———. 2004. *L'Énigme argentine. Images d'une société en crise*. Montreal: Athéna.

Armony, Victor, and Elena Bessa. 2002. Emerging Social and Ethnic Identities in Latin America. Paper presented at the 15th World Congress of Sociology, Brisbane, Australia, July 7–13.

Auyero, Javier. 2002. *La protesta: retratos de la beligerancia popular en la Argentina democrática.* Buenos Aires: Centro Cultural Rojas-UBA.

Bruce, James. 1953. *Those Perplexing Argentines.* New York: Longmans and Green.

Carrier y Asociados (Buenos Aires). 2002. Informe telecomunicaciones residenciales. June.

Cheresky, Isidoro. 2002. La bancarrota. *La Ciudad Futura* (Buenos Aires) 51 (August): 6–8.

———. 2003. En nombre del pueblo y de las convicciones. Posibilidades y límites del gobierno sustentado en la opinión pública. Paper presented at the conference "Building the Americas," University of Quebec, Montreal, November 5–7.

Clarín (Buenos Aires). 2001. El voto bronca llegó a casi cuatro millones. October 16.

———. 2003. Los Kirchner, al tope de las preferencias de la gente. December 1.

———. 2005. Kirchner encabezó los actos por el Día de la Independencia. August 9.

Corrales, Javier. 2002. The Politics of Argentina's Meltdown. *World Policy Journal* 19, 3 (Fall): 29–42.

Cox, Robert. 1996. A Perspective on Globalization. In *Globalization: Critical Reflections*, ed. James H. Mittelman. Boulder: Lynne Rienner. 21–33.

Cullen, Jim. 2003. The American Dream: *A Short History of an Idea that Shaped a Nation.* New York: Oxford University Press.

Cuore Consumer Research (CCR). 2002. Survey (N = 4,500). March. Cited in Sociedad: el impacto de la crisis, *Clarín*, August 19.

De Ipola, Emilio. 2002. Debate. *La Ciudad Futura 51* (August): 17–30.

DeLaney, Jeane H. 2002. Imagining *El Ser Argentino*: Cultural Nationalism and Romantic Concepts of Nationhood in Early Twentieth-Century Argentina. *Journal of Latin American Studies* 35: 625–58.

Devoto, Fernando. 1992. Idea de nación, inmigración y "cuestión social" en la historiografía académica y en los libros de texto de Argentina (1912–1974). *Estudios Sociales* 2, 3: 9–30.

Feinman, José Pablo. 2003. Poder y contrapoder. *Página 12.*

Filmus, Daniel, ed. 1999. *Los noventa: política, sociedad y cultura en América Latina y Argentina del fin de siglo.* Buenos Aires: Eudeba/FLACSO.

Frondizi, Arturo. 1959. Desarrollo económico y unidad nacional. Buenos Aires: Servicio de Prensa de la Presidencia de la Nación. November 5.

Gayol, Silvia, and Kessler, Gabriel. 2002. *Violencias, delitos y justicias en la Argentina.* Buenos Aires: UNGS-Manantial.

Giarracca, Norma, and Karina Bidaseca. 2001. Introducción. In *La protesta social en la Argentina. Transformaciones económicas y crisis social en el interior del país*, ed. Norma Giarraca et al. Buenos Aires: Alianza Editorial. 19–40.

Guemureman, Silvia. 2002. Argentina: la "medición" de la inseguridad ciudadana. Una lectura de la encuesta victimológica a través de los indicadores sociales. Paper presented at the Canadian Association for Latin American and Caribbean Studies Conference, Montreal, October 24–26.

Hanke, Steve H. 2002. Argentina: Caveat Lector. Paper prepared for the Cato Institute's 20th Annual Monetary Conference cosponsored with *The Economist*, New York City, October 17.

Iñigo Carrera, Nicolás, and María Celia Cotarelo. 2003. Social Struggles in Present-Day Argentina. *Bulletin of Latin American Research* 22, 2: 201–13.

International Monetary Fund (IMF). 2002. *World Economic Outlook.* Washington, DC: IMF. September.

Jozami, Angel. 2003. *Argentina. La destrucción de una nación.* Buenos Aires: Mondadori.

Kaiser, Susana. 2002. *Escraches*: Demonstrations, Communication, and Political Memory in Post-dictatorial Argentina. *Media, Culture and Society* 24: 499–516.

Kirchner, Néstor. 2003. Mensaje ante la Asamblea Legislativa. May 25. Presidencia de la Nación Argentina. <www.presidencia.gov.ar>.

———. 2006. Palabras en el acto de inauguración del ciclo lectivo 2006 en la provincia de Córdoba. February 27. Presidencia de la Nación Argentina. <www.presidencia.gov.ar>.

Krueger, Anne. 2002. Crisis Prevention and Resolution: Lessons from Argentina. Paper presented at the conference "The Argentina Crisis," Cambridge, MA, July 17.

Lanata, Jorge. 2002. *Argentinos. Desde Pedro de Mendoza hasta la Argentina del centenario.* Buenos Aires: Ediciones B.

Laufer, Rubén, and Claudio Spiguel. 1999. Las "puebladas" argentinas a partir del "santiagueñazo" de 1993. Tradición histórica y nuevas formas de lucha. In *Lucha popular, democracia, neoliberalismo: protesta popular en América Latina en los años de ajuste*, ed. Margarita López Maya. Caracas: Nueva Sociedad. 15–44.

Levitsky, Steven, and María Victoria Murillo. 2003. Argentina Weathers the Storm. *Journal of Democracy* 14, 4 (October): 152–66.

Mahon, James E., Jr., and Javier Corrales. 2002. Pegged for Failure? Argentina's Crisis. *Current History* (February): 72–75.

Menem, Carlos. 1989. *Discursos del presidente*. Buenos Aires: Secretaría de Medios de Comunicación. December 9.

———. 1990a. March 8.

———. 1990b. September 3.

———. 1992. April 14.

———. 1993. May 1.

———. 1999. March 1.

Miami Herald. 2003. It's too early to judge Kirchner's "miracle." November 30.

Minujín, Alberto, and Gabriel Kessler. 1995. *La nueva pobreza*. Buenos Aires: Planeta.

Mocca, Edgardo. 2002. Debate. *La Ciudad Futura* 51 (August): 17–30.

O'Donnell, Guillermo. 1994. Delegative Democracy. *Journal of Democracy* 5, 1 (January): 56–69.

Ollier, María Matilde. 2003a. Argentina: Up a Blind Alley Once Again. *Bulletin of Latin American Research* 22, 2: 170–86.

———. 2003b. De la bipolaridad maltrecha a las incógnitas de la dispersión. *Textos* (Buenos Aires) 2, 2 (April): 4–11.

Oviedo, Luis. 2001. *Una historia del movimiento piquetero*. Buenos Aires: Ediciones Rumbos.

Pérez-Liñán, Aníbal S. 2003. Pugna de poderes y crisis de gobernabilidad: ¿hacia un nuevo presidencialismo? *Latin American Research Review* 38, 3 (October): 149–64.

Perón, Juan. 1973. *Habla Perón*. Buenos Aires: Editorial Freeland.

Peruzzotti, Enrique. 2002. Civic Engagement in Argentina: From the Human Rights Movement to the *Cacerolazos*. Washington, DC: Woodrow Wilson International Center for Scholars.

Pharr, Susan J., and Robert D. Putnam, eds. 2000. *Disaffected Democracies: What's Troubling the Trilateral Countries?* Princeton: Princeton University Press.

Pharr, Susan J., Robert D. Putnam, and Russell J. Dalton. 2000. A Quarter-Century of Declining Confidence. *Journal of Democracy* 11, 2 (April): 5–25.

Portantiero, Juan Carlos. 2002. Los desafíos de la democracia. *TodaVIA* (Fundación OSDE, Buenos Aires), September. <www.revistatodavia.com.ar/ notas2/Portantiero/textoportantiero.htm>

Rock, David. 1992. Racking Argentina. *New Left Review* 17 (September–October): 55–86.

Schamis, Hector E. 2002. Argentina: Crisis and Democratic Consolidation. *Journal of Democracy* 13, 2 (April): 81–94.

Schnapper, Dominique. 2002. *La démocratic providentielle. Essai sur l'égalité contemporaine*. Paris: Gallimard.

Smith, Peter H. 2000 (1996). *Talons of the Eagle: Dynamics of U.S.–Latin American Relations*. 2nd ed. New York: Oxford University Press.

Stiglitz, Joseph. 2002. Argentina, Shortchanged. *Washington Post*, May 12.

Svampa, Maristella. 2002. Las nuevas urbanizaciones privadas. Sociabilidad y socialización: la integración social "hacia arriba." In *Sociedad y sociabilidad en la Argentina de los 90*, ed. Luis Beccaria et al. Buenos Aires: Biblos. 55–96.

Taddei, Emilio. 2002. Crisis económica, protesta social y "neoliberalismo armado" en America Latina. *Revista del Observatorio Social de América Latina* 3, 7 (June).

Tedesco, Laura. 2002. Argentina's Turmoil: The Politics of Informality and the Roots of Economic Meltdown. *Cambridge Review of International Affairs* 15, 3 (October): 469–81.

Wall Street Journal. 1992. Argentine "Miracle": Talk of Buenos Aires is that Latest Revival in Economy Is for Real. September 11: 1.

Chapter 18

Democracy Without Parties? Political Parties and Regime Change in Fujimori's Peru

Steven Levitsky
Maxwell A. Cameron

In much of Latin America, democracy faces a critical problem: one of its central pillars, the political party, is increasingly viewed with dissatisfaction by citizens and, in some cases, by politicians. Yet most students of Latin American politics continue to share E. E. Schattschneider's view (1942, 1) that democracy is "unthinkable" without parties. Indeed, recent scholarship suggests that parties remain critical to the achievement (Corrales 2001), performance (Mainwaring and Scully 1995; Mainwaring 1999), and stability (Mainwaring and Scully 1995; Gibson 1996; McGuire 1997) of democracy in Latin America.

Few countries highlight the difficulties of achieving and sustaining democracy in the absence of parties more clearly than contemporary Peru. In the 1990s, the Peruvian party system decomposed to a degree that surpassed even the most notoriously fragmented systems in Latin America (Tanaka 1998, 1999; Lynch 1999; Conaghan 2000; Planas 2000). Throughout the decade, electoral politics was dominated by political "independents" and candidate-centered parties, many of which did not survive beyond a single electoral cycle. At the same time, Peru's democratic regime succumbed to a 1992 *autogolpe*, or self-coup, led by President Alberto Fujimori. Over the course of the decade, a weak and fragmented opposition failed to prevent Fujimori from dismantling institutional checks on his power; ultimately, internal tensions caused by a corruption scandal brought about Fujimori's fall.

This article analyzes the relationship between party collapse and political regimes in Peru. It examines three central questions. First, it seeks to explain the decomposition of the Peruvian party system. It argues that although the deep structural crisis of the 1980s weakened established parties and created an opening for antipolitical establishment outsiders, the full-scale decomposition of the party system and its replacement with an atomized, candidate-centered system were ultimately the product of Fujimori's political success in the wake of the 1992 *autogolpe*.

Peruvian politicians drew two lessons from this success: that public opinion would not reward the defense of formal democratic institutions; and that parties were not necessary for (and might impede) career advancement. In light of these lessons, scores of politicians abandoned both established parties and the democratic opposition in favor of an "independent" strategy centered on individualized and short-term electoral goals.

The second question is the regime implications of party system collapse. This article argues that although the established parties had clearly lost democratic support in Peru (in the sense that they were massively rejected by voters), their demise had far-reaching implications for Peruvian democracy. Party collapse and the proliferation of political "independents" weakened the democratic opposition in two ways. First, by focusing on short-term electoral gain rather than challenging the increasingly authoritarian regime, key political figures ceased to serve as instigators of what O'Donnell (1994) calls horizontal accountability. Second, the proliferation of candidate-centered movements, furthermore, eroded the opposition's capacity to act collectively or mobilize against the regime.

The third question in this study concerns the prospects for rebuilding parties in post-Fujimori Peru. In contrast to scholarly approaches that locate the roots of party failure in either government repression or institutional design—both of which offer potential remedies in the post-Fujimori period—we present a more cautious, historical-structural view. Strong parties are products of particular historical, sociological, and technological conditions that are absent or only weakly present in the contemporary period. Because of long-term structural changes, such as the growth of the urban informal sector and the increased influence of mass media technologies, contemporary politicians may lack both the incentive and the capacity to build new party organizations. Although these structural changes did not cause the collapse of Peru's party system, they may inhibit its reconstruction.

WHY PARTIES MATTER IN A DEMOCRACY

Political parties, to paraphrase John Aldrich, make democracy "workable."[1] For voters, parties make democracy workable by providing critical information about what candidates stand for and how they can be expected to govern (Downs 1957). Voters use party labels and platforms as cues or shortcuts, and parties may be evaluated based on their past performance, either in government or in opposition. Where parties are weak or noninstitutionalized, voters must confront a dizzying array of (often short-lived) electoral options, which limits their capacity to evaluate candidates retrospectively, associate them with known labels or ideologies, or even differentiate among them (Mainwaring and Scully 1995, 25; Mainwaring 1999, 324–27).

Parties also make democracy workable for politicians (Aldrich 1995). Politicians are self-centered and shortsighted animals who, when left to their own devices, have little incentive to think beyond the next election or their own electoral district. Consequently, they confront a variety of coordination problems, both in their pursuit of public office and in government (Aldrich 1995). Parties are critical to solving these problems.[2] Because they exist beyond a single election and must compete on a national scale, parties develop longer-term priorities and broader goals than individual politicians do. To the extent that parties discipline politicians, then, they can reshape politicians' incentives in ways that induce them to act in a more farsighted and collective manner.

Yet parties do more than simply make democracy "workable" for voters and politicians. They also help make democracy viable for society as a whole. In Latin America, parties have contributed to democratic stability in a variety of ways. They help to protect the interests of socioeconomic elites who have the capacity to "kick over the chess board" (Borón 1992, 76). When powerful socioeconomic actors cannot protect their interests in the electoral arena, they are more likely to support non-democratic alternatives or engage in praetorian tactics that put democratic institutions at risk. Parties serve as an important means of protecting powerful interests in the electoral arena. As Edward Gibson (1996) has argued, when strong conservative parties have protected elite economic interests in Latin America, democratic regimes have tended to be stable. Similarly, when organized working classes are strong, links to labor-based parties may be critical to regime stability (Collier and Collier 1991; McGuire 1997).

Strong parties are also essential to democratic governability. By serving as a bridge between executives and legislatures, parties provide a critical mechanism for overcoming gridlock. Without the disciplining function of parties, legislatures may degenerate into chaos or, worse, a marketplace for influence peddling. In Latin America, weak parties have been associated with legislative inefficiency, executive–legislative conflict, policy ineffectiveness, and, not infrequently, regime crises (Mainwaring and Scully 1995; Mainwaring 1999). By contrast, where parties have been strong and party systems institutionalized (Chile, Costa Rica, and Uruguay), executive–legislative relations have tended to be smoother and governability crises less frequent (Mainwaring and Scully 1995).

Parties help hold elected leaders accountable to democratic institutions. Many Latin American democracies are characterized by weak or ineffective systems of checks and balances (or "horizontal accountability"), which allow executives to govern at the margin of other democratic institutions and actors (O'Donnell 1994, 1998). Caesarist behavior is strongly associated with weak parties and poorly institutionalized party systems (Mainwaring and Scully 1995, 22–23; Mainwaring 1999, 328). Parties are important instigators of horizontal accountability. Where they are weak and politicians gain power through direct, unmediated appeals, executives tend to govern in a personalistic and anti-institutional manner, often violating the "unspoken rules of the game" that underlie Republican institutions (Mainwaring and Scully 1995, 22). Where parties are strong, by contrast, politicians must work through them in order to obtain higher office and, when in office, must cooperate with them in order to remain there.

The primary arena through which parties check executive power is the legislature. By resisting the tendency to fuse legislative and executive power, parties provide a bulwark against the despotism of an over-weening executive. Through the right of inquiry, censure, and oversight, they use the legislature to constrain executive power and prevent its abuse. Autonomous legislatures also help to guarantee the independence of the judiciary by ensuring that courts are not stacked and judges not summarily dismissed. They may even help to ensure the integrity of the electoral process by defending the independence and transparency of electoral institutions.[3]

Parties play an important role in recruiting and socializing democratic elites, and thus in limiting the space available to political outsiders. They provide the foundation for a democratic political class. Political classes vary considerably with respect to their openness, their coherence, and their links to society, and this variation may have important consequences for democracy. When they are oligarchic or cartellike, channels of access and the scope of competition are reduced, and the gap between elites and mass publics tends to widen. In such a context, citizens may conclude that politicians are unrepresentative, corrupt, or unconcerned with the public interest, and this perception may erode democratic legitimacy.[4] Yet when a political class is absent, politics becomes a world of amateur or "outsider" politicians, many of whom lack experience with—and in some case, commitment to—democratic institutions.

Historically, the most effective means of maintaining a political class that steers clear of both oligarchy and amateur politics has been the political party. Strong parties broaden and diversify the elite recruitment process. In many European countries, for example, social democratic parties played a central role in recruiting members of the working class into the political system; and in the United States, urban Democratic Party machines provided channels of access to various immigrant and ethnic groups.[5]

Parties also socialize office seekers into democratic politics and provide them with training and experience. Although party politicians are hardly exempt from irresponsible and even authoritarian behavior, on the whole, they are more likely than outsiders to have experience with (and be oriented toward) democratic practices, such as negotiation, compromise, and coalition building. They are also more likely to value democratic institutions, or at least to have a stake in their preservation. The absence of strong parties often gives rise to outsider or "neopopulist" candidates who are elected on the basis of direct and often antisystem appeals (Roberts 1995; Weyland 1999). Because they are amateurs at democratic politics, outsiders constitute a "shot in the dark" in terms of their capacity to govern and their commitment to democracy. Indeed, in Latin America, the election of political outsiders has frequently resulted in ineffective, irresponsible, and in some cases undemocratic governments.

Beyond democratic viability, political parties may play an important role in achieving democracy (Corrales 2001; Franklin 2001). They do so in at least two ways. They facilitate collective action; the ability of democratic oppositions to maintain a united front is often critical to their success (Corrales 2001). Fragmented opposition movements tend to be weak, to lack coherence, to have limited mobilizational capacity, and to be highly vulnerable to cooptation and the "divide and rule" strategies of autocratic incumbents (Corrales 2001, 95–96). By facilitating coordination among and, when necessary, imposing discipline on individual leaders, strong parties help to avoid such problems. Strong parties also serve as "mobilizing structures" for opposition movements (Tarrow 1994; Franklin 2001), providing them with the organizational resources necessary to sustain a mass-based democracy movement. When parties are weak, prodemocratic elites often lack national-level infrastructures or strong ties to society, and civic groups tend to lack the kind of horizontal ties that facilitate macrolevel collective action (Roberts 1998, 72–73).

In summary, political parties are essential to achieving, maintaining, and improving the quality of democracy. Where they are weak, class actors tend to have less of a stake in electoral politics, legislatures are less able to oversee the executive, antisystem candidates are more common and more successful, and societies are less well equipped either to resist authoritarian encroachments or to remove autocratic governments.

DEMOCRATIC BREAKDOWN AND PARTY SYSTEM COLLAPSE IN PERU

During the early 1990s, Peru experienced the collapse of both its party system and its democratic regime. Each of these developments can be traced largely to the profound political and socioeconomic crisis that hit Peru in the late 1980s. Yet party weakness and the *Fujimorazo* also interacted in important ways. Party weakness made Fujimori's election possible, and the election of an antipolitical–establishment outsider exacerbated Peru's political–institutional crisis and increased the probability of a coup. In turn, Fujimori's success in the wake of his 1992 *autogolpe* accelerated the process of party system decomposition by creating an incentive for politicians to abandon existing parties and pursue office as "independents." These defections decimated an already debilitated party system.

Party Crisis, Outsider Politics, and the 1992 Autogolpe

Throughout most of the 1980s, Peru possessed a relatively coherent (if weakly institutionalized) four-party system, consisting of the leftist United Left, the populist American Popular Revolutionary Alliance (APRA), the centrist Popular Action (AP), and the conservative Popular Christian Party (PPC). Although the strength of these parties has been the subject of debate, all possessed national structures, discernible programs or ideologies, and identifiable social bases.[6] In the 1985 presidential election and the 1986 municipal elections, the four parties collectively accounted for more than 90 percent of the vote (Tanaka 1998, 55).

Beginning in the late 1980s, however, Peru's established parties fell into crisis (Cameron 1994; Cotler 1994; Tanaka 1998; Lynch 1999; Planas 2000). The demise of the old party system is attributable to a variety of factors, including aspects of the electoral system (Schmidt 1996; Tuesta Soldevilla 1996b, 1998) and the mistakes of the parties themselves (Lynch 1999).[7]

The principal roots of the crisis, however, lay in the profound structural challenges the parties faced during the 1980s. The elimination of the last barriers to full suffrage, large-scale urban migration, and the expansion of the urban informal sector radically altered the electoral landscape. The growth of the informal economy, which encompassed more than 50 percent of the economically active population by 1990, weakened class-based organizations, eroded collective and partisan identities, and produced a growing pool of politically unattached voters (Cameron 1994; Lynch 1999, 160).

At the same time, a deep economic crisis and the brutal insurgency of the Shining Path guerrilla movement limited the capacity of the established parties to build enduring linkages to this emerging electorate. In the wake of the successive failures of the AP government of Fernando Belaunde Terry (1980–85) and the APRA government of Alan García Pérez (1985–90), the political center collapsed, leaving a large sector of the electorate available for outsider appeals (Cameron 1994, 1997, 45–50).

The first manifestations of party system crisis emerged in the 1989 municipal elections, when Ricardo Belmont, a radio personality who had formed an "independent movement" called *Obras* (Works), was elected mayor of Lima. A year later, the top two finishers in the first round of the 1990 presidential election, novelist Mario Vargas Llosa and the virtually unknown Alberto Fujimori, were both political amateurs who appeared from outside the established parties. Vargas Llosa, whose candidacy was backed by AP and the PPC, finished first in a fragmented field in the first round, but Fujimori overwhelmingly won the runoff.

Although it was facilitated by the crisis of the late 1980s, Fujimori's victory was also, however, the result of several other contingent factors. The, which might otherwise have capitalized on the crisis of the centrist parties, suffered a debilitating schism in 1989—Fujimori received behind-the-scenes support from Alan García, who sought to weaken APRA candidate and internal rival Luis Alva Castro (Schmidt 1996, 342; Lynch 1999, 191). Fujimori also benefited from the mistakes of Vargas Llosa, whose radical neoliberal platform and alliance with traditional conservative elites helped to consolidate an "anyone but Vargas Llosa" vote.[8] Finally, the election of an outsider was facilitated by Peru's majority runoff system, which allowed Fujimori to capture the presidency despite finishing second in the first round (Schmidt 1996; Tanaka 1998).

Fujimori's election had devastating consequences for democracy. The election of an antipolitical–establishment outsider exacerbated what had already become a serious regime crisis (Kenney 1996; McClintock 1996; Cameron 1997, 1998). Hyperinflation and mounting political violence had generated broad public dissatisfaction with the political status quo. Although such conditions would have posed a severe challenge to any government, Fujimori was particularly ill equipped to respond to them in a democratic manner. A political amateur, he had no real party behind him, no program ready for implementation, and no team to staff the government. His supporters held less than a fifth of the seats in the congress, and his initial support from the left and APRA quickly evaporated. He was opposed, moreover, by leading sectors of the political, economic, and religious establishment.[9]

Lacking experience with the give and take of democratic politics, Fujimori opted for an authoritarian strategy for political survival, designed by his security adviser, Vladimiro Montesinos: the April 1992 *autogolpe*. Although there is no guarantee that the regime would have survived under a party-backed politician, it is reasonable to suggest that Fujimori, an antipolitical–establishment outsider without any socialization in the political process, was particularly open to an authoritarian alternative.

Authoritarian Success and the Rise of Political "Independents"

Although the crisis of the 1980s badly weakened the Peruvian party system, it was Fuji-mori's success in the wake of the 1992 *autogolpe* that proved more devastating. Although widely discredited, the established parties survived the 1990 election (Tanaka 1998, 194–95; Planas 2000, 337). APRA won a surprising 25 percent of the legislative vote, and AP, the PPC, and the all retained an important presence in the congress.

What ultimately sealed the fate of the party system was the outcome of Fujimori's high-stakes battle with the established parties. As Martín Tanaka (1998, 198–200) has argued, outsider presidents Fernando Collor de Mello of Brazil and Jorge Serrano of Gua-temala lost similar battles during this period. Had Fujimori been impeached like Collor, or had he failed in his *autogolpe* attempt like Serrano, Peru's party system might have ended up similar to those of Brazil and Guatemala: weak and discredited but essentially intact.[10]

Fujimori, however, succeeded. His claim that the *autogolpe* was necessary to rid Peru of a "false democracy" (Paredes Castro et al. 1992) dominated by party cliques was, by and large, accepted by Peruvians. Public support for Fujimori jumped from 53 percent in March 1992 to 81 percent after the *autogolpe* (Tanaka 1998, 219), and over the next three years, the president's average approval rating was a whopping 66 percent (based on data from Tanaka 1998, 219). Fujimori's popularity helped to create a broad base of support for the new regime. *Fujimorista* forces easily won the constituent assembly elec-tions held in November 1992: Fujimori's New Majority/C-90 won 49 percent of the vote, compared to 9.8 percent for the second-place PPC. The following year, a new constitu-tion was approved—albeit with greater difficulty—via referendum. In 1995, Fujimori was easily reelected, winning a stunning 62.4 percent of the vote and gaining an absolute majority in the new congress.

The *autogolpe's* success was based largely on its timing (Tanaka 1998, 220–21). During the months immediately preceding and following the coup, Fujimori vanquished two forces that Peruvians had come to find unbearable: hyperinflation and the cycle of protest and violence that had culminated in the terrorism of Shining Path. The *autogolpe* was carried out at a time when economic stabilization was taking hold and Fujimori's popularity was on the rise (Tanaka 1998, 220–21). The capture of Shining Path leader Abimael Guzmán several months later helped to consolidate that support. By late 1992, a clear majority of Peruvians had decided that Fujimori represented the sort of strong leader for whom they had been yearning.

This success distinguished Peru from other Latin American cases in the 1990s. Other elected outsiders in the region (Collor, Serrano) failed to resolve their countries' deep political and economic crises and were ultimately defeated, and other hyperinflationary crises in the region (Argentina, Bolivia, Brazil) were resolved by established parties. Only in Peru was an antiparty president responsible for ending the crisis (Tanaka 1998, 52–53).

Fujimori's successes effectively buried the established parties. The *autogolpe* created a new partisan cleavage: Fujimori versus "the opposition." Given the president's popularity, this cleavage worked to the parties' great detriment. Anti-Fujimori politicians became col-lectively known as *la oposición*, a derogatory moniker connoting self-serving opponents of the government. Worse, established parties found themselves on the wrong side of public opinion when they defended democratic institutions. Although surveys found substantial opposition too many of the abuses committed by the Fujimori government (Tanaka 1999, 10–14; Carrión 2000), it is also clear that much of the electorate viewed those abuses as the price of strong and effective leadership. This was particularly true of working-class and rural Peruvians, many of whom had experienced only limited access to justice and tended to associate the preexisting rule of law with corrupt judges and police officers. In general, then, a staunch defense of the rule of law was a priority only for relatively privileged sectors of society (students, professionals, unionized workers), and mainly in Lima.

The opposition's defense of democratic institutions in the immediate aftermath of the coup thus failed to win mass support. When Congress, meeting in secret, impeached Fujimori and appointed vice president Máximo San Román to replace him, San Román's presidential aspirations made him a laughingstock, and legislators were derided when they appeared in public. When constituent assembly elections were held in late 1992, APRA, AP, and the boycotted them as illegitimate; yet the boycott failed to prevent the constitutional process from moving forward, and the vacancy left by the established parties was quickly filled by political newcomers. Eighty-five percent of the vote went to either *Fujimorista* or "independent" candidates.

Although the established parties participated in subsequent elections, they fared poorly. In the 1993 municipal elections, APRA, AP, the PPC, and collectively won just 33.3 percent of the vote, and in the 1995 presidential election, the four parties accounted for just 6.3 percent of the vote. In the 1995 race, no candidate who ran under an established party label won even 5 percent of the vote. Many regime opponents rallied behind the candidacy of former U.N. Secretary-general Javier Pérez de Cuéllar, who headed the *Unión por el Perú* (Union for Peru, or UPP). Although it presented itself as independent, the UPP was widely perceived as another incarnation of *la oposición*. Pérez de Cuéllar received just 21.8 percent of the vote, barely a third of Fujimori's total.

Peruvian politicians drew two lessons from the initial failures of the democratic opposition, both of which had far-reaching implications for the party system and for democracy. First, they concluded that a defense of the political *status quo ante* was not a viable electoral strategy. Not only did public support for Fujimori make the defense of democratic institutions unprofitable, but such a strategy associated politicians with the discredited old guard elite that led the oposición. Confronted with this problem, ambitious non-*Fujimorista* politicians began to distance themselves from prodemocratic forces and to define themselves as "independents." Many of them adopted an ambiguous position in regard to the Fujimori regime, refusing to condemn the *autogolpe* and avoiding, whenever possible, direct conflict with the president. Instead of challenging the regime itself, they sought to advance their careers within it, focusing on developing personal reputations as effective administrators. In so doing, the new "independents" essentially foreswore their role as agents of horizontal accountability.

The second lesson politicians drew was that they no longer needed parties. During the 1980s, independent, candidate-centered electoral strategies were rarely an effective alternative to parties. Politicians who defected from major parties, such as Hugo Blanco, Miguel Angel Mufarech, and Andrés Townsend, generally failed in the electoral arena (Tanaka 1998, 96–97). This situation changed considerably in the 1990s. Fujimori's success suggested that established party labels and organizations were no longer necessary for (and might be a hindrance to) a successful political career.

Fujimori himself invested little in party organization. His original party, *Cambio 90* (Change 90, or C-90), lacked a program, a national structure, and a minimal activist base. Although Fujimori might have used his popularity to transform C-90 into an organized party, he ignored C-90 and even actively impeded its consolidation (Planas 2000, 347–51). Instead, he substituted state agencies for party organization (Roberts 1995, 2002; McClintock 1999).[11] With the assistance of friendly television networks, he also relied heavily on direct mass appeals (Roberts 1995; Conaghan 2000, 282). In preparation for the 1992 constituent assembly elections, Fujimori created a second, equally personalistic party: *Nueva Mayoría* (New Majority, NM). Neither C-90 nor NM ever developed an organizational life of its own. Three years later, Fujimori created a third party, *Vamos Vecino* (Let's Go Neighbor), to compete in the 1998 municipal elections. The pattern was repeated in 2000, when the creation of Perú 2000 brought the total number of *Fujimorista* parties to four.

Fujimori thus established a new model of electoral organization: the disposable party. Although often referred to as "independent movements," such parties were actually little more than electoral labels or candidate-centered vehicles. During the 1990s, this model became generalized as politicians of all ideological stripes borrowed Fujimori's organizational strategy. The result was a massive hemorrhaging of the established parties and the proliferation of personalistic vehicles. Many of the new independents were defectors from established parties.

The most important of these was Alberto Andrade of the PPC. A successful three-term mayor of the prosperous Lima district of Miraflores, Andrade quickly detected the antiparty mood of the electorate and, in anticipation of the November 1995 metropolitan Lima mayoral election, declared himself an independent. "No candidate affiliated with a party had a chance of winning the mayoralty of Lima," he bluntly told PPC leader Luis Bedoya Reyes later (*Diario La República* 2000). Andrade created a personalistic organization with an apolitical label: *Somos Lima* (We are Lima). The move succeeded: Andrade defeated Fujimori ally Jaime Yoshiyama in the 1995 election and established himself as the country's leading non-*Fujimorista* politician.

Central to Andrade's initial success was his ambiguity in relation to the regime. During his first term as mayor, he avoided taking positions on national issues, particularly those related to democracy, and instead sought to build a reputation as an effective administrator. Anticipating a 2000 presidential bid, Andrade transformed *Somos Lima* into *Somos Perú* (SP), which, despite some effort to create a national organization, remained personalistic and largely without programmatic content.

Other politicians who became independents in the 1990s include former Social security Institute director Luis Castañeda Lossio, an ex-AP member who created the National Solidarity Party (PSN) as a vehicle for a 2000 presidential bid; and former APRA senator Javier Valle Riestra, who briefly served as Fujimori's prime minister in 1998. At the local level, influential mayors, such as Alexander Kouri of Callao (PPC), José Murgia of *La Libertad* (APRA), Michel Azcueta of Villa El Salvador, and Angel Bartra of Chiclayo (AP), formed independent movements. Many legislators also became free agents, switching parties at each election to ensure reelection. Examples include Henry Pease (to UPP to *Perú Posible*, PP), Beatrix Merino (FREDEMO to the Independent Moralizing Front [FIM] to SP), Máximo San Román (C-90 to Obras to UPP), Anel Townsend (UPP to SP to PP), and Alberto Borea (Hayista Base Movement to PPC to UPP).

At the same time, many new and aspiring politicians began to create their own parties instead of joining existing ones. The most important of these was Alejandro Toledo, a business school professor and political amateur who created *País Posible* in preparation for a 1995 presidential bid. He resurrected the organization before the 2000 elections, changing its name to *Perú Posible* (PP). PP had no *raison d'etre* other than Toledo's presidential candidacy. Another example was Federico Salas, who was elected mayor of Huancavelica as an independent and who cofounded (but later abandoned) *Perú Ahora* (Peru Now) in anticipation of a presidential bid.

By the end of the decade, the "independent movement" had emerged as the dominant mode of electoral organization in Peru. As Catherine Conaghan observes, presidential hopefuls "do not see their relationship to parties as especially integral to their own ambitions for power. What they do regard as crucial is their relationship to the media establishment and the cultivation of a positive public image, preferably as a political independent" (2000, 182). Indeed, all the country's successful parties in the late 1990s—including both progovernment parties and opposition parties, such as *Somos Perú* and *Perú Posible*—were personalistic, candidate-centered vehicles that lacked national structures or even minimal links to civil society. Without programs or ideologies to identify themselves, many of these parties simply adopted the name of the territory they sought to represent. At the national level, *Somos Perú, Perú Posible, Perú Ahora*, UPP, and *Perú 2000* emerged between 1995 and 1999. At the local level, parties such as We Are Huancayo, Forward Chiclayo, Ayacucho 95, Eternal Cuzco, and Let's Save Huaraz proliferated.

Thus, in the 1990s, electoral politics reached a degree of fluidity and atomization that surpassed any other country in Latin America, including notoriously fragmented party systems such as those of Brazil and Ecuador. Peru's party system was created anew at each election: in 1990, the leading parties were C-90, FREDEMO, and APRA; in 1995, they were New Majority and UPP; in 1998, *Vamos Vecino* and SP; in 2000, Perú 2000 and PP. In 2000, the parties that had dominated electoral politics in the 1980s together received less than 2 percent of the vote; and each of the top five presidential candidates—Fujimori, Toledo, Andrade, Salas, and Castañeda Lossio—presided over a candidate-centered party. This pattern was reproduced at the local level. Each municipality developed its own party system. The number of independent mayors increased from 2 in 1986 to 79 in 1993 (Planas 2000: 268); and in 1998, independent lists proliferated to such a degree that the overall number of parties soared into the hundreds.

A few attempts to build national parties were made in the 1990s. In 1998, Andrade built alliances with mayors and regional leaders in an effort to expand his movement nationwide (Planas 2000, 289–93), but this party-building process never really took hold. After the 1998 municipal election, SP quickly fell victim to a government campaign to coopt pro-Andrade mayors. In August and September 1999, 23 mayors abandoned him (Planas 2000, 390). Many of these mayors were swayed by bribes or promises of future positions in the government; others despaired of governing without the support of the national executive.

Although some scholars have cited these developments as evidence that government repression made party building impossible in the 1990s (Planas 2000, 394), the failure of the SP party-building project is probably best understood as a product of the incentives and constraints facing Peruvian politicians. Because Andrade could use the media instead of party organization to launch a national candidacy, his organizational efforts never even remotely approached those that went into building parties such as APRA or AP. Local politicians, moreover, had few incentives to join or remain with SP. Like Andrade, many of them were independents who had won (or could win) office without national party affiliation. Lacking a well-oiled party machine or a coherent identity, SP could not establish enduring linkages to these local leaders. Without either the resources or the disciplinary mechanisms to ensure that SP members remained in the fold, Andrade's coalition was inherently unstable.

PARTY WEAKNESS, CAESARISM, AND THE FAILURE OF THE DEMOCRATIC OPPOSITION

The consolidation of an atomized system of candidate-centered politics seriously inhibited efforts to restore democracy in Peru.[12] Between 1992 and 2000, opposition parties repeatedly failed to check the Fujimori government's autocratic behavior. They played, moreover, only a marginal role in the regime's eventual collapse. Scholars differ considerably in their explanations of these failures. Some analysts argue that the opposition parties failed to seize opportunities to promote a democratic transition (Tanaka 1998, 1999). Others point to the repressive tactics of the Fujimori regime (Lynch 2000).

This study offers a somewhat different assessment. Like Lynch, it views the opposition's failure to check Fujimori's autocratic behavior as rooted more in its political weakness than in its strategic mistakes; yet in this view, the opposition's weakness was a product not of government repression but of politicians' adaptation to an environment in which both the defense of democracy and party building were widely perceived as unprofitable.

The "independent" politicians who abandoned anti-authoritarianism in favor of individualized efforts to win elections ceased to serve as instigators of horizontal accountability. Without vigorous opposition to the abuse of power, the network of public institutions responsible for upholding the rule of law became increasingly degraded and ineffectual. This inaction ultimately eroded vertical accountability as well. To ensure that elections are fair, electoral institutions must be transparent, and Congress and the judiciary must be able to check executive abuses. The unwillingness or inability to defend these institutions ultimately left opposition politicians defenseless as the conditions for free and fair elections eroded.

The collapse of parties also eroded the opposition's capacity for collective action and mobilization. Key decisions, such as whether or not to participate in a questionable election, how to select a single opposition candidate, and whether or not to negotiate with the regime (and on what terms), require organizations that can speak for (and discipline) large numbers of politicians across the national territory. The "independent movements" that emerged in Peru in the 1990s lacked such organizations. With no *raison d'etre* other than the election of their founder, they had short time horizons and lacked an encompassing interest in the preservation of democratic institutions. Lacking national infrastructures, strong roots in society, or linkages to important civic and social organizations, parties were reduced to narrow circles of elites, which left them, and the democracy movement they spearheaded, without much mobilizational muscle.

Destruction of Mechanisms of Horizontal Accountability

Between 1995 and 2000, the Fujimori government grew increasingly authoritarian. It circumvented, abused, or dismantled many of the mechanisms of horizontal accountability that the regime itself had established in the 1993 Constitution, while expanding the powers of the National Intelligence Service (*Servicio de Inteligencia Nacional*, SIN) (Mauceri 2000; Rospigliosi 2000; Conaghan 2001). The process of regime hardening began with an issue that had been at the center of the *autogolpe* decision: presidential reelection. In August 1996, the congress passed the Law of Authentic Interpretation of the Constitution, which stated that Article 112 of the 1993 Constitution could not be applied retroactively and therefore that Fujimori had only been elected once under the new constitution. This law established the legal foundations for his 2000 reelection bid.

Despite the clear unconstitutionality of Fujimori's effort to legalize his reelection bid, the opposition was unable successfully to challenge it through institutional channels. Fujimori's legislative majority limited the utility of the congress as a vehicle for checking executive power. Other mechanisms of horizontal accountability, such as the courts and the electoral authorities, were corrupted by the vast network of espionage, bribery, and extortion operated by Vladimiro Montesinos out of the SIN offices. The judicial branch was brought to heel via the systematic removal of independent judges and their replacement by Montesinos agents and "provisional" judges whose tenure hinged on government discretion (and who therefore tended to rule in the government's favor). The government also effectively subordinated Peru's highest electoral authority, the National Election Board (JNE). In December 1997, the congress passed legislation (popularly known as the Fraud Law) that allowed recently appointed "provisional" judges to elect members of the JNE. This rule change allowed the government to stack the JNE with Fujimori allies, and in 1998, elections for five members of the JNE produced a solid progovernment majority.

The institution that perhaps posed the greatest threat to Fujimori's reelection bid was the Constitutional Tribunal (TC), Peru's highest authority on constitutional matters. In January 1997, the TC ruled, in a 3–2 vote, that the Law of Authentic Interpretation did not apply to Fujimori. In response, the government effectively dismembered the TC. On May 28, 1997, the *Fujimorista* congress voted to impeach the three TC members who had voted against the government in January. The justices were never replaced, leaving the country without its highest constitutional authority for more than three years.

Without recourse to the legislature, the courts, or the electoral authorities, the opposition attempted to call a referendum on the reelection issue.[13] This effort was undermined by another act of Congress. In April 1996, the congress had approved the so-called Siura Law III (named after a lawmaker close to Montesinos), which required 48 votes in Congress before a referendum could be held. This law, which was initially adopted to stop an opposition-led referendum on privatization, clearly violated the spirit of the referendum provision in the constitution. It effectively meant that because the opposition lacked 48 votes in the legislature, only the government could use referenda. Nevertheless, opposition forces, under the umbrella of a civic association called the Democratic Forum, launched a campaign to collect the 1.2 million signatures needed to call a referendum on the reelection. It gathered more than 1.4 million signatures, but in August 1998, Congress voted 67–45 to block the referendum. In December 1999, the JNE, now dominated by *Fujimorista*, officially approved Fujimori's candidacy.

A large majority of Peruvians opposed the government's abuses, and the blocking of the referendum provoked nationwide protests.[14] This opposition, however, was not channeled into a sustained prodemocracy movement. The protests soon fizzled, and the TC and referendum issues quickly faded from the national agenda. These opposition failures were rooted largely in party weakness. The demise of organized parties left the democratic opposition without effective mobilizing structures or strong roots in society. Umbrella groups, such as the Democratic Forum, were supported by parties from across the political spectrum, but because the parties lacked infrastructures and activist bases, these organizations never became more than heterogeneous assortments of individual political elites. They provided forums for individual politicians but not channels for public participation or vehicles for large-scale mobilization.

Party collapse also eroded the opposition's capacity to act collectively. The UPP, which had brought together a large portion of the anti-Fujimori opposition in 1995, was decimated by defections after the election. The UPP congressional bloc dwindled from 17 to just 7 members, and the party quickly lost credibility as a serious opposition vehicle (Conaghan 2000, 279). The plethora of loosely organized and personalistic groups that emerged in its place seriously undermined opposition cohesion. Efforts to create a single opposition bloc in the legislature, such as the Parliamentary Democratic Opposition Bloc and the National Coordination Front, failed repeatedly. In the former case, the bloc disbanded soon after its formation because none of the leaders could find time to meet (*Latin American Weekly Report* 1997).

The opposition was further weakened because the leading non-*Fujimorista* politicians, such as Andrade, Castañeda Lossio, Toledo, and Salas, shied away from confrontation with the government and kept their distance from the democracy movement as they prepared their presidential bids. For example, although Andrade clearly aspired to the presidency, before 1998 he generally limited his public statements to municipal issues, such as traffic congestion and the remodeling of Lima's historic center.[15] The other three stayed so far from the democracy movement that it was often difficult to tell if they represented the government or the opposition. Consequently, even as support for the government fell significantly between 1996 and 1998, no credible alternative to Fujimori emerged.

The 2000 Transition: Opposition Weakness and Collapse from Within

Having failed in the effort to block Fujimori's unconstitutional bid for a third term in 2000, opposition parties were not the protagonists in the collapse of the Fujimori regime. Only the implosion of the regime itself brought about its demise.

After nearly four years of preparation, Fujimori's December 1999 decision to register his name as a candidate in the 2000 election was anticlimactic. Fujimori knew his presence was needed to ensure that the political system he had built did not collapse in disarray, leaving key members to defend themselves against accusations of corruption and human rights abuses. Opinion polls, moreover, suggested that his chances of winning were good. The government hastily formed a new "electoral alliance" called the *Frente Independiente Perú 2000*, which nominally included (but in reality circumvented) C-90, *Nueva Mayoría*, and *Vamos Vecino*. Despite sharp internal differences, *Fujimorista* leaders agreed on the need to achieve reelection. There was no question about where ultimate power lay: Montesinos was the undisputed mastermind behind the reelection campaign.[16]

Opposition candidates faced formidable challenges in their efforts to defeat Fujimori. Beyond the president's continued popularity (which hovered near 40 percent), they confronted an electoral playing field mined with dirty tricks and unfair incumbent advantages. Fujimori enjoyed a virtual monopoly over network television, an array of tabloid newspapers (many of which were later revealed to be subsidized and directed by SIN) that systematically assaulted opposition candidates, and the vast resources of the state. For example, SIN spied on opposition candidates and hired thugs to organize counterdemonstrations at opposition rallies; and state employees, including the armed forces, campaigned for progovernment tickets. Although opposition leaders complained bitterly about these conditions, the government's control over the judicial branch and electoral authorities, such as the JNE and the National Office of Electoral Processes (ONPE), left no means of redress.

The absence of institutional checks on government electoral abuses was made particularly manifest by the 1999–2000 signature scandal involving Fujimori's newest electoral vehicle, Perú 2000. Because Perú 2000 lacked even a minimal activist base, it was unable to collect the nearly five hundred thousand signatures needed to register a new party. An investigation by the newspaper *El Comercio* (2000) showed that as many as one million signatures had been forged by hundreds of people working in "signature factories" in late 1999, apparently under the supervision of Fujimori ally Absalón Vásquez. The scandal should have led to the disqualification of Perú 2000, but the JNE and ONPE stonewalled and downplayed the issue. The government promised to investigate itself, but a congressional investigation by *Fujimorista* Edith Mellado and a judicial investigation by the notoriously biased judge Mirtha Trabucco found nothing pointing to higher-ups.

Under these conditions, the opposition's best strategy might have been either to withdraw from the race or to form a broad coalition behind a single candidate (Bazo and Cameron 2000), as anti-authoritarian forces did in Chile in 1989 and Nicaragua in 1990. Yet the major parties never held serious negotiations toward either of these goals. Indeed, the leading candidates never once met in person to discuss the matter. Andrade, who led the field in many opinion polls in 1997 and 1998, was the least willing to join a common anti-Fujimori front. Thus, in April 1999, when eight opposition parties signed an accord to oppose Fujimori's reelection and work toward a single opposition candidacy, Andrade demurred.

There are several reasons for the opposition's failure to unite behind a common strategy. Each of the major opposition candidates was an "independent" who, having abandoned the struggle to defend democratic institutions, simply sought to replace Fujimori in the new political system. The candidates also faced a collective action problem: although the best options may have been for all candidates to boycott the election or to run united, each individual candidate preferred the option to run while all the others stood down. This problem was exacerbated by the extreme volatility of the electorate, which, by making it difficult to calculate candidates' electoral prospects, convinced all candidates that they had a chance of winning. It was further exacerbated by Peru's majority runoff electoral system, which allowed for the possibility that a marginal candidate could finish second in the first round and then win in the second round (as Fujimori did in 1990).

Most fundamentally, however, the candidates' collective action problem was rooted in party weakness. Had the major candidates belonged to institutionalized parties, longer time horizons might have encouraged the adoption of a coordinated strategy, and mechanisms would have existed to impose a single candidacy. Yet SP, PSN, and PP were little more than candidate-centered electoral vehicles. Lacking collective identities or goals beyond the personal ambitions of individual leaders, their time horizons did not extend much beyond the 2000 elections. They therefore had virtually no incentive to give up the chance to participate in those elections.

Divided, the opposition stood little chance of defeating Fujimori in 2000. Andrade, who had long been the most popular opposition candidate, suffered repeated and intense attacks by the progovernment media and saw his support decline precipitously in 1999.[17] After a similar wave of government attacks weakened Castañeda Lossio, Toledo emerged from the pack as the most viable opposition candidate; and as soon as he did, support for Andrade and Castañeda Lossio evaporated—a clear sign of the fragility of their parties and electoral bases.

The official results of the first round gave Fujimori 49.9 percent of the vote—tantalizingly close to the 50 percent needed to avoid a second round—and Toledo 40.2 percent. Fujimori's vote total was almost certainly inflated (Interview, Senior Electoral Officer 2002), and many observers suspect that the ONPE would have awarded Fujimori a first-round victory had it not been for intense scrutiny by national and international observers and massive election-night demonstrations in support of Toledo. The outcome, however, was not inconsistent with what polls had predicted.[18] The government's refusal to establish a level playing field for the second round led Toledo, now free of the collective action problems that had hindered opposition candidates in the first round, to withdraw from the race. Running unopposed, Fujimori won the second round with 51 percent of all ballots cast (including blank and null votes) and 74 percent of the valid votes.[19]

Party weakness also contributed to the opposition's failure to prevent Fujimori's reconsolidation of power after the contested election. Following the reelection debacle, the Fujimori government faced intense protest both in Peru and in the international arena. On the domestic front, Toledo led a large-scale protest, called the March of the Four Suyos, to coincide with Fujimori's July 28, 2000, swearing-in ceremony. On the international front, both the U.S. government and the Organization of American States observer mission declared the election unfair. Although the OAS General Assembly voted not to invoke Resolution 1080 and expel Peru on the grounds that its unfair election constituted an interruption of the democratic institutional order, it sent a high-level mission to Peru to recommend ways of improving the democratic process (Cooper and Legler 2001).

None of these sources of pressure was sufficient to dislodge Fujimori from power. Although the March of the Four Suyos constituted the largest opposition protest of the Fujimori period, the government ably used the violence (later shown to have been the work of SIN agents) to discredit the opposition and discourage further protest. By August 2000, OAS-sponsored negotiations had stalled and the government was showing little inclination to carry out the democratizing reforms the opposition demanded.

Fujimori not only survived the immediate postelectoral protests but also managed to reconstruct a new governing majority. Pro-Fujimori forces won only 52 of 120 seats in the congress in 2000. Without a legislative majority, the government risked losing control over key committees that could begin to investigate abuses committed by the executive branch. To avoid this, Montesinos employed the same strategy he had used to weaken *Somos Perú* in 1998: he used a combination of bribery and blackmail to coopt individual opposition members. In the weeks following the 2000 election, as many as 18 legislators changed their partisan affiliation. Toledo's PP was the hardest hit by defections, losing nearly a third of its 29-member caucus. Popularly known as *tránsfugas*, or turncoats, these defectors provided Fujimori with an ample legislative majority.[20]

The *tránsfugas* justified their opportunism in a variety of ways. Many said they wanted to distance themselves from the March of the Four Suyos and to avoid extreme positions. They stressed their desire to work "for the country" rather than for a party. Most insisted that they were not joining the government but sitting as "independents" (although this, of course, freed them to vote routinely with the government). In reality, most of the *tránsfugas* were making deals with Montesinos, and many signed letters of adherence to the government side in the SIN headquarters. Typically, tránsfugas were paid handsomely for their defection, usually substantial monthly sums in cash. Others were given important legislative committee assignments, positions that brought power, prestige, and additional perquisites. In other cases, Montesinos used his influence in the judiciary to call off investigations of members of Congress in exchange for their abandoning their party. Max Weber once noted that in the absence of parties, parliaments would become "a mere marketplace for compromises between purely economic interests, without any political orientation to overall interests." In such a context, he argued, "any public control over the administration would be vitiated" (1978, 1397). This characterization aptly fits Peru's 2000–2001 Congress.

The "purchase" of turncoats thus effectively substituted for partisan coalition building in a context of extreme party weakness. *Perú Posible* spokesperson Luis Solari attributed the wave of defections to a lack of "responsibility" among individual legislators, declaring, and "this is not a crisis of a party, but of persons" (*El Comercio* 2000). It was a crisis of party nonetheless. The defections reflected the tenuous nature of the linkages between "independent movements" and individual politicians. Because the "independent movements" were based almost entirely on the distribution of short-term selective incentives, a substantial number of elected legislators lacked even minimal ideological or affective ties to their parties (Grompone 2000, 145–46). They were essentially free agents; their party loyalties were virtually nil. Many legislators viewed elections as a commercial venture, involving an up-front investment to get onto a winning list. Once in power, they would recover their investment through the perquisites of office and the opportunities for illicit enrichment it would present.[21]

The parties themselves, moreover, lacked mechanisms to induce or compel their representatives to remain in the fold. Indeed, given that unsuccessful candidate-centered parties were unlikely to survive until the next election, their representatives had no incentive at all to remain with them.

As of August 2000, then, Fujimori appeared to have survived the reelection debacle. Antiregime protests had largely subsided, opposition forces had been discredited and demoralized, and Fujimori had constructed a new legislative majority that would enable him to govern securely for another five years. Both the United States and the OAS, moreover, had accepted the third term as a fait accompli. Domestic and international pressure was decisive only after cracks appeared in the regime.

The fall of the regime primarily stemmed from internal divisions; it was, in the words of former military president Francisco Morales Bermúdez, a "monster destroyed from within" (Mariella Balbi 2000). Fujimori's reliance on Montesinos both to control the armed forces and to manage his reelection campaign blurred the boundaries between intelligence activities and partisan politics. The use of the security apparatus rather than an organized party reinforced the president's penchant for illegal and covert campaign activities (such as espionage, bribery, and blackmail, as well as forging signatures for *Perú 2000*). Yet these tactics eroded the regime's legitimacy and hurt the electoral chances of those running for Congress on Fujimori's ticket. The failure to win a majority in Congress induced the government to engage in further illegality: the SIN's purchase of members of Congress, the exposure of which destroyed the regime.

The September 2001 release of a video showing Montesinos paying off a *tránsfuga* (McClintock 2001; Cameron 2002) exposed the dark side of the regime by providing irrefutable evidence that Montecinos was running a secret "government within the government"; it effectively destroyed the congress as a functioning institution and damaged the president's already questionable electoral legitimacy; and, above all, it undermined the relationship between Fujimori and Montesinos. Montesinos had accumulated a video archive documenting his control over much of the political establishment—members of Congress, senior judges, election officials, journalists, and media magnates. The purpose was to ensure his own indispensability, so that Fujimori could not remove Montesinos without bringing clown the entire political system they had constructed. This meant that even after the video's release—which convinced Montesinos that he was "destroyed" (Interview, Former Intelligence Officer 2002)—he retained the ability to blackmail Fujimori. Seeing no other way out, Fujimori resigned, and within weeks the entire regime collapsed. As opposition leaders themselves acknowledged, if the "Vladivideo" had not been released, the Fujimori government might well have survived.[22]

THE PROSPECTS FOR PARTY (RE)BUILDING IN POST-FUJIMORI PERU

Peru underwent a successful democratic transition in 2000–2001. Under the leadership of Interim President Valentín Paniagua, democratic institutions were thoroughly reformed. Functionaries of integrity replaced Montesinos agents in the ONPE and the JNE. A judicial renovation eliminated many members of the "Montesinos Mafia," and hundreds of military officers were purged or were obliged to offer *mea culpas* for their relationship with Montesinos. In addition, media independence increased enormously. The transition culminated in new elections in 2001, in which Toledo fended off a surprisingly strong challenge from ex-president Alan García to win the presidency. The vestigial *Fujimorista* forces were virtually wiped out, gaining just 4 of 120 seats in the congress.

What are the prospects for rebuilding political parties in post-Fujimori Peru? Answers to this question vary, often hinging on scholars' explanations of the party system's collapse. For some analysts, the failure of party-building efforts in the 1990s was largely a product of the repressive tactics of the Fujimori regime. As the government's assault on Somos Perú in 1998 and 1999 seemed to suggest, party building was exceedingly difficult while Fujimori was in power (Planas 2000, 389–94; also Lynch 2000). Moreover, given that democratic institutions, such as the legislature, had been rendered ineffective under Fujimori, normal party-building incentives may have been weakened. Such an approach yields a relatively optimistic prognosis for party development in the post-*Fujimori* era. If the primary problem in the 1990s was Fujimori's authoritarianism, then democratization should clear the way for new party-building efforts.

Institutionalist approaches locate the roots of party weakness and party system fragmentation in electoral rules, such as open-list proportional representation (PR), the single national district and minimal threshold for election to Congress, and the majority runoff system, that weaken incentives for politicians to build strong organizations (Schmidt 1996; Tuesta Soldevilla 1996b, 1998). To the extent that these rules persist, institutionalists argue, there is little reason to expect the emergence of strong parties. However, electoral rules can be changed, potentially reshaping politicians' incentives in ways that encourage party building.

A third approach, which might be characterized as historical–structural, yields a more pessimistic forecast. According to this approach, strong parties are products not of electoral engineering but of particular historical, sociological, and technological conditions, many of which are only weakly present in the contemporary period. Stable party systems are often rooted in deep societal cleavages or intense political struggles (Lipset and Rokkan 1967; Collier and Collier 1991). Indeed, many of Latin America's strongest and most enduring parties emerged from civil wars (the traditionally dominant parties in Colombia, Costa Rica, and Uruguay), social revolutions (Bolivia's MNR, Nicaragua's FSLN, Mexico's PRI), or periods of sudden or dramatic expansion of the electorate (Argentine Peronism and Democratic Action in Venezuela). As Michael Coppedge (1998) has argued, these party-building episodes were in many respects historically bound. Most stable party systems either took shape before the advent of mass suffrage (Chile, Colombia, Uruguay) or emerged from the process of mass enfranchisement (Argentina, Mexico, Venezuela). After this period, the crystallization of party loyalties and the absence of large groups of new voters limited the electoral space available to new parties (Coppedge 1998, 175). Thus, with the exception of cases in which civil wars or revolutions created new mass identities (for example, El Salvador), few stable party systems have emerged in Latin America after the establishment of full suffrage.

Moreover, long-term changes in class structures and technology have reduced politicians' need for party organizations and have increased the cost of building and sustaining them. Many of Latin America's largest and most socially rooted parties built their electoral bases on large peasantries or emerging industrial working classes. Because of their geographic concentration and lower levels of education and social mobility, these social classes were both relatively easy to organize and relatively stable in terms of their political loyalties. With the decline of peasantries and industrial working classes and the expansion of the informal sector, the social bases of party politics have grown increasingly unstable. Geographically fragmented and extremely heterogeneous in terms of their work, interests, and identities, informal sector workers are difficult to organize and encapsulate (Cameron 1994; Roberts 1998). Indeed, few new parties in Latin America have built stable electoral bases on these sectors.

Technological change also militates against contemporary party-building efforts. Most large-scale party organizations were established before the spread of television.

In the absence of mass media and communications technologies, politicians were often compelled to build and maintain extensive territorial organizations in order to reach voters. Although politicians' ability to substitute state resources or corporatist structures for party organization inhibited party development in some countries (Mainwaring 1999), party organization was nonetheless critical to electoral success in most countries. In the contemporary period, the increased influence of mass media technologies has weakened politicians' incentive to invest in party organization (Katz 1990; Perelli et al. 1995). As the success of media-based candidates, such as Fernando Collor de Mello and Vicente Fox, suggests, contemporary politicians may reach millions of voters through television and may do so more quickly and at lower cost (in terms of human and organizational resources) than through party organizations. Local party structures therefore have become increasingly "vestigial" (Katz 1990; for a critique of this view, see Scarrow 1996).

These structural changes do not spell the imminent demise of party organizations. In many countries, the persistence of strong partisan identities and the significant human, organizational, and patronage resource advantages enjoyed by existing parties continue to serve as important barriers to entry for political outsiders. As long as politicians believe that the benefits of remaining in an existing party outweigh the benefits of defecting and competing as an outsider, established parties may endure. Once established parties fail, however, the incentives for politicians change dramatically. Mass media and the volatility of contemporary electorates may remove individual politicians' incentive to build new party organizations from scratch. Consequently, contemporary party systems may prove to be somewhat like Humpty Dumpty: in the absence of crisis, they may persist, but if they happen to collapse (for any number of historically contingent reasons), all the institutional engineering in the world may be insufficient to put them back together again.

The challenges of party building are exceptionally great in the Andes, where exclusion from citizenship rights is an enduring legacy of colonialism and where local, indigenous cultures coexist uneasily with the individualistic notions of citizenship that underpin representative democratic institutions. There, where the gap between the *país oficial* (formal political institutions) and the *país real* (established habits and customs) is greatest, the obstacles to consolidating mass partisan linkages are particularly imposing (Van Cott 2000).

A historical–structural analysis thus suggests that the prospects for rebuilding parties in Peru may be rather bleak. According to this approach, the 1990s may constitute a critical juncture for the Peruvian party system. Although the collapse of the old party system was in many ways a historically contingent outcome, the opportunities and constraints posed by the new social, structural, and technological context are such that politicians lack both an incentive and the capacity to build new party organizations (see also Conaghan 2000, 280–82). In other words, although long-term structural changes did not cause the collapse of Peru's party system, they may inhibit its reconstruction.

Two additional factors may help to reinforce or "lock in" the post-1992 party system configuration. First, the contemporary environment "selects for" candidates (such as Toledo) who can succeed at media-based, candidate-centered politics, while the kinds of politicians that are critical to building and sustaining parties—good party bureaucrats or machine politicians—find little demand for their services. To the extent that this is the case, aspiring politicians will invest in the skills necessary to win as "independents." Second, electoral rules may become an endogenous variable in this context. Most elected offices are currently held by nonparty politicians who know how to win by electoral rules that favor weak parties. Such politicians are less likely than party politicians to support reforms aimed at strengthening parties.

This is not to argue that no party rebuilding should be expected in post-Fujimori Peru. Just as relatively stable parties were built from scratch in many Central European countries in the 1990s, stronger parties may well re-emerge in contemporary Peru. Given the alternative electoral strategies available to local and national politicians, however, contemporary party-building efforts are likely to encounter greater obstacles than they did in the past. To the extent that new parties emerge, these parties are likely to be loosely structured organizations with fluid electoral bases and tenuous linkages to society. Like many other new parties in the region (such as the Argentine Front for a Country in Solidarity and the Chilean Party for Democracy), they would rely more on media-based and candidate-centered appeals than on organization and activists. Although such parties would be far better for democracy than the independent movements that dominate contemporary Peruvian politics, their capacity effectively to channel societal interests, recruit and socialize elites, and facilitate collective action and social mobilization remains open to question. Therefore, although it would be premature to predict the demise of political parties in Peru, party system decomposition may prove substantially more enduring than the regime that provoked it.

The empirical record since 2000 lends initial support to this more pessimistic approach. Democratization initially generated hope for a rebirth of party activity. Not only did party-oriented politicians (Paniagua of AP, García of APRA, Lourdes Flores of the PPC) take center stage, but APRA and (to a lesser extent) AP and the PPC launched drives to rebuild their organizations. The transition also triggered a series of institutional reforms aimed at strengthening parties. For example, the single electoral district was replaced with a multiple-district system prior to the 2001 elections. In addition, a new Political Parties Law, passed in 2003, sought to limit the proliferation of flash parties by establishing more demanding criteria for legal registration and entry to Congress. According to the new law, legal registration would require that parties establish committees—made up of at least 50 registered voters—in two thirds of Peru's 24 departments. The law also established a new minimum threshold for entry into Congress: in 2006, only parties winning at least four percent of the vote (and in subsequent elections, at least five percent) would gain legislative representation.

Through 2006, however, the record of party rebuilding was not encouraging. The 2001 election remained strikingly candidate-centered (for a different view, see Kenney 2001). All presidential candidates except García ran on tickets that did not exist before 1990, and most of these were little more than candidate-centered vehicles.[23] Of the 11 parties that won seats in Congress, eight could readily be classified as personalist. The election was also marked by the low quality of the candidates. Although Toledo was more committed to democratic institutions than Fujimori had been, in other ways his rise was remarkably similar to that of his predecessor. Like Fujimori, Toledo had little experience in politics and had never held elected office. He was a marginal candidate whose second-place finish in 2000 was virtually accidental—a product of a wave of strategic voting by anti-*Fujimoristas* desperately seeking a viable candidate. Like C-90, Toledo's PP was little more than a vehicle for his presidential bid. As occurred with *Fujimorismo* in 1990, PP fell well short of a legislative majority, winning only 45 of the 120 seats in Congress.

In short, although Toledo was less autocratic than Fujimori, he was an outsider whose electoral strategy faithfully reproduced the Fujimorista style. Toledo's inexperience caused repeated mistakes during the campaign (and throughout his presidency). Indeed, a major reason for his victory was simply the weakness of the rest of the candidate field.

Problems of party weakness persisted under the Toledo government (2001–2006). Party switching remained rampant. The governing PP never established itself as a viable political force. Lacking an effective organization or platform, and tied to an unpopular president, PP fell immediately into disarray, and it deteriorated to the point where it was unable to even field a presidential candidate in 2006.

The 2006 election was characterized by extraordinary party system fragmentation. The Political Parties Law was not seriously enforced, and as a result, an unprecedented 36 parties were eligible to compete in the 2006 election. Of these, 20 parties fielded presidential candidates (up from eight in 2001, and a record high) and 24 parties (also a record) fielded legislative lists. Most of these parties were candidate-centered vehicles for individual politicians seeking to emulate the success of Fujimori and Toledo. Of the major presidential candidates, only Alan García ran on a party label. Lourdes Flores of National Unity (UN) (a coalition of Flores' PPC, the conservative National Renovation, and Castañeda Lossio's National Solidarity) ran what she called a "hyper-personal campaign,"[24] based on direct contact with voters. Though a longtime PPC member, Flores marginalized party operators within the UN and ran a campaign that centered almost entirely on her character.

The 2006 election also witnessed the emergence of another neopopulist outsider: Ollanta Humala. A nationalist former military officer who led a controversial military rebellion during the final months of Fujimori's presidency, Humala modeled himself on Hugo Chávez. Like Fujimori and Toledo before him, he was an amateur politician who invested little effort in party building. With a small group of supporters, many of whom were military reservists, he created the *Partido Nacionalista Peruano*, but failed to register it in time for the election. Seeking an electoral vehicle, he joined—or rented—the UPP (soon throwing that party into internal crisis). Like Fujimori, Humala ran a personalistic, anti-political establishment campaign. He mobilized considerable support among the poor, particularly in the southern highlands. Out of nowhere, he rose from the low single digits to the top of the polls. Humala captured a plurality of the first round vote, and García narrowly edged Flores to place second.[25] A second round victory by Humala might have placed Peru on a path to yet another regime crisis. However, Garcia won the runoff by appealing to UN voters—especially those who were less poor and in Lima—who feared Humala. Viewing the APRA candidate as the lesser evil, UN voters flocked to García.

García's victory thus narrowly averted the election of yet another political outsider and brought an institutionalized party into office for the first time since 1990. As a result, prospects for democratic governability improved considerably. Although APRA held only 36 of 120 seats in Congress, the combination of APRA discipline and programmatic alliances with the UN and *Fujimorista* factions generated favorable prospects for building working majorities in the legislature.

Nevertheless, parties nevertheless remained strikingly weak. Humala's UPP/PNP, which finished first in the 2006 legislative election, imploded almost immediately. Moreover, the November 2006 municipal and regional elections brought a level of party failure that was unprecedented even in Peru. All parties lost badly. Despite Garcia's presidential honeymoon, APRA suffered a major defeat, winning only two of Peru's 25 regions (down from 12 in 2002), and even losing its historic stronghold of Trujillo. Other parties fared still worse.[26] Twenty-one of 25 regional governments were captured by "independent" movements. Moreover, the winning party in one region almost invariably lost in neighboring regions and even in municipalities *within* that region (Tanaka 2006). The resulting "political archipelago" (Tuesta Soldevilla 2006) would likely limit the opposition's capacity to serve as a check on presidential power, with negative consequences for the quality, if not the stability, of democracy.

DEMOCRACY WITHOUT PARTIES?

Peruvian democracy rebounded in 2001, but—at least through 2006—political parties did not. Despite considerable institutional engineering, mechanisms of political representation remained weak, and personalism, electoral volatility, and party switching remained high. At both the local and national levels, political outsiders continued to dominate elections. As Sinesio López (2006) put it, Peru had "no national parties." Indeed, there is reason to think that the era of well-organized and socially rooted parties is over. If this is the case, then what are the prospects for post-Fujimori democracy? Here the lessons of the 1990s are sobering.

The challenge of making democracy work in a context of fluid and fragmented electoral politics will be difficult. To govern effectively, politicians will be compelled to innovate, particularly in the areas of coalition building and legislative organization. Yet even in the most optimistic of scenarios, the likelihood of executive–legislative conflict, executive abuse of power, corruption, personalism, and successful outsider and even antisystem candidacies will remain high. Peru may not be alone in this challenge: the Venezuelan party system also decomposed in the 1990s, and long-established party systems in Argentina and Colombia showed signs of severe erosion in 2001 and 2002.[27]

These developments highlight a paradoxical aspect of the relationship between parties and democracy: although parties are essential to the effective functioning of modern democracies, they are not typically created for that purpose. Parties are created by politicians in an effort to resolve coordination problems and further their own careers (Aldrich 1995). To an extent, then, parties' various contributions to democracy are felicitous byproducts of organizations that are created for other purposes. As long as politicians believe that they can advance their careers through parties, then the "democratic goods" provided by parties will be provided. But if politicians (or voters) decide they are better off without parties, then those democratic goods may be underprovided. In such cases, it unclear what kinds of institutions or organizations would provide those goods.

This returns us to the conundrum mentioned at the beginning of this article: parties are among the least credible democratic institutions in Latin America today, yet democracy without them is nearly inconceivable. The Peruvian experience offers stark evidence of the indispensability of parties as mechanisms of representation. Whether recognition of this evidence stimulates a renewed interest in party building in the region, however, remains to be seen.

NOTES

We appreciate comments from Manuel Alcántara, Fabiola Bazo, Charles Kenney, Scott Mainwaring, Cynthia McClintock, David Scott Palmer, Gregory Schmidt, and three anonymous referees. Max Cameron is grateful to the Social Sciences and Humanities Research Council of Canada for research grants that enabled him to conduct work in Peru from December 2001 to January 2002, and from January to June 2006. Research assistance was provided by Annabella España, Mikala Grante, and Lissette Torres. The authors alone are responsible for the content of this article.

1 Modifying Schattschneider's oft-cited claim that "democracy is unthinkable save in terms of parties" (1942, 1), Aldrich writes that "democracy is unworkable save in terms of parties" (1995, 3).

2 According to Morris Fiorina, "the only way collective responsibility has ever existed, and can exist, given our institutions, is through the agency of the political party" (1980, 26).

3 In this sense, horizontal accountability is critical to what O'Donnell (1994) calls "vertical accountability," or free and fair elections.

4 Such a phenomenon occurred in Venezuela in the 1980s and 1990s (Coppedge 2003).

5 Although Latin American parties have functioned less well as channels for political recruitment, parties such as Venezuela's Democratic Action, the Chilean Socialist and Communist Parties, and the Brazilian Workers' Party have served as important channels of access to the political arena for working classes.

6 For example, Planas (2000, 399) and Levitt (2000) argue that Peru's traditional parties have always been weak and personalistic, while Tanaka (1998) contends that the parties were relatively strong in the 1980s.

7 Relevant features of Peru's electoral system include a proportional representation system with no minimum threshold for legislative representation; a majority runoff system for presidential elections; a single national district for legislative elections, which eliminated the need for national party structures; and the double preferential vote system (in which voters cast preferential votes for two candidates on party lists), which encourages candidate-centered campaigning (Schmidt 1996; Tuesta Soldevilla 1996b, 1998).

8 Indeed, Fujimori's stunning rise in the polls in the clays before the election is best explained by strategic shifts in voting intentions by Peruvians desperate to avoid a runoff between Vargas Llosa and APRA (Schmidt 1996, 344–46).

9 Fujimori also faced the real possibility of a military coup. A military cabal began preparing a coup in 1989 and had planned to prevent Fujimori from taking office (Rospigliosi 2000, 74–82).

10 Even though the opposition parties were widely discredited during the 1990–92 period, Fujimori's success was far from assured. Established parties won battles with presidents in Brazil, Guatemala, and Ecuador during the 1990s, even though they lacked broad public support. Fujimori, moreover, was not in a particularly strong position during 1990 and 1991. For much of 1991, Fujimori's public approval rating was below 40 percent (Tanaka 1998, 219).

11 These included the ministry of the presidency, the armed forces (which, in lieu of party activists, were used in electoral campaigns to paint pro-Fujimori electoral graffiti), the tax collection agency, the National Intelligence Service, municipal governments, and social welfare agencies, such as the National Food Assistance Program and the National Compensation and Development Fund (FONCODES).

12 According to David Scott Palmer (2000), in regions such as Ayacucho, emerging civil society organizations effectively substituted for parties in channeling citizen participation and meeting local needs.

13 The right of citizens to initiate a referendum was enshrined in the 1993 Constitution.

14 For example, a survey conducted by the Instituto de Desarrollo e Investigación de Ciencias Económicas (IDICE) found that 77.6 percent of Peruvians disapproved of the dismissal of the three TC justices (Flores 1997, 2).

15 Andrade became more active in opposing the regime beginning in 1998.

16 To make this clear, congressional candidates were required to sign letters of adherence to the movement in the SIN headquarters.

17 Although this decline was largely a product of government-sponsored attacks, it may also be attributed to Andrade's gradual abandonment of a non-confrontational "independent" strategy and his increasing association with the democratic opposition.

18 The "fraudulent" character of the election lay less in the vote-counting process than in the unfair and unfree conditions leading up to the vote, which fell well short of internationally accepted norms.

19 Toledo instructed his supporters to write "no to fraud" on their ballots.

20 The exact number of turncoats is not clear because the defectors were often ambiguous about their intentions, and some defected and then repented (the so-called *tránsfugas arrepentidas*). A new vocabulary emerged to describe the alchemy though which the government converted members of the opposition. In addition to turncoats, there were reverse turncoats (those who abandoned one side and then another), repentant turncoats (*arrepentidos*, those who abandoned their party and then thought better of it), neoturncoats (those who abandoned the government party after it began to lose its grip on power) and moles (*topos*, or double agents who remained in an opposition party while taking orders from the government).

21 One member of Congress committed a Freudian slip during his swearing-in ceremony, declaring his allegiance to "God and money" (*Dios y la plata*) instead of "God and homeland" (*Dios y la patria*).

22 Interviews were conducted with four of the most important party leaders in Congress: one representing the PPC, one from APRA, and two from the FIM. They were asked, "Which was more important in bringing down Fujimori: the opposition (parties, Congress, civil society, marches, the independent media, international organizations and foreign states) or the regime's internal problems (the Vladivideo and the dispute between Fujimori and Montesinos)?" All agreed that the latter was more important, saying "the video was the detonator," "were it not for the video we would still be under the Fujimori regime," or "the video brought Fujimori down" (interviews conducted with various party leaders January 8–14, 2002). This is consistent with survey results reported in McClintock 2001, 139.

23 It is noteworthy that Flores, despite being a PPC member, chose to create a new ticket called National Unity for her presidential bid.

24 Lourdes Flores used this phrase to describe her campaign in a meeting with the foreign press in Lima on February 9, 2006. See: http://weblogs.elearning.ubc.ca/peru/archives/022846.php

25 Party organization was probably decisive in this contest. Given that García's margin of victory was only 62,578 votes (less than one vote per poll), the capacity of APRA to pull and defend its vote was critical. Flores complained that she had lost votes in the process of ballot counting, but the UN simply did not have enough agents on the ground to scrutinize the vote.

26 AP, the UN, and Toledo's PP failed to win a single region. The UPP won one region, as did the small New Left Movement.

27 Alcántara and Freidenberg (2001) offer a more optimistic perspective on Latin American party systems.

REFERENCES

Alcántara Saez, Manuel, and Flavia Freidenberg. 2001. Los partidos políticos en América Latina. *América Latina Hoy 21* (April): 17–35.

Aldrich, John H. 1995. *Why Parties? The Origin and Transformation of Political Parties in America.* Chicago: University of Chicago Press.

Balbi, Mariella. 2000. Entrevista. Ex presidente Francisco Morales Bermúdez afirma que el Perú está gobernado por una mafia. *La República.* Domingo (Lima). September 17.

Bazo, Fabiola, and Maxwell A. Cameron. 2000. Dilemmas of the Opposition, Peru Election 2000: A Public Education Website. <http://qsilver.queensvi.ca/peru/in-site/insite4.shtml> Accessed June 2003.

Borón, Atilio. 1992. Becoming Democrats? Some Skeptical Considerations on the Right in Latin America. In *The Right and Democracy in Latin America, ed. Douglas A. Chalmers,* Maria do Carmo Campello de Souza, and Atilio Borón. New York: Praeger. 68–95.

Cameron, Maxwell A. 1994. *Democracy and Authoritarianism in Peru: Political Coalitions and Social Change.* New York: St. Martin's Press.

———. 1997. Political and Economic Origins of Regime Change in Peru: The Eighteenth Brumaire of Alberto Fujimori. In *The Peruvian Labyrinth: Polity, Society, Economy,* ed. Cameron and Philip Mauceri. University Park: Penn State University Press. 37–69.

———. 1998. Self-Coups: Peru, Guatemala, and Russia. *Journal of Democracy* 9, 1: 125–39.

———. 2002. Endogenous Regime Breakdown: The Vladivideo and the Fall of Peru's Fujimori. Paper prepared for the conference "The Fujimori Legacy and Its Impact on Public Policy in Latin America," sponsored by the Dante B. Fascell North-South Center and the University of Delaware Department of Political Science and International Relations. Washington, DC, March 14.

Carrión, Julio. 2000. La campaña electoral y la opinión publica en el Perú actual. Paper presented at the 22d Congress of the Latin American Studies Association, Miami, March 16–18.

Collier, Ruth Berins, and David Collier. 1991. *Shaping the Political Arena: Critical Junctures, the Labor Movement, and Regime Dynamics in Latin America.* Princeton: Princeton University Press.

El Comercio (Lima). 2000. Aseguran que no hay crísis de partido dentro de Perú Posible. August 3.

Conaghan, Catherine M. 2000. The Irrelevant Right: Alberto Fujimori and the New Politics of Pragmatic Peru. In *Conservative Parties, the Right, and Democracy in Latin America*, ed. Kevin J. Middlebrook. Baltimore: Johns Hopkins University Press. 255–84.

———. 2001. Making and Unmaking Authoritarian Peru: Re-Election, Resistance, and Regime Transition. North-South Agenda Paper No. 47. Coral Gables: North-South Center.

Cooper, Andrew, and Thomas Legler. 2001. The OAS in Peru. *Journal of Democracy* 12, 4: 123–36.

Coppedge, Michael. 1998. The Evolution of Latin American Party Systems. In *Politics, Society, and Democracy: Latin America*, ed. Scott Mainwaring and Arturo Valenzuela. Boulder: Westview Press. 171–206.

———. 2003. Venezuela: Popular Sovereignty versus Liberal Democracy. In *Constructing Democratic Governance*, 2d ed., ed. Jorge I. Dominguez and Michael Shifter. Baltimore: Johns Hopkins University Press. 165–192.

Corrales, Javier. 2001. Strong Societies, Weak Parties: Regime Change in Cuba and Venezuela in the 1950s and Today. *Latin American Politics and Society* 43, 2 (Summer): 81–114.

Cotler, Julio. 1994. *Política y sociedad en el Perú*. Lima: Instituto de Estudios Peruanos.

Diario La República (Lima). 2000. Especial de elecciones: Alberto Andrade Carmona. February 6. <http://www.laRepública.com.pe/SUPLEMEN/ DOMINGO/2000/0206/domingo10.htm> Accessed June 3, 2002.

Downs, Anthony. 1957. *An Economic Theory of Democracy*. New York: Harper and Row.

Fiorina, Morris. 1980. The Decline in Collective Responsibility in American Politics. *Daedalus* 109 (Summer): 24–45.

Flores, Inés. 1997 Desaprobación a destitución de magistrados sube al 77.6% Solo el 39.5% aprueba a Fujimori. *Diario La República*, June 1: 2.

Franklin, James C. 2001. The Role of Party-led Dissent in Redemocratization. *Party Politics* 1, 5: 567–80.

Gibson, Edward. 1996. *Class and Conservative Parties: Argentina in Comparative Perspective*. Baltimore: Johns Hopkins University Press.

Grompone, Romeo. 2000. Al día siguiente: el fujimorismo como proyecto inconcluso de transformación política y social. In *El fujimorismo: ascenso y caída de un régimen autoritario*, eds. Grompone and Julio Cotler. *Lima*: Instituto de Estudios Peruanos. 77–174.

Katz, Richard S. 1990. Party as Linkage: A Vestigial Function? *European Journal of Political Research* 18: 141–61.

Kenney, Charles. 1996. ¿Por qué el autogolpe? Fujimori y el congreso, 1990–1992. In Tuesta Soldevilla, ed. 1996. 75–104.

———. 2000. Presidents, Parties, and Horizontal Accountability in Latin America. Paper presented at the 22d Congress of the Latin American Studies Association, Miami, March 16–18.

———. 2001. Guess Who's Coming to Dinner: the Death and Rebirth of Traditional Party Politicians in Peru, 1978–2001. Paper presented at the 23d Congress of the Latin American Studies Association, Washington, DC, September 6–8.

Latin American Weekly Report. 1997. Fujimori Promises Big Social Projects: President seeks to Halt Decline in Popularity. June 24: 297.

Levitt, Barry Steven. 2000. Continuity and Change in Peru's Political Parties, 1985–2000. Paper presented at the 22d Congress of the Latin American Studies Association, Miami, March 16–18.

Lipset, Seymour Martin, and Stein Rokkan. 1967. Cleavage Structures, Party Systems, and Voter Alignments: An Introduction. In *Party Systems and Voter Alignments: Cross-National Perspectives*, ed. Lipset and Rokkan. New York: Free Press. 1–64.

López, Sinesio. 2006. Suerte para García, desgracia para el Perú. La Primera (Lima). November 20. Available at: http://weblogs.elearning.ubc.ca/peru/archives/2006_11_20.php.

Lynch, Nicolás. 1999. *Una tragedia sin héroes. La derrota de los partidos y el origen de los independientes*. Peru 1989–1992. Lima: Fondo Editorial Universidad Nacional Mayor de San Marcos.

———. 2000. Los partidos en los noventa en el Peru: ¿qué pasó y qué pasara? Paper presented at the 22d Congress of the Latin American Studies Association, Miami, March 16–18.

Mainwaring, Scott. 1999. *Rethinking Party Systems in the Third Wave Democratization: The Case of Brazil.* Stanford: Stanford University Press.

Mainwaring, Scott, and Timothy R. Scully. 1995. Introduction: Party Systems in Latin America. In *Building Democratic Institutions: Party Systems in Latin America*, ed. Mainwaring and Scully. Stanford: Stanford University Press. 1–34.

Mauceri, Philip. 2000. Unchecked Power: The Presidency Under Fujimori and Beyond. Paper presented at the 22d Congress of the Latin American Studies Association, Miami, March 16–18.

McClintock, Cynthia. 1996. La voluntad política presidencial y la ruptura constitucional de 1992 en el Perú. In Tuesta Soldevilla, ed. 1996. 53–74.

———.1999. Es autoritario el gobierno de Fujimori? In *El juego político: Fujimori, la oposición y las reglas*, ed. Fernando Tuesta Soldevilla. Lima: Fundación Friedrich Ehert Stiftung. 65–95.

———. 2001. The OAS in Peru: Room for Improvement. *Journal of Democracy* 12, 4: 137–40.

McGuire, James. 1997. *Peronism Without Peron: Unions, Parties, and Democracy in Argentina.* Stanford: Stanford University Press.

O'Donnell, Guillermo. 1994. Delegative Democracy. *Journal of Democracy* 5, 1: 55–69.

———. 1998. Horizontal Accountability in New Democracies. In *The Self-Restraining State: Power and Accountability in New Democracies*, ed. Andreas Schedler, Larry Diamond, and Marc Plattner. Boulder: Lynne Rienner. 29–51.

Palmer, David Scott. 2000. Direct Democracy at the Grassroots in Peru: "Informal Politics" in Ayacucho. Paper presented at the 22d Congress of the Latin American Studies Association, Miami, March 16–18.

Paredes Castro, Juan, Hugo Guerra Arteaga, and Juan Zuñiga Sañudo. 1992. Entrevista al presidente Alberto Fujimori: "ni falsa democracia, ni dictadura militar." *El Comercio*, May 3: 4–5.

Perelli, Carina, Sonia Picado, and Daniel Zoviatto, eds. 1995. *Partidos y clase política en América Latina en los 90.* San José: Instituto Interamericano de Derechos Humanos.

Peru. Former Intelligence Officer, member of SIN. 2002. Author interview. Lima, January 9.

Peru. Senior Electoral Officer with ONPE. 2002. Author interview. Lima, January 8.

Planas, Pedro. 2000. *La democracia volátil: movimientos, partidos, líderes políticos y conductas electorales en el Peru contemporáneo.* Lima: Fundación Friedrich Ebert.

Roberts, Kenneth M. 1995. Neoliberalism and the Transformation of Populism in Latin America. *World Politics* 48, 1: 82–116.

———. 1998. *Deepening Democracy? Modern Left and Social Movements in Chile and Peru.* Stanford: Stanford University Press.

———. 2002. Do Parties Matter? Lessons from the Fujimori Experience. Paper prepared for the conference "The Fujimori Legacy and Its Impact on Public Policy in Latin America," sponsored by the Dante B. Fascell North-South Center and the University of Delaware Department of Political Science and International Relations. Washington, DC, March 14.

Rospigliosi, Fernando. 2000. *Montesinos y las fuerzas armadas.* Lima: Instituto de Estudios Peruanos.

Scarrow, Susan. 1996. *Parties and Their Members: Organizing for Victory in Germany and Britain.* New York: Oxford University Press..

Schattschneider, E. E. 1942. *Party Government.* New York: Rinehart.

Schmidt, Gregory D. 1996. Fujimori's 1990 Upset Victory in Peru: Electoral Rules, Contingencies, and Adaptive Strategies. *Comparative Politics* 28, 3: 321–55.

Tanaka, Martín. 1998. *Los espejismos de la democracia: el colapso del sistema de partidos en el Perú.* Lima: Instituto de Estudios Peruanos.

———. 1999. *Los partidos políticos en el Peru, 1992–1999: sobrevivencia, estatalidad y política mediática.* Lima: Instituto de Estudios Peruanos.

———. 2006. Impresiones sobre los resultados del domingo. *Peru.21* (Lima). November 21. Available at: http://weblogs.elearning.ubc.ca/peru/archives/2006_11_21.php.

Tarrow, Sidney. 1994. *Power in Movement: Social Movements, Collective Action, and Politics.* New York: Cambridge University Press.

Tuesta Soldevilla, Fernando, ed. 1996a. *Los enigmas del poder. Fujimori 1990–1996.* Lima: Fundación Friedrich Ebert.

Tuesta Soldevilla, Fernando. 1996b. El impacto del sistema electoral sobre el sistema político peruano. In Tuesta Soldevilla, ed. 1996. 129–68.

———. 1998. Instituciones, reformas, y representación política en el Perú. Paper presented at the 21st Congress of the Latin American Studies Association, Chicago, September 26–30.

Van Cott, Donna Lee. 2000. Party System Development and Indigenous Populations in Latin America: The Bolivian case. *Party Politics* 6, 2: 155–74.

Weber, Max. 1978. *Economy and Society.* Vol. 2. Ed. Guenther Roth and Claus Wittich. Berkeley: University of California Press.

Weyland, Kurt. 1999. Neoliberal Populism in Latin America and Eastern Europe. *Comparative Politics* 31, 4: 379–401.

Chapter 19

Social Correlates of Party System Demise and Populist Resurgence in Venezuela

Kenneth M. Roberts

The landslide election of Hugo Chávez to the presidency of Venezuela in 1998 provided perhaps the most clear-cut evidence yet of the enduring vitality of populism in contemporary Latin American politics. A short decade earlier, populism—conventionally understood to be a form of personalistic leadership that mobilized diverse popular constituencies behind statist, nationalistic, and redistributive development models—had been considered all but extinct in the region. A variety of scholars had written its epitaph or extolled its demise, consigning populism to an earlier stage of historical development (Drake 1982) or condemning its association with economic instability (Dornbusch and, Edwards 1991).

The crisis-ridden denouement of Alán García's ill-fated government in Peru, arguably the most ambitious populist experiment of the 1980s, seemed to provide a symbolic endpoint to the region's populist cycle. After the initial promise and charisma of García's administration, the Peruvian debacle reinforced the view that populist mobilization and heterodox economic nationalism were followed, almost inevitably, by inflationary spirals and political upheaval. García's exit from office thus coincided with the scholarly proclamation of an emerging "Washington Consensus" around an antipopulist, technocratically managed vision of political and economic liberalism (see Williamson 1990).

The much-heralded demise of populism, it turns out, was premature. Although the debt crisis of the 1980s bankrupted the nationalist, state-led development models pursued by traditional populist leaders, it also undermined the party and labor institutions that had been constructed to represent popular sectors during the era of import substitution industrialization (ISI). This deinstitutionalization of mass representation left a political void that was quickly filled, in some nations, by new personalistic leaders who cultivated a direct, unmediated relationship to unorganized mass constituencies. In response, scholars resurrected and reformulated the populist concept, highlighting its political connotations—in particular, direct leader-mass relations that bypass intermediary institutions—while downplaying its historical association with the ISI model of development. Some scholars even argued that "unexpected affinities" existed between neoliberal economic reforms, an atomized social landscape, and populist styles of political leadership (Weyland 1996; see also Roberts 1995). With the rise of Chávez at the end of the 1990s, moreover, it became clear that even more traditional statist and nationalist variants of populism retained a capacity to mobilize mass support where established party systems had been undermined by acute political and economic crises and deepening social inequalities.

Clearly, the populist concept remains subject to an uncommonly broad array of connotations, in large part because of its multidimensionality (Roberts 1995; Berins Collier 2001; Weyland 2001). When populism is understood first and foremost as a top-down, personalistic mode of mass political mobilization, however, its relative autonomy from any given model or phase economic development can be established, and the political correlates of its resiliency become more readily apparent. Indeed, there appears to be a dialectical relationship between the demise of traditional representative institutions and the eruption of new forms of populist leadership, whether they come attached to statist or market-oriented development policies.

The most distinctive features of this new leadership are its implacable hostility to the political establishment and an aversion to intermediary institutions that can hold a leader accountable to mass constituencies. In the Venezuelan case, Chávez proved to be a master of "the politics of antipolitics." As a former military coup leader, he was the consummate political outsider, a man of action who was untainted by the rampant corruption, political patronage, and collusive pactmaking that bred disillusionment with the post-1958 democratic regime. Chávez denounced the party leaders who dominated Venezuelan democracy, accusing them of squandering the nation's oil bonanza and draining the political system of its democratic content through their monopolization of power. These attacks both capitalized on and deepened the public antipathy toward established institutions, encouraging Chávez to rely on personal charisma rather than organizational bonds to consolidate mass support.

What are the conditions under which such a populist strategy can tap a responsive chord in a nation with a long democratic tradition and a highly institutionalized party system? Populism is clearly a durable and adaptable political phenomenon in Latin America, one that is capable of emerging in diverse and unexpected contexts. It arises most forcefully, however, in periods of political and economic crisis or transition, when established patterns of representation are strained or breaking down, and new ones have yet to be consolidated. In such contexts, traditional representative institutions may lose their capacity to appeal to large sectors of the populace, or they may be eclipsed by the mobilization of new groups by emerging leaders or political movements.

Not surprisingly, then, there have been two primary periods of populist upheaval in the political development of Latin America. The first period coincided with the demise of oligarchic sociopolitical orders and the onset of mass politics after the 1920s and 1930s, when urbanization and industrialization transformed the social landscape. The rapidly growing urban middle and working classes were not easily absorbed into the rural-based patron-client networks of traditional oligarchic parties, and in much of the region they were available for mobilization by populist figures—including Juan Perón, Gertúlio Vargas, Lázaro Cardenas, and Victor Raúl Haya de la Torre—or new populist parties that advocated grassroots organization, social reform, and nationalistic ISI policies (see Conniff 1982).

Acción Democrática (AD) was one of the most prominent of these new parties, and its emergence in the 1940s fundamentally transformed the elitist and authoritarian character of Venezuelan politics. New lines of political cleavage were drawn, and a magnum leap occurred in the levels of both social and political organization. AD built the first-ever mass political party in Venezuela, and its social outreach efforts reconfigured Venezuelan civil society, endowing the party with organic ties to mass labor and peasant associations. For nearly half a century, these sociopolitical bonds helped weave the fabric of a political system whose central cleavage pitted a mass-based, labor-mobilizing party against its more conservative arch-rival, the Christian Democratic COPEI (Comité de Organización Política Electoral Independiente).

A second period of populist upheaval was initiated across much of Latin America, however, when the "state-centric matrix" (Cavarozzi 1994) left behind by the first phase of populism began to decompose in the 1980s. Despite their personalistic leadership patterns, the first wave of populist movements eventually constructed an institutional edifice—including mass-based party organizations, powerful trade union movements, and state corporatist modes of interest intermediation—that was deeply imbedded in the ISI model of development and the opportunities it provided to mobilize political support around varied forms of state intervention or patronage distributions. When this development model collapsed in the 1980s, it struck a severe blow to the representative institutions that had grown up alongside it. Labor movements were decimated by economic crises and structural adjustment policies; their corporatist linkages to states and parties were shredded by market reforms and economic austerity; and populist parties were shaken by the loss of their development strategies, the disarticulation of their social bases, and the political costs associated with crisis management. The net result was a fragmented social landscape and a more independent, detached electorate that was less bound to traditional parties and thus more fluid in its electoral behavior.

This context was tailor-made for the eruption of new expressions of populist leadership that appealed directly to the masses while bypassing representative institutions. With traditional parties discredited by corruption scandals and economic mismanagement, independents and political outsiders could easily mobilize popular support by adopting an antiestablishment line. Some of these challengers were new to the national political stage, such as Alberto Fujimori in Peru, whereas others were familiar to the body politic in one form or another, such as Fernando Collor de Mello in Brazil and Rafael Caldera and Hugo Chávez in Venezuela. All, however, eschewed party organization and formed independent movements to represent *el pueblo* against the partisan establishment, and they often clashed with labor movements and other interest groups that were affiliated with the old order. Although the economic policies adopted by these leaders were markedly different, the similarities in their political logic were striking.

This populist resurgence was especially astonishing in Venezuela, given the strength of the established institutions that had to be displaced to create political space for new populist figures. Indeed, for most of the 1980s, as other Latin American nations were struggling to establish or consolidate democratic regimes and rebuild party systems following periods of authoritarian repression, Venezuela surely would have been considered a "least likely case" for a regime-threatening party system breakdown and populist resurgence. The Venezuelan case is therefore highly instructive for theoretical and comparative purposes; causal factors that are strong enough to undermine even the most highly institutionalized of party systems are likely to exert more general effects throughout the region.

What, then, explains the surprising breakdown of Venezuela's party system and the populist resurgence that it spawned? This article argues that these unexpected outcomes are best understood through an analysis of the social bases of political representation in Venezuela and how they were eroded by the prolonged crisis and demise of the state-centric matrix of development. Venezuela's powerful representative institutions were founded on a mixture of corporatist and clientelistic linkages to social actors that were unable to withstand the secular decline of the oil economy and several aborted attempts at market liberalization. Successive administrations led by the dominant parties failed to reverse the economic slide, with devastating consequences for the party system as a whole. The party system ultimately rested on insecure structural foundations, and when its social moorings foundered in the 1980s, the institutional edifice of the old order began to crumble. As Chavismo filled the political void, it both capitalized on and accelerated the institutional decomposition of the old order.

THE PUZZLE OF PARTY SYSTEM DECADE IN VENEZUELA

The decomposition of the Venezuelan party system in the 1990s poses a significant challenge to the scholarship on political institutions and representation. In a region notorious for the shallow institutional development and ephemeral character of its political parties, Venezuela was thought to be different. The post-1958 democratic regime was anchored by two dominant parties that were electorally stable, internally disciplined, and deeply embedded in civil society. AD and COPEI were hierarchically and bureaucratically structured parties, and their organizational tentacles penetrated every nook and cranny of Venezuelan society, generating powerful political loyalties and cohesive collective identities. A far cry from the patrimonial networks and personalistic vehicles that masqueraded as political parties in many other Latin American nations, Venezuela's party organizations were formidable governing institutions that were built to last. Their demise therefore raises unsettling questions about the sustainability of representative institutions in modern Latin American democracies.

To be fully understood, the Venezuelan case needs to be viewed from a comparative perspective that includes the interaction between representative institutions, their social constituencies, and the evolving structural context in which parties try to mobilize support. The crisis of ISI and the shift to neoliberalism in the 1980s and 1990s were a turning point in Latin America's political development, as they shredded the social bonds that many traditional parties had relied on and created a new socioeconomic matrix for political representation. Although some traditional party systems survived and adapted to the new social landscape, the period of transition proved to be especially traumatic and politically disruptive in the Venezuelan case. By the end of the 1990s, when Hugo Chávez and his upstart Movimiento Quinta República (MVR) had swept to a series of electoral victories, not only the party system but the entire constitutional order of the post-1958 democratic regime had decomposed in Venezuela.

The demise of the Venezuelan party system is hardly unique in the Latin American region. Traditional party systems have also been eclipsed in Peru, Ecuador, Bolivia, Colombia, and Brazil over the past 20 years, while many other nations have experienced high levels of electoral volatility or major electoral realignments. In other cases of party system decomposition, however, traditional party organizations were generally noted for their debility; what is distinctive about the Venezuelan case is the fortitude of the institutions that decomposed.

This decomposition could hardly be more at odds with the general thrust of contemporary research on political institutions. Scholars have devoted considerable attention to explaining how institutions are generated, how they structure and stabilize political behavior (Lijphant and Waisman 1996; March and Olson 1989; Shugart and Carey 1992), and how they adapt to changes in their external environment (Kitschelt 1994; Mair 1997; North 1990) Among Latin Americanists, the institutionalization of party systems is often considered vital for the consolidation and healthy functioning of democratic regimes (Mainwaring and Scully 1995). Theorizing about the causes and process of institutional breakdown, however, remains at a rudimentary stage, despite its obvious relevance for the contemporary political scene (Remmer 1997, 52 -53) In short, a great deal is known about how institutions emerge, evolve, and shape political behavior, but the tendency to associate institutions with fixed relationships, standard operating procedures, and the rule-based reproduction of patterned behavior leaves their potential for decay shrouded in mystery.

The valuable work of Mainwaring and Scully (1995) party systems, for example, places the primary emphasis on institution building rather than institutional decay. The authors recognize that institutionalization "is neither unilinear, nor irreversible" (1995, 21), and they identify a number of factors that can erode established party systems. Nevertheless, their main concern is the inchoate nature of party systems in much of Latin America, which they associate with political instability, ineffective legislating and policymaking, populist and patrimonial practices, and underrepresentation of popular sectors in the political process (see also Mainwaring 1999). The construction of more institutionalized party systems is thus understood to be a primary challenge for effective democratic governance, and even after the political turmoil of the late 1980s and early 1990s Venezuela ranked very high on Mainwaring and Scully's index of party system institutionalization (1995, 17). In their eyes, Venezuelan parties had stable electoral constituencies, solid roots in civil society, legitimate political functions, and strong internal organizations.

Once established, such parties are not expected to collapse. In their seminal study of partisan cleavage patterns, Lipset and Rokkan (1967) assert that the social cleavages structuring electoral competition at the onset of universal suffrage tend to become frozen in place, encouraging party system stability. Similarly, but from a more micro level of analysis, Converse (1969, 139) claims that once party institutions survive the initial threats that accompany their founding, they are expected to "accumulate a deepening stability with the passage of time" through processes of habituation, socialization, and political learning. Although the political turmoil of the 1960s, the emergence of new social movements, and the social changes that accompanied the rise of postindustrial society spawned a flurry of studies on electoral realignment and party system change in advanced industrial democracies (Crewe and Denver 1985; Inglehart 1990; Dalton. et al. 1984), established party systems and their underlying cleavage structures proved to he highly resilient (Bartolini and Mair 1990). And even if social and economic changes or political crises induce electoral realignments or the weakening of traditional parties, it hardly follows that highly institutionalized party organizations will simply collapse as serious political competitors.

Dominant theoretical perspectives thus provided little reason to anticipate the decomposition of Venezuela's formidable party institutions. As Converse declares, "the timing of . . . terminal events, embedded as they will be in a complex nexus of change, seems almost impossible to forecast" (1969, 139). Nevertheless, political scientists love an empirical anomaly, and the Venezuelan case has spawned a range of efforts to interpret and explain its apparent singularity. Indeed, the four leading theoretical approaches to the study of comparative politics—institutionalism, structuralism, rational choice, and political culture—have all generated interpretations of the crisis, if not necessarily the demise, of the Venezuelan party system. These four approaches have focused attention on two critical variables in the development of the Venezuelan crisis: the design of political institutions, and the impact of oil on the country's economic development, political culture, and patterns of political representation.

Institutional explanations have attributed the crisis to the characteristics of Venezuelan political institutions, both at the level of the political regime and at the level of party organizations. The important study by Coppedge (1994), for example, suggests that the overinstitutionalization of a party system may be as problematic as the underinstitutionalization stressed by Mainwaring and Scully. According to Coppedge, Venezuela's hierarchically controlled, bureaucratically organized parties so thoroughly dominated electoral campaigns, legislative proceedings, and civic organizations that they destabilized democracy and generated disillusionment by "blocking off most of the informal channels through which citizens voice their demands" (1994, 158). When combined with presidentialism at the regime level, this *partidocracia* undermined democratic accountability and flexibility while encouraging unprincipled political factionalism within the parties. Corrales (2000, 136–38) and Levitsky (2001, 50–51) concur that the "cartelization" and bureaucratic routinization of the AD directorate created organizational rigidities that impeded the adoption of economic reforms.

In a related vein, Crisp (2000) argues that the electoral and consultative arrangements established during Venezuela's democratic transition in 1958 produced political stability, but at the price of institutional rigidities that culminated in crisis by blocking adaptation to a changing social and economic context. Dominant parties and interest groups thus "became a frozen status quo," with institutional safeguards that allowed them to "control policymaking, exclude new groups from participating, and keep new issues off the agenda indefinitely" (Crisp 2000, 173). Efforts to reform these institutions in the midst of crisis failed to reinvigorate them, and may have even hastened their demise. Explanations drawing on rational choice and game theoretic models of political behavior have argued that post-1989 decentralizing reforms weakened AD and COPEI by lowering barriers to the entry of new parties and encouraging political entrepreneurs to abandon or assert their autonomy from traditional parties (Benton 1997; Penfold Becerra 2000).

A second variable that has been stressed by scholars working from a variety of theoretical perspectives is the political and economic impact of oil. This emphasis is most explicit in the structural approach of Karl (1997), who argues that developing states and their affiliated models of political representation are heavily shaped and constrained by their dominant export commodities and strategies for revenue extraction. According to Karl, the availability of extraordinary (yet undependable) oil revenues engendered a highly interventionist but grossly inefficient state, erratic economic performance, and a patronage-ridden party system that entered into crisis as it progressively lost its capacity to provide public services and distribute benefits to a broad range of clients. Likewise, political culture approaches have emphasized the role of oil in creating a "rentier mentality" among Venezuelan citizens, who supported democracy on purely instrumental grounds and thus turned against democratic institutions when they failed to deliver the mythological bounty from the nation's oil wealth (Romero 1997). According to Romero, the illusion of affluence encouraged demagoguery and "pathological learning" among political elites, along with a popular aversion to economic reforms that could have addressed the nation's deepening crisis

Even institutional and rational choice approaches have acknowledged the structural importance of oil revenues, which fueled the political pacts (Penfold Becerra 2000), patronage distributions (Benton 1997), and semicorporatist consultative mechanisms (Crisp 2000) that upheld Venezuela's democratic regime. The decline in oil revenues in the 1980s and 1990s thus undermined the material foundations by which Venezuelan democracy had generated support and conciliated interests (Kornblith 1998).

These works have contributed greatly to theoretical understanding of the Venezuelan experience, and there is no denying the centrality of the oil-institutions nexus in the genesis and evolution of the nation's multilayered crisis. Too often, however, the literature on Venezuela leaves the impression that the nation is a political outlier, a singular case with an exceptional, *sui generis* trajectory of economic and political development. Romero, for example, defends the notion of Venezuelan exceptionalism by claiming that the availability of oil rents to facilitate political compromise created a deeply flawed, "country-specific" process of democratic development (1997, 9). Other works are more careful to locate Venezuela within a comparative theoretical framework, but nonetheless emphasize the nation's extreme characteristics. This can be seen in Coppedge's assertion that "there is no other pluralistic system in which parties control so many aspects of the democratic process so completely," making Venezuela "probably the most extreme case of a pathological kind of political control" known as partyarchy (1994, 2). Likewise, Karl sees Venezuela as the one full-fledged "petrostate" in the Latin American region, which helps to explain why it developed a "permanent predominance of the public sector matched in Latin America only by Socialist Cuba" (1997, 90).

Venezuela's post-1958 political order certainly boasted a number of distinctive attributes that contributed to the crisis and decomposition of its party system, but these should not be allowed to obscure the commonalties the nation shares with others in Latin America. The main distinctions that did exist reflected differences of degree rather than differences of kind, and the challenges Venezuela confronted during the shift from ISI to neoliberalism were comparable to those of its neighbors. For this reason, there may be significant theoretical payoffs in locating the Venezuelan experience in a region-wide comparative framework for analyzing the relationship between socioeconomic and political change.

CORPORATISM, CLIENTELISM, AND PARTY–SOCIETY LINKAGES

To understand why a seemingly stable party system rapidly decomposes, it is necessary to explore the bonds that link parties to their social constituencies and to analyze how the bonds become eroded or severed at particular political conjunctures. Venezuela's dominant political parties may have been more highly developed in their bureaucratic organization than their counterparts in most other Latin American countries, but they did not differ significantly in the nature of their societal bonds. These societal bonds were forged during the ISI era of state-led development, and they were severely strained by the crisis of ISI and the shift (however incomplete in the Venezuelan case) toward market liberalism, with its emphases on economic austerity and diminished state intervention.

Historically, parties in Latin America have relied on two principal modes of societal linkage to mobilize constituency support. Patron–clientelism, which entails an exchange of material benefits for political support, is a nearly universal linkage mechanism in Latin American party systems. Vertical patronage networks managed by political brokers link individual clients to a party machine by means of discretionary and selective distribution of political favors, public employment or services, and government contracts or subsidies. Patron–clientelism was the primary linkage mechanism in nineteenth-century oligarchic party systems, and it was frequently used by both elite and mass-based parties to mobilize lower-class electoral support following the onset of mass politics in the twentieth century.

In contrast, the second main linkage mechanism, corporatist or encapsulating bonds, was a creation of the ISI era and the mass political participation it unleashed. These bonds were less universal than clientelism, as they developed in some Latin American party systems but not in others. Although corporatist, bonds may also entail an exchange of material benefits for political support, they differ from clientelism in their organizational basis—they are collective rather than individual in nature. That is, corporatist bonds are established between parties and group constituencies that are organized outside the partisan arena, such as labor and peasant confederations, giving parties a horizontally organized, grassroots base of mass support that purely clientelistic machine parties generally lack (see Kaufman 1977).

A basic differentiating feature of Latin American party systems was whether they developed encapsulating corporatist bonds during the ISI era to complement clientelism, or whether they relied more exclusively on the latter. In some Latin American countries, most notably Argentina, Brazil Bolivia, Chile, Mexico, Nicaragua. Peru, and Venezuela, party systems were reconfigured during the ISI era by the rise of a mass-based, labor-mobilizing populist or leftist party with encapsulating linkages to lower-class constituencies. In these nations parties were linked to society through a combination of corporatist and clientelistic bonds, and a central political cleavage typically developed between the labor-mobilizing party (or parties) and conservative defenders of the socioeconomic and political status quo. In other countries, however—namely Colombia, Costa Rica, the Dominican Republic, Ecuador, Honduras, Panama, Paraguay, and Uruguay—either traditional oligarchic parties remained electorally dominant throughout the ISI era, or new elite or personality based parties emerged that provided little impetus for social mobilization. Party systems in these nations continued to rely overwhelmingly on clientelistic rather than corporatist bonds.

Countries that developed a strong labor-mobilizing party and a combination of corporatist and clientelistic linkage mechanisms shared a number of other characteristics. Unionization levels were much higher in these countries, as labor movements were invigorated by aggressive ISI strategies (Argentina, Brazil, Chile, Mexico, and Venezuela), strategic mining or extractive industries (Bolivia, Chile, Mexico, Peru, and Venezuela), periods of leftist or revolutionary government (Bolivia, Chile, Mexico, Nicaragua, and Peru), or some combination of these factors. All these countries adopted extensive forms of state economic intervention before the onset of the debt crisis in the 1980s, and all suffered severe economic crises during the transition from ISI to neoliberalism. Indeed, all the hyperinflationary cycles that plagued Latin America between the 1970s and 1990s occurred in this set of cases.

Venezuela, like Mexico, managed to avoid hyperinflation partly because labor demands and distributive conflicts were tempered by the close historical ties between the dominant party and organized labor. Nevertheless, crises plagued both countries during this period of economic transition. By contrast, in countries that retained more elite-based party systems during the ISI era, union movements were weaker, development strategies generally were less interventionist, and economic crises during the transition to neoliberalism tended to be less severe (see Roberts 2002).[1]

Not only were economic crises more severe in the countries with strong labor-mobilizing parties, but the political trauma associated with the shift from ISI to neoliberalism was also more disruptive. The most electorally stable party systems in Latin America during the 1980s and 1990s were not those boasting strong mass-based party organizations, as the European literature would lead us to expect (Bartolini and Mair 1990), but rather those rooted in nineteenth-century oligarchic forms of domination (see Roberts and Wibbels 1999). The average Pedersen electoral volatility score between 1980 and 1998 in countries lacking a strong labor-mobilizing party was 19.3, compared to 29.8 in the countries that possessed such a party (Roberts 2002).

In part, this reflects the greater political costs and sharp anti-incumbent vote swings that accompanied acute economic crises in the countries with a strong labor-mobilizing party. High levels of electoral volatility in these party systems, however, also suggest that the demise of ISI and the shift toward neoliberalism was more disruptive of their party-society linkages. Although it is often assumed that the state retrenchment and economic austerity prescribed by neoliberal formulas threaten the patronage networks that allow elite-based parties to expand their electoral constituencies (Geddes 1994), these parties were often highly resilient and capable of retaining (or adapting) their societal linkages. Indeed, an extensive body of research suggests that clientelistic linkages remain a highly salient political resource in the neoliberal era (Dresser 1991; Levitsky 1998; Roberts 1995). Because patron clientelism tends to thrive under conditions of scarcity that preclude universal programs of social assistance and force a resort to particularistic criteria, clientelistic linkages may remain strong even in a context of resource constraints, and the individualized exchanges on which they are built certainly conform to a neoliberal social landscape where large-scale collective actors have been notably weakened.

In contrast, the encapsulating corporatist linkages that existed in countries with a strong labor-mobilizing party have clearly weakened as a result of the crisis of ISI and the adoption of structural adjustment policies. Social and economic change have eroded the foundations of this pattern of political representation; and while this does not in itself preordain a collapse of the party system, it ensures that large social blocs will increasingly detach themselves from the collective organizations that previously bound them to political parties. The hold of parties on encapsulated social constituencies weakens; to survive, parties must forge new, less organic and more contingent linkages to an increasingly individualized electorate. Survival thus becomes heavily dependent on parties' ability to adapt and generate instrumental support through their performance in office.

THE VENEZUELA CRISIS IN COMPARATIVE PERSPECTIVE

The challenges posed to traditional party–society linkages by the economic crisis and transition of the 1980s and 1990s can be clearly seen in the Venezuelan case. As in other countries with a strong labor-mobilizing party, the post-1958 party system in Venezuela developed extensive clientelistic and corporatist linkages to social constituencies. Both AD and COPEI cultivated networks of party clients as they distributed public sector jobs and or economic favors in exchange for political support. The steady expansion of the public sector after 1958 helped to extend these clientelistic networks, which swelled to unsustainable levels in the 1970s as the petroleum windfall entered state coffers and the government invested heavily in industrial and infrastructure projects, private sector credits, and social programs.

Total government expenditures increased 150 percent between 1970 and 1981, while the public sector share of GDP ballooned from 14.6 percent in the early 1970s to 37.6 percent in 1978 (Karl 1997, 249, 142). By the mid-1970s, public funds accounted for nearly 90 percent of industrial investments. Public sector employment also swelled, from only 6.7 percent of the workforce in 1950 to 19.1 percent in 1971 and 24.4 percent in 1981 (Crisp 2000, 170). Given the existence of a highly interventionist state that, as Karl put it, "had the power to distribute raw materials, grant tariff exemptions and subsidies, finance private firms, set price controls, and decide who might enter an industry" (1997, 158), the private sector became highly dependent on rent-seeking ties to public officials. Likewise, ordinary Venezuelans increasingly relied on government jobs, consumer subsidies, and social programs. Clientelism was complemented by the more collective, corporatist linkages forged between the dominant parties and national labor and campesino confederations (see Ellner 1995). Strong ties had existed between organized labor and AD since the 1940s, when the populist party beat out the Communist Party for leadership of the labor movement (Collier and Collier 1991, 252–62). After 1958, the Venezuelan labor movement developed into one of the strongest and most politically influential in Latin America, although its autonomy from the AD was heavily restricted. By the 1980s, more than a quarter of the workforce belonged to labor unions (well above the regional norm), and over 80 percent of these unions were incorporated into the Confederation of Venezuelan Workers (CTV), which was dominated by AD but included representatives from COPEI and minor parties as well.

Organized labor was well represented inside the AD through the party's Labor Bureau, which Coppedge calls "probably the most important broker in the party, because of its size and impressive ability to mobilize its membership" (1994, 112). Labor was also represented in AD's congressional delegation, and it had a voice in public administration and policymaking through seats on the governing boards of bureaucratic agencies and tripartite advisory commissions (see Crisp 2000). Although these political linkages limited organized labor's militancy and autonomy, they also produced substantial material rewards: Venezuelan workers benefited from some of the highest wages and the most heavily protected labor market in Latin America (Márquez and Pagés 1998, 6). The state established extensive legal restrictions on job dismissals, and union members received privileged access to social security and government subsidies for food, transportation, and health care (Coppedge 1994, 33; see also Davis and Coleman 1989). The government heavily subsidized the national labor movement and made major contributions to a workers' bank that financed its own enterprises and "established a virtual financial empire under the control of the CTV" (Crisp 2000, 171).

The nature of these corporatist and clientelistic linkages and the mechanisms by which they were reproduced broadly resembled those in other Latin American countries with a strong labor-mobilizing party. Comparatively speaking, however, petroleum revenues gave the Venezuelan state, and by extension AD and COPEI, greater resources to create and sustain these linkages, and they probably expanded the range of individuals and social actors incorporated in materially based partisan networks. Capitalists, workers, campesinos, and middle-class citizens all participated in the distribution of Venezuela's oil rents. Over the course of Venezuela's democratic experience, these corporatist and clientelistic networks crowded out other types of bonds between parties and their constituencies, leaving political representation contingent on highly instrumental forms of attachment. For example, programmatic and ideological bonds had been prominent during the gestation of the modern Venezuelan party system in the 1930s and 1940s, and the ambitious social reforms promoted by AD during the short-lived democratic trieno between 1945 and 1948 so polarized the political arena that they stimulated the counterorganization of conservative and elite forces behind COPEI. The negotiated political pacts that ushered in the 1958 democratic transition, however, required that AD tone down both its reformist objectives and its support for lower-class social mobilization (Karl 1987), and over the course of the next several decades both AD and COPEI gravitated to the political center in a competitive struggle to capture the median voter (Downs 1957). Likewise, the party system in its formative years possessed a significant class cleavage, with working and lower classes offering staunch support to AD and elite sectors linking to COPEI. This cleavage dissipated, however, as the parties converged programmatically and were transformed into multiclass, catchall electoral parties that sought to appeal to a broad cross-section of Venezuelan society (Myers 1998).

Consequently, by the 1970s the political arena was dominated by two party organizations that were virtually indistinguishable in their programmatic stances and relatively undifferentiated in their social make-up, despite AD´s ongoing corporatist ties to organized labor and peasant groups. Political loyalties based on class identities and ideological appeal had clearly waned (Alvarez 1996), and parties had lost their capacity to represent distinct social groups or policy alternatives. What remained was a struggle for power between competing machines that possessed alternative networks of individual and collective clienteles. As Karl states, the two dominant parties had evolved into "machines for extracting rents from the public arena" (1997, 93) and distributing them as political patronage.

The structural bases for this pattern of political representation were gradually undermined by social and economic changes after the early 1980s, when the global debt crisis and plunging oil prices created severe fiscal and balance of payments problems in Venezuela. First, the corporatist linkages were weakened by the combination of prolonged economic hardship and changes it the labor market. Both labor and campesino movements, historic allies of the AD, were emasculated in the process. An oil-inflated currency undermined the competitiveness of Venezuelan agriculture; combined with other structural changes in the economy, this caused the portion of the workforce devoted to agricultural activities to plummet from 40.3 percent in 1961 to a mere 10.8 percent in

1996 (Wilkie et al. 1999, 365, 377), neutralizing the political significance of AD's ties to campesino organizations. The flight from agriculture was especially dramatic during the first four years of market-oriented reform between 1989 and 1992, when an estimated six hundred thousand people abandoned the countryside (Bolívar and Pérez Campos 1996, 52).

Similarly, according to data provided by the International Labour Organization (1997, 235), union membership fell by nearly one-third between 1988 and 1995, a period of deepening economic crisis punctuated by market reforms and a heterodox retrenchment. The percentage of the workforce belonging to trade unions was cut nearly in half, declining from 26.4 percent to 13.5 percent over the same period. Over the course of the 1980s and 1990s, employment gradually shifted from heavily unionized formal sectors of the economy—the public sector and large-scale private enterprises—to informal sectors where unionization was less common. Indeed, the portion of the workforce engaged in informal activities surged from 34.5 percent in 1980 (Sunkel 1994, 155) to 53 percent in 1999 (Economist Intelligence Unit 2000, 16). The CTV did not effectively articulate the political identities or represent the interests of these informal workers. Even among workers who did belong to trade unions, the CTV became less representative, as a powerful independent union movement emerged in the southern industrial state of Bolívar with political ties to a rising leftist party, La Causa R (López-Maya 1997).

Corporatist bonds were frayed even further by the initiation of neoliberal reforms by AD president Carlos Andrés Pérez in 1989. Pérez, a populist figure renowned for extravagant public spending during an earlier stint in the presidency during the mid-1970s oil boom, had been supported by the AD Labor Bureau against the preferred candidate of the party hierarchy in the 1988 election. Once reelected, however, he broke with AD's statist tradition and his own populist image by implementing a harsh stabilization and structural adjustment program. The reform package triggered a violent backlash, with widespread urban riots in February 1989 that were repressed by the military, leaving hundreds dead. The economic reforms and popular protests trapped the CTV between its political loyalty to AD and its need to maintain legitimacy with rank and file workers. Frontal opposition to the reforms would have endangered organized labor's political access, which was already being challenged by Pérez's technocratic style of policymaking and the growing rift between the president and AD. An overly conciliatory stance, on the other hand, could cause the labor leadership to be outflanked by the more militant opposition tactics of independent leftist unions and civic protest groups. The CTV therefore declared one general strike and expressed moderate criticism of the reforms before returning to a more collaborative stance and negotiating with the government for concessions in specified areas (see Ellner 1995; Burgess 1999).

In the process, however, organized labor lost its capacity to channel the growing popular resistance to neoliberal reform. New grassroots protest movements sprang up among the urban poor, where AD's organizational penetration was less thorough. An increasingly complex and diversified civil society was largely excluded from traditional corporatist consultative institutions (Crisp 2000), while the labor and business associations that did participate came to be perceived as narrow, politically compromised interest groups whose rent-seeking demands clashed with the realities of dwindling public resources, market reforms, and technocratic policymaking.

The loosening of encapsulating corporatist linkages, which followed the earlier erosion of ideological bonds and social cleavages, left the Venezuelan party system highly dependent on patronage distributions, socialized partisan identities, and performance criteria to reproduce its electoral support. The remarkable durability of traditional parties in countries like Uruguay, Colombia, and Honduras through the 1990s suggests that this formula can sustain some party systems indefinitely. Nevertheless, such continuity reflects a delicate balance that is difficult to establish and maintain, because it requires that parties provide sufficient benefits to reproduce collective identities and preempt alternative forms of social mobilization, without such payoffs becoming so costly that they undermine macroeconomic performance or so arbitrary that they provoke a backlash against endemic corruption.

In a context of secular economic decline, Venezuela's parties failed to maintain such a delicate balance. With partisan patronage added to the costs of corporatist distributions and massive generalized subsidies for business and consumers, the Venezuelan state borrowed heavily even in the midst of the oil boom of the 1970s, then sank into fiscal crisis in the 1980s, when global interest rates tripled and oil prices plunged. A prolonged period of economic stagnation punctuated by short-lived boom-and-bust cycles began, with gradually accumulating inflationary pressures. By the mid-1990s, per capita GDP had declined by 20 percent from its late 1970s peak (Crisp 2000, 75). This smaller economic pie also was distributed more unequally; whereas the income share of the poorest 40 percent of the population fell from 19.1 percent in 1981 to 14.7 percent in 1997, that of the wealthiest decile increased from 21.8 to 32.8 percent (CEPAL 1999, 63). Real industrial wages in 1996 stood at less than 40 percent of their 1980 level (International Labour Organization 1998, 43), while per capita social spending by the state in 1993 was 40 percent below the 1980 level (República de Venezuela 1995, 40f). Between 1984 and 1993, the percentage of the population living below the poverty line increased from 36 percent to 62 percent, while the percentage living in extreme poverty tripled, from 11 percent to 33 percent (República de Venezuela 1995, 23).

Clearly, the Venezuelan party system had ceased to distribute generalized material benefits, making it incapable of mobilizing support on the basis of instrumental performance criteria. Furthermore, the parties' ongoing efforts to dispense selective patronage in a context of acute economic hardship merely contributed to their delegitimation, as public revulsion against political corruption spread. Public opinion surveys placed political parties last (and labor unions second from last) in confidence ratings of national institutions, and repeatedly showed that Venezuelan citizens blamed the political establishment and rampant corruption for creating an economic crisis in an oil-rich nation (see Romero 1997).

The combination of prolonged economic crisis and social change eroded both the corporatist and clientelistic linkages that Venezuelan parties had created in their mediation between the state and society. This erosion is certainly not unique to the Venezuelan case; clientelism is under pressure throughout Latin America in an era of market liberalization, and corporatist bonds and labor movements have been seriously weakened by economic crisis and reform in virtually all the nations that used to possess a strong labor-mobilizing party (Roberts 2002). In most of these other nations, however, established party systems were shaken but found ways to survive and adapt in a realigned form. Indeed, many of them suffered economic crises that were even more severe, by some measures, than that of Venezuela, which never experienced hyperinflation like that in Peru, Bolivia, Nicaragua, Argentina, Chile, and Brazil. Why, then, did established party systems in nations like Venezuela and Peru decompose in the midst of economic crises in the 1990s, whereas party systems in much of the region found ways to hold on?

These divergent outcomes are heavily contingent on the distribution of political costs and dividends associated with economic crisis, stabilization, and reform during the transition from ISI to neoliberalism. Where party system adaptation occurred, acute economic crisis was typically of shorter duration, imposing political defeats on an incumbent party while giving an opposition party the opportunity to take office and reap political rewards from economic stabilization. This dynamic contained the political costs associated with economic crisis and internalized the political dividends attendant to stabilization within the party system, facilitating adaptation and realignment.

In contrast, party system decomposition is more likely when a crisis endures through successive administrations, spreading the political costs more widely across the party system as a series of parties fail to achieve stabilization. Established parties thus bear the full brunt of the political costs associated with economic crisis, and the electorate is increasingly inclined to turn to a political outsider as a potential solution, giving outsiders the opportunity to reap the political rewards of stabilization. The political economy literature has often stressed the severity of crises in creating political conditions that are conducive to structural adjustment, but when it comes to the fate of party systems, the duration of an economic crisis may well be the more important consideration.

This dynamic can clearly be seen in Venezuela and Peru, the most prominent cases of party system decomposition during the transition from ISI to neoliberalism in the 1980s and 1990s. In Venezuela, the economic crisis gradually deepened but never engendered a hyperinflationary spiral with such immense short-term costs that it would induce public support for the bitter medicine of structural adjustment policies (see Weyland 1998). Consequently, the dominant parties chose to "'muddle through" and resist painful economic reforms, a pattern that was reinforced by AD's aforementioned inflexible bureaucratic structure (Corrales 2000; Levitsky 2001). The crisis therefore lingered on, politically damaging COPEI and AD administrations in succession for their failure to reverse the slide. When Pérez defied his populist campaign message by adopting a harsh neoliberal package to preempt a deepening foreign exchange and inflationary crisis, the public turned on the party system with a vengeance, and the groundswell of support for political outsiders commenced.

The electorate first opted for a familiar and safe outsider in former COPEI leader and ex-president Rafael Caldera, who broke with his party to win an independent bid for the presidency in 1993. By the end of the decade. however, when a series of independents vied for the presidency, voters sided overwhelmingly with Chávez, who offered the most thorough break with the traditional order and the most virulent anti-neoliberal line. A prolonged crisis produced systemic political costs that were only exacerbated by the long tradition of collusion between AD and COPEI; the two parties were held jointly responsible for the secular decline in economic performance, and neither could throw a lifeline to the party system by restoring prosperity.

In Peru, a prolonged economic crisis elicited a similar corrosive political effect as first one party and then another tried but failed to manage a recovery in the 1980s, causing the electorate to punish the entire political establishment and search for an outside savior. Fujimori could then reap the political dividends from economic stabilization, furthering the demise of the traditional party system.

It is not surprising that Peru and Venezuela had by far the worst scores in Latin America on one of the clearest indicators of long-term changes in popular living standards, the decline in real industrial wages. In 1996, Venezuela's real wage index stood at only 38.8 percent of its 1980 level, while Peru's stood at 42.4 percent, compared to an average of 102.6 percent in the rest of the region (International Labour Organization 1998. 43:). A party system with reserves of support drawn from recent struggles to defend human rights or restore democratic governance might be able to survive such a negative economic performance. For the Venezuelan party system, however, whose societal linkages and political legitimacy were so heavily dependent on the delivery of material benefits, the secular decline in popular living standards proved devastating.

CONCLUSION: FROM CRISIS TO PARTY SYSTEM DEMISE

According to Converse, the more entrenched a party system is, the more severe a shock must be to induce fundamental systemic change (1969, 167). In Venezuela, the demise of ISI and the aborted shift to neoliberalism proved to be just such a shock. Venezuela's party system stood at the apex of a mode of representation that was deeply embedded in a state-led ISI model of development, and the demise of this development model eroded the social and economic moorings of representative institutions. As the economy settled into an endemic crisis and the social landscape became increasingly informalized and impoverished, both the corporatist and clientelistic bonds that linked established parties to social constituencies were emasculated. The parties lost their capacity to distribute generalized material benefits, making their resort to more selective forms of patronage increasingly vulnerable to an anticorruption backlash. Economic reforms were diluted by entrenched interests and popular hostility, leaving the Venezuelan economy increasingly out of step with regional trends. By the mid-1990s, both orthodox and heterodox programs had failed to reverse the economic slide, and both AD and COPEI were seriously discredited by their cumulative economic mismanagement. The electorate eventually turned on the political establishment with a vengeance, placing its trust in an insurgent populist who promised to sweep aside the *partidocracia* and refound the Venezuelan republic.

Under Chávez, party-based mediation of state-society relations gave way to a direct, personalistic relationship between the masses and a charismatic (though often polarizing) leader. His party, the MVR, was a weakly institutionalized, personality-based movement. Although *Chavismo* spawned a plethora of grassroots groups that organized around election campaigns and social programs, especially in low-income communities, these often existed on the margins of the official party. Consequently, the personalism of executive authority tended to impede the reconstruction of national-level representative institutions, despite very high levels of grassroots social mobilization (see Ellner and Hellinger 2003).

This mobilization only intensified as Chávez's supporters rallied behind their leader in response to a series of opposition attempts to drive him from power. Between 2002 and 2004 opposition groups organized mass protests that demanded the president's resignation, a military coup that briefly removed him from office, a two-month oil strike that wreaked havoc on the national economy, and a recall campaign aimed at the revocation of Chávez's electoral mandate. Chávez relied heavily on popular mobilization to counter these opposition strategies and consolidate his authority; he broke the oil strike, augmented state control over a booming oil economy, redirected oil revenues to new social programs, and dealt his opponents a crushing defeat in the recall referendum.

These cycles of mobilization and countermobilization deepened Venezuela's political cleavage, but they did little to institutionalize it. Opponents of Chávez coalesced against his populist rule, but they did not unify behind a new or revived party organization. The anti-Chávez side of the cleavage was organizationally shallow, fluid, and fragmented; more movement than party, the opposition failed to translate social and political mobilization into more institutionalized channels of political representation. Likewise, grassroots *Chavista* organizations emerged in many low income communities, but their linkages to the national party were often informal or tenuous. Consequently, as Chávez launched a successful re-election campaign in 2006, neither government nor opposition sectors were effectively represented by partisan institutions. A new party system was slow to arise from the ruins of the old, despite a relatively durable cleavage alignment and high levels of social mobilization and political conflict.

Following several decades of highly institutionalized and relatively consensual politics, this progressive slide towards personality and movement-based politics provides an instructive counterpoint to the status quo biases of most conventional approaches to the study of political institutions. The Venezuelan case demonstrates that institutions are not fixed and confining determinants of political behavior; although designed for reproduction, they are subject to decay under certain conditions. As such, institutions should be treated as dependent variables as well as independent ones, and scholars should strive to identify the contingent outcomes of sociopolitical processes that lead to both institution building and institutional decay. Although the process of decay in Venezuela manifests a number of distinctive features, it still corresponds to a broader causal logic that is best illustrated through comparative analysis.

NOTES

Portions of this article were published in slightly different form in Spanish as "La descomposición del sistema de partidos en Venezuela vista desde un análisis comparativo." *Revista Venezolana de Economía y Ciencias Sociales* 7, 2 (May–August 2004): 183–200.

1 Costa Rica and Uruguay, which development strong welfare states by Latin American standards are partial outliners on this particular dimensional, but in other respects they fit the general pattern. Uruguay was the only country in his category to experience triple-digit inflation. but it did not fall prey to hyperinflation like most of the countries with a labor-mobilizing party system.

REFERENCES

Alvarez, Angel Eduardo. 1996. La crisis de hegemonía de los partidos políticos venezolanos. In *El sistema político venezolano: crisis y transformaciones*, ed, Alvarez. Caracas: Universidad Central de Venezuela. 131–54.

Bartolini, Stefano, and Peter Mair. 1990. *Identity, Competition and Electoral Availability: The Stabilization of European Elections. 1885–1985*. Cambridge: Cambridge University Press.

Benton, Allyson Lucinda. 1997. Patronage Games: The Effects of Economic Reform on Internal Party Politics and Party System Stability in Latin America. Paper presented at the 1997 meeting of the American Political Science Association, Washington, DC, August 28–31.

Berins Collier, Ruth. 2001. "Populism," in *International Encyclopedia of the Social and Behavioral Sciences*. Amsterdam and New York: Elsevier Science Ltd.

Bolívar, Ligia, and Magaly Pérez Campos. 1996. El sistema de derechos humanos en la constitución de 1961 y propuestas de reforma. In *El sistema político venezolano: crisis y transformaciones*, ed. Angel Eduardo Alvarez. Caracas: Universidad Central de Venezuela.

Burgess, Katrina. 1999. Loyalty Dilemmas and Market Reform: Party-Union Alliances Under Stress in Mexico, Spain, and Venezuela. *World Politics* 52, 1 (October): 105–34.

Cavarozzi, Marcelo. 1994. Politics: A Key for the Long Term in South America. In *Latin American Political Economy in the Age of Neoliberal reform*, ed. William C. Smith, Carlos E. Acuña, and Eduardo A. Gamarra. New Brunswick: Transaction. 127–55.

CEPAL (Comisión Económica para América Latina). 1999. *Anuario estadístico de América Latina y el Caribe*. Santiago de Chile: United National Economic Commission for Latin American and the Caribbean.

Collier, Ruth Berins, and David Collier. 1991. *Shaping the Political Arena: Critical Junctures, the Labor Movements, and Regime Dynamics in Latin America*. Princeton: Princeton University Press.

Conniff, Michael L., ed. 1982. *Latin American Populism in Comparative Perspective*. Albuquerque: University of New Mexico Press.

Converse, Philip F. 1969. Of Time and Partisan Stability. *Comparative Political Studies* 2, 2 (July): 139–71.

Coppedge, Michael. 1994. *Strong Parties and Lame Ducks: Presidential Partyarchy and Factionalism in Venezuela*. Stanford: Stanford University Press.

Corrales, Javier. 2000. Presidents, Ruling Parties, and Party Rules: A Theory on the Politics of Economic Reform in Latin America. *Comparative Politics* 32, 2 (January): 127–49.

Crewe, Ivor, and David Denver, eds. 1985. *Electoral Change in Western Democracies: Patterns and Sources of Electoral Volatility*. New York: St. Martin's.

Crisp, Brian. 2000. *Democratic Institutional Design: The Powers and Incentives of Venezuelan Politicians and Interest Groups*. Stanford: Stanford University Press.

Dalton, Russell, Scott C. Flanagan, and Paul Allen Beck, eds. 1984. *Electoral Change in Advanced Industrial Democracies: Realignment or Dealignment?* Princeton: Princeton University Press.

Davis, Charles L., and Kenneth M. Coleman. 1989. Political Control of Organized Labor in a Semi-Consociational Democracy: The Case of Venezuela. In *Labor Autonomy and the State in Latin America*, ed. Edward C. Epstein. Boston: Unwin Hyman.

Dornbusch, Rudiger, and Sebastian Edwards, eds. 1991. *The Macroeconomics of Populism in Latin America*. Chicago: University of Chicago Press.

Downs, Anthony. 1957. *An Economic Theory of Democracy*. New York: Harper and Row.

Drake, Paul VT. 1982. Conclusion: Requiem for Populism? In Conniff 1982. 217–45.

Dresser, Denise. 1991. *Neopopulist Solutions to Neoliberal Problems: Mexico's National Solidarity Program*. San Diego: Center for U.S.-Mexican Studies, University of California.

Economist Intelligence Unit. 2000. Country Profile 2000: *Venezuela*. London: Economist.

Ellner, Steve. 1995. *El sindicalismo en Venezuela en El contexto democrático (1958–1994)*. Caracas: Fondo Editorial Tropykas.

Ellner, Steve and Daniel Hellinger, eds. 2003. *Venezuelan Politics in the Chávez Era: Class, Polarization, and Conflict*. Boulder, Col.: Lynne Rienner.

Geddes, Barbara. 1994. *Politician's Dilemma: Building State Capacity in Latin America*. Berkeley: University of California Press.

Inglehart, Ronald. 1990. *Culture Shift in Advanced Industrial Society*. Princeton: Princeton University Press.

International Labour Organization. 1997. *1997 Labour Overview: Latin America and the Caribbean*. Lima: International Labour Organization.

———. 1998. *1998 Labour Overview: Latin-America and the Caribbean*. Lima: International Labour Organization.

Karl, Terry Lynn. 1997. Petroleum and Political Pacts: The Transition to Democracy in Venezuela. *Latin American Research Review* 22, 1: 63–94.

———. 1997. *The Paradox of Plenty: Oil Booms and Petro-States*. Berkeley: University of California Press.

Kaufman. Robert R. 1977. Corporatism. Clientelism and Partisan Conflict: A Study of Seven Latin American Countries. In *Authoritarianism and Corporatism in Latin America*, ed. James Malloy. Pittsburgh: University of Pittsburgh Press. 109–48.

Kitschelt, Herbert. 1994. *The Transformation of European Social Democracy*. Cambridge: Cambridge University Press.

Kornblith, Miriam. 1998. *Venezuela en los noventa: las crisis de la democracia*. Caracas: Ediciones IESA.

Levitsky, Steven. 1998. Crisis, Party Adaptation, anti Regime Stability in Argentina: The Case of Peronism, 1989–1995. *Party Politics* 4. 4:445:70.

———. 2001. Organization aid Labor-Based Party Adaptation: The Transformation of Argentine Peronism, in Comparative Perspective. *World Politics* 54 (October): 27–56.

Lijphart, Arend, and Carlos H. Waisman, eds. 1996 *Institutional Design in New Democracies: Eastern Europe and Latin America*. Boulder: Westview Press.

Lipset, Seymour Martin, and Stein Rokkan. 1967. Cleavage Structures, Party Systems, and Voter Alignments: An Introduction. In *Party Systems and Voter Alignments: Cross-National Perspectives*, eds. Lipset and Rokkan. New York: Free Press. 1–64.

López-Maya, Margarita. 1997. The Rise of Causa R in Venezuela. In *The New Politics of Inequality in Latin America: Rethinking Participation and Representation*, ed. Douglas A. Chalmers,

Carlos M. Vilas, Katherine Hite, Scott B. Martin, Kerianne Piester, and Monique Segarra. New York: Oxford University Press. 117–43.

Mainwaring. Scott P 1999. *Rethinking Party Systems in the Third Wave of Democratization: The Case of Brazil.* Stanford: Stanford University Press.

Mainwaring, Scott P., and Timothy R. Scully, eds. 1995. *Building Democratic Institutions: Party Systems in Latin America.* Stanford: Stanford University Press.

Mair, Peter. 1997. *Party System Change: Approaches and Interpretations.* Oxford Clarendon Press.

March, James C., and Johan P. Olsen. 1989. *Rediscovering Institutions: The Organizational Basis of Politics.* New York: Free Press.

Márquez, Gustavo, and Carmen Pagés. 1998. Ties That Bind: Employment Protection and Labor Market Outcomes in Latin America. Working Paper 373. Washington, DC: Inter-American Development Bank.

Myers, David J. 1998. Venezuela's Political Party System: Defining Events, Reactions, and the Diluting of Structural Cleavages. *Party Politics* 4, 4: 495–521.

North, Douglas. 1990. *Institutions, Institutional Change and Economic Performance.* Cambridge: Cambridge University Press.

Penfold Becerra, Michael. 2000. El colapso del sistema de partidos en Venezuela: explicación de una muerte anunciada. Paper presented at the 22nd meeting of the Latin American Studies Association, Miami, March 16–18.

Remmer, Karen L. 1997. Theoretical Decay and Theoretical Development: The Resurgence of Institutional Analysis. *World Politics* 50 (October): 34–61.

República de Venezuela. 1995. *Venezuela ante la cumbre mundial sobre desarrollo social.* Caracas.

Roberts, Kenneth M. 1995. Neoliberalism and the Transformation of Populism in Latin America: The Peruvian Case. *World Politics* 48 (October): 82–116.

———. 2002. Social Inequalities Without Class Cleavages in Latin America's Neoliberal Era. *Studies in Comparative International Development* 36, 4 (Winter): 3–33.

Roberts, Kenneth M., and Erik Wibbels. 1999. Party Systems and Electoral Volatility in Latin America: A Test of Economic, Institutional, and Structural Explanations. *American Political Science Review* 93, 3 (September): 575–90.

Romero, Aníbal. 1997. Rearranging the Deck Chairs on the Titanic: The Agony of Democracy in Venezuela. *Latin American Research Review* 32, 1: 7–36.

Shugart, Matthew Soberg, and John M. Carey. 1992. *Presidents and Assemblies: Constitutional Design and Electoral Dynamics.* Cambridge: Cambridge University Press.

Sunkel, Osvaldo. 1994. La crisis social de América Latina: una perspectiva neoestructuralista. In *Pobreza y modelos de desarrollo en América Latina,* ed. Eduardo S. Bustelo, Félix Bombarolo, and Horacio E. Caride. Washington, DC: Economic Development Institute.

United Nations. Comisión Económica para América Latina (CEPAL). 1999. *Anuario estadístico de América Latina y el Caribe.* Santiago de Chile: CEPAI.

Weyland, Kurt. 1996. Neoliberalism and Neopopulism in Latin America: Unexpected Affinities: *Studies in Comparative International Development* 31 (Fall): 3–31.

———. 1998. The Political Fate of Market Reform in Latin America, Africa, and Eastern Europe. *International Studies Quarterly* 42: 645–74.

———. 2001. "Clarifying a Contested Concept: Populism in the Study of Latin American Politics," *Comparative Politics* 34 (October): 1–22.

Wilkie, James W., Eduardo Alemán, and José Guadalupe Ortega, eds. 1999. *Statistical Abstract of Latin America.* Vol. 35. Los Angeles: UCLA Latin American Center.

Williamson, John, ed. 1990. *Latin American Adjustment: How Much Has Happened?* Washington, DC: Institute for International Economics.

LaVergne, TN USA
04 December 2010
207293LV00002B/1-28/P